THE TIMES
Survey
of
Foreign
Ministries
of the
World

THE TIMES
Survey
of
Foreign
Ministries
of the
World

Selected and edited by
ZARA STEINER

TIMES BOOKS
LONDON

First published by
Times Books Ltd,
16 Golden Square,
London, W.1

© Times Books Limited, London 1982

British Library Cataloguing in Publication Data
The Times survey of foreign ministries of the world.
  1. Foreign offices
  I. Steiner, Zara
  351.01   JX1687

  ISBN 0-7230-0245-2

Published in North America by
Meckler Publishing Inc.
Westport, Connecticut 06880, U.S.A.

Printed and bound in Great Britain by
Biddles Ltd, Guildford and King's Lynn

Contents

Introduction

ZARA STEINER

Dr Zara Steiner is Fellow and Director of Studies in Modern History at New Hall, Cambridge. She was born in New York City and studied at Swarthmore College, Penn., at St Anne's College, Oxford, and Harvard University. She is author of *The Foreign Office and Foreign Policy, 1898–1914* (1969), *Britain and the Origins of the First World War* (1977), and two studies of the Department of State under the auspices of the Center of International Studies, Princeton University, *The State Department and the Foreign Service* (1958) and *Present Problems of the Foreign Service* (1961).

Diplomacy is an old and flexible profession. Primitive people sent emissaries to open negotiations. The ancient world had a recognizable system of diplomatic discourse. The Venetians, Florentines and members of the Hanseatic League developed their own forms of diplomatic exchange. As national states evolved and their relations with each other became more complex, there developed a specialized corps of men to handle such matters, sharing a common code of behaviour and obeying rules accepted by the participating states. By the time of the Peace of Westphalia (1648), an international system had evolved that, despite changes in the forms and behaviour of states, proved to be surprisingly durable. Without the establishment of any supranational authority or law, there has grown up since that time a series of arrangements that the nationals of the world acknowledge and accept and that have, until the present time, survived individual offenders and the disruption of major wars.

This has been a slow and irregular development, dependent on national needs and international requirements. There has been continuity, but also breaks and even reversals. Different states and governing groups have come to power that have fashioned alternative styles of diplomatic intercourse. Changed configurations in the relations between states have produced new kinds of international institutions. Historians point to a number of key events: the Congress of Vienna (1815) and the establishment of the concert system, the Hague Peace Conference (1899 and 1907) and the codification of the laws of war and peace, the Treaty of Versailles (1919) and the creation of new states according to the principles of self-determination, and a new form of multinational organization, the League of Nations. The arena of action has also been expanded. Compare the number of states represented at Vienna (8), in the League of Nations (63 at various times in its history), and in the United Nations (154 in 1981).

This is a book about Foreign Ministries, those institutions in each state that were developed to manage the conduct of foreign affairs. The volume has been compiled in the hope of filling an important gap in our knowledge. Though there have been many manuals of diplomatic instruction, some still read today, and numerous histories of diplomatic negotiations, there have been surprisingly few studies of foreign policy institutions. The sources are often difficult to trace: negotiations between states are recorded and kept; administrative memoranda, sometimes personal, often outlining only *ad hoc* and temporary arrangements, are frequently destroyed. Few clerks write memoirs, though diplomats did and do. Moreover, until the present day, historians have not been attracted to this field of enquiry. Bureaucratic historians have excluded departments of external affairs because they do not fit easily into general patterns of administrative developments. Diplomatic historians were far more interested in 'what one clerk said to another clerk' as G. M. Young disparagingly commented. There has been a sharp change of focus in recent years. The students of administration have turned to comparative studies and have begun to cross national lines. The current interpenetration of domestic and foreign affairs has increasingly diminished the gap between domestic and foreign departments, making the exclusion of the latter from any administrative survey an anomaly. This same breakdown in older categories has led diplomatic historians to consider the shaping influences of internal factors in the making of foreign policy. Increasingly, they ask not only about who makes policy but what factors determine the decision-makers' choice of options. Foreign Ministries and diplomatic services are part of this internal complex. The scope of diplomatic history has altered as radically as diplomacy itself.

Each of the authors in this book has written about a single Ministry. Most have dealt with primary material that is scattered and incomplete. Few have had the advantage of published sources centrally relevant to their concerns; at best there have been monographs about specific periods of ministerial history. There appeared to be special advantages in presenting a multinational study, despite the inevitable incompleteness of each chapter. It is the need to communicate between states that provides the *raison d'être* of all diplomatic institutions. However strongly influenced by internal forces, all Foreign Ministries must respond to changes in the international environment, which is itself in constant flux. A comparative study alerts the reader to this shifting pattern of international relations, providing an additional vantage point from which to view its evolution.

These chapters reveal striking parallels and contrasts in the experiences of the different countries, most of which were included because they had pre-1919 histories and were part of a European system of international relations. What is common to the development of their respective foreign policy institutions derives not only from similar patterns of administrative growth but also from their participation in a common field of diplomatic action. What differentiates them are just those domestic characteristics that have produced the modern, independent, sovereign state. Institutional differences reflect the size, power, governmental structure and political leadership in each state. Few nations, moreover, have had continuous lines of political evolution. Most have been subject to radical and even revolutionary changes of government. These, of course, have affected the shape and evolution of government departments. Though shared international experiences create common forms, each Ministry, developing within a separate political system, will have its own distinctive characteristics. Only by placing the Foreign Office within a national framework could one judge the degree to which its development diverged from that of domestic counterparts. The study of Foreign Ministries is exemplary just because they are shaped by both internal and external forces.

The historical patterns are almost everywhere the same. All Foreign Ministries, like the leading domestic departments, trace their origins to the ruling household. But sovereigns, whether sultans, tsars or kings, retained their interest in foreign affairs long after their powers diminished in other fields. This was as true in the great as in the smaller nations. The Emperor Franz Joseph remained central to the decision-making process in Austria–Hungary right up until his death in 1916. Even where constitutional monarchies were established and royal powers curtailed, as in Great Britain, Belgium and Norway, the king continued to intervene in foreign matters and took an active interest in the appointment of diplomatic representatives. Leopold II even used the Belgian Foreign Ministry for his own private fiscal purposes in the Congo. Nor was this tendency reversed when republics were established. In France under the Third Republic, both before and after the First World War, and in recent times as well, the President has been an active participant in foreign affairs. And while the United States must be treated in a special category, the unique position of the President in the policy-making process was recognized by the Constitution and proved in practice to be the most important factor in the conduct of American diplomacy.

When chancellors and prime ministers emerged, it was natural that they should have inherited their sovereign's interest in foreign matters. Inevitably, where strong monarchies survived, there were clashes between sovereigns and first ministers; that between William II and Bismarck is only the most famous of numerous examples. But chancellors, too, where they could, kept a close control, often presiding directly over the Foreign Ministry. In France and Italy (Francesco Crispi being a prime example) and even in Great Britain, the same man held both the prime ministership and the portfolio of foreign affairs. Lord Salisbury much preferred the Foreign Office to his duties as Prime Minister. It was not even necessary actually to assume the office; Bismarck was very much the chief of the Wilhelmstrasse even though there was a State Secretary. One could appoint a protégé, use personal envoys or intervene in the daily business of the office.

Despite the continuing interest of sovereigns and chancellors, Ministers for Foreign Affairs did emerge as men of influence, particularly, as was so common in the nineteenth century, when they were former diplomats and experienced in their craft. Even when they were party politicians, as in Britain, they commanded considerable respect and, apart from the Prime Minister, occupied the most prestigious position in the Cabinet. Neither the Cabinet nor parliamentary bodies proved adequate checks on the power of the Foreign Secretary, for only he could keep abreast of the daily flow of diplomatic activity. Many Foreign Secretaries held office for considerable periods of time (though Joseph Bech's 33-year term at the Luxembourg Ministry was somewhat exceptional), returning to the Ministry under different prime ministers, as did Carlo Sforza in Rome after an interval of almost 30 years.

The office was important enough for Foreign Secretaries to be retained as symbols of continuity and stability. Even Hitler was to treat the Wilhelmstrasse (like the army) differently from other departments, keeping Neurath in office until 1938 to provide just such a semblance of continuity, which was only partly justified by events. On the other hand, political bargaining over appointments, a rapid turnover in ministerial heads or the deliberate appointment of a weak Minister were signs of domestic instability or a reduced international role. There were exceptions. In France under the Third Republic, for instance, neither politicians nor diplomats were anxious to assume responsibilities that provided little political leverage and yet were never free from political intervention. While in Imperial Germany the State Secretary was either bullied by Bismarck or subject to the capricious will of the Kaiser. Switzerland, too, appears to have been a special case. The administration of foreign affairs was of so little importance that for much of the period between 1848 and 1920 it could be entrusted to the President of the Confederation, who held his office for one year only.

By the end of the nineteenth century all Foreign Secretaries were assisted by bureaucracies of considerable sophistication. The professionalization of ministerial staffs, who enjoyed considerable security of tenure, balanced the tendency of political Ministers to come and go. They represented not only a reservoir of expertise but a departmental memory bank upon which the

Foreign Minister could draw. It is sometimes forgotten that some of these Ministries had exceedingly short histories. Only a few date their evolution to the sixteenth and seventeenth centuries; most only began their independent existence in the late eighteenth or the nineteenth centuries. Evolution depended not only on the achievement of full political maturity (hence the late starting dates for Norway, Finland and the British Commonwealth countries) but also on the capacity of rulers and the extent of foreign involvements. Smallness of size, geographic isolation, protected neutrality, might equally delay the development of diplomatic agencies. The case of Spain is of particular interest: a very early development was followed by alternating periods of expansion and contraction paralleling the political instability of that country.

At the start, the king's clerks were loyal and discreet scribes who could master foreign languages and write a good hand. Like their royal masters, early officials handled domestic and foreign correspondence until the latter became too voluminous and some form of division was necessary. As Ministers took over the conduct of affairs, they inherited and expanded these writing offices, though penmanship and language facility remained the paramount requirements. In states like Russia, Greece, Denmark and Turkey, foreigners were employed until natives could be trained to the necessary level of language competence. The Dutch made excellent use of the French Huguenots in their own country for the same purpose. As is indicated in almost every chapter in this book, these staffs were small and its members personally known to their chiefs. Gradually, positions came to be handed down from generation to generation. The same family names appeared – father and sons, brothers, uncles and nephews. There were many 'closed shops'. Successive generations of civil servants were often related to one another through descent or marriage.

Ministries remained tight organizations right up until the First World War. Russia was the outstanding exception; here 'feather-bedding' was a common practice and the granting of office sinecures part of the tsarist structure. Elsewhere, few foreign offices, even among the great powers, employed more than 50 officials at mid-century, or between 100 and 150 men on the eve of the Great War. The French, for instance, increased the number of their clerks from 80 in 1870 to 170 (excluding doorkeepers, typists, etc.) in 1914. The Danish Foreign Ministry increased from nine officials in 1848 to 21 in 1914, the Dutch from 23 in 1849 to 45 in 1914. As Ministries grew, they came to be divided into departments and bureaux. The arrangement of business was either functional (political and commercial) or geographic (with the main emphasis on the European nations). Administrative offices, dealing with legal matters, protocol, archives and internal administration, proliferated. The type of work done in such departments was not fundamentally different, though the political and European divisions were by far the most prestigious. The pace was leisurely in the nineteenth century: time for 'stump cricket' at the Foreign Office in London and for *'le thé de cinq heures'* at the Quai d'Orsay.

Titles and distinctions were of considerable importance. A senior permanent official (secretary-general, assistant state secretary, permanent under-secretary) emerged as the highest-ranking officer, in some cases coordinating all the activities of the Ministry. In countries such as France (the position emerged late in the Department's history) and Italy he might share power with the political director and the head of his Minister's cabinet. There was also an under-secretary responsible for relations with parliamentary bodies, a post that became increasingly important after 1880 when such bodies began to take a more active interest in foreign affairs. Below this often mixed group of permanent civil servants and ministerial appointees, there developed a career ladder that men climbed slowly, 'Hackney coach-like from bottom to top, by dint of mere living'. Men spent their whole lives in these institutions. Some remained throughout their careers nothing more than glorified clerks; others had a real place in the policy-making apparatus. As the volume of business increased and the subject matter of diplomacy became far more complex, some devolution of responsibility became inevitable. Foreign Secretaries could not manage the tide across their desks; increasingly the senior clerks and heads of bureaux handled questions of secondary importance.

Foreign Ministers needed efficient clerks; this contributed to the professionalization of their departments. Though some form of caste patronage persisted in many nations, minimum requirements for entering the bureaucracy were raised everywhere during the course of the nineteenth century. Examinations were introduced – little more than a formality in some states but with a real element of competition in others. Even those who counted on family and political connections were expected to have a university degree (often in law) and considerable language competence. Men were specially prepared to sit these papers, but the preparation itself presupposed a certain social background.

In most states there were distinct differences between the Foreign Ministry and the diplomatic service. Although this book centres on the development of the former, there were, of course, intimate links between the two. In countries where there was only a relatively small pool of prospective diplomats, interchanges between the Ministry and the diplomatic service were common and a single man might even simultaneously hold a position in each. In most European states, however, there were two distinct career services as well as a consular service, differently recruited and each with its own career ladder. For the most part, the diplomatic service attracted those who enjoyed the benefits of high birth and good incomes. It was certainly the more glamorous career for the old aristocracy when they could afford it. The great European embassies – London, Paris, Rome (for its glittering social life), Vienna, St Petersburg (if one could stand the cold), Madrid and Constantinople were the ultimate prizes. They might be awarded to those who had served in the Foreign Office or had climbed the diplomatic ladder. More often they were used as rewards for faithful supporters or, on occasion, as places to send a dangerous rival.

The hierarchy of overseas posts had been established at the Congress of Vienna. Embassies and legations began as familial affairs but, as at the central office, career services with qualifying examinations, promotion ladders and pay scales were gradually established for all but the very top appointments. The independence of ambassadors depended upon the personalities of incumbents and their distance from home. Austrians were expected to carry out orders; the British and French ambassadors were often men of considerable influence. It was not until the increased use of the telegraph after the 1880s restricted the initiative of the diplomat, and an increasing number of posts were opened outside Europe, that the overseas service began to lose its attraction. Towards the end of the century, the able and ambitious looked more favourably at the positions at home, where one was closer to the real centres of decision-making.

There was a certain amount of rivalry between the incumbents of the Ministry and the diplomats overseas. The gulf between the 'pen pushers' and the 'social butterflies' mirrored their somewhat different functions. The bureaucrats were often irritated by the narrow views of their colleagues abroad, the common disease of 'localitis', the remoteness from the concerns of the home country. More than one head of chancery was chided for his untidy administrative habits or his involvement in the social whirl of the embassy world. The archives, then as now, contained numerous complaints from diplomats that their dispatches remained unread and their advice disregarded. Those unfortunate enough to find themselves in remote parts of the world believed, with some reason, that they were totally forgotten. Neither group favoured the creation of a single service; the work and the life-styles were far too different. Clerks could live on their earned incomes; diplomats could not – often they were not paid at all during their first years of service. Even ambassadors, who were seemingly well-rewarded, spent their own funds to maintain the 'dignity of their table'. In Britain, Austria–Hungary, Russia, Germany and Italy, candidates for the diplomatic service were required to give evidence of their independent means. The sums required were considerable; with the downward turn of agricultural prices in the 1880s and 1890s the expense of the diplomatic life deterred those of the landed classes who had to look to their estates for income. It was cheaper, if more restricting, to live and work at home.

The gap between the home and diplomatic service narrows if one compares their structures and rewards with those of the consuls. Even states where consular services were older and more important than their diplomatic counterparts did little to improve the career prospects for those who performed commercial duties. The Belgians, for instance, only took the necessary steps to create a professional service in 1896. Wherever it was possible, honorary consuls were employed, while the fee system postponed the development of proper salary scales. The result was a poorly organized, though often extensive, career service with few rewards for the enterprising. There were transfers from the consular to the diplomatic service (exceptional in the British case, more frequent in Imperial Russia) but the differences between the two could be sharp. In some cases, diplomats and consuls were recruited from different social classes, entered through different examination systems (when consular services were created), and rarely mixed socially even outside the European circuit. These consular corps were the Cinderellas of the diplomatic world. Only pressure from business and commercial groups, as well as parliamentary protests, led to improvements and a breakdown of deeply entrenched snobberies. In the Netherlands, at least, the pressure was so strong that between 1825 and 1850 the diplomatic missions were down-graded, the consular service augmented and the Ministry staff increased to handle commercial rather than political affairs. The reduction of the Netherlands after 1830 to a third-class power meant a diminished interest in power politics and favoured a sustained shift of attention to economic and colonial affairs that lasted right up to the end of the First World War.

The differences between the incumbents of the Foreign Office and the diplomatic service were often only marginal. With but few exceptions (Denmark, where the Foreign Ministry was staffed by middle-class officials) the Ministries as well as the diplomatic services attracted the well-born. Both favoured sons from noble and gentry families: the Political Division in the Auswärtiges Amt, and the Eastern Department in the British Foreign Office were as aristocratic as any embassy. The professional and successful business families who entered were already moving in upper-class circles. Where the pool of entrants was broader, as in Austria–Hungary, the middle-class recruits took on the colouring and attitudes of their social superiors. The Ballhausplatz was no less aristocratic because of its middle-class contingent.

Moreover, there were numerous contacts and even interchanges between the two services even before the outside pressure for amalgamation mounted. Diplomats began in the Ministries; it was the officials there who were responsible for their subsequent appointments and promotions. There was a continuous correspondence between the two groups, visits, exchanges arranged for both personal and professional reasons, and at the top of the career ladders, appointments to the more coveted positions in both services.

Judging from the evidence presented in this book, it is not unfair to see the diplomatic establishment as a closed caste representing a relatively narrow social élite. Foreign Ministries and diplomatic services alike projected a common image that obscured any differences between them. Foreign Ministries were both socializing and nationalizing institutions. In Turkey, Austria–Hungary and Switzerland, for instance, recruits stemmed from various national, religious and linguistic groups, but represented a single nation. It was at the Ballhausplatz, despite a period of Magyar domination, that the imperial ideal found its strongest supporters. In Russia, foreign names were still found in the Ministry at the end of the nineteenth century even when the Great Russians dominated the service. And in Germany the Prussian aristocracy was forced to share the Office and the diplomatic service with increasing numbers of non-Prussians. There were states, Britain for one, where only the dominant national groups were represented, while certain exclusions on religious grounds were not uncommon. Nevertheless, Foreign Ministries represented a single state and were in themselves symbols of unification.

There was another side to the coin. However self-enclosed or socially exclusive, this was a professional élite whose interests went beyond national borders. Because, with few exceptions, the same kind of men staffed the departments of all the states, they understood each other, spoke the same language, read the same books. Members of the diplomatic establishment were the multinationals of their time. William Tyrrell, Sir Edward Grey's pre-war private secretary, spent his vacations from 1900 to 1910 at the home of Prince Hugo von Radolin, the German ambassador in Paris, whose mother-in-law was in turn a Talleyrand. Members of the profession, despite the occasional chauvinist, thought of themselves as members of a cosmopolitan, culturally homogeneous, European family. Bismarck refused to read dispatches from St Petersburg not written in French. But more than a common language linked the diplomats of the pre-war world. They were the defenders of the same institutions, national and international. They were conscious of the common lines that kept the peace between them and had a vested interest in their preservation. There were unspoken assumptions about the way diplomacy should be conducted that influenced behaviour at home and abroad.

Such cohesiveness affected the decision-making process. Officials tended to represent conservative forces within their own societies. The French Chamber of Deputies had to be reassured that the Quai d'Orsay had become republicanized and the number of noble recruits drastically reduced; even then individual deputies remained suspicious. There was in every Ministry a strong inclination to serve the ruling monarch and to preserve the *status quo*. There was a sense of professional superiority, intense objections to outsiders (the 'amateurs' and 'busybodies' who concerned themselves with foreign affairs), suspicion about professional rivals (including the military) who might intrude where they were not wanted. Above all, it was generally believed that neither the public nor its representatives could understand the workings of a complex and intricate system that was best left to the diplomats to run.

Though diplomacy was a high art, it was a narrow one. Wherever possible diplomats chose to ignore the fact that there were competitors in their field of action. The realities of the situation, even before the war, did not escape contemporary notice. Edward Goschen, British ambassador in Berlin, wrote to London: 'What I do find is more muddle – more confusion – than I have found in any country during my 35 years of experience. Chaos is the only word for it – . . . .' Sir Edward Grey avoided any knowledge of the actual details of the Anglo-French military conversations because of their uncomfortable political implications. Few Foreign Ministers were students of Carl von Clausewitz, and only rudimentary steps were taken to coordinate diplomatic and military planning. More often than not, there was a certain amount of rivalry between Foreign Ministries and military departments (where even the military and naval chiefs pulled in opposite directions). At best, planning for peace and war were treated in separate compartments. With regard to intelligence services, there was more competition than cooperation between the diplomats and the military even in such countries as France and Russia, where cipher-breaking techniques were well advanced and could have been more effectively exploited.

The diplomats, though recruited from the same social groups as their military colleagues, neither appreciated the political implications of the new techniques of war nor understood the extent to which military planning curtailed their own freedom of action. It is true that after 1900 diplomats became more aware of the rising costs of maintaining ever more elaborate and expensive war machines. But just as they resented military interference in their affairs (though on occasion they were forced to give way to such pressures) they were equally reluctant to intervene in the planning of the general staffs. Just because the civilian statesmen believed that no state could sustain a long war under twentieth-century conditions, they accepted and shared the short-war illusions of the military high command. It was the function of the army and navy to fight wars, the function of the diplomats to preserve the peace. Thus, though many of the same conditions that were to undermine the position of the inter-war foreign offices already existed in pre-1914 Europe, in those self-confident times the diplomats believed they could avoid the disastrous consequences of conflicting aims and contending authorities in their own governmental circles.

There were less far-reaching but equally important difficulties arising from the professional and social élitism of the diplomatic caste. Because of their backgrounds and education, their tendency to move in restricted circles, officials thought in formally political terms. The political departments were the heart of the Ministry; economic and commercial affairs were of secondary importance. There was a certain contempt for trade and traders. Curiously enough, this anti-commercial bias was possibly strongest in Britain, where world-wide economic interests were balanced by a powerful *laissez faire* tradition that left the pursuit of loans and markets to the exporters and financiers. It was usually in the non-European capitals that diplomats became involved in loan operations and concession-hunting. Even in those nations where economic interests were paramount and political questions of secondary importance, diplomats tended to leave such 'bread and butter' issues to others. In the Netherlands, Belgium and the Scandinavian countries, the parliament repeatedly argued that expensive diplomatic services served little purpose. The legalistic training and political orientation of diplomatic representatives were unsuited to the needs of commerce.

Most Foreign Ministries were far more concerned with European questions than those of the extra-European world. Though some departments spawned colonial divisions, these often became, or co-existed with, semi-independent or independent Ministries. Colonial issues tended to be viewed in European terms. As for the rest of the world – the Far East, Latin America, the United States – these were areas of secondary importance whose affairs could be left in the hands of experienced counsellors or senior clerks. There were signs of change at the turn of the century, but they appeared minimal to those involved in the competition for influence and markets and for whom imperial questions were of overriding importance.

It was for these reasons that the periodic critiques heard throughout the nineteenth century became a loud chorus after 1880. As the bourgeoisie gained political power, they grew increasingly critical of a diplomatic service that represented aristocratic interests. But though they deplored the exclusive character of the career services, they proved to be exceedingly niggardly when it came to financing them. Complaints about the prevailing diplomatic myopia brought the first stirrings of reform towards the end of the century; by 1914 few Foreign Ministries remained unaffected by the demand for change.

Representative bodies insisted that diplomatic establishments should be made more democratic and responsive. This meant a more broadly based approach to the problems of recruitment and staffing. There was a need for more information and publicity (press departments had been small or non-existent) and greater accountability to the electorate. Industrialists, manufacturers and exporters argued that economic diplomacy had to be up-graded and that political and commercial questions should be treated as of equal importance. This meant strengthening the commercial departments at home, improving the consular services abroad, and above all integrating all those responsible for the making and execution of policy into a single career service that would represent the multiple interests of the whole nation. Each group of critics pointed to the more energetic tactics of their foreign rivals. There were, moreover, the administrative critics, both outside and in the departments, who pointed to the outdated methods of handling an ever-increasing load of dispatches and telegrams and who argued for a more systematic and rational distribution of assignments.

The reforming impulse lasted into the 1920s. Ministers and bureaucrats – men like Philippe Berthelot in France, Eyre Crowe in Britain, Edward Schüler in Germany – restructured their respective Ministries. The French reforms of 1907 began a process of reconstruction that changed the organizational habits of the Department, strengthened the commercial competence of the Ministry and the embassies and initiated the first steps towards the integration of all the services. The pre-war British reforms, freeing the diplomatic establishment from its purely secretarial duties, affected only the Foreign Office. The earliest moves towards formal amalgamation took place during 1919–21, but the consular service was not brought in from the cold until the Eden reforms of 1943. Reform was delayed at the Wilhelmstrasse until 1919. Then, with incredible energy, Schüler attacked the citadel of Imperial Germany. The area of recruitment was widened; outsiders were appointed to leading positions, a Department for Foreign Trade was created. Other states, before, during and after the war, introduced similar measures, strengthening career structures, expanding economic and commercial competencies, creating press departments, forging firmer links with parliamentary bodies. More hesitantly, states began to merge their home and overseas services and to break down the barriers between the diplomatic and consular career structures. Practices varied from state to state. The Italians abolished their internal administrative service in 1907 but did not create a single diplomatic–consular list until Mussolini's time (1927). The Swedish services were all integrated in 1976; in the Netherlands, a dual service structure (Ministry and foreign service) still exists in practice today.

The critiques and the reforms were markedly similar whether we are speaking of London, Paris, Rome, Brussels, The Hague, Stockholm or Copenhagen. Change was very much the order of the day. The timing differed, as did the importance of the reforms and the success of the innovations, but everywhere men were conscious of a changing environment to which they had to adapt. Physically, too, Foreign Ministries entered the twentieth century. Electric lights replaced smoking oil lamps, typewriters and female typists were introduced, and the telephone, that most radical of innovations, made its appearance in a few chosen rooms. In 1910 a new item appeared in the Quai d'Orsay budget, 'machines et moteurs'. It was a sign of the times.

The war represents an important watershed in this history. Relegated to a secondary place by their political and military leaders, Foreign Ministries were soon involved in commercial, maritime and propaganda activities, which had become central to the war effort. Foreign Secretaries and their officials suffered a diminution in prestige and reputation. The failure to prevent war weakened the confidence of the public and the professionals in the virtues of the 'old diplomacy'. Woodrow Wilson's appeals above the heads of traditional Foreign Ministries evoked a positive response not only in the Anglo-Saxon world but in continental Europe as well. The Bolshevik revolution, with its slogan of 'open diplomacy', further undermined those common assumptions shared by the upper classes in the pre-war world and raised fundamental doubts about the old system.

Yet there was no radical break with the past. The Germans continued to use the name Auswärtiges Amt, as they were to do again in 1950 when the

Wilhelmstrasse no longer existed. The new Ministry was to be revived but in a reformed guise. In Austria a vast imperial legacy had to be liquidated; though some officials continued to serve the new Republic, they were a shrunken group led by a succession of political Ministers. In Communist Russia, under Ivan Zalkind a new Commissariat emerged, staffed not by Tsarist diplomats but still by educated men with considerable foreign experience. Much was salvaged from the older structure. It was the purges of the 1930s that produced the sharpest break in the history of the new organization. An entirely different generation of officials had to be recruited and trained, men of modest backgrounds and little education who had never been abroad but were loyal Stalinists. One such figure, Andrei Gromyko, would rise to the very top of the ministerial ladder.

Among the victorious powers, during the early 1920s efforts were made to re-equip Ministries along new lines. Battles were fought to gain greater control over the conduct of economic affairs, which was already becoming the centre of European debate. Individual reformers sought to implement the recommendations of the business community and to carry out long-overdue changes in recruitment and staffing policies. Against a background of public criticism, the professionals attempted to re-establish their authority at home by expanding their competences and enlarging their spheres of influence. There were moments of success when Foreign Secretaries (e.g. Austen Chamberlain) regained effective control over the conduct of affairs, and ambassadors (e.g. Joseph Grew, the American ambassador in Japan) influenced the formulation and execution of policy.

The war and the peace, particularly the creation of the League of Nations, had an even more positive effect on the smaller powers. Belgium, the Netherlands, Luxembourg, Switzerland and the Scandinavian countries were all forced to reconsider their neutral positions and isolationist traditions. Many strengthened and expanded their Ministries and overseas services. Most joined the League and sent representatives to Geneva who achieved international prominence on this larger and more public stage. The League experience was of considerable importance; League of Nations departments were far more influential in such states than those at the British Foreign Office and the Quai d'Orsay, which became bureaucratic backwaters. At Geneva, delegates became familiar with the techniques of multinational negotiations and, during the subsequent decade, dealt with social and economic questions that required a new and different form of international cooperation.

But these positive achievements could not reverse the loss of pre-war positions. Even at the Paris Peace Conference, the contributions of the Foreign Ministers and their officials were of secondary importance. The new form of 'summitry' left the professionals in the back rooms. The heads of states (often without their Foreign Ministers) met to settle post-war problems. Nor were the politicians the only successful rivals. Foreign Ministry officials were forced to contend with competing domestic departments and a whole range of specialists, in financial, economic, military and intelligence matters, over whom they had no control. The politicians increasingly called upon the services of private bankers, industrialists and even academic mandarins to arrange matters far too complicated for less expert negotiators.

There were other reasons why the promise of the immediate post-war period was not fulfilled. The public pressure that had forced Foreign Ministers to reform began to recede as domestic issues crowded out less immediate international problems. Financial stringency led to reduced budgets everywhere; new posts were abolished and reorganizations postponed or abandoned. Some reforms looked more impressive on paper than they proved to be in reality. Many did not survive the demand for retrenchment or the resistance raised by the older generation of officials who had only grudgingly accepted the new changes. Schüler's innovations, for instance, proved far too radical for those who had come of age in imperial days.

There was already in the 1920s a reaction in diplomatic circles against the illusions of Woodrow Wilson. In the major European capitals, Foreign Ministers were ambivalent towards the Geneva system and anxious to return to more conventional means of negotiation. The dangers of the 'new diplomacy' seemed far greater than those of the 'old'; it was easy to retreat when the issues were not dramatic and when concern could be limited to the professionals. Apart from the Soviet Union, there were few significant changes in the Foreign Ministries of Europe and many lost opportunities. Only some of the attempts to improve financial and economic competence proved to be successful. Such matters, so important in the inter-war period, were left to those outside. The action was elsewhere. The diplomats proved to be most successful when they could handle problems in the old way and by the old means. But they were not adequately equipped to face the complexities of a period in which new forms of international behaviour were being forged.

In a sense, the challenge of Hitler represented a backward step in the history of international relations. There was a return to balance of power thinking and bilateral diplomacy. Europe again became the chief focus of attention; the Sino-Japanese conflict faded in importance when measured against the German threat. American isolationism seemed to preclude any European role. Attention was focused on Germany and a new security system. Colonial and economic arrangements were only means by which the British hoped to arrive at a new political understanding with Hitler. The League of Nations had lost its political *raison d'être*, though delegates continued to assemble and the public, at least in Britain, continued to talk of collective security. The Manchurian and Ethiopian crises had revealed Geneva's political impotence; it was not only the great but the small powers who turned to traditional means to preserve their independence. There was a general retreat to older patterns of international behaviour.

This return did not result in a revitalization of the European Foreign Ministries. Mussolini and Hitler made use of their Ministries, where many shared their diplomatic aims. Franco and Salazar assumed control over the conduct of foreign affairs with little difficulty; almost the entire corps of the Spanish Republic joined the Franco forces. Neither in Britain nor in France did the professionals give a strong lead to their political heads. There were warnings and even sharp insights into what was happening, but when it came to the formulation of policy the bureaucrats spoke in uncertain terms and in muted voices. There were exceptions, but they were few and could be easily by-passed. As the crisis deepened, so did the divisions among officials. Even good professional advice would not have compensated for the weakness of the political leadership in France, nor would Chamberlain have been dissuaded from taking the diplomatic initiative if faced with greater opposition from the Foreign Office. The latter contributed to the decision-making process but never played the dominant role. It was the Treasury and the service departments who determined strategic priorities. Lord Halifax, the Foreign Secretary, and his permanent under-secretary read the European scene in the same way as Chamberlain, at least until after Munich.

During the Third Reich the Auswärtiges Amt became an instrument of Nazi diplomacy; in 1933 its members joined the Nazi party, and reaffirmed their allegiance in 1944 after the original records of their party membership were burnt. The Consulta followed Mussolini despite individual doubts about Italy's preparedness. The Austrian Foreign Ministry was closed; the Germans did not need Austrian diplomatic assistance abroad. Among the states defeated by the Nazis, some Ministries continued to function throughout the war, acting as channels of communication between the occupier and the occupied. Almost everywhere, there were two Foreign Ministries in existence – one at home, the other attached to governments in exile. The Belgians, Poles, Dutch, French, Greeks, Luxembourgers and Norwegians reconstituted their departments in Britain or in the western hemisphere. It was necessary to preserve a symbolic presence (archives were frequently removed from occupied countries), though these small groups of diplomats were rapidly involved in practical matters of more than a symbolic importance. Readers will find the treatment of the wartime experiences of particular interest; some of the accounts have been written by participants in the events recorded. Neutral countries, too, adjusted to the new order in Europe, though here there were fewer divisions and general support for political leaders.

As in the 1914–18 war, diplomatic questions gave way to military needs. With regard both to the planning of the war and the peace, the American State Department and the British Foreign Office had limited influence. In the case of the former, its officials put their mark on the United Nations and on the Japanese peace treaty but had far less to say when it came to the European settlements. There were the towering figures of Roosevelt and Churchill, to say nothing of Stalin. Roosevelt listened to many but took few into his confidence, and certainly not his ailing Secretary of State. The President enjoyed a certain amount of bureacratic competition, but he made his own decisions. Churchill was often at odds with Eden and reserved certain matters for his personal perusal. There was an impressive flow of papers from the Foreign Office. Nevertheless, Britain's weakness curtailed its ability to implement these policies and checked any major initiative of its own. In fact, the Foreign Office was later to be blamed for attempting to sustain too ambitious a role for a power of the second rank. The wartime meetings between the Big Three already suggested that the post-war world would look very different.

Thus far we have been speaking primarily of the European states covered in this volume. There are, however, a few nations about which something more needs to be added. China, Japan, Turkey and the United States were all, in some sense, peripheral to European affairs. Each, despite early contacts with foreigners, enjoyed relatively long periods of self-imposed isolation assisted by geographic and racial and religious distinctions. In the Turkish and Chinese cases, there was a certain contempt for the foreigner and deep reluctance either to recognize their presence or to go abroad to learn their ways. It was, apart from the United States, pressure from outside, from nations anxious to establish trading links, that forced each state in turn to recognize the need to regularize its external relations.

The acknowledged foundation dates for the Turkish (1836), Chinese (1861) and Japanese (1869) Foreign Ministries hardly do justice to the great differences in their rate of development. It was from the Interpreter's Room of the Grand Vizier that the Turkish Foreign Ministry traces its origins. But the highly centralized form of the Turkish government delayed any distinction between domestic and foreign affairs until the second half of the nineteenth century, and though the Ministry proved to be an extremely durable department, surviving ministerial and even revolutionary changes, it only slowly achieved the status of an independent and self-contained department of state. The Japanese evolution was far more rapid. A high degree of professionalism had been achieved even before the First World War, and in the subsequent decade there existed a well-structured department. The Foreign Minister was an experienced diplomat, supported by an élite that had been carefully recruited and trained and that was influenced by the internationalist sympathies of teachers and mentors. In the 1930s the Foreign Ministry proved unable to withstand the pressure from the military; outsiders came to rule the Department and inner conflicts weakened its position in the debates that preceded Japan's decision for war. In China, where the whole process of bureaucratic growth was far more erratic and incomplete, improvements in organization were repeatedly frustrated by the lack of a strong central authority, by internal upheavals and foreign interventions. Political turbulence continued to restrict the efforts made after the establishment of the Republic. And again, while important changes were introduced under the Nationalists, the outbreak of war led to dramatic cuts in the size of the Ministry (from 317 officials in 1930 to a staff of only 128 in 1938). The subsequent civil war weakened the potentially more efficient structure created in the interval.

In all three nations, linguistic problems remained central to the staffing of these departments. As all had to move in a European-dominated world (though American advisers had an important influence in China), they had to respond to alien cultures. The Turks recruited foreigners and subsequently benefited from their multinational composition. Competence in French, the official working language of the Ministry, was a *sine qua non* for entrance into the bureaucracy. In China, and above all in Japan, Americans and Englishmen played key roles as advisers and interpreters, though linguistic difficulties continued to complicate relations with outsiders throughout the inter-war period.

The American case is *sui generis*. After a brief flurry of diplomatic activity during the early years of the Republic, Americans took the advice of their first President and, guarded by the high seas and their ability to preserve and extend their hemispheric interests, turned their backs on European concerns. The United States was to be the Garden of Eden, untainted by the quarrels and corrupting influence of the Old World. Highly respected men served as

Secretaries of State, including future Presidents, but their departments were small (five in 1779, 15 in 1820, 52 in 1870) and diplomats exceedingly few. Almost from the start, there were democratic prejudices against the very concept of professional diplomacy. Consuls (whom the Republic was loath to pay) were more appropriate to a nation whose main interest in the outside world was commercial, a belief that persisted until the Second World War. Under such conditions, it is hardly surprising that the Department of State had an arrested development, and that only a few long-serving and devoted officials (W. W. Hunter, 1829–86, A. A. Adee, 1878–1924, W. Carr, 1892–1937) enabled it to handle an increasing workload. The Department was not totally exempt from the pressures for civil service reform in the Theodore Roosevelt era; in subsequent years, the merit principle was more extensively applied and the divisions were regrouped along geographical lines. It was only in the pre-war period (1905, 1909 and 1915) that the consular service was put on a career footing and the first steps were taken to professionalize the diplomatic service. There were serious setbacks, and the President continued to fill (with the Senate's approval) posts with political appointees and financial supporters.

As in the case of the European Ministries, and further stimulated by the expanding commercial interests of the nation, the period of the First World War was a time of considerable expansion and reconstruction. By the 1920s a competitively chosen, Ivy League-educated (Princeton, Harvard, Yale, but also Stanford), wealthy, cohesive body of professional diplomats had emerged that was much like its European model. In 1924 the Rogers Act laid the basis for a fused consular and diplomatic service, though it took some years for this amalgamation to be effected and for an increasing number of senior posts in the Department and abroad to be filled by Foreign Service officers. In the 1920s as well the Department, under successive Secretaries of State – Charles Evans Hughes, Frank Kellogg and Henry Stimson – enjoyed considerable influence in the shaping and execution of policy. Its subsequent eclipse under Franklin Roosevelt again paralleled European experience, though the career structure established under the Rogers Act was strengthened. There remained marked differences from practices elsewhere. Patronage continued to play an important part in the assignment of posts. The separation of powers and uneasy balance between the President and Congress complicated the formulation of foreign policy and involved a much wider domestic constituency in the conduct of foreign affairs than was customary in Europe. Thus the public prejudice against the 'cookie pushers' and 'striped pants brigade' was only reinforced by the professionalization of the service.

A word should be added about the histories of Ireland, Canada and Australia, all of which were slow to achieve diplomatic independence. The Irish Free State sent its first permanent representative to Washington in 1924; Canada opened its first legation in 1927, Australia only in 1940. Influence was exercised through the high commissioners and the Dominions Office in London. Even when international events underlined the need for foreign policy institutions of their own, development depended upon the will of the Prime Minister, who generally held the ministerial portfolios. In the Irish Free State, too, where the Department of Foreign Affairs began as a Propaganda Department during the Anglo-Irish war of 1919–21, it was the

President who conducted foreign policy; external affairs was only a part of the chief executive's entourage. Departments in all three states were small. Progress resulted from the efforts of a few pioneering officials (Joseph Pope and O. D. Skelton in Canada, Lt.-Col. W. R. Hodgson in Australia, Joseph Walshe in Ireland) who had to contend with powerful political heads and with considerable public hostility against diplomatic agents ('Iveagh House types', as they were called in Dublin). For all three, particularly Canada, it was the Second World War that proved to be the watershed in their respective diplomatic evolution.

The post-1945 world looked dramatically different from its pre-war predecessor. The attainment of super-power status by the United States and the Soviet Union and the eclipse of Britain ended the long period of European domination. The ideological differences and conflicting aims of the two Titans shaped the domestic struggles in Continental Europe. The division into two blocks shattered what remained of a Eurocentric consciousness and history, however divisive and tragic. The rapid post-war transformation in the balance of power took the diplomats by surprise. But the immediate problems of reconstruction left little time for future speculation.

Foreign Ministries were rapidly reconstituted. Old buildings were reopened and libraries and archives reassembled. Exiles returned home; such was the shortage of qualified staff that some wartime behaviours were forgotten and men with doubtful pasts returned to their old desks. By 1948, when the Marshall Plan was announced, the Foreign Ministries were prepared to take an active role. In time, and after a number of false starts, a new Auswärtiges Amt appeared in Bonn, with Chancellor Konrad Adenauer at its head. When the occupiers left Vienna, the Ballhausplatz was well prepared to resume the full range of its activities. In Tokyo, a purged Foreign Ministry was given a new legal status in the Constitution of 1947.

It was already clear that some form of internal reorganization would become necessary (the Eden reforms of 1943 in Britain were a beginning, as were General Marshall's unsuccessful efforts to streamline the Department of State). But in that immediate post-war period there was a tendency to look back with a certain sense of nostalgia to pre-war days. Despite their enhanced importance after Roosevelt's death, American foreign service officers were reluctant to take on new responsibilities in far-flung fields.

The period between 1945 and 1948 was one of transition as the Soviet Union and the United States sought to define their post-war positions. The United Nations, which was to provide a new focus for international debate, had barely begun to function when the breakdown of the American–Soviet relationship stifled its growth. In a very short time, it was this rivalry that extended the area of competition. Economic, financial, cultural, intelligence and military weapons were marshalled for use in the 'Cold War', the term itself unknown to an earlier generation. The Communist victory in China and the Korean War further enlarged the area of geographic involvement. The subsequent transformation of the former colonial territories into the Third World gave a new meaning to global diplomacy.

The impact of these events was greatest on the two super-powers. Despite its initial resurgence, the State Department could not sustain its claim to a dominant role in foreign policy-making. President Truman took advice, but it was not always the Secretary of State who had the President's ear. New and competing executive departments, much favoured by Congress, sprang into existence. The Department's unwillingness to accept the experts within its walls in the intelligence and cultural fields created a void that was rapidly filled. A new hierarchy of command was established outside Foggy Bottom, with the National Security Council, on which the Department had only one seat, as its apex. Poor leadership, unsuccessful reorganization, cuts in personnel and the attacks of Senator Joseph McCarthy led to the demoralization of the Eisenhower years. It was somewhat paradoxical that at a time when the country embarked on a new world role, the Department of State should have been entering a period of passivity and decline.

The Soviet case was somewhat different. Neither Stalin nor Khrushchev relinquished his tight control over the management of foreign affairs. Molotov and Gromyko were kept on short leads. Foreign negotiators complained of Soviet inflexibility and of long delays arising from the need to consult Moscow even on minor points. Yet it is clear that in the post-Khrushchev period the Soviet Foreign Ministry was visibly strengthened, its diplomats groomed for wider international responsibilities. The amount of formal training given to Soviet officials surpassed that offered to diplomats in the West. Under Gromyko's leadership, and assisted by a group of long-serving and highly experienced officials, Soviet diplomacy achieved senior status. Whatever the special problems resulting from its political and ideological orientation (a study of East European Ministries would be fascinating in this respect), it would be surprising if Soviet administrators did not share some of the same bureaucratic problems as their Western counterparts.

During the last thirty years, there have been repeated shifts in the international scene. The pace of change has been dizzying. The super-powers, instead of existing in a bipolar world, have had to adapt to a multi-national situation. There was China to be considered, and a multitude of middle and small powers who, either alone or in groups, now make their voices heard in the corridors of international power. There are, as we have said, 154 members of the United Nations, a far greater number than those represented at the League. And unlike those Geneva meetings, the delegates who come to New York represent states of entirely different cultures with sharply contrasted economic and political requirements. There is only a fragile consensus. There is no real *lingua franca,* the phrase itself having an ironic ring.

The striking rise in the number of national entities has been matched by the proliferation of subjects of international interest. The 1920s provided but a foretaste of the multitude of economic and social questions to be considered by multinational bodies. The diplomatic process has been broadened to include almost every field of human concern. A whole range of new fields, many stemming from the most recent advances in technology and science, appear on international agendas. Foreign Ministries, usually in cooperation with other government agencies, have become involved in aid and development programmes that demand new forms of expertise. Political reporting and negotiations, the heart of nineteenth-century diplomacy, now represents but one part of the diplomatic function.

The modes of negotiations have also multiplied. States are simultaneously engaged in bilateral, regional and multinational conversations, not to speak of a bewildering variety of *ad hoc* conferences lasting days, weeks or even months. There are embassies (the inflation of titles since 1945 corresponds to the inflation in number) to be maintained, permanent delegations to be staffed, regional meetings and specialized conferences to attend. In this profusion of bodies and subjects, traditional distinctions between domestic and foreign policy have become increasingly blurred. We have returned to the past, when home and foreign affairs were essentially one. Effective diplomacy depends on the mobilization of a home consensus as much as foreign agreement. This means the cultivation of contacts within and outside government circles and with a variety of interest groups, both public and private. For the negotiating process has even gone beyond national lines, and non-governmental groups are operating in the international arena. With the proliferation of states, subjects and actors, older categories, though not necessarily older primacies, have disappeared. Marcel Proust's M. Norpois would find himself in a bewildering world should he enter the doors of the Quai d'Orsay today, though the building and titles might strike him as familiar, and one of his technocratic grandsons might be receiving him.

The first response to these new conditions was an increase in the size of all diplomatic establishments. The rise in numbers continued throughout the next decades, despite temporary freezes on recruitment and often savage cuts in personnel. By 1978 the French were employing 6637 officials, more than 2000 serving at home, a fourfold increase in 30 years. The Austrian Foreign Ministry grew from 428 officials in 1947 to 1426 men and women in 1980, including 348 persons in the senior government service. Though others did not match this massive increase, even the less populous states were forced to expand, particularly as the Scandinavian and Benelux countries entered a far wider range of diplomatic responsibilities. This increase, inevitable as the number of independent states and multinational organizations proliferate, has altered the character of the élites of the past. Though the process of expansion has levelled off as a result of better administrative methods and legislative demands for economy (the Swiss Foreign Ministry has a legislative limit of 1756 employees), the sheer size of most present establishments precludes the familiarity of a previous age. Personnel offices and computers, organizational charts with multiple boxes connected by lines existing only in the administrator's imagination, have replaced the rule of a private secretary's office.

It was, of course, not sufficient to add men and departments to post-war establishments. Swollen complements and budgets created their own problems without solving old ones. The concluding sections of each of our chapters look arrestingly alike. Regardless of size or form of government, all Ministries face similar problems of organization and staffing. Indeed, it is somewhat surprising that they have not learnt more from each other's experiences. The commentators in this book have stressed certain areas of general concern: planning and coordination, the internal organization of business, the generalist–specialist division, reform and morale. They harbour few illusions about the present and future roles of Foreign Ministries. The world's leaders will continue to conduct negotiations at the highest levels; summit meetings and roving diplomacy have become a permanent part of international relations. The Foreign Ministry will remain only one of a multitude of governmental organizations concerned with foreign issues, while the number of private groups even of a non-national order can only increase. How can the prestige and bargaining position of the Foreign Minister and his department be strengthened?

The *ad hoc* and pragmatic nature of most decision-making in the international field has mitigated against the development of any long-range or predictive planning. Departments have attempted to correct this deficiency in various ways. Policy planning councils staffed by officials relieved of their departmental responsibilities have rarely fulfilled the hopes of their founders. Comprehensive reviews of foreign policy have been no more successful. Few have the time or the desire to read such weighty memoranda. Decision-makers prefer quick and immediate answers. Repeatedly such efforts have been abandoned despite the knowledge of the importance of long-range forecasting.

The problems of coordination are more immediately pressing. No Foreign Ministry has sole control over foreign affairs; all must engage in a bargaining process at home. A dynamic Foreign Secretary, it is true, can make all the difference; so can a good committee man. It is not only that the Ministry needs to be represented on key committees, it must make its presence felt if the claim to being *primus inter pares* is to be sustained. In particular, the coordination of political and economic negotiation has become central to the position of the Ministry. In a country like the Federal Republic of Germany, the use of economic power is often a substitute for political diplomacy. Elsewhere, the whole range of economic and commercial negotiations represents a major part of the states' international interests. Leadership in this domain has taken on a new and continuing importance.

The Ministry must also maintain a presence in the intelligence, military, cultural and information fields, where independent agencies are both producers and users of Foreign Ministry information. The intelligence-gathering that used to be a traditional function of Foreign Ministries has generated numerous, partly esoteric organisms. The life of those organisms with or on the fringe of the open diplomatic fabric is proving one of the principal sources of current *malaise* and has put diplomatic staff directly in the line of fire. All Ministries are acutely aware of relations with parliamentary bodies and the citizenry at large. These requirements have produced a mass of joint committees, which in turn have created their own hierarchies and offshoots that, in the United States at least, have ultimately reduced the power of the Department of State.

A parallel situation exists in the overseas mission: a major embassy reproduces in miniature the complex organization of the central department. The large number of experts (often reporting to different agencies) attached to most embassies, and the rapid growth and importance of operational programmes, have weakened the traditional authority of the ambassador and placed a new weight on his managerial skills. At the same time, the explosion of tourism (in every sense of the word) has brought the pressure of the home constituency directly to bear on the representatives abroad.

Within the department, the tendency is to rely on senior officials to create coherent policies. The older forms of functional or geographic organization have given way everywhere to experiments in mixed organizations. Some states (Germany, Italy, Belgium, Holland) tend to favour the functional approach where political, economic, cultural–scientific–technical, developmental, and administrative business is divided into separate directorates, underlining the importance of the subject to be handled and the need to concentrate the expertise of the department in subject areas. Other states (Britain traditionally, France and Portugal currently) have moved towards a geographic division where *all* questions (particularly the political and economic ones) with regard to one country or area can be seen as a whole. Even in these Ministries, there must be functional departments where expert knowledge is available with regard to subjects that need to be treated multilaterally – i.e. international organizations, strategic and atomic affairs, overseas nationals, and some forms of commercial negotiation.

All states, moreover, have a series of technical directorates associated with the running of the diplomatic machine where the mechanics of diplomacy (people as well as processes) are handled. In practice, most states have opted for the system that provides some degree of flexibility. A comparison of organizational charts illustrates not only the high number of departments or directorates, sometimes with some seventy major subdivisions, but the variety of approaches to the functional/geographic problem. Whatever system is adopted, cross-referencing becomes essential for any unit of direction. It is not always the largest Ministries that have the most complicated substructures. Some charts border on the ludicrous; the Ministry functions despite them. Others obscure the fact that it is at the top of the chart, in the expansion of the Minister's cabinet or the secretary-general's office, that the real concentration of responsibility and influence is to be found.

It is a truism that no department is better than the men who staff it. It is for this reason that the generalist/specialist issue has raised the most heat in professional circles. Staffs everywhere are now recruited by competitive examinations. Even where the 'old boy network' survives and Ministries have failed to shed their upper-class (now upper middle class) image, it has proved necessary to open the doors and seek a wider pool of entrants. There remains a considerable debate about what kind of recruit is needed, with what form of training and at what level of entrance. Most Ministries still look for the generalist, university-educated but with broad interests; states like the Soviet Union have their own pre-entrance educational programmes.

Nevertheless, all have had to recruit an increasing number of specialists, and administrators everywhere are seeking for ways to keep and reward such men in a service where the top positions still tend to go to the all-rounder. Again, most departments have opted for a compromise solution; the consequences are an uneasy hybrid that endlessly complicates the problem of staffing. One can appreciate the feelings of that Canadian 'who waits for the brief glorious hour or day, seldom longer, when everyone is in place and the system is in equilibrium'.

Admittedly, these problems are hardest for the larger states. The smaller powers are forced to restrict their range. They have developed ways to economize on personnel while fulfilling their own needs and international obligations. Multiple postings have become common, mini-missions established, consular networks, often using honorary consuls, expanded. Some have developed specialized competences – the representation of states who have closed their embassies under duress, the servicing of specific regional or technical organizations. As, everywhere, parliamentary pressures for economy mount, these practices are increasingly being copied by more powerful neighbours as well.

The search for answers to these questions has led to endless investigations and reorganizations in recent years. Some of the Ministries covered in this book have been the object of too many surveys (eight committees in four years goes beyond even bureaucratic tolerance) with few positive results. Too often change has complicated the administrative apparatus at the expense of departmental morale. There have been times when necessary reforms have been blocked by small groups or when even departmental reformers have been defeated by bureaucratic inertia. But it is equally clear that some Ministries have suffered from an overdose of administrative experimentation. Even the most talented men will find the lines of communication, both vertical and horizontal, seriously blocked. News from the field does not reach the desk of the decision-maker; departmental decisions are modified or reversed as they move upward and outward. The leaders of the nations make decisions that do not really benefit from the mass of expertise at their disposal.

The problems of reorganizing staff are compounded by the present state of morale in Ministries subject to political harassment and administrative revolutions. At best, the diplomatic life has shed its nineteenth-century image. Only the chosen few, and then they may not be career men, live on the scale of their aristocratic ancestors. The large number of posts in remote, unhealthy or hostile states more than balance the advantages of life abroad. The rise of terrorist attacks and the collapse of rules, accepted everywhere in the Europe of the past, pose security problems of an entirely different order than those of protecting safes and ciphers from spying valets or master cryptologists. There is the natural wish to be where the action is, at the central Ministry, rather than at the end of the telex machine. There remains a serious gap between the popular image of diplomacy and the reality. Politicians still attack those 'who feed at the public trough and see exotic places at government expense'. Though demanding a wide range of men and services, legislatures are rarely generous with men whose highest achievements are often of a negative kind. Foreign services have limited domestic constituencies and are natural targets for budgetary cuts.

Though we rightly speak of diminished influence and multiple rivals, Ministries everywhere have outgrown their inter-war quarters. Where the once palatial buildings are still in use, as in London, the rooms are over-crowded, halls used for storage, the library and archives miles away. The Quai d'Orsay houses only part of its Department; offices are located elsewhere – with one even in Nantes. In Washington, and more recently in Canada, the Netherlands, and in Copenhagen new, purpose-built structures have been erected so that all the work can be centralized in a single place. The Syngros residence in Athens has a Neo-classical extension built in 1933 and an ultra-modern wing opened in 1979. This is more than a commentary on Greece's new international role, it is symbolic of the present diplomatic situation everywhere. The older edifices are used for those social functions that are still part of the embassy scene; the new wings reflect the more utilitarian concerns of the modern period.

Does all this matter? Will these new buildings house future dinosaurs? The Cassandras may be wrong. No state is strong enough or weak enough to live in splendid isolation. All will need negotiating agents. The old forms and skills will be preserved though new techniques and functions will be developed. The new requirements will not eliminate those of the past. On the contrary, recent events have underlined their centrality. The advice given to aspiring diplomats in the works of Abraham de Wicquefort (1679) and François de Calliéres (1716) is as pertinent today as when these manuals of instructions were first written. It is with good reason that Ernest Satow's *Guide to Diplomatic Practice* (1919) was updated and reissued in 1979. The old and new coexist in an uneasy relationship – political departments with functional ones, bilateral with multilateral negotiating agents. The flying mission has not replaced all resident posts, few ambassadors have become hoteliers and amateur travel agents, the trade promotion expert has failed to unseat the political analyst. The spread of American English has not reduced the importance of language competence. No state has as yet permanently closed its Foreign Ministry.

The attempts at adaptation will persist. There can be no ideal solutions in a context of ever-accelerating planetary change. Administrative structures do not create. They can only speed or inhibit the flow of new ideas. But it is clear that the current situation exhibits a fascinating coexistence of continuity and experiment. This is why a comparative study of the evolution and operation of Foreign Ministries will have its relevance for the practitioner as well as the theorist, for the sociologist as well as the historian.

Only a small number of the world's Foreign Ministries are included in this volume. In this sense, it is only the start of what should be a much larger enterprise. Apart from the wish to build on a core of states with long histories and European connections (the omission of the Latin American countries was due only to lack of space), my selection has been influenced, above all, by the availability of experts with access to the material willing to produce concise chapters instead of books.

The men who have contributed to this volume represent different disciplines and backgrounds. As the biographical entries indicate, some are historians, others archivists and librarians, practising or retired civil servants, and diplomats. Some are nationals of the countries studied while others are specialists working from outside. This variety of interests and outlooks, as well as the often fragmentary quality of the archival material, explains the wide variety of approach and coverage. There are, consequently, gaps in the narrative. Nevertheless, the book has been enriched by this multiplicity of approaches to the study of diplomatic institutions. Apart from providing the original brief and raising inconvenient questions, I have left each author free to handle the problem of coverage in his own way.

It is fitting that in such a book the most difficult problem has been one of translation. Too often, the cadence and nuance of the original text has been lost. It has proved, moreover, exceedingly difficult to find the right equivalents for official nomenclatures and technical terms. The standardization and translation of ministerial charts, generously provided by the Ministries, only illustrates the importance of the ability to understand, interpret correctly and render accurately – one possible definition of the diplomatic art. I wish to acknowledge the very special contribution of Mrs

Candida Hunt, the sub-editor of this volume, who has had to contend with the vagaries of the English language, the world post, and the general editor. Barry Winkleman of Times Books has sustained this project in every way from its inception until its completion and Dörthe Henning of Times Books has carried more than her share of the secretarial labours. Above all, I want to thank all the contributors, for without them a long-cherished idea could not have been brought to fruition. For many, these essays should be a starting point for future research. The editor, at least, has considerably enlarged her working horizons.

Australia

The Department of
Foreign Affairs

ALAN WATT

Sir Alan Watt has enjoyed a distinguished career at the Department of
Foreign Affairs in Canberra, Australia. Sir Alan was born in 1901
and was educated at Sydney and Oxford Universities. After practising
as a barrister, he joined the Department in 1937 and served as first
secretary in Washington (1940–5), as delegate to the UN General
Assemblies, 1946 and 1947, as minister (1947–8) and then ambassador
(1949–50) to the USSR, and as ambassador to Japan (1956–60) and to
the Federal Republic of Germany (1960–2). He also served as Assistant
Secretary (Political) and Secretary (1950–3) in the Department of
External Affairs, Canberra. He was awarded the CBE in 1952. His
publications include *The Evolution of Australian Foreign Policy 1938–
1965* (1967), *Vietnam* (1968), *Memoirs* (1972) and *The United Nations*
(1974).

Although Canada opened a legation in Washington within a year of the Balfour Declaration of 1926 and South Africa established embassies in Washington, Rome and The Hague in 1929, it was not until 1940 that Australia opened in Washington its first diplomatic mission to a foreign country. Why this long delay?

The fundamental reason was the different ethnic composition of the population of Australia. Unlike Canada and South Africa, there were in Australia during the 1920s and 1930s no large, politically influential, non-British groups speaking a European-derived language other than English, with strong and persistent sympathies for the land of their forbears making them less disposed to remain tied to British apron-strings. Australia had been settled and developed predominantly by people from the British Isles. Until the Second World War, many Australians still thought of Britain as 'home', despite the fact that the Irish brought with them anti-British feelings and that the discovery of gold in the 1850s attracted a proportion of non-British Europeans and Americans and a number of Chinese. There were, of course, approximately 100 000 people of aboriginal descent, but they were scattered, without central organization, and without votes or any influence upon the direction of Australian foreign policy until a more recent period in Australian history.

In 1914, it was a Labor Party leader, Andrew Fisher, who promised to support Britain to 'the last man and the last shilling'. Hundreds of thousands of Australians volunteered to fight in Europe and the Middle East during the First World War, and more Australians were killed on the battlefield than Americans. Australia's future was seen as part of the British Empire, whose overall security was regarded as essential to Australia's survival.

The attitude of non-Labor Party governments towards separate diplomatic representation overseas was expressed most clearly by R. G. Menzies, then Attorney-General in the Lyons Government, during the Munich debate in 1938. 'I have always believed', he declared, '. . . that the British Empire exercises its greatest influence in the world . . . when it speaks with one concerted voice.' It would be 'suicidal' for a Dominion to formulate a foreign policy and announce it, whether or not it was in line with that of Great Britain. Australia should be able to 'say useful things at the right time' to the United Kingdom for consideration in determining Empire policy as a whole.

The Labor Party was not anti-British, but by 1938 it had become more isolationist. During the Munich debate John Curtin, leader of the Labor Party opposition, declared that '. . . the Labor Party . . . is opposed in principle and in practice to Australians being recruited as soldiers in the battlefields of Europe.' The best service Australia could render to the British Empire was 'to attend to its own business', manage Australia effectively and be able to rely upon itself in emergency.

Australia fully supported Neville Chamberlain's policy, which led to the Munich agreement. However, Hitler's subsequent entry into Prague and Australian fears of Japanese expansionism forced an important reappraisal of the Government's attitude towards the establishment of diplomatic missions overseas. In his first broadcast to the nation as Prime Minister, delivered on 26 April 1939, Menzies coined a significant new phrase: 'What Great Britain calls the Far East is to us *the near north*.' 'In the Pacific,' he added, 'we have primary responsibilities and primary risks . . . I have become convinced that in the Pacific Australia must regard herself as a principal, providing herself with her own information and maintaining her own diplomatic contacts with foreign powers . . .' This was the authoritative statement following which Australia began, in 1940, its long-delayed voyage upon the wide seas of international diplomacy.

The trend towards an independent Australian foreign policy was greatly strengthened when Japan entered the Second World War and its forces moved south with unexpected speed and success. The Labor Party came to power in Canberra in October 1941, some two months before Pearl Harbor. France had fallen; Australian army divisions were far from home, fighting in the Middle East; Britain's power to reinforce and hold Singapore had been greatly reduced. On 27 December 1941 Prime Minister Curtin made a public appeal to the United States that offended Winston Churchill and caused uneasiness in sections of Australian opinion. 'Without any inhibitions of any kind,' he declared, 'I make it quite clear that Australia looks to America, free of any pangs as to our traditional links of kinship with the United Kingdom.' The contrast between this statement and that made by Andrew Fisher in 1914 is self-evident. In the meantime, the world had suffered a sea-change. In the Far East British power and prestige was being undermined and the Australian continent was under direct threat for the first time in its history; Australia had to fight for its life, concentrate its own resources and seek military help wherever it could be found.

The Department of External Affairs, renamed the Department of Foreign Affairs in 1970, was born early but had an arrested childhood. When the six Australian states federated to form the Commonwealth of Australia in 1901, Section 51 of the Constitution provided that exclusive powers granted to the Commonwealth should include 'External Affairs' and 'Relations of the Commonwealth with the Islands of the Pacific'. External Affairs was one of the seven original Departments of State created. Not surprisingly, its political head was the first Australian Prime Minister. The British government had responsibility for the conduct of foreign policy for the Empire, and Australian Prime Ministers were regarded as the appropriate members of Cabinet to communicate Australian views to London. After 1932 it became the rule for a separate Minister for External Affairs to be appointed, and since that date Prime Ministers have held the External Affairs portfolio, for limited periods, on only two occasions.

The first Secretary (permanent head) of the Department of External Affairs, selected by Prime Minister Barton, was Atlee Hunt, a practising barrister aged thirty-six. An Australian historian, Professor La Nauze, has described him as an 'intelligent, well-educated man', 'the permanent official most closely associated throughout with the Prime Minister' for the first decade of the Commonwealth. Hunt held the respect of successive Prime Ministers, Alfred Deakin praising him as a man of 'judgement, loyalty and unflagging zeal'. With minimal staff, he drafted for consideration by his political masters 'dispatches' to the governor-general (then the channel of communication with London), while his private correspondence with organizations and individuals, especially regarding Papua, provide further testimony to the active part he played in the execution of government policy.

In 1904 a Prime Minister's 'Office' was created within External Affairs, but it was not until 1911 that a distinct Prime Minister's Department was established. The Department of External Affairs was abolished in 1916, but in 1919 a Pacific Branch was created within the Prime Minister's Department to deal with mandates under the League of Nations and other matters relating to the Pacific. Although Prime Minister W. M. Hughes re-established External Affairs as a Department in 1921, he assumed that portfolio in addition to the Prime Ministership, while the Secretary of the Prime Minister's Department also acted as Secretary of the Department of External Affairs until 1935. During this period, therefore, External Affairs was in effect merely a branch of the Prime Minister's Department.

An Australian High Commission was created in London as early as 1910, responsible to the Prime Minister's Department after the latter's establishment, but the functions of the High Commissioner were largely concerned with financial and commercial matters until the second half of the 1930s. The Chanak crisis of 1922, however, raised doubts about the adequacy of existing consultative relations with the British Government, and Prime Minister S. M. Bruce made arrangements for Allen Leeper, an Australian-born member of the British Foreign Office, to visit Australia to report on improved machinery for the conduct of Australia's external relations.

Following Leeper's report, two senior appointments were made to External Affairs from a strong field of applicants who could satisfy stated criteria, though not by way of special examination. Walter Henderson, who had earned a doctorate of law at the Sorbonne and studied political science in Paris, was based in Melbourne, then the seat of the Commonwealth Government. R. G. Casey, a Cambridge graduate in mechanical engineering with a good war record and considerable overseas experience, was sent to London in 1924 as Australian liaison officer and ensconced in the British Cabinet Office in Whitehall. His primary task was to keep in close touch with British officials and to report direct to the Australian Prime Minister on British policy in the formative stage, in order to allow time for Australian views to be expressed in London before such policy crystallized and became virtually a *fait accompli*. In due course, after Australia had established a number of diplomatic posts abroad, External Affairs representation in London was concentrated in the office of the High Commission, External Affairs officers functioning as members of the High Commissioner's staff without direct responsibility for reporting to the Australian Prime Minister.

In 1937 F. K. Officer, who had acted as External Affairs officer in London for three and a half years, was appointed Australian counsellor on the staff of the British ambassador in Washington, who had the right to see all communications sent to Australia. This arrangement held until Australia opened a legation in Washington in 1940, when he was transferred to the staff of the Australian minister, Casey, who had by then resigned a Cabinet post to take up the Washington appointment.

Meanwhile, in Australia the Department of External Affairs had finally been divorced from the Prime Minister's Department in 1935. Lt.-Col. W. R. Hodgson, a career army officer who had been badly wounded at Gallipoli, and who subsequently concentrated upon intelligence work and acquired law and accountancy qualifications, was appointed Secretary and began to build up a fully fledged foreign office, staffed by men with tertiary training and, where available, overseas experience. An organization chart of 1936 (Appendix A) shows that the Department then consisted of a Secretary and seven career officers, all with tertiary qualifications. They included some officers already in the public service, but also two graduates of the University of Oxford recruited without examination. By this time the Department was offering serious advice on foreign policy to the Government, and drafting parliamentary speeches for the Prime Minister and for the Minister for External Affairs.

During the early stages of the Department's development, while its officers were acquiring experience at home and abroad, Australian governments chose as heads of overseas missions non-officials who had made their mark in politics, law or other professions. For many years London and Washington were regarded as 'Cabinet' posts, at least when suitable men were available. Ex-Prime Minister S. M. Bruce served his country with great distinction as High Commissioner in London from 1933 to 1945. Following Casey's appointment to Washington Sir John Latham, Chief Justice of the High Court and a former Minister for External Affairs, was sent to Tokyo (1940) and Sir Frederic Eggleston, a Victorian solicitor and parliamentarian, was appointed to China (1941). It was not until 1945 that the first departmental career officers became heads of mission in Paris and Ottawa respectively. Since 1970 four senior Foreign Affairs officers have served as ambassador in Washington, while in 1975 a career public servant (not from Foreign Affairs) was appointed High Commissioner in London.

The development of the Department of External Affairs after 1936 is best seen against the background of the Second World War, the foreign policies of the main political parties and the personalities of three significant Ministers for External Affairs: Dr H. V. Evatt, P. C. (later Sir Percy) Spender and R. G. (later Lord) Casey.

Labor Party policy during its period in office from 1941 to 1949 was dominated by its Minister for External Affairs and Attorney-General, Dr Evatt. Until 1943, Evatt's primary preoccupation was to secure maximum military aid from the United States and Britain for the defence of Australia. Thereafter, he fought to secure an appropriate voice for Australia in post-war settlements, especially in the Pacific, while during and after the formation of the United Nations Organization he concentrated largely upon its activities.

Most leading Labor Party politicians have graduated into politics from the trade union movement. Evatt, a 'white-collar' man, was atypical. After a brilliant academic record in arts and law, he was appointed to the High Court Bench by a Labor government at the unprecedented early age of thirty-six. He resigned this position in 1940 to enter federal politics.

In 1943 Evatt decided to introduce an External Affairs 'cadet' scheme, under which non-graduates were selected after written examinations higher than those required for entry to the public service Clerical and Administrative (Third) Division as a whole, and were given special training courses – first at Sydney University and later at the Canberra University College – before appointment to the Department as third secretaries. Such watering down of qualifications on entry may possibly have been unavoidable during a period of acute civilian manpower shortage, but the results were not always satisfactory. By 1948 recruitment of university graduates became the rule once more, the written examination for entry was dispensed with, and selection was based upon extensive personal interview, although a minor essay and précis test is still given to a small group among applicants from which final selections are made.

Evatt had an almost pathological suspicion of anyone who had had close political or official relations with the previous government. Before his first visit to Washington as Minister in 1942, he sent a message by secret telegram to the legation with instructions that it was to be deciphered and delivered by the most junior diplomatic officer to an influential American. By implication, no one else was to see it – including the head of mission, R. G. Casey, who a few months later decided to accept Winston Churchill's offer of appointment as British Minister of State in the Middle East, with a seat in the British War Cabinet.

After Evatt's arrival in Washington, legation diplomatic staff were not informed of the results of his interviews with American political leaders or officials, nor allowed to see telegrams sent by him to Canberra. A second secretary who had served briefly as private secretary to R. G. Menzies was removed from Washington to wartime Kuibyshev (USSR) before the year ended. The effect upon departmental morale of this kind of treatment can easily be imagined.

When Lt.-Col. Hodgson was appointed head of mission in Paris in 1945, Evatt selected W. E. Dunk to succeed Hodgson as Secretary of the Department of External Affairs. This was a curious appointment, as Dunk's previous public service experience had been in financial and auditing fields, though during the war he had been in charge of reciprocal lend-lease, which involved detailed relations with the United States. After two years Dunk found that he could not work under Dr Evatt, and became chairman of the powerful Public Service Board. In his place the Minister appointed an External Affairs officer, aged thirty-two, who had been his private secretary but had never served at a diplomatic post overseas. He held this position for three years, became High Commissioner to Ceylon, but resigned after a couple of months to stand for federal Parliament as a member of the Labor Party. Defeated in the election, he chose not to exercise his option to apply for re-entry into the public service.

In December 1949 the Liberal–Country Party Coalition came to power and held office for no less than twenty-three years, during seventeen of which R. G. Menzies was Prime Minister. It was during this period that the Department of External Affairs became a coherent and effective foreign office and achieved a notable degree of stability and self-confidence. By this time able and experienced Australians, including several Rhodes scholars, had been attracted to its ranks and were beginning to make their mark. They were recruited on their record and after interviews, not by examination; promotion was based upon conceived merit; there was speedy opportunity for advancement during a period of expansion of overseas posts. Despite occasional charges that the Department's selection process favoured candidates from private (fee-paying) schools, there is no credible evidence that officers from state schools were disadvantaged in their careers. Indeed, since 1950 no less than four out of six heads of the Department were educated at 'state' schools.

Since 1950 all those appointed to the post of Secretary of the Department have been senior career officers from its own ranks with substantial overseas experience. Most heads of diplomatic missions overseas have been selected from the same group, though occasional appointments are still made of ex-Cabinet ministers and senior armed forces personnel.

With the change of government in 1949, relations between Ministers for External Affairs and their departmental advisers improved greatly, while relations between External Affairs and the Department of Defence, which had been mutually suspicious and minimal during the Evatt regime, drew much closer. In the early 1950s the Secretary of the Department of External Affairs was made a member of the Defence Committee when defence issues that involved foreign policy were being considered. This arrangement led to direct contact with the three chiefs of staff, as well as the Secretary for Defence.

The new Government had come to power on a strongly anti-Communist platform, following upon a disastrous strike at home by Communist-controlled coalminer unionists and, abroad, Communist victories and insurgencies in Asia and the Cold War in Europe and across the Atlantic, which led to the formation of NATO. Whereas Dr Evatt had aspired to be the leader of the small and middle powers within the United Nations, seeking to limit a great power dominance in the world at large, Menzies was far more sceptical of UN activities and preferred to rely more upon 'the support of great and powerful friends' – primarily Britain and the United States. His first Minister for External Affairs was Spender, a successful Sydney barrister, whose initiatives and achievements were impressive even though he held the portfolio for only sixteen months before being appointed to Washington as Australian ambassador.

Spender was substantially responsible for negotiation of the ANZUS security treaty with the United States and New Zealand and for devising the Colombo Plan, under which economic aid and technical assistance was to be granted to developing countries in South and South-East Asia. Under this plan, literally thousands of students, mainly from Asian countries, have spent extended periods in Australian educational establishments, while overseas development assistance is now an important function of the Department of Foreign Affairs, with a staff in Australia of 468.

It was inevitable that Australian foreign affairs priorities should change after the Second World War. Diminishing attention was given to Middle East security problems, and much more to similar problems in the Pacific and in eastern Asia. Australia contributed land, sea and air forces during the Korean War; became a party to the South-East Asian Collective Defence Treaty Organization (SEATO); took the unprecedented step of stationing military forces in Malaya in time of peace: and participated in the war in Vietnam. After a short, goodwill visit to South-East Asia in 1951, Casey, who had succeeded Spender as Minister for External Affairs and who held that portfolio until 1960, recommended to the Government that diplomatic relations with all the countries of the area should be built up. This recommendation was approved, and while it was gradually being carried out a former head of the Department was sent to Singapore for two years (1954–6), with direct representational responsibilities in Singapore, Malaya and the British Borneo Territories, and a degree of coordinating responsibility for South-East Asia as a whole.

A restructuring of the Department in February 1951 reflected the new governmental priorities and pointed the way to future departmental expansion in more specialist directions. Three assistant secretaries were appointed, responsible respectively for (1) a number of divisions, each dealing with a particular geographical region, with emphasis on the Pacific area; (2) United Nations questions, questions of international organization and policy aspects of economic relations (including the Colombo Plan); and (3) administration of the Department and its overseas posts, consular matters and protocol. There was also provision for appointment of a counsellor to deal with questions of international law and treaties. In the words of the Minister of the day, 'The new arrangement gives the permanent head greater freedom to concentrate on major questions and by making possible an appropriate delegation of authority in other matters, will relieve him of many routine responsibilities.'

During the 1950s relations with Japan were a primary preoccupation of Australian governments. Harsh Japanese treatment of Australian prisoners during the Second World War had created great bitterness against Japan in Australian public opinion, which would have resented strongly the 'soft' peace treaty with Japan negotiated by John Foster Dulles if Australians had not been substantially reassured by the concurrent negotiation of the ANZUS treaty. When a soft treaty had become a *fait accompli*, however, and against the background of the Korean War and instability in South-East Asia, the Australian government, without public announcement, made a deliberate decision to try to improve relations with Japan within the gradually extending limits that public opinion would be likely to tolerate. One of the important steps taken that is often overlooked was the posting to Tokyo of a succession of senior and experienced career ambassadors, which coincided with the appointment of similar Japanese ambassadors in Canberra. Together they made a significant contribution to the establishment of the close working relations at both ministerial and official levels that today characterize consultation between the two countries. Signature of a trade agreement in 1957, leading to a vast increase in mutual trade, marked a watershed in post-war Australian attitudes to Japan.

The developments outlined above vastly improved the flow of information available to governments regarding the problems of Australia's 'near north', and substantially increased the expertise of foreign service officers in Asian affairs, while at the same time providing many career opportunities. Yet, although conditions of service overseas for Australian diplomats improved considerably during the Menzies regime, the Department of External Affairs was not without its problems.

The Public Service Board, established by Act of Parliament at the time of federation, was given and has retained the responsibility of making all decisions of substance upon staffing and conditions of service not only of all departmental officers serving in Australia, but also for those serving abroad. The Board's natural instinct is to lay down uniform conditions for all public servants without sufficient understanding of the special problems that arise overseas, despite periodic visits to overseas posts by Board inspectors. Further, the old-established Department of the Treasury continued to impose strict and rigid financial controls on overseas missions, and to grant minimal discretion to heads of mission.

In its detailed submission to the Royal Commission on Australian Government Administration, appointed in 1974, the Department of Foreign Affairs gave examples of the frustration experienced in carrying out its functions because of delays caused by the need to secure Public Service Board and Treasury approval for alterations in staff numbers and conditions of service made necessary by sudden changes abroad, such as devaluation of the currency. In addition, the Department expressed dissatisfaction with the degree of recognition and acceptance of its coordinating functions in regard to foreign policy by a few well-established departments with overseas responsibilities, such as those dealing with trade, energy and immigration matters. It argued that, whereas in the earlier years after the Second World War the Department was concerned principally with politico-security problems, changes in the international environment had now increased the importance of economic problems, regarded by other departments as their primary responsibility. The Department of Foreign Affairs found the 'present system of consultation' with such departments 'too spasmodic, incomplete and dependent upon voluntary initiatives' for efficient co-ordination of foreign policy as a whole.

Further, the submission claimed that some officers of other departments attached to overseas missions tended to 'regard themselves at a post as merely an overseas extension of their own Department', failing to keep the head of mission properly informed of their activities. In its report, the Royal Commission recommended that the Department of Foreign Affairs 'should be more fully informed and should be consulted or given the opportunity to contribute to policy formation whenever, in its opinion, there are significant international considerations'. At the same time the Commission warned against any exaggeration of international aspects and advocated 'negotiation and persuasion' as a means of settling interdepartmental differences. However, problems of coordination have continued since 1974, the extent of the department's influence varying with the nature of the economic subject-matter.

The resignation of Prime Minister Menzies in 1966 marked the start of a severe decline in the fortunes of the Liberal–Country Party coalition. Within a period of six years there were no fewer than three Liberal Prime Ministers, none of whom proved able to match the parliamentary or general political skill of Menzies. Instead, E. G. Whitlam, who became leader of the Labor Party in 1967, succeeded in establishing a personal dominance in debate. A barrister by training, like Dr Evatt, he had two qualities that Evatt lacked: the gift of effective speech, and a somewhat mordant wit that he used upon his political opponents with devastating effect. In addition, he was able to devise new policies that appealed to middle-of-the-road voters as well as to traditional Labor Party supporters.

The Labor Party came to power in the House of Representatives (though it did not control the Senate) in December 1972. No member of its large Cabinet had ever held ministerial office before, and many members were deeply suspicious of public servants who had advised more conservative governments for so long.

The new Prime Minister was his own Foreign Minister for almost a year, and speedily announced that his Government would move towards a 'more independent Australian stance in international affairs, an Australia . . . less militarily oriented and not open to suggestions of racism.' The Government recognized the People's Republic of China and withdrew its mission from Taiwan; completed withdrawal of Australian forces from Vietnam; downgraded SEATO and took steps in the United Nations and elsewhere to build closer links with Third World countries. Several new posts were opened abroad, including diplomatic missions in Hanoi and Pyongyang. The Prime Minister made extensive journeys overseas, becoming the first Australian Prime Minister to visit Peking and Moscow.

During the three-year regime of the Labor Party Government public service morale declined. Ministerial suspicion, fed by numerous ideologically committed advisers appointed to the personal staffs of Ministers, led to the side-tracking and replacement of several heads of departments and tension between such advisers and departmental officers. There was a marked increase in 'leakage' by public servants to the media of confidential information, which has increased considerably since the Whitlam Government lost office.

The Royal Commission on Australian Government Administration, dealing with the public service as a whole, recommended *inter alia* limitation of periods of tenure for departmental heads, better training in 'management' techniques, staff rotation of officers between departments and statutory bodies to gain wider experience and to stimulate initiative, and more lateral recruitment above junior levels. Although these recommendations may be justifiable as applied to 'home' departments, and some action along these lines had already been taken by the Department of Foreign Affairs, their suitability to a Foreign Office requires careful consideration. In particular, the primary function of the head of the foreign office is to act as his Minister's principal adviser on international issues, and managerial ability can be no more than a secondary function. To fulfil his primary role the head must have *lived* in a range of countries outside Australia.

In November 1975 the Government was dismissed from office by the governor-general, although it still had a majority of votes in the House of Representatives. Inflation had risen substantially; the budget was in large deficit; senior Ministers thought to have misled Parliament had been dismissed by the Prime Minister; for the first time in Australian federal history the Senate failed to grant Supply, whereupon the Government sought unorthodox means of obtaining finance. At the election the Liberal–Country Party Coalition was returned to office with majorities in both Houses of Parliament, and the new Liberal Party leader, Malcolm Fraser, became Prime Minister. He was firmly pledged to reduce inflation, cut government expenditure and reinvigorate private business activity, and these objectives have been pursued single-mindedly, despite a heavy increase in unemployment.

Fraser, a grazier with an Oxford degree in history, has accentuated the quasi-presidential style of government which began to be noticeable under Prime Ministers Gorton and Whitlam. His expanded Department can no longer be regarded as mainly a coordinating body as it now provides advice on a wide range of subjects, including economic matters and foreign affairs. The new Office of National Assessments, headed by a senior career Foreign Affairs officer, is under his jurisdiction, and was quickly directed to provide a new strategic assessment. Fraser travels overseas frequently, and himself announces most important Government decisions.

This Government, preoccupied with economic problems, has made no dramatic changes in other aspects of foreign policy. It is more sympathetic to the United States than its predecessor, and more critical of the USSR. Relations with the People's Republic of China have been maintained and developed, while Foreign Minister Andrew Peacock displayed a sensitive understanding of Third World problems and has tried to strengthen Australian ties with ASEAN. Close ties remain with Britain, despite the latter's entry into the EEC, diminished trade between Australia and the United Kingdom, and the substantial increase in the proportion of Australians of non-British origin.

Since the Fraser Government gained office, staff ceilings have been imposed each year throughout the public service. These have borne with particular severity on the Department of Foreign Affairs, the overall reduction in numbers amounting by 1979 to no less than 17.38 per cent.

As of 31 October 1978 total staff of the Department numbered 4530. Of these, 1648 were located in Australia, including 192 Foreign Affairs officers, 745 consular and administrative staff, 242 keyboard and technical staff, and 468 members of the Australian Development Assistance Bureau. Overseas there were 2882, consisting of 65 heads of mission, 204 Foreign Affairs officers, 227 consular and administrative staff, 26 engaged on development assistance work, and 2108 locally engaged staff. An organizational chart as of 16 May 1978 (Appendix B) shows the great expansion of the Department to cover present needs, including a small policy planning unit at present headed by an academic, a nuclear affairs division and a historical research unit. By February 1979 Australia was represented overseas by 49 embassies, 19 high commissions, 5 consulates-general, 2 commissions and 6 consulates.

Funds provided under the 1977–8 budget totalled approximately $A466 million, but no less than $A376¼ million of this sum was assigned for bilateral and multilateral economic aid abroad – a large proportion for now-independent Papua-New Guinea. Of the remaining approximately $A89 million, $A48 million was provided for overseas service. This amount has been insufficient for effective performance of an increased range of departmental functions; in Australia, all recruitment of junior officers to the Department was stopped for two years and was then resumed on only a minor scale.

Social changes in Australia have reduced the readiness of some officers to face a life abroad of constant change, isolation from friends, educational difficulties for children, climatic illnesses and, recently, physical risks from terrorists and hijackers. Employment opportunities in Australia for women have greatly increased; families have fewer children, and some wives pursuing professional careers of their own are reluctant to follow their husbands overseas where suitable employment might not be available. The divorce rate for Foreign Affairs officers has increased and some good young diplomats have resigned from the public service or have transferred to other departments or agencies.

In 1979 about one million Australians travelled overseas, putting great pressure upon limited numbers of consular and administrative staff at missions abroad, who are recruited originally to the Third Division of the public service at standards lower than those required for Foreign Affairs officers. While some have university degrees, and a few have attained high rank, the sufficiency of their training has been questioned and limitations upon their career opportunities tend to create dissatisfaction.

Finally, the Department of Foreign Affairs has been subjected to no less than eight reviews or inquiries since 1975, sometimes as part of inquiries into wider aspects of the public service. To sustain a sense of the importance of their role, its members badly need encouragement and support. Fortunately, the latest inquiry by the Senate Standing Committee on Foreign Affairs and Defence, while not uncritical of some aspects of departmental administration, has issued a report showing considerable sympathy for current departmental problems, including staff ceilings and finance. It has recommended, *inter alia*, greater use of middle and junior rank Foreign Affairs officers in the decision-making process, and better training and career structures for both consular and administrative and development assistance staff. In the Committee's opinion, the Department's role on interdepartmental committees should be reassessed to ensure better coordination of Australian overseas policy objectives.

It is to be hoped that the Government accepts and acts upon these recommendations. Australia, with a population of about 15 million people of predominantly European cultural traditions inhabiting a vast continent with significant resources, is permanently anchored off the south-eastern rim of Asia – one of the most turbulent areas of the world. Maintenance and encouragement of an effective diplomatic service is one of the vital elements in its continued survival in recognizable form.

BIBLIOGRAPHY

Documents on Australian Foreign Policy 1937–49, Vol. 1 (Canberra 1975), 544–55.

Submission by the Department of Foreign Affairs to the Royal Commission on Australian Government Administration (Canberra 1974).

Report of the Royal Commission (Canberra 1976).

Submission by the Department of Foreign Affairs to the Senate Standing Committee on Foreign Affairs and Defence (Canberra 1978).

Report of the Senate Standing Committee (Canberra 1979).

Geoffrey Hawker, R. F. I. Smith and Patrick Weller, *Politics and Policy in Australia* (Queensland 1979).

W. J. Hudson, *Australian Diplomacy* (Melbourne 1970).

W. J. Hudson and Jane North (eds), *My Dear P.M.; R. G. Casey's Letters to S. M. Bruce 1924–1929* (Canberra 1980).

Alan Watt, 'The Australian Diplomatic Service', in Gordon Greenwood and Norman Harper (eds), *Australia in World Affairs (1961–65)* (Melbourne 1968).

Alan Watt, *Australian Diplomat: Memoirs of Sir Alan Watt* (Sydney 1972).

AUSTRALIA – APPENDIX A

DEPARTMENT OF EXTERNAL AFFAIRS
(February 1936)

Secretary: Lt.-Col. W.R. Hodgson

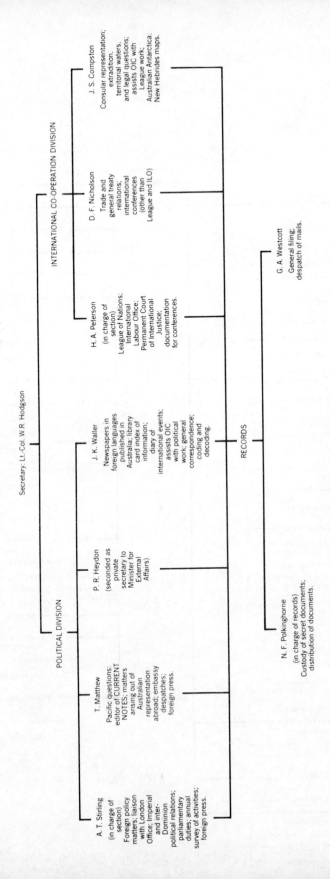

POLITICAL DIVISION

A. T. Stirling
(in charge of section)
Foreign policy matters; liaison with London Office; Imperial and inter-Dominion political relations; parliamentary duties; annual survey of activities; foreign press.

T. Matthew
Pacific questions; editor of CURRENT NOTES; matters arising out of Australian representation abroad; embassy despatches; foreign press.

P. R. Heydon
(seconded as private secretary to Minister for External Affairs)

J. K. Waller
Newspapers in foreign languages published in Australia; library card index of information; diary of international events; assists OIC with political work; general correspondence; coding and decoding.

INTERNATIONAL CO-OPERATION DIVISION

H. A. Peterson
(in charge of section)
League of Nations; International Labour Office; Permanent Court of International Justice; documentation for conferences.

D. F. Nicholson
Trade and general treaty relations, international conferences (other than League and ILO)

J. S. Compston
Consular representation; extradition, territorial waters, and legal questions; assists OIC with League work; Australian Antarctica; New Hebrides maps.

RECORDS

N. F. Polkinghorne
(in charge of records)
Custody of secret documents; distribution of documents.

G. A. Westcott
General filing; despatch of mails.

Deputy Secretaries

Defence
Defence Coordination
Liaison
Assessment
Defence Projects
Defence Policy
Plans & Policy
Joint Planning Staff
Disarmament

Management & Foreign Service
Administrative Services
Property & Office Services
Overseas & General Accounting
Audit
ADP
Personnel
Staffing Training & Heads of Mission
Conditions of Service
Administrative Post Liaison & Organization
Technical Services
Information Systems
Engineering & Development
Diplomatic Security
Communications
State Offices
Foreign Service Adviser

Adviser on Science, Technology & the Environment
Science, Technology & Environment

Chief of Protocol
Protocol

Editor of Historical Documents
Historical Research

Executive Secretariat
Policy Planning
Post Liaison & Guidance

Nuclear Affairs
Nuclear Safeguards
Nuclear Policy
Divisional Pool Positions

Legal & Treaties
General Legal & Treaties
General Legal
Treaties
International Legal
Law of the Sea & Antarctica
UN Legal

International Organizations & Consular
Consular, Immigration & Passports
Passports
Immigration
Consular
International Organizations
UN Social & Technical
UN Political
Commonwealth & Multilateral Organizations

Economic
Economic Policy
Transport & Resources
Commercial Policy
Economic Organizations
UN Economic Agencies
OECD/EC

SENATE STANDING COMMITTEE ON FOREIGN AFFAIRS & DEFENCE

DEPARTMENT OF FOREIGN AFFAIRS (May 1978)

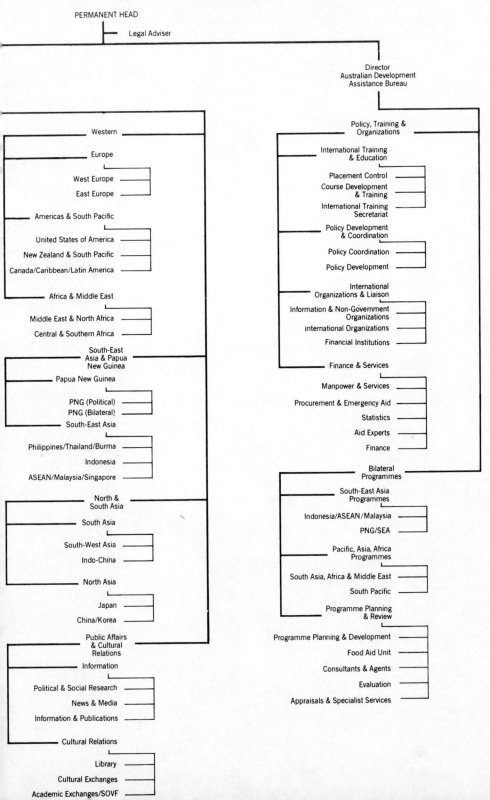

PERMANENT HEAD

Legal Adviser

Director
Australian Development
Assistance Bureau

Western

Europe

West Europe

East Europe

Americas & South Pacific

United States of America

New Zealand & South Pacific

Canada/Caribbean/Latin America

Africa & Middle East

Middle East & North Africa

Central & Southern Africa

South-East
Asia & Papua
New Guinea

Papua New Guinea

PNG (Political)
PNG (Bilateral)

South-East Asia

Philippines/Thailand/Burma

Indonesia

ASEAN/Malaysia/Singapore

North &
South Asia

South Asia

South-West Asia

Indo-China

North Asia

Japan

China/Korea

Public Affairs
& Cultural
Relations

Information

Political & Social Research

News & Media

Information & Publications

Cultural Relations

Library

Cultural Exchanges

Academic Exchanges/SOVF

Policy, Training &
Organizations

International Training
& Education

Placement Control

Course Development
& Training

International Training
Secretariat

Policy Development
& Coordination

Policy Coordination

Policy Development

International
Organizations & Liaison

Information & Non-Government
Organizations

International Organizations

Financial Institutions

Finance & Services

Manpower & Services

Procurement & Emergency Aid

Statistics

Aid Experts

Finance

Bilateral
Programmes

South-East Asia
Programmes

Indonesia/ASEAN/Malaysia

PNG/SEA

Pacific, Asia, Africa
Programmes

South Asia, Africa & Middle East

South Pacific

Programme Planning
& Review

Programme Planning & Development

Food Aid Unit

Consultants & Agents

Evaluation

Appraisals & Specialist Services

The Foreign Ministry of Austria and Austria–Hungary 1848 to 1918

HELMUT RUMPLER

Dr Helmut Rumpler is Professor for Modern and Austrian History at the Universität für Bildungswissenschaften Klagenfurt, Austria. He was born in 1935 and was educated at the University of Vienna where he completed his Habilitation in 1973. His books include *Das Völkermanifest Kaiser Karls vom 16 Oktober 1918* (1966), *Ministerrat und Ministerratsprotokolle 1848–1867* (1970) and *Die deutsche Politik des Freiherrn Friedrich Ferdinand von Beust 1848–1850* (1972). He is editing *Protokolle des österreichischen Ministerrates 1848–1867* (1970) and *Kärntens Volksabstimmung 1920* (1981).

The palace at 19 Ballhausplatz in Vienna was built in 1717 by Lukas von Hildebrandt, architect to Prince Eugene, on the site of the court dairy farms as a Secret Court Chancery (Geheime Hofkanzlei). In 1753, when Count Kaunitz assumed leadership of the State Chancery (Staatskanzlei), which had been founded in 1742, the 'Ballhausplatz', which took its name from the ball park that had been constructed there in 1743, became the centre of Austrian foreign policy. Metternich turned the bureaucratic apparatus, which Kaunitz had already organized superbly, into a perfectly functioning machine. Thus from 1753 Austrian foreign policy, at least, was centrally controlled under a Minister who was personally responsible for it. In accordance with the great importance of foreign policy for a multinational state, based on Germany, Italy and the Balkans, the State Chancery, and from 1848 the Foreign Ministry, increasingly became the intellectual, and in part also the institutional, fulcrum of Austrian – in the sense of Austrian imperial – policy. The Ballhausplatz was, probably to a greater extent than elsewhere in Europe, the field of action for the socially and politically dominant ruling classes in the Habsburg monarchy, i.e. those groups who identified themselves with the existence of the state as a great power in Europe, whether on economic, political or cultural grounds. The Austro-Hungarian 'Ausgleich' of 1867 and the intensification of the political and social divisions within the two halves of the empire, 'Cis- and Transleithanien', further increased the need for a centre of coordination for the collective policy of the empire. It was exactly because after 1867 there was no longer an 'imperial' government that the Ballhausplatz took on the role of imperial decision-making, in an informal yet effective manner.

In these political circumstances the Ballhausplatz was naturally the institution in which political continuity, from the European policy of a Prince Eugene up to the last struggles for existence during the First World War, found its most powerful expression. If there had been any changes in the state under Emperor Franz Joseph, it was least evident in the Foreign Ministry; so it was that the Ministry continued until 1918 in the organizational form in which it had been constituted in 1848. And the organization of 1848 by Foreign Minister Johann Philipp Wessenberg (1848) and then under Felix Schwarzenberg (1848–52) did not fundamentally produce anything new. In fact, the pre-revolutionary State Chancery simply received the new title of Ministry. The chancery directive of 1849 and the statute of organization of 1854 established a working procedure that was already standard practice in the pre-1848 State Chancery. And, despite a few restructurings, which continued into the 1890s, the Ministry remained until 1918 as it had been in 1848. The Foreign Ministry was also characterized by the principle of continuity in the policy regarding its employees. Just as Kaunitz had once retained Ignaz Koch, Prince Eugene's private secretary, as one of his most important colleagues, and as Metternich protected the famous decoder Wenzel Löschner in his circle of employees, so the changes of Ministers after 1848 hardly brought about any greater breaks in personnel. Not even in 1871, when the greatest and strictly speaking the only basic change in the Austro–Hungarian system of foreign policy occurred under Gyula Andrássy (1871–9), were new people brought in to handle the new course of cooperation with Germany, or those who had executed Friedrich Ferdinand Beust's (1866–71) confrontation policy dismissed. Only Richard Metternich in Paris, the cornerstone and centre of the pro-French orientation since 1866, was forced to make a demonstrative departure. And in 1895, when Agenor Goluchowsky (1895–1906) changed his first two department heads, this did not represent a change either in ministerial style or in the political line of its leadership. The many proofs of continuity are far more characteristic than the occasional alterations in personnel. While the '*homo novus*' did exist, occasionally in the Ministry and more rarely still in the diplomatic service, he was an exception. Normally, employment in the foreign service was almost a family affair. Indeed, once a new family had gained a foothold in the Foreign Ministry it was almost a rule that the sons, and even the grandsons, remained in this profession.

Thus the Ballhausplatz had no real history in the sense of a development during the nineteenth century. It was an institution so well established that it neither could nor needed to be substantially changed. In so far as there were any minor changes, the process stopped in 1870.

The stagnation and rigidity of the Ministry and its policy was evident from the fact that Ministers stayed in office for relatively long periods: Andrássy for eight years, Gustav Kálnoky for fourteen (1881–95), Goluchowsky for eleven and Aloys Aehrenthal for six years (1906–12) until his death. From 1912 to 1918 four ministers succeeded each other in quick succession. This was very different from the period before 1871, when with the exception of Carl Ferdinand Buol-Schauenstein no Minister remained in office for longer than five years. Only one decisive change occurred after 1870, which reveals the general political importance of the Ministry: the number of civil servants increased dramatically. The number of higher officials (department heads, ministerial advisers, department counsellors, ministerial secretaries, clerks) rose from 42 in 1860 to 51 in 1895, 92 in 1911 and 146 in 1918. Until the 1890s the Ministry had managed with the same number of officials as had worked at the State Chancery in 1848 (39 higher officials in the last year of its existence). The doubling of staff took place only after the turn of the century. This striking increase is not explained simply by an increase of work. Certainly, the number of written settlements amounted to 150000 per annum. But a ministerial official reports in his memoirs that the officials in his department were 'so numerous' that 'hardly more than three or four files reached them from among the daily receipts' (Cormons, *Schicksale und Schatten*, p. 77). It seems, however, that this staff expansion in what was, after all, the most important centre of imperial policy, was connected with the critically intensified internal and external crisis of the Habsburg Empire after the turn of the century.

Corresponding to the special position of the Foreign Ministry within the framework of the state administration as a whole was the rather special position of the Foreign Minister. He was the highest ranking minister of state and, because of his office, possessed considerable political influence. To be sure, the moral weight of his office was of greater practical effect than the legal power he was entitled to use. There were, repeatedly, strong tendencies to safeguard the dominant position of the Foreign Minister in an institutional manner as well. This was most successfully realized at the beginning of the official history of the Ministry of Foreign Affairs: Felix Schwarzenberg was Minister of Foreign Affairs and Prime Minister. Although the office of Prime Minister was pointedly abolished in 1852 after Schwarzenberg's death, the Foreign Minister remained chairman of the Council of Ministers, and under the pressure of international defeat, Johann Bernhard Rechberg (1859–64) again became Prime Minister for two years in 1859. It was Emperor Franz Joseph himself who counteracted this concentration of power in his Foreign Secretary – more successfully – by creating a Ministry of State under Anton Schmerling and by appointing Archduke Rainer as president of the Ministerial Council.

The sphere of activity of the Ministry of Foreign Affairs underwent a decisive change through the constitutional Austro-Hungarian 'compromise' (Ausgleich) of 1867, which divided the existing corporate body of the monarchy as a whole into two separate states. Like the army and the imperial finances, foreign policy belonged to 'common' *('gemeinsam')* matters. But only part of this common foreign policy, the imperial policy, belonged to the so-called 'pragmatic common' *(pragmatisch gemeinsam)* policy. All questions of export trade were covered by the term 'agreed common' *(paktiert gemeinsam)* matters and had to be pre-negotiated and decided in state treaties between Austria and Hungary. Though the Foreign Minister still represented the real union of Austria-Hungary in the 'pragmatic' and 'agreed' common affairs, there were a not inconsiderable number of questions where Austria and Hungary were completely autonomous, and in such questions as legal aid, extradition of criminals, postal, telegraph and railway contracts, the Minister of Foreign Affairs represented each of the two states separately. Doubtless, the highly inflexible and conservative basis of Austro-Hungarian foreign policy was caused by the complexity of the decision-making behind it. The more the vague terms of the Ausgleich were, in the interests of decentraliza- tion, differently interpreted and practised in the two halves of the empire, the more inflexible did foreign policy itself become. A concept of foreign policy different from that of simply parrying the activities of other states or of adapting to international developments as they occurred might have been worked out in Austria-Hungary, but it was extremely difficult given the strange structure of the foreign policy leadership, which was different from that of any other European country.

It was natural that an attempt should be made after 1867 to expand the sphere of activity of the Foreign Minister by strengthening his authority. Beust had himself appointed Chancellor of the empire (Reichskanzler) and the existence of an 'Oberstaat' – a concept of the empire that included both parts of the dual monarchy – was postulated in this gesture. From the Austrian side, continuous attempts were made to establish and institutionalize this remnant of the imperial idea, but Hungary successfully seized the oppor- tunity to protest against any such attempts. The term 'Austro-Hungarian government' was used frequently, though in reality it did not exist. Goluchowsky in 1895 was the last Foreign Minister, and Moritz Auffenberg in 1911 was the last Minister of War, to be appointed Imperial Ministers (Reichsminister). But in this struggle for the imperial idea, Hungary did not assume a consistently negative attitude – it just formally denied a common empire. Until 1918 the words that the Hungarian Josef Eötvös wrote in a letter to Andrássy in 1865 were true: 'Above all, not only our administrative autonomy but also our national independence must be secured; we must, however, also see to it that ways and means are provided to preserve the powerful position of the empire – which is also our empire and whose position is connected with our well-being' (Komjáthy, *Protokolle des Gemeinsamen Ministerrates der österreichisch-ungarishen Monařchie*, p. 12).

This conditional acceptance of a political commonality was the basis from which the mutual Foreign Minister could build up his office as the unofficial nucleus of government for the whole monarchy. An important contribution to this was the fact that the Foreign Minister was always in addition, indeed primarily, a 'Minister of the Imperial House'. As such, he was not only the highest ranking minister but he had immediate access to the Emperor. The business of the Foreign Ministry did not go through the Imperial Cabinet Chancery. The Ministry was, to a greater extent than the Imperial Cabinet Chancery, the advisory and executive organ for the general policy of the empire, a policy that was ultimately determined by the monarch. From 1867, the most important subsidiary function of the Minister for Foreign Affairs was chairing the Common Council of Ministers (Gemeinsamer Ministerrat). There were heated constitutional discussions about this council. It was decided between Goluchowsky and the Hungarian Prime Minister István Tisza (1903–05, 1913–15) that there was no question of a Common Council of Ministers, but only common ministerial conferences. But this was merely a legal classification, which was superseded in everyday political practice, especially in the years before and during the First World War. Although scholarly opinion is divided on this point, one can cite Miklós Komjáthy's convincing evidence that in the Common Council of Ministers 'a leading government authority was created, superior to the Austrian and the Hungarian ministries' (Komjáthy, p. 149). And it was a government responsible to no one but the monarch. The Foreign Minister was obliged to submit a report and to answer questions from the so-called Delegations, which met once a year and were deputed by the Austrian and Hungarian parliaments. But because of the procedures and the composition of these Delegations, they did not constitute a genuine counterweight to the wishes and powers of the Ministry of Foreign Affairs.

In view of the legal position and the possibilities for action connected with it, each Foreign Minister of the Habsburg monarchy could have had a considerable impact on politics. Astonishingly, hardly any head of the Ballhausplatz made use of such opportunities. Only Schwarzenberg, the senior Andrássy and Aehrenthal developed a political programme and carried it out with their full personal commitment. Almost every other Minister took up office not from any inner calling but out of obedience to the wish or command of the monarch. Alexander Mennsdorff-Pouilly (1864–66) and Leopold Berchtold (1912–15) were the most disastrous examples of this. A fair verdict on the passive role of the heads of the Ballhausplatz must at any rate take into account the fact that Emperor Franz Joseph considered foreign policy his own exclusive domain, and that in his capacity as the highest and most responsible civil servant of his state the Emperor involved himself closely with the running of the Foreign Ministry. From the mid-1870s the famous stroke on the lower left hand corner, a sign of their being put before the Emperor, can be found on a large number of the more important dispatches. And most draft copies for the attention of foreign missions carry the note 'copied for His Majesty'. One can surely draw the conclusion from this that no foreign policy decision of any importance was taken without the express consent of the Emperor, and that he was kept fully informed of all transactions.

In the long history of foreign policy between 1848 and 1917 there was never any real attempt made by the Ministers or the Ministry to stand in the way of imperial influence. And the Emperor, as he has often been criticized for doing, never tolerated any politician of prominence near him, perhaps with exceptions in Budapest. Those three Foreign Ministers – Schwarzenberg, Andrássy, Aehrenthal – who one can say developed a personal initiative in foreign policy, were called to their office in characteristic fashion because of a special crisis.

Despite the Foreign Minister's comprehensive official power and despite Emperor Franz Joseph's personal authority, the influence of leading officials at the Ballhausplatz on even basic international decisions was not insignificant. Almost all Foreign Ministers of the monarchy had access in some measure to the advice of their assistants, and often depended upon it. It is certainly true that even here the period before 1870 left more elbow-room for such actions, whereas after that date, activities even of leading Ballhausplatz officials were limited on account of the single-track Austro-German friendship.

The civil servants of the Foreign Ministry reflected the political complexity of the Habsburg states. The majority of officials came from the Theresianum, an institution founded by Maria Theresa as a centre of education for patriotic imperial officialdom. Every candidate for the foreign service had to be a university graduate, had to have practised at court or in the administration for a year, and, moreover, had still to take a relatively difficult diplomatic examination in constitutional and international law, political economy, history and foreign languages. It is true that some of the most efficient officials in the diplomatic service came from the Consular Academy, but this means of qualification was generally used only by those who did not belong to the diplomatic corps because of inferior birth and social position; by going through the Consular Academy a number of applicants from the middle classes gained acceptance. But the actual training of diplomats took place neither in the Theresianum nor in the Consular Academy. Their social and intellectual training occurred either in the diplomatic missions or in Vienna. Even admission to the foreign service was not in the first place decided by the obligatory diplomatic examination but by social status; for a leading position in the foreign service proof of a fixed income, which made it possible to fulfil the duties of representation, was also required. But a lack either of income or of high social position was not an absolute hindrance for a career as a diplomat. A middle-class background was no disqualification for the entrance examination to the diplomatic service. In the socially prestigious diplomatic corps we already find between 28 (1847) and 44 (1918) per cent of commoners in leading positions; in the Viennese Ministry the percentage was between 50 (1847–97) and 66 (1918) per cent. Only the Hungarian contingent in the Ballhausplatz drew almost exclusively on the aristocracy for recruits, taking as many from the magnate class as from the gentry. Admittedly such social statistics do not reveal very much; the spirit of the Ballhausplatz always remained aristocratic even for those who were commoners. The relatively numerous memoirs of Austrian diplomats provide a vivid picture of the special social and spiritual world of this highest and noblest category of Austrian officialdom. It was a world of culture and elegance, of generosity and even indifference towards important political issues, a world of inter-nationalism. Entry to the diplomatic service did not merely modify social differences but even dissolved the bonds of nationality. Yet despite the common bond of the supernational ideal, the national affiliations of the officials in the Ballhausplatz had a considerable effect on the way and the direction in which they gave meaning to this imperial ideal in foreign policy. Beust's leading assistants – Leopold Hofmann, Ludwig Biegeleben, Otto Rivalier-Meysenbug, Max Gagern, Roger Aldenburg – came from the small and middle-sized German states, and were as such rooted in the tradition of 'großdeutsch' politics. With Andrássy began the great time of Hungarian influence in the Ministry. In 1914, six of ten ambassadorships (Berlin, Constantinople, Paris, Rome, Tokyo and St Petersburg) were occupied by Hungarians. This Hungarian influence was most strongly personified by the head of department, Béla Orczy. He was called to the Foreign Ministry in 1868 as confidant for the Hungarian government in compensation for the request (which Vienna had refused) for Hungarian under-secretaries of state in the joint ministries. But as a rule the Hungarians in the foreign service were also representatives of the empire as a supranational institution. The Ballhausplatz, as far as its officials were concerned, was a centre of imperial attitudes, and it was from the Ballhausplatz that the idea of a supranational empire was most strongly championed.

It is surprising, and in comparison with other nations unique, that Austro-Hungarian diplomats at foreign missions took no part whatever in the making of the monarchy's foreign policy. Their job was simply to report and to act as mediators. There was no place in the organization of Austro-Hungarian foreign policy for the 'insubordinate' ambassador. Personalities like Ignatiev, Stratford Canning, Cambon, Barrère, Münster or Goltz would have been unthinkable as Austro-Hungarian diplomats. The absence of personal participation was one of the distinctive characteristics of an Austro-Hungarian diplomat. In these circumstances, the centre of decision-making lay entirely with the central administration in Vienna. Admittedly, this was of relatively minor significance because the internal and external services were, practically speaking, parts of the same whole even in matters of staff. Only a few diplomats, such as Minister Berchtold or the ambassadors to London, Rudolf Apponyi (1856–71) and Albert Mensdorff (1904–14), had never served in the centre. There were, on the other hand, some officials who served their entire careers at the Ballhausplatz. In senior posts it was, however, the rule that officials should alternate between the internal and external services. Almost always the first and second departmental heads came from the diplomatic service, and the next ambassadorial appointments were reserved for them. A great number of active officials at foreign missions were recalled to serve at the centre.

The central administration of the Ballhausplatz was divided into three main sections: the Minister's Cabinet, the administrative departments and the political sections. The greatest share in formulating the objectives of foreign policy fell naturally to the five political sections. Four of these sections were assigned a specific geographical region (I, the Balkans, Turkey and Russia; II, the Vatican; III, Germany and Scandinavia; IV, Western and south-west Europe and countries overseas). Only section V was organized super-regionally, and served as a police information service abroad; it was a continuation of Metternich's police department at the State Chancery. Beust placed it under the direct charge of the Minister, and from 1877 until 1908 it existed as an independent Office of Information (Informationsbüro). This organization, dating from Metternich's time, was so flexible that it could be adapted to new political needs. The most important section at all times – in terms of the overall foreign policy of the monarchy – was the Oriental Section (I), where the 'active political business was pursued'. It was here that the personal leadership of the Ministers had its strongest effect. Generally, however, the political correspondence and the implementation of decisions reached by the Minister and Emperor in consultation with the Ministerial Council lay completely in the hands of the heads of sections. For certain periods, we may speak of 'the rule of the great Privy Counsellors' on the Ballhausplatz. It is again true that the sphere of decision-making was greater for officials before 1867. The *gross-deutsch* policy of hegemony, which led to 1866, was determined by Privy Counsellors Biegeleben, Gagern and Meysenbug in cooperation with the Minister of State, Schmerling, and carried out against the will of Foreign Secretary Rechberg. In the Chancery regulations of 1868 Beust had tried to arrange that drafts of documents were submitted to departmental heads for revision. Yet this system worked only under Beust and his personal confidant and first departmental head, Hofmann. After 1871, the influence of heads of sections again increased. It was, however, very rarely that a single man gained a dominating influence. Though he was relatively unknown, one of Andrássy's most important assistants, especially with regard to Balkan questions, was Joseph von Schwegel. He was one of the Austro-Hungarian delegates to the Berlin Congress and was thought to be a possible successor to Andrássy. Kálnoky was the exception among Ministers; almost pedantically, he attended to the entire correspondence himself. It was exactly for this reason that the Emperor Franz Joseph thought so highly of him. Under Goluchowsky, Julius Zwiedeneck–Südenhorst was the dominating personality first as head of the Oriental Section, then as first departmental head and director of all political sections. Later on, a changing team of section heads cooperated when drafting important documents so that belonging to a specific section was no longer of any importance. The classic example of such a team decision is the story about the wording of the ultimatum to Serbia. While it was the head of the Balkan Section, Alexander Musulin, who did the drafting, the decisions that intensified the political conflict came from the first department head, Johann Forgách, and from the head of the Minister's Cabinet, Alexander Hoyos. It is typical that only in 1914, with the administrative innovation of the so-called 'section sheet', was it clearly established who had dictated the draft, written and revised it. Before 1914, the writer was hardly ever named and his identity can only be deduced from his handwriting, though the files show that the writer was usually not the author of the draft and that revisions were made by several officials; the person who probably had the fullest insight into the administration of the Ballhausplatz was the Emperor himself. According to the general concentration of business, this became standard practice only in the time after Andrássy.

Every day part of the diplomatic reports and orders were submitted to the Emperor, documents he returned with the greatest punctuality, even the next day, but as a rule without comment. The first department head decided what was presented to the Emperor from the 'political reading matter'. It was most probably during Kálnoky's time that under the direction of the first departmental head, who was in charge of the four political sections, the incoming political documents were sifted and given a political classification. After that time, the first departmental head held a key position, for he was in practice the one to decide what would be submitted to be dealt with and inspected, and when.

The administrative departments were no less important than the political sections being almost supplementary offices of foreign policy for the Minister. Almost all political fields were treated from the diplomatic aspect by these departments, which had increased from five to 17 between 1849 and 1914. The most important was the Press Department which before 1870 was the centre for all press matters, even at home, and where the press review for the monarch was compiled. Equally important as a coordinating centre was the Political Department of Trade. The most important political tool for the Minister was the Presidential Office. Beust tried to make it into an Imperial Chancery with comprehensive political tasks. As 'Cabinet of the Minister' under Kálnoky, it was authorized to deal with only a limited field of activities, yet he made it an enlarged centre for the determination of foreign policy. It dealt with the personal correspondence of the Minister, especially with the Austrian and Hungarian governments, took down the minutes in the Common Ministerial Council and prepared negotiations with the Delegations. The Presidential Office was the place of contact with the joint Minister of Finance with regard to all questions concerning Bosnia and Herzegovina. Finally, the Presidential Office compiled the diplomatic reports for submission to the Minister and the Emperor. This multiplicity of competencies explains why under Aehrenthal and Berchtold the departmental heads, Friedrich Szápáry (1902–12) and Alexander Hoyos (1912–15) were the most influential officials of all.

Apart from the informal ways through which the Foreign Minister could effectively intervene in the overall policy of the state, there was the official apparatus of the Ballhausplatz, an instrument about which it has rightly been said that it comprised 'almost all branches of public life in their effects upon foreign relations' (Bittner, *Das österreichisch-ungarische Ministerium des Äußern. Seine Geschichte und Organisation*, p. 131). And the Ballhausplatz made use of these possibilities of intervention and coordination, though always in such a way that the Minister's leading position and the ultimate authority of the Emperor were never questioned.

The organizational, social, and also no doubt political, exclusiveness of the Foreign Ministry in Vienna was the most important reason why neither the military nor any economic institution had any influence worth mentioning on the postings of the Foreign Ministry. Nevertheless, the Foreign Ministry and its policy were caught up in the overall tasks of Austrian politics in the nineteenth century. The Ballhausplatz was increasingly and ultimately an instrument of power for the dominant peoples and social classes in the monarchy. It served to uphold the *status quo* in domestic politics, which had been established in 1867. On the one hand, in its bureaucratic efficiency, on the other, in its political submissiveness, the Ballhausplatz was an almost perfect reflection of the state under Franz Joseph as it neared its dissolution.

BIBLIOGRAPHY

For the institutional history of Austrian foreign policy before 1848, Josef Karl Mayr, *Geschichte der österreichischen Staatskanzlei im Zeitalter des Fürsten Metternich* (Invertare Österreichischer staatlicher Archive Bd. 5/2, Vienna 1935) offers a sound foundation.

Peter Cordes, *Die obersten Staatsorgane und die Leitung der auswärtigen Angelegenheiten, 1792–1852* (typewritten thesis, Graz 1978). A broadly laid out thesis that supplements the above history of officialdom with more precise details, and brings out these relationships with the development of the central administration as a whole.

Erwin Matsch, *Geschichte des auswärtigen Dienstes von Österreich-Ungarn 1720–1920* (Vienna 1980) gives a good comprehensive survey; also Georg Schmid, *Der Ballhausplatz 1848–1918*, Österreichische Osthefte, 23 (1981), 18–37.

There is no general history of the development and organization of the Ballhausplatz during the period 1867 to 1918. The only comprehensive work is: Ludwig Bittner, 'Das österreichisch-ungarische Ministerium des Äußern. Seine Geschichte und Organisation', *Berliner Monatshefte*, 15 (1937), 819–843. It may be supplemented by Rudolf Wiedermeyer, Geschäftsgang des k.u.k. Ministeriums des Äußern 1908–1918, *Archivalische Zeitschrift*, 40 (1931), 131–152.

Friedrich Engel-Janosi, 'Der Ballhausplatz, 1848–1918', *Geschichte auf dem Ballhausplatz. Essays zur österreichischen Außenpolitik, 1830–1945* (Graz 1963), 9–28, brilliantly illustrates the relationships between the characteristics of the bureaucratic machinery and the content of the political decisions. The most successful example of an analysis of the process of decision-making in foreign policy, apart from studies of individual cases, is the introduction by Miklós Komjáthy, *Protokolle des Gemeinsamen Ministerrates der österreichisch-ungarischen Monarchie (1914–18)* (Publikationen des ungarischen Staatsarchivs, Bd. II/10, Budapest 1966), 1–137.

Robert Paula, *Der Einfluß Kaiser Franz Josephs auf die Außenpolitik der Monarchie mit besonderer Berücksichtigung der Orientpolitik* and Walter Wagner, *Kaiser Franz Joseph und das Deutsche Reich von 1871–1914* (typewritten theses, Vienna 1952 and 1950) look at the influence of Kaiser Franz Joseph. A good essay on the relationship between military and foreign policy is found in a chapter in Antonio Schmidt-Brentano, *Die Armee in Österreich. Militär, Staat und Gesellschaft 1848–1867* (Wehrwissenschaftliche Forschungen/Militärgeschichtliche Studien Bd.20, Boppard/Rhein 1955), 169–228. There is little on the connections between the economy and foreign policy (e.g. Karl Heinz Werner, 'Österreichs Industrie- und Außenhandelspolitik 1848–1948' in *Hundert Jahre österreichische Wirtschaftsentwicklung, 1848–1949*, ed. Hans Mayer (Vienna 1949). The influence of the Foreign Ministry on the shaping of public opinion is well covered in Barbara Krebs, *Die westeuropäische Pressepolitik der Ära Beust, 1865–1871* (Göppinger Akademische Beiträge Bd. 5, Göppingen 1970) and Margarete Kossina, *Die Rotbücher der österreichisch-ungarischen Monarchie* (typewritten thesis, Vienna 1946). There is little on the direct effect of public opinion, press and parliament on foreign policy.

The unsatisfactory state of research is astonishing given the excellent sources available. The 'Administrative Registratur' of the Vienna Haus-, Hof- und Staatsarchiv contains all the substantive documentation needed for a history of the organization of the Foreign Ministry. Material relating to the personal history of the official class in the state schemes and in the yearbooks of the foreign service (published yearly since 1897) is both rich and detailed and is still far from exhausted. The numerous memoirs of various diplomats are a similarly unexplored source. Only the work of the editor of the 1914 ultimatum, Alexander von Musulin, *Das Haus am Ballplatz* (Munich 1924) has been amply appreciated. For other important references see Ludwig von Przibram, *Erinnerungen eines alten Österreichers* (Stuttgart/Leipzig 1910); Ernest U. Cormons, *Schicksale und Schatten. Eine österreichische Autobiographie* (Salzburg 1951). The organizational foundation of consular life is portrayed by Leopold Neumann in his *Handbuch des Konsularwesens* (Vienna 1854) and Joseph Piskur, *Manuale dell'istituzione consolare austriaca* (Vienna 1862). The question of the organization and arrangements of work in the Foreign Ministry is recalled by Robert Stropp, 'Die Akten des k.u.k. Ministeriums des Äußern 1848–1918' *Mitteilungen des österreichischen Staatsarchivs*, 20 (1970), 389–506.

Austria

The Foreign Office
since 1918

MICHAEL DERNDARSKY

Michael Derndarsky is Universitätsassistent at the Universität für Bildungswissenschaften Klagenfurt, Austria. He was born in 1949 and studied at the University of Vienna. His articles include 'Einführung in die Methodik der Geschichtswissenschaft', *Grundstudium Geschichte*, edited M. Derndarsky, G. Hödl, H. Rumpler, E. Weber (1978), 'Welcher Zeit Geschichte? Zum Versuch, Zeitgeschichte einzugrenzen', *Geschichte in Wissenschaft und Unterricht* 30 (1979), 'Die Diskussion um eine 'Doktrin' für die Aussenpolitik Österreichs', *Zeitgeschichte* 7 (1979–80), 'Die Kärntner Volksabstimmung im Spannungsfeld von Wissenschaft, Politik, Ideologie und Publizistik', *Österreichische Osthefte* 22 (1980).

With the end of the First World War came the dissolution of the Austro-Hungarian monarchy, which had grown into a multinational state formed from different groups of countries upon whose territory the 'successor states' were founded. For the German Austrian countries, which now constituted a small republican state, the impression of a completely new beginning emerges in view of the far-reaching governmental reforms and changes in the composition of the state and its territories. But despite this break with the past, some continuity can be observed, not least in the governmental offices. Because the administrative centre of the former empire was on Austrian soil, in Vienna, the Cisleithian ministries were taken over as the administrative offices of the new state in a practically unchanged form. Only the Foreign Office was an exception because one had to go back, in contrast to other ministries, to what had been common to both halves of the Empire.

As early as 30 October 1918 the provisional National Assembly had erected a government formed of representatives from all parties under State Chancellor Karl Renner, a Social Democrat. The last joint Foreign Minister, Count Julius Andrássy the younger, did not resign until 2 November. Emperor Karl then entrusted the leadership of the Foreign Ministry to its first departmental head, Ludwig von Flotow; basically this meant giving him the job of liquidation. In theory, the imperial career diplomat thus presided over 433 government clerks of all nationalities, 142 of whom came from the Hungarian half of the Empire and about whose fates a decision had to be taken. They had to find new professions, or to be pensioned off if they were not accepted into the diplomatic services of one of the successor states. This proved to be the case for about half the former employees. Barely a quarter (105) entered the Austrian foreign service, in which they represented the lion's share of the whole civil service, which numbered 122 men in 1921. With regard to the officials taken over by Austria, a sharp drop in the proportion of representatives from the diplomatic career is particularly noticeable: 31.4 per cent of the old Ministry and only 18.1 per cent of the new. There was less willingness to serve the Republic among the aristocracy, who had mainly entered this career, than among other social classes. Another reason for their departure might be sought in the property they owned in the successor states, which forced them – unlike other foreign service officials who were not necessarily wealthy men – to take the nationality of the state in question. Moreover, leaders of the new state disliked having aristocrats as representatives of the Republic.

The abolition of the old imperial diplomatic network stretched out over two years. One reason why this took so long was the fact that Switzerland did not recognize Austria and Hungary until 1920, and until this date diplomatic contact was maintained via the old joint Austro-Hungarian Ministry; for a few months both the imperial envoy, Léon de Vaux, and the Republic's chargé d'affaires, Leo di Pauli, were recognized in Bern. It was not until 8 November 1920 that Flotow completed the liquidation, which was partially carried out with the Republic's Foreign Office, now also situated on the Ballhausplatz. The provisional government, in naming its administrative offices, apparently adopted the usages of the German state for the goal of Anschluss was official policy. The office was originally named the State Office of Foreign Affairs (Staatsamt des Äussern) and was established 'with the authority of the former imperial and royal Foreign Ministry and with the task and the power to govern and to foster external relationships, including those of the national states that had come into being on the territory of the former Austro-Hungarian monarchy'. The grand old man of Austrian social democracy, Victor Adler, was appointed as the first Secretary of State but he died a few days later, before the Republic had even been proclaimed. He was replaced by his fellow party member, the former Under-Secretary of State Otto Bauer, who was given two further under-secretaries, Leopold Waber and Egon Pflügl, as assistants. From the very beginning the constituent National Assembly, installed after the first post-war elections (held on 16 February 1919), confirmed, and thereby legitimized, the legislative and administrative powers of its predecessors and thus secured the continuing existence of the State Office for Foreign Affairs (Staatsamt für Äusseres).

The Constitution, which was decided upon by the National Assembly in the autumn of 1920 and put into effect about one year after the signing of the Treaty of Saint Germain (which contained a clause forbidding an Anschluss), defined the Austrian Republic as a federal state whose most important administrative business was henceforth to be carried out by a federal government. Correspondingly, the law by which the Constitution came into effect determined that the state offices were to continue to exist with the same spheres of effective power as federal ministries. From this point on, foreign policy was determined by the Federal Ministry for Foreign Affairs (Bundesministerium für Äusseres).

This was hardly to last any longer than its predecessor. In return for the international credit that was needed by a war-weakened Austria, further ravaged economically by the dissolution of its formerly large and unified economic area, the country had to agree to measures for a wide-ranging reorganization, under international supervision, which entailed substantial reductions in its extensive administrative apparatus inherited from the old monarchy. As a result of this cutback the Foreign Ministry, like the Ministries of the Interior and of Justice, was curtailed and made part of the Federal Chancellery Office (Bundeskanzleramt) which was transferred to the Ballhausplatz, which thus became the centre of political power for the Republic, where formerly only the Foreign Ministry and the head of state, the Federal President – who transferred his seat to the Hofburg after 1945 – had resided.

This meant some changes in the organization of external affairs. While the State Office and the Ministry had, albeit to a limited extent, remained similar to the former joint Ministry, and had four sections at their disposal which also dealt with the economic agenda and with the affairs of the League of Nations – foreign policy itself was now reduced to a single department within the Federal Chancellery Office. In addition, matters of commercial policy were transferred to the Federal Ministry for Trade and Commerce, a move that constituted a diminution in the Foreign Ministry's sphere of competence and brought about a further reduction in personnel and agencies.

In this way, Austria's already small number of diplomatic missions became even smaller. The agency in Madrid had already been abolished in 1922; now the legation in The Hague, which also dealt with Belgium, was changed into a chargé d'affaires post. In addition, eight of the fifteen consulates (Brno, Cracow, Czernowitz, Hamburg, Lemberg, Moravska-Ostrava, Stuttgart and Zurich) and two of the four passport offices (Sarajevo and Venice) were turned into honorary positions. This left only the consulates in Bratislava, Cologne, Ljubljana, Milan, Munich, New York and Trieste and the passport office in Cracow. The office in Zagreb was lifted to consular status in the reshuffle but was closed again in 1932; in 1927 a further consulate was established in Jerusalem.

All the other Austrian missions had the rank of legation; the First Republic never filled more than 21 of them. (In 1914 there were 29 embassies and legations and 112 consulates.) Apart from legations in neighbouring and successor states (Bern, Berlin, Prague, Warsaw, Bucharest, Budapest, Belgrade and Rome) there were still missions in the capitals of the great powers – London, Paris, Washington and Moscow, the last being merely an authorized agency until 1925. There were others in Athens, Constantinople, Ankara, and Sofia, as well as in the Holy See and at the League of Nations. Outside Europe there was only one more legation, in Rio de Janeiro. This one (apart from an interval when there was a second one in Buenos Aires in 1928–34) was also assigned almost all the other South American states. Elsewhere, too, envoys were recognized in several states. Thus the envoy in Berlin was accredited for a long time to all the Scandinavian countries. Though there had been an attaché in Stockholm since 1924, he only became independent from Berlin in 1927 and took over dealings with Finland and Norway and, in 1932, with Denmark. Such countries as Albania, Cuba, Estonia, Latvia, Persia and Spain, and during the thirties (when attempts were apparently made to widen the sphere of diplomatic contacts), Iraq, Lithuania and Mexico, were entrusted to other Austrian legations. Egypt, in which the legation established in 1931 was directed by the head of the mission in Greece, was a special case.

The Republic was represented in Asia and Africa by Swedish, Dutch and German embassies; the last continued to exercise protecting functions even after the intensification of tension with Hitler's Reich. On the other hand, honorary consulates were numerous; both supply and demand for such offices seems always to have been high. In 1932, there were 172 honorary consulates (six unoccupied). Eight of the most popular (one may assume the agencies dissolved in 1923) were in the hands of honorary consuls who presided over clerks from the Austrian diplomatic staff. The number of professional consulates was further reduced during the thirties. Trieste, like Zagreb, became an honorary consulate.

When the government was reorganized in 1923, an ordinance left the possibility of appointing a Federal Minister for Foreign Affairs despite the suppression of the Ministry. The 1920 Constitution further created the posts of secretaries of state (whose functions were not comparable to those of their namesakes before 1920, but to the under-secretaries of that time!) who were placed at the Minister's disposal for handling the business of the Ministry and for parliamentary representation. They were subordinate to him and bound to his directives, and were therefore, if not members of the government *de jure,* yet involved in the running of the department. If one takes a general view of the official leaders of Austrian foreign policy from 1918 to 1938, they present themselves as a merry-go-round of persons and functions in colourful succession.

The 20 years between 1918 and 1938 – and this can be taken as a symptom of the political instability of that time – saw no less than 27 governments, while there were 15 succeeding heads of government (12 individuals) and 24 foreign policy leaders (19 individuals). When Bauer resigned in 1919, State Chancellor Renner took over the Foreign Office, too, a post that he retained when Michael Mayr replaced him as Chancellor. After the elections of 17 October 1920 the Socialists left the Government and remained in opposition for the remainder of the inter-war period. The Christian Socialists became the dominant political power, but they still needed the support of the third force in Austria's political spectrum, the so-called 'national camp'. Nevertheless, they generally filled the Chancellor's post, with only three exceptions when Josef Schober became the head of the Government. When he took Mayr's place he was at first both Chancellor and Foreign Minister, like his predecessor, but he soon had to hand foreign policy over to the Christian Socialist Leopold Hennet because of differences with the *gross-deutsch* groups. In the three cabinets under Ignaz Seipel, who succeeded Schober, Alfred Grünberger became Foreign Minister both before and after the dissolution of the Foreign Ministry. The next Chancellor, Rudolf Ramek, gave the Foreign Minister's post to Heinrich Mataja, who because of several political awkwardnesses left at the next reshuffle. Ramek now took over the Foreign Office himself, as did the following three Chancellors – Seipel, Ernst Streeruwitz and Schober. Then Seipel became Foreign Minister under Carl Vaugoin; two months later it was Schober's turn to preside over foreign affairs in his capacity as Vice-Chancellor, first under Otto Ender and then under Karl Buresch. The latter (the case seems to be a little complicated!) formed his second cabinet without Schober; as a result, control over foreign policy fell back to the Chancellor. This remained the state of affairs under Engelbert Dollfuss, who directed the Republic's transformation into a corporate state. Trying to get a broader political basis Dollfuss, who had dissolved Parliament, finally appointed the envoy in Berlin, Stephan Tauschitz from the Landbund, as his Secretary of State. A short time after the murder of Dollfuss by the Nazis in 1934, Kurt Schuschnigg formed the next (and last) governments before the Anschluss. At first he took Egon Berger-Waldenegg from Home Defence to be Foreign Minister, then dismissed him after internal differences with his political colleagues. Finally, after the July Agreement of 1936 with Hitler, he took Guido Schmidt as Secretary of State, who was to become Foreign Minister in February 1938. One month later, Schuschnigg had to resign because of Nazi pressure, and handed the government over to Arthur Seyss-Inquart, who made a clerk of the Foreign Office, Wilhelm Wolf, Foreign Minister. One day later, Austria was declared part of the German Reich, and after two more days, on 15 March 1938, Wolf's affairs were handed over to the German Reichsaussenminister.

This heterogeneity in the foreign policy leadership, not easy to survey but underlining only too clearly the general point, makes it difficult to trace any kind of pattern. Prominent party members, after first managing the foreign sections, later coveted posts in other offices that were seen as key areas. Several foreign ministers claimed other departments. This applied to Mataja in Renner's first cabinet, Grünberger in Mayr's first and second as well as in Schober's first two cabinets, Hennet in Schober's first and second cabinets, and also Berger-Waldenegg in Schuschnigg's cabinet. The Under-Secretary of State in the first Republican cabinet, Waber, claimed other departments under Schober, Seipel and Ramek. On the other hand, the post of Foreign

Minister itself, which was not even occupied for several years, lost some of its importance and sometimes served only to make up a party balance. The so-called specialist minister was a rare occurrence – only Berger-Waldenegg and Under-Secretary of State Pflügl came from the diplomatic service, and Schmidt had been a provisional attaché before becoming Secretary of State and then Foreign Minister. More frequently, foreign ministers and even professional politicians were used in the diplomatic service.

While changes in the leadership of the Foreign Ministry were frequent, there was more continuity in the general membership of the house. The officials who were taken over from the monarchy during the process of liquidation occupied the new foreign sections in such a way that it was difficult for the office to take on new young colleagues, a tendency accentuated by the reduction in the number of officials and the spirit encouraged by the economy programme. The Consular Academy, intended for the training of diplomats, continued to exist, but in the end it served more to school candidates for the Foreign Ministries of other nations. Austrian graduates had little prospect of being accepted into their own foreign service. Only in 1933 was there a sizeable number of appointments, under Dollfuss who recalled several envoys from their posts. At first, however, this hardly changed anything in the ranks of the diplomats, who were characterized by two main features. In the first place, there was the continuing domination of civil servants who had begun their service in the monarchy; in 1938, 15 of the 20 Austrian envoys were former imperial and royal diplomats, and some of these were to serve the Second Republic as well. Secondly, and in contrast to this imperial link, important posts were given to certain politically trust-worthy men. The perfect example was that of Berlin, first given to the historian, Ludo Moritz Hartmann, who strove hard for an Anschluss but who left the service after the Social Democrats stepped down from the government. His successor was Richard Riedl, former head of department in the Imperial Ministry of Commerce, who had collaborated with the *gross-deutsch* groups which had implemented the policy of Anschluss in a coalition agreement with the Christian Socialists. Riedl made increasing difficulties for the Christian Socialist Government as it turned away from this policy. In the end he was recalled, with difficulty, by Mataja. After him, the former Vice-Chancellor Felix Frank took over, who despite his sympathies with the *gross-deutsch* platform was more skilful, before Tauschitz was finally appointed. Thus, a professional diplomat never became head of the diplomatic mission in Berlin. Sometimes, foreign posts were placed at the disposal of ex-ministers for their maintenance; in Budapest, for instance, former members of the Government, Hennet, Odo Neustädter-Stürmer and Eduard Baar-Baarenfels, were accredited diplomats, while Grünberger had a period of official residence in Paris. A posting abroad was also a method of getting politicians out of the way. Thus, the former Home Defence director, Richard Steidle, was made consul-general in Trieste, and Anton Rintelen, the former ruler of Styria who was involved in the leadership struggle within the Christian Socialist party, became minister in Rome. This did not, however, prevent him from participating in the July *putsch* against Dollfuss. In Rome at the Holy See the church historian, Ludwig von Pastor, was appointed during the early twenties, though he used his office more for academic than for political purposes.

Compared to the practice under the monarchy, a distinct change had taken place in the old tripartite structure of the service. The differences between the diplomatic, consular and ministerial career ladders were abolished. According to a custom that is fully established today, diplomats began to be appointed alternately to foreign and home posts, and had their periods of residence abroad shortened. This was by no means done systematically; in most places between the wars only two or three heads of missions were alternated in this way. At the League of Nations (Emmerich Pflügl), in London (Georg Franckenstein), in Washington (Edgar Prochnik) and New York (Friedrich Fischerauer), in Prague (Ferdinand Marek) and in Rio de Janeiro (Anton Retschek) the same representative served throughout the entire inter-war period. The last named should be specially mentioned as he became Austria's first envoy in Brazil after the Second World War, as well as having been vice-consul in Rio de Janeiro before the First World War.

In 1938 the question of what course to take was once again raised. Heads of missions had been immediately recalled to Vienna after the German entry into Austria. Although there was at first no clarity about the future fate of the Austrian diplomatic machinery, there followed a little later the dissolution of the entire external branch and the handing over of legations and their staffs to the German heads of mission. The decision fully to integrate the Austrian representatives into the German diplomatic service came after a thorough examination during 1938. Although there are hardly any records of investigations or statements on this doubtless delicate question, one can nevertheless ascertain that there were only a small number of such mergers, first because the German need for diplomats had hardly been increased by the Anschluss, and second because the Austrian diplomats were essentially characterized by their 'nostalgia' for the Habsburg state. Among the envoys of the other successor states were many former colleagues from the old imperial service, a fact that led to convivial relationships though not exactly along official lines. So these diplomats were far more inclined towards a Danubian Confederation than towards an Anschluss with Germany; besides which, the diplomats had been weeded out by the leadership of a corporate state that had pursued an independent Austrian policy. The Ballhausplatz later on became the domicile of Gauleiter and Reichsstatthalter Baldur von Schirach.

At the end of the Second World War, when the National Socialist regime collapsed before the advance of the Russians, former officials reassembled at their old posts in the heavily bomb-damaged building even before a provisional government was formed, a government that, as after the First World War, was established under Renner as State Chancellor. Admittedly, the Government had to wait almost half a year for recognition as representing all of Austria. Karl Gruber from the Austrian People's Party (ÖVP), the successor to the Christian Socialists, was appointed Under-Secretary of State for Foreign Affairs as the representative of Austria's western federal lands. Gruber's entry into the Government had been one of the conditions for its recognition. After the election of 25 November 1945, in which the ÖVP became the strongest political power (a position they were to maintain for twenty-five years), Gruber was given the post of Foreign Minister in a coalition government under his fellow party member Leopold Figl.

The tasks of the Foreign Office in the State Chancellery consisted initially of a clearing-up operation, preparatory activities and maintaining contact with the Soviet occupiers while seeking connections – informal at first – with the other conquering powers, who were at first suspicious of Renner, whom they regarded as a Soviet puppet. Because of the military occupation of Austria, a considerable part of its foreign policy during the next decade took place on home soil. The reconstruction of the Foreign Office was, if troublesome, basically speedily attained. As early as January 1947 the personnel of the Foreign Office, which during the previous year had stood at 197 officials (including 66 diplomats) had increased to 428 officials (including 110 diplomats). This was markedly higher than the figures for 1938 (379 officials, including 98 diplomats). Of these 98, 37 were re-employed in the Office by the end of 1946. The other diplomats in the new office were new appointees who either transferred from other branches or returned from abroad, where they had made valuable contacts or were confidants of the various political parties. Officials who had been taken into the German Foreign Office could not be considered, though later there were a few such re-appointments. But attempts were made to accept only qualified candidates, whatever the difficulties; studies in jurisprudence and a knowledge of both English and French were, like taking the diplomats' examination, mandatory requirements for entrance.

After recovering from the 'lean patch' of the first post-war years, diplomatic legations could be quickly established despite difficulties created by the lack of foreign currency. In 1945, indeed, there was only one envoy's office abroad, the office of the Austrian representative in Prague, which was built up by the former envoy, Marek. Without any action on the part of the Ballhausplatz, legations were formed in other cities by émigrés, which sometimes resulted in conflict with the official legations. At the end of 1945, the Allied Commission had accepted the Government's request to recognize political legations in the capitals of the victorious powers. By the Second Control Agreement, of 28 June 1946, Austria was granted the right to open diplomatic relations with countries belonging to the United Nations. Thereafter, a network of missions was developed to link Austria with these nations. At first, a great number of representatives were accredited to several countries, but the inter-war position was in this respect soon superseded. The increased need for personnel, together with the new appointments made in the immediate post-war period, meant that the continuity between the First and Second Republics was much less strong than that between the Empire and the First Republic. The first missions were established as early as 1946 – apart from the United States and France – Brazil, the Netherlands, Sweden, Switzerland and Turkey. For some time, only political relations existed with other countries, such as Great Britain (until 1947), the Soviet Union, Yugoslavia and Poland (1953) and Romania (until 1955). In Hungary and Czechoslovakia, until 1947 and 1948 respectively, consulates attended to diplomatic relations, which were normal from the start. Germany was a special case. Austria first had a consulate and then, from 1948, a contact point in each of the three Western zones, to which an 'Austrian representation' in Bonn was added in 1953. Austria could not establish normal diplomatic relations with the Federal Republic until 1955, when the occupying troops withdrew from Austria after the State Treaty and Austria obtained its liberty and independence; only then was an embassy installed in Bonn. The establishment of such highest ranking diplomatic missions had begun in 1951 (with the United States, France and Great Britain), followed in 1952 with the Holy See,

Italy, Argentina, Brazil, Chile and in 1953 with Belgium, Yugoslavia and the Soviet Union. In the course of the fifties and sixties, according to international custom, all missions were given embassy status or established as such. The last and only legation was, for a long time, that in Prague, which was finally promoted in 1974, after the settlement of differences over property. Austria currently has over 98 missions subordinate to the Foreign Ministry, consisting of 66 embassies (whose heads often also deal with affairs in other countries), five permanent legations with international organizations, 16 consulates-general or consulates, a delegation in Berlin and 10 cultural institutes. The number of honorary consulates has meanwhile passed the figures of the inter-war period and now exceeds 180.

Paralleling this increase, the number of civil servants in the Foreign Ministry has also increased. By 1960, the 1947 figure had doubled. There were 847 officials in all, 164 in the higher foreign service, as the separate branch, with its special official titles and entry requirements outlined in an administrative act of 1948, was called. A further increase in the early sixties was followed by a period of stagnation, caused by a devolution of responsibility and economy measures, which led even to a slight cutback in personnel. In the seventies there was once again a steady increase, which mounted sharply in 1974 because of a new distribution of authority under a law relating to the federal ministries; 1326 government officials, of whom 267 were in the higher foreign service. The growth continued; in 1980 the number of officials had risen to 1426, including 348 senior government officials (as the academic civil servants were called after the introduction of a new office law in 1978 – this figure includes other government officials and not just diplomats). This increase took place despite the fact that the proportion of the budget that goes towards maintaining the Foreign Office was practically unchanged in the First and Second Republics; it represents between 0.4 and 0.5 per cent of total expenditure.

With regard to training and to the pattern of an official's career, the model of the inter-war period was perfected and standardized. A university degree is required of all aspiring diplomats, and the requirements have been altered to include recognition of studies in economic science as well as in law. For other academics a period of training at the Diplomatic Academy, founded in 1964 as a successor to the Consular Academy (which was closed during the Second World War and not reopened) was required. This serves as a preparation for the *examen préalable*, which all candidates are required to take and which covers both the general and specific needs of the service. Accepted examinees then undergo a basic training in the departments of the Ministry and must pass a diplomat's examination before definitive acceptance. The career pattern provides for an alternation between posts abroad, where the most comprehensive administrative and geographic diversity is sought, and domestic service, in a time-ratio of about two to one. In contrast to what happened during the First Republic, the selection of diplomats actually followed this pattern. The only important exceptions were Karl Waldbrunner, later Transport Minister, who was Austria's first envoy in Moscow for a short and unsuccessful period, and Gruber, who after his retirement as Minister was employed in the diplomatic service. Similarly, in most cases, heads of diplomatic missions were regularly alternated: the only exceptions were Norbert Bischoff in Moscow (1947–60), Joseph Kripp at the Vatican

(1951–61), Albin Lennkh in Rio (1960–70) and Max Löwenthal-Chlumecky in Rome (1955–74). In relation to the total number of personnel and in comparison with the inter-war period, these cases are hardly significant. In general, one can say that equal treatment of diplomats genuinely exists even if certain posts can be bestowed for political reasons. It can also be said that in general the personnel of the Foreign Office, not least because of the special entry requirements, is less politically saturated than that of other ministries.

In the management of foreign policy, too, there are considerable differences between the First and Second Republics. In the constancy of cabinets and politicians alone one sees a greater political continuity. There have been 15 governments involving a total of six Chancellors and eight Foreign Ministers; some of these changes were determined by the results of parliamentary elections that altered the balance of political power. The first Foreign Minister, Gruber, who because of his marked Western orientation (which ran against Austria's actual neutral policy at the time) and also because of a leadership struggle with the ÖVP, was removed and was, as it were, packed off abroad. He was succeeded by the former Federal Chancellor Figl, who had to step down as head of government in favour of Julius Raab. In 1953, the 'great coalition' was jointly in power, the ÖVP and the SPÖ (the Socialist Party of Austria), but after an election result that much favoured the latter party, the 'black' Foreign Minister was given a 'red' Secretary of State in Bruno Kreisky as compensation for the altered power positions of the parties. He, however, corresponding to political practice, was more a watchdog than, in accordance with the provisions of the Constitution, a subordinate. The elections of 1956 swung the other way, after which a second Secretary of State, Franz Gschnitzer, was appointed, again as a counterweight, with special responsibilities for the South Tyrol. The elections of 1959, on the other hand, gave power afresh to the SPÖ, who in the course of the coalition dealings were allowed the post of Foreign Minister and filled it with Kreisky, while Gschnitzer remained the only Secretary of State. Since, after all that, Chancellor and Foreign Minister no longer belonged to the same party, a separate Foreign Ministry was finally re-established (29 July 1959), as before situated, like the Federal Chancellery, on the Ballhausplatz.

After this date, Chancellors of the coalition government changed, Alfons Gorbach and Josef Klaus, and with them the Secretaries of State, Ludwig Steiner and Carl Bobleter under Kreisky. After the elections of 1966, Bobleter remained Secretary when Klaus left the coalition and set up a single-party government, in which Lujo Tončic-Sorinj became Minister for Foreign Affairs. As a result of disagreements with the Chancellor, his leadership of the Foreign Ministry came to an end in the governmental reshuffle of 1968, and it was entrusted to one sole Minister, Kurt Waldheim. Waldheim, like all Foreign Ministers since that time, belonged to no political party. This constitutes an exception in the post-war political system. The elections of 1970 brought the SPÖ into power, which they have retained until today. Under Chancellor Kreisky, Rudolf Kirchschläger became Foreign Minister. He was elected as the SPÖ's candidate for Federal President in 1974, being succeeded by Erich Bielka-Karltreu, who was seen from the beginning as an interim appointment and who came from the Foreign Ministry, like his two predecessors. Finally, in 1976, after internal discussions in the Socialist Party, in which several quarters demanded a party member as the next Minister,

Kreisky, who admittedly is helping to mould foreign policy and who acquired professional, as well as political, experience in the Foreign Office, had his way and appointed a top-ranking official from the Federal Chancellery Office (Bundeskanzleramt), Willibald Pahr, as Minister, an appointment that can also be viewed as the result of an effort to keep foreign policy out of the inter-party struggle and as a matter of political consensus. It seems remarkable, however, that the post of Foreign Minister was always occupied by a party politician in the period of coalition government, while in times of single-party government it has become almost a matter of course to have the Foreign Ministry run by non-party members.

In terms of organization and the delegation of authority, the Foreign Ministry has been the subject of several changes during the Second Republic. Directly after the war, the Foreign Office constituted one part of the Ballhausplatz, called Federal Chancellery Office – External Affairs (Bundeskanzleramt–Auswärtige Angelegenheiten). Its agenda was dealt with according to the political needs of the day in newly established departments whose task it was to deal with immediate problems of foreign policy. As mentioned earlier, section IV of the Federal Chancellery became a separate Federal Ministry for Foreign Relations (Bundesministerium für Auswärtige Angelegenheiten) in 1959, for it was in this section that the Foreign Office had been re-established since the end of the 1940s. Not least because of the different political affiliations of the Federal Chancellor and the Foreign Minister, authority in matters pertaining to the OEEC and the ERP remained within the Federal Chancellery. Similarly, less attention was paid to the removal of authority from other ministries than to securing their cooperation. Differences between the government parties with regard to the policy for European economic integration policy led in 1963 to a transfer of authority from the Foreign Ministry to the Ministry of Commerce, which was headed by the vigorous pro-Common Market Fritz Bock. In 1966 the Foreign Ministry underwent a further restriction of its authority. It entailed above all the transfer of responsibility for cultural contacts abroad to the Ministry of Education, while the Ministry of Commerce was granted new privileges. These restrictions led to reductions in the organization and in the personnel of the Foreign Ministry. Since its reestablishment, it had been divided into sections and departments, like all Austrian governmental offices, with the Federal Minister and the Cabinet, and, up to 1968, the Secretary of State with his secretariat at the top. Following other countries' examples, in 1923 a secretary-general was placed at the head of the Office, and he dealt with all the external agendas; he was retained in the reestablished Ministry, where he embodies a kind of super-head of department and holds an appointment unique in the Austrian administration. He and his agents have under them the General Secretariat. The agenda of the Ministry is prepared in the departments, which for the most part consisted of sections, though some matters, principally protocol and international law, were dealt with outside the departmental structure. The number of sections was at first four, then five. In the post-war Foreign Office there has been the same tendency as in the period between the wars (and, indeed, during the monarchy as well) to delegate mainly to the three principal sections (formerly departments) matters concerning general politics, economic politics and questions of law.

In 1973 there followed the last important change, caused by the Federal

Ministries Act of 1973, in which the general spheres of responsibility for all ministries were determined by one single law. For the Foreign Ministry this brought with it an increase in status. While it was only allotted 'external affairs, as long as they do not come under the authority of another Federal Ministry', this limitation clause was applied to the spheres of nearly all ministries. Furthermore, the OECD agenda remained with the Federal Chancellery, while EFTA and GATT matters, as well as important bilateral economic relations remained under the authority of the Ministry of Commerce, which, however, had to deal with Austrian legations abroad via the Foreign Ministry (to whom 'matters of economic integration' are expressly reserved) just like any other Ministry. In addition, the press and cultural attachés and the cultural institutes were placed under the authority of the Foreign Ministry. As a result of this redistribution, the number of personnel rose considerably. In 1974 it took over 101 government officials from other branches, to whom the special conditions of entry into the senior foreign service were not applied.

According to the clauses of the law the Ministries, without exception, had to be divided up into sections. The power of organization in this matter lies with the Minister, who thus retains his leadership of the administrative apparatus in the Austrian governmental system. As well as the three major sections already mentioned, there are now three more: (I) Section of General Affairs, (II) Political Section, (III) Section for Economic Policy, (IV) Legal and Consular Section, (V) Cultural Section, (VI) Administrative Section. The organizational chart (Appendix A) shows their subdivisions. Moreover, departments and within them 'referats' can be set up or disbanded according to demand. In spite of continual changes – thus, for instance, the present 'Science/Education' referat of the first department of Section V used to be a separate fifth department; the fifth department of Section III was split off from the former first department of that section – the current form of organization will, in its basic structure, remain as it is for a long time to come.

BIBLIOGRAPHY

For general information and bibliographical specifications concerning Austrian history, see Erich Zöllner, *Geschichte Österreichs. Von den Anfängen bis zur Gegenwart*, 6th edn (Vienna 1979); Heinrich Benedikt (ed.), *Geschichte der Republik Österreich* (Vienna 1954); Erika Weinzierl and Kurt Skalnik (eds), *Österreich. Die Zweite Republik*, 2 vols (Graz, Vienna, Cologne 1972); Peter Malina and Gustav Spann, *Bibliographie zur österreischischen Zeitgeschichte 1918–1978. Eine Auswahl* (Politische Bildung 28–30, Vienna 1980) (2nd edn, completed up to 1980); Lilly-Ralou Behrmann, Peter Proché and Wolfgang Strasser, *Bibliographie zur Außenpolitik der Republik Österreich seit 1945* (Schriftenreihe der Österreichischen Gesellschaft für Außenpolitik und Internationale Bezeihungen 7, Vienna/Stuttgart 1974).

Specific information about the Foreign Ministry, a field of study not much explored, can be taken from Erwin Matsch, 'Die Auflösung des österreichisch-ungarischen Auswärtigen Dienstes 1918/1920', in *Mitteilungen des Österreichischen Staatsarchivs*, 30 (1977), 288–316, a pioneer study, but with some superficial conclusions; Erich Zöllner (ed.), *Diplomatie und Außenpolitik Österreichs. 11 Beiträge zu ihrer Geschichte* (Schriften des Institutes für Österreichkunde 30, Vienna 1977) contains several interesting allusions. Josef Schöner, 'Der österreichische Diplomat' in *Diplomatie unserer Zeit. Beiträge aus dem Internationalen Diplomatenseminar Kleßheim,* Karl Braunias and Gerald Stourzh (eds) (Veröffentlichungen der Österreichischen Gesellschaft für Aussenpolitik und Internationale Beziehungen, Graz, Vienna, Cologne 1959) 250–63, is almost the only detailed study about Foreign Office personnel, but tends to avoid delicate historical points. Former diplomats' memoirs by Lothar Wimmer, *Zwischen Ballhausplatz und Downing Street* (Vienna, Munich 1958), and by Clemens Wildner, *Von Wien nach Wien. Erinnerungen eines Diplomaten* (Vienna, Munich 1961) are mainly of value for the psychological framework of the 'k.u.k.-republican diplomats'. In general, statements and memoirs of the different Foreign Ministers provide some information. Chronological facts about administration and personnel are to be found in the *Österreichisches Jahrbuch* (Vienna 1918 onwards, with interruptions) and the *Österreichischer Amtskalender* (Vienna 1921–1936 and 1949 onwards), the continuation of the *Hof- rnd Staats-Handbuch*. Since 1975 the Foreign Ministry has edited an *Außenpolitischer Bericht*, which gives the official interpretation of Austrian policy in the events of the year.

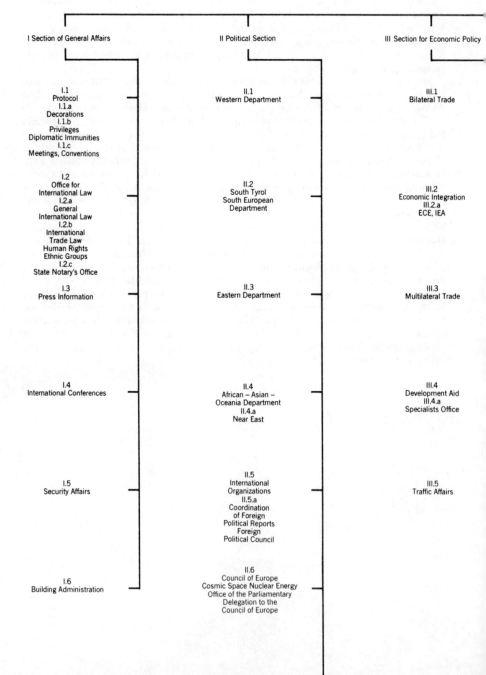

I Section of General Affairs

II Political Section

III Section for Economic Policy

I.1
Protocol
I.1.a
Decorations
I.1.b
Privileges
Diplomatic Immunities
I.1.c
Meetings, Conventions

II.1
Western Department

III.1
Bilateral Trade

I.2
Office for
International Law
I.2.a
General
International Law
I.2.b
International
Trade Law
Human Rights
Ethnic Groups
I.2.c
State Notary's Office

II.2
South Tyrol
South European
Department

III.2
Economic Integration
III.2.a
ECE, IEA

I.3
Press Information

II.3
Eastern Department

III.3
Multilateral Trade

I.4
International Conferences

II.4
African – Asian –
Oceania Department
II.4.a
Near East

III.4
Development Aid
III.4.a
Specialists Office

I.5
Security Affairs

II.5
International
Organizations
II.5.a
Coordination
of Foreign
Political Reports
Foreign
Political Council

III.5
Traffic Affairs

I.6
Building Administration

II.6
Council of Europe
Cosmic Space Nuclear Energy
Office of the Parliamentary
Delegation to the
Council of Europe

II.7
Security Policies
Disarmament

AUSTRIA – APPENDIX A

THE FOREIGN MINISTRY
(January 1981)

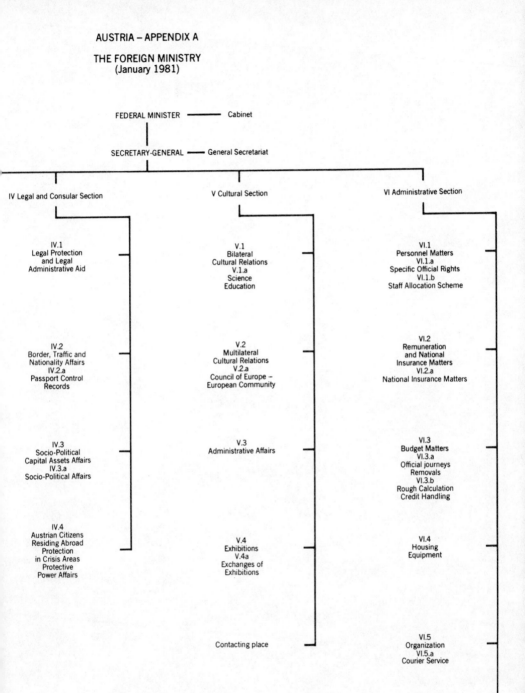

FEDERAL MINISTER —— Cabinet

SECRETARY-GENERAL —— General Secretariat

IV Legal and Consular Section

V Cultural Section

VI Administrative Section

IV.1
Legal Protection
and Legal
Administrative Aid

V.1
Bilateral
Cultural Relations
V.1.a
Science
Education

VI.1
Personnel Matters
VI.1.a
Specific Official Rights
VI.1.b
Staff Allocation Scheme

IV.2
Border, Traffic and
Nationality Affairs
IV.2.a
Passport Control
Records

V.2
Multilateral
Cultural Relations
V.2.a
Council of Europe –
European Community

VI.2
Remuneration
and National
Insurance Matters
VI.2.a
National Insurance Matters

IV.3
Socio-Political
Capital Assets Affairs
IV.3.a
Socio-Political Affairs

V.3
Administrative Affairs

VI.3
Budget Matters
VI.3.a
Official journeys
Removals
VI.3.b
Rough Calculation
Credit Handling

IV.4
Austrian Citizens
Residing Abroad
Protection
in Crisis Areas
Protective
Power Affairs

V.4
Exhibitions
V.4a
Exchanges of
Exhibitions

VI.4
Housing
Equipment

Contacting place

VI.5
Organization
VI.5.a
Courier Service

VI.6
Telecommunications

Belgium

The Ministry of Foreign Affairs

JACQUES WILLEQUET

Professor Jacques Willequet is Professor at the University of Brussels where he lectures on European and diplomatic history. He was born in 1914 and studied at Luxembourg, Stuttgart and Brussels where he received his doctorate in history. He served as historical adviser to the Ministry of Foreign Affairs from 1947 to 1949. Among his many books and articles in the field of diplomatic history are *Le Congo Belge et la Weltpolitik 1894–1914* (1962), *Les relations militaires franco-belges, de mars 1936 au 10 mai 1940,* travaux d'un colloque d'historiens belges et français (1968) and a number of biographies, including *Le baron Lambermont* (1971) and *Paul-Henri Spaak, un homme, des combats* (1975).

It would be wrong to assume that there was no independent Belgium before 1830. In fact, by as early as the fifteenth century, leaving aside the principality of Liège, a Belgian 'area' had taken shape, with Brussels as its own capital. Known first as the Spanish Netherlands then the Austrian Netherlands, it had a separate administrative structure and in particular a Conseil d'Etat, which was a real Ministry of Foreign Affairs, and in the eighteenth century possessed the essential attribute of a sovereign state: diplomatic representation, both active and passive. The main European courts were represented in Brussels and, conversely, 'Belgian' diplomats protected the interests of Brussels abroad as either permanent or temporary representatives.

The French invasion of 1794 made the Belgian provinces part of the Republic, then of the Napoleonic Empire; later on, from 1814 to 1830, they were amalgamated with Holland as the Kingdom of the Low Countries, but this solution did not withstand the Revolution of August–September 1830, which gave birth to an independent Belgian state in which all central administrative bodies had to be created, or even improvised, *ex nihilo*. We shall therefore begin our account from this date, describing the evolution and organization of a Ministry that, true to an old tradition, calls itself the Département, with a capital D.

There are considerable gaps in the story. Men are moved to action both by noble causes and by less noble ones, but the emphasis has always been put on the former. In administrative history there is always evidence of the logical and functional justifications for the various organizations and reorganizations, whereas traces of the personal motives (friendship, animosity, political interventions) that were often their real cause are very rare. Although many things were known or guessed by contemporaries, their echo scarcely reaches the historian. Thus royal decrees justifying changes in the administrative framework almost invariably call upon 'the interest of the service' or the necessity to 'ensure a prompt and smooth progress' of affairs – phrases that hide under their banality the real reasons for those reorganizations.

It is true, nevertheless, as was remarked by one of the few observers to have examined this matter, that 'administrative organization depends only to a very small extent on the will of more or less informed political reformers . . . its main features are determined by the fluctuation of collective needs . . . The dynamics of administrative institutions are actually no more than a concrete translation of collective needs, which become greater and more varied as social interdependence gets stronger because of technical progress.'[1]

In order to understand clearly the development of the Ministry of Foreign Affairs, therefore, it seems safer to start from the general situation. Several broad chronological sections correspond to the internal and external activities of the state: the first fifty years (1830–80), during which a young and neutral Belgium, ruled by an enfranchised bourgeoisie, strives to defend and strengthen its international position; the period of worldwide economic expansion (1880–1914); the Great War and its consequences (1914–40); and finally, the profound transformations that have characterized the last four decades. These divisions cannot but be general, of course: attitudes evolve more slowly than events, some constants remain, variables come into play or cease to operate for reasons that are sometimes fortuitous. Within each of those four main divisions the same series of themes will be examined: internal and external requirements of the country, the organizational structure of the

Department, the diffusion of and changes in its diplomatic and consular services, their recruitment and membership, the material and moral situation of its officers – in short, the ways and means of a policy.

1830 to 1880

The Ministry began on a small scale, first as a 'Diplomatic Committee' (18 November 1830), then as a 'Ministry of Foreign Affairs' (25 February 1831); politically, of course, it fell under the authority of a Minister, but it was, and still is, administered by a high-ranking official with the grade of secretary-general. The secretary-general can be compared in some respects to the 'permanent secretary' in Great Britain, though his range of competence is more limited. The Belgian secretary-general prepares the budgets and coordinates the various services, but he only exercises direct control over sectors specifically designated as his own. The general officials have always had direct access to the Minister, whereas the secretary-general is only entitled to information. This, of course, leaves him power to initiate, propose and advise. That outline is true in theory; because of personal elements concerning both the Minister and the secretary-general himself, there have been some all-powerful secretaries-general (Baron Lambermont, for example),[2] and others who kept strictly to administration, staying out of the field of high politics.[3]

The Department's first organization charts[4] show that the Minister has had his private secretary from the very beginning. At first, he was only a personal secretary, but this service was to grow considerably. In 1939 there were no more than four, but at present the secretariat numbers some forty officials, no longer chosen by the Minister but by the party. These secretaries are of course temporary, and in the Department they are actually less prone to become substitutes for the permanent administration than elsewhere.

The secretary-general is responsible for bodies whose official names vary (offices, divisions and boards), which deal with the general index, dispatch, orders, nobility, translations, archives and library.

Further down, there are three major divisions. At that time, the chief of an office or of a division used to be someone important. The Division of Political Affairs (known to this day as 'P') became the first directorate in 1841; a director was therefore responsible for it, as we shall see, until 1905. The Commercial Division became the second directorate in 1841, and was divided into two separate directorates (External Trade and Consulates; Internal Trade) in 1846. Later, the Directorate of Internal Trade moved to another ministry, and until 1895 there was just the Directorate of Trade and Consulates, still known in departmental jargon as 'B'. The third division also became the third directorate in 1841; it consisted of all the services of the Chancery: finances, accountancy, legalization and disputed claims. Finally, there was a specific Directorate of the Navy, whose titles and fortunes varied and which was handed over to the Ministry of Public Works in 1872.

The royal decree of 15 December 1875[5] reveals that staff numbers had already increased. It lists one private secretary, one secretary-general, seven directors or chiefs of division, six chiefs of office, five first-class clerks, four second-class clerks, twelve third-class clerks and six dispatching clerks (forerunners of our typists). This adds up to 42 officials, whose earnings were 10 000 and 8000 francs for the secretary-general and the director respectively;

below them, salaries ranged between 8000 for the head of division at the top of the scale to 1400 for the first-year dispatching clerks.

The origins of diplomacy in Belgium reveal an attitude that has fortunately not yet completely disappeared, according to which serving the state is an honour not necessarily connected with a reward. Only members of the wealthier social classes could offer their services to the king without expecting to make a living. The choice of the words 'the king' is deliberate. Immediately after what had been a bourgeois revolution part of the nobility remained wary, and this occasioned a brief democratic progress. Having played a part in the bourgeois guard during the revolutionary troubles was a proof of patriotism, and it was impossible to enter the civil service without bona fide references on that score. Later, some of these commoners were ennobled, and the whole of the landed aristocracy rallied to the new state. Of the 169 diplomats that can be accounted for in the period between 1830 and 1850, 120 were noblemen, ten per cent officers, and the remainder consisted of wealthy members of the upper bourgeoisie. There were exceptions, of course, but many valuable officials were compelled either to resign or to accept a mediocre standard of living in an inferior position because they could not afford the expenditure demanded of a chief of mission, which included the rent of lodgings and office, assistance to needy compatriots and status spending.[6] From the beginning there were some salaried legations, but as Parliament voted on general budgets and these were unevenly distributed between the various capitals it is difficult to assess each individual share of these credits. One thing is certain: the attaché received no remuneration, and the second secretary was paid only in some cases. Although it would be premature to speak of salary scales at that time, the data for 1873 indicate that a secretary received between 5000 and 8000 francs, a counsellor between 10 000 and 12 000 francs; a chargé d'affaires between 12 000 and 21 000 francs, a resident minister between 15 000 and 30 000 francs and a plenipotentiary minister between 25 000 and 58 000 francs. A comparison with the salaries of 'home' civil servants at the time must have shocked ill-informed people: a first judge at the Supreme Court of Appeal would earn 16 000 francs, a grammar school teacher 4000 francs and a university professor 7000 francs.[7]

Diplomats' salaries were indeed vehemently attacked every year, when the foreign affairs budget was discussed in Parliament. Yet we know for a fact that most chiefs of mission considerably depleted their own fortunes (we also know that during the war of 1914–18 many of them complained of the loss of their private resources, which were blocked in enemy-occupied Belgium). The very need for a diplomatic service was far from obvious, and doubts about it grew stronger with the century. Why should this little neutral country need diplomats? Each time, the Ministry of Foreign Affairs was forced to defend itself – to show the importance of observations and reports, of strengthening the presence and prestige of the country and also of protecting it from dangers that because of their very nature had to remain veiled with prudence and discretion. Historians know what threats the independence of Belgium was under during the reign of Napoleon III.[8]

Until 1858, when the diploma of candidature in philosophy and arts became compulsory,[9] no university degree was required. Attachés were appointed on a mere recommendation. Although there is a royal decree of 1841[10] that mentions an examination for promotion to the grade of second secretary, we do not know at all to what extent it was enforced. Only in 1857 were these promotion examinations clearly defined. From then on they included general history (including the main treaties), the history of Belgium, statistics and political economy, German or English language (the candidate's choice), law of nations, public law, both Belgian and foreign, a basic knowledge of civil law, diplomatic style (drafting a report), commercial system (laws, tariffs, etc.) and commercial facts (movements, exchanges, etc.), consular regulations.[11]

As for the distribution of missions, a glance at the *Almanach royal* for 1875 reveals that Belgium had thirteen legations in Europe (including the Ottoman Empire), one in the United States, one in Brazil, one in China and one in Japan, with 60 diplomats (including some interpreters) and twelve diplomats on non-active service.

The historian of institutions might tend, rather naïvely, to consider 1830 as a kind of zero year. But we must not forget that in spite of revolution commercial circuits remain active, industries still produce, traders still buy and sell, and ships still sail the seas. It is not surprising, then, that one of King Leopold's first acts, as early as July 1831, was to sign two decrees naming two consuls, one in Liverpool and the other one in Messina. Very soon afterwards there were other nominations, made under the pressure of Antwerp businessmen. As soon as they had settled down, diplomats were careful to extend a network that by 1833 already numbered thirty-seven consuls, who were appointed on the recommendation both of diplomats and of the chambers of commerce.[12] The organization of this profession, which at first only included honorary consuls, was laid down in a statute dated 27 July 1831,[13] which was completed by the law of 31 December 1851.[14] These honorary consuls were unsalaried Belgians or foreigners, but this does not mean that their work was unpaid – on the contrary, a series of decrees fixed the tariffs they were allowed to charge for services rendered, such as the preparation of maritime documents and legal acts, both administrative and private. The system worked, but it soon appeared to be in some respects both incomplete and unfair. In European countries where Belgian trade was already well established the honorary consuls lived well with little effort, while in far-off regions, where their services were rarely called upon but where they were legitimately expected to perform the much more arduous task of exploration and prospecting, they received little or nothing. Thus the necessity of appointing salaried consuls or consuls-general became obvious. It was thought at first that their appointments would only be temporary and that they would later be able to hand over to honorary consuls. This was wishful thinking, of course: as early as 1855, there were one vice-consul (in Cologne) and four consuls-general (in Valparaiso, Singapore, Australia and what is now The Gambia), whose guaranteed annual salaries ranged between 3600 and 25 000 francs.[15]

In this field, as in many others, the powerful activity of Baron Lambermont was to be felt. This remarkable secretary-general of the Ministry redirected his country's customs policy towards free trade, and at the same time created a wide network of consular agents who would gather the fruits of this new policy. His system remained resolutely 'liberal', including an overwhelming majority of *consuls-marchands*, but at the same time the state intervened either by giving indemnities to some of the consuls or by paying full salaries to consular officials whose task was to pioneer regions where private initiative was not yet able to come into play. Thus in 1865 there were already seven such consuls-general (Cape Town, Valparaiso, Smyrna, Calcutta, Constantinople, Athens and Sydney); the total number of consular posts reached 361, of which 221 were in Europe, 23 in the Ottoman Empire, eight in Africa, 26 in South America, 18 in the United States, 18 in Mexico and Central America, three in China, one in the Pacific and 43 in European-controlled colonies (of which 23 alone were in British possessions as a result of free-trade agreements contracted with London). The general structure of the consular service was established; henceforth it only underwent functional readjustments.[16]

It was all very well to make enquiries, canvass opinions and write reports, but how could this information be brought to the notice of those most concerned, the businessmen? It was published at first in the *Moniteur Belge* and distributed to the chambers of commerce. Then Lambermont stepped in; he ordered the publication of the *Recueil Consulaire Belge* (that inexhaustible source of information for exporters – and for future historians) and the creation of a 'Musée de l'Exportation',[17] which was later to expand under various names to become the 'Office Belge du Commerce Extérieur', whose present organization is based on the law of 16 July 1948. (We are getting well ahead of chronology here, but in order to finish with this subject, let me say that the activity of this office was later complemented by the Office National du Ducroire, which gives financial guarantees to exporters – but which in fact depends upon the Ministry of Economic Affairs.[18]

1880 to 1914

It is probably worth recalling that if Belgium was the first country in continental Europe to become industrialized, it had some advantages that in this particular period contributed to push it into the first rank of the world's economic and commercial powers: its geographical position, its coal, the port of Antwerp, its skilled manpower and liberal doctrine. Belgium was therefore an economic giant but a political dwarf. This became an additional argument that was often used. In the keen competition for the conquest of world markets, was it not preferable for countries such as China, Siam or Persia to choose the partnership of Belgium, rather than of great powers whose imperialist aims were far from reassuring? Not that Belgium was itself totally devoid of such imperialist aims, but circumstances were such that King Leopold II himself took responsibility for these ambitions. It is well known that he used his genius and obstinacy to carve a personal empire in central Africa that he could use as he pleased, with the intention of finally leaving it to Belgium, which he did in 1908. Between 1876 and 1908 the King was able to make use of very strong tactical support, among others from the Ministry of Foreign Affairs. The secretary-general, Lambermont, and the librarian-archivist, Banning, collaborated closely with the King, especially before the 1890s, when royal management methods began to be criticized both at home and abroad. The same ambiguity appears in the services Leopold II frequently requested of Belgian diplomats for his Congolese enterprises, which often put them in a delicate position. Who, after all, did they represent – small, neutral Belgium, or this fearsome potentate whose undertakings aroused such a variety of reactions? Finally, it is clear that some consulates, such as that in Zanzibar for example, were only created or developed in relation to and for the benefit of activities that could not be clearly identified either as national or as personal to the sovereign.[19] This unusual, if short-lived, situation created a new dimension that permanently affected the Department's work.

A quick look at the Ministry's organizational structure illustrates this growth. In the sector of the secretary-general, the division in charge of orders and the nobility became a directorate in 1873, as did the Archives, translation and the library.[20] In 1905, 'P' and 'B' became directorates-general, as did the Chancellery, known to this day as directorate-general 'C', which took over the Accountancy Department in 1910. In 1896 the post of departmental lawyer (1873) was amalgamated with the Directorate of Protocol and Disputed Claims, which became a directorate-general in 1905.[21]

As for manpower and salaries, let us look at the royal decree of 27 February 1912. Henceforth there were: one secretary-general (12000 francs), one private secretary (4000 to 9000 francs), four directors-general (10000 to 11000 francs), 15 directors and chiefs of directorates (6000 to 9000 francs), 14 chief and deputy chiefs of bureaux (4300 to 5400 francs), 38 clerks, 25 dispatching clerks and attachés (1600 to 4300 francs), and one supernumerary clerk. On the eve of 1914, therefore, there were 98 officials in the Home (Brussels) Department.[22] Many decrees, the most important being those of 11 December 1873, 9 November 1895 and 30 December 1905,[23] had laid down the conditions of appointment and the examinations or exemption from examination for passing from one grade to another. Similarly, the law of 21 July 1844 created a scheme of superannuation that was very favourable compared to that in the private sector, where there was nothing similar at that time. Retirement at the age of sixty-five remained optional until 1914.[24]

The number of diplomats did not increase at a similar rate during this period: there were only sixty-nine in 1909.[25] Among the preoccupations of the Department economic expansion came first; it even pushed national susceptibilities into the background. This can be seen in the relentless efforts made to renew relations with Mexico (from which the Belgians had been ignominiously driven out in 1867 as a consequence of their interference in the Civil War), in the attempts to gain access to the Transvaal (at the risk of antagonizing Great Britain) and in similar events in Iran and China.[26] In fact, during this long period of peace in Europe, Parliament and newspapers had attacked the diplomatic corps more sharply than ever. 'Nearly two and half million francs for the budget of foreign affairs, exclaimed the *Ami de l'Ordre* on 2 October 1892. 'This is a high price to pay for the pleasure of knowing that some of our compatriots are enjoying themselves in foreign capitals. A good consular corps, active and watchful, would easily fulfil all our needs – among which we do not include the need for showing off.[27] Every attack used the same comparison: twice as much money for diplomats as for consuls, whereas in France the proportion was reversed.[28] This did not take into account the fact that French consuls were civil servants. In Parliament, ministers stressed the countless 'invisible' services performed by the external staff[29] and, on 18 April 1902, Favereau remarked in the Senate: 'It is claimed that diplomats do nothing but parade in salons. Well, our Paris legation alone sends off 9000 letters every year: is that a sinecure?' 'That would depend on the letters', was the retort.[30] The arrival of enormous numbers of socialists in the House did not improve the situation. Why not get rid of these diplomats, after all?

This campaign had a significant effect at the consular level, and led to demands for more stringent commercial training of diplomats. An internal note of 14 June 1887 suggested the organization of an additional test[31] in this subject and resulted in the royal decree of 4 February 1888. Henceforth, second secretaries of legation would still be chosen from among attachés who had passed the examination mentioned earlier, but they would also have to pass the 'commercial' examination[32] in order to become first secretaries. The broad lines of this formula have remained the same to this day, with the addition of training courses and higher linguistic demands. Since 1924, however, the first examination has become a compulsory qualification for an attaché, and the second is required for the grade of second secretary.

Despite some protests, a knowledge of Flemish was not considered necessary. 'There have been no complaints from people using our services', was the Minister's response.[33] As regards foreign languages, the examination demanded a 'thorough' knowledge of English or German, and a 'basic' knowledge of Spanish.[34] Salaries remained stationary (as did the cost of living), but the payment of various costs of representation and indemnities became customary. Since 1887 the Department had also embarked on a property-buying programme.

The critics mentioned above, who without saying it in so many words were aiming at a fusion of the diplomatic and consular careers, did at least bring about an improvement in the consular system. The great instigator of this reform, both in word and in deed, was the deputy (later senator) Andrimont. He pointed out that in 1889 there were twenty-five career consuls out of a total of about 500 officials scattered all over the world: no examinations, no probationary periods, no career, no hierarchy – all appointments were at the discretion of the Minister. Why not add above this body of honorary consuls a structure of permanent and qualified consuls?[35] A royal decree was finally promulgated on 25 September 1896 that created a paid consular career, hierarchical in structure, and requiring that competence be proved. Vice-consuls, consuls and consuls-general were chosen from among those holding a diploma of higher commercial education, and they were paid between 6000 and 14000 francs. As for the honorary consuls, they were still appointed by the Minister, but only on presentation of a 'diploma of aptitude'.[36] On 15 May 1900 another decree clarified this last point: career consuls were to be graduates in commercial and consular sciences from a Belgian university.[37]

Thus the service was greatly improved and better structured. By 1903 there were already 32 career consuls and 20 career vice-consuls outside Europe; by 1909 a total of 63 career consuls and 591 honorary consuls (the ex-*consuls-marchands*) had been reached.[38]

1914 to 1945

Caught in an unprecedented whirlwind, in August 1914 the Belgian Government withdrew, first to Antwerp, then to Le Havre, where it spent the four years of the war. Two mistakes were made on that occasion: only a few (15 to be precise) higher officials left,[39] and the archives remained in Brussels. That was a windfall for the Germans, who installed a team of historians (headed by Dirr and Schwertfeger) in the offices of the rue de la Loi. They studied the archives and then used them for propaganda, a step that soon appeared to be highly ambiguous. On the one hand, they would have liked to prove that Belgium had broken its obligatory neutrality well before 1914; on the other, they discovered many reports that, when selected and abridged, spotlighted some very critical evaluations of the external policies pursued by London and Paris. The neutral diplomats could not have known that Britain and France would become allies in 1914, nor could they have expected their texts to be used later as enemy propaganda! These reports were first published in the press, then in five volumes under the title *Zur Europäischen Politik 1897–1914*. (This opened the huge question of responsibility for the war, a subject that became crucial in the polemical debates of the twenties and thirties, where, on the Belgian side, Alfred de Ridder, the departmental archivist, distinguished himself.)

In Le Havre, the Department's skeleton staff faced an increase in their workload, which was swollen both by preparations for the post-war period and by the intense activity of awakening the world's conscience to Belgium's plight. The psychological and moral importance for the Allies of the image of little David, neutral and innocent, attacked by a Goliath who had broken his word of honour, is common knowledge. New staff, recruited in the free world, were taken on in Le Havre, and by 1918 175 officials were employed.[40] This was also a period of reflection for the ministers, and we shall soon see its fruits.

There is no need to stress the multiple responsibilities that were to burden these officials after 1918: the peace treaty and its execution, the problems of the Rhine area, reparations, Locarno . . . all fields where the political, economic, monetary and financial elements were so intricate that it was decided as early as 1919 to form a 'diplomatic committee' whose chairman would have to coordinate the work of 'P' and 'B'.[41] This committee was dismantled a year later to allow the merger of the two directorates into the Directorate-General of Politics and Trade, which contained fifteen sections – eight 'geographical' and seven 'technical' ones.[42] It soon became obvious that this instrument was too unwieldy for practical purposes; besides, the secretary-general was now entrusted with the control of the protocol and orders service, of dispatch, of the Directorate-General of Chancellery and Disputed Claims, of Accountancy, and of a new Directorate-General of Archives, Nobility and Translations (which constituted a significant promotion). The superior grade conferred on de Ridder allows us to infer that the utmost importance was given from then on to historical studies, whose extensive relevance had suddenly come to light in the polemics about Belgian neutrality and the origins of the First World War.

These changes are reflected in the post-war organizational structure: with one chairman of the diplomatic committee (soon to be dismantled), one secretary-general, one private secretary, five directors-general (including that for accountancy, which was also short-lived), 25 directors and chiefs of division, 22 chiefs of bureaux, 37 deputy chiefs of bureaux and drafters, 107 clerks, 40 'lady typists' (an innovation!) and, in special posts, 20 accountants, five archivists, six librarians and 18 translators – a total of 286 officials, paid between 3000 francs for a first-year typist and 20 000 francs for the chairman of the diplomatic committee, though these salaries soon changed as a result of high inflation in the early twenties.[43] As for conditions of recruitment, provisions were made for an entrance examination, with promotion by seniority in the lower grades but by selection in the upper ones.[44]

It is not necessary to list all the new services that developed during the post-war period, except for the creation within 'P' of a modest Office of the League of Nations; at a time when external relations were still exclusively bilateral, this was the first sign of the multilateralism that was to proliferate later on. By the end of 1925 the merger of 'P' and 'B' had proved unworkable and the two were again separated. This reorganization brought the total number of staff to 351 agents.[45] The reorganization of 'B', where collaboration with the business world had become crucial, was now so essential that an unusual step was taken: the appointment as (temporary) director-general of an industrialist from the private sector, G. Hannecart, who proved to be extremely successful.[46] In 1934 the Department took the official title of Ministry of Foreign Affairs and External Trade.[47]

Important changes resulted from the creation in 1936 of a Commission for Administrative Reform. These were: a new status for all state officials in 1937, the establishment of a permanent secretariat for recruitment, which was in charge of entry examinations and promotions and of the classification of the diplomas the candidates must hold. By 1939 the whole administrative corps was subject to a hierarchical structure based on the level of education reached – university, upper and lower secondary, and primary.[48]

Another whirlwind hit the Ministry after 10 May 1940. The ambassador in London, Cartier de Marchienne, and the secretary-general, F. van Langenhove (who had been the first to hasten, with remarkable determination, to the capital of Britain), reorganized the services in a building in Eaton Square, where Minister Spaak came to resume his position in October. This time, however, the archives had long been stored in what were called 'mobilization' boxes, and it was thus possible to keep those precious papers at Caernarvon Castle in Wales for the duration of the war.

The First World War had at least one fortunate consequence: it finally put an end to traditional criticism of the diplomatic corps. It was possible, before 1914, to think that its only use was observation; the importance and complexity of post-war problems forced it to assume an active role, the necessity for which was no longer questioned. Moreover – and this is why we now group diplomats and consuls in the same paragraph – these years marked the beginning of the integration of the two careers, which were to merge completely during the next period.

Yet it is striking that the number of diplomats remained absolutely stationary during these years: in 1939 there were only 64 diplomats in missions abroad, plus a few who had been detached, temporarily or permanently, to serve in the home services. Some of them, however, had been promoted to the grade of ambassador after 1918: in Paris, London, Rome, Rio, Washington, at the Vatican and, in 1938, in Berlin. By contrast, the number of career consuls had almost doubled (to 115), whereas the figures for honorary officials remained stable (at 543).

Although the two traditional examinations became compulsory in the 1920s,[49] as mentioned earlier, there were no fundamental changes in the status of diplomats. However, a decree of 15 July 1920 noted that the low salary level was forcing diplomats to draw on private sources of income, and that salaries must therefore be raised. The salary range was henceforth 6000 to 40 000 francs, but these figures were gradually increased to 24 000 and 100 000 francs respectively, to which not only the varying indemnities of missions (written into the annual budgets) were added but also many additional costs that were now to be borne by the state. Besides, this decree of 1920 forsaw the 'possibility' that a diplomat might assume consular duties.[50]

The most decisive reforms were made on the consular side, following the work of a commission set up in 1919. The decree of July 1920 maintained the distinction between honorary and salaried staff; like the diplomats, the latter would now have to pass an entrance examination, which gave them the grade of consular aide. After a period of two years they would become consular attachés, and eventually vice-consuls, consuls and consuls-general. The great innovation was that these officials might be called upon to carry out diplomatic functions.[51] This opened the way for the organization, after 1924, of a single recruitment examination for both legation attachés and consular attachés.[52] By the end of the thirties the two careers were – at least in theory – equal: first class plenipotentiary minister or first class consul-general (salary: 80 000 to 100 000 francs), second class plenipotentiary minister or second class consul-general (65 000 to 75 000 francs), councillor or third class consul-general (50 000 to 58 000 francs), first class secretary or consul (40 000 to 46 000 francs), second class secretary or first class vice-consul (32 000 to 37 000 francs), third class secretary or second class vice-consul (27 000 to 29 500 francs), legation attaché or third class vice-consul (24 000 to 25 000 francs).[53] In spite of this apparent comparability, it was impossible not to acknowledge that there were differences between those two categories of officials, still based on considerations of fortune and social level, that cooperation did not always work very well, that promotion was much more rapid on the one side than on the other, and that there were not in fact two careers but 'two castes'.[54] Why not, in the end, have a single career service, a single promotion table – which the Commission for Administrative Reform had in fact just suggested? This question was being studied in 1939.[55]

1945 to 1980

Enormous changes have taken place in the duties, responsibilities and powers of the Department since the Second World War in response to the changing world to which all nations are having to adapt. Rather than presenting the successive developments in chronological order, it will be simpler to describe the present organization of the services, which have greatly increased in size. There are now some 1460 officials (there were three dozen when the Ministry was first established!), a large proportion of whom work in multilateral relations – a reflection of today's world. There is also, of course, an unprecedented need for technical specialization in the staff.

Since 1961 the overall administrative body, still called the Department, has been reunited in a single building in the rue des Quatre-Bras, under the orders of three Ministers. External trade ('B') was entrusted to a special Minister in 1946. After the independence of the Congo in 1961 a new step was taken: the Ministry of Cooperation and Development was formed out of the former Ministry of the Colonies and the colonial services of the Ministry for Foreign Affairs.

Cabinets have all swollen in size, partly as a result of growing politicization. In Foreign Affairs there are 47 officials, of whom nine are administrators; in Cooperation 42 officials, including four administrators; in External Trade 37 officials (five administrators). The general secretariat (42 officials, seven administrators) covers the legal service, European coordination, the Centre for Analysis and Forecasts, special missions and the Diplomatic Commission. A new directorate-general 'A' (Administration) has been established, with 577 officials of whom 98 are administrators. It includes two directorates of staff (for home and abroad), the department in charge of probation, the Medical Centre, the Directorate of the Budget and Accountancy, the Directorate of Home Services, Intendancy, Cipher, Organization and Training, the Inspectorate of Diplomatic and Consular Posts, the Administrative Directorate of Documents and Treaties, the archives, the library, translation, orders, nobility, overseas social security, the Inspectorate of Staff in Services Abroad, protocol, security and restaurants. The Directorate-General of Economic Relations Overseas (134 officials, 81 administrators) covers the geographical sectors and three administrative directorates – foreign markets, multilateral relations and economic relations of various kinds. The Directorate-General of the Chancellery and of Legal Affairs, which is divided into four administrative directorates, has 134 officials and 61 administrators. The Directorate-General of Politics also includes general bilateral services, such as the Administrative Directorate for African Affairs, but it consists mainly of multilateral sections: Western, international and European organizations, and East–West coordination. A scientific service, a historical service and services of General Affairs and of the Environment also belong to this directorate.

In the meantime, an Administrative Directorate for Information and Cultural Relations (with 65 officials, including 22 administrators) has separated from the Division of Political Affairs ('P'). (This directorate publishes, among other things, an interesting collection of multilingual brochures entitled *Textes et Documents*.) The General Administration for Cooperation and Development (with 247 officials, of whom 131 are administrators) includes a Directorate-General for the Preparation and Evaluation of Policies and several administrative directorates – geographical and sectional planning, multilateral cooperation, educational and social cooperation, economic cooperation, and general services including finances, study grants, laws covering guarantees and reinstatement, recruitment and voluntary service, etc.

A century ago Belgium was a nation ruled by an exclusively French-speaking bourgeoisie. The increase in democracy gave rise to claims that resulted in reforms in favour of Dutch, which is the written language of the Flemish region; but foreign affairs – like the army – did not attract many Dutch-speakers, so the Department has been slow to respond to laws that gradually imposed a better linguistic balance in the administration. Since the laws of 1963, which initiated a kind of federalization by dividing the country into strictly homogeneous linguistic regions, 40 per cent of employees in all ministries must be monolingual Flemish (i.e. Dutch-speaking) and 40 per cent monolingual French-speaking, with the remaining 20 per cent perfectly bilingual. A different balance was reached in the case of officials in missions abroad (see below).

The condition of state officials, reflecting a general change in attitudes, has changed in many other respects since 1945. The state has lost its sacred aura and its officials have become more integrated into society, adopting some of its positive and some of its less desirable characteristics – politicization being counted among the latter. For example, while the entrance examinations of the permanent secretariat for recruitment are scrupulously fair, it is unfortunately true that the higher the candidates climb in the hierarchy the more their promotion will be based not on merit but on political con-siderations. This can even apply to the appointment of a secretary-general. Trade unionism has greatly increased, and the unions now participate in the organization and administration of the services. During the 'golden sixties' the unions demanded that civil servants should benefit from the greatly increased prosperity enjoyed by the private sector. 'Social programming' (i.e. negotiations between the state and the unions) was introduced into the Department, as it was in other areas of the administration, bringing such benefits as family allowances, extra holiday pay, health service benefits, annual bonuses, etc.[56] This brings us to the question of salary. In these days of inflation and indexation, and with a sliding scale of taxation that in some cases reduces the salary by more than half, a straightforward list of current figures would not reflect the true situation. It is better demonstrated by observing that the *net* salary of the lowest-paid official is about 21 000 francs per month; in Belgium, salary scales vary by a factor of 4:7, so to obtain the net salary of the secretary-general one has only to multiply by this figure the earnings of the porter-messenger.

There is no need to describe in detail what is a general phenomenon: the tremendous changes undergone by the diplomatic profession in the post-war period. These modifications, caused partly by the figurative shrinking of the world and also by the new balance of power and wielding of influence that most nation-states are able to exert, are perhaps felt most sharply by small countries. In 1940 the world could still hold its breath in anxious expectation of a political decision to be taken in Brussels. Those days are gone, but the workings of a diplomacy that has been compared to a board of directors allows small states and strong personalities much greater influence than in the days of bilateral relations. In Belgium's traditional role as mediator – in the construction of Europe, in East–West relations, or in helping the Third World – its ministers have often played a vital part. Diplomats prepare for and extend this action. Today, every head of post is an ambassador (an indirect consequence of so many states becoming independent); the diplomatic and consular careers have now been united – reform that was being considered before 1940.[57]

There have been adjustments to the language requirements, so important in Belgium. Today, all officials in missions abroad must be perfectly bilingual in French and Dutch, a situation rather different from that of their colleagues at home. The first recruitment examination in Dutch was apparently held in 1937;[58] at that time the Minister believed that he had given full satisfaction to the Flemish people. In 1962 a law made compulsory the listing of officials on two separate rolls according to language.[59] This division showed a clear imbalance in favour of French-speakers, so the Minister, M. Fayat, intro-duced a simplified examination for Dutch-speaking candidates.[60] French-speaking officials who wanted to retire were allowed to do so (on their full salary until the age of sixty-five, then on a normal pension), though only about forty of them took advantage of this offer,[61] possibly because they were little impressed by a state that – rather strangely, one must admit – interfered with established rights and unilaterally modified the statutes controlling recruitment. Finally, a decree of 1968 established the present structure of overseas careers, fixing a maximum number of posts for each grade and confirming that there should be the same number of officials on the two language lists.[62]

In other respects the conditions of the recruitment examination (now open to women) have hardly changed, except for a strengthening of the language demands; a perfect knowledge of French, Dutch and English is required, and at the end of the training period, in addition to the traditional commercial examination there is now an examination in a fourth language to be chosen from German, Spanish, Italian, Russian, Arabic, Chinese and Japanese. Diplomats are paid the same as their 'home' collegues, with the addition of field allowances. There are 248 diplomats in all, of whom a hundred are ambassadors or heads of mission (some of them holding several posts simultaneously) either in foreign capitals or at the headquarters of international organizations. There are also 160 chancellors and about 300 consuls, three-quarters of whom hold honorary posts, various scientific and agricultural advisers, locally recruited general staff and many unpaid commercial agents.

Conclusion

During the 150 years' existence of the Belgian state, the Ministry for Foreign Affairs has seen great changes and expansion that have been the result of continuing adaptation. Whereas in 1830 a small, neutral country could, in a context of economic liberalism and within a framework of strictly bilateral relations be satisfied with a few dozen agents to fulfil its international commitments, it now needs nearly three thousand of them. Today's multilateral diplomacy encompasses political, economic, social, military and scientific activities, and even countries with a limited population must devote to them an ever-increasing part of their resources. The few aristocrats and members of the gentry who originally esteemed it a point of honour to 'serve the king' in a disinterested manner have given way to less privileged career officials. In spite of the disadvantages that all vast administrations suffer, the awareness of being useful, of serving the country, of defending legitimate material and moral interests, is unquestionably felt more among the officials of this Department than in other offices with more specific attributions. The Belgian Ministry for Foreign Affairs cannot, of course, compare with either the Foreign Office in London or the French Quai d'Orsay, which are supported by five centuries of tradition, but its own tradition nevertheless gives it a strength, a cohesion, a sense of the state that makes it a special body within the Belgian administration.

NOTES

[1] H. Janne, *Dynamique des institutions. Naissance et Développement des ministères belges des origines à la guerre de 1914–1918* (Brussels 1952), 454.

[2] J. Willequet, *Le Baron Lambermont* (Brussels 1970).

[3] A. Molitor, *L'Administration de la Belgique* (Brussels 1974), 239–40.

[4] These organization charts have been carefully established and analysed by Y. Peemans in *L'Organisation de l'administration du Ministère des Affaires étrangères de 1830 à 1914,* an unpublished typewritten memoir accepted with distinction in 1979 by the Faculté des Sciences sociales, politiques et économiques of the Université Libre de Bruxelles.

[5] *Moniteur belge,* 29 December 1875.

[6] M. Delsemme, *Agents diplomatiques belges et étrangers aux XIXe et XXe siècles* (Brussels 1968), 33–48.

[7] M. Delsemme, op. cit., 38, 53.

[8] In the Archives of the Ministry of Foreign Affairs (henceforth referred to as AEB) there is a sub-file of file 12.978 with, for that period, a telling indication: 'On the usefulness of the diplomatic corps'.

[9] Royal decree of 1 April 1858, in *Recueil des Lois et Arrêtés royaux de la Belgique* (1858), 271.

[10] Royal decree of 10 October 1841, in *Recueil des Lois et Arrêtés royaux de Belgique* (1841), 891.

[11] Royal decree of 26 June 1857, in *Recueil des Lois et Arrêtés de Belgique* (1857), 206–7.

[12] J. Willequet, 'Un facteur d'expansion commerciale: le système consulaire sous Léopold I', in *Expansion belge 1831–1865* (Brussels 1965), 32–40.

[13] *Moniteur belge,* 30 September 1831.

[14] *Moniteur belge,* 7 January 1852.

[15] J. Willequet, 'Un facteur d'expansion commerciale: le système consulaire sous Léopold I', in *Expansion belge 1831–1865* (Brussels 1965), 49.

[16] J. Willequet, op. cit., 50–5.

[17] J. Willequet, op. cit., 52–3.

[18] Royal decree of 31 August 1939 in *Moniteur belge,* 4 October 1939.

[19] J. Stengers, *Combien le Congo a-t-il coûté à la Belgique?* (Brussels 1957), 57–66.

[20] For the Archives, there is an excellent study by Daniel H. Thomas in *The New Guide to the Diplomatic Archives of Western Europe* (Pennsylvania 1975), 40–42; and another by J. Willequet, 'Les archives du Ministère des Affaires étrangères', in *Archives, Bibliothèques et Musées* (Brussels 1951).

[21] See the organization chart in Y. Peemans, op. cit.

[22] Royal decree of 27 February 1912 in *Moniteur belge,* 9 March 1912.

[23] *Moniteur belge,* 13 December 1873, 25 November 1895 and 28 January 1906.

[24] M. Delsemme, op. cit., 35.

[25] AEB 13.162. Brochure: *Ministère des Affaires étrangères. Agents diplomatiques et consulaires* (1909).

[26] See the study by N. Carcan-Chanel in M. Delsemme, op. cit., 67–102.

[27] AEB 1509 Pers.

[28] AEB, *Le Commerce et l'Industrie de Gand,* 28 January 1893.

[29] See, for example, AEB 10.988, note of 31 December 1896 on the board of Chancellery.

[30] AEB 12.938. Criticism of the role of diplomacy.

[31] AEB 11.926. Reorganization of examinations.

[32] Royal decree of 4 February 1888 in *Moniteur belge,* 15 February 1888.

[33] AEB 12.938. Yet apparently, already in 1901 (AEB 12.937) a note of the Commission on the diplomatic examination listed a basic knowledge of Dutch among the compulsory subjects.

[34] Royal decree of 25 May 1914 in *Moniteur belge,* 14 June 1914, which in fact confirmed the text of many former decrees.

[35] See AEB, the whole of file 1509 Pers, the parliamentary debates of 1886 and the following years, and the articles in *L'Etoile belge* of 29 November and 7 December 1889.

[36] Royal decree of 25 September 1896 in *Moniteur belge,* 14 October 1896.

[37] Royal decree of 15 May 1900 in *Moniteur belge,* 26 May 1900.

[38] AEB 13.162, brochure quoted before (note 25).

[39] AEB 12.207, note from the secretary-general, Costermans, on 15 September 1925.

[40] AEB 12.207, ibid.

[41] Royal decree of 29 December 1919 in *Moniteur belge,* 29 February 1920.

[42] Royal decree of 20 January 1921 in *Moniteur belge,* 29 January 1921.

[43] See in AEB 12.207 the brochure *Barème des Départements ministériels 1924,* and a series of readjustments that eventually fixed the minimum salary at 9000 francs, and the maximum salary at 125000 francs. In 1935, all salaries were linked to the index of prices (A. Molitor, op. cit., 386).

[44] Royal decree of 29 December 1919 in *Moniteur belge,* 29 February 1920.

[45] Royal decree of 28 December 1925 in *Moniteur belge,* 6 January 1926.

[46] On this subject, see in AEB 11.542 an interesting article of the *Echo de la Bourse,* 1–3 April 1926.

[47] Royal decree of 20 November 1934 in *Moniteur belge,* 21 November 1934.

[48] On all those reforms, see M. Halewyck de Heusch, *Le Recrutement des agents de l'Etat* (Brussels 1945).

[49] Royal decree of 30 November 1924 in *Moniteur belge,* 14 January 1925. One should note that in accordance with the linguistic law of 1921, this decree was introducing 'spoken and written' knowledge of Dutch in the entry examinations.

[50] Royal decree of 15 July 1920 in *Moniteur belge,* 25 July 1920.

[51] Royal decree of 15 July 1920 on the reorganization of the consulates in *Moniteur belge,* 25 July 1920.

[52] Royal decree of 5 December 1924 in *Moniteur belge,* 14 January 1925.

[53] Table, without date, in AEB 12.159.

[54] AEB 12.978. Note from Consul-General Moulaert, 19 June 1925, and AEB 14.455, unsigned and undated memorandum (apparently of 1944).

[55] AEB 12.159, *passim*, and article in *Nation belge*, 18 December 1936.

[56] See the perceptive reflections by A. Molitor, op. cit., 278–83 and *passim*.

[57] Royal decree of 16 October 1946 in *Moniteur belge*, 18 December 1946.

[58] Perhaps already in 1936, but certainly not in 1935: the information of the Ministry is incomplete for 1936.

[59] Law of 5 April 1962 in *Moniteur belge*, 10 April 1962.

[60] Dubbed 'Fayat-boys' in the jargon of the Department. Law of 6 April 1962 in *Moniteur belge*, 10 April 1962.

[61] A. Molitor, op. cit., 366.

[62] Royal decree of 30 March 1968 in *Moniteur belge*, 3 May 1968.

BIBLIOGRAPHY

M. Delsemme, *Agents diplomatiques belges et étrangers aux XIXe et XXe siècles* (Brussels 1968).

M. Halewyck de Heusch, *Le recrutement des agents de l'Etat* (Brussels 1945).

H. Janne, 'Dynamique des institutions. Naissance et développement des ministères belges' in *Mélanges Georges Smets* (Brussels 1952).

A. Molitor, *L'administration de la Belgique* (Brussels 1974).

Y. Peemans, *L'organisation et l'administration du Ministère des Affaires Etrangères de 1830 à 1914* (unpublished typewritten memoir, University of Brussels 1979).

D. Thomas, *The new Guide to the Diplomatic Archives of Western Europe* (Pennsylvania 1975).

J. Willequet, *Le Baron Lambermont* (Brussels 1970).

J. Willequet, 'Un facteur d'expansion commerciale: le système consulaire sous Léopold I' in *L'Expansion belge* (Brussels 1965).

BELGIUM – APPENDIX A

MINISTRY FOR FOREIGN AFFAIRS, FOREIGN TRADE AND DEVELOPMENT COOPERATION

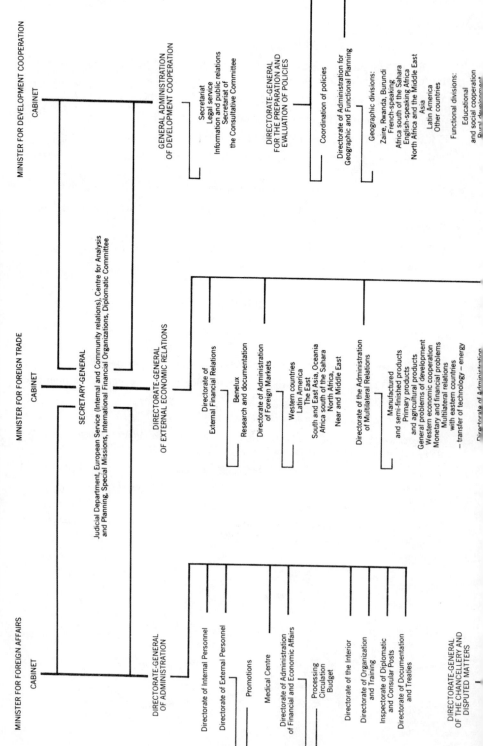

Fourth Directorate of Administration

DIRECTORATE-GENERAL OF POLITICAL AFFAIRS

General Services

Bilateral Sectors

Western countries
Near East, European-Arab dialogue
Eastern European sector
Far Eastern sector

Directorate of African Affairs

Zaire, Rwanda, Burundi
Africa south of the Sahara
Pan-African and regional organizations
Latin America

Multilateral Sectors

Politico-military affairs
Security
Disarmament and control
International organizations
Belgian Committee for UNESCO
Commission on Women's Conditions
Scientific service
Services of the European organizations
East-West coordination
Environment
Historical service
General Affairs

DIRECTORATE OF ADMINISTRATION FOR INFORMATION AND CULTURAL RELATIONS

Secretariat
Cultural relations
General documentation
Films
Postal information

Development Bank
OECD
Inspectorate-general
Evaluation of programmes and projects
Means and methods of cooperation
Organization and methods
Statistical studies

DIRECTORATE-GENERAL FOR THE PREPARATION AND EXECUTION OF PROGRAMMES

Secretariat
Coordination of programmes

Directorate of Administration for Social and Educational Cooperation

General information
Planning for social and technical development
Technical instruction and professional development
Social and co-financial development
Medical development

Directorate of Administration for Economic Cooperation

Agricultural development
Industrial development
Administration and promotion
Infrastructure

DIRECTORATE-GENERAL OF CENTRAL SERVICES

Documentation and library   Printers
General affairs   Financial services
Central services   Supplies
Translation   Funds
Plant

Directorate for the Administration of Personnel

Personnel for cooperation
Advisory personnel   Non-advisory personnel
Health, travel   Recruitment

Consultative Council for Development Cooperation

(Throughout this chart, the details on administrative sections have been abridged.)

Canada

The Department of External Affairs

JAMES EAYRS

James Eayrs is presently Eric Dennis Memorial Professor of Government and Political Science at Dalhousie University, Halifax, N.S. He was formerly Professor at the University of Toronto and is the author of many books on international, Commonwealth and Canadian affairs. Professor Eayrs has recently completed *Growing Up Allied*, the fourth volume in his series *In Defence of Canada*; he hopes two more will follow. A Fellow of the Royal Society of Canada and co-editor of *International Journal*, in 1950 he declined appointment in the Department of External Affairs for life in the academy and has since sustained from the sidelines his interest in 'conditions of foreign service'.

A foreign office, while not necessarily a frill of government, is an optional part of a state apparatus. Any government could conduct its foreign affairs without a ministry created expressly for that purpose. Its leaders could rely instead upon their own resources and those of their staffs to supervise and coordinate departments of trade, defence, immigration, agriculture, fisheries and any others doing the country's business abroad, resorting again to their own resources to attend to any residue that might show up as 'foreign policy' pure if not so simple. As the agenda of diplomacy changes (with issues of high statecraft displaced by those having less to do with the structure of peace and the balance of power than with the transfer of technology and the balance of payments); as the pace of diplomacy quickens (with world-wide instantaneous communications and no capital more than a day's flight distant); and as the level of diplomacy rises (with more and more world leaders developing an appetite and sometimes an aptitude for conducting foreign policy themselves), critics contend that it is no longer necessary to entrust the management of external relations to an élite sector of the public service. They even contend that the foreign office is obsolete.

Despite such contentions, not one of scores of newly independent countries has seen fit to dispense with its ministry of foreign affairs under whatever name. It may be that their leaders consider such ministries useful still. Or that they are merely copying their former metropoles. But it is certain that they find them valuable as symbols. Foreign offices of new states proclaim their sovereignty, their status, their capacity to enter into relations with other states under conditions of formal equality – however miniscule their power may be.

By creating a foreign ministry for Canada, Sir Wilfrid Laurier and his cabinet had not intended to mint a symbol of sovereignty, still less to seek a role in world affairs. The birth on 1 June 1909 of the Department of External Affairs ('External' rather than 'Foreign' in deference to the principle of diplomatic unity of the British Empire) predates by a decade Canada's acquisition of international personality through founding membership of the League of Nations, by nearly two decades its first exercise of the right of legation, by three decades its assertion of sovereignty in declaring war against Germany a week after the United Kingdom. Their objective had been more modest.

The Department of External Affairs (hereafter 'the Department', 'External', or 'DEA') was the brainchild of the leading public servant of the time, Sir Joseph Pope. Pope took a keen and solitary interest in the drafting and filing of official papers, and lamented the lack of attention to both in the conduct of Dominion business. To provide for the orderly preparation and collection of government documents, he proposed the creation of a department with 'a small staff of young men, well educated and carefully selected,' so as to 'acquire an organized method for dealing with international questions which at present we wholly lack.'[1] A more substantial role than that Pope neither desired nor claimed for the Department. Or for the government: '. . . [L]eave European questions such as the Bessarabian frontier &c to our Imperial statesmen and the trained experts of Downing Street.'[2] North American questions could be safely left to the judgement of the British ambassador to the United States (guided from time to time by Pope's shuttle diplomacy via the overnight train to Washington).

Plant and personnel were for some years as modest as the pretensions of the founder and original under-secretary of state for external affairs (USSEA). Quarters were found over a barbershop in downtown Ottawa. Only when Prime Minister Sir Robert Borden became Secretary of State for External Affairs (SSEA) in 1912 – so starting the practice (which lasted until 1946) of having the Prime Minister of the day hold the External Affairs portfolio – did the Department move, two years later, to its long-time home in the East Block on Parliament Hill. (The Prime Minister's office was also in the East Block: DEA's proximity to it, both of place and of personnel, was the source of much of its durable influence, which began to wane as distance grew between them.) The staff were few and, Pope apart, feeble. 'We have only three men in the Government Service who have any knowledge of details connected with Canada's foreign relations,' a governor-general complained to London. 'One drinks at times, [another] . . . has a difficulty expressing his thoughts. . . .'[3]

Out of these unpromising origins there would develop over the next half century what a former British ambassador has called 'one of the highest-powered foreign services in the modern world.'[4] How this came about it is not the purpose of this chapter to relate. (An official history of the Department of External Affairs, commemorating the 75th anniversary of its founding, is under preparation by its historical division for publication in 1984.) Rather, it will attempt to identify the main problems confronting the Department since that accolade was bestowed upon it in 1960; to assess to what extent its vicissitudes have been the tribulations of the profession of diplomacy at large, to what extent peculiar to its own milieu; and to examine its efforts to respond by adjusting to, resisting or surmounting its plethora of challenges.

Bureaucracy and personality

A small bureaucracy with large responsibility is shaped more by the personality of its managers than by its organization chart. So it proved for the Department, at least before the sprawl.

O. D. Skelton, the Department's adviser in 1923–4, its councillor in 1924–5, and its USSEA from 1925 until his death on the job early in 1941, imparted to it through his character and his ways of looking at the world an ethos that outlasted him. If Pope put the Department on the map of government, Skelton created contours that endured for decades. If Pope had been content to leave 'the Bessarabian frontier &c' to 'the trained experts of Downing Street', Skelton, driven by his obsession that they would drag, through their folly, ineptitude or perfidy, an innocent Dominion into trouble, sought to create in Canada some countervailing expertise. He set in place at the East Block and in a succession of legations and high commissions (at Washington in 1927, Paris in 1928, Tokyo in 1929, The Hague, Brussels and Canberra in 1939, Dublin, Wellington and Pretoria in 1940) the machinery for foreign policy. Among his early recruits, plucked from junior donships (as he himself was plucked from deanship) were Norman Robertson, Hume Wrong and Lester Pearson. Their apprenticeship was uneventful, but the trio providentially reached the apogee of their formidable if varied talents just when the utmost was required of them – the shaping of peace by a Canada made strong in war.

In due course, this new policy community would leave its mark upon the institutions of the United Nations system for collective security; upon those of the North Atlantic Treaty Organization when regional security came to seem the only feasible objective; upon the practice of peacekeeping, which by 1956 was sufficiently refined to permit that initiative during the Suez crisis which British officials in their memoirs call 'the Canadian lifeline' and which earned for the man most responsible for throwing it a Nobel Prize for peace. Nor was that all. 'We for the first time in our history,' writes a former member of the Department who played an active part in these events, 'contributed out of our taxes to the economic development of poor countries.'[5] Here was Canadian diplomacy's 'golden age'.

Sustaining this impressive performance – its initiation had been political, the crusading spirit of L. S. St Laurent (SSEA from 1946 to 1948, Prime Minister thereafter to 1957) and Lester Pearson (who entered politics in 1948 by switching from USSEA to SSEA, in which capacity he remained until 1957) prevailing over the revived suspicions of Skelton's patron, W. L. Mackenzie King (Prime Minister for all but a few weeks from late 1921 to 1930, and from late 1935 to late 1948), who only grudgingly acquiesced in their internationalist initiatives – was a corps of foreign service officers whom an Australian scholar could describe as 'articulate, worldly-wise yet earnest, seeking few favours but determined to be active'.[6]

During this decade of ascendancy – say from 1947 to 1957, though others might pick other dates – the Department exhibited in relief bolder then than before or since five main features of organization and ethos.

First, the Department was a rotational service. Its foreign service officers were moved between headquarters and field at periodic intervals, usually from place to place in the field before a stint at home. Second (and in consequence of such rotation), the Department prized the 'generalist'. All-rounders were preferred to specialists, for whom little scope was offered. Third, the Department was pragmatic in its approach, and sceptical alike of long-range planning and grand designs. Fourth, the Department, questioning the worth of new management techniques and organization theory, tended to resist administrative innovation. Fifth, the Department retained into the 1950s a reputation and self-image as the élite sector of the public service.

During the past decade or so, each of these departmental characteristics – its rotational process, its bias towards generalists, its neglect of long-term planning, its down-grading of experiments at reorganizing, and its position as the ranking department within the federal service – has come in for criticism; in some cases the criticism has led to change. How, why, and with what results the Department has responded to its critics the remaining sections of this chapter will explore.

Station and rotation

The most durable of the Department's five main features has proved to be its practice of rotating its foreign service officers from country to country, abroad, punctuated by periods in Ottawa.

Rotational service imposes wear and tear on all concerned – the itinerant diplomats and their families, the personnel managers who oversee their transfers. Even as a small foreign office with only a few posts to man, External felt the strain. '[H]e is taking the whole business very hard,' wrote a colleague of a member of an embassy staff ordered to return to Ottawa just after having learned the ropes in Washington.[7] Today, staff must be found for missions of varying size in some 150 countries (although often the ambassador or high commissioner will be accredited to two, or even three, different governments); for some forty consular offices; for more than a dozen missions or delegations at international organizations; and for countless *ad hoc* multilateral conferences, some lasting for only a week or two while others (such as the Conference on the Law of the Sea) go on indefinitely.

Rotating officers among so many and such far-flung assignments is a costly process, preoccupying keepers of the public purse with such questions as whether offspring studying in Canada should visit their diplomat parents free of charge. Moreover, the family whirled from Yaoundé to Islamabad to Bogotá to Ottawa, and overseas once more, will have more than its fair share of strain. A brochure warns prospective foreign service officers about the emotional toll that such a career will be likely to take, and counsels them to 'consider very carefully the effects . . . on personal lifestyle. Spouses and dependents . . . should be consulted.'[8]

If the foreign service officer is lucky enough to keep health and family intact while moving around the diplomatic firmament, is he able to make a worthwhile contribution when so constantly in motion? How can he drum up trade, report on the state of play in the capital, during so short a sojourn? Critics contend that he can't. A year to get one's bearings, three years of full productive effort, another year in which to wind things up, would seem to be a realistic flow-chart for fieldwork. But the average posting is closer to two years' duration than to five.

And yet the rotation game continues to be felt worth the candle, its toll on players notwithstanding. 'Despite the difficulties, we still manage every year, after terrible struggles and agonizing decisions, to fill all positions at headquarters and abroad,' the USSEA remarked in 1979. 'For one brief, glorious hour or day, seldom longer, everyone is in place and the system is in equilibrium. We all take a deep collective breath and then the whole process of reassignment and posting begins again.'[9]

Why does it seem worthwhile? Sending personnel from headquarters to posts equips officers with first-hand knowledge of missions in the field, so that on returning they will be aware of their problems and opportunities and sensitive to their concerns. At posts abroad, particularly if heads of them, foreign service officers confront situations that test and develop their executive skills to a greater degree than does more staid departmental life at Ottawa; it is partly for this reason that so many External Affairs members reach the commanding heights of public service. Conversely, field hands are thought to benefit by being returned periodically to Ottawa. Their renewed immersion in Canadian affairs keeps them in touch with their own country, purges them of 'localitis' (that occupational malady marked by excessive sympathy for foreign causes to which diplomats are prone), and helps reinvigorate the headquarters. For these reasons, the Department remains convinced that, as one of its senior members reported, 'the system of rotational foreign service cannot, *of course*, be abandoned . . .' [my italics].[10]

But it may be modified. The rotational principle can now be satisfied when an officer is moved functionally rather than geographically – that is, from task to task instead of from place to place. A cadre of managers remains permanently at headquarters. But the real power, both in policy-making and in administration, still rests with rotational senior officers. The USSEA, accordingly, wants to slow the process, offering two reasons why the brakes should be applied. 'Foreign service officers are often at a disadvantage in the "interdepartmental game" because they usually serve in a particular job in headquarters only for a few years and then they are posted. It is thus difficult for them to develop the contacts in the domestic departments that are essential to help alert them to emerging issues. While I recognize the serious consequences of a change in rotational personnel policies,' A. E. Gotlieb admitted, 'the Department must, at a minimum, slow up significantly the rotational process if our officers are to achieve the necessary level of effectiveness in Ottawa.' The USSEA here recognizes how much more variegated and populated has the foreign policy community become in recent years. The fact that there is now a constellation of people and influences drawn from many parts of government, from the Prime Minister down, all having a legitimate stake in the planning, formulation and carrying out of foreign policy, means that External can seldom plan, formulate or carry out policy on its own. Practically everything it does is part of a collective endeavour, and the premium for being heard – never mind prevailing – is spending more time at home. The other reason for braking proffered by the USSEA was the need to 'enable officers to increase their specialist expertise'.[11]

Generalist and specialist
Of the five traits of the Department outlined above, the bias in favour of the generalist derived in part from its compact size of earlier days, in part from the personal predilections of its senior personnel who, themselves former students of the humanities (Skelton, Wrong and Pearson were historians), sought in their recruits much the same attributes Rhodes Scholar selection committees looked for in theirs (and in consequence recruited a disproportionately large number of Rhodes Scholars). Traditionally, a prospective foreign service officer has been judged on his ability to bring to the varied activities of his job intelligence, a sense of adventure, poise and common sense – assets most recently reformulated as 'a high degree of adaptability, versatility, initiative and good judgement . . .'[12] A candidate versed in, say, Slavonic culture or the law of extradition would not be disqualified on that account – so long as acquisition of such expertise had left undiminished all-round ability and zest for general knowledge.

'Nothing excites the foreign service more than the generalist–specialist debate,' asserted the USSEA in 1979, and he made this contribution to it: 'I think that both the pure generalist and the pure specialist, if there were such people, would not be very useful in a contemporary foreign service. The good foreign service officer must be both.'[13]

Producing such a hybrid is the purpose of what is called 'mid-career streaming'. In this process, foreign service officers are encouraged, after five or so years spent as jacks-of-all-trades, to focus their attention on one or two specialized fields: fisheries, energy, technology transfer, maritime boundaries, space law, arms control (to name a few). If the apprentice-specialists show an aptitude for gaining and applying such expertise, the Department attempts to arrange the pattern of their careers so that their knowledge will be deepened rather than dissipated. A further formalizing of 'streaming', made necessary by the consolidation of 1980 (see below), is among the newly designed four main foreign service functions – aid and development, commercial and economic, political and economic, and the so-called 'social affairs' stream comprising immigration and consular business. 'Officers will serve much of their careers in one or two functional streams,' the SSEA explained to inquiring parliamentarians, 'and will have to have served in at least two streams to qualify for advancement in the executive group'[14] – whether as heads of posts abroad or as senior managers at home.

There may be less in this than meets the eye for, like M. Jourdain speaking prose, the Department has been streaming its personnel for years. 'Although "streaming" has been formalized of late, there was always, in fact, a certain amount of this going on,' a former senior foreign service officer recalls. 'People with legal training did concentrate on law and likewise those with economics. Those with Asian or Eastern exposure also tended to be diverted to those areas. As for myself, I was certainly regarded as primarily a UN and Commonwealth officer and was streamed in those directions.'[15]

Another way of providing scope for specialists is through cross-posting. The Department proposes to allow its own officers to seek secondment to other parts of government where they might add to their store of lore. Thus, a foreign service officer working on energy policy might spend three or four years in the Department of Energy, Mines and Resources. The Department has also announced its willingness to appoint experts from elsewhere in the public service to temporary positions in its own ranks. (Lateral entry from business or academic life is, however, rare: the Department, like other professions, prefers to rear its own.)

These devices – the slowing of rotation, mid-career streaming, cross-posting – are intended to create 'an officer group retaining a generally well-rounded background but with a greater depth of knowledge in selected fields.'[16] To that extent the Department has been willing to defer, however belatedly, to the dictum that jacks-of-all-trades are masters of none.

Planning and prediction

Detailed in November 1945 to write a memorandum on the political consequences of the atomic bomb, the official charged with the assignment subsequently admitted of his reaction to it: 'This I was naturally reluctant to accept.'[17] His 'naturally' betrays the Department's rooted distaste for peering too far ahead of events. Its approach to policy has been pragmatic. It prefers 'making policy on the cables' to drafting grand designs, the patched-up compromise to the perfect formula whose time might never come.

Such an approach is common to foreign offices at large (save those in thrall to burning ideology) wherein the 'task of diplomacy', as George F. Kennan has described it, is seen as 'essentially . . . menial . . . , consisting of hovering around the fringes of a process one is powerless to control, tidying up the messes other people have made . . .'.[18] In Canada, that code has been strongly reinforced by the brokerage style of politics imposed upon its policy-makers by the fragility of the coalition of cultures, regions and polities of which their country is composed. '. . . [N]o one who reaches to so high a place as the office of the Secretary of State for External Affairs will be ignorant of the broker's game,' a leading student of Canadian foreign policy has written. 'Nor, for that matter, will the senior officials of the bureaucracy over which he nominally presides . . .'[19] Officials freely own up to such a style: 'It is always a case of realizing as fully as you can the implications of what you propose to do,' a high-ranking foreign service officer once explained to a group of academics, 'and of doing it according to the best judgement you can make in a single circumstance at the moment . . .'[20]

This tradition was brought into question by the advent of the prime ministership of Pierre Elliot Trudeau in 1968. The Cartesian Trudeau, schooled by Jesuits and trained at law, seemed restive with the notion (about which his pragmatic predecessor, Lester Pearson, had been happy enough) that foreign policy consisted of a succession of expedients. Policy for him required a corpus of doctrine and fundamental principle of which its measures should be the offspring. Far from averse to long-range planning, Trudeau was dismayed to discover how little aptitude the policy community possessed for it, and he resolved to use his time in office to develop procedures and institutions that could enable government, if not to know the future, at least to be less unprepared for its usually cruel surprises.

Certain officers in the Department, alert to these new vibrations, did not wait to be told what to do. A Policy Analysis Group (PAG) was contrived in 1969. It was not a new idea but it was an innovation at External: a handful of experienced officials were to be relieved of the daily administrative and operational chores to devote their full attention to identifying long-range policy objectives and supplying a rationale for their priority. Those familiar with the experience of other foreign offices with such esoteric apparatus will be able to predict PAG's fate: like the Policy Planning Council of the US Department of State, it withered on the vine.

A related enterprise was the preparation of a comprehensive review of Canada's foreign policy. After much effort, a consensus acceptable to the diplomats sceptical of the need for change and the politicians desirous of it was published by the government in 1970 as a white paper. *Foreign Policy for Canadians* (as the document was called) is remarkable for its attempt to get back to basics (how often do foreign offices pause to ask what their foreign policy should be, let alone to ask by what principles it should be guided?) and for the arid level of abstraction at which its argument proceeds. Predictably, it provoked derision where it did not evoke indifference: '[T]o convince a harried desk officer that taxonomies of objectives serve any purpose . . . is a formidable task.'[21] But its relentless depiction of national goals, and of the inescapable 'trade-offs' among them (e.g. 'economic growth' calls for doing business with South Africa, 'social justice' for economic sanctions), impressed where it counted: at the Privy Council Office where the Prime Minister commanded and at the Cabinet where he presided.

Planning on a less cosmic scale – for the allocation of resources rather than for the formulation of policy – is done by the Department's desk officers and bureau directors, in conjunction with posts and other parts of government. The exercise is guided by an interdepartmental committee (discussed below) of which the USSEA is chairman. Its product is a series of 'country papers', eventually one for each of the eighty or more countries where Canada has resident representation. It would be misleading to think of the country paper as an instrument of policy planning, but it is a device for policy coordination and, as one senior foreign service officer describes it, for 'organizing the allocation of human and financial resources'. Within these limitations, that officer considers, 'it has developed quite usefully . . .'.[22] The USSEA under whom the country paper programme was introduced in 1971 indicated that it was intended to provide guidance for missions, but not too rigidly. 'You cannot fix and freeze positions in a great variety of countries around the world within concrete or ice, as may be, without allowing a good deal of flexibility as requirements shift and change during the year.' As country papers are secret – it would not do to tip Canada's hand to foreign governments – an outsider cannot comment on their quality. A former USSEA has emphasized, however, that 'they are not great strategic documents . . .'.[23]

Organization and accountability

In 1942, Lester Pearson despaired of his Department ever being able to organize itself efficiently. 'It's pathetic,' he wrote to a colleague, 'to see [the USSEA] . . . involved in some trifling detail concerning a stenographer's overtime.'[24] It had by then acquired at least an organization chart, wrung by an importunate Civil Service Commission from a protesting USSEA: '. . . [T]he Department cannot easily be broken up into branches.'[25] O. D. Skelton's chart, devoid of divisions, depicted under him an associate USSEA, a legal adviser, three counsellors, eight third secretaries, a protocol officer, a passport officer, a translator, and four clerks. By 1945 the chart was of the usual 'boxes and string' variety, showing eight divisions – diplomatic, economic, information, legal, plus three 'political' divisions, the first charged with 'special political affairs, including international organization and peace settlements', the second with 'political affairs relating to British Commonwealth, Europe, Middle East and Africa', and the third with 'political affairs relating to United States, Latin America and Far East'. Down the years more divisions were added to this core. Treaty and administrative divisions appeared in 1946; the diplomatic division split into protocol and consular divisions; a personnel division was created to deal with the Department's growing staff and rapidly expanding posts; and in 1949, the year of the North Atlantic Treaty, a defence liaison division was formed. During the next two decades, sixteen more boxes sprouted on the chart, bringing the total number of divisions within the Department to twenty-eight; there was also a press office, an inspection service, and a political coordination section. The good ship External, with a complement in 1960 of some 300 officers, seemed seaworthy enough.

But not to the Royal Commission on Government Organization. The Commissioners, chaired by J. Grant Glassco, an eminent chartered accountant, brought to their assignment the same faith in the techniques of cost-benefit analysis, planning–programming–budgeting and accountability as was then being displayed by the US Secretary of Defense, putting in place at the Pentagon the style and system of administration that had improved productivity and profitability during his presidency of the Ford Motor Company. Reporting in 1963, they found something to praise and more to criticize in External's past performance. 'New forms of organizations, new techniques and special skills are now required and continued reliance on practices and procedures appropriate only to a small-scale organization significantly limits the effectiveness of performance.'[26] The Glassco Commissioners recommended that the Department's 'substantive work' be hived off from its administrative and support services; that the positions of deputy USSEA (Political) and deputy USSEA (Administrative) be created to take charge of these activities; that rotation of personnel be confined mainly to the political divisions; that professional managers, streamed in their own career service and exempted from rotation, be recruited to improve the administration of the Department; and that the position of head of post, hitherto accountable to the Department, be made responsible for all overseas activities of the Government.

These proposals were not as sweeping as they might have been; even so, the Department was slow and even loath to implement them. The Glassco Commission's report appeared in time to greet the return of a Liberal government under the leadership of the man who, more than any, had guided the Department with the same controls as those that the Commission proposed to alter. In the absence of zeal for organizational change on the part of Prime Minister Pearson and his colleagues, the Department remained content with what it considered to be methods tried and true. Its spokesman in the Cabinet was fond of quoting Viscount Falkland: 'When it is not necessary to change, it is necessary not to change.'

There was a modicum of tinkering. In 1964, External retained a firm of management consultants 'to identify weaknesses of administration . . . and to propose means of correcting them', as well as 'to recommend an appropriate organizational structure'.[27] This brought forth an Organization and Methods Unit to improve management techniques, and the appointment of a senior officer in the new position of inspector-general to keep missions cost-efficient. But these cautious innovations fell short of what even the Glassco Commission had envisaged. 'Our philosophy of management in the Department', its assistant USSEA explained in 1967, 'cannot be that of a business enterprise.'[28]

Foreign Policy for Canadians, the white paper issued in 1970, contained in its brief but pregnant section on 'Organizing for the Seventies' a passage on which the Trudeau imprimatur is clear: 'To meet the challenge of coming decades, to be equipped to take advantage of new opportunities, to keep abreast of the rapid evolution of events, the Government needs strong and flexible organization for carrying out its reshaped foreign policy.' Any presumption that the Government believed that in the Department as already structured it possessed an organization sufficiently 'strong and flexible' for its purposes was laid to rest by the white paper's proposals for reform.

To give expression to the Government's view that foreign policy ought to be the pursuit of national interests abroad, the white paper proposed to admit other departments to the process of making it.

Within the Cabinet, a system of committees already set in place under Prime Minister Pearson required policy emanating from External Affairs to clear the Committee on External Policy and Defence (as it was called in 1979: incoming governments tend to change its name), composed of members of the Cabinet whose departments perform major duties overseas: the Ministers of National Defence, Employment and Immigration, Industry, Trade and Commerce and, as its *ex officio* chairman, the SSEA. 'I had to be rigorously scrupulous not to allow my departmental interests to prejudice my impartiality as chairman of the committee,' Flora MacDonald, the Department's Minister from June 1979 to March 1980, has recalled.[29]

The white paper's principal device for bringing departments other than External Affairs into the making of foreign policy is the Interdepartmental Committee on External Relations (ICER), of which the USSEA is chairman. An ICER subcommittee, the Personnel Management Committee, was to set 'uniform standards for recruiting, evaluating and promoting the staffs of departments (other than National Defence) with operations in other countries. The white paper announced the Government's decision 'that the head of post must represent and be accountable for all department's interest in his area of jurisdiction. This implies,' the white paper pointedly added, 'as regards the selection of heads of posts, increasing emphasis in future on managerial capabilities . . .'[30]

ICER came to consist of the deputy ministers of the three civilian departments with major operations abroad (Industry, Trade and Commerce, Employment and Immigration, and External Affairs), the president of the Canadian International Development Agency, the secretary to the Cabinet, the secretary of the Treasury Board, with the USSEA as chairman. All these mandarins have different constituencies to serve and most have vested interests to defend: in-fighting ensued (reportedly sometimes over trivial concerns), and then, as the protagonists grew weary of the fray, there was a wary truce. An in-house appraisal, assessing six years' experience, concluded that ICER had 'not become a policy coordinating instrument to any significant degree'. The critic (then a senior foreign service officer) reports that some officials in and outside the Department believe that the Government's insistence on coordination at all costs could 'stifle creativity and initiative . . . [and] also lead to preoccupation with the form rather than the substance of policy'.[31] A more recent assessment by another senior foreign service officer sees ICER as no more than 'the symbol of the crossfire. In the real world, the weapons and the ammunition still rest with individual departments, and that is not likely to change.'[32]

Such a prediction could prove premature. In 1980, Pierre Trudeau was restored to prime ministership. Beholden to no one – party, caucus, colleagues – for his triumph at the polls, Trudeau at once began a final fling at shaping Canada to his liking. Overlooked in the ensuing hubbub at his attempt to 'patriate' its constitution and to repatriate its oil and gas was what his SSEA described as 'a fundamental change for the conduct of . . . external relations'.[33]

The fundamental change, announced by the Prime Minister on 21 March when barely a fortnight into power, was to be 'a programme for consolidation of Canada's foreign service . . . to improve the economy and efficiency of foreign operations without affecting the policy and program-development roles of the departments involved; to unify the management of Canada's foreign posts and the image of Canada which they project; and to improve the career prospects and broaden the experience of foreign service personnel.'[34] Thus was begun a merger of the foreign service officers of the two departments of Industry, Trade and Commerce and Employment and Immigration, together with the officials of the previously separate Canadian International Development Agency (CIDA), with those of DEA, under the auspices of the latter. The measure was sudden and unexpected and, in the opinion of a retired foreign service officer, deliberately so: 'While government organization is recognized as a prerogative of the Prime Minister, well-entrenched ministers are likely to be resistant to changes which affect the size and scope of their departments. Clearly the best tactic for the Prime Minister was to act as early as possible in the life of his new government.'[35]

The consequences of consolidation are not yet apparent. If Big is Beautiful,

External appears the winner, its influx from its rivals' ranks confirming its role as a department of supply and services abroad – perhaps at the expense of the traditional foreign office skills of intelligence analysis, policy formulation and the conduct of negotiation. 'Some officers both in and out of External speculate that foreign service consolidation may not be the last step in the department's evolution,' a knowledgeable former member of it comments: '. . . that at some future date there may be a need to designate a ministry of foreign affairs to deal with policy matters separate from a department of external services designed to implement government programmes abroad. Others oppose such a separation, arguing that the best place to work up new policy ideas is in a corner of the workshop, not an ivory tower.'[36]

Distinct from DEA's engorgement through consolidation is its re-equipment through organization. The most far-reaching organization of its history was begun on 1 February 1971. The structure, with its modifications since, may be described as follows.

An apex is formed by the USSEA, a recently added associate USSEA, four deputy USSEAs and five assistant USSEAs; the latter are responsible respectively for (1) inter-country relations, (2) international peace and security affairs, (3) economic and social development areas, (4) legal, constitutional and public affairs, and (5) administration. To this directorate report the directors-general of ten headquarters bureaux. Four of these are grouped according to the geographic area for which they (and the country or regional desks within them) are responsible: European Affairs, African and Middle East Affairs, Asian and Pacific Affairs, and Western Hemisphere Affairs. The remaining six bureaux are functionally defined, with responsibilities for United Nations Affairs, Public Affairs, Legal and Consular Affairs, Defence and Disarmament Affairs, Economic and Science Affairs, and a so-called Coordination Bureau concerned with Commonwealth relations, relations with French-speaking countries ('La Francophonie'), and federal–provincial relations in their growing external context.

One of the purposes of this scheme is to provide the head of post with the most helpful support system from headquarters. '. . . [I]n establishing the regional bureaux which we now have in the Department and in delegating more responsibility to the directors-general of those bureaux,' the USSEA explained on 12 May 1971, 'we have tried to establish a more intimate contact between a senior officer of the Department and each of the missions abroad. We would hope that this would permit those senior officers to keep closer to missions abroad, to correspond with them more regularly, to respond more promptly to their communications than has perhaps been true under our previous organizations.'[37] And a departmental memorandum explains further: 'Each regional bureau, in its capacity as the coordinating centre responsible for the shaping and management of country plans and programmes, ensures that the functional interests are appropriately reflected in post operations. Similarly, functional bureaux respect in the management of their operations the interests of the regional bureaux. The two perspectives are complementary, and in union generate a sensitive and thorough approach to the complexities of the Department's operations.'[38]

If saying so could make it so, it would be so. 'I am told that the management experts call this "matrix management",' the first USSEA to whom it fell to operate the new machinery observed in 1971, 'but those of us who are trying to work it in the Department of External Affairs are finding that it makes just good practical sense whatever lofty titles may be applied to the particular administrative method.'[39]

The chart needed to depict the Department's organization today (see Appendix A) is a bewilderingly intricate document, as is that 'imaginative attempt' (as a USSEA has described it) to show diagrammatically 'how the thing really works'[40] (see Appendix B). What would Sir Joseph Pope have made of it? Would he repeat his comment, quoted approvingly from Lord Morley, on a document of his own era: 'It's not worth the paper it is written on. To the end of time it will always be a case of "Thy head or my head"; I have no faith in such schemes'?[41] There may still be foreign service officers who hold, doubtless deep within themselves, the same unflattering opinion of their Department's administrative structure as their founder reserved for the League of Nations covenant.

Mood and morale

'I can assure you . . . that members of the Department of External Affairs are not sitting around feeling sorry for themselves . . . [B]ut to what extent their morale is at a peak or in the depths is . . . something that is hard to measure': so the USSEA told a parliamentary committee on 7 April 1970.[42] Here, more likely than not, was bad news. When a spokesman for a finance ministry rules out the prospect of a devaluation, it is often opportune to sell short its currency; so, too, when a spokesman for a foreign ministry declines to comment on its morale, there may be reason to diagnose malaise within the ranks.

A decade ago, Canada's foreign service officers had reason to feel sorry for themselves, and there may be some who did. Diplomacy everywhere had new anxieties to contend with – fears of supersession via telex and high-flying superiors à la Kissinger, the daunting accumulation of world problems seemingly beyond control by the traditional techniques of statecraft, not least the targeting of diplomats for terrorist attack. Added to these troubles of the profession were those peculiar to it in Canada.

The Department had always hitherto been secure in its assumption that, while it might now and then become the butt of populist agitators, it could count on the full support and confidence of the Prime Minister of the day and therefore of the Government. During the period 1957 to 1963, a small but influential number of its members had resigned. Speculation had it that their departure had been due to a temperamental incompatibility between the fiery and vindictive Prime Minister, John G. Diefenbaker, and the polished sophisticates – 'Dief's' so-called 'Pearsonalities' – distrusted by him for alleged Liberal (with a capital 'L') loyalty.

It is easy to make too much of this. The exodus from External was neither a case of abandoning ship nor a case of purge, rather one of moving to the greener pastures of the expanding universities. The Diefenbaker government was done in not by sabotage from bureaucrats but by its own members' loss of confidence in their leader. External's officers seem to have relished Diefenbaker's arrival at the East Block (and that of Howard Green, the second and more durable of his two Foreign Ministers, who since returning from Europe at the end of the First World War had seldom left his country) as an invigorating challenge to their skills of adaptation.

But by the style of Prime Minister Trudeau, External's officers were caught off guard. At first welcoming the new star of the Liberal galaxy, they were taken aback by his uninhibited assertions of their irrelevance (as when, during a TV interview, he mused on the outmodedness of the diplomatic profession: 'I believe it all goes back to the early days of the telegraph when you needed a dispatch to know what is happening in country A, whereas most of the time you can read it in a good newspaper').[43] The Department's morale was further buffeted by Trudeau's contemptuous rejection of its advice, and by his insistence on economies that meant closing seven missions and cutting personnel by seven per cent. As the Prime Minister added austerity to insult, his Cabinet appeared to egg him on.

The Department became alienated from more than its political constituency during the 1970s. Sniping from academic critics, coming at a time of adversity, proved wounding where in the previous era of External's invulnerability shots from such light artillery would have bounced harmlessly off the bureaucratic hide. The media, too, jumped on a department all too obviously down: a choice example, an article mischievously titled 'Where Are You, Mike Pearson, Now That We Need You?', led with a punishing blow: 'Some people will tell you, when you ask whatever happened to Canada's Golden Age of Internationalism, that the beginning of the end was a couple of long, hot, sunny days in Belgrade in 1948, when Pierre Trudeau languished in jail – he'd flown in without a visa – and no one at the Canadian Embassy bothered to lift a finger.'[44]

But there are signs of resurgence. To the challenge of the managerial revolution, the Department has responded not as a counter-revolutionary but as an enthusiast determined to make a go of it and the best of it. 'To be frank, the magnitude and pace of change require an extraordinary effort':[45] its USSEA was referring to the international environment with which his officers now deal, but his statement is applicable to the magnitude and pace of the attitudinal adjustments that have been required of them.

The Department's capacity to adjust to the magnitude and pace of change was tested as never before by the consolidation policy announced by the Prime Minister in 1980 – a decision taken without consultation with either the Professional Association of Foreign Service Officers or with other Cabinet ministers. 'People are very much upset and concerned,' the former SSEA in the preceding Conservative government (which had not acted on the report recommending consolidation) alleged from her place in opposition. 'I would urge you, Mr Minister, to pay greater attention to the state of low morale that exists in your department.'[46] That the sudden addition to the 750 External Affairs foreign service officers of 300 from Industry, Trade and Commerce, 250 from Employment and Immigration, and 150 from CIDA would adversely affect morale at External – not least because the influx seemed likely to impair career choices and slow promotion – could hardly have been overlooked. The Prime Minister's announcement concomitantly with that of consolidation of his intention to create a Royal Commission on Conditions of Foreign Service suggests that it was not overlooked.

The Royal Commissioner, deputy minister of National Health and Welfare at the time of her appointment and as such the most senior female in the public service, and who had served in the Department of External Affairs in a career that had taken her from clerk to ambassador, was instructed to identify the causes of what Pierre Trudeau had described as 'the dissatisfaction which seems to be prevalent in the foreign service'. The Prime Minister cautioned Commissioner Pamela McDougall that her study should not be 'an inquiry into the role of the foreign service' but rather into 'how changes in that role should be reflected in how we relate to those who carry it out'. Part of the problem, Trudeau speculated, 'may be that general perceptions of the foreign service, as well as perceptions within the ranks of that service, are based on a concept of diplomatic practice grounded in an age which has disappeared . . . Traditional concepts of foreign service have diminished relevance in an era of instantaneous, world-wide communications, in which there is increasing reliance on personal contacts between senior members of governments . . . I am not convinced,' the Prime Minister added pointedly, 'that our approach to foreign service adequately reflects this new era.'[47] So blunt a reminder that the head of their government had not renounced his earlier strictures about the obsolescence of the diplomatic profession can only have added to the dissatisfaction the causes of which the Royal Commission had been created to uncover; and foreign service officers, at External at least, had reason to wonder whether the Prime Minister's solution was not itself part of the problem.

As is customary in royal commission work in Canada, the inquiry was begun by inviting submissions: members of the foreign service in Ottawa and abroad, their families, ex-foreign service officers and 'persons or organizations who make direct use of the foreign service' were asked to submit their views. No more intensive user of the foreign service might be found than the Minister who presided over the Department of External Affairs from July 1979 to February 1980. Flora MacDonald felt as much used by its senior officials as user of their services. She complained publicly, after her defeat, of the 'entrapment devices' that External's mandarins had perpetrated on her: 'The unnecessary numerous corridor-decisions I was confronted with . . . here is the situation (breathless pause), let us have your instructions.' 'The unnecessarily long and numerous memos.' 'The late delivery to me of my submissions to Cabinet, sometimes just a couple of hours (or less) before the meeting took place. On a number of occasions my aides resorted to obtaining bootleg copies of such documents on their way through the overly complex bureaucratic approval system.' And: 'The one-dimensional opinions put forward in memos. I was expected to accept the unanimous recommendation of the Department . . . Seldom, if ever, was I given the luxury of multiple choice options on matters of major import.'[48] Ministerial confessions of such candour had not been heard since R. H. S. Crossman's in the United Kingdom; but Crossman's were published posthumously. The appearance of Miss MacDonald before Miss McDougall as a witness at the Royal Commission on Conditions of Foreign Service would be an event for *cognoscenti* of Cabinet government greatly to enjoy, but the appearance need not take place: MacDonald had testified already.

Ethos and milieu
Early in 1973 the Department's headquarters, which over the years had spilled from the East Block into almost a dozen other buildings, were moved under one roof. The Palais des Nations, the Viceroy's Palace, even the edifice at the United Nations Plaza in New York City, might be held to validate a

cynic's rule: 'The more resplendent the building, the less puissant the institution.' But the Department's leaders are determined to make theirs an exception.

An architectural critic, writing of the Lester B. Pearson building set so spectacularly across the Ottawa River from the Gatineau Hills with the spires of Parliament to the west and the British High Commission, the French Embassy and the Prime Minister's residence nestling below, wonders whether its design might not well have made 'some historic reference to the classical columns and courtyards of the Foreign Office in Whitehall, or some recollection of the ornate . . . good manners of the Quai d'Orsay, or even, perhaps, a bow to that crusty stylistic monster, the old State Department building in Washington.' At any rate, this temptation was resisted; instead, External has been settled in a distinctive structure of its own – 'an enormous stratified sculpture with interesting and unexpected projections'.[49] An architectural expression, it may not be too fanciful to say, of the policies fashioned within – and of the personnel within.

For if the building is a bit exotic, so is the department that it houses. Its spokesmen in recent years have been at pains to dispel the notion that its members are an irrelevant élite. 'I would like to lay at rest,' its Minister felt impelled to declare in 1970, 'the tiresome and unfounded myth that External Affairs is engaged in some arcane, nineteenth-century gavotte of little meaning to Canada';[50] and his successor a decade later expressed the same thought pithily: 'Bread and butter issues are our meat and potatoes.'[51] All the same, Canada's diplomats occupy a special place in the service of their country. Like the armed forces (to which External's operations, physically more hazardous each year, make it analogous), foreign service officers acquire by reason of the missions they perform – formulating policy, communicating with foreign leaders and publics, managing External's business and (in its recently confirmed capacity as a central agency of government) that of other departments, too – a distinctive character and outlook. This is probably as it should be, undoubtedly as it is.

If distinctiveness is ensured by the nature of its work, exclusivity is fostered by the process of selection. When the budget allows recruitment (and there have been years when it does not), about 4000 minimally qualified – by citizenship, a university degree and the desire to join up – will sit the annual foreign service examination (in English or French) common to the three departments (Industry, Trade and Commerce, Employment and Immigration, and External Affairs) offering careers in the foreign service. Candidates attempt a *précis* to assess their skills of comprehension and expression, a series of multiple choice questions that probe their knowledge of Canadian and international affairs, and a further series of multiple choice questions to gauge their powers of judgement. A sample of the last of these may be of interest.

> You are the senior officer in charge of a Canadian embassy abroad. You have only one other officer as your subordinate. An important question has arisen on which you must make a recommendation to Ottawa and after thorough discussion, your subordinate continues to disagree with your considered decision on how to deal with it. The best thing to do is to
>
> (1) take the decision you think is right
> (2) report both views to Ottawa in a fair and balanced way

(3) discuss the matter with your subordinate until a consensus of views has been reached

(4) seek the advice of a senior official of the local government whose judgement you respect.[52]

The Department deems the correct answer to be (1).

Depending on the number of foreign service officers to be recruited for the three departments, between the top 5 to 15 per cent of the examinees are interviewed; and from these, since 1975, an annual average of about twenty foreign service officers have been chosen. 'Because the work is sensitive and complex,' the Government's brochure cautions prospective candidates, 'the men and women selected to serve in Canada's Foreign Service must be of the highest calibre.'[53]

Such a system is only as fair as the educational system that feeds it, and Canada's is far from egalitarian. The under-representation of Canadians of French descent, statistically verifiable in 1968, has since been overcome, but not that of Canadians who are of other than Anglo-Saxon origin, who come from families whose breadwinner is not in the professions, or who happen to be women. The Department, in keeping with government hiring policy, eschews quotas and other forms of 'affirmative action'. While one has heard it said, privately, and perhaps not entirely in jest, that its ideal candidate these days is a female Métis, she has yet to qualify.

Still distinct, despite efforts to homogenize, within the public service, does Canada's Department of External Affairs differ significantly from other foreign offices?

Perhaps the most striking feature is the Department's ability to draw on the bicultural inheritance of Canadians of British and French descent to field officers proficient in the two official languages that are the major diplomatic languages. (It was partly for this aptitude that Canadians were selected to serve on the Indo-China truce supervision commissions in 1954.) But is there more than that? 'I am pretty sure that we are well ahead of many other foreign services in our acceptance of the idea of public diplomacy,' a senior foreign service officer responds in answer to the question. 'No longer are diplomats encouraged to avoid contact with the media. Indeed, opportunities to tell the story to the media and influential audiences are actively sought and exploited by our best practitioners abroad.' Commenting on the expanding role of Canada's representatives, this authority observes: 'The ambassador will still have to be capable of broad political analysis and hotel-keeping but on top of that – and in most countries more important than that – he will have to be at home in the bread and butter aspects of the Canadian interest. This combination is what the Department is working towards.'[54] Rejecting the notion that telex and jet aircraft have eroded ambassadorial responsibility, the USSEA asserted in 1979 that 'the ambassador has a task that is today more important than any time in the past. And therefore he, or indeed she, should be a remarkable person.'[55]

Nearly twenty years ago, a future USSEA, in the course of defining the nature of the Canadian diplomat, pointed to his opportunities 'for travel abroad, . . . for promotion, varied duties, and the stimulus of competition' – all of which, he considered, 'create a psychological milieu peculiar to the Department'. But there was a rough side to the smooth, 'a certain tenseness, an uneasiness, which can be occasionally glimpsed beneath the unruffled exterior of the diplomat whose profession consists in a curious blending of freedom and restraint, of the changing and the stable, of splendour and simplicity, of crests and hollows, of coming and going.'[56] Today, more than yesterday, when the calm of chanceries can at any time be shattered by the whine of bullets and the shriek of the mob, the expression of a foreign service officer is justifiably a worried frown, even if his composure may not let it show; and it appears unmasked on the features of a candidate pondering the question bluntly put by the prospective employer: 'Are you prepared to accept the very real hardships and difficulties that foreign service life sometimes entails?'[57]

I gratefully acknowledge the helpful comments of H. B. Robinson and Don M. Page of the Department of External Affairs; John W. Holmes of the Canadian Institute of International Affairs; Professors Don Munton, Paul Pross and Denis Stairs of Dalhousie University; and Professor Kim Nossal of McMaster University. Errors of fact or faults of interpretation are mine alone.

NOTES

[1] Quoted in James Eayrs, 'The Origins of Canada's Department of External Affairs', in Hugh L. Keenleyside et al., The Growth of Canadian Policies in External Affairs (Durham, N. C. & London 1960), 17.

[2] Quoted in James Eayrs, In Defence of Canada, I, From the Great War to the Great Depression (Toronto 1964), 11.

[3] Quoted in Eayrs, 'The Origins . . .', 21.

[4] Sir William Hayter, The Diplomacy of the Great Powers (London 1962), 65.

[5] Escott Reid, 'Canada and the Struggle Against World Poverty', International Journal, xxv, 1, Winter 1969–70, 142.

[6] J. D. B. Miller, The Canadian Forum, August 1959.

[7] L. B. Pearson to Vincent Massey, 9 June 1942, Massey Papers.

[8] Public Service Commission of Canada, Careers in the Foreign Service (Ottawa 1979), 13.

[9] A. E. Gotlieb, 'Canadian Diplomacy in the 1980s: Leadership and Service' (Ottawa 1979, mimeographed), 38.

[10] A. S. McGill, 'The Role of the Department of External Affairs in the Government of Canada' (Ottawa 1976, mimeographed), Part III, 44.

[11] Gotlieb, 'Canadian Diplomacy . . .', 33–4.

[12] Careers in the Foreign Service, 11.

[13] Gotlieb, 'Canadian Diplomacy . . .', 32.

[14] Canada, House of Commons Standing Committee on External Affairs and National Defence (SCEAND), Minutes of Proceedings and Evidence, 17, 28 October 1980, 2.

[15] Letter of 2 October 1979.

[16] Gotlieb, 'Canadian Diplomacy . . .', 32.

[17] Lt.-Gen. Maurice A. Pope, *Soldiers and Politicians* (Toronto 1962), 276.

[18] George F. Kennan, 'History and Diplomacy as Viewed by a Diplomatist', in Stephen D. Kertesz and M. A. Fitzsimonds (eds.), *Diplomacy in a Changing World* (Notre Dame, Ind. 1959), 107–8.

[19] Denis Stairs, 'Unity, Diversity and Foreign Policy', *Transactions of the Royal Society of Canada, 1978*, Fourth Series, xvi (Toronto, Buffalo, London 1979), 101.

[20] Quoted in Burton Keirstead, *Canada in World Affairs*, VII, *1951–1953* (Toronto 1956), 37.

[21] Daniel Madar and Denis Stairs, 'Alone on Killers' Row: The Policy Analysis Group and the Department of External Affairs', *International Journal*, xxxii, 4, Autumn 1977, 728.

[22] Letter of 19 October 1979.

[23] SCEAND, *Minutes of Proceedings and Evidence*, 26, 12 May 1971, 29.

[24] L. B. Pearson to Vincent Massey, 1 April 1942, Massey Papers.

[25] USSEA to Secretary, Civil Service Commission, 16 September 1940, DEA files.

[26] The Royal Commission on Government Operations, 4, *Special Areas of Administration* (Ottawa 1963), 103.

[27] SCEAND, *Minutes of Proceedings and Evidence*, 8, 9 June 1966, 248.

[28] Ibid., 4, 22 June 1967, 75.

[29] Flora MacDonald, 'Cutting Through the Chains', *The Globe and Mail* (Toronto), 7 November 1980.

[30] *Foreign Policy for Canadians*, I (Ottawa 1970), 39–40.

[31] McGill, 'The Role of the Department . . .', 15.

[32] Letter of 19 October 1979.

[33] SCEAND, *Minutes of Proceedings and Evidence*, 17, 28 October 1980, 3.

[34] Quoted in ibid., 3, 10 June 1980, 12–13.

[35] Jack Maybee, 'Foreign Service Consolidation', *International Perspectives*, July/August 1980, 17.

[36] Ibid., 19.

[37] SCEAND, *Minutes of Proceedings and Evidence*, 26, 12 May 1971, 13–14.

[38] DEA memorandum, 'Headquarters Organization', in ibid., 24, 5 May 1971, 32.

[39] Ibid., 7.

[40] Ibid.

[41] Quoted in Maurice Pope (ed.), *Public Servant: The Memoirs of Sir Joseph Pope* (Toronto 1960), 287.

[42] SCEAND, *Minutes of Proceedings and Evidence*, 21, 7 April 1970, 15.

[43] Quoted in Peter C. Dobell, *Canada's Search for New Roles: Foreign Policy in the Trudeau Era* (London, New York, Toronto 1972), 19.

[44] Sandra Gwynn, 'Where Are You, Mike Pearson, Now That We Need You?', *Saturday Night* (Toronto), April 1978, 27.

[45] Gotlieb, 'Canadian Diplomacy . . .', 7.

[46] SCEAND, *Minutes of Proceedings and Evidence*, 17, 28 October 1980, 8–9.

[47] Prime Minister Pierre E. Trudeau to Pamela A. McDougall, 28 August 1980 (mimeograph release).

[48] MacDonald, 'Cutting Through the Chains'.

[49] Humphrey Carver, 'A Fresh Architectural Face to Fit External Affairs' Role', *International Perspectives: A Journal of the Department of External Affairs*, Nov./Dec. 1972, 49–50.

[50] SCEAND, *Minutes of Proceedings and Evidence*, 20, 24 March 1970, 6.

[51] 'Notes for a Speech by the Secretary of State for External Affairs, Flora MacDonald, to the Men's Canadian Club, Vancouver, B.C., September 13, 1979, at 12.15' (Ottawa, 1979, mimeographed), 4.

[52] *Careers in the Foreign Service*, 18.

[53] Ibid., 5.

[54] Letter of 19 October 1979.

[55] Gotlieb, 'Canadian Diplomacy . . .', 28.

[56] Marcel Cadieux, *The Canadian Diplomat: An Essay in Definition* (Toronto 1963), 110.

[57] *Careers in the Foreign Service*, 13.

BIBLIOGRAPHY
(does not include works cited in references)

Colin Campbell and George J. Szablowski, *The Superbureaucrats: Structure and Behaviour in Central Agencies* (Toronto 1979).

'Canada and the United States: Transnational and Transgovernmental Relations', special issue of *International Organization*, vol. 28, no. 4, Autumn 1974.

Canada in World Affairs. Biennial survey published under the auspices of the Canadian Institute of International Affairs (Toronto 1941–).

'Canada's Foreign Policy', special issue of *International Journal*, vol. xxvi, no. 1, Winter 1970–1.

Centre for Foreign Policy Studies, Dalhousie University, *The Changing Role of the Diplomatic Function in the Making of Foreign Policy* (Occasional Paper, June 1973).

Department of External Affairs, Annual Review.

Jean-Yves Dionne, 'Des professionnels sans profession: les agents du Service extérieur', *Perspectives Internationales*, Winter 1981, 41–7.

G. Bruce Doern and Peter Aucoin (eds), *Public Policy in Canada: Organization, Process and Management* (Toronto 1979).

James Eayrs, *The Art of the Possible: Government and Foreign Policy in Canada* (Toronto 1961).

——, *In Defence of Canada*, IV, *Growing Up Allied* (Toronto 1980).

R. Barry Farrell, *The Making of Canadian Foreign Policy* (Scarborough, Ont. 1969).

J. L. Granatstein, *A Man of Influence: Norman A. Robertson and Canadian Statecraft 1929–68* (Ottawa 1981).

Norman Hilmer, 'The Anglo-Canadian Neurosis: The Case of O. D. Skelton', in Peter Lyon (ed.), *Britain and Canada: Survey of a Changing Relationship* (London 1976), 61–84.

——, and Garth Stevenson (eds), *A Foremost Nation: Canadian Foreign Policy and a Changing World* (Toronto 1977).

John W. Holmes, *The Better Part of Valour: Essays on Canadian Diplomacy* (Toronto 1970).

——, *Canada: A Middle-Aged Power* (Toronto 1976).

——, *The Shaping of Peace: Canada and the Search for World Order, 1943–1957*, 2 vols (Toronto 1979, 1981).

T. A. Keenleyside, 'Career Attitudes of Canadian Foreign Service Officers', *Canadian Public Administration*, vol. 19, no. 2, Summer 1976, 208–26.

——, 'Lament for a Foreign Service: The Decline of Canadian Idealism', *Journal of Canadian Studies*, 12, 4, Winter 1980–1, 75–84.

Peyton V. Lyon and Brian W. Tomlin, *Canada as an International Actor* (Toronto 1979).

Richard A. Preston, 'Canadian External Relations at the Centennial of Confederation', in Richard A. Leach (ed.), *Contemporary Canada* (Durham, N.S. 1967), 271–96.

H. Gordon Skilling, *Canadian Representation Abroad* (Toronto 1945).

Bruce Thordarson, *Trudeau and Foreign Policy: A Study in Decision-Making* (Toronto 1972).

Brian W. Tomlin, *Canada's Foreign Policy: Analysis and Trends* (Toronto 1978).

'Trudeau and Foreign Policy', special issue of *International Journal*, xxxiii, 2, Spring 1978.

Michael Tucker, *Canadian Foreign Policy: Contemporary Issues and Themes* (Toronto 1980).

CANADA – APPENDIX A

DEPARTMENT OF EXTERNAL AFFAIRS
(November 1979)

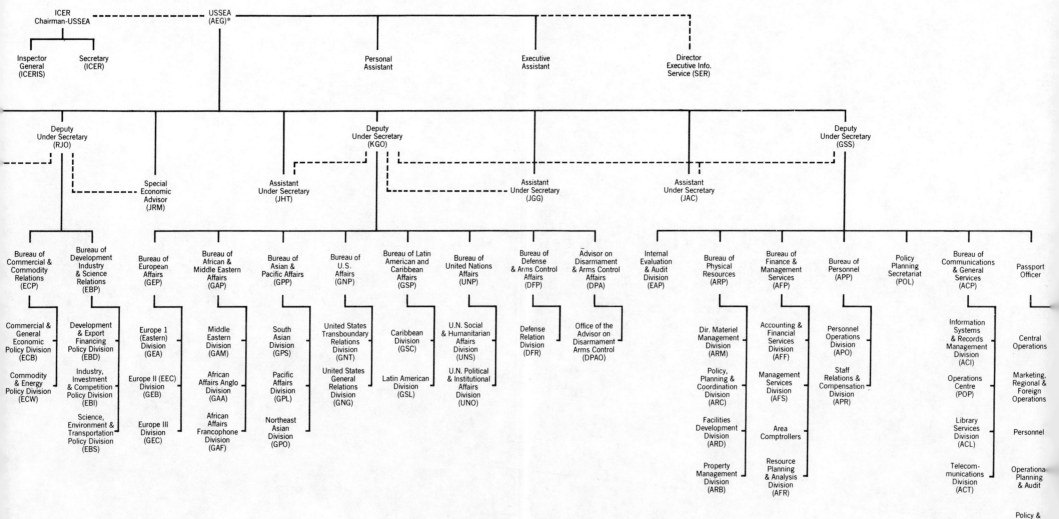

ICER
Chairman-USSEA

USSEA
(AEG)*

Inspector General (ICERIS)

Secretary (ICER)

Personal Assistant

Executive Assistant

Director Executive Info. Service (SER)

Deputy Under Secretary (RJO)

Deputy Under Secretary (KGO)

Deputy Under Secretary (GSS)

Special Economic Advisor (JRM)

Assistant Under Secretary (JHT)

Assistant Under Secretary (JGG)

Assistant Under Secretary (JAC)

Bureau of Commercial & Commodity Relations (ECP)

Bureau of Development Industry & Science Relations (EBP)

Bureau of European Affairs (GEP)

Bureau of African & Middle Eastern Affairs (GAP)

Bureau of Asian & Pacific Affairs (GPP)

Bureau of U.S. Affairs (GNP)

Bureau of Latin American and Caribbean Affairs (GSP)

Bureau of United Nations Affairs (UNP)

Bureau of Defense & Arms Control Affairs (DFP)

Advisor on Disarmament & Arms Control Affairs (DPA)

Internal Evaluation & Audit Division (EAP)

Bureau of Physical Resources (ARP)

Bureau of Finance & Management Services (AFP)

Bureau of Personnel (APP)

Policy Planning Secretariat (POL)

Bureau of Communications & General Services (ACP)

Passport Officer

Commercial & General Economic Policy Division (ECB)

Commodity & Energy Policy Division (ECW)

Development & Export Financing Policy Division (EBD)

Industry, Investment & Competition Policy Division (EBI)

Science, Environment & Transportation Policy Division (EBS)

Europe 1 (Eastern) Division (GEA)

Europe II (EEC) Division (GEB)

Europe III Division (GEC)

Middle Eastern Division (GAM)

African Affairs Anglo Division (GAA)

African Affairs Francophone Division (GAF)

South Asian Division (GPS)

Pacific Affairs Division (GPL)

Northeast Asian Division (GPO)

United States Transboundary Relations Division (GNT)

United States General Relations Division (GNG)

Caribbean Division (GSC)

Latin American Division (GSL)

U.N. Social & Humanitarian Affairs Division (UNS)

U.N. Political & Institutional Affairs Division (UNO)

Defense Relation Division (DFR)

Office of the Advisor on Disarmament Arms Control (DPAO)

Dir. Materiel Management Division (ARM)

Policy, Planning & Coordination Division (ARC)

Facilities Development Division (ARD)

Property Management Division (ARB)

Accounting & Financial Services Division (AFF)

Management Services Division (AFS)

Area Comptrollers

Resource Planning & Analysis Division (AFR)

Personnel Operations Division (APO)

Staff Relations & Compensation Division (APR)

Information Systems & Records Management Division (ACI)

Operations Centre (POP)

Library Services Division (ACL)

Telecommunications Division (ACT)

Central Operations

Marketing, Regional & Foreign Operations

Personnel

Operational Planning & Audit

Policy & Advisory Services

Financial & Administration Services

* These initials, and all others in brackets, are the acronyms by which each bureau or administrative unit are identified within the departmental bureaucracy

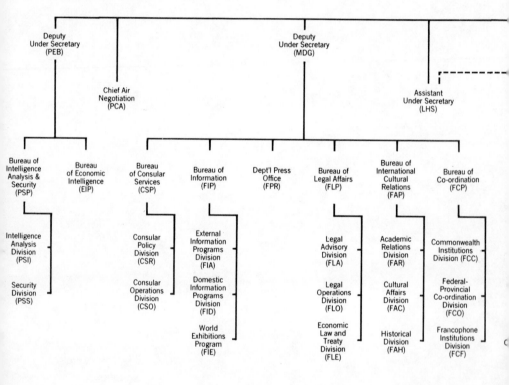

Deputy
Under Secretary
(PEB)

Deputy
Under Secretary
(MDG)

Chief Air
Negotiation
(PCA)

Assistant
Under Secretary
(LHS)

Bureau of
Intelligence
Analysis &
Security
(PSP)

Bureau
of Economic
Intelligence
(EIP)

Bureau
of Consular
Services
(CSP)

Bureau of
Information
(FIP)

Dept'l Press
Office
(FPR)

Bureau of
Legal Affairs
(FLP)

Bureau of
International
Cultural
Relations
(FAP)

Bureau of
Co-ordination
(FCP)

Intelligence
Analysis
Division
(PSI)

Security
Division
(PSS)

Consular
Policy
Division
(CSR)

Consular
Operations
Division
(CSO)

External
Information
Programs
Division
(FIA)

Domestic
Information
Programs
Division
(FID)

World
Exhibitions
Program
(FIE)

Legal
Advisory
Division
(FLA)

Legal
Operations
Division
(FLO)

Economic
Law and
Treaty
Division
(FLE)

Academic
Relations
Division
(FAR)

Cultural
Affairs
Division
(FAC)

Historical
Division
(FAH)

Commonwealth
Institutions
Division (FCC)

Federal-
Provincial
Co-ordination
Division
(FCO)

Francophone
Institutions
Division
(FCF)

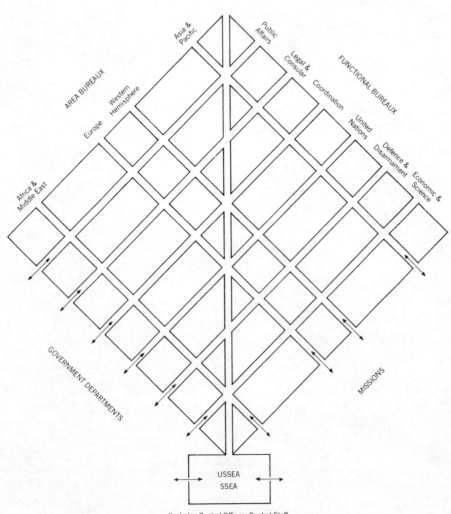

AREA BUREAUX

Asia & Pacific

Public Affairs

Legal & Consular

Coordination

FUNCTIONAL BUREAUX

Western Hemisphere

Europe

United Nations

Defence & Disarmament

Economic & Science

Africa & Middle East

GOVERNMENT DEPARTMENTS

MISSIONS

USSEA
SSEA

(Includes Central Offices: Central Staff,
Operations Center, & Policy Analysis Group)

Note: omitted from diagram are Administrative Bureaux –
Finance & Administration, Personnel & Communications & Information Systems –
and special units reporting directly to USSEA – Bilingualism Advisor.
Press Relations, Protocol, Inspection Service & Security & Intelligence.

China

The Development of the Chinese Foreign Office in the Ch'ing Period

IMMANUEL C. Y. HSÜ

Professor Immanuel C. Y. Hsü is Professor of History at the University of California, Santa Barbara. Born in Shanghai in 1924, now an American citizen, Professor Hsü holds a Ph.D. from Harvard University. His major work, *The Rise of Modern China* (1970, 1975) was given the Commonwealth Literary Prize of California (1971). He is also the author of *China's Entrance into the Family of Nations* (1960); *The Ili Crisis: A study of Sino-Russian Diplomacy, 1871–1881* (1965) and has edited *Readings in Modern Chinese History* (1971).

Traditional China was a universal empire. The ancient classic, the *Book of Odes*, declared, 'Under the wide heaven, there is no land that is not the emperor's, and within the sea boundaries of the land, there is none who is not a subject of the emperor.'[1] Ruling with a Mandate of Heaven, the Chinese emperor claimed jurisdiction over all mankind. As the mediator between man and nature, he was figuratively known as the Son of Heaven. The Chinese world consisted of the eastern part of the Asian continent and China unhesitatingly regarded itself as the Middle Kingdom surrounded by a group of smaller states. The highest political ideal in traditional China did not stop with ruling China well, but extended to the ordering of the whole known world, East Asia.

China of old was thus not a nation-state as understood in the modern West. In fact there was a conspicuous lack of national sentiment among the Chinese. There was no national flag, only dynastic or imperial banners. The boundaries of the country were indistinct; only a vague notion existed about a northern frontier somewhere in the Mongolian desert, a western border in the Central Asian massif, a southern frontier dissolved into the jungles of what is today South-East Asia, and an eastern border at the sea coast. The people exhibited no strong feelings of nationalism though they took immense pride in their culture. Some sinologists boldly asserted that traditional China was not so much a state as a cultural entity.[2]

For nearly 2000 years before the mid-nineteenth century China stood resplendent in a state of 'glorious isolation'. As its political, social and economic institutions were stable and self-contained, it felt no need for foreign intercourse. The land of the sages Yao and Shun was the source of civilization; who among civilized men would associate with other outlandish peoples? With this political culture and philosophical heritage, foreign relations were impossible. Indeed, what could be 'foreign' in a universal state? The lack of awareness of other equal states and of the need for intercourse with them precluded the existence of a foreign office. Nonetheless, China did develop relations with barbarian tribes that intermittently invaded; hence there was recognition of barbarian relations. In addition, China maintained ritualistic relations with peripheral states such as Korea, Liu-ch'iu (Ryūkyū), Annam (Vietnam), Siam (Thailand) and Burma that involved the giving and receiving of gifts. These were known as tributary relations.[3] Lastly, maritime trade since the sixteenth century with European countries and overland trade with Russia evidenced a recognition of trade affairs. Each of these types of relations was directed by a special agency of state, but there was no recognition of formal diplomatic relations between China and any other equal state. It was not until the intrusion of the West in the mid-nineteenth century that the Chinese were forced to realize that powerful states did exist outside China. Only then were efforts made to create a foreign office to cope with the unprecedented situation.

Early institutions of foreign intercourse

The absence of a foreign office does not mean that there were no institutions in China to deal with external affairs. During the Ming dynasty (1368–1643) there were the Common Residence for Envoys (Hui-t'ung-kuan) and the Residence for Barbarian Envoys (Ssu-i-kuan) under the Court of Sacrificial Worship. In 1748 the Ch'ing emperor Ch'ien-lung combined the two into a

Common Residence for Tributary Envoys (Hui-t'ung ssu-i-kuan) under a senior secretary of the Board of Rites. As indicated by its title, the new office handled the receiving and lodging of tributary envoys. The more serious matter of proper ceremonies was left to the Court of State Ceremonial (Hung-lu ssu).

Relations with Russia were a special case. Because of its position as a northern neighbour with overland trade relations, Russian affairs, together with Mongolian, Tibetan and Muslim affairs, were under the charge of the Court of Colonial Affairs (Li-fan yüan).[4] By the Treaty of Kiakhta of 1727, Russia was permitted to send periodic trade caravans and to establish a religious mission with a language school in Peking. Groups of Russian priests and language students came to China every ten years. The mission performed semi-diplomatic functions, while the returned language students began what were probably the first sinological studies in Europe.[5]

There were several related organizations concerned with Russian affairs. The Superintendent of Russian Affairs (Tsung-li O-lo-ssu shih-wu) in Peking was established in about 1709 with Ma-ch'i (Maci) as its first appointee. It managed commercial affairs such as the reception of the caravans. A language school under the control of the Grand Secretariat and the Court of Colonial Affairs was established in 1757 to translate Russian documents, with a permanent body of twenty-four students selected from the Eight Banners. In the outposts, from 1762, two Imperial Residents at Urga, Outer Mongolia, superintended overland trade with Russia, while the general of Ili in Sinkiang and that of Heilungkiang in Manchuria were sometimes authorized to negotiate treaties with their Russian counterparts (e.g. the Treaty of Kuldja of 1851 and the Treaty of Aigun of 1858). The Russian government institutions in charge of relations with China were the Senate and the governor at Tobolsk.

Though the Western maritime nations did not fit into the Chinese pattern either as Russia or as the tributary states, the Ch'ing dynasty insisted that the uninvited westerners accept tributary status and perform the *kowtow* to the emperor. Of the seventeen Western missions to Peking between 1655 and 1795, only Lord Macartney's mission of 1793 was exempted from this ritual; the other sixteen yielded under protest. Western traders were allowed to reside in Macao and Canton as a special favour from the emperor toward men from afar. They were governed by the governors and governors-general at Canton through the Customs Superintendent, the Hoppo, and the monopolistic Hong merchants. When foreign problems grew out of control, the emperor might appoint an imperial commissioner to investigate the situation. Thus Lin Tse-hsü was sent to Canton in 1838 to investigate the opium question. During the Opium War the governors and governors-general of the coastal provinces became part of the system of foreign intercourse, as they were authorized to receive and transmit foreign communications. After the war, in 1842, when Imperial Commissioner Ch'i-ying was appointed governor-general of Canton, files on foreign affairs were deposited in his *yamen* (office building) and it became a 'foreign office' in all but name. This practice of using Canton to shield Peking from direct contact with the Western powers was called by foreigners the Canton Viceroy System. After the Opium War, as trade moved northwards with the opening of Amoy, Foochow, Ningpo and Shanghai, the governor-general of Liang-Kiang became a sort of 'deputy foreign minister'. Institutionally, the rise in power of the governors-general at Canton and Nanking in managing foreign affairs presaged the establishment of a foreign office.

Foreign diplomats and traders were, of course, unhappy with this practice of using governors-general and imperial commissioners to keep them from Peking. Though Article 11 of the Treaty of Nanking (1842) authorized them to correspond directly, on an equal footing, with high Chinese officials in the capital, foreign diplomats found their correspondence to Peking sidetracked or returned to Canton, and their representations to local high officials unanswered. Peking was still inaccessible. The conviction grew in foreign circles that Peking must be forced to take up the responsibility of transacting its own foreign affairs, and that diplomatic residence in the capital was essential. During the *Arrow* War of 1856 and the negotiations of the Treaties of Tientsin in 1858, England and France sought to end the foreigners' being 'tossed to and fro like a shuttle between Imperial and Provincial authorities' under the Canton Viceroy System by insisting on diplomatic residence in Peking.[6] They won the right, which was later reaffirmed in the Conventions of Peking in 1860, and foreign legations were established in the following year. A totally unprecedented situation arose in Chinese external relations, necessitating a complete reexamination of the existing system.[7]

The establishment of the Tsungli Yamen

This reexamination, which led to the creation of a foreign office in 1861, was affected by both external and internal factors. Externally, there was the Western powers' constant demand for a centralized foreign affairs organ in the Chinese government. The establishment of foreign legations in Peking in 1861 raised the questions of the allocation of legation quarters, the reception of foreign representatives, the payment of indemnities, the opening of new ports, and a host of other issues requiring immediate attention. What office was to handle these problems?

After the conclusion of the Conventions of Peking, the first British minister to China, Frederick Bruce, on 8 November 1860, indicated to Prince Kung, who had negotiated on behalf of China, that in the future he expected to deal with him (Prince Kung) or with the 'foreign minister at the capital'. On the same date, the head of the British expedition, Lord Elgin, wrote to Prince Kung that he expected the administration of Chinese foreign relations to remain in Kung's hands.[8] Baron Gros, head of the French expedition, similarly expressed his wish that the prince would head a forthcoming 'Department of Foreign Affairs'.[9] Meanwhile, the Russians insisted on communicating only with the Grand Council, thereby negating the power and status of the Li-fan yüan. If Britain, France, and the United States followed suit, the Grand Council would be overburdened. Clearly, there was a need for the creation of a separate office to bear the brunt of foreign intercourse.[10]

Domestically, the rise in government of Prince Kung made possible the realization of his ideas on diplomatic and military modernization. It may be recalled that during the Anglo-French occupation of Peking in 1860, Emperor Hsien-feng fled to Jehol in Manchuria, and left his younger brother, Prince Kung, to negotiate with the enemies. By staying in the capital at great personal risk and achieving a peace settlement, he came to be regarded as the 'saviour' of the dynasty and his prestige soared. Though formerly anti-foreign, Prince Kung's first-hand dealings with Lord Elgin and Baron Gros led him to a new understanding of the 'barbarian' situation. He developed a degree of secret admiration for British power and found that these new barbarians were different from China's historical invaders. They had their own logic and good faith, and their prompt evacuation of Peking was evidence that they had no territorial designs on China. Thus, Prince Kung deduced, if China treated foreign powers with good will and kept her treaty obligations, peace would prevail. He devised a two-pronged approach to China's future: in the short-term (piao), maintain peace with the foreign powers to gain a respite in which to achieve the long-term goal (pen) of self-strengthening. Western governments and traders welcomed the new Chinese attitude; and, satisfied with the new treaty concessions, they adopted a cooperative policy toward China. They looked to Prince Kung as the symbol of friendliness and progress, and decided to support him against the conservative elements in the Chinese government.

Peace had returned but the emperor, ashamed of his flight from Peking and afraid of foreign demands for audience without kowtow, had not. He soon died in Jehol leaving behind a son, Ts'ai-chün, aged five (six sui by Chinese counting), and two empresses. Tz'u-hsi, mother of the boy emperor, and Tz'u-an, the childless first wife, now became Empresses Dowager. At the same time, eight Manchu princes and high officials concocted a 'Council of Regency' in Jehol, which left the Dowagers and Prince Kung out in the cold. In the ensuing power struggle the Dowagers and Prince Kung, with British support, joined forces to topple the Regency. Emerging victorious from the coup of 1861, the Dowagers and Prince Kung became co-regents, with the prince serving as the front man while the Dowagers administered state affairs from behind a screen (ch'ui-lien t'ing-cheng). Added titles were bestowed on Kung as Prince Regent (I-cheng Wang), chief grand councillor, minister of the Imperial Household, presiding controller of the Imperial Clan Court, and head of the new foreign office.[11] The British role in this palace revolution was revealed in several dispatches from Peking by its minister: '. . . it is no small achievement within twelve months to have created a party inclined to and believing in the possibility of friendly intercourse, to have effectually aided that party to power. To have established satisfactory relations at Peking and become in some degree the advisors of a government with which eighteen months since we were at war.' Again: 'The downfall of the violent party, and the language of the decree of arrest amount to a real ratification of the Treaty of which the formal ratification was executed last year. . . . I shall be certainly mortified, if the Prince (Kung) does not administer foreign affairs in a more reasonable and intelligent spirit than has hitherto characterized the proceedings of the Chinese Government.'[12] A. H. Layard, British under-secretary for foreign affairs, spoke before the House of Commons on 18 March 1862: 'Within a very short time a great change had taken place; a coup d'état had been effected which led to a change of Ministers . . . Prince Kung and the two empresses had called together a new Ministry and had inaugurated a new policy; for the first time a Chinese Government had admitted the rights of foreigners, and consented to treat them as equals.'[13]

Supported both by the British and by the two Dowagers, Prince Kung felt confident enough to carry out his diplomatic reforms and self-strengthening programmes. On 11 January 1861 he and his associates submitted a six-article proposal to the court recommending the establishment of a 'foreign office' called the Tsung-li ko-kuo shih-wu ya-men (office for the general administration of the affairs of the different nations).[14] The court approved this proposal on 20 January but added the words *t'ung-shang* (commerce) to the title, which suggested that the new office was to deal with trade relations only. After some deft manipulation by Prince Kung this addition was finally omitted in foreign correspondence but remained in Chinese documents.[15] The long title was abbreviated to Tsungli Yamen. The office was temporarily housed in a Buddhist temple, the Chia-hsing ssu, to await the renovation of the deserted office of the Department of Iron Coins in the eastern section of the Imperial City. The Board of Rites made an official seal of the office on 11 March 1861, at which time a formal ceremony was held marking the inauguration of China's first foreign office. On 11 November 1861, the Yamen moved into the renovated building of the former Department of Iron Coins.

The organization and procedure of the Tsungli Yamen

The Tsungli Yamen, conceived of as a temporary office to settle immediate foreign and military concerns, did not enjoy a status equal to that of the Six Boards or ministries – Civil Appointments, Revenue, Rites, War, Punishment and Public Works. For thirty years it went unlisted in the official Red Book (Chin-shen ch'üan-shu) that registered government offices and officials.[16] It had no official charter to spell out its organization, function and procedure, but only the initial appointment of three *wang ta-ch'en*, or prince and high officials – Prince Kung, the grand secretary, Kuei-liang, and the grand councillor and vice-president of the Board of Revenue, Wen-hsiang. Nevertheless, from the various memorials and documents we see that the Tsungli Yamen gradually took on the appearance of a government office. Though commonly known to foreigners as the foreign office, in reality it functioned more like a sub-committee of the Grand Council.

At the apex of the Yamen was the Controlling Board, whose members, known as ministers, were appointed by the emperor. A prince of the blood usually presided over the Board while the other members were concurrent high metropolitan officials such as grand councillors, grand secretaries, presidents or vice-presidents of the boards, or leading officials of the Li-fan yüan and the Censorate. Being concurrent appointees they received no salaries from the Yamen, which could thus operate on the low budget of 600 taels per month for general expenses.[17] The prestige and status of the Yamen were largely determined by those of the presiding prince and leading ministers. The greater the number of grand councillors serving in the Yamen, the greater its political clout. From 1869 to 1875 Prince Kung had succeeded in getting four of the five members of the Grand Council appointed to the Yamen, and between 1876 and 1881 all of them (five to seven).

As a temporary office with no statutory basis, the Yamen had no power to make foreign policy, only the duty to execute it. The power of decision rested with the emperor and the Grand Council. In practice, however, since both Prince Kung and Wen-hsiang were grand councillors, the recommendations of the Yamen were usually approved as long as they were members. Prince Kung presided over the Controlling Board from 1861 to 1884, and Wen-hsiang served as the backbone of the Yamen from its inception until his death in 1876. Thus, the Yamen enjoyed a high status during the first fifteen to perhaps twenty years of its existence. Thereafter, its influence waned steadily.

The size of the Controlling Board was determined by the emperor, varying from the original three men in 1861 to thirteen in 1884, but averaging about ten. The Board usually met in the afternoon as its members, as concurrent appointees, had work elsewhere, but emergency meetings could be held at any hour. The Yamen memorials represented the consensus of the Board members; no individual or separate opinions were allowed. In matters of utmost importance the ministers themselves had to write, copy or orally transmit secret memorials to the throne. Routine matters were discharged by the secretaries.

Originally, the Tsungli Yamen had sixteen secretaries *(chang-ching)*, half of them Manchu and half Chinese. They were chosen from the secretaries of the Grand Secretariat, the Court of Colonial Affairs, and the Boards of Rites, Revenue, and War. They too were concurrent appointees and could not work full time in the Yamen, but attended by rotation, day and night. Among them, two Chinese and two Manchus served as secretaries-general *(tsung-pan)*, and two others as assistant secretaries-general. In addition, eight secretaries from the Grand Council served as supernumerary secretaries at the Yamen. The position of secretary sometimes led to promotion; in time, eight secretaries rose to be ministers, and two ultimately became grand councillors.[18]

Below the secretaries were sixteen clerks, chosen from the State Historiographer's Office and the Military Archives Office for their integrity and ability to maintain secrecy, who worked as copyists.[19] Below them were some servants and soldiers who served as messengers and guards.

In the beginning, the division of labour among secretaries was based on the function each had performed in his former office. Thus Russian affairs were handled by secretaries from the Li-fan yüan, and maritime customs by those from the Board of Revenue. In practice, however, such alignment often resulted in the separation rather than the coordination of the functions of the Yamen. By 1864, through trial and error, the general division of labour was fixed and several bureaux were created, each with specific functions. The English Bureau was in charge of affairs concerning England, Austria, international commerce and maritime customs; the French Bureau of affairs relating to France, Holland, Spain, Brazil, religion and emigration; the Russian Bureau of matters concerning Russia, Japan, overland trade, frontier defence, boundaries, protocols, reception of guests, official transfers and examinations; the American Bureau of affairs relating to the United States, Peru, Germany, Italy, Sweden, Norway, Belgium, Denmark, Portugal, treaty ports, labour protection and international conferences; the Maritime Defence Bureau of matters concerning the northern and southern coastal defence, the Yangtze River police force, the navy forts, dockyards, purchase and maintenance of steamships, arms and ammunitions, machine manufacture, telegraphs, railways, and mines in the provinces. This bureau was created in 1883 and abolished after the Sino-Japanese War of 1894–5.[20] There is no apparent logic behind the separation of functions in these bureaux. The arrangement can only be described as haphazard, ensuring confusion and inefficiency while demonstrating Chinese ignorance of foreign countries.

The Yamen comprised several administrative units: the General Affairs Office (Ssu-wu t'ing), in charge of the supervision of the official seal, presentation of memorials and the transmission of dispatches; the Archives (Ch'ing-tang ch'u or Ch'ing-tang fang), in charge of the care of official documents and training of the Yamen's new recruits; the Office of Telegraph (Tien-pao ch'u), created in 1884 to handle the transmission and reception of telegrams during the Sino-French War over Vietnam; and the Treasury (Yin-k'u), to take care of the financial affairs of the Yamen.

Two other offices were attached to the Tsungli Yamen, the T'ung-wen kuan, a foreign language school, and the Inspectorate-General of Customs (Tsung shui-wu-ssu). The former, under the charge of the American educational missionary W. A. P. Martin, became, in the 1870s, a small liberal arts college with a printing press. The latter was put under the charge of the Irishman Robert Hart.

The activities of the Tsungli Yamen involved not only foreign affairs but also the promotion of modernization and defence projects. The office was concerned with the introduction of Western science and industry, modern schools, customs and the purchase of ships and guns. Its influence rose and fell with the political fortunes of its presiding prince and leading ministers. Its prestige was greatest in the 1860s when Prince Kung was riding high, but waned somewhat after his second chastisement from the Dowager Tz'u-hsi in 1869–70. When Li Hung-chang became concurrently governor-general of Chihli and superintendent of trade for the three northern ports in 1870, he enjoyed the patronage of the Dowager and increasingly eclipsed the Tsungli Yamen. After the death of Wen-hsiang in 1876, the Yamen began its downward course.

The superintendents of trade and local governors-general

When Prince Kung and his associates recommended the creation of the Tsungli Yamen in 1861, they also suggested, and received approval for, the appointment of a superintendent of trade at Tientsin to oversee the three northern ports of Tientsin, Newchwang and Chefoo. This post paralleled the commissionership at Shanghai, which oversaw the five original ports opened by the Treaty of Nanking in 1842 and the new ports along the Yangtze River and the southern sea coast opened by the treaties of 1858–60. In 1866 the Shanghai commissionership became a concurrent appointment of the governor-general at Nanking, and in 1870 the Tientsin superintendency became a concurrent appointment of the governor-general of Chihli. These two superintendents of trade became known as the high commissioner for the northern ocean (Pei-yang ta-ch'en), and the high commissioner for the southern ocean (Nan-yang ta-ch'en) – 'ocean' here meaning ports.

The Chinese created these trade superintendencies secretly hoping to direct business away from Peking so as to leave foreign diplomats little reason to stay there. 'If Tientsin can manage properly, then even though the barbarian chieftains live in the capital, they must be depressed with having nothing to do and finally think of returning home.'[21] So Prince Kung soothed the wounded pride of the court! The stratagem did work to the extent that foreigners were vexed by the endless cross-reference of matters between the Yamen and the superintendents. Needless to say, however, they would not leave Peking after having fought two wars to get there. But when Li Hung-chang, enjoying the Dowager's favour, became the high commissioner for the northern ocean, his office in Tientsin was frequented by foreign diplomats, traders and military experts to such an extent that he increasingly appropriated the functions of the Tsungli Yamen. It was Li who settled the Tientsin Massacre case in 1870 and the Margary Affair in 1876. It was Li also who conducted peace negotiations with France in 1884 and Japan in 1895. For the quarter century after 1870, Li was virtually the 'foreign minister' of China.[22]

The decline of the Tsungli Yamen

With Li Hung-chang's growing influence, the Tsungli Yamen could do nothing to stem the tide of its decline. Provincial authorities followed Li rather than the Yamen in foreign matters, and the Yamen could only appeal to the throne when it sought adherence to a specific policy. Frequently, the Yamen sought the advice of the powerful provincial authorities and metropolitan officials, as their support or lack of it determined the ultimate decision of the throne and its closest adviser, the Grand Council. Also, by tradition, imperial commissioners negotiated important treaties, leaving only minor issues such as trade regulations and immigration for the Yamen to negotiate. The one treaty of substance that it did negotiate, the Alcock Convention of 1869, was rejected by Britain. It has been estimated that during the life of the Yamen it signed only four of the forty-eight treaties of that period.[23] As the imperial commissioners maintained direct communications with the throne, the Yamen was often left in the dark even as to the contents of a treaty.

With the dismissal of Prince Kung in 1884 the Yamen's status deteriorated rapidly. The Dowager appointed Prince Ch'ing, a distant relative of the Imperial Household, as his successor. Ch'ing had neither the ability nor the will to administer the office. His main qualification seemed to be his good relations with Prince Chün, father of the boy emperor, Kuang-hsü. Though prohibited by tradition from exercising state power outright, Prince Chün nevertheless did it behind the scenes by receiving Yamen ministers and their reports in his private residence where decisions were made. From 1884 until his death in 1891 he acted as 'prime minister' of China.[24] A further negating influence came in 1885 with the establishment of the Board of Admiralty (Hai-chün yamen), which assumed part of the Tsungli Yamen's role in national defence.

The shrinking influence of the Tsungli Yamen left it with only a perfunctory role in the capital. The Yamen's duties included mostly the arrangement of dates for imperial audiences, the supervision of ceremonies, paying visits to the legations, the receipt of foreign communications passed directly at the capital, and the translation, transmission, coding and decoding of telegrams between the central government and the provincial authorities, foreign representatives, and Chinese legations abroad. Because of this last function, the Yamen acquired the designation of I-shu, or Office of Translation. The progressive decline of the Yamen was not stemmed by the reappointment of Prince Kung in 1894 as the presiding member. His vitality and drive spent, he died in that office in 1898. With the appointment of the xenophobic Prince Tuan during the Boxer Rebellion of 1900, the Tsungli Yamen's doom was sealed. The peace settlement, by specifying that the Tsungli Yamen be replaced by a regular foreign office, marked the end of an era in Chinese foreign relations.

Criticisms of the Tsungli Yamen

A product of time and circumstance, the Tsungli Yamen was a compromise between the old and the new, the progressives and conservatives, and a concession to the stark fact that China must face the new international situation thrust upon it. Though an improvement over the previous system, the Yamen, as a temporary organization devoid of a constitutional, i.e. statutory, basis, suffered many shortcomings.

Functionally, the Yamen handled many duties far beyond the normal limits of a foreign office. In addition to diplomatic affairs, it coordinated almost the entire range of 'Western affairs' *(yang-wu)* such as foreign trade, customs, education, overseas affairs, postal service, national defence and cultural affairs. It oversaw the work of the Inspectorate-General of Customs and indirectly supervised the port commissioners in consultation with the two trade superintendents. It was involved in mining, machine factories, telegraph construction, Chinese labourers abroad, missionary incidents, and the manufacture and purchase of guns and ships. Further, the Yamen supervised the T'ung-wen kuan for the training of language students and future diplomatic and consular personnel. After 1867, when astronomy, chemistry, mathematics and physics were added to the curriculum of the school, the Yamen defended its development against conservative opposition. All in all, the Yamen's activities were too diverse to be functionally efficient.

The internal organization of the Yamen was haphazard. The establishment of the various bureaux followed neither geographic nor linguistic nor any other logical principle. The English Bureau handled Austrian affairs; the American Bureau, German affairs and those of six other European countries; the French Bureau, Dutch and Brazilian affairs; and the Russian Bureau, Japanese affairs. A more logical arrangement would have been to transfer the German and other European affairs from the American Bureau to the French or English, and to move emigration problems from the French Bureau to the American.[25] Similar confusion surrounded the appointments of Chinese envoys, who were frequently accredited to two or more countries. The minister to the United States held concurrent posts in Spain and Peru. In 1880, Marquis Tseng Chi-tse was minister to England, France, and Russia, while Li Feng-pao was minister to Germany, Austria, Italy, and Holland.[26] Inefficiency was built in.

Though most of the Yamen's early leaders were the progressives of Chinese officialdom, most had never been outside China and had limited knowledge of foreign diplomacy, politics, economy, history or geography. They little recognized the importance of developing an overall, positive foreign policy that aimed at the abolition of the unequal treaties and the improvement of China's international standing. For example, a policy of alignment with certain countries against certain others might have broken up the frequent group actions of the foreign powers. Preoccupied with pressing daily issues, they bogged down in granting, refusing and bargaining about foreign demands. Nonetheless, the Yamen was a step forward in Chinese diplomacy, as peaceful negotiations marked an improvement over gunboat dictations by foreign powers.

The concurrent appointment of the princes and ministers who received added responsibilities without compensation was another source of inefficiency in the Yamen. Absenteeism was common, sometimes exceeding half the total number of ministers.[27] Appointment to the Yamen was viewed not so much as promotion, rather as punishment, and clever politicians such as Li Hung-chang managed to avoid it. Conversely, the appointment of xenophobic, unsympathetic officials such as Grand Councillor Wo-jen, though an attempt to involve them in foreign affairs so as to neutralize their criticisms, worked to the detriment of the Yamen. Too clever to miss the point, they secretly obstructed the Yamen from within.

Foreign criticisms of the Yamen abounded. In 1875, during the Margary Affair, British minister Thomas Wade ridiculed the dilatory tactics of the Yamen as the behaviour of a fifteen- or sixteen-year-old boy acting like a one-year-old.[28] Others described the Yamen as 'an India rubber-ball-like body', and dealing with it as 'as useful as addressing a row of books'.[29]

The inability to keep its deliberations confidential was another shortcoming of the Yamen. Foreigners bribed its staff or even the ministers so that often the substance of a discussion was known to outsiders before a formal representation was made to the emperor. Furthermore, the ministers worked as a committee to reach a consensus of opinion; but collective responsibility resulted in evasion of individual responsibility, hence delay or inaction. No foreign office in any major country was run as a committee.

Powerful local authorities infringed on the Yamen's activities. As governor-general of Chihli, superintendent of trade for the northern ports, and confidant of the empress dowager, Li Hung-chang maintained what amounted to his own 'foreign office' in Tientsin. From 1870 to 1901, by negotiating most of China's important treaties, he usurped the functions of the Yamen. At times powerful foreign employees also overshadowed the Yamen. Robert Hart, inspector-general of customs, served as a foreign adviser to the court. It was he who, through his London agent, James D. Campbell, helped settle the Sino-French conflict over Vietnam in 1885.

The Tsungli Yamen was an unfortunate buffer between aggressive foreigners and conservative Chinese officials. It satisfied neither and was ridiculed by both. For most of its forty-year existence (1861–1901) it lived an unsettled life as a temporary office. The demise finally came during the Boxer Rebellion, when its members dispersed: three ministers accompanied the court in an unheroic flight to Sian, four were dismissed, and three others were assigned to unrelated posts. The Yamen for all intents and purposes ceased to function. The Boxer Protocol of 1901 specified the reorganization of the Tsungli Yamen into a regular Ministry of Foreign Affairs (Wai-wu pu) and ushered in a new day in Chinese foreign relations.

The Wai-wu pu

In accordance with article XII of the Boxer Protocol, an imperial edict was issued on 24 July 1901 that established a foreign office called the Wai-wu pu. This office took precedence over the Six Boards. It was headed by a comptroller-general and an associate comptroller-general, followed by a president who also carried the title of associate comptroller, two vice-presidents, two deputy vice-presidents and two councillors. There were five divisions to handle translation work in Russian, German, English, French and Japanese. Later, the first two were combined into a Russo-German Division, while two new departments, the Secretariat and the Division of Confidential Affairs, were added. Each division had a chief assisted by a number of staff members, but all divisions were under the direct supervision of the two deputy vice-presidents.[30]

The Wai-wu pu had four bureaux: Protocol, Arts (railways, mines, shipping, etc.), Customs and Accountancy, and General Affairs (boundaries, travel, missionaries, foreign claims, etc.). In addition, there were the offices of Archives and Telegraph. However, with the establishment of the Office of Maritime Customs (Shui-wu ch'u) in 1906 and later of the Ministries of Posts and Communications and the Navy, the Wai-wu pu was increasingly relieved of its charge of maritime customs, postal, telegraph and railway services, and naval matters. It became more of a foreign office in the regular sense. In 1910, the posts of comptroller-general and associate comptroller-general were abolished in favour of a single president of the Ministry of Foreign Affairs.

The Wai-wu pu was forced upon China by the Western powers. China's lack of enthusiasm for the office was in reverse proportion to the imperialist powers' high expectation of it. Nevertheless, the first appointees were all men of high standing. Prince Ch'ing (I-kuang) was the comptroller-general, Grand Secretary Wang Wen-shao served as the associate comptroller-general, and Ch'ü Hung-chi, president of the Board of Public Works, was made president and associate comptroller.[31] In spite of these appointments, the new office functioned listlessly in the rapidly sinking dynasty. In 1912 the Ch'ing dynasty fell and the short life of the Wai-wu pu ended.

NOTES

[1] The *Book of Odes*, 'Hsiao-ya: Pei-shan', Chapter II. Translation taken from James Legge, *The Chinese Classics* (London 1861–72), Vol. IV, Part II, 360, with minor changes by me.

[2] Yano Jinichi, *Kindai Shina ron* (On modern China) (Tokyo 1927), 3–4, 24–6, 114.

[3] For a study of China's management of the barbarian and tributary relations, see Immanuel C. Y. Hsü, *China's Entrance into the Family of Nations: The Diplomatic Phase, 1858–1880* (Cambridge, Mass. 1960, 1968), chapter 1; John K. Fairbank and S. Y. Teng, 'On the Ch'ing Tributary System', *Harvard Journal of Asiatic Studies*, 6:2: 135–246 (June 1941); John K. Fairbank (ed.), *The Chinese World Order: Traditional China's Foreign Relations* (Cambridge, Mass. 1968).

[4] For a study of Li-fan yuan, cf. an unpublished dissertation by David Miller Farquhar, 'The Ch'ing Administration of Mongolia up to the Nineteenth Century', Ph.D. thesis, Harvard University 1960.

[5] Immanuel C. Y. Hsü, 'Russia's Special Position in China during the Early Ch'ing Period', *Slavic Review*, 13:4:688–700 (December 1964). The best study of early Chinese institutions of foreign relations may be found in Fang Hao, *Chung-kuo chin-tai wai-chiao shih* (Modern Chinese diplomatic history) (Taipei 1955), chapter I, dealing with the organizations, functions and procedures of Chinese institutions of foreign relations during the last two hundred years. See also Eric Widmer, *The Russian Ecclesiastical Mission in Peking during the Eighteenth Century* (Cambridge, Mass. 1976).

[6] Horatio Lay, *Our interests in China* (London 1864), 49.

[7] For a study of the Western determination to break down the 'Canton Viceroy System' and force the court at Peking to take up foreign affairs itself, see Hsü, *China's Entrance*, op. cit., Part I, 'The Establishment of Foreign Legations in China, 1858–1861', 21–118.

[8] Masataka Banno, *China and the West, 1858–1861: The Origins of the Tsungli Yamen* (Cambridge, Mass. 1964), 210.

[9] Ibid., 211.

[10] S. M. Meng, *The Tsungli Yamen: Its Organization and Functions* (Cambridge, Mass. 1962), 16.

[11] For the *coup d'état* of 1861 and the evolution of Prince Kung's new policies, see Immanuel C. Y. Hsü, *The Rise of Modern China* (New York 1975), 2nd edn, 325–33; also Kwang-ching Liu, 'The Ch'ing Restoration', in John K. Fairbank (ed.), *The Cambridge History of China*, Vol. 10 (Cambridge 1978), 418–23.

[12] Quoted in Banno, 241. Italics added.

[13] Ibid., 240–1.

[14] A title apparently borrowed from, or influenced by, an expression in the 1858 Treaty of Tientsin with Russia, in which the 'Russian Minister for Foreign Affairs' was rendered as 'O-kuo tsung-li ko-kuo shih-wu ta-ch'en', Meng, 22.

[15] Banno, 228.

[16] Meng, 26.

[17] Ch'en T'i-ch'iang, *Chung-kuo wai-chiao hsing-cheng* (China's administration of foreign affairs) (Chungking 1943), 20.

[18] Hsü Keng-shen and Hsü Yung-i, cf. Meng, 37, 105.

[19] Banno, 230–1.

[20] Ch'en T'i-ch'iang, 18–19.

[21] *Ch'ou-pan i-wu shih-mo* (The complete account of the management of barbarian affairs) (Peiping 1930), Hsien-feng period, 71:27.

[22] For the rise of Li Hung-chang, see Ting-yee Kuo and Kwang-ching Liu, 'Self-strengthening: the Pursuit of Western Technology', in *The Cambridge History of China*, op. cit., 507–11.

[23] Meng, 43.

[24] Ibid., 124.

[25] Ch'en T'i-ch'iang, 30–1.

[26] Meng, 74.

[27] Ibid., 75.

[28] Ch'en T'i-ch'iang, 33, quoting a conversation between Thomas Wade and Li Hung-chang, 3 August 1875.

[29] E. H. Parker, *China Past and Present* (New York 1903), 217; Stanley Lane-Poole, *The Life of Sir Harry Parkes* (London and New York 1894), II, 389.

[30] Yü-chuan Chang, 'The Organization of the Waichiaopu', *The Chinese Social and Political Science Review*, I:1:34–5; Ch'en T'i-ch'iang, 48.

[31] Ch'en T'i-ch'iang, 45–6.

BIBLIOGRAPHY

Masataka Banno, *China and the West, 1858–1861: The Origins of the Tsungli Yamen* (Cambridge, Mass. 1964).

Knight Biggerstaff, 'The Establishment of Permanent Chinese Diplomatic Missions Abroad', *Chinese Social and Political Science Review*, Vol. 20, No. 1 (April 1936), 1–41.

H. S. Brunnert and V. U. Hagelstrom, *Present Day Political Organization of China* (Shanghai 1912).

Chang Chung-fu, 'Ya-p'ien chan-ch'ien Ch'ing-t'ing pan-li wai-chiao chih chi-kuan yü shou-hsü (The office and procedures for dealing with diplomatic affairs of the Ch'ing court before the Opium War), *Wai-chiao yüeh-pao* (Foreign Affairs, Peiping), Vol. 2, No. 2 (1933), 1–7.

——, 'Tzu Ya-p'ien chan-cheng chih Ying-Fa lien-chün ch'i-chung Ch'ing-t'ing pan-li wai-chiao chih chi-kuan yü shou-hsü' (The office and procedures for dealing with diplomatic affairs of the Ch'ing court during the period between the first and second Anglo-Chinese wars), *Wai-chiao yüeh-pao*, Vol. 2, No. 5 (1933), 43–51.

——, 'Tsung-li ko-kuo shih-wu ya-men chih yüan-ch'i (The origins of the Tsungli Yamen), *Wai-chiao yüeh-pao*, Vol. 3, No. 1 (1933), 1–11.

Chang Yü-chuan, 'The Organization of the Waichiaopu', *The Chinese Social and Political Science Review* (CSPSR), Vol. I, No. 1 (April 1916), 21–39.

Ch'en T'i-ch'iang, *Chung-kuo wai-chiao hsing-cheng* (China's administration of foreign affairs) (Chungking 1943).

Ch'ou-pan i-wu shih-mo (The complete account of the management of barbarian affairs) (Peiping 1930), Hsien-feng period (1851–61), 80 *chüan*; T'ung-chih period (1862–74), 100 *chüan*.

John King Fairbank (ed.), *The Chinese World Order: Traditional China's Foreign Relations* (Cambridge, Mass. 1968).

——, and S. Y. Teng, 'On the Ch'ing Tributary System', *Harvard Journal of Asiatic Studies*, Vol. 6, No. 2 (June 1941), 135–246.

——, (ed.), *The Cambridge History of China*, Vol. 10 (Cambridge 1978).

Fang Hao, *Chung-kuo chin-tai wai-chiao shih* (Modern Chinese diplomatic history) (Taipei 1955).

Fu Tsung-mou, 'Ch'ing-tai Tsung-li ko-kuo shih-wu ya-men yü Chun-chi-ch'u chih kuan-hsi' (The relationship between the Tsungli Yamen and the Grand Council during the Ch'ing period), *Chung-shan hsüeh-shu wen-hua chi-k'an*, Vol. 12 (Nov. 12, 1973), 285–324.

Immanuel C. Y. Hsü, *China's Entrance into the Family of Nations: The Diplomatic Phase, 1858–1880* (Cambridge, Mass. 1960, 1968).

——, 'Russia's Special Position in China during the Early Ch'ing Period', *Slavic Review*, Vol. 13, No. 4 (Dec. 1964), 688–700.

Liu, Kwang-ching, 'The Ch'ing Restoration', in John K. Fairbank (ed.), *The Cambridge History of China*, Vol. 10 (Cambridge 1978), 409–90.

S. M. Meng, *The Tsungli Yamen: Its Organization and Functions* (Cambridge, Mass. 1962).

Wu Ch'eng-chang, *Wai-chiao-pu yen-ko chi-lüeh* (A brief account of the development of the Ministry of Foreign Affairs), 2 vols, Ministry of Foreign Affairs (Peking 1913).

China

The Ministry of Foreign Affairs during the Republican Period 1912 to 1949

DAVID PONG

Dr David Pong is Associate Professor of East Asian History at the University of Delaware. He was born in Hong Kong and educated at the University of London, taking his Ph.D. in 1969. He has recently been Research Fellow at the Australian National University (1978–82) and has written numerous articles on Chinese administrative and political history as well as a critical guide to the Kwangtung Provincial Archives deposited at the Public Record Office in London.

During the Republican era the Ministry of Foreign Affairs continued its evolution into a modern governmental organ. Internally there were discernible changes for the better. On the other hand, many of these changes, as well as the authority the Ministry enjoyed, were closely related to the particular needs of the government in power. That being so, it is best to deal separately with the Ministry's development under the Peking Government and under the Kuomintang (Nationalist Party) tutelage.

The Ministry of Foreign Affairs under the Peking Government, 1912–28

Internal organization After several administrative changes in the first year of the Republic, the Ministry's organizational structure finally took shape in November 1912. In contrast to its Ch'ing predecessor, with its top-heavy leadership of comptrollers and presidents (seven in all), the new Ministry was headed by a single minister and a vice-minister. They were assisted by a council of four and a secretariat, while the functions of the Ministry were carried out by a Chancery and four departments. The Chancery, consisting of five sections, dealt with classified information (including a telegraph bureau), documents, statistics, accounts, translation, general administration, archives, a library, a reading room and publications.

The four departments were:

1. The Department of Diplomatic Relations, made up of four sections, handled legal disputes, boundaries, extradition, treaties, protection of foreigners, nationalization and prohibitions.

2. The Department of Commercial Relations, composed of five sections, was in charge of trade agreements, treaty ports, protection of Chinese traders and labourers abroad, foreign commercial and industrial enterprises in China, customs, foreign loans, employment of foreigners, and commercial affairs in general.

3. The Protocol Department, consisting of four sections, handled letters of credential, ceremonial matters, reception of foreign representatives and dignitaries, and the awarding and receiving of decorations.

4. The General Affairs Department, made up of four sections, dealt with missionary affairs, passports, diplomatic and consular expenditures, sending of delegations overseas, legal matters relating to Overseas Chinese, and international exhibitions.

In principle, the departments were organized according to function rather than to countries, a precedent set by the Ch'ing Ministry. This organizational principle was adhered to throughout the Peking Government period, though the departments themselves were modified three times.

By 1914 it was recognized that the duties performed by the General Affairs Department were too diverse and unrelated for it to function efficiently. It was therefore abolished and its functions assigned to the Chancery and the remaining departments. The Ministry's organization became more rational: the Chancery now had exclusive control over personnel and the financial affairs of the Ministry and its diplomatic and consular services, while the Department of Diplomatic Relations also acquired the oversight of missionary affairs, passports, and legal matters regarding Chinese overseas.

In 1921 a Treaty Department comprised of four sections was added to cope with increased activities in this area after the First World War, divesting the

Department of Diplomatic Relations of some of its charges. Unfortunately, its creation also produced large areas of overlapping responsibilities, especially regarding the interpretation and revision of treaties as well as the investigation of international disputes. The 1921 reorganization also saw the addition of administrative sections to the Chancery and the Departments of Diplomatic and Commercial Relations. Now each had six sections, signalling another step towards expansion and specialization. By this time, the professional staff of the Ministry had grown from a meagre fifty or so in 1912 to 120.

The final reorganization of the Ministry took place in July 1927 with the abolition of the Protocol Department, whose functions were now taken over by the Chancery. In its place was created the Intelligence Department, headed by the vice-minister himself with the assistance of two deputy department heads. Its four sections were designed to collect, study and translate vital information, in addition to the handling of certain aspects of public relations. This, then, was the state of the Ministry when the Peking Government came to an end in mid-1928.

Diplomatic missions The early Republic divided diplomatic missions into embassies and legations, but because of prohibitive costs and the reluctance of the powers to exchange ambassadors with China only legations were maintained. Deteriorating relations with the Soviet Union also prevented the implementation of the 1924 agreements that provided for the exchange of ambassadors. At the beginning of the Republican period the Peking Government maintained legations in the capital cities of sixteen nations, and the number steadily increased except for the few years following China's declaration of war against Germany and Austria. By 1928 China had diplomatic relations with twenty-three states that were either important in themselves or where large numbers of Overseas Chinese were found. A noticeable omission was Thailand, despite the huge Chinese community there.

To keep expenses to a minimum, the legations remained small. A typical mission in a major country would have a staff of seven, made up of a minister, three secretaries (one for each grade), two attachés, a chancellor and, in some cases, one or two student attachés. A legation in a minor country, however, could have as small a staff as four, including the minister. Compared with late Ch'ing practices, this represented an addition of one staff member for small legations and a reduction of two to three for major ones.

Special delegations were sent to represent China in international conferences and organizations. At the Paris Peace Conference (1919) the Chinese delegation consisted of fifty-two persons led by the Minister of Foreign Affairs and the Ministers to the United States, Great Britain and Belgium. The delegation to the Washington Conference (1922) was even larger, with 132 persons headed by equally distinguished figures. At the League of Nations China was regularly represented from the very beginning by her envoys in Europe.

Consular establishments In 1912 the Peking Government inherited some fourteen or so consular establishments from the Ch'ing dynasty, but their number soon increased. Towards the end of 1913 there were already thirteen consulates-general, nine consulates and two vice-consulates. By 1925 their

numbers were twenty-three, twenty-eight and one respectively. In contrast
to the legations, which were mostly in Europe, most of China's consular
establishments were to be found in North and South-East Asia. In 1925, for
example, China had five consulates-general and nine consulates in the USSR
alone. All except the consulate-general in Leningrad were located on or near
the Chinese border. In Korea, then part of Japan's empire, the Chinese had a
consulate-general and five consulates, whereas in Japan itself there were two
consulates-general and a consulate. Finally, there were four consulates-general
and seven consulates in various parts of South-East Asia. The rest (eleven
consulates-general, six consulates and a vice-consulate) were scattered among
Western European countries, the white dominions of the British Empire, the
United States, Mexico, Cuba, Panama and South Africa.

It was the existence of sizeable Chinese settlements that largely explains the
establishment of these consulates. The contribution made by the Overseas
Chinese to the overthrow of the Ch'ing dynasty and their continuing support
for the new state led to a more positive approach to these emigrants, whom
the Peking Government regarded as Chinese nationals. Generally speaking,
traders from China doing business abroad were numerically insignificant.
They were not of central concern to the Chinese government except in Soviet
Asia, where the land frontier permitted more frequent movement of Chinese
traders – an additional reason for the large number of consular establishments
in that area.

The size of the consular staff was kept to a minimum. The regulations
promulgated in 1916 provided for a consul-general or a consul in each
establishment, a vice-consul for some of the consulates-general, one student
attaché or none at all, and one or two chancellors. In 1923 there were five
members each at the consulates-general in Vladivostok and Blagoveshchensk;
the majority of the consulates-general had a staff of four, and consulates a
staff of three.

The operation of the Ministry of Foreign Affairs The Ministry of Foreign
Affairs was indebted to the Ch'ing for cultivating, directly or indirectly, many
of its talents. It therefore did not have to fill its key posts with men unfamiliar
with public service or foreign affairs. For instance, the first Minister of
Foreign Affairs, Lu Cheng-hsiang (1871–1949), was a student at the
Kiangnan Arsenal School (Kuang-fang-yen kuan) and the Tsungli Yamen's
T'ung-wen kuan. Before he joined the Peking Government he had been
China's minister to the Netherlands (1906–11) and to Russia (1911). His
vice-minister, Yen Hui-ch'ing (1877–1950), though basically American-
trained, had also studied in the T'ung-wen kuan and had had a foreign service
career under the Ch'ing.

Of the senior officials of the Ministry and the more prominent diplomats,
all but one – Wellington Koo or Ku Wei-chün – had served under the Ch'ing.
Indeed, the Ministry's provisional regulations of 1912 specifically required
that all ministerial appointees must have had previous experience at a ranking
level in either the foreign or the diplomatic service. While a necessity at the
time, this policy was no guarantee that the Ministry's personnel would be of
high quality, for it was the Ch'ing's practice to select diplomats mainly on
their linguistic skill. To improve their knowledge of the conditions in China
and to enhance their status in the international diplomatic community, the

Peking Government often transferred its foreign service personnel between posts in Peking and abroad. In fact, few of the senior diplomats did not serve as a minister or vice-minister of the Ministry at some point. A number of the councillors and department chiefs were also given experience overseas.

The idea was well conceived, but it was nullified by the political turbulence of the time. During the short period of sixteen years the Ministry changed hands no less than twenty-four times, while ten different people held the post of vice-minister, a position that was supposed to provide administrative stability within the Ministry. Although membership in the council was less frequently changed, true stability of personnel was not found until the level of department chief. In any event, the frequent shifts at the top seriously undermined the morale and efficiency of the Ministry.

Little is known of the background and training of the lesser officials of the foreign service. The regulations laid down in 1915 (revised in 1919) prescribed a special examination for those aspiring to join the service and, as pointed out earlier, some of the major legations and consular establishments also had trainees attached to them, although they were often treated as clerks rather than student diplomats. The early efforts of Minister Lu Cheng-hsiang to create a modern foreign service apparently came to little, so China's very few truly great diplomats were left with little staff support.

Many of the Ministry's weaknesses resulted from domestic political conditions. Throughout this period the position of the Ministry *vis-à-vis* that of the president or the legislature was weak. As the Provisional Constitution (in force during March 1912–November 1913 and June 1916–October 1923) did not require Cabinet ministers to be chosen from among party leaders, under a strong President like Yüan Shih-k'ai the Minister of Foreign Affairs and his Ministry could easily be reduced to an administrative agent. At times the Ministry was simply ignored. During the negotiations with the Five-Power Consortium for the Reorganization Loan in 1913 Yüan used as chief negotiator his long-term associate Chou Hsüeh-hsi, whom he had earlier appointed Finance Minister, and the Loan was concluded without reference to the Ministry. After Yüan assumed dictatorial powers in late 1913 the power of the Ministry withered. In 1915, after Yüan and Ts'ao Ju-lin (Vice-Minister of Foreign Affairs) had negotiated with the Japanese over the Twenty-One Demands, Minister Lu Cheng-hsiang was compelled to sign the agreement, which, as he protested to Yüan at the time, was tantamount to signing the 'death sentence' to his diplomatic career.

After the death of Yüan in June 1916, despite the revival of the Provisional Constitution, real power rested with the militarists, who whether in direct control of the Peking Government or not virtually dictated China's foreign policy. The declaration of war against Germany in 1917, which had met with considerable opposition in the National Assembly, was forced upon that legislative body after Premier Tuan Ch'i-jui, himself a warlord, had secured a unanimous agreement from the provincial military governors. Then, under the pretext of sustaining China's war efforts, Tuan negotiated in utmost secrecy a series of loans (the Nishihara loans) from Japan in exchange for vast railway and mining concessions in Shantung and other parts of China. The Ministry of Foreign Affairs was not apprised of the proceedings.

Peking did not, however, control the rest of China, and some of the more powerful warlords did not hesitate to use their power to influence China's foreign policy: in 1922, for example, Wu P'ei-fu denounced the Premier for his pro-Japanese policy. The political division also invited exploitation by the foreign powers. Again, the relationship between Wu and the British and Americans is well known. After the organization of the military government in the south by Sun Yat-sen the power of the Peking Government, and hence the authority of the Ministry, was further eroded. The USSR dealt with both Peking and Canton, as though they were two independent governments.

Deprived of its proper role, the Ministry remained under-financed and understaffed. At times staff salaries were two to three years in arrears, causing considerable demoralization. Throughout the period the Ministry never succeeded in developing an intelligence service, which, if efficient, would have rendered it more powerful. While such vital services were left unattended its council was allowed to be taken over by time-servers.

The principal objectives of China's foreign policy since the closing decades of the Ch'ing had been the abolition of the 'unequal treaties' and the preservation of administrative and territorial integrity. The period 1912–28 saw some gains in this direction, but the major successes were achieved not so much by the efforts of the Ministry, though it cannot be faulted for not trying, as by the conjuncture of international events and the interplay of big power politics. The first treaty signed on the basis of equality was with Germany, the vanquished, in May 1921, putting an end to extraterritoriality as far as the Germans were concerned. In dealing with the victors the Chinese were less successful, as shown by their failure to regain possession of Shantung at the Paris Peace Conference. When retrocession finally came in 1922, at the Washington Conference, it was essentially the product of the concern of the great powers to curb the rising Japanese, although the Chinese delegates also performed creditably.

The importance of the powers is best illustrated by China's timid reaction to the Karakhan Manifesto of 1919, whereby the USSR offered to repudiate the 'unequal treaties' and return all territories taken by the Tsarist regime. The Chinese, realizing that this would not be viewed favourably by the interested powers, dared not respond openly and accept the generous offer, although the skilful diplomacy of Minister Yen Hui-ch'ing did manage to ward off the attempts of the great powers to step into the Sino-Russian diplomatic vacuum and provide extraterritorial protection for the citizens of old Russia. In any case, much valuable time was lost and when the Chinese and the Russians finally reached an agreement in 1924 the USSR whose international status had become greatly strengthened, was in a position to retract some of the more generous offers made five years before.

The Ministry of Foreign Affairs under the Nationalist Government, 1928–49

Internal organization A Ministry of Foreign Affairs was formed in July 1925 when the Nationalists established a government in Canton to challenge the government at Peking. As the Canton regime was not recognized internationally, and as its 'foreign relations' were restricted to local matters in the limited areas it controlled, the organization of the Ministry was kept simple. Even the post of vice-minister, which existed under its predecessor government (Sun Yat-sen's military government), was abolished. After the establishment of the Nationalist Government in Nanking in May 1927, however, two vice-ministerial posts were created, one to take care of political matters and the other administrative matters. Below the ministers was a council (two to four members) whose job was to provide legal advice, particularly with reference to administrative matters though they often took part in policy-making as well. Next came the secretariat, which had among its responsibilities the scheduling of meetings (both intramural and with the diplomatic corps), the recording of their proceedings, translation, and the custody of important documents.

In the organization of the departments, the Nationalists adopted a more regionally oriented model. As of December 1928, there were five departments whose functions were as follows:

1. The Department of General Affairs, consisting of seven sections, dealt with the transmission of documents and telegraphic messages, radio transmission, protocol, budgets, accounts, general administrative matters, archives and library resources.

2. The Department of International Affairs, incorporating five sections, had under its charge commercial relations and intelligence, consular affairs, passports and visas, legal matters concerning aliens and international settlements, the registration and protection of Overseas Chinese and their business enterprises, Chinese students studying abroad, Kuomintang (Nationalist Party) activities abroad, the League of Nations and other international organizations, international agreements and conventions, international expositions, aviation and contraband.

3. The Department of Asian Affairs was given charge of all diplomatic affairs relating to Japan (First Section), the USSR (Second Section), and Turkey, Persia, Afghanistan, Thailand, Finland, Latvia, Lithuania and Estonia (Third Section). A Fourth Section dealt with matters concerning two or all three of the above sections as well as other special problems.

4. The Department of European and American Affairs paralleled the Department of Asian Affairs in internal organization. Its First Section handled relations with France, Germany, Austria, Italy, Belgium, Switzerland, Poland, Czechoslovakia and the Balkan states; the Second Section dealt with matters concerning Great Britain, the Netherlands, Spain, Portugal, Denmark, Sweden and Norway; the Third Section concerned itself with the USA and countries in Central and South America. The functions of the Fourth Section were the same as those of its counterpart in the Department of Asian Affairs.

5. The Intelligence and Publicity Department had four sections. The First Section dealt with reports from diplomatic and consular sources, the press, statistical data of the Ministry and publication; the Second Section concerned itself exclusively with intelligence on Europe and the American continents; the Third Section handled domestic intelligence, press releases and their publication in the Chinese press; the Fourth Section covered intelligence on Japan and the USSR.

In addition to these departments there was a Treaty Commission headed by the Minister himself. Its special duties were to look into the legal aspects of treaty agreements, their interpretation and revision. At a time when the Chinese were trying to abolish the unequal treaties this was an important commission, and its working committees were all chaired by full-time specialists and former senior diplomats.

Only minor modifications were introduced until October 1936 when, as a result of the Government's attempt to tighten its financial control over the entire bureaucracy, an Accounting Office and an Office of Statistics were created. The former, with a staff of sixteen to twenty-five, was placed under the Department of General Affairs; the latter, with a much smaller staff of four to seven, under the Intelligence and Publicity Department.

In general the internal organization of the Ministry as it was largely conceived in December 1928 had a number of drawbacks. To assign the responsibility for all diplomatic affairs around the world to two average-sized departments (Asian Affairs, and European and American Affairs) meant, at the very least, an excessive demand on their resources. Nor was the division of labour within the departments always logical, to wit, the grouping of the various countries handled by the Third Section in the Department of Asian Affairs. The functions of the Department of International Affairs were also far too encompassing and demanding. On the other hand, some of the duties that would have been best performed by a single department were carried out by separate departments: for example, the gathering of intelligence on Japan and the USSR would have been more efficiently conducted by the Department of Asian Affairs.

Many of these drawbacks were recognized, and appropriate changes were introduced when the Ministry was reorganized in September 1939. By this time the size of the Ministry had been drastically cut because of the war with Japan. In 1930 the entire staff of the Ministry stood at 317, and its number was increasing; as the Nationalist government moved to Chungking in 1937, 80 per cent of the Ministry's personnel were retrenched and, despite some increases in the following year, it had a staff of only 128 in 1938, of which forty-three were lowly employees who did not even enjoy civil service status. The reorganization of 1939 was therefore aimed at the redeployment of the limited human resources and at rationalizing some of the departments' organizational inconsistencies. In place of the two old regional departments there were now four:

1. The Department of East Asian Affairs had two sections dealing with Japan and a third section with Thailand (which had the largest Overseas Chinese community in an independent country) and the rest of Asia.

2. The Department of West Asian Affairs also had three sections, two handling affairs with the USSR and one those with the rest of West Asia.

3. The Department of European Affairs consisted of four sections: the first three were in charge of relations with Britain, France and Germany respectively; the last had under its charge Italy, the rest of Europe and all the African states as well as Overseas Chinese affairs.

4. The Department of American Affairs was made up of only two sections: the first concerned itself with the USA and the second Central and South American nations. But the latter also handled contributions from Overseas Chinese towards China's war efforts, thus relieving the Department of General Affairs of some of its responsibilities for Overseas Chinese.

Another feature of the reorganization was the creation of a Treaty Department. (Its predecessor, the Treaty Commission, which had rapidly deteriorated into a haven for time-servers, was disbanded in the retrenchment of 1937.) The need for a fully fledged Treaty Department was now greatly felt, as the changed conditions brought by the war called for an overhaul of

China's treaty relations. Anticipation of post-war requirements also played a part in its creation. It had two sections: the first dealt with international organizations, agreements and conventions; the second with new treaties, treaty revision and interpretation. Attached to this Department was a Research Office for the study of international law, economics and commerce.

The new departments rendered the Department of International Affairs redundant – it was duly abolished. Some of its remaining functions, e.g. consular affairs, international expositions, aliens in China, passports and some matters relating to Overseas Chinese, were taken over by the Department of General Affairs, now somewhat expanded. The war and the severely reduced area under Nationalist control also made it necessary to suspend many of its functions.

Other changes introduced in 1939 included a slight expansion of the Secretariat and the appointment of so-called specialists, an unfixed number to the Council and one or two to each of the departments. Few, if any, were real specialists, but their appointment as supernumeraries helped to solve some of the personnel problems in a much contracted Ministry. The practice was, however, open to abuse.

The reorganization did not remedy all the organizational ills of the Ministry, but it was a potentially more efficient system. The staff also gradually built up again after 1939. By the early 1940s there were 236 persons in the Ministry, but the intensification of China's own civil war after 1945 prevented a return to its former size before the Nationalists retreated to Taiwan.

Diplomatic missions When the Nationalists assumed power in mid-1928 they also inherited the twenty-three permanent diplomatic missions set up by the Peking Government. Of these only the one at Moscow was at ambassadorial level, but poor relations between China and the Soviet Union precluded the exchange of ambassadors until early 1933. Up to then the 'embassy' at Moscow was left in the hands of a chargé d'affaires and a small staff of two to three persons. The size of the staff remained practically unchanged even after 1933.

As it was the policy of the Nationalist Government eventually to abolish the unequal treaties, it considered the setting up of new diplomatic relations on the basis of equality and reciprocity a desirable step in this direction. It was partly on this account that China signed the treaties of amity and commerce with Poland (1929) and Czechoslovakia (1930). Legations were then opened in Warsaw and Prague in 1932. By 1942 another eleven nations had entered into diplomatic relations with China at the ministerial level. Among these were Turkey (1935), Egypt, Canada, Australia, Colombia, Venezuela, several Central American states (all in 1941), the Vatican and Iran (1942). In addition, China had a commercial commissioner in Thailand and a commissioner in India (1942).

There is no doubt that this diplomatic 'offensive' was hastened by the increasingly tense international situation in the post-Depression years. After the Japanese set up the Manchukuo puppet state there was an even more urgent need to seek broader international support and to isolate Japan. Such a move was also intended to improve the Nationalists' image at home and abroad, to bolster their struggle against the Japanese and to strive towards equality in the international community. To this end, the Nationalist Government also chose to elevate its diplomatic relations with the major powers to ambassadorial level. The up-grading of the legations in London, Paris, Washington, Tokyo, Rome and Berlin took place between 1934 and 1936. Later, ambassadors were also exchanged with Belgium.

As regards staffing policy, the Ministry under the Nationalist Government generally followed the guidelines set by its predecessor in 1916, but there were some increases, especially for the embassies and a couple of the larger legations. Thus the diplomatic missions at Washington and London had a staff of ten to fourteen. The one at Moscow increased its staff from eleven to seventeen in 1936, although it was deliberately kept small before 1935. In 1935 military attachés were for the first time sent to all the embassies, except London (which had a naval attaché) and Japan (which had both). A commercial counsellor was also appointed to the Japanese embassy in 1936.

From July 1937, when the Japanese openly attacked north China, to the end of the Second World War, a number of China's diplomatic missions were seriously affected. First, the embassy in Tokyo was closed in June 1938 although war was not declared until December 1941. Then in July 1941, after the recognition of Manchukuo by Germany and Italy, China severed diplomatic relations with them. The majority of the embassies and legations in countries that had fallen to the Axis Powers were suspended while a few were moved, mostly to London.

After the war old diplomatic ties were restored, new ones established, and a number of legations were up-graded to embassies. By June 1946 the Nationalist Government had seventeen embassies and ten legations. In addition, it was represented in Allied occupied Germany and Japan by a military delegation. By 1948 the number of embassies was increased to twenty-four, whereas that of legations jumped to nineteen.

In the League of Nations China was represented by a delegation of three plenipotentiaries chosen from the senior and most experienced ambassadors (ministers before 1935) and always including the ambassador to the United States or Great Britain, or both. In 1933 a permanent office was set up in Geneva. Its tasks were carried out by the staff of the Chinese legation there, with the minister to Switzerland also serving as secretary-general of the delegation. This remained so until the League practically ceased to function after the outbreak of war.

After the war China took an active part in the founding of the United Nations. As one of the Five Powers China had a permanent seat in the Security Council and a permanent delegation was appointed, headed first by the experienced Kuo T'ai-ch'i and then by the famous diplomatic historian T. F. Tsiang (Chiang T'ing-fu).

Consular establishments During the two decades of Nationalist Government the consular service experienced a number of changes. First, there was a marked increase in the number of consular establishments. Between 1925 and 1935 the number of consulates-general grew from twenty-three to twenty-eight, that of consulates from twenty-eight to thirty-five, and that of vice-consulates from one to ten. While a large number of these were affected by the war, the post-war recovery was remarkable. By 1947 there were thirty-two consulates-general, forty-eight consulates and five vice-consulates.

Again, the protection and the promotion of Overseas Chinese interests were the key factor behind this growth, but international trade, not just trade handled by Overseas Chinese, was also beginning to be important, as shown in the establishment of the consulate at Portland (Oregon), the removal of the vice-consulate at Galveston to Houston (Texas) in 1933, and the request by the consul-general at Manila for the appointment of an expert on international trade to his staff.

A second change involved tighter control over the consular service by the Ministry. Until 1933 the five consular establishments in the USSR across the border from Sinkiang had been financed and its staff appointed by that province; after some lengthy negotiations the province finally agreed to surrender its control over them. To improve supervision and coordination among consulates, the director of the Department of International Affairs was sent in 1933 on an inspection tour to South-East Asia. On his recommendation the consulates in Malaya were placed under the supervision of the consulate-general in Singapore. Similar arrangements for the consular service in the Dutch East Indies and in Korea soon followed (1934 and 1935 respectively). In 1936 two inspectors were despatched to South-East Asia and to Europe. Because of the war, no inspectors were sent after that.

The 1930 regulations stated that in addition to the clerical staff, the staff of a consulate-general should consist of a consul-general, one or two vice-consuls and an assistant or two; the consulates should have a consul and one or two assistants; the vice-consulates should consist of a vice-consul and one or two assistants. This meant a possible increase of one or two persons over the quota set in 1916 by the Peking Government. During the Nationalist period Vladivostock remained the largest consulate-general, with six members. Most consulates-general had a staff of four or five and consulates a staff of two to four, whereas a vice-consulate might have had nobody other than the vice-consul himself.

The Ministry in action Two major factors contributed to the development of the Ministry of Foreign Affairs under the Nationalists. First, its predecessor in Peking, despite its many defects, was more modern in outlook than any other government organ. Under the Nationalists the Ministry continued this tradition. Second, during their years in Canton the Nationalists had had a small but active Ministry of Foreign Affairs, and when they moved to Nanking they could with relative ease expand the Ministry into a fully fledged organ by availing themselves of talent from Peking. Nanking's first Minister of Foreign Affairs, Wang Cheng-t'ing (C. T. Wang, 1882–1961), was a case in point. Having served the Peking Government as Minister of Foreign Affairs three times, dealt with Russia and Japan and represented China in international conferences, Wang could be regarded as a foreign affairs man. Yet he was deeply sympathetic to Sun Yat-sen's cause: in 1918 he was in the United States seeking diplomatic recognition and financial aid for the Canton government, and in 1919 he was among Canton's representatives to the Chinese delegation at the Paris Peace Conference. Similarly, the Ministry's first political vice-minister, Chu Chao-hsin, had served as minister to Rome and twice as officiating minister at the Court of St James (London) before 1928. Examples of this type abounded and can be found even among those who joined the Ministry much later.

In addition to job experience, the Ministry's staff were also highly educated. In 1929, for instance, among its staff of 267, 25.6 per cent had studied abroad and an additional 65.3 per cent had had a university education at home. This compares extremely favourably with the averages for the entire civil administration in the central Government, which in the same year had only 16.47 per cent of its employees with a foreign degree and 36.64 per cent with a home degree.

On the other hand, despite the Ministry's preference for university graduates who had studied political science, law, economics and history, none of the aspiring career foreign servicemen or diplomats had any training in international studies, which were not taught by the universities. Even the preparation course for candidates of the Higher Civil Service Examination had only twenty hours' worth on international studies. To remedy the situation the Ministry urged the universities to modify their curricula and the civil service examinations their syllabuses. Within the Ministry, study sessions were organized and the staff were encouraged to take advantage of overseas postings to broaden their horizons. Aspiring diplomats were also sent to embassies, legations and consulates as student attachés. In 1929 there were five such attachés; by 1932 the number had gone up to nineteen and remained at about that level until 1937.

The Ministry had many of the attributes needed to develop it into a modern and efficient branch of the government, yet in the end it fell victim to forces that were largely beyond its control. Greater political stability allowed the ministers to enjoy longer terms of office than under the Peking Government – over twenty years there were only thirteen ministers and eleven political vice-ministers, but the post of administrative vice-minister still changed hands far too frequently for the Ministry's good. The old vice of firing existing staff to make room for one's own followers affected the Ministry and its overseas services as much as other branches of the Government. The preference given to Kuomintang party members, provided for by statutes, was also open to abuse. The debilitating effects of these practices must have been greatly amplified when the Ministry underwent drastic staff retrenchments in 1937.

The persistence of bureaucratism, too, plagued the Ministry's various services. Once secure in their jobs the employees of the Ministry made little effort to improve their proficiency. In the various diplomatic missions and consulates the student attachés were often treated as lowly paid clerical staff. At the same time, their superiors were often indolent. Most consulates failed to promote China's foreign trade, while some did not exert themselves in protecting Overseas Chinese interests even in the height of anti-Chinese activities in the early and mid-1930s.

China's civil servants were not well paid, and for those posted abroad it was hard to function socially, especially in the more developed countries, even with allowances twice the size of their basic salary. China's own weakness and poverty further hampered the effectiveness of the Ministry at home and abroad. Partly because of funding problems and partly because of its lack of vision, the Ministry's intelligence and propaganda services remained superficial. Yet the Ministry's budget, amounting to a mere 1.11 per cent of the National Government budget, often came under question.

China's top diplomats were often accused of being ignorant and naïve. In

1935 a critic claimed that only Yen Hui-ch'ing, Wellington Koo and Kuo T'ai-ch'i were diplomats of high calibre. Though exaggerated, there is an element of truth in this criticism, reflected by the repeated plea that China should step up its training of staff in the foreign and diplomatic services. The appointment of such internationally known scholars as Chiang T'ing-fu to the Soviet Union in 1936 and Hu Shih to the United States in 1938 was probably a response to these calls, but there was no long-term policy in this direction.

Finally, the Ministry did not enjoy a healthy degree of independence, and it had to contend with rival agencies in the government. Its responsibility for Overseas Chinese, for example, had to be shared with the Overseas Chinese Affairs Commission and certain organs within the Kuomintang. Its budget, accounting and personnel offices were all subject to supervision by agencies either above the Executive Yuan (e.g. the Budgetary Office) or in other ministries (e.g. the Ministry of Personnel in the Examination Yuan).

As for policy decisions, real power rested with the Central Supervisory and the Central Executive Committees of the Kuomintang, both dominated by Chiang Kai-shek after 1935. From 1939 these were superseded by the Supreme National Defence Council, chaired by Chiang himself. Wartime contingencies also called for diplomatic dealings at the highest levels. Chiang, for example, went to India in 1942 in an unsuccessful attempt to win Gandhi's support for his war efforts, and attended the Cairo Conference in 1943. At other times he would send his own personal emissary, as was the case with T. V. Soong, who in 1940–1 negotiated two US$50-million loans with the United States.

During the Republican era the Chinese scored significant gains in their relations with the powers: the retrocession of a number of foreign concessions, the recovery of tariff autonomy, and most important of all, the abolition of extraterritoriality – the cornerstone of the unequal treaties. But credit must go first to the rising tide of Chinese nationalism, the initial success of the Nationalists to harness such popular sentiments, and the modernization of China's legal code. Undoubtedly, Nationalist China enjoyed greater international prestige than its predecessor had done, yet it was the interest of the powers in China's anti-Japanese position that finally turned the tide. Meanwhile, the Ministry of Foreign Affairs struggled to keep abreast of international developments, trying its best to further China's foreign policy as an essential administrative organ. At the same time, like everything else in China in that fateful epoch, it aspired to be modern, battling against the ills of old China as best it could.

The author wishes to thank Dr Tim Wright for his many valuable comments and suggestions.

BIBLIOGRAPHY

Abbreviation: *WCPL* – *Wai-chiao p'ing-lun* (The Foreign Affairs Review), Vols 1–8 (1932–7).

Biographical Dictionary of Republican China, Howard L. Boorman and Richard C. Howard (eds), 5 vols (New York 1967–79).

Chang Ch'ün and Ch'en Hsiang-mei, *Chang Yüeh-kung hsien-hua wang-shih* (Chang Ch'ün chatting about his past) (Taipei 1978).

Chang Tao-hsing, 'Wai-chiao hsing-cheng chi-k'ou ti t'iao-cheng lun' (On reforming the administrative organs for China's foreign affairs), *Wai-chiao yen-chiu* (Foreign Affairs), I, 3/4 (July 1939), 29–31.

Ch'en Chih-mai, 'Kai-shan wai-chiao hsing-cheng ti i-chien' (Proposals on improving the administration of China's foreign affairs), *Wai-chiao yen-chiu*, I, 3/4 (July 1939), 21–6.

Ch'en T'i-ch'iang, *Chung-kuo wai-chiao hsing-cheng* (China's administration of foreign affairs) (Chungking 1945).

F. T. Cheng, *East and West, episodes in a sixty-years' journey* (London 1951).

Madeleine Chi, *China Diplomacy, 1914–1918* (Cambridge, Mass. 1970).

Ch'ien Tuan-sheng, *The Government and Politics of China* (Cambridge, Mass. 1967).

Chin Wen-ssu (Wunsz King), *Wai-chiao kung-tso ti hui-i* (Recollections of my diplomatic career) (Taipei 1968).

Ch'iu Tsu-ming, 'Chung-kuo wai-chiao chi-kuan chih yen-ke' (A history of institutions for handling foreign relations in China), *WCPL*, IV, 5 (May 1935), 73–90.

Chou Huan, 'Ju-ho chih-hsin wai-chiao chen-yung' (How to strengthen China's foreign and diplomatic services), *WCPL*, IV, 4 (May 1935), 20–4.

——, 'Wai-chiao hsing-cheng shang chih tung-t'ai' (Recent developments concerning the administration of foreign affairs), *WCPL*, VII, 3 (October 1936), 1–9.

Chung-kuo wai-chiao chi-kuan li-jen shou-chang han-ming nien-piao (A chronological table of the titles and names of the successive heads of the Chinese foreign office), Ministry of Foreign Affairs, comp. (Taipei 1967).

Wesley R. Fishel, *The End of Extraterritoriality in China* (Berkeley 1952).

Edmund Fung, 'China's Foreign Policy, 1912–49', in Colin Mackerras (ed.), *China: The Impact of Revolution* (Hawthorn, Victoria 1976), 185–207.

Franklin W. Houn, *Central Government of China, 1912–1928: an Institutional Study* (Madison 1957).

Hsing Chien, 'Chung-kuo yü ko-kuo shih-chieh sheng-ke' (The elevation of diplomatic status between China and several foreign states), *WCPL*, IV, 5 (May 1935), 151–6.

Hsü Ching-wei, 'Wai-chiao jen-ts'ai chih hsün-lien yü p'ei-yang' (Training and fostering foreign service personnel), *WCPL*, II, 11 (November 1933), 19–24.

Immanuel C. Y. Hsü, *The Rise of Modern China*, 2nd edn (New York 1975).

Hsü Kung-hsiao, 'Wai-chiao chen-yung yu cheng-ch'ih chih pi-yao' (The necessity to strengthen China's diplomatic front), *WCPL*, VI, 3 (April 1936), 18–22.

Ku Ping-lin, 'Chung-O fu-chiao chih mien-mien kuan' (Views on the restoration of Sino-Russian relations), *Shen-pao yüeh-k'an*, II, 1 (15 January 1933), 5–10.

Ku Wei-chün, *V. K. Wellington Koo and China's wartime diplomacy* (New York 1977).

Werner Levi, *Modern China's Foreign Policy* (Minneapolis 1953).

Li Ting-i, *et al.* (eds), *Pu-p'ing-teng t'iao-yüeh yü p'ing-teng hsin yüeh* (The 'Unequal Treaties' and the new 'Equal Treaties'), in the series entitled *Chung-kuo chin-tai-shih lun-ts'ung* (A collection of articles on Modern Chinese history), second series, Vol. 1 (Taipei 1958).

Liu Ch'iu-nan, *Chung-kuo chin-tai wai-chiao shih* (Diplomatic history of modern China), (Taichung 1972).

Lo Hsiang-lin, *Fu Ping-ch'ang yü chin-tai Chung-kuo* (Fu Ping-ch'ang and Modern China), (Hong Kong 1973).

Min-kuo jen-wu chuan (Biographies of Republican China), Li Hsin and Sun Ssu-pai (eds), Vol. 1 (Peking 1978).

Robert T. Pollard, *China's Foreign Relations, 1917–1931* (New York 1933).

Sun Huai-jen, 'Chung-O fu-chiao yü tung-pei wen-t'i' (The problem of the North-East in the restoration of Sino-Russian relations), *Shen-pao yüeh-k'an*, II, 2 (15 February 1933), 27–33.

William L. Tung, *China and Some Phases of International Law* (London and New York 1940).

——, *China and the Foreign Powers* (New York 1970).

Min-ch'ien T. Z. Tyau (Tiao Min-ch'ien), *Two Years of Nationalist China* (Shanghai 1930).

Wang Cheng-ming *et al.*, *Chung-kuo wai-chiao shih lun-chi* (An anthology on the history of China's foreign relations), 2 vols (Taipei 1957).

Wang Ching-wei, *China's problems and their solution* (Shanghai 1934).

Wu Paak-shing, 'China's diplomatic relations with Mexico', *The China Quarterly* (Chungking), IV, 3 (Summer 1939), 439–59.

——, 'China's diplomatic relations with Panama', *The China Quarterly* (Chungking), V, 1 (Winter 1939), 129–40.

——, 'China and Peru: a study in diplomatic history', *The China Quarterly* (Chungking), V, 2 (Spring 1940), 275–93.

——, 'China's diplomatic relations with Brazil', *The China Quarterly* (Chungking), V, 4 (Supplementary, Winter 1940), 857–68.

Yang Kung-ta, 'Kai-ke wai-chiao hsing-cheng wen-t'i' (Issues in reforming China's administration of foreign affairs), *Wai-chiao yen-chiu* (Foreign Affairs), I, 3–4 (July 1939), 27–8.

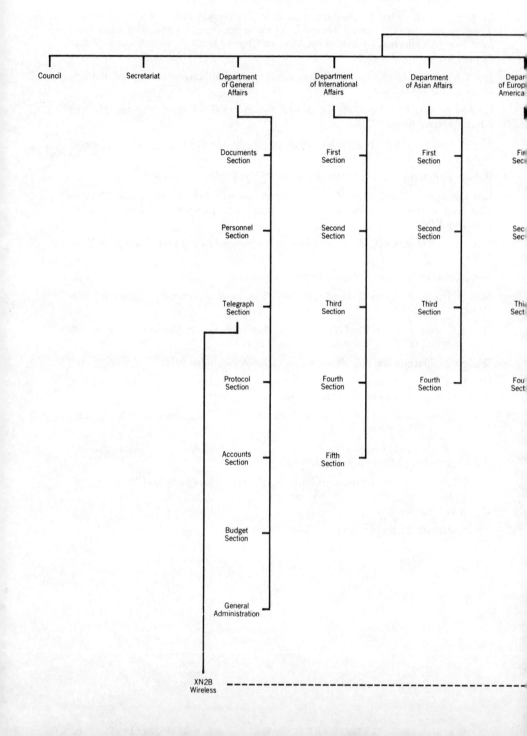

Council   Secretariat   Department   Department   Department   Depar
                            of General   of International   of Asian Affairs   of Europ
                            Affairs   Affairs   America

                            Documents   First   First   Fir
                            Section   Section   Section   Sec

                            Personnel   Second   Second   Sec
                            Section   Section   Section   Sec

                            Telegraph   Third   Third   Thi
                            Section   Section   Section   Sect

                            Protocol   Fourth   Fourth   Fou
                            Section   Section   Section   Sect

                            Accounts   Fifth
                            Section   Section

                            Budget
                            Section

                            General
                            Administration

                XN2B
                Wireless

APPENDIX

REPUBLICAN CHINA

HE ORGANIZATION OF THE MINISTRY OF FOREIGN AFFAIRS IN 1931

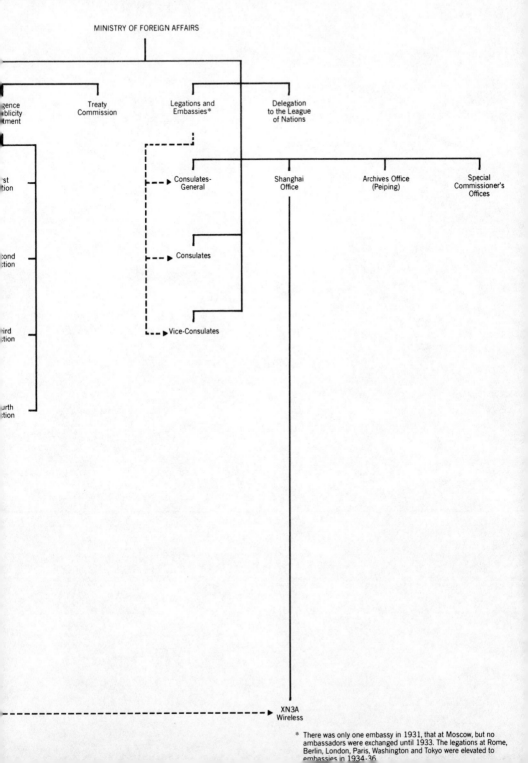

MINISTRY OF FOREIGN AFFAIRS

gence
blicity
tment

Treaty
Commission

Legations and
Embassies*

Delegation
to the League
of Nations

st
tion

cond
ction

ird
ction

urth
ction

Consulates-
General

Shanghai
Office

Archives Office
(Peiping)

Special
Commissioner's
Offices

Consulates

Vice-Consulates

XN3A
Wireless

* There was only one embassy in 1931, that at Moscow, but no
ambassadors were exchanged until 1933. The legations at Rome,
Berlin, London, Paris, Washington and Tokyo were elevated to
embassies in 1934-36

China

The Ministry of Foreign Affairs of the People's Republic of China

M. B. YAHUDA

Michael Yahuda is Senior Lecturer in the Department of International Relations at the London School of Economics and Political Science. He is the author of *China's Role in World Affairs* (1978) and he has published many articles in books and scholarly journals. He also broadcasts frequently for the BBC External Service.

The Chinese Ministry of Foreign Affairs can be regarded as very much the creation of the late Premier Zhou Enlai. In addition to his heavy domestic responsibilities as Premier he held the post of Foreign Minister for the first nine years following the establishment of the state, and he retained overall control over the execution of foreign policy until his death in January 1976. Beginning virtually from scratch in 1949, Zhou built up an administrative apparatus endowed with an *esprit de corps* that was able to weather the enormous storms of the Cultural Revolution (especially in 1967), and that barely a few years later proved itself capable of meeting the challenge of a sudden and unprecedented expansion of its activities in the early 1970s.

The major issues of foreign policy in the People's Republic have always been taken by the most senior political leaders. Indeed, given the high degree of political centralization in China, it often seems as if minor decisions, too, are taken at the highest levels. It is best, therefore, to consider the Foreign Ministry as primarily the executor of decisions taken elsewhere. It is by no means certain that the Foreign Ministry even supplies the briefings on which the leaders decide upon policy. China's leaders seem to rely upon a comprehensive translation service of a wide selection of the world's newspapers. A daily issue is produced. It is not known to what extent this is supplemented by information from intelligence, diplomatic or other services.

Unfortunately, little is known about the processes of decision-making in China especially in the field of foreign affairs, which has tended to be insulated from domestic politics except for a brief period during the Cultural Revolution. Thus it is not possible to throw much light on the institutional links between the Foreign Ministry and other ministries and organizations concerned with foreign relations. Likewise, it is difficult to ascertain its relationship with the Communist Party and with the departments of the Party's Central Committee that deal with foreign relations. Nevertheless, observation of the conduct of the Ministry over a period of more than thirty years combined with analysis of its senior personnel, organizational changes, the training of diplomats, etc., have ensured that accounts of the structure and performance of the Ministry need not be unduly speculative. Moreover, it is also possible to exaggerate the limits of what is knowable. Particularly since China's entry to the United Nations and the unprecedented expansion of its diplomatic activities (both quantitatively and qualitatively) in the 1970s, it has been possible to acquire first-hand knowledge from many sources of Chinese diplomacy in practice. However, it must be recognized at the outset that it is simply not possible to give as full an account of the organization and performance of the Chinese Foreign Ministry as is possible of, say, the British Foreign Office, let alone the American State Department.

The development of the Ministry
In establishing the Ministry of Foreign Affairs in 1949–50, Premier Zhou Enlai relied essentially on the clutch of young men in their late twenties and early thirties who had served on his staff during his various negotiations in the 1940s, or had been journalists commenting on international affairs for Communist papers. These formed the nucleus of the senior personnel of the nascent Foreign Ministry in Beijing. Having been based for so long in China's hinterland, the newly victorious Communists were short of people with significant international experience. China's relative diplomatic isolation

in the early 1950s meant that its rather limited qualified diplomatic corps was not over-stretched. Indeed, it was possible to discern a pattern in the 1950s by which China's diplomats were deployed for maximum effectiveness. The countries of the Soviet bloc (with whom China was closely allied in this period) were used as a kind of testing ground for putative diplomats whose experience hitherto had been largely military or confined to domestic affairs. The more experienced personnel were used either for the few Western countries or the Afro-Asian countries in which China had diplomatic missions. It should be noted that the more important aspects of relations with Soviet bloc countries were conducted through Communist Party channels. Negotiations or conferences of any significance were conducted by senior Party leaders. Moreover, any inexperienced behaviour by a Chinese diplomat on Socialist 'friendly' territory would obviously matter less than in the West or in Afro-Asia, where Chinese diplomats were expected to be on their mettle. This meant that by the late 1950s and early 1960s, when relations with the Soviet bloc were souring and relations with Afro-Asia were expanding, China already possessed a sizeable body of diplomats of counsellor level and above who had served in various countries and who could be relied upon to represent the country well and with appropriate dignity.

The structure of the Foreign Ministry and the establishment of related organizations can also be seen as related to the paucity of personnel who were both politically reliable and experienced in international affairs. In this context it is as well to recognize that the Chinese Communist leadership in 1949 considered itself isolated and inexperienced in the face of a hostile, Western-dominated world. The inexperience applied also with regard to the urgent domestic tasks of building the structures of state administration and in carrying out economic construction. For all these questions the Chinese leadership turned to the Soviet Union for succour and as an example to emulate. The influence of the Soviet model can also be seen in the structuring of what might be called China's early foreign affairs system. Thus a foreign language, publications and distribution bureau was set up under the dual control of the Ministry of Culture and the Communist Party's Central Committee Propaganda Department. Likewise, a commission was established for cultural relations with foreign countries and the Chinese People's Association for Friendship with Foreign Countries. Both of these were patterned on what are sometimes called Soviet popular front organizations. But these soon acquired a special significance for China because of its diplomatic isolation. They became the instruments for what has been called 'people's diplomacy'. This was the diplomacy that China conducted with many countries with whom no formal governmental relations existed, or with non-governmental personnel in countries with which diplomatic relations had been established. There was frequent exchange of personnel between these organizations and the Foreign Ministry. The New China News Agency (like its Soviet equivalent) has long had close informal links with the Foreign Ministry. Its journalists have often carried out quasi-diplomatic functions of the more clandestine variety.

As to the Foreign Ministry itself, the principles of its organizational subdivisions have been followed ever since they were established by Zhou Enlai in 1949. These were the establishment of geographic and functionalist departments. Both have expanded considerably since the early days of

1949–50. Alongside them, on the Soviet model, there was also a political department run by the Communist Party. This, however, ceased functioning in January 1974. One feature of the Ministry as established by Zhou that has survived is the institution of vice-minister. There have usually been at least eight of these; at present there are ten, with three assistant ministers. These may be regarded as the cream of China's professional foreign service personnel, most of whom have served as ambassadors in countries of key importance to China and who have been entrusted with delicate negotiations.

As in the past, the usual initial training for putative diplomats in China is learning a foreign language. Thus from the outset a close institutional link was established between the Ministry of Foreign Affairs and the two foreign language institutes in Beijing. The best graduates of these institutes are normally recruited into the Ministry and into other foreign related organizations, including trade and tourism. In a country as closed from the outside world as China, it is considered important to expose aspiring diplomats to experience in embassies abroad. Since the 1970s an interesting feature of the training of the most promising of the foreign language students is that they are sent for at least two years to complete their studies in those countries where their particular language is spoken.

Another feature of the foreign affairs establishment set up by Zhou Enlai that has endured and greatly expanded is the research and training institutes. The Chinese People's Institute of Foreign Affairs was established in 1949, partly to conduct research and partly to act as host to foreign visitors. Other institutes established in due course include those of diplomacy and of international problems (both of which are directly under the Foreign Ministry and serve as training as well as research centres), and those of international relations, world politics, world economy (before the Cultural Revolution they were under the Academy of Sciences, suspended for the period 1966–76 and finally reestablished under the Academy of Social Sciences inaugurated in 1977).

It should be noted that two major areas of significance to China's foreign relations do not organizationally even come under the aegis of the Ministry of Foreign Affairs. These are inter-Communist Party relations, which are controlled by the International Liaison Department of the Central Committee, and relations with Overseas Chinese, which are organized in the first instance by a special Commission of the State Council but are in fact directed by the Central Committee's United Front Department. Both of these, interestingly, are concerned with areas of activity in which domestic and foreign affairs overlap considerably. The former necessarily involves intimate ideological questions, and the latter is concerned not only with Overseas Chinese who are foreign citizens but also with Chinese citizens residing abroad and the relatives of both sets who reside in China. Their treatment includes providing them with special educational, occupational and residential facilities. This is also related generally to China's treatment of its intelligentsia and former bourgeoisie. It also extends to relations between the Han Chinese and China's national minorities, many of whom are also to be found in neighbouring countries.

Very little is known about the institutional relationship between the Foreign and Defence Ministries. Obviously these can be coordinated at the level of the State Council or, perhaps more pertinently, at the Party's Political

Bureau. But it is not known how their activities are coordinated operationally. It is known, however, that the various military attachés of China's embassies come directly under the institutional authority of the Ministry of Defence.

The Foreign Ministry and the Cultural Revolution

Having gradually built up a proficient administration and a corps of trained personnel with a coherent career structure that had proved itself sufficiently flexible to adapt to the changed circumstances of China's foreign relations following the break with the Soviet Union, China's Foreign Ministry was brought almost to a standstill by the Cultural Revolution. This was a case of China's domestic politics spilling over into its foreign relations rather than a genuine dispute over foreign policy itself. In essence the issue concerned the politics of the Foreign Minister, the late Marshal Chen Yi. A brave and outspoken critic of the Red Guards, he had (like several other senior leaders) squashed in his Ministry the early manifestations of Red Guard activities during the early part of summer 1966. By late 1966, with the Red Guards and the ultra-left in full cry, he became a target of their criticisms. He also figured as a target for some of those involved in the power struggles behind the scenes at the highest levels in Beijing. Things came to a head in the spring and summer of 1967. In an atmosphere reminiscent of the Boxer Uprising at the turn of the century, Chinese radicalism veered towards an ugly Sino-centricism and xenophobia. Amid the hysteria of the adulation of Mao, revolutionary zeal and disdain for all things foreign, all but one of more than forty ambassadors were recalled to Beijing, relations with thirty-two countries were disturbed by incidents arising out of the Cultural Revolution, and Chen Yi was so affected by Red Guard persecution that Mao himself intervened to save him by complaining that the Marshal was too ill to be shown to foreign visitors. Indeed, at one point in the summer of 1967 the Foreign Ministry itself was taken over by the ultra-left. That takeover culminated in the burning of the British mission. Fortunately for the Ministry, the ultra-left had overplayed its hand at this point by seeking to extend its activities into the military high commands. The axe then fell swiftly upon it and the Ministry of Foreign Affairs was restored to its normal stewardship.

It is interesting, however, to recall the charges that were laid against the Foreign Ministry and its personnel. The Ministry was accused of not supporting foreign revolutionaries, in particular among the Overseas Chinese. Furthermore, it had not promoted Mao's thought to the mass of the people of the world, who were said to be avidly seeking guidance from it. The diplomats themselves were accused of having succumbed to the decadent attractions of the foreign bourgeois style of life. These charges appear grotesque, particularly in retrospect, and it can be argued that the entire episode was of only passing significance, since from 1969 onwards China had no difficulty in reaching out once more to the rest of the world. Nevertheless, the episode is representative (perhaps in a rather lurid way) of a particular aspect of the Chinese response to the outside world. These self-righteous Sino-centric cultural xenophobes who at the same time feel that their message is of universal significance can be said to have their antecedents in the reactionary anti-foreign Confucian scholars and officials of the nineteenth century and in the superstitious peasant Boxers of the turn of this century. At a deeper level they may be said to reflect in an exaggerated form the ambivalence of the attitude of modern Chinese to the outside world in general and to the West in particular. China is highly nationalistic and the Chinese world (even in 1980) is still very much cut off from the world outside. The story of China's external relationships over the last hundred years or more can thus be seen almost as alternate patterns of exaggerated xenophilia and xenophobia. Even in the thirty-year period of the People's Republic it is possible to detect the same phenomenon. Not entirely through its own fault, China threw itself into a close friendship with the Soviet Union in the early 1950s in the context of hostile relations with the West. This was followed by a period of isolation and hostility to both East and West, which in turn has been followed by a period of opening out, to the West in particular, in what superficially seems to be a most thorough-going way. To be sure, this is an over-simplified account, but there is sufficient truth in it to indicate something of the ambivalence and tensions that underlie China's dealings with the outside world. In many respects the Ministry of Foreign Affairs is located in the eye of the storms of this complex relationship. Thus its experiences during the Cultural Revolution should not be written off too lightly.

The long-term consequences of the Cultural Revolution, which have proved so damaging to China as a whole, curiously have not proved to be so damaging to the Ministry of Foreign Affairs itself. After the ravages of 1967 both Mao and Zhou took particular care to protect and insulate it from further damage. That is perhaps why the Ministry was able to cope so well with the problem of staffing the numerous embassies and missions at international organizations that were rapidly established in the early 1970s. It will be recalled that in the space of three years, between 1969 and 1972, China reappointed more than forty ambassadors and opened more than fifty new foreign embassies, as well as joining the United Nations and its various agencies. Indirectly, however, the Ministry has had to pay a heavy price. Against a background in which properly trained young talent is spread very thinly in China, the various research and support institutions that had developed in the 1950s but had ceased operations to a considerable extent in the ten-year Cultural Revolution period of 1966–76 have recently been painfully restored. The shortage of researchers with experience and a genuine understanding of the workings of other countries is all too evident to anyone who has visited these newly established institutes. Enquiries about the precise functions of Chinese embassies abroad suggest that all too many of them simply lack sufficiently competent staff to file back to Beijing adequate analysis of the social, economic and political conditions of the countries in which they are located. Against this, China's embassies have the reputation of conducting the business of representing their country efficiently and with dignity while at the same time respecting the independence and dignity of their hosts.

The organization of China's foreign affairs system
From the outset the basic pattern of what might be called the foreign affairs system of the People's Republic of China followed broadly along Soviet lines. Separate institutional systems were set up for the conduct of (Communist) Party to Party, state to state and people to people relations. A separate organizational arrangement of Chinese Communist origin existed

for the management of relations with the Overseas Chinese. This was managed under the aegis of the United Front Work Department of the Party's Central Committee, and its state arm was the Commission for Overseas Chinese Affairs. This aspect of foreign affairs was intimately connected with the domestic question of handling relations with intellectuals and the remnant bourgeoisie in China itself as well as with the extensive family connections in China of the Overseas Chinese. Those related to Overseas Chinese, as already mentioned, received preferential treatment within China and much of the work of the Overseas Chinese Commission was in fact concerned with domestic administration. This peculiarly Chinese link between domestic and external affairs in this regard has developed and expanded considerably since the conclusion of the Cultural Revolution. With the renewal of the drive towards modernization the Overseas Chinese have been regarded as people with an exceptional role to play and special efforts have been made to attract their capital and their expertise in modernization.

Of course, overriding the various separate institutional systems has been the Political Bureau (and its Standing Committee) of the Communist Party. It is here that the major decisions are made, and indeed a persistent complaint of these most senior leaders is that they have to take the minor decisions as well. Too little is known about the pattern of decision-making regarding foreign and strategic questions to provide a clear account of the relationship between the various organs concerned. Nevertheless, it is worth reiterating that it is best to consider the Foreign Ministry as an executor rather than an initiator of foreign policy. Thus China's last three Foreign Ministers (including the present incumbent, Huang Hua) have held a Party ranking no more senior than Central Committee membership. The foreign affairs organizations are represented in the eleventh Political Bureau by two newly elected veteran Party figures who are not known to have played a significant part in China's foreign policy to date: Geng Biao, Director of the International Liaison Office (an organization responsible for relations with foreign Communist parties – in recent years this has meant primarily the tiny splinter Marxist–Leninist parties) and Ulanfu, head of the United Front Work Department (which deals with China's national minorities and with non-Communist Chinese both inside and outside China).

It is thought that aspects of China's foreign policy involving strategy are deliberated in the powerful Military Affairs Commission of the Central Committee, which normally includes the most significant members of the Political Bureau and the military establishment. The Ministry of Defence also has an important foreign affairs department. *Inter alia* this administers the military attachés posted to various embassies.

Little is known about the extent to which the Ministry of Foreign Affairs actually influences major policy decisions. Although it is known that individual ambassadors of political weight and possessed of diplomatic experience were given considerable leeway in the execution of policy in Africa in the early 1960s, by and large it is safe to assume that the Ministry performs more as an expert body in charge of implementing policy decided by China's major leaders. Insofar as China may be said to be still torn between the impulses of isolationism and of expansiveness regarding the outside world the Ministry is the main expression of the latter impulse. However, in the new period of greater opening out to the external world the

Ministry is facing new challenges. Perhaps the most notable of these is widening the functions of its embassies abroad to include information gathering and in-depth reporting of their host countries. The relatively passive role of simple representation of China in foreign countries is no longer sufficient.

BIBLIOGRAPHY

CIA, *The Foreign Affairs Organisations of the People's Republic of China* (Washington, D.C. 1980).

Radiopress, *The China Directory* (Tokyo 1979).

Donald W. Klein, 'Peking's Evolving Ministry of Foreign Affairs', *The China Quarterly* No. 4 (October–December 1960).

Melvin Gurtov, 'The Foreign Ministry & Foreign Affairs During the Cultural Revolution', *The China Quarterly*, No. 40 (October–December 1969).

PEOPLE'S REPUBLIC OF CHINA FOREIGN AFFAIRS SYSTEM

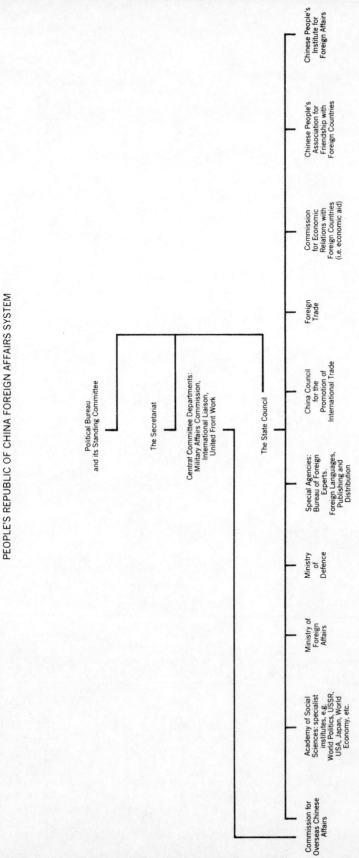

Political Bureau and its Standing Committee

The Secretariat

Central Committee Departments: Military Affairs Commission, International Liaison, United Front Work

The State Council

Commission for Overseas Chinese Affairs

Academy of Social Sciences: specialist institutes, e.g. World Politics, USSR, USA, Japan, World Economy, etc.

Ministry of Foreign Affairs

Ministry of Defence

Special Agencies: Bureau of Foreign Experts, Foreign Languages, Publishing and Distribution

China Council for the Promotion of International Trade

Foreign Trade

Commission for Economic Relations with Foreign Countries (i.e. economic aid)

Chinese People's Association for Friendship with Foreign Countries

Chinese People's Institute for Foreign Affairs

Denmark

The Royal Danish
Ministry of Foreign Affairs

KLAUS KJØLSEN

Klaus Kjølsen is currently head of the Archives Division of the Royal
Danish Ministry of Foreign Affairs and Librarian to Her Majesty the
Queen's Reference Library. He was born in 1927, obtained a degree
in history from the University of Copenhagen and entered the
general service of the Danish foreign service in 1956. He is the author
of a number of books and articles on the history of the Danish
administration of foreign affairs, including *Den danske Udenrigstjeneste
1770–1905*, vol. 1 of *Den danske Udenrigstjeneste 1770–1970* (1970),
The Foreign Service of Denmark 1770–1970 (1970), *Livet på det andet
Christiansborg*, vol. 2 of *Christiansborg Slot* (1975).

An independent kingdom for more than a thousand years, Denmark has nevertheless been highly dependent on other countries in several respects. First, its geographical situation greatly affects national security. Then there are strong economic ties, resulting in particular from a large volume of foreign trade; and thirdly, religious and cultural influences, especially from the south. Consequently, the collective – and unified – foreign service (which the legislators in Copenhagen, in an unusual burst of poetic licence in 1921, called a tree with three branches – the Ministry of Foreign Affairs, the diplomatic and the consular missions) has a place in the history of Danish public administration.

The old Foreign Ministry prior to 1770

The Royal Chancellery, headed by the Chancellor, was the core of the central administration in the Middle Ages. He also supervised the clerks or secretaries who conducted foreign correspondence. In the late Middle Ages this was in German for Germany, Danish for Sweden and Latin for the rest of Europe. The clerks were often employed for negotiations with foreign powers.[1]

Events during the years after the mid-fifteenth century form a starting point for the Danish foreign service. In 1460 the Danish king was elected ruler of the duchy of Schleswig and the county (soon after duchy) of Holstein; and so occurred the amalgamation with the two predominantly German provinces that endured for some 400 years. It was not until 1920 that a definitive border was found between Danish and German. The two duchies were administered in German, the language that underlay the gradual division in the administration. The central administration of the German Chancellery comprised the German provinces and foreign affairs, insofar as they were conducted in foreign languages – that is to say, with countries to the south and west. The Danish administration came under the Danish Chancellery, which in foreign affairs conducted correspondence in Danish, i.e. with Sweden and Russia. The chancelleries were by no means clearly distinguished: a special head of the German Chancellery did not exist until 1523, and the office of German Chancellor remained unoccupied for long periods in both the sixteenth and seventeenth centuries.

Considerable enlargements also took place in respect of diplomacy in about 1450. They were with the Western powers, Poland, Bohemia and the Empire, plus the old connection with the Papacy. Danish noblemen lacked both an interest in and the required knowledge of languages (Latin as well as the increasingly important national languages) to be capable of working abroad. For this reason churchmen of Danish or foreign origin were appointed in the Chancellery and posted as diplomats. Later, the officials of the German Chancellery were often middle-class lawyers, mostly appointed from Germany.

The introduction of absolutism in 1660 was momentous in the history of the Danish central administration. Until 1770 the foreign policy of Denmark–Norway was conducted, for the monarchy as a whole, through the German Chancellery, whose activities were extended in about 1680 to include Swedish and Russian matters.

Apart from the economy, the Chancellery remained in charge of the internal civil administration of the predominantly German lands of

Schleswig, Holstein, Oldenburg and Delmenhorst. In 1676 the Privy Registry (Geheimeregistratur) came into use. This was, for each foreign country, a common copy-book for outgoing communications appertaining to foreign affairs, and was kept without a break until the end of the nineteenth century.

The importance ascribed by the king to the central administration was outwardly expressed by the erection in 1721 of an administrative building where the German Chancellery was also housed. The Chancellery Building, or the Red Building as it is called, is thus contemporary with the corresponding Baroque building, the Ballhausplatz, in Vienna. To this day it remains unchanged externally and is still used by the central administration.

It is not clear what carried most weight in the German Chancellery's sphere of activity: internal German or external affairs. They were not sharply differentiated. This has something to do with the complex constitutional affairs of the German lands; in the case of the German provinces this involved a fluid transition between internal and external matters because although under the Danish Crown, Holstein was also part of the Holy Roman Empire. Some of the so-called national (Reich) matters were handled by the German Chancellery together with internal affairs, and there was permanent multilateral representation by a Danish envoy at the Reichstag in Regensburg. This mixture of internal and external affairs under one administration was nothing exceptional in eighteenth-century Europe. It was known in Great Britain before 1782, and the foreign affairs administration of France administered a few French provinces. Nor does an elected Foreign Minister today make much distinction between domestic and foreign affairs, and may well work on the former in the morning in Parliament and his constituency and on the latter in the afternoon in his ministry or when travelling. EEC matters, too, seem increasingly to become cross-frontier extensions of domestic affairs.

Königl. Teutsche Cantzeley der in- und ausländischen Affairen in Copenhagen, is the full title given the Chancellery in the Hof- und Staats Calender, which has been published annually (first in German and Danish, now only in Danish) since 1734. Yet in the hundred years before 1770 there was no German Chancellor, the administration of the German Chancellery being in the charge of a chief secretary, who normally belonged to the king's inner circle and was a member of the government. The duality of the German Chancellery's functions is indicated by the chief secretary's official title, taken from a Franco-Danish commercial treaty of 1742: Premier Secrétaire d'Etat des affaires étrangères et de la Chancellerie Allemande. One might have expected the insertion of 'du Département' in front of 'des affaires étrangères', but that was not then customary. Administratively, for example in respect of appropriations, the German Chancellery functioned as one unit. What started as a practical division of work in the handling of foreign and domestic affairs gradually acquired a firmer organizational framework. In 1736, soon after the accession of J. von Schulin as chief secretary, there is mention of a foreign department as distinct from a domestic one. The foreign department came under the direction of J. von Klinggraf, with the style, known from French external administration, of 'premier commis des affaires étrangères'. By the close of the period the division into two departments had also been formally effected. The situation at about the mid-eighteenth century, from 1751 under Schulin's successor Johan Hartvig Ernst Bernstorff, the outstanding statesman and head of the German Chancellery, has been described by J. Wasserschlebe, his close associate for many years, as follows:

> 'Depuis le 1751 M. le Bernstorff étoit Ministre et Secrétaire d'Etat des affaires Etrangères et de la Chancellerie Allemande: Les Bureaux des Affaires Etrangères étoient en tout separés de ceux des Affaires de l'interieur du Royaume, ou des Provinces dites Allemandes. Il n'y avoit ni Seances ni déliberations; ceux qui y étoient employés travailloient, en qualité de Commis, sous les Ordres du Secrétaire d'Etat'.[2]

This is an allusion to the collegiate system that was general in the Danish central administration and was also employed in the German Chancellery in German matters, as distinct from that employed in foreign affairs.

The chief secretaries of the German Chancellery were predominantly immigrant Germans. This is true of almost the entire succession from C. Biermann (ennobled as von Ehrenschild) in 1664 to A. P. Bernstorff, who died in 1797; and all of them were the absolutist king's highly trusted, top-level associates. The German element, whether immigrant Germans or natives of the German provinces, also dominated the ranks of civil servants. There are examples of men from outside having to bind themselves on their appointment to remain permanently in the king's service. Nearly all of them came from the middle class. It is not surprising that, alongside diplomatic French, German was the administrative language of the German Chancellery for both domestic and foreign affairs.

From the German Chancellery there was a link both to the local administration in the king's German lands and to the diplomatic missions abroad. The Dano-Norwegian monarchy was one of the states that in this period spread a network of permanent missions throughout Europe. The problem of when permanent diplomatic missions were established in Europe with regard both to chronology[3] and to the exact definition of 'permanent mission'[4] is still being debated. In the case of Denmark-Norway, the greatest expert on early Danish diplomacy, the late Emil Marquard, puts the establishment of permanent missions in the decades around 1700 (1680–1730), and he bases his assessment on long-standing and comprehensive studies.[5] By permanent missions he understood that posting was for a lengthy period, that the envoy was not withdrawn until a successor had been appointed, and that his mandate was general and not restricted to a particular assignment. When establishing permanent missions, special attention was directed to an order of 1680, which said that envoys should employ royally appointed civil servants as secretaries of legation as distinct from privately appointed secretaries. This was put into practice by royal letters of appointment being issued for six secretaries of legation, all destined for foreign service, with the style chargé d'affaires when deputizing for the envoy in his absence.[6] The essence was the royal appointment, whereby the secretary was committed to the king through obedience, loyalty and secrecy by oath. It was clearly found insufficient at the time to maintain a succession of envoys without deputies. In 1716, the then chief secretary strongly advocated the importance of continuity in the foreign service by means of secretaries who would carry on in the envoy's absence. Although isolated permanent missions are known from before the mid-seventeenth century, including the post in Stockholm

(1621), the evidence favours the dating of permanent missions as an established form of administration in the Danish foreign service between 1680 and 1720.

A Dano-Norwegian consular system comprising up to a score of consuls and consular posts was established in the final decades before 1700, especially in western and southern European ports, including the Mediterranean.[7] It was organized to support the Dano-Norwegian trade and shipping that was carried on under cover of the policy of neutrality during the great European wars from 1688 to the war with Sweden in 1709.

The old Foreign Ministry after 1770

The separate history of foreign service administration begins in 1770.[8] On 24 December the king signed two orders setting up the Department for Foreign Affairs as a fully independent administration separate from the German Chancellery, which continued to administer the monarchy's German territories. The reform was permanent, and although the change was not based directly on foreign models it must be seen in the light of the general trend in Europe during the eighteenth century to establish departments of moderate scope with the special object of conducting foreign affairs. The quite brief order came into being without much preliminary work and sprang from an idea to appoint Adolph Siegfried, Count von der Osten, as Minister of the Department and at the same time to separate foreign affairs of state from the Germany Chancellery. Only four days later a plan lay ready for implementing the orders, which did not involve any difficulties. The reform passed quite unnoticed and failed to evoke the interest of foreign envoys. The reason is simple: as it was only a change of form, foreign affairs being conducted, as already stated, by a special department of the larger Chancellery, the reform did not appear to be of particular interest.

The reason for the change of 1770 must be sought in domestic political developments, as it is clear that the reform was politically and not administratively motivated. In September 1770 J. H. E. Bernstorff had been overthrown by Struensee, who by dominating the mentally deranged king had arrogated to himself absolute power. As a British envoy rightly put it, Struensee was 'a mushroom minister', and his rule was short but dramatic. Bernstorff's position rested, among other things, on the fact that he combined a leading place in the Government with the administration both of foreign policy and of a considerable part of domestic policies, and Struensee wanted to abolish this combination of offices. It was essential, however, to get foreign policy under firm direction. For this reason Osten was appointed to the office, under Struensee's control but with foreign affairs as his sole concern.

The Department for Foreign Affairs was, continuing the tradition, a secretariat for the minister, and unlike the colleges of other administrations, which employed the collegiate method of work, its civil servants were entirely controlled by the minister. They were a firmly welded professional hierarchy with fixed standards of titles, promotion and remuneration, this last at a fairly high level, partly because there were no perquisites. To a Foreign Ministry official of today, working with 750 colleagues in buildings at Asiatisk Plads, it is a striking thought that the Department consisted of nine men all told in 1770. They were the Minister, three secretaries, one archivist, two minor officials and two messengers, all concentrated in a handful of rooms in the Chancellery building at Slotsholmen, where the conversation, probably chiefly in German, was accompanied by the scratching of quill pens on paper and in winter the crackling of logs in the stove. All the officials were middle class and their careers had until then been in the domestic administration. None had served for any length of time at a mission abroad, though several had some experience of foreign countries from other work. The German element still predominated, two of the three secretaries being immigrant Germans and the third a Holsteiner.

The conditions of the foreign service changed in the course of the nineteenth century. Domestically, this was due to the fall of the autocracy in 1848 and the introduction of a liberal constitution and a parliament. Externally, the monarchy was curtailed by the cession first of Norway to Sweden in 1814, and then of Schleswig and Holstein in 1864 and their incorporation shortly afterwards into Prussia. Relations with Germany became the great issue, primarily because of the antipathy between the national movements in Germany and Denmark, whereas a non-aligned policy of neutrality was pursued with regard to the Great Powers. Before 1848 the administration of foreign policy rested with the king and the heads of the central administration, and after 1848 with a small group of successive politicians (often former civil servants) and senior civil servants. The influence of parliament on foreign affairs was very limited until shortly before the turn of the century.

The Department, renamed from 1848 the Foreign Ministry (Udenrigs-ministeriet), continued on the whole to be a static administrative apparatus. This becomes especially apparent when it is compared with the development that has taken place in the twentieth century. The total number of personnel, from minister to messenger, expanded from nine to twenty-one by about 1900, though the growth was accounted for by an increase in junior staff, the number of senior officials, four, remaining unchanged. Within this framework, innovations of lasting importance occurred. The most important of these were the establishment of the office of director (which still exists) and the extension of the field of operations to include foreign economic matters.

In the Danish as in other foreign services, the central administration at that time occupied a different place in the overall foreign service administration from the one it does today. In the first hundred years after 1770, the centre of gravity lay as before with the envoys, whereas more recently the balance has shifted to the Ministry. The domestic and diplomatic services offered separate careers, and civil servants were seldom transferred from one to the other. Formerly, the Minister chiefly obtained guidance from envoys' reports, whereas now the basis of study is reports, other papers and their analysis in the Ministry, the latter being now of relatively greater importance. The Department's personnel resources in the past excluded such analyses, which were only occasionally carried out by the director. In foreign negotiations the Minister's principal assistants were the envoys, whereas important business would be unthinkable nowadays without preparation and active participation by civil servants from the Ministry.

The first enlargement of the Department happened before the application of technological inventions in the field of communications began to have practical effect (for example, the telegraph in the 1850s). The starting point was the establishment of the post of director in 1800. This occurred in a rather special way, caused by the death of the experienced Foreign Minister A. P. Bernstorff a few years before and his replacement by his sons Christian and Joachim, the former as Minister, the latter as director. They both retired in 1810, and a few years later Christian Bernstorff entered the German service as Prussian Minister for Foreign Affairs. The office of the director was reestablished in 1831, originally under another name, with the Holsteiner Frederik Dankwart as director until 1848. After a lapse of ten years it was reintroduced gradually from 1858, formally in 1864, and was retained, with Peter Vedel in the post, for the rest of the century. Down to the beginning of the twentieth century any important matter not dealt with by the minister was settled by the director. In the Minister's absence, the director usually conducted oral negotiations with foreign envoys in Copenhagen, maintained the overall direction of the Ministry and checked all the more important communications personally before despatch. He also signed all important letters not signed by the minister himself and handled matters of a special political and confidential nature.

The consular system and commercial matters came under the economic administration until 1848 when all foreign affairs, including consular ones, were made subject to the Foreign Ministry. Foreign economic affairs incorporated assistance to shipping and the commercial administration that followed from foreign trade, although no significant state aid was given to trade and exports. As the Government refrained from establishing a permanent Ministry of Trade, the Foreign Ministry was given the task of filling the vacuum left by the abolished Commercial College. The civil servants who had previously done this work were transferred to the Foreign Ministry, where they were organized in a special department that was only gradually integrated with the security policy departments, whose work was considered to be more important. Later, when a demand arose for greater weight to be given to foreign economic affairs, the 1848 reform acquired a special importance as a tradition had been created for assigning these matters to the foreign service, abroad and at home. Foreign economic affairs were not transferred to the Ministry of Trade and Shipping that had been set up in 1908, and at no time has a Ministry for Foreign Economic Affairs (see p. 176) been created within the Danish administration.

The reform of assembling all foreign affairs under one administration became permanent; but an attempt in 1848 (at the same time as the introduction of parliamentary democracy) to reshape the organization of the Foreign Ministry proved abortive. Because the autocracy had been distinctly a regime of civil servants, the king's authority in practice being limited in scope, the men of the new regime sought to influence the Foreign Ministry by trying to get the position of civil servant changed from a royal to a government servant. The Foreign Minister wanted to concentrate all power in his own hands. The post of director was abolished and the senior secretary was dismissed. In their place four secretaries, equal in status and individually responsible directly to the Minister, were appointed. The arrangement failed to function properly and a gradual return to the organizational form of the autocracy was sought. Senior officials were against being reduced from policy initiators to mere promoters of political decisions; the post of director was recreated, and by the close of the nineteenth century the organizational form of the Ministry did not differ materially from that of the pre-1848 one.

Under the autocracy an able and trustworthy class of officials had been created. The middle-class officials of Copenhagen depended both on the king's favour and on their salaries. With loyalty to the Crown as the point of departure, they were expected to offer all the basic virtues of the civil servant: a combination of professional knowledge and high morality, zeal, conscientiousness and capability. The civil servants of the old Foreign Ministry were generally both conscientious and efficient, and often they had considerable cultural ballast. Someone who knew both the old Foreign Ministry and the new one after the First World War maintained that minor matters were handled better by the new Ministry but doubted whether the same could be said of major affairs. Above all, the civil servants were honest, and corruption entirely unknown. No civil servant in the Foreign Ministry was dismissed or penalized for abuse of office in the period 1770–1905, and premature discharge for inefficiency was extremely rare. Even during the straitened economic conditions at the beginning of the nineteenth century, they were commended for loyalty and integrity. No formal qualifications were required for appointment to the foreign service, but from the final decades of the autocracy it became general for applicants to hold a law degree from Copenhagen University. Importance was attached to the applicant's knowledge of languages, and relationship with someone in the service was an advantage. The personnel was drawn from the secure middle class, often sons of civilian officials and clergymen. There were still some immigrant Germans in the eighteenth century, but the great majority in this period were Danish-born, the number of Holsteiners and (before 1814) Norwegians being extremely low in the home service.

'Not even the most eminent qualities can make up for lack of confidence in their officials by the rulers', Niels Rosenkrantz, head of the department, wrote in 1811, and he expressed something fundamental about the *liens de dépendence* which is valid even now. Mutual trust is the note usually struck by foreign ministers today when meeting their civil servants for the first time. Some common approach to basic issues by rulers and officials is a prior condition of this trust; whenever the trust has broken down, the consequence has been replacements among senior civil servants. This occurred in 1848 because of a change in the form of government, and again in the late 1850s when supporters of the old Danish-German unitary state had to make way for civil servants whose approach was to serve a Danish national state comprising Denmark and Schleswig. One such civil servant was Peter Vedel, who was to influence the old Foreign Ministry for a generation.

The scope of the foreign service is shown by the following tables.[9]

Diplomatic service

	1774	1797	1823	1838	1847	1853	1860	1870	1880	1890	1900
Envoys	14	14	11	8	7	7	8	7	7	8	8
Resident Ministers	3	0	1	2	3	2	3	1	1	0	0
Chargés d'affaires	0	0	3	4	6	1	1	0	0	0	0
Secretaries of Legation	9	11	9	8	8	7	7	5	5	5	5
Career Consuls General/Consuls	6	9	5	1	1	0	0	0	0	0	(1898) 6
Other Career Officials (Chaplains, Attachés)	8	10	6	2	3	1	1	1	1	1	1
Total	40	44	35	25	28	18	20	14	14	14	20

Honorary Consulates

	1770	1800	1825	1848	1875	1900	1920
Consuls General	2	3	16	24	28	28	20
Consuls	33	52	52	78	127	143	164
Vice-consuls	12	175	213	261	411	402	350
Total in Europe	43	221	233	299	392	386	361
Total outside Europe	4	9	48	64	174	187	173
Overall total	47	230	281	363	566	573	534

It will be seen that after 1848 the foreign diplomatic service was halved, and that the number of career personnel at no time exceeded fifty. The reason for the reduction was the country's contraction and consequently reduced international status and activity. Two important changes occurred. One was the change from German to Danish personnel, in particular the departure from the service of pro-German and loyalist Holstein landowners in the 1850s and 1860s, which was undoubtedly a qualitative loss to the administration. Among others, there was the conservative supporter of the Danish-German unitary state and opponent of nationalism, Bernhard Bülow, Danish envoy to the Federal Diet at Frankfurt, who chose to go south and was later employed by Bismarck as Foreign Minister of the Reich. The other change was a reversion to the practice of attaching greater importance to economic functions in the overall work of the foreign service. This occurred by means of a law of 14 April 1893 on the consular service, authorizing the establishment of new posts for career consuls in support of foreign trade. This type of office, comprising an element of aid for trade and shipping, had previously been known in the Danish foreign service only in the Mediterranean, c. 1750–1830. The law is also significant in that this was the first time that Parliament set its stamp on the organization of the foreign service.

The number of unsalaried honorary consuls grew rapidly throughout the period, especially at the end of the eighteenth century and from the mid-nineteenth century onwards, when the service became global. Honorary consuls occupied a relatively more important place in the overall foreign service in this period than they did after the First World War. In 1900 80 per cent of this group were foreign nationals, and the work was only a sideline, carrying a measure of prestige, to their local business. They were, therefore, guided by a set of general instructions, issued for the first time in 1749 and then in revised form in 1824, 1868 and 1893.

The new Foreign Ministry

Three times in the present century Parliament, the central administration, and trade and industry have together tried to determine the best organization for discharging the foreign service's functions. The means were the commissions of 1906, 1919 and 1957, the results of which, after discussions in Parliament and by the Government, were embodied in the laws of 27 May 1908, 6 May 1921 and 26 April 1961.[10] A few other enactments in the intervening and subsequent years introduced further modifications in the structure of the foreign service. Common to all these was a basic desire to create a foreign service, at home and abroad, that would support the economic interests of the nation, trade, industry and individuals in their relations with other countries. On the other hand, there have been considerable differences in the conception of its political functions, the special concern of the Ministry's political department, which with no sectional limitations had a coordinating and evaluating function with a core of security policy. In 1906 the economic point of view predominated. The same applied in 1921, but with an awakening, though transitory and inadequate, appreciation of the political (security policy) functions, whose importance was frankly acknowledged in 1957. As defined somewhat pointedly by a former director of the Foreign Ministry, the economic approach inclined to the view that the foreign service should think in terms of cheese and that the head of a diplomatic mission was only an outsize commercial traveller. According to the political view, the economic aspect was worthless if there was nothing to contain it – and the container was national security, which would ensure the country's continued existence. After the Second World War there was a change of direction in Danish foreign policy. The old post-1720 neutrality policy changed to one of non-alignment after 1814 and did not involve any major foreign policy activity between 1870 and 1900. On the other hand, after 1870 there occurred a great economic expansion in agriculture, industry and shipping, which naturally led to demands for the foreign service to be employed for economic ends. In the inter-war years, especially from the late 1920s, the country's foreign policy was principally an economic one. By adhering to the NATO treaty in 1949, Denmark returned to a policy of alliance, involving an active engagement in foreign policy and, for the first time since the First World War, with a military element.

Never in a short space of years has the foreign service undergone such a transformation as regards the actual work done than that which took place between 1905 and 1919. The Ministry's total personnel trebled to fifty-eight in 1919, the career personnel abroad being doubled to fifty-one. The aristocratic element in the service abroad was replaced by the middle class, who remained dominant in the Ministry. At the close of the First World War, 'new types', as they were called, entered the Ministry. They were officials in shirt sleeves who strove for efficiency. The reorganization of the service, aimed at strengthening its economic functions, did not immediately entail a change in the personnel structure. Under the 1908 law, the Ministry itself was organized in two departments, one of them concerned with political, legal and other questions, the other with trade and industry and the consulates. The post of director was abolished and replaced by heads of departments, a post that in Danish administrative practice carries direct responsibility and access to a minister. The law reflected a deep and widespread distrust of the efficiency of the diplomatic service and looked to the employment of commercially trained personnel – i.e. commercial attachés. The commercial bias did not, however, prevail in recruitment. The traditional service, whose core was formed by academics with legal training, proved to be viable, and was able to adjust to the new requirements and functions. This was so during the First World War, which involved a greatly increased workload for the whole service because of the many economic questions that arose in connection with Denmark's policy of neutrality.

The inter-war years began with an expression of optimistic faith in the future. The 1921 law laid the framework for a big expansion of the service just when the idea of an integrated foreign service was becoming acceptable. In consequence, the principle of rotation for career members of the civil service was implemented. The 1921 law involved lasting innovations. It established a special office (more came later) with grade promotion as its particular jurisdiction, and economic considerations took precedence in the Ministry's work. Under a law of 1923 a permanent foreign policy committee was set up in Parliament. Optimism soon gave way to a demand for economy, restrictions and stagnation, abroad and at home. This was the general theme for the inter-war period. The result was a law in 1927 that fixed the Ministry's structure for more than a generation. The core of this was the establishment of two chief sections: the economic–political one and the political–legal one, with a director, whose post had been restored in 1921, as coordinator. In 1935 the statutory siting of missions was discontinued, enabling them to be located as and where required, one indication that the old parliamentary mistrust of the foreign service was on the wane. An important contributory factor was that P. Munch, Foreign Minister 1929–40, had the confidence of Parliament as the first real parliamentarian in the post, which in the past had normally been occupied by men drawn from the service itself. For example, the Foreign Minister during the two world wars, Erik Scavenius, the most outstanding Danish Foreign Minister in recent times, was from the service. (He was Foreign Minister 1909–10, 1913–20, 1940–2 Prime and Foreign Minister 1942–5.)

The German occupation of Denmark from 9 April 1940 until 5 May 1945 is a special chapter in the history of the foreign service, since its work then was of a quite special and, one may hope, unique character. There was considerable scope for diplomats, both at home in relation to the occupying power and abroad with the Allied governments in Washington and London, to exercise their skill in the difficult art of negotiating from the worst possible position. There were two political currents at the time. One called for a policy of negotiation, the other was the Resistance, supplemented by a Danish effort in the Allied camp. At the time they were sharply opposed to one another, but were in fact complementary and equally patriotic in their basic views, which by different ways and means were directed at the recovery of Danish freedom and independence.

Negotiation was the key word in Denmark's official policy towards the Germans in occupation, and it involved an effort to avoid German interference in internal Danish affairs in return for acceptance of the occupation and maintenance of tranquillity and order, so as to place no obstacles to the German war machine. This policy, which was pursued by the king, the lawful government and the freely elected Parliament, and originally had the broad support of the population, endeavoured to preserve independence as far as possible and to carry the Danish people safely through the war's miseries. In this way a Nazi satellite government was avoided and internal administration was kept in Danish hands. The policy of negotiation ceased on 29 August 1943, when its broad basis crumbled because of unacceptable German demands. The powers and functions of the king were suspended, the Government ceased to function and Parliament was shut down; but negotiations with the Germans continued on a limited scale at the administrative level. Meanwhile, the Resistance movement grew in all its different forms.

The Foreign Ministry became the Government's most important instrument in the negotiating policy, by deliberately channelling contacts through diplomatic means and at the same time keeping a certain distance between German authorities on the one hand and the Government and the internal Danish administration on the other. Through their knowledge of German ways and language, and by general diplomatic skills, the civil servants were specially qualified for negotiating and opposing German demands with counter-demands and counter-arguments. Among them the director, Nils Svenningsen, returned to the same office in 1951. By unremitting negotiating tactics time was won, German demands were limited, German extortions from the country's economy impeded, and Danish nationals assisted.

While nearly every leading civil servant in the Ministry backed the official policy of negotiation, a substantial number of Danish diplomats in Allied countries declared themselves free; that is, they broke with the home Government and supported the government where they served. Consequently, they were dismissed by the Government in Copenhagen, and reinstated after the war. They were the envoys and subordinate civil servants mainly in the United States and the British Commonwealth, headed by the ministers H. Kauffmann and E. Reventlow in 1940 and 1941. The minister to the United States, in an agreement with the American Government, obtained confirmation of Danish sovereignty in Greenland, the Americans in return getting the formal provision needed for establishing bases there.

With the return to ordinary life in 1945 it soon became evident that conditions had changed since 1939. In the next few years a great expansion occurred in Denmark's international relations, and with them an expansion in the functions of the foreign service. The significance of this became apparent when Parliament's foreign affairs committee obtained authority in the Constitution of 1953 for providing Parliament with the maximum influence on the country's foreign policy. The principal innovation was the continuing intensification of multilateral international cooperation. Conferences and travelling became commonplace for civil servants as a result of Denmark's membership of the NATO collective security pact of 1949, the Council of Europe, the OEEC (later OECD), and the wealth of activity that followed the plans for integrating European markets from the end of the 1950s, with Danish membership of EFTA and then the EEC, in addition to a long succession of other international organizations. The United Nations, from 1945, was not strictly an innovation in terms of diplomatic representation but a continuation of the League of Nations, yet together with participation in the special agencies it was immeasurably more comprehensive and administratively burdensome. In more recent years Denmark has belonged to forty multilateral international organizations, of which fewer than half – though the biggest and most important of them – are covered by a locally based delegated mission. Other activities followed from decolonization and the great increase in the number of independent states in Asia and Africa, including several developing countries. The extra work was not only on an unprecedented scale but to some extent of an unfamiliar nature. In addition, there is the work of the foreign service resulting from increased cross-frontier mobility (tourism, immigrant workers, crime, etc.).

In 1945 it was clear that the foreign service would have to expand. Whereas a corresponding expansion after the First World War soon slowed down, after 1945 expansion continued both at home and abroad. To enable the foreign service to discharge its many tasks there were two important laws passed in the period, in 1945 and 1961. Common to both was an adjustment to and extension of the service both at home and abroad, though neither embodied basic innovations of great consequence. The law of 26 April 1961, amended by that of 24 December 1970, developed the departmental structure, under the general coordination of the director, from the two old sections of 1927 and the administrative section of 1945. In the 1961 law all were divided into seven sections: Economic, Commercial, International Development Cooperation (under a law of 1962), Political, Legal, Administration, and Press and Cultural, besides units such as Protocol, Archives and the Foreign Service Inspectorate. The 1961 law refers to the missions as bodies directly subject to the Foreign Ministry, thus marking a long line of development transferring the centre of gravity in the service from the missions to the Ministry.

This expansion is reflected in the fact that the general service (abroad and at home) i.e. the university personnel in the top salary grades as provided for by these various laws, comprised 172 posts in 1921 (of whom only 146 were actually appointed), 113 in 1927, 158 in 1945 and 246 in 1961.[11] The number of university personnel in the period 1960–75 was as follows:

	Serving at home	Serving abroad	Total
1960	90	120	210
1965	130	155	285
1970	155	155	310
1975	195	160	355

The figures show an increase of about 70 per cent, the bulk of it accounted for by the home service, whose share of the total rose from 43 per cent in 1960 to 55 per cent in 1975. The real growth is even greater: the 1961 arrangement facilitated an expansion and increased differentiation of specialist personnel, notably commercial and press experts, who in 1968 numbered sixty, and in addition there is a large office staff. The foreign service as a whole expanded during the 1960s and early 1970s from about 560 persons to about 1100.

Quantitatively, the growth can be ascribed to two large areas. One is export promotion (Danish exports doubled during the decade 1960 to 1970) and the other the administration of Danish aid to developing countries. The number of foreign missions has been constantly increased until 1980. There were forty-two diplomatic and consular missions in mid-century including five embassies, the title of ambassador having been introduced in 1947 for the permanent missions. In 1960 there were sixty-three, in 1970 seventy-six, and in 1980 ninety-eight missions. The number of honorary consuls in all three grades has remained stationary at about 500. To stimulate cooperation and to render thanks for their voluntary and unpaid work they were all invited, for the first time, to a large and festive gathering in Copenhagen in 1955.

The present foreign service

In the relationship between political leaders and the administration, in Denmark as predominantly in Western Europe, the principle of ministerial rule prevails. There are, however, variants in Danish practice.[12] At the political level, in addition to the Foreign Minister and the Prime Minister as head of the Government, there is often a further minister who relieves the Foreign Minister of certain special areas of concern – among them, in recent years, foreign economic affairs, European Community affairs and development assistance. These are not junior or deputy ministers but Government members in their own right, and they are indispensable if the overall field, with travel and conferences abroad, becomes too great for one person. There has not been any corresponding division of the Foreign Ministry, though work and offices are directed to the minister for the special sphere. For example, there has been a Minister for Foreign Economic Affairs without any corresponding institution of a Foreign Economic Affairs Ministry. In spite of the political ups and downs of recent years departmental services have continued to be found in the Foreign Ministry. The foreign service is integrated. The Foreign Minister is responsible for the organization and administration of the service while the top civil servant, the director, is the service's supreme administrative head and supervises coordination in the Ministry and between the home and foreign-based service. The director also heads the Department for Foreign Affairs (Department I), while a head of department directs the Department for Foreign Economic Affairs (Department II). Another circumstance peculiar to Denmark is strong parliamentary control exercised by the Folketing, in particular over Common Market policy. The peculiarity is that the control is anterior through a special Market committee, which fixes the negotiating mandate that is binding on a minister at meetings in Brussels.[13] A third factor that may be mentioned is an established Danish tradition in the whole of the central administration, including the Foreign Ministry, of being a wholly non-political, that is to say a non-party political, administration. This means the absence of any controlling elements other than ministers, such as Cabinets, secretaries of state or political assistants who come and go with the minister. The tradition is for a senior official (director or head of department) to have direct access to the minister and to serve with unchanging loyalty successive political currents and persons, provided the Constitution and legislation are observed. This ensures continuity, with years of office frequently running into double figures.

The present structure of the Foreign Ministry (based on current law of 26 April 1961 with latest amendments 29 March 1974) consists of two departments, each having a number of sections divided into offices, which are the Ministry's working core (see Appendix A). The staff functions of administration, archives and protocol are available to the whole of the Ministry. There is no single criterion underlying the division of the department into sections and offices, the division being governed by functional, geographical and institutional considerations. Of the greatest importance is the internal coordination across the established units, in the form of regular meetings at various levels, appointments of *ad hoc* groups, internal circulation of general written information, proper distribution of incoming mail and, not least, informal personal and telephone contacts.

The Foreign Ministry's functions are wide-ranging. Apart from the service's administration of itself, they can be divided into political functions – in the broad sense – of security and economics, plus functions of aid and service. Unlike the organization, these functions are not prescribed by any law or regulation. The field of operations is not technically delimited, and has no formal criterion other than the relation of the case to another country or countries. As Danish membership of the EEC has developed the technical ministries, especially the economic ministries covering agriculture, trade and tariffs, are being increasingly drawn into this aspect of European policy where technical expertise is necessary. New issues, replete with problems, seem destined to continue to be assigned to the Foreign Ministry. One measure of the scope of the functions is the mail, which amounts to 514 000 incoming and outgoing items, including 110 000 telegrams. (Figures for incoming and outgoing items in previous years are: 1907 25 000–30 000, 1913 44 000, 1921 105 000, 1938 148 000, 1961 408 000.)

The present organization was created when the major concern in foreign affairs was Denmark's entry into the EEC. The current law is a good example of how administrative laws codify already existing practice. In 1966 the Foreign Ministry's Common Market affairs were placed under a special Market Secretariat, and it was with this secretariat as the point of departure, and with the same head, that the Department for Foreign Economic Affairs functioned in 1971. In the spring of 1972 the Government laid down procedures for dealing with EEC matters in order to ensure, through the Department for Foreign Economic Affairs, a centralized control in relation both to other administrations and to the Ministry in general. In the autumn of 1972 the Folketing's finance committee endorsed the change in the Ministry's structure, with effect from 1 January 1973; the Market Secretariat's status was thus changed to that of a section, the Ministry's sections being distributed according to their subject range in the two departments. Since then, European political cooperation (EPC) outside the framework of the Treaty of Rome has increased unexpectedly fast, the emphasis today being on a concerted European policy.

With regard to personnel, the foreign service has 1500 employees in all categories, about half of them at home and the other half abroad at the ninety-eight missions. The running costs (1980) are about 400 million kroner, about 60 per cent of this being spent on overseas costs. The total number of personnel increased with the creation of new posts at home and abroad, with a view to export promotion, the entrance into the Common Market and the expansion of development aid. In addition there are about sixty attachés posted at the missions from other ministries (Defence, Agriculture, Fisheries, Finance).

The general service consists mainly of academically trained personnel serving as secretary, principal, office (division) or sectional head at home and as embassy secretaries and counsellors, consuls, consuls-general and ambassadors abroad. Appointment is not subject to the holding of a particular degree, but theoretical education at university level is assumed. In practice, the traditional law degree still predominates, though the corresponding economics degree has made great strides in recent decades. Many other equivalent degrees are also represented, e.g. in political science, history and languages. Theoretical training is assumed to have been acquired before appointment, so that what follows is training on the job, through transfer from section to section and through home and overseas service, in addition to language tuition in the Ministry's school of languages, over a two-year trial period.

Foreign Service (1980)	Total numbers of personnel	Staff at missions
General service		
Heads	119	69
Staff	242	89
Specialist staff		
Commercial and industrial attachés	87	68
Journalists	20	10
Danida (development aid) staff	90	26
Consular secretaries	32	32
Clerical staff	540	197
Messengers	87	9
Other personnel	42	0
Locally appointed office personnel	299	299
Total	1558	799

Social criteria play no part at all in recruitment. In the general service, totalling 357 persons at 1 June 1978, just over 10 per cent were women, and the proportion of women has been rising in recent years. *Primavera diplomatica.* There are no women among the forty-five senior officials in the two top salary grades at present. Head posts are normally filled by civil servants. This is the traditional method of appointment in the Danish central administration, under a set of laws that in practice make discharge, apart from normal retirement, an extremely difficult proposition. Personnel from this group are appointed by royal warrant, and qualify for a pension at the age of sixty-seven, as a rule, with the possibility of earlier retirement from the age of sixty. Personnel in the general service, specialist staff and a considerable proportion of the remainder are subject to transfer between service at home and abroad. For junior staff, this is normally at intervals of between two and four years, in the case of head posts on an average of four to seven years but without any fixed rules so that service periods can be relatively longer. The specialist staff consist of commercial, industrial and press experts, together with specialists in international development aid (Danida). At home they normally serve in the Commercial, Press and Cultural Section or in Danida, a few being in the Market Section. When serving abroad they rank as commercial, industrial and press secretaries, attachés or counsellors. A special group is that of translators of English, German and French. Office staff forms by far the biggest group. They cover a great many jobs, such as case-working, archive work, book-keeping and typing. Some are liable to transfer and serve as attachés and vice-consuls. It is generally the case that jobs which only a few years ago would have been done as a matter of course by academically trained personnel are today done by clerical personnel, who now have the possibility of advancement. The messenger staff are responsible for watch duty, driving, mail despatch, duplicating, etc., and act as guards abroad. Consular secretaries are recruited among junior office workers. After a short course in the Ministry they are posted abroad for two to three years' service at missions; they may be attached to honorary consuls. The large group of locally appointed staff at missions comprises translators, case-workers, shorthand typists, guards, etc.

Of the ninety-eight missions, six are at international organizations (EEC, NATO, the UN in New York and Geneva, OECD and Council of Europe), about nineteen are consulates or consulates-general and the rest embassies. The multilateral missions are mostly comparable to an office or a section of the Ministry and are controlled from there. The service abroad, however, consists predominantly of quite small missions, living a life relatively independent of the Ministry with a broad area of external contact, and normally with four or five delegated staff members, of whom three are usually case-workers. Typically, a Danish embassy comprises an ambassador (or consul-general), a counsellor or secretary, a commercial attaché and two office workers, plus locally appointed personnel. A few are considerably larger: the embassies in London, Paris, Bonn and Washington. Geographically, nearly half the case-workers abroad work at missions in Europe, and half of these in EEC countries. The embassies are responsible both for political work and for aid, the consulates give only aid and assistance, and the multilateral missions have chiefly political functions. A general profile of a bilateral mission shows the following functional pattern (expressed in percentages): protocol 3, commercial, consular assistance and development aid 61, general political and economic reporting 19, administration 15, others 2. The greater part of the aid work clearly consists of assistance rendered to Danish trade and industry; in the case at almost all bilateral missions this is the largest and the fastest growing single activity in the overall work of the service abroad.

The great expansion of the service at home has led to a growing need to find a rational solution to the accommodation problem of the Ministry in Copenhagen, where (as in other European capitals) there are clear dis-advantages in having the functions scattered over several buildings. In 1923, when the Ministry moved to Christiansborg Palace in the centre of Copenhagen (which also accommodated the king, the Folketing and the Supreme Court), the entire Ministry could be housed in an apartment that had originally been intended for the king but was eventually made available to the Foreign Minister and his staff of 130. With the growth in functions and consequent increase in personnel the palace became too cramped, and from the 1940s one branch of the service after another had to be accommodated at different places – eventually eight – in the vicinity. Only the senior staff, one section and some technical functions remained at Christiansborg. The spread entailed an irrational and cumbersome work flow that has impeded vital coordination at all levels – quite apart from the extra costs, which ran into millions of kroner.

In 1961 the Ministry's political and departmental heads decided to assemble the whole Ministry under one roof, and after various vicissitudes and abortive projects a new complex of buildings rose at Asiatisk Plads across the water at Christianshavn, to which the entire Ministry moved in March 1980.[14] The Folketing, which has granted the allocations, took over the premises at Christiansborg. The site is a combination of new buildings (80 per cent) and the restoration of old buildings (20 per cent). The situation is both central and attractive, close to the rest of the central administration, with rapid access to the airport and by the quayside in an old quarter. In the old buildings, which includes a large eighteenth-century warehouse, a spacious conference and meeting sector will be provided, offering every modern facility in the traditional atmosphere of the massive old timbered structure that has been preserved. The new building, with a gross area of 25 000 square metres, comprises an office complex of three parallel blocks standing at right-angles to the harbour entrance, one of seven storeys and two of four storeys, partly joined together and all of them interconnected.

There is some symbolic value in siting the new Foreign Ministry at Asiatisk Plads, which in the eighteenth century was the centre of Danish overseas trading and shipping companies. It offers an inspiration for the continued support of Danish trade and industry abroad, and the fact that the buildings combine old and new will perhaps encourage staff to emulate those many members of the foreign service who in the past earned the reputation of being a 'trusty man of the realm'.

NOTES

[1] There is no overall account of the Danish foreign service prior to 1770. The principal work on the central Danish administration begins at the mid-seventeenth century. It is *Den danske Centraladministration*, Aage Sachs (ed.) (Copenhagen 1921). The Rigsarkiv has published a register of external affairs in English: *Danish Department of Foreign Affairs until 1770* (Copenhagen 1973).

[2] J. Wasserschlebe, *Memoire* (transcript). Fol.711b. Ny kgl. Samling. Det kongelige Bibliotek, Copenhagen. cf. Aage Friis, *Bernstorfferne og Danmark*. I–II Copenhagen. 1903–19, II, 81 ff.

[3] *Repertorium der diplomatischen Vertreter aller Länder seit dem Westfälischen Frieden (1648)* by L. Bittner, L. Gross et al. I–III. 1936–65. I, XIV.

[4] Klaus Müller, *Das kaiserliche Gesandtschaftswesen im Jahrhundert nach dem Westfälischen Frieden (1648–1740)*. (Bonn 1976), 60 ff, in the series Bonner Historische Forschungen, vol. 42. Butterfield: 'Diplomacy' in *Studies in Diplomatic History. Essays in Memory of David Bayne Horn*, R. Hatton & M. S. Anderson (eds) (London 1970), 362 ff.

[5] Studies for *Danske Gesandter og Gesandtskabspersonale indtil 1914* by Emil Marquard (Copenhagen 1952).

6 Dated 24.1.1680. T.K.I.A. Patenten Registratur 1680.

7 D. Jørgensen, *Danmark-Norge mellem Stormaktene 1688–1697. Dansk-norsk sjøfart og utenrikspolitik under den pfalsiske arvefølgekrig* (Oslo n.d.), 224 ff.

8 *Den danske Udenrigstjeneste 1770–1970* (Copenhagen 1970), I–II.

9 *Den danske Udenrigstjeneste 1770–1970* (Copenhagen 1970), I, 121, 238, 288 ff.

10 The reports and laws are all fully described in the Foreign Service's history (see note 8).

11 *Den danske Udenrigstjeneste 1770–1970*, II, 340. There are no entrance examinations for the Danish foreign service. A university education was considered necessary in the Ministry from about 1830.

12 Since 1890, with a few exceptions, an annual *Udenrigsministeriets Kalender* has been published, giving information about the Ministry, missions and service records.

13 Carsten Lehmann Sørensen, *Danmark og EF i 1970'erne* (Copenhagen 1978). *Studier i dansk Udenrigspolitik, tilegnet Erling Bjøl*, Niels Amstrup & Ib Faurby (eds) (Århus 1978).

14 *Asiatisk Plads. The Danish Foreign Service's new headquarters in Copenhagen* (Copenhagen 1980). English and French editions.

BIBLIOGRAPHY

The principal work on the Danish foreign service is *Den danske Udenrigstjeneste*, I–II (Copenhagen 1970). Abbreviated editions were published by the Ministry of Foreign Affairs in 1970–1 in English, French and German. The English language edition is entitled *The Foreign Service of Denmark 1770–1970*.

With regard to literature published in recent years, reference is made to a selected bibliography in Danish and foreign languages on Danish foreign policy after 1945, including the nature and functions of the foreign service, published in *Studier i dansk Udenrigspolitik, tilegnet Erling Bjøl* (Studies of Danish Foreign Policy, dedicated to Erling Bjøl), Niels Amstrup and Ib Faurby (eds) (Århus 1978).

Very little has been written about the nature and functions of the foreign service before 1770, but a survey of source material on Danish foreign policy, including the nature and functions of the foreign service, has been published in English: *Danish Department of Foreign Affairs until 1770* (Copenhagen 1973).

There exists a synopsis of Danish diplomats entitled *Danske Gesandter og Gesandtskabspersonale indtil 1914* (Danish Envoys and Legation Staffs up to 1914) by Emil Marquard (Copenhagen 1952). Biographies are found in *Dansk Biografisk Leksikon* (Danish Encyclopedia of Biographies), (new edition 1979 onwards). Among major biographies are Aage Friis, *Bernstorfferne og Danmark* (The Bernstorffs and Denmark), I–II (Copenhagen 1903–19); Viggo Sjøqvist, *Peter Vedel*, I–II (Copenhagen 1957–62), with a summary in English; and Viggo Sjøqvist, *Erik Scavenius*, I–II (Copenhagen 1973).

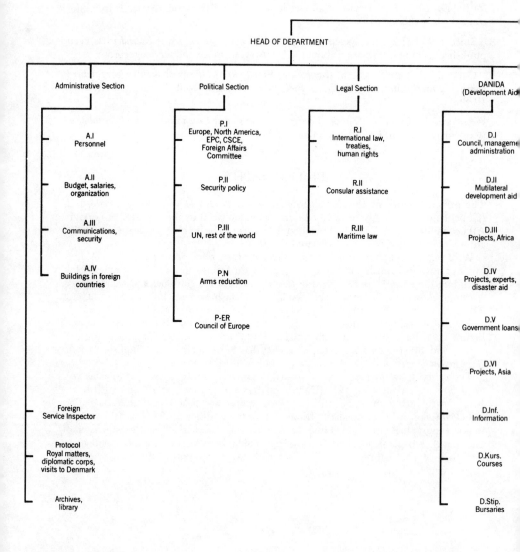

HEAD OF DEPARTMENT

Administrative Section

A.I
Personnel

A.II
Budget, salaries,
organization

A.III
Communications,
security

A.IV
Buildings in foreign
countries

Foreign
Service Inspector

Protocol
Royal matters,
diplomatic corps,
visits to Denmark

Archives,
library

Political Section

P.I
Europe, North America,
EPC, CSCE,
Foreign Affairs
Committee

P.II
Security policy

P.III
UN, rest of the world

P.N
Arms reduction

P-ER
Council of Europe

Legal Section

R.I
International law,
treaties,
human rights

R.II
Consular assistance

R.III
Maritime law

**DANIDA
(Development Aid**

D.I
Council, manageme
administration

D.II
Mutilateral
development aid

D.III
Projects, Africa

D.IV
Projects, experts,
disaster aid

D.V
Government loans

D.VI
Projects, Asia

D.Inf.
Information

D.Kurs.
Courses

D.Stip.
Bursaries

DENMARK – APPENDIX A

THE MINISTRY OF FOREIGN AFFAIRS (1979)

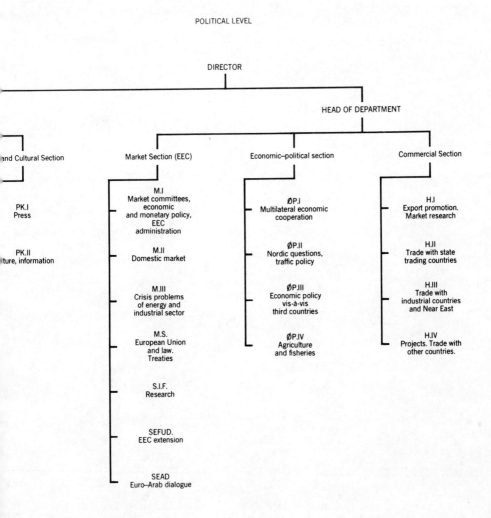

POLITICAL LEVEL

DIRECTOR

HEAD OF DEPARTMENT

and Cultural Section

Market Section (EEC)

Economic–political section

Commercial Section

PK.I
Press

PK.II
lture, information

M.I
Market committees,
economic
and monetary policy,
EEC
administration

M.II
Domestic market

M.III
Crisis problems
of energy and
industrial sector

M.S.
European Union
and law.
Treaties

S.I.F.
Research

SEFUD.
EEC extension

SEAD
Euro–Arab dialogue

ØP.I
Multilateral economic
cooperation

ØP.II
Nordic questions,
traffic policy

ØP.III
Economic policy
vis-à-vis
third countries

ØP.IV
Agriculture
and fisheries

H.I
Export promotion.
Market research

H.II
Trade with state
trading countries

H.III
Trade with
industrial countries
and Near East

H.IV
Projects. Trade with
other countries.

Finland

The Finnish Foreign Service

JUKKA NEVAKIVI

Professor Jukka Nevakivi is Professor and Chairman of the Department of Political History at the University of Helsinki. He was born in 1931 in Finland, educated at the University of Helsinki and at the London School of Economics (Ph.D. 1963). From 1963 to 1979, he was a member of the Finnish foreign service, serving in Budapest and Cairo, and in the Finnish delegation at the Conference of Security and Cooperation in Europe, 1974–5. He was head of CSCE affairs at the Ministry for Foreign Affairs and counsellor and minister counsellor at the Finnish embassy in Paris, 1976–9. His publications include *Britain, France and the Arab Middle East 1916–1920* (1969), *The Appeal That Was Never Made – The Allies, Scandinavia and the Finnish Winter War, 1939–1940* (1976) and other works in Finnish. He is currently working on an official history of the Finnish foreign service.

In the period between its separation from Sweden in 1809 and the achievement of full independence in 1917, Finland had enjoyed internal autonomy within the limits of its status as a Grand Duchy under the crown of Russia. But the tsarist government was in charge of the external affairs of the Grand Duchy, so Finland did not have a foreign ministry or a diplomatic service of its own. The office of the Minister Secretary of State representing the Finnish Government in St Petersburg, and the few Finns acting as official trade agents under diplomatic status but attached to Russian consulates abroad, did not really establish a Finnish tradition of diplomacy during the period of autonomy.

In December 1917, when the first government of independent Finland had to improvise the administration of its foreign affairs and to find persons to be sent as its official representatives abroad, it badly lacked men of experience. Most delegates sent abroad during the following months in order to acquire recognition and to establish permanent representations of the new foreign service were university teachers, businessmen and journalists, who knew foreign languages and happened to have some practice in international intercourse.

During the very first phase, characterized by a civil war (in January to May 1918) against local Reds and some remnants of Russian troops stationed in Finland, a Bureau of Foreign Affairs, supervised directly by the head of government, directed the activities of Finnish diplomacy. The preliminary task of the representations abroad was to help the White Finnish government with transmitting arms and food supply orders wherever this was possible. Because of the military and political character of these needs, the personnel serving in Finnish diplomatic missions to the Central and even to neutral powers were recruited overwhelmingly from pro-German Activists circles. This bias remained even after the armistice of 1918 and was only slowly balanced by new appointments, particularly those made by the pro-Entente Foreign Minister Rudolf Holsti in 1919.

An example of the earlier German influence was the invitation made to the Auswärtiges Amt to assist in organizing the Finnish Ministry for Foreign Affairs, which was established officially on 1 July 1918. In fact, the mission of the officially appointed counsellor, Karl Müller, was to be of short duration. The Finnish Ministry never became a replica of the German Foreign Ministry. Instead, the development of its organization and practice was from the outset influenced by Scandinavian, especially Swedish, example.

On the other hand, the presidential character of the Finnish foreign service was accentuated by the new Constitution Act of the Republic, which came into effect on 19 July 1919. According to the Constitution – valid to this day – special emphasis is laid upon the strong executive power with which the President of the Republic is invested. As the highest authority in foreign affairs, he is in a position to influence all activities of the administration, not least by his right of nomination, which covers all career vacancies, from top to bottom.

The Foreign Affairs Committee of the Cabinet has occasionally, during the tenures of weaker Presidents, had a decisive say on questions of nomination. Similarly Parliament, especially in earlier times, has affected developments in the foreign service by means of budgetary policy. Still, the past of this branch of administration is closely connected with Finnish history in general, with the first uncertain years of independence, with the trials of the Second World War and its aftermath, with the country's slow return to the international community and with the consolidation of the policy of neutrality thereafter. Relatively little affected by twists and turns in national politics, the history of the Finnish foreign service offers an image of continuity largely due to its constitutional link with the highest executive and, during the second half of its existence, to the exceptionally long tenures of the last two Presidents.

Still, during the first half of its existence, this history can hardly be explained solely by the length of the presidential terms. Until 1939, Finland had two temporary heads of state and four regular Presidents, yet the structure and the forms of activity of its foreign service remained much the same. For the second period, from 1939 to 1959, when the country again had four Presidents, the foreign service was in nearly constant crisis, shaken by the war and by post-war problems. For the third and fourth periods, running from 1956 to 1970 and from 1970 to the present, there has been only one President, Urho Kaleva Kekkonen; the development of the foreign service is nevertheless marked by a continuous effort towards reform, more far-reaching than earlier attempts.

1918 to 1939

During the years between the two world wars Finnish foreign policy had in principle, despite changes in execution, the same general aims: to win recognition for the newly independent state and to safeguard its prosperity and security. Yet the changes – from the so-called Baltic orientation of the early 1920s to the League of Nations line, and finally, from the mid-thirties, the neutral Nordic orientation of its foreign policy – made execution problematic and occasionally contradictory. Though their loyalty in general was beyond doubt, Finnish civil servants had in the early years of independence some of the same difficulties in respecting their young republican régime as they had had in obeying the monarchies.

The way in which heads of state handled the foreign service differed greatly according to their personalities. During his short term as regent in 1918–19, the then General C. G. E. Mannerheim intervened on many occasions in the everyday activities of the Foreign Ministry and the overseas missions. Even later, especially during his chairmanship of the Defence Council in the 1930s, his influence was felt in diplomatic appointments. As an example of 'weaker Presidents' L. K. Relander (1925–31) is sometimes mentioned, but in fact he was very active in diplomacy, exchanging, for the first time in Finnish history, state visits with several neighbouring Nordic and Baltic countries. One of the least active Presidents with regard to foreign affairs was Kyösti Kallio (1937–40), but he too was sensitive to parliamentary and even to outside criticism of the foreign service and had a tendency to intervene in nominations.

Nevertheless, in Finland as elsewhere in the new European states, the foreign service quickly made itself indispensable to the head of state for the simple reason that he did not have a staff capable of managing even his personal public relations. The Foreign Office had to assist the presidential staff as well as Parliament in the field of official ceremonies, social events and visits, not to speak of foreign correspondence.

The predominant role of the foreign service in the years before 1939 in formulating Finnish foreign policy is demonstrated by the fact that, out of 11 men appointed as Foreign Ministers, no fewer than eight were active or former members of the service. The first of these, Carl Enckell, was appointed Foreign Minister three times (during the years 1918–19, 1922 and 1924) for short periods; he was Foreign Minister for a fourth time in 1944–50, and then for an extended period.

His successor in 1919, Rudolf Holsti, stayed in office for three years (1919–22), and was later to be Foreign Minister for another two years (1936–8). A third prominent member of the service, Hjalmar Procopé, was appointed as Foreign Minister twice (1924–5 and 1927–31). The last head of the office of Minister Secretary of State under the former Russian Provisional Government, Karl Gustaf Idman, in his turn held the post of Foreign Minister for a short period (in 1925), then stayed in the service until his retirement.

Though not a career diplomat, the first Finnish minister to the Soviet Union, Antti Hackzell, served a long period as Foreign Minister (in 1932–6) and then as Prime Minister before suffering a fatal illness while he was head of the Finnish armistice delegation in Moscow in 1944. Another envoy to Moscow, Aarno Yrjö-Koskinen, was appointed Foreign Minister (in 1931–2) to negotiate the Finnish–Soviet treaty of non-aggression. Later, in 1939, he had to leave the new legation in Krapotkinskii Pereulok, two days after his host government had renounced the treaty. Even the last Foreign Minister before the war, Eljas Erkko (1938–9), had spent a number of years in diplomatic service. All in all, for more than three-quarters of the period under review the office of Foreign Minister was held by men coming from, or at least having had experience in, this branch of administration.

The need for competent personnel in the foreign service became evident in the very first years of independence when Finland, besides building up its diplomatic representation, had to pay attention to its litigation within the framework of the League of Nations (the questions of Åland in 1920 and of Eastern Karelia in 1922–3). The fact that in the case of Åland Finland had been able to secure its national interest by means of multilateral diplomacy was an achievement of a magnitude sufficient to quiet those critics who, at the dawn of independence, had claimed that there was no need for the country to create a foreign service of its own, or that it should at least be limited merely to a consular representation.

According to the first charter, given in 1918, the Ministry for Foreign Affairs was divided into political, commercial, juridical and archives departments and a separate bureau of press affairs. During the first year the career personnel consisted of 17 civil servants, six of whom were senior ones; K. G. Idman served as first secretary-general. In principle, the staff were obtained not by transferring suitable officials from other branches of the administration but by recruiting a totally fresh nucleus selected personally by the first Foreign Minister, Otto Stenroth. The candidates came mainly from among young lawyers with foreign language ability – the average age of the first group did not exceed 30 years. The bureaux of the new office were located in the former Imperial Palace. In 1920 it moved to the Government Palace Building, with the main access from Ritarikatu (Riddargatan).

Representation abroad during the first year was limited to Stockholm, Oslo, Copenhagen and Berlin. The missions in London and Paris had no official status. After the recognition of Finland by Great Britain and the

United States in May 1919, and the re-establishment of diplomatic relations between Finland and France, the missions in London, Washington and Paris were given the status of legation.

In establishing diplomatic missions, the Finnish government did not at the outset aim at universal representation, nor did it in general follow a formal reciprocal principle. Still, during the following three years it opened additional legations in Tallinn, Moscow, Warsaw, Rome, Madrid, The Hague, Bucharest (closed for financial reasons in 1923) and Tokyo, making a total of 15. Meanwhile another diplomatic mission, established in Kiev in 1918 in order to assist Finnish subjects and trade refugees in southern Russia, had already ceased its activities. During the same year (1922) a consulate-general was established in Leningrad, with a career officer in charge. At that time the total number of Finnish honorary consuls abroad was nearly two hundred.

With the exception of Berlin and Paris, where the Finnish legations had four or five officials, most missions had no more than two or three members on the diplomatic list. In all, in 1922 the Foreign Ministry had 19 permanent and 18 temporary vacancies for career officials, as well as four permanent posts for clerks. Correspondingly, the number of permanent career officials in the diplomatic service had increased to 45.

Hitherto, the organization and the activities of the Finnish foreign service had been improvised according to the needs of each particular situation. The efficiency of the administration had been criticized, especially by business interests. Parliament had been rather indifferent to its needs for development. In order to study its responsibilities and performance thoroughly, as well as to consider suggestions for possible reforms of the foreign service, a committee under the chairmanship of Rafael Erich (an authority on international law, a former Finnish Prime Minister and a future member of the Permanent International Court of Justice) was appointed in 1921. During the following four years this committee was to give guidelines on the reorganization of the foreign service and on the selection of career officers.

In accordance with the recommendations of the Erich Committee, and following a recent Swedish example, the Foreign Ministry was reorganized in 1923. The political and commercial departments were combined and their work redivided, on a geographical basis, into the Western and Eastern sections. The second department was made responsible for juridical and (until 1928) League of Nations matters; a third dealt with administrative affairs.

From 1928, when the principle of geographic division was abandoned, political and commercial (e.g. trade policy) affairs were once more dealt with in two separate units; two years later these units were re-established as two departments. The Political Department was by then divided into three sections, responsible for political, press and League of Nations affairs. From 1936 until the war even the press and League of Nations affairs were operated as separate departments. Otherwise the basic division into political, commercial, juridical and administrative departments remained until the establishment of a protocol department in 1951.

The year 1922 represents the peak year, when the foreign service share of the national budget was just over 48 million marks, or 1.9 per cent of total state expenditure. The lowest allocations (0.6 per cent) did not coincide with the great economic depression but corresponded to those years when the country was governed by Centre–Labour coalitions, which were usually cool to foreign service needs. In fact, during that period the Finnish foreign service had relatively little reason to complain about its allocations compared with those made in the other Nordic countries, with the exception of Denmark.

All the same, the expansion of the foreign service was handicapped by the recession to the extent that neither the network of posts nor the number of career officials abroad increased significantly before the Second World War. Notable new legations of the 1930s were Riga, Bern, Buenos Aires and Rio de Janeiro. All were very small, with the exception of a diplomatic mission established in 1936 in Budapest to deal with representation not only in Hungary but also Austria, Bulgaria, Yugoslavia and even Turkey. The work of this mission came to an end during the final phase of the Second World War, when even its newly purchased legation palace was destroyed.

The Finnish diplomatic service was, before the war, very much concentrated on the Continent, with the result that in 1939 the only European states with which Finland did not have diplomatic relations were Albania, the Holy See and the Irish Free State. The lack of universality in foreign representation was partly compensated for by the Finnish presence in the League of Nations and its specialized agencies. Remarkably active in those circles, and represented by men of the stature of Erich and Holsti, Finland was elected for the term of 1927–30 as a member of the Council of the League. As a result of Finland's increased interest in the League, the legation in Bern, hitherto responsible for the relations with it, was transferred to Geneva in 1932 (until 1940).

At its high point before the war, in 1938, Finland had 20 diplomatic representations abroad with 54 officials. At the Foreign Ministry, the number of career vacancies was at the same time not more than 31. Limited as these numbers are, they compare fairly well with the corresponding figures for Norway, Sweden and Denmark. Whether these vacancies were filled by the best possible men is another question. In any case, the selection and training in general were less advanced in Finland than in the other Nordic countries.

During the first years of the Finnish foreign service the candidates for career nomination had been selected personally by the responsible Minister or the secretary-general. As the result of this kind of recruitment, over half of the career officers up to July 1919 (the end of Mannerheim's regency) were of Finno-Swedish background, although the part of the Finnish population speaking that language as their mother tongue was even then only one-tenth. The tendency to favour the highest class of society in general, and higher academic degrees in particular, was obvious. More than three-quarters of the officials selected in that period came from the upper class, which represented not more than some 5 per cent of the population, and nearly one quarter of them had higher degrees. (The role of the Finnish nobility in the administration being very limited, the 'upper class' means here only the well-to-do, the first of the four basic social groups classified by Finnish sociologists. The others are the middle class, the peasants and the workers.) It is worth noting that a dozen of this first year's vintage did not end their service until the end of the Second World War, by which time most of them had become ambassadors.

After the establishment of the Republic, and especially as a result of the new foreign service system introduced by the Erich Committee, the social background of the nominees slowly began to change. A selection committee of three to five members, most of them representatives of political and economic circles outside the service, examined the candidates for nomination. The basic qualifications included a university degree – either LL.B. or M.A. (the latter with additional examinations in economics, political sciences and international law) – as well as knowledge of two foreign languages, the first of which, in principle, had to be French. The suitability of the candidates was determined during a two-year probation period. During this time they had to serve both in Helsinki and abroad. According to the practice adopted in the 1930s, candidates ended their probation with an additional examination in everyday administrative knowledge and procedures.

Because the country had two official languages, civil servants had to have a fluent command of both Finnish and Swedish. During the first two decades of independence, this obligation was used as a weapon in the 'Finnization' of the administration. As a result, the number of officials speaking Swedish as their mother tongue fell in the 1930s to about 10 per cent of the career personnel, which was in harmony with the approximate proportion in the total population of Finland.

Besides the language quarrel, which gave a noisy background to certain higher nominations, politics always tended to interfere with foreign service affairs. The storm centre usually moved around Rudolf Holsti who, having eliminated the old pro-German and conservative elements during his first term as Foreign Minister, had during his second term, in the late 1930s, to deal with even more dangerous rivals belonging to a younger generation with radical right-wing views. These elements found backing above all in the Agrarian Party, which played an *avant-garde* role in the Finnization of the administration. Labour influence in the foreign service at that time was almost non-existent; only one envoy was a Social Democrat, appointed by the minority government of Väinö Tanner in 1927.

The general reduction in salaries and Finland's abandonment of the gold standard in 1931 caused a deterioration in the economic situation of officials both at home and abroad. Recovery was slow, and it handicapped the recruiting of candidates with talent but of modest economic background. Although in the thirties the proportion of upper-class recruits was reduced to little more than half of all nominations, the number of those selected who had a peasant or worker's background fell during this decade from 15 to 10 per cent. This tendency certainly did not please the two main parties in power by the end of the thirties, the Agrarians and the Social Democrats.

On the other hand, the earlier uncertainty in the Finnish foreign service gave way to self-confidence during that decade. It now looked like the corresponding administration in any respectable state, though the obligation of officials to be transferred to another post or even *en disponibilité* was introduced in Finland only in the wake of more recent reforms. There were surely reasons even then for criticizing its shortcomings and lack of efficiency. At least public opinion had begun to understand why even a small state like Finland needed diplomats.

1939 to 1956

In order to preserve its independence during the Second World War, Finland was compelled to change its foreign policy several times. Despite its declaration of neutrality the country was twice forced into war with the Soviet Union; it was also compelled into an alliance of a sort (the Finns called it 'co-belligerency') with Germany in 1941. For Finland the war ended in September 1944, in an armistice with the Soviet Union and in armed conflict with Germany. Finland had been in a state of war with Great Britain since December 1941 and had no diplomatic relations with the United States after June 1944.

The trials and tribulations of the Finnish foreign service, put to a severe test by these changing conditions, were not over with the ending of the war. The burden of diplomacy in the period preceding the final peace settlement (in Paris in March 1947), when Finland's suzerainty was in fact limited by the presence of the Soviet-led Allied Control Commission in Helsinki, fell heavily upon the foreign service. Since the country had both to reconstruct and to recover its production, all in fulfilling the severe terms of war reparations, the main emphasis was on re-establishing trade relations. In addition, the foreign service was, though to a lesser degree, charged with the formulation and execution of the policy of better relations with the Soviet Union, initiated and conducted personally by J. K. Paasikivi, Prime Minister from 1944 and President from 1946 to 1956. The service had understandable difficulties in meeting the growing tasks of the post-war years, not least since its resources were reduced to a minimum because of many material and personnel cutbacks.

From the outset the foreign service was closely connected with the Finnish war effort. Risto Ryti, President between 1940 and 1944, had earlier, as Prime Minister, made extensive use of diplomatic missions for securing arms supplies for Finland. As President he kept up active contacts with his envoys, especially in Berlin and Washington, relying on their political information more than any of his predecessors had done. One of the envoys, T. M. Kivimäki, a former Prime Minister and minister in Berlin in 1940–4, was later in a war crimes trial charged with having promoted a pro-German foreign policy line in Helsinki. Ryti's successor, Marshal Mannerheim, was actively assisted in his diplomacy by a senior member, a relative and his confidant in the foreign service, G. A. Gripenberg. In fact, as an envoy to Stockholm Gripenberg was in 1944 able to reopen the decisive peace talks with the Soviet representatives.

The next President, Paasikivi, was not only a former Prime Minister (he had been the head of government in 1918, when the Finnish foreign service was established), he was also a diplomat, having represented his country both in Stockholm and in Moscow – in the latter post during both the crucial negotiations in the autumn of 1939 and the peace talks of 1940 and early 1944. He was above all a man with knowledge of and interest in international relations. Had he not taken the initiative of founding a foreign policy association, the first of its kind in Finland, before the war?

As a consequence, Paasikivi had more confidence in himself than in the career officials. An exception was, of course, Carl Enckell, who because of his familiarity with things Russian was called back to the post of Foreign Minister, where he remained until 1950. But otherwise, even the main missions abroad tended to be filled by political nominees of the old President, who preferred to remove them, for one reason or another, from the home scene. It did not matter that many of them were leftist in sympathy. In his patriarchal way, Paasikivi preferred to deal with questions he considered important not through his envoys abroad but by personal talks with foreign representatives in Helsinki.

Even where legations suffered materially (the legations in Berlin, Budapest and London were destroyed by bombs), the Finnish foreign service suffered no career personnel casualties. Nor were more than two or three officers compelled to leave the service for political reasons. With a very few exceptions, the rank and file remained cool to fascist ideologies. Those in positions of responsibility when, in 1944, Finland had to sue for peace, never waivered in their loyalty to the government. Finnish diplomacy therefore proved its fitness as a channel for conducting foreign policy, in war as well as in peace.

The first Finnish diplomatic missions to be reopened in 1945 were the legations in London, Moscow, Oslo, Paris, Warsaw and Washington. Five years later Finland already had more diplomatic missions than before the war, and in 1955 their number totalled 25. In Berlin and Cologne (later Bonn) Finland, faithful to its German policy, had only a commercial representation. As a notable opening to other continents, legations were established in Canberra, New Delhi, Ottawa and Pretoria, as well as in Peking and Tel Aviv. From 1955 onwards most of the Finnish diplomatic missions abroad, with only one exception (that in South Africa), have been promoted on a reciprocal basis to the rank of embassies.

At the end of 1955 the foreign service totalled 124 officials, with 70 serving abroad. Over 30 officials who had begun their service in the 1920s, mostly the first year's appointees among whom were former Ministers Erich, Idman, Holsti and Procopé, were by now retired. Despite the change, the social background of career personnel remained much the same. The only exception was that the proportion of officials representing the Swedish-speaking minority rose again to more than a quarter of the total number of career officers in the 1940s, though the number was decreased subsequently. Besides this phenomenon, which was due to the lessening of the pressure for Finnization in the administration, recruitment during the crisis period seemed to favour candidates with an upper-class background (63 per cent in the 1940s and well over half even in the 1950s). Another trend of the war and post-war years was to select older candidates than before. As a consequence, at the end of the period the heterogeneity of the foreign service was well below pre-war standards, and there was a real need for reform. This was, however, delayed until the following decades.

A basis for educating future Finnish diplomats was created with the establishment of the Faculty of Political Sciences in the University of Helsinki immediately after the war. Although other university degrees, especially in law, have maintained their place as basic qualifications for selection, candidates graduating from this faculty were to take the numerical lead in nominations from the 1950s onwards.

1956 to 1970

The year 1956 was in many respects a turning point in Finnish post-war history. 'Finland's desire to stay outside the conflicting interests between the great powers', noted in the preamble of the Finnish–Soviet Treaty of

Friendship, Cooperation and Mutual Assistance of 1948, was given a real chance by the Soviet evacuation of the Porkkala military base in 1956 (it had been occupied as a condition of peace since 1944). Moreover, since the beginning of that year, Finland has taken a full member's part in the activities both of the Nordic Council and of the United Nations. The country's return to the international community was underlined on 1 March 1956 with the accession to the presidency of Urho Kaleva Kekkonen. Remaining in office until this year, he has given a remarkable continuity to Finnish foreign policy during the last 25 years.

The main aims of that policy during the early years of Kekkonen's presidency were the development of good neighbourly relations with the Soviet Union as well as with the Nordic countries, the safeguarding of the country's commercial interests in an integrating Europe (associating with the EFTA in 1962) and, above all, the recognition and affirmation of Finnish neutrality. In 1956 Finland had diplomatic relations with 50 states; by 1969 this number had increased to 80. In the United Nations, Finland's active role was accentuated by its membership of the Security Council in 1969–70. At the same time the country had become a member of other international organizations: UNESCO (1956), IAEA (1958), ICAO (1959) and UNCTAD (1965). The growth in the responsibilities of Finnish diplomacy is reflected by the unprecedented increase in the quantity of Foreign Ministry correspondence; during the period from 1956 to 1970 it nearly doubled.

Still, in pursuing its mission, the foreign service was by now more than ever a tool in the hands of the President. Taking full advantage of his long experience not only as Prime Minister (five times in the early 1950s) and Foreign Minister (1952–3 and 1954), but also as an experienced analyst of international politics, President Kekkonen followed the line initiated by his predecessor: he kept the reins of foreign affairs firmly in his own hands.

The role of the foreign affairs committees of both the Cabinet and Parliament was reduced to a minimum. As Ministers the new President preferred political appointees such as Ahti Karjalainen, a long-time protégé, who served as Foreign Minister for nine years during this period. Another confidant, the then secretary-general for foreign affairs, Jaakko Hallama, served as a member of the non-parliamentary caretaker Cabinet (in 1963–4). He was, after P. J. Hynninen (in 1957–8), the second Foreign Minister with a career background appointed by President Kekkonen. The last, but not the least, of his advisers in the field of foreign affairs was Eero A. Wuori, the only prominent post-war political envoy nominee, who after seven years as head of mission in London served as head of the Political Department in the Foreign Ministry, then for eight years as ambassador in Moscow and died as secretary-general of the office of the President in 1966.

In 1964 an attempt was made to respond to the pressure for reform when an *ad hoc* committee appointed by the Cabinet gave its report on the most urgent needs for developing the Finnish foreign service. As a result the resources of the Ministry were increased by creating new posts, among others the posts of an inspector of the diplomatic service and of an adviser recruited from outside the service, specializing in questions of international law. The press, archives and translation services were expanded; and a nucleus for the future administration of aid to developing countries – starting with a staff of five officials only – was established in 1965.

In contrast to the Ministry as a whole, the diplomatic service experienced a spectacular expansion. Most of the new missions in this period were established in Africa and the Near East (Addis Ababa, Algiers, Cairo, Lagos, Baghdad, Beirut) and in Latin America (Mexico City, Lima). Altogether the number of Finnish diplomatic missions abroad at the end of 1969 stood at 39. With secondary accreditations their network covered nearly a hundred countries.

As a result of this expansion, by 1969 the number of officials in the Ministry had increased to 80 and in the diplomatic service to 127. These figures do not include military attachés and other corresponding personnel but do cover press and development assistance officials as well as commercial secretaries. Here, above all, the committee report of 1964 inspired both change and expansion: the number of commercial secretaries charged with the promotion of export trade, which had been limited to between two and four positions before the war and after it was practically non-existent, began to increase rapidly and grew to 20 postings by the end of this period. To coordinate the activities of the commercial secretaries, an export promotion bureau was established in the Commercial Department.

The turnover of personnel, especially in higher posts, was rapid: nearly thirty of the veteran diplomats of the pre-war generation left the service between 1956 and 1970, most of them holding the rank of ambassador. One of them, G. A. Gripenberg, had served continuously for over forty years; he ended his career as the first Finnish ambassador to the UN. The need to fill openings on some occasions led to outside recruitment. For instance, Max Jacobson, who was later Finnish ambassador to the UN and a serious candidate for the post of Secretary-General, entered the Finnish foreign service in this way; Risto Hyvärinen, later a high official at the UN (the Secretary-General's special representative in the disarmament negotiations at Geneva); Matti Tuovinen, the secretary of state (in other words the secretary-general) of the Ministry for Foreign Affairs; and Keijo Korhonen, later Foreign Minister (in 1976–7) and under-secretary of state for political affairs.

Although these individuals were undoubtedly fully qualified, the nomination system nevertheless gave precedence to more political appointments. This generated criticism both inside and outside the foreign service. Despite attempts at reform, the pattern of recruitment remained throughout the 1960s very much the same as it had been earlier. Nominations of candidates with upper-class backgrounds did to a certain extent give way to those of candidates from the middle class (40 and 45 per cent respectively in the 1960s). However, the possibilities for candidates from farming or working-class families remained as limited as before the war. Instead, nominations of female officials, not unknown but certainly uncommon during the earlier period, now began to increase, with the result that the career service in 1969 included nine women, four of them abroad.

In order to carry on the reform of the foreign service, which was considered insufficient especially after 1966 when the Left returned to the government, a new committee was appointed in 1968 to prepare a report on this question. The committee was composed of experts and representatives not only of the Foreign Ministry but also of the main political parties under the chairmanship of Olavi Mattila, a former Minister for Foreign Trade and a future Minister for Foreign Affairs. Its report, published in 1969, gave an impetus to the deep changes that took place during the coming decade.

1970 to 1980

A new dimension in Finnish foreign policy, later termed active neutrality, became apparent in the early 1970s when *détente* was beginning to affect the rigid structures of the blocs. Its main tenet was that the lessening of tension in Europe, as well as in the whole world, was very much in the Finnish national interest and gave the country a better opportunity to safeguard its rights and to defend its independence by political means than would be the case under more hostile conditions. 'The application of our policy of neutrality changes as the world changes', President Kekkonen pronounced in 1971, and he added, 'although the bases of the policy itself remain the same.'

This approach was to underline the basic tone of the foreign policy of Finland during the following decade, not only with regard to its neighbours but also in its approach to its bilateral relations in general. This was the line of policy even *vis à vis* the United Nations, the specialized organizations as well as toward SALT, CSCE, the Nuclear Non-Proliferation Treaty Review Conference and similar initiatives for the control of mass destruction and disarmament. These activities, among them the duties of hosting the Conference on Security and Cooperation in Europe, prepared, opened and closed in Helsinki in 1972–5, were in fact a test for the Finnish foreign service. In order to pass that test, it was forced to mobilize its capacities and to renew its resources in an unprecedented way. It is indeed not exaggerating to call this decade a period of great reform and modernization.

The grip of the aged President on foreign affairs has remained as tight as ever. With the exception of two terms of rather short duration when Kalevi Sorsa, a Social Democrat, was Foreign Minister, control of the service has remained firmly in the hands of men representing the President's party. Continuity is emphasized by the fact that Matti Tuovinen, a former head of press and political affairs of the Ministry, who has served as secretary of state for most of this time, is known as a particularly trusted colleague of the President. Moreover, with Keijo Korhonen as the under-secretary of state in command of political affairs and another personal friend and former Foreign Minister, Jaakko Hallama, as ambassador in Moscow, Mr Kekkonen is considered to have his own men in the key positions.

A notable recommendation of the committee in 1974 was to establish the posts of under-secretaries of state. Each of these high officials, now numbering four, has under his supervision one sector of foreign affairs: administrative, political, foreign trade or development cooperation. Together with the secretary of state they form the directorate of the Ministry. The organization as a whole is still based on the earlier concept of concentrating related matters in the same department. Still, the political, foreign trade and development cooperation departments include units that are responsible for dealing with different areas or groups of states. In some cases this geographic division of organization is promoted by permanent coordination of matters relating to cooperation – e.g. with Nordic and Socialist states and with Western industrialized countries – and supervised by senior officials of ambassadorial level.

Since 1972 the Ministry has had a department of its own for affairs relating to international development cooperation. Besides the six departments, there are the Inspectorate-General of Diplomatic and Consular Missions (since 1974) and the Press and Cultural Affairs Centre, both directly under the supervision of the secretary of state. Whereas the former is a rather small unit the latter has grown to departmental size and consists of 10 officials and a secretarial staff of 20.

Another novelty in the organization of the Ministry, the creation, in 1971, of bureaux between the department and section levels, has among other things improved the Ministry's capacity to deal effectively with visitors, enquiries and other everyday routine. The expansion of the Ministry's administration has also offered possibilities for carrying out work based on a longer time scale. To this end, the Political Department has a special research unit of its own. The organization of bureaux has finally permitted the establishment of more than a dozen higher vacancies for officials who have served abroad as counsellor and could next expect a post as minister counsellor or as a lower-ranking ambassador. The reorganization has assisted the integration of the vacancy-filling systems of the Ministry and the diplomatic service, which were separate until 1977. Candidates serve a five-year probation period divided between home and abroad and, after securing a permanent nomination, make their way up the hierarchy circulating between posts and functions. Ambassadorial level is seldom reached before 18 to 20 years of service. The age of retirement is relatively high; officials may retire at 63 but are not obliged to leave until 67.

The diplomatic service has expanded relatively little in recent years. One of the basic observations of the reform committee of 1968 was, indeed, that for the time being Finland would need, not more missions, but missions with efficient and more numerous personnel. The normal number – two career officers per mission – was reached in 1973; now the target is three officials. This would allow a larger worldwide representation with a smaller financial effort through additional accreditation. During the last ten years the main effort in expanding the mission network has taken place outside the European continent. Since the establishment of embassies in both Berlin and Bonn in 1973, Finland now has a diplomatic mission in all the European capitals with the exception of Dublin, Reykjavik and Tirana. Altogether their number at the end of 1980 was 50 embassies, legations or permanent delegations and five consulates-general. The network of representations is completed by nearly five hundred honorary consuls all over the world.

The recent expansion of the foreign service is indeed better reflected by the increase in its personnel. The number of officials serving at the Ministry has more than doubled in ten years, reaching 258 in 1979. The number of career officials in the diplomatic service has since increased to 261. The number of other personnel is even more impressive. The non-career staff at the Ministry increased during the last ten years from 178 to 332, and in the service abroad from 240 to 323. Altogether the personnel of the Finnish foreign service is well above a thousand – without counting persons recruited abroad and not included in the above statistics.

Compared with the statistics of earlier periods, these figures reveal the fact that numerically the staff of the Ministry is now larger than the staff of the diplomatic service. Usually the opposite has been the case, even though some development might have taken place in order to increase the resources of the Ministry at the expense of the diplomatic service. The main reason for this seems to be the appearance of the development cooperation administration, which has surpassed in size all the other departments of the Ministry.

The most important reform of the past decade in the Finnish foreign service was the adoption of a new recruitment and training system. Since 1970, candidates for the foreign service have been selected (annually about 6 to 7 per cent of all the persons applying) according to an open selection process. The basic criterion of selection is nowadays much more liberal. University degrees are no longer a necessity, or at least they no longer automatically open the doors to a career. Among the languages, French has lost its hegemony. The psychological suitability of the candidate seems to be the most decisive factor of selection; even the probation time of two years is still retained primarily to give training service abroad and to provide further opportunities to test the candidate before he is finally accepted into the career se.vice. As a result of the democratization of the nomination policy, the social background of the generation of officials of the 1970s seems to be far less homogeneous than earlier, though there is unfortunately no information available to confirm this impression.

Purely political appointments have not been numerous, but nevertheless have given grounds for criticism both inside and outside the service. It is customary to claim that politicians, especially the most influential members of the usual government coalitions, the Centre (formerly Agrarian) Party and the Social Democratic Party, have had a decisive say in selecting candidates for the Foreign Ministry, at least to positions of importance. An employees' association, comprising not only officers but representatives of all categories of foreign service personnel, has been active since 1969. In spite of difficulties because of its broad representation (of both career and clerk-level personnel), the association has not been without success in promoting the interests of both groups and acting as a vanguard for modern, impartial personnel policies.

As has happened elsewhere, in Finland the Ministry for Foreign Affairs had to cede to other ministries part of the management of external relations that was earlier concentrated exclusively under its jurisdiction. For example, the Ministry of Education has carried out its own foreign relations in an active and rather independent way for nearly twenty years. A ministry for foreign trade, under consideration for some time, has not come into being; as a compromise, governments have sometimes agreed on the appointment of a Minister for Foreign Trade who has, in fact, worked as a second Minister at the Ministry for Foreign Affairs. The separation of foreign trade matters, as well as development assistance, into ministries independent of the Ministry for Foreign Affairs seems difficult for the time being. In reality, not only technical reasons but also rivalries among the coalition parties interested in manning top positions in these new administrations make this change improbable.

BIBLIOGRAPHY

No history of the Finnish foreign service has been published except a study in French and in Finnish dealing with its birth and development until the Second World War by Professor Juhani Paasivirta: *L'administration des affaires étrangères et la politique extérieure de la Finlande. Depuis le début de l'indépendence nationale en 1917 jusqu'à la guerre russofinlandaise de 1939–1940* (Annales Universitaties Turkuensis B:99, Turku 1966). There is also a Finnish edition, *Suomen ulkomaanedustus ja ulkopolitiikan hoito* (Porvoo–Helsinki 1968). Professor Paasivirta, together with Dr Juhani Mylly, has also published in Finnish a study on the background of the career officers of the Finnish foreign service until the year 1968: *Suomalaiset ja diplomaattiura (1918–1968)* (Poliittisen historian laitos Turun yliopisto, Julkaisuja C:3, Turku 1969).

Other studies and memoirs relating to the history of the Finnish foreign service and diplomacy include:

Ossian Donner, *Åtta år. Memoiranteckningen från åren 1918–1920* (Oxford 1926).

G. A. Gripenberg, *Finland and the Great Powers: Memoirs of a Diplomat* (Lincoln, Nebraska 1965).

Max Jakobson, *The Diplomacy of the Winter War* (Cambridge, Mass. (1961).

Jukka Nevakivi, *The Appeal That Was Never Made. The Allies, Scandinavia and the Finnish Winter War 1939–1940* (London 1976).

J. K. Paasikivi, *Toimintani Moskovassa ja Suomessa 1939–41* (Porvoo 1958), German: *Meine Moskauer Mission 1939–41* (Hamburg 1962).

Otto Stenroth, *Ett halvt år som Finlands första utrikesminister. Händelser och minnen* (Helsingfors 1931).

Väinö Tanner, *The Winter War* (Stanford, Calif. 1957).

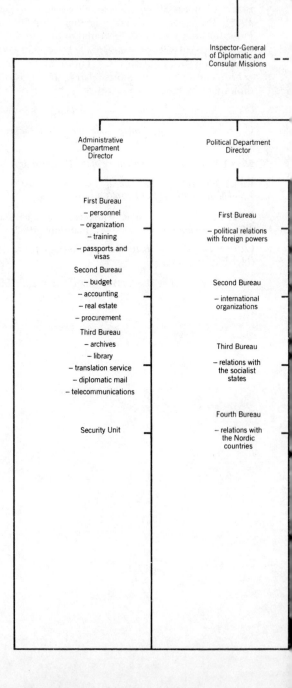

Inspector-General
of Diplomatic and
Consular Missions

Administrative
Department
Director

Political Department
Director

First Bureau
– personnel
– organization
– training
– passports and
 visas

First Bureau
– political relations
with foreign powers

Second Bureau
– budget
– accounting
– real estate
– procurement

Second Bureau
– international
organizations

Third Bureau
– archives
– library
– translation service
– diplomatic mail
– telecommunications

Third Bureau
– relations with
the socialist
states

Fourth Bureau
– relations with
the Nordic
countries

Security Unit

FINLAND – APPENDIX A

MINISTRY FOR FOREIGN AFFAIRS

(March 1981)

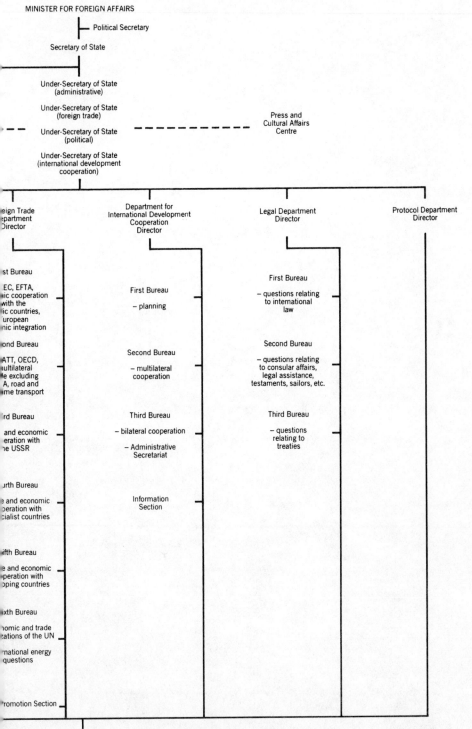

MINISTER FOR FOREIGN AFFAIRS

– Political Secretary

Secretary of State

Under-Secretary of State
(administrative)

Under-Secretary of State
(foreign trade)

Under-Secretary of State
(political)

Under-Secretary of State
(international development
cooperation)

Press and
Cultural Affairs
Centre

eign Trade
epartment
Director

Department for
International Development
Cooperation
Director

Legal Department
Director

Protocol Department
Director

st Bureau

EC, EFTA,
ic cooperation
with the
ic countries,
uropean
nic integration

ond Bureau

ATT, OECD,
ultilateral
e excluding
A, road and
me transport

rd Bureau

and economic
eration with
e USSR

urth Bureau

e and economic
peration with
cialist countries

ifth Bureau

e and economic
peration with
oping countries

ixth Bureau

omic and trade
ations of the UN

rnational energy
questions

Promotion Section

First Bureau

– planning

Second Bureau

– multilateral
cooperation

Third Bureau

– bilateral cooperation

– Administrative
Secretariat

Information
Section

First Bureau

– questions relating
to international
law

Second Bureau

– questions relating
to consular affairs,
legal assistance,
testaments, sailors, etc.

Third Bureau

– questions
relating to
treaties

Diplomatic Missions

Consular Missions

Special Missions

The Ministry of Foreign Affairs since the Nineteenth Century

GEORGES DETHAN

Georges Dethan is Chief Librarian at the French Ministry of Foreign Affairs and editor of the *Revue d'histoire diplomatique*. He has formerly served as archivist at the Quai d'Orsay. M. Dethan is the author of several books, *Gaston d'Orléans* (1959), *Mazarin et ses amis* (1968) (*The Young Mazarin*, 1977), *Mazarin, un homme de paix à l'âge baroque* (1981) and articles about seventeenth-century France, Franco-Italian connections during the time of the Risorgimento and Stendhal. As a member of various European commissions, he is closely associated with recent work in the study of international relations.

The French Ministry of Foreign Affairs was installed in the Quai d'Orsay at the beginning of the Second Empire period in 1853. It already had a long and glorious history, about which a few words must be said at the beginning of this study, which attempts to trace the evolution of the 'Department' (the name that diplomats and agents of the 'Quai' give to their administration) since the last century.

At the beginning of the sixteenth century King François I, by making it normal practice to send ambassadors to foreign courts, provided French diplomacy with a permanent means of execution. Moreover, by entrusting important negotiations to certain 'secretaries of finance', he began to build up the structure of a central administration. It was not until 1589, however, that one of the four deputies, who had become 'secretary of state' under Henry II, was given overall command of foreign affairs. Even then, Louis de Révol's appointment to the post was made only because of his personal devotion to the king. The institution of Secretary of State for Foreign Affairs, a direct adviser to the sovereign assisted by a separate service, was finally consolidated by the regulation of 11 March 1626.

During the seventeenth century, under such First Ministers as Richelieu and Mazarin, who were passionately interested in diplomacy and concerned with France's position in Europe, the office took on growing importance, even though its holders were at that time nothing more than humble servants and mouthpieces of the Cardinal-Ministers. In 1657 Hugues de Lionne, who was not yet appointed, judged it 'the best public office of the kingdom and the most important, just as it is the most confidential'. The holder of the office in fact shared the secrets of the head of government, at that time Mazarin, whose principal ambition (realized shortly before his death) was to establish general peace in Europe, based on a just and lasting agreement. These principles of equity and balance were henceforward to govern French diplomacy; as François de Callières wrote in 1716, 'the secret of negotiation is to harmonize the actual interests of the parties in question'.

The eighteenth century saw the French diplomatic set-up perfected and installed at Versailles, where it would remain until the Revolution. Under Louis XV, the office of the Secretariat of State for Foreign Affairs saw its effective force quadrupled since the time of Louis XIV; it included about twenty deputies, a consultant lawyer and several archivists, cipherers, interpreters and translators. This body of staff, subject in 1971 of a work by M. J. P. Samoyault, was recruited on recommendation, settled with a regular salary, and subject to a strict hierarchical order.

The French Revolution, under which this administration became the Ministry for Exterior Relations with a great deal of disorder (as is described in the somewhat ill-disposed book by Frédéric Masson), brought to it two important reforms. A decree in 1793 gave the Ministry authority over the consulates, formerly governed by the naval Secretary of State; and in 1795 the School of Oriental Languages was founded, destined to send competent directors to consular posts in the Middle East. This 'Division of Consulates', with the same civil servants, is called in the year 9 (1800–1) the 'Division of Commercial Relations'. For several decades this remained the only lasting measure concerning the recruitment of diplomatic agents, which during the greater part of the nineteenth century was subject to chance and to the favour of successive and often opposing regimes. Despite the praiseworthy efforts of the Comte d'Hauterive under the Restoration to establish an examination for entry into the profession, the first examination, that of 1826, was also the last. It at least permitted Lamartine to be nominated ambassadorial secretary. He was doubtless thinking of the former school when, as Minister for Foreign Affairs in the Second Republic, he had a part in the founding of the short-lived School of Administration, created in 1848.

The government under Napoleon III limited itself to a requirement that attachés in the Ministry of Foreign Affairs should hold a law degree (1853). At the Quai d'Orsay palace, specially built for the Department, where it settled in 1853 after numerous diverse lodgings since the time of the Revolution, the bureaux were divided according to a rough geographical order into two divisions, called North and South (Midi), essentially of Europe; offices were created in 1844 for America and the Far East, to be replaced in 1856 by a double subdepartment of America and Indo-China. One consulate division was concerned specifically with those commercial affairs that, along with naval business, had remained the prerogative of consular agents.

It was at this stage, after the fall of the Empire in 1870, that the Third Republic founded the Quai d'Orsay. Its natural head was the political director, placed at the head of the North and South divisions. He represented an element of stability during the time of Napoleon III, when the other ministers had been forced to conform to the politics of the Emperor, which were both personal and fluctuating. The new regime, headed by Adolphe Thiers, was so anxious not to disturb the established order of the Department that it kept the majority of the staff, above all, the political director. During the first ten years of its existence the Third Republic brought few changes to the workings of the Quai d'Orsay; and it is now appropriate for the machinery, as it functioned and was modified during the course of the last century, to be described in detail.

1870 to 1914: The Minister and the limits of his power

In the forty-four years between September 1870 and August 1914 thirty individuals became head of the Ministry of Foreign Affairs. The most notable and lasting ones were the Duc Decazes (1873–7); Freycinet, promoter of the Franco-Russian alliance, who exercised a dominating influence over exterior politics during the 1880s both at Foreign Affairs and as the Président du Conseil; Gabriel Hanotaux, who despite a brief gap between two long periods at the Quai d'Orsay remained there for nearly four years (1894–8); Delcassé, who stayed for seven years (1898–1905); and Stephen Pichon who, in several different governments between 1906 and 1913, was at Foreign Affairs for nearly five years. In fact the continuity of French foreign politics hardly suffered at all from the brevity of some terms of office.

Does this mean that during this period foreign politics only happened at the Quai d'Orsay? The constitution of 1875 recognized the prerogatives due to the President of the Republic in this matter. If we are to believe it, it is he who negotiated and ratified the treaties, according to the usage established by the first of the nouveau régime Presidents, Adolphe Thiers, even before there was a written constitution. As soon as he came to power, Thiers had gone over the head of his Minister for Foreign Affairs, Jules Favre, and had dealt directly with the foreign diplomats, giving orders to the French heads of mission. Was it this precedent that caused the stipulation in the Constitution that the President of the Republic should himself direct important negotiations, that ambassadors should be accredited to him as though to a sovereign, and that he was to appoint France's representatives abroad?

In any case, Thiers' successors did not abuse the privileges that the Constitution gave them, and even Grévy limited his own powers, not wanting the violent measures undertaken by MacMahon in May 1876 to be re-enacted. But it was this same Grévy who declared to Flourens: 'My Minister of Foreign Affairs is myself', while fifteen years later Félix Faure, in a discussion with the tsar of Russia, confided 'We have no need of intermediaries.'

The fact remains that certain Presidents of the Third Republic, such as Grévy, Félix Faure and above all Poincaré, exercised an influence of no little importance. They sometimes played a part in the election of the head of the Quai d'Orsay (Grévy chose Freycinet, for example, and Félix Faure chose Delcassé) and they intervened to play the part of mediator in case of crisis: for example, Grévy disentagled the Schnaebele incident and himself directed the instructions to the French ambassador in Berlin. Félix Faure persuaded Delcassé to give the order to evacuate Fashoda; Loubet deserted Delcassé under the German threat, which he judged to be even more dangerous as the French army was not ready. The role of the President of the Republic increased in importance when the new French alliance policy came into force, which involved official visits to St Petersburg in 1877 and 1914, to London and to Rome in April 1904; but the communications the President had with the host sovereign were not always of a political nature, and the task more often fell to the representative of the Quai d'Orsay.

This representative also had to reckon with the Président du Conseil; Foreign Ministers such as Pichon and de Selves were in fact created by the man in this post, the first by Clemenceau and the second by Joseph Caillaux (the agreement negotiated by the latter with Germany, after the Agadir coup, was done without the knowledge of the Quai d'Orsay). There were no instances of jurisdictional conflicts when the same statesmen held the post of Foreign Affairs as well as that of the Président du Conseil: this was the case with Gambetta, Freycinet, Ribot, Casimir Périer and, above all, Poincaré during the whole of 1912.

Finally, the Constitution stated that the most important agreements should be approved by Parliament. This was Parliament's opportunity to intervene in foreign politics. This rarely happened, but on two occasions occurred in a decisive manner: a protest (by the right as well as the left) against a colonial policy that seemed dangerous to them, when Freycinet was overruled on the subject of Egypt (on 29 July 1882); and Jules Ferry with regard to Tonkin (30 March 1885).

Another occasion when the deputies had a significant influence over the arrangements of the Quai d'Orsay occurred during discussions of the budget of the Department, which had long been kept at a derisory figure – between 1871 and 1915 it fluctuated between 12 and 20 million francs (of which 1 600 000 was for the staff of the central administration), but was not really raised until 1898, and then particularly in favour of French cultural and social establishments abroad (les 'oeuvres françaises'). Many representatives of the people, remembering the Second Empire, saw only excessive spending in the expenses of the French missions: they considered French diplomacy to be an institution hostile to the Republic and people with reactionaries. They did not begin loosening the nation's purse-strings until after 1880, when the Minister for Foreign Affairs was able to assure them that from now onwards the Quai, 'in order to help services dependent upon it to stay alive, would call upon a certain number of men devoted to republican opinion'.

The cabinet and the political director
During this period it was rare for the Ministers for Foreign Affairs to have a diplomatic past, and only the Duc Decazes, Stephen Pichon and Hanotaux had been part of the framework of the Quai d'Orsay before becoming its head (and even then the last named had only spent a few months abroad, as councillor in Constantinople). To tell the truth the post was not particularly coveted either by career diplomats, who were suspicious of its instability and who frequently refused it (for example, Barrère and the Cambons), or by the lawyers and journalists who made up the majority of the deputies and who knew the limited electoral interests the Minister for Foreign Affairs inspired.

The Minister was supported and advised by that master of the administration of the Quai d'Orsay, the director of political affairs, to whom he turned for the execution of French foreign policy, if not constantly for his explanations and guidance. The Minister himself chose a 'cabinet', which over the years became more and more important. Composed of five agents in 1875, the Minister's cabinet numbered around forty in 1883 when Jules Ferry was Minister, though this figure did include several technical offices that were gradually attached, enabling the Minister to be the first to be informed on various matters: correspondence, ciphers, translation, and above all personnel, which gave him a command over the nominations of diplomats, and the press, through which he could influence public opinion (the press office alone grew from seven agents in 1863 to fifteen in 1906). Protocol itself became annexed to the cabinet until 1893.

In fact, the heads of cabinet received or introduced to the Minister more Parliamentary deputies than heads of diplomatic mission. It was they who were responsible for relations with Parliament and dealt with the electoral interests of the Minister (who was himself often a deputy). This did not prevent them from occasionally encroaching on inside territory and finding themselves rivals to the political director, except when these two posts were held in conjunction (as was the case with Pierre de Margerie in 1914). Thus the Minister's cabinet was sometimes regarded with a mistrustful eye by members of the 'profession'; they were suspicious of the 'young lions' (the expression is Paul Cambon's) who were attached to it and who took advantage of their connections to leap at highly placed posts: for example, Philippe Berthelot, who entered the cabinet of his father Marcellin Berthelot in 1895, and Dutasta, a personal friend of Clemenceau. But in fact the Minister generally chose to be surrounded by competent men, and of the 34 heads of cabinet in the years 1870 to 1914, 24 were career diplomats (Crozier, Beau, Paléologue, Daeschner, Herbette, etc.).

The principal official in the Quai d'Orsay was the director of political and disputed affairs (more often called the political director), who from 1907 also took on commercial affairs (the Directorate of Consular and Commercial Affairs), which until then had been the other big department of the Ministry. He was always in the Minister's confidence, and even had a functional apartment at the Quai d'Orsay. His post was a stable one and often outlasted the falls of Ministers: between 1870 and 1914, for thirty Ministers only thirteen political directors held office, of which the first, Desprez, was the incumbent for nearly fifteen years (from 1866 to 1880). Although a former *préfet* (Decrais) and several journalists (Weiss, Charmes) are to be found among their number, the great majority were professional diplomats. We will mention those whose personal role was most important: Baron de Courcel (1880–1), who managed the Tunis affair and was principally responsible for the Treaty of Bardo; Albert Billot (1883–5), who entered the Ministry as a supernumerary in 1865, and who in less than twenty years climbed all the rungs of the administrative ladder – he was the consistently approved collaborator of Challemel-Lacour and Jules Ferry, and sometimes even the principal player in the affairs of Madagascar and especially of Indo-China; Nisard (1889–98), who organized the new subdirectorate of the Protectorates and was the favoured adviser of Ribot and Hanotaux regarding the Franco-Russian alliance; Cogordan (1902–4), who died at his desk in the post of political director after having laid the foundations for the Entente Cordiale along with Delcassé and the ambassador to London, Paul Cambon; Georges Louis (1904–9), who managed French interests in the Moroccan affair at the time of the Algeciras Conference; Maurice Paléologue (1912–13), a protégé of Poincaré, who kept a journal of his particularly active director-ship; and finally Pierre de Margerie (1914–19), who took part in the last attempts to prevent war in August 1914.

The papers of certain high-ranking functionaries have been preserved. They enable us to affirm that the political director had command (with the approval of his Minister) not only over French exterior politics but also over the entire diplomatic personnel; this is shown, for example, in the numerous letters of recommendation received by Albert Billot, his direct correspondence with the principal ambassadors, and the various notes that show his control over the different offices of the Quai d'Orsay.

Bureaux and their personnel

The bureaux of the Quai d'Orsay have always influenced foreign policy, if only because they themselves resolve the majority of secondary affairs and the way in which these matters are decided cannot fail to shape policies on a more general level. Although the Minister signs the replies to the leader of posts, these replies are prepared by his staff. As a consequence, in so far as politics are guided by routine, the bureaux of the Quai d'Orsay have, since the nineteenth century, taken a predominant role.

Apart from the Minister's cabinet and the various offices dependent upon it, there were within the two major departments of the Ministry – the Directorate of Political Affairs and the Directorate of Commercial and Consular Affairs – two further subdivisions: the North, which received and sent out all correspondence dealing with Germany, the Austro-Hungarian Empire, Great Britain, Russia and other northern countries; and the South (Midi) and East, covering the Mediterranean states (Italy, Spain, the Balkans, Turkey, etc.), Africa and Asia. A subdirectorate for America also comprised, apart from the New World (excluding the United States), certain international questions (commissions for the Pyrenees, the Danube, etc.). Finally, the subdirectorate for disputed matters dealt with questions of public and naval rights.

This was the state of the administration of the Quai d'Orsay when Billot, for example, came to it, organized according to Decazes' decree of 1 February 1877 and Freycinet's decree of 1 February 1880. The following years saw the creation of a Far Eastern sub-department in 1885, and in 1886 of a Consultative Committee for the Protectorates, for which the administration was taken from the naval and colonial ministries. A more massive reform of the Quai was initiated by Pichon's decree of 27 April 1907, prepared by a report of Philippe Berthelot: the division between political and commercial affairs was abandoned, and all this business, under one director, was henceforward redivided into four geographic subdirectorates: Europe and Africa–Oceania, the Levant, Asia, and America. Specialist services were attached to this combined directorate, such as the legal advisory service, commercial counselling, archives, the offices of communications (ciphers and secretariat) and of French Works Abroad (embryo of the future Cultural Relations Office). The two other departments, handling administrative and technical affairs and accounts, appear more like poor relations.

To run this important administrative machine in Paris the Quai d'Orsay had only eighty employees in 1870. At this time the number of officials in all the ministerial administrations totalled only 3000 (of whom 1500 were employed in the Inspectorate of Finances). In 1914 the effective force in the central administration of the Quai d'Orsay doubled in number, jumping from 80 to 170 (excluding 'service personnel', an extra 64 persons: doorkeepers, office caretakers and typists, a profession that women could join from 1912). These numbers were still modest, though the evolution was slow and subject to harsh criticism from Parliament. In 1891 the Commission of Finance found that the personnel of the Department was both too numerous and underpaid: the salaries were derisory, and the jobs were taken by young people with a personal fortune at their disposal. 'A republican administration should make this vice disappear', the Commission protested virtuously.

How, then, were the Ministry's employees recruited? Before 1877 it was common for them not to have spent any time abroad: this was the case in 1872 for two directors and five out of six subdirectors. Having entered at the lowest end of the scale, they had moved slowly up the hierarchy and passed from being supernumeraries to salaried attachés, writers *(redacteurs)* and heads of office before finally reaching the post of director. Leaving aside the political directors, such was the case for Meurand, who was director of consulates and commercial affairs from 1867 to 1880. There was no rule governing their engagement. Recommendations counted for more than diplomas, except for the law degree, which permitted the non-renumerated articled clerks to call themselves 'editorial candidates' and not simply 'copywriters'. Decazes' reform of 1 February 1877 had created a double examination system (embassies and consulates), which became one examination between July 1880 and September 1913. At this later date an 'examination for the post of consular attaché' was instituted; it was this *petit concours* that doubled with the *grand concours* or diplomatic examination for 'admission into the diplomatic and consular professions' until 1945. The new reform encouraged a gradual but steady integration of the staff of the central administration with members of the overseas services. Decazes had already brought the two staffs closer together by assimilating the subdirectors of the

Quai with consuls-general and ambassadorial secretaries, first class; office heads with consuls and ambassadorial secretaries, second class; and the paid attachés with student-consuls and ambassadorial secretaries, third class. The decree of 31 March 1882 (supported and made precise by that of 12 May 1891) took a new step forward in this integration, providing the same promotion table for all those who had taken the examination and who were from now onwards to fill all the posts of the central administration. The Minister's cabinet, on the other hand, would henceforth be made up only of persons recruited from outside the diplomatic examination, apart, of course, from such specialists as archivists, palaeographers, geographers, cipherers, accountants and other 'service personnel'.

The results were excellent. This blending of administrators within the Ministry with members of the diplomatic corps abroad permitted the Department to limit the intrusion of agents from the prefectorial administration (such as Barrère, Cambon) whom 'the profession' (la Carrière) was in fact remarkably capable of absorbing. The Quai did not then have to complain, like so many other administrations, about seeing its most important directorships entrusted to officials from other major government bodies (like the Inspectorate of Finance or the Council of State). But above all, thanks to the presence of officials within the central services and in diplomatic and consular posts who had been recruited by the same examination and were all successively called upon to fulfil the same functions, a remarkable cohesion was achieved between the central administration and the external services – the one bringing experience of foreigners and the other a greater sensitivity to French public opinion.

1914 to 1944

While the Quai d'Orsay lived through the Great War of 1914–18 at a somewhat slower pace, as some of its staff were mobilized, these years were no less profitable for the development of the Department. Indeed, it was at this time that its directorship was strengthened by the creation in 1915 of a General Secretariat. Established because of the needs of French propaganda in the neutral countries, the Maison de la Presse was the embryo of what was later to become the Press Service.

When peace was re-established, the Department drew on the lessons to be learnt from the new state of the world, and above all of Europe as it had been remodelled by the peace treaties. It was the period when multilateral diplomacy was introduced, characterized by the number and importance of international conferences and assemblies. There then developed more open relations between nations, which the Anglo-Saxons call 'open diplomacy', and from this came the growing interest given to the press and to cultural activities.

Ministers, President and the secretary-general

Diplomacy, that guarantor of peace, was so young that from 1915 to 1933 the post of Minister for Foreign Affairs was for the most part held by the Prime Minister (Président du Conseil). This was true of Aristide Briand and Raymond Poincaré, as it would be in 1932 of Pierre Laval, André Tardieu and Edouard Herriot, and from 1939–40 for Edouard Daladier; but was no longer the case for Joseph Paul-Boncour in 1933, Louis Barthou in 1934,

Pierre Laval in 1935, or Yvon Delbos or Georges Bonnet from 1936 to 1939. For twenty years, fourteen Ministers for Foreign Affairs (in forty-one governments) held often differing or unsteady political views. The historian, J. B. Duroselle, has recently shown (in *La décadence*, 1979) to what extent the diplomacy of the time was affected by ministerial instability and hesitancy, even sometimes a changing of sides, with fatal consequences for French diplomacy.

The part played by the President of the Republic in foreign politics was gradually reduced until, at the time of Albert Lebrun (1932–40), it was limited to a merely representative role. (An exception must be made for Alexandre Millerand, who in 1923 gave Poincaré the idea of the occupation of the Ruhr, after having brought about his fall by recalling Briand.)

Although the deputies were not interested in foreign politics (except when they had Briand, a prestigious orator, as their spokesman), the Commission for Foreign Affairs of the Chamber was often more exacting, especially when Poincaré was presiding. It was the Commission again, in October 1938, that wanted to examine the text of the Munich agreements, when it was a little late to contest them as they had already been sanctioned by the Chamber.

The office of Secretary of State developed after 1914; the first in the Ministry of Foreign Affairs was Abel Ferry in 1914–15. Among those Secretaries of State (called under-secretaries of state until 1940 and much less numerous – there were only ten – in the period up to 1940 than thereafter) closest to the Minister should be mentioned Pierre Viénot who, in 1936–7, tried to settle the question of French mandates in the Levant.

The Minister, who was frequently absent on official journeys abroad or in his electoral constituency, had to be able to count on a large and efficient cabinet. During this period the head, who in 1934 became the director of the cabinet, was for the most part an agent of the Department. One such head was Alexis Léger, head of Briand's cabinet from 1925 to 1932, who for some time combined this office with that of director of political and commercial affairs. In addition, the Information and Press Service and the Telegrams Office were directly dependent on the cabinet. One imagines that under these conditions Léger's influence might well have overshadowed that of the secretary-general himself, Philippe Berthelot, who had, moreover, preceded him to the headship of the cabinet.

The prestigious office of secretary-general had been created in October 1915 for Jules Cambon, who had been entrusted with the permanent and general assignment of the signature of the Minister (who was Briand at that time). His prerogatives, when they passed to Maurice Paléologue in January 1920, were defined as follows: 'The secretary-general exercises, under the authority of and in the name of the Minister, the top superintendence of all the services of the Ministry.'

After Paléologue, the post was occupied by Philippe Berthelot from September 1920 to February 1933 except during the period from January 1922 to April 1925, when it remained vacant as Berthelot had been disgraced by Poincaré. The post thus became the sole domain of this brilliant man, who had inspired the reform of the Department from as long ago as 1907 and was the creator of the Maison de la Presse and a favourite of Aristide Briand. After Berthelot's death it fell to Alexis Léger (whose literary name was Saint-John-Perse), who held office until May 1940. Léger, less closely linked to his successive Ministers than Berthelot had been to Briand, divided his collaborators (there were four or five) among three sections, charged respectively with liaison with the Chamber, with the personal secretariat and with the secretariat for political dispatches. The respective power of the head of Cabinet, the political director and the secretary-general, when these posts are held by different men, depends very much on their personal influence with the Minister.

The central administration and exterior posts

The reform of April 1907 was confirmed by the decree of 23 July 1918, which, because of the many earlier innovations, was restricted to the transfer of Oceania from the subdirectorate of Europe to that of Asia, and with giving Africa a subdirectorate of its own (regrouped with the Levant in 1925).

Before long, however, new needs were to bring about the formation of new organisms. Some were born of stipulations in the peace treaties: the Office for Private Goods and Interests, which was charged with dealing with questions relating to French property in former enemy countries; the Service for Reparations and the Ruhr, which lasted from 1923 to 1927; above all, the French Service of the League of Nations, founded in 1919 and directed by René Massigli from 1928 to 1935, when it embraced the General Secretariat for the Conference of Ambassadors, another post-war creation.

Other innovations answering recent needs were the Service of Press and Information (headed for a time by the writer-diplomat Jean Giraudoux), established in 1920 with about twenty agents. The Service of French Works Abroad dates from January 1920; it was charged with 'French intellectual expansion outside the country' and had no more than ten agents working for it. In England it served as a model for the British Council (only created in 1934), and redoubled its activity after Jean Marx came to direct it in 1933.

It should finally be noted that the Legal Consultancy Office became a real service in the Department, and the re-establishment of relations with the Papacy gave rise in 1926 to the founding at the Quai d'Orsay of a post of councillor for religious affairs, to which Louis Canet was appointed.

The number of agents functioning abroad in 1939 was 585. This had not changed for twenty years, nor had the number of posts; on the eve of the Second World War there were 16 embassies, 38 legations, 28 consulate-generals, 123 consulates and 574 consular agencies. In contrast to this, the number of specialized attachés had grown. So had the military attachés, whose status, until then based on instructions dating from 1899 and 1903, was fixed by a decree in 1936; there were then about 50 of them, spread over 42 countries. Besides these there were four financial attachés, charged with certain important posts (in London, New York, Berlin and Rome) for the management of French Treasury funds abroad and the reimbursement of war debts; in these posts the names of Jacques Rueff in London and Emmanuel Monick in New York were particularly illustrious.

The main novelty was the post of commercial attaché, established with the law of 25 August 1919. The law clearly specified that their activity should take place 'under the control of the head of the diplomatic mission', but the destination of their reports was the Ministry of Commerce, which was also responsible for choosing them. Nominated for five years they were, according to the terms of the law that created them, 'agents abroad working for the expansion of French commerce'. It was not until after the Second World War, however, that a body of professional commercial attachés was formed. They had taken over a considerable part of the consuls' power (though the consuls could still be useful informants), and though both consuls and even heads of diplomatic missions often found this invasion of the technical into the political domain excessive, the practice continued to develop to an even greater extent over the years.

The ordeal of the Second World War
The long parenthesis of the Second World War had so many consequences that a few words must be said about those four years, which after the military defeat of May 1940 saw France occupied by the enemy and divided between two governments: one based in Paris under the control of Marshal Pétain and dependent on the Germans, and the other directed from London and then from Algiers by General de Gaulle, trying to maintain contact between the territories of the French empire. Each had its own diplomatic procedure and attempted to pursue an independent foreign policy.

Once the 'ministère-croupion' was installed at Vichy, at the Hotel du Parc, he was unable to take the departmental archives, which had remained in the Quai d'Orsay or had been evacuated to Touraine. This gave him almost as much difficulty as the problems of communicating with posts abroad (in order to reach Washington, for example, it was necessary to go via Madrid or Geneva). His first appointed Minister, Paul Baudouin, elected on 17 June 1940 by the new head of the French state, only remained in the post for four months. He was replaced by Ministers who gradually became more and more resigned or disposed to collaboration with Germany: the first two, Pierre Etienne Flandin and Admiral Darlan, attempted to limit collaboration by leaning on Great Britain and the United States respectively, while the last, Pierre Laval, let himself be drawn into collaboration almost without restriction. It is true that numbers of their diplomatic colleagues refused to follow them and tried to temper their excesses; some, grouped around Jean Chauvel and Jean Fouques-Duparc and devoted to the Resistance, even used the diplomatic bag to send clandestine messages.

As the war developed and the Occupation weighed more and more heavily on France, diplomatic correspondents at Vichy became increasingly scarce, as did speakers at the government headquarters of the 'French state' (32 powers represented in July 1940, only 22 in June 1944). The resignations by agents multiplied, especially after the occupation of the so-called 'free' French zone in November 1942. Moreover, the Vichy government had itself struck off those diplomats of whom it disapproved, and to replace them, Pierre Laval chose politicians sympathetic to collaboration with the Germans or military men (especially admirals). Representatives of the Vichy government were kept at Moscow (until June 1941), Washington (until the end of 1942), and still at Tokyo, Nanking, Ankara, Ottawa, Pretoria, Dublin, Madrid, Rome, the Vatican and Bern; this permitted them to keep a foot in the other camp, which often worried the Germans, who always suspected the Vichy representatives of Gaullist sympathies.

Meanwhile, General de Gaulle had established in London (on 26 September 1941) the French National Committee (Comité National Français), for which the Commissioners for Foreign Affairs were successively Maurice Dejean,

René Pléven and René Massigli. The Committee took over the tasks of the Ministry of Foreign Affairs in countries where the Vichy government was unable to operate, and after obtaining immediate recognition by Great Britain and the USSR also received it from the United States in 1942.

The first Commissioner, Maurice Dejean, collected a total of half a dozen career agents in order to set up a central administration, to direct the delegations of Free France, support the actions of the 500 committees spread around the world, participate in the Inter-Allied Commission in London, save French establishments (lycées, hospitals, etc.) abroad, protect French people living outside France, and so on. Such work demanded a great deal of improvisation and the assistance of new energies to be found outside the diplomatic profession; but it was not until its installation in Algiers in June 1943 that the Free French government was able to take the necessary recruitment measures.

On that date even those countries that, like Spain and Portugal, had kept up relations with the Vichy government opened up more or less official communications with the French National Liberation Committee. All the powers at war on the side of the Allies were represented at Algiers, where the personnel of the various commissariats of Fighting France flocked in great numbers. Mixed in with the rare career diplomats, they brought new blood to the profession and are the origins of the 'lateral staff' (recognized by decree on 26 April 1944), later called the 'complementary staff': between August 1944 and November 1945 almost 200 people were integrated into the Department in this way.

It was thus a renewed team that René Massigli sent to Georges Bidault, first Minister for Foreign Affairs of liberated France after the liberation of Paris on 10 September 1944. It had been formed by the trials of the motherland even more than by the 'spirit of the house'; and it was ready to face the crippling task that, in an overturned world and in a France that had to be rebuilt, awaited the Quai d'Orsay.

1945 to 1980: The organs of management

From September 1944 to September 1980, in the course of thirty-six years, the number of Ministers for Foreign Affairs (excepting four whose command lasted hardly a month and who rather held interim power) can be established as twelve, which gives the remarkable average of three years each. The most durable was Maurice Couve de Murville, who stayed for ten years as the head of the Quai d'Orsay (1958–68); but even in the Fourth Republic the duration of office of Georges Bidault and Robert Schumann, who alternated between 1944 and 1954, was fairly exceptional. The last years of the Fourth Republic (1954–8) certainly constituted a less stable period, and saw, in rapid succession, Pierre Mendès-France, Edgar Faure, Antoine Pinay and Christian Pineau (the latter managed to stay more than two years at the Quai). After the long proconsulate of M. Couve de Murville, there were six ministers in 12 years: more precisely, setting aside the politicians – Michel Debré (1968–9) and Maurice Schumann (June 1969–March 1973) – there have been four top officials of the Quai or the Elysée: Jobert (1973–4), Sauvagnargues (1974–6), de Guiringaud (1976–8), and Jean François-Poncet since November 1978.

Since the beginning of the Fifth Republic and the 1958 Constitution, which strengthened the powers of the head of state, 'guarantor of national independence, or territorial integrity, and of respect for the agreements of the Community and treaties' (art. 5), the direct influence of the President of the Republic on foreign politics has considerably increased, up to the point of becoming, it has been said, his 'personal domain', whether this is applied to General de Gaulle or to his successors, Georges Pompidou and Valéry Giscard d'Estaing. In the field of diplomacy the secretaries-general of the Elysée have at times rivalled in influence those of the Quai d'Orsay when, for example, they were Michel Jobert or Jean François-Poncet and were themselves destined soon to become Ministers for Foreign Affairs. But even during the Fourth Republic, President Vincent Auriol was, as his *Journal du Septennat* reveals, becoming most anxious to have his say in foreign matters, and was somewhat concerned to see the politics of Robert Schumann 'laying France open to Germany' (June 1952).

If it can be argued that politics does not seem to have greatly influenced the choice of Minister, that influence does appear in the election of the Secretaries of State – of whom there were 24 in 36 years (or rather in 28 years, for there were none in the first years of the Fourth or Fifth Republics). These posts have served as trial positions for statesmen who have later acquired ministerial responsibilities, generally outside the Quai d'Orsay (except for Maurice Schumann and Jean François-Poncet, Secretaries of State in the Department before becoming Ministers there). They were often charged with following up certain important matters: Franco-Algerian relations, the European Community, French cooperation with the Third World (which was eventually entrusted to a new Ministry of cooperation). They are not appointed by the Minister for Foreign Affairs but by the president of the appropriate council at the time of the formation of the ministerial cabinet.

The directors of the cabinet were career diplomats (sometimes, as in the time of Robert Schuman and Maurice Schumann, they were inspectors of finance), which did not prejudice the development of their career: thus, M. de Beaumarchais became political director, M. Soutou and M. Bruno de Leusse, secretaries-general and M. Jean-Bernard Raimond, director-general of cultural relations.

In these same 36 years the Department has known only ten secretaries-general who have remained true heads of administration for Foreign Affairs. Some of these, like Jean Chauvel (1945–9) or Hervé Alphand (1965–73) have left memoirs of their years as head of the Department that give some idea of the importance and diversity of their functions as well as of the limits of their personal influence. M. Alphand was formerly director-general of economic affairs; Louis Joxe, who preceded him (from 1956 to 1959) – before Eric de Carbonnel – at the General Secretariat, had previously been the first director-general of cultural relations. Since 1945, no political director has become secretary-general, though one of them, M. Couve de Murville, was to become Minister, a post he held for ten years.

The offices and their reform

It was to the Political Directorate, the most prestigious of the divisions in the Department, that the big geographic subdirectorates were until recently attached; and the titular head often appeared as the most influential official of the Quai d'Orsay after the secretary-general, or even alongside him. This domination was not to last.

Its preponderance had already been diminished by the creation in 1945 of a Directorate-General of Economic, Financial and Technical Affairs, which soon had a counterpart, in the field of propaganda and French intellectual and artistic influence abroad, in the Directorate-General of Cultural Affairs (which included scientific and technical affairs when it became responsible in 1957 for assistance to developing countries). After the liberation, the Quai d'Orsay decided to take a resolute step towards the methodical or functional division of the offices, favouring in this way the specialization of both tasks and agents.

The inconvenience arising from this functional division soon became apparent. As early as 1954, a diplomat who had reached the end of his career, Amedée Outrey, denounced 'the claim to reduce all political questions to technical questions'. According to him, 'the special abilities needed to regulate matters where the right solution is more or less obvious do not qualify one to make the right decision when a choice has to be made between two unsatisfactory solutions. In such a case, knowledge and theoretical experience is no longer sufficient for the agent responsible; he has to weigh and appreciate, attempt to forecast and often lay bets. It is this choice, this bet, this risk, that makes up the political act.' Above all, a theoretical organization like this, wrote Jacques Chazelle in 1962, 'compromises the unity of politics with regard to a given country or region'; it is unnatural to dissociate the economic or cultural factors from those regarded as truly political in order to establish policy and to put it into practice.

Such arguments led the Quai to a radical reform, the 'geographization' of the Department, in a manner that was more experimental than theoretical. No text has at present sanctioned the changes, which have nevertheless proved to be effective ones. This reform has been introduced gradually. First, from July 1976 it was tried out on the old Asian subdirectorate. It was then extended two years later to the whole of the Quai d'Orsay, though the changes that it introduced into the structure of the Ministry do not appear in the *Diplomatic Annual* until 1978.

One can summarize them as follows. The geographic subdirectorates, which until then (apart from African and Madagascan affairs) depended on the Political Directorate have become autonomous directorates (Europe, Asia–Oceania, North Africa and the Middle East, America) responsible for all questions, political or economic, of a bilateral nature between France and those countries or groups of countries of which they are in charge. The old Directorates of Economic Affairs and of Political Affairs (plus Atomic Affairs, which formerly fell under Cultural and Technical Relations) are qualified to deal with multinational questions, international organizations, the common problems of French-speaking people throughout the world, the 'European-Arab dialogue', strategic and atomic affairs for the Political Directorate, economic cooperation and commercial relations for the Economic Directorate.

In certain cases, the division remains a delicate one. Thus, the new European Directorate deals with everything concerning the European Community, though the political director, not its own director, represents the Quai d'Orsay at the (political) EEC Commission. On the other hand, the heads of the Political and Economic Directorates are kept up to date with bilateral affairs by the responsible geographic departments. The Directorate-General of Cultural Relations, which should also be undergoing reform, seems to be adapting itself more slowly to this new course and has no representatives in the new geographic directorate.

The present basic structure of the Department includes, besides the large administrative and geographic directorates, some specialized services. The Service for the French Abroad (previously called Administrative Conventions and Consulate Affairs) attends both to the French colonies scattered around the world and to foreigners resident in France; it is autonomous, like the Directorate of Judicial Affairs and the Service of Protocol, of Information and the Press, and of Archives and Documentation; like them, it depends only upon the secretary-general and the Minister. This is also the case for the important Directorate of Personnel and General Administration, which is in charge of the practical organization (financial, real estate, social) of the Ministry and above all of recruitment, of promotion and of the interests of those staffing it, from the lowest levels of the hierarchy to the summits of the profession.

The personnel and their new tasks

It is of these people we must speak in conclusion, for it is upon them, the 'agents of the Department', that the future of the Quai d'Orsay depends, the success or the failure of its attempt to adapt to the needs of today's world. In the last thirty or forty years the profession has evolved and changed more than it was able to do during the whole of the last century. Since 1945, in fact, it has had to bend to the consequences of the Second World War and of decolonization, just as much as to the reorganization of the French administration and to contemporary social transformations.

Its tasks have multiplied and diversified. There is no longer any activity of a nation that is not of interest to its agents posted abroad. Certainly, they are assisted by technicians of all kinds, not only councillors, military attachés, commercial agents and traditional financiers, but also by cultural, scientific and agricultural specialists, experts in social affairs, in the press, transport, the merchant navy and even atomic questions. Nevertheless, these technical advisers, while becoming more and more numerous in the major posts (France has about fifty such specialists in the United States, divided between the embassy in Washington and the principal consulates) do not exist in all the secondary posts. The diplomatic and consular agents must, however, omit nothing in their efforts to ensure the development of good relations between their own country and that to which they are accredited. These tasks can be of very different kinds according to whether they are carried out in another industrialized nation or in a developing nation, in which the truly political action of the embassy has but a small place compared to the economic, technical and cultural assistance dispensed by developmental personnel who are far more numerous than the diplomats, and whose efforts penetrate much more deeply into the heart of the country. In fact, in the socialist republics, such as the East European countries, the possibilities of political action on the part of French representatives are few, if not non-existent, and they are compelled to confine themselves to information work and a few economic or cultural exchanges, which have been in constant development for the last decade. The diplomat's mission at international organizations and commissions is also very different, for here the qualities of an orator and negotiator are required; and in specialized institutions such as those of education, science and culture (UNESCO), of food, agriculture, health and work, the business is so specific that it eclipses the political aspect.

A few statistics will give a more precise idea of the new needs facing the personnel of the foreign affairs administration. In 1978 the Ministry employed four times as many agents as it had done thirty years before in Paris and all round the world: a total of 6637 agents (of whom rather more than 2000 were based in the central administration), compared with a total of 1548 in 1948. During the same period the number of diplomatic representatives rose from 65 to 149, and that of posts abroad from 213 to 317. It was above all the proliferation of new business that caused the hundred thousand telegrams received at the Quai or sent out by the Department in 1948 to have multiplied by fourteen by 1978; and the same applies to the twenty international conferences in 1948, which had become 290 by 1978. During the same period, the number of French residing abroad rose from 500 000 to 1 300 000; while the considerable growth of business travel and tourism has seen more and more people having recourse to their country's representatives abroad, and their numbers increase every year, which puts a considerable extra load on the work of the French missions, particularly at the consulates.

The multiple and diverse nature of diplomacy today is matched by the variety of backgrounds from which the staff are recruited. The profession could at one time have been considered a kind of caste (see the novel by Abel Hermant, *La Carrière*, dated 1904), an aristocracy that was permitted to elect its own members by certain practices in the *grand concours*, as for example the 'probationary stage'. There have been in France, both before and since the Revolution, dynasties of diplomats, but they have rarely gone through more than two generations, (e.g. Sainte-Aulaire, Bourée, Chodron de Courcel, Lefebvre d'Ormesson, Jacquin de Margerie, Seydoux). There have also been cases of brothers following parallel diplomatic careers, Gerard de Rayneval (Conrad and Joseph) at the end of the eighteenth century, Latour-Maubourg (Florimond and Septime) and the Cambon brothers (Jules and Paul) in the nineteenth century, d'Ormesson (André and Wladimir) and Seydoux (François and Roger) in the twentieth century. It should be pointed out that this hereditary or family attachment was not just the prerogative of the aristocracy and upper bourgeoisie (often Protestant). Such dynasties also existed in the nineteenth century in the most modest ranks of the central administration and in the consulates, above all in the posts of the Orient (for example the Outreys, a family of interpreters, at least originally).

The older system has been left behind. The end of recruitment by recommendation and the growing difficulty of the examination has almost put an end to this phenomenon, even if the diplomatic career still attracts the sons of families in which relatives and ancestors have been or are in 'the career'. Since 1945 the diplomatic corps has been upset by successive integrations. The 'lateral staff', for example, whose agents had begun their service in London or Algiers or had been engaged after their exploits in the Resistance, in 1950 made up a good third of the senior staff in the Quai d'Orsay. After the period of decolonization (1955–64) many officials from the old Ministry of France beyond the Seas or from the civil control of Morocco and Tunisia, deprived of their old jobs, steamed into the Quai (there were over 300 of them), and enabled the Department to overcome its personnel difficulties. Traditional recruitment to the various parts of the Ministry was reformed after the liberation as part of the general reform of the public administration. The traditional diplomatic and consular examinations were last held in 1945, being replaced by interministerial training entrusted to the newly established National School of Administration (Ecole National d'Administration, ENA). For several years the ENA admitted recruits specifically for the Ministry of Foreign Affairs, but in 1958 this arrangement was ended and the destination of future diplomats was decided only at the end of their training period.

It was in 1947 that the first ENA pupils, or *enarques* as they are known, entered the Quai d'Orsay. There were eleven of them, but recruitment was less numerous in the following years. Their training was different from that of their predecessors; they were given a wider range of knowledge through theoretical as well as practical courses in administration or business, which helped to make them worthy successors to their elders, men of action conscious of the needs of a new world. The need remained, however, for some specialized top-level agents, particularly those with knowledge of foreign languages. The recruitment of secretary-interpreters for the East and the Far East was retained, and the examination now provides about eight agents a year for the Department. In order to provide the diplomats with properly qualified assistants several categories of 'agents supérieurs' have been created (for which candidates sit a series of examinations graded in difficulty): secretaries and assistant administrative secretaries, administrative attachés, chancellors, chancery secretaries, administrative secretaries and agents.

The ENA and other approaches have opened the career service to young men of relatively modest backgrounds (well-off peasants and lower middle class), though few from the working classes are tempted to apply.

The rise in the number of agents in the Department has forced the Quai d'Orsay to break out from its original premises. It now has several annexed headquarters in Paris, of which the principal one is the old Majestic hotel on the Avenue Kléber, taken over by the Department after its occupation by the Germans from 1940 to 1944: and even an office in the provinces in Nantes where the 'services de l'Etat Civil' have now taken refuge. The transformation of a body of the 'happy few', often proceeding at a fairly slow pace, to an army of labouring and often anonymous ants cannot be effected without creating certain changes of spirit. The trade becomes somewhat vulgarized, especially in the embassies; contacts at the highest level between heads of state, as well as the proliferation of specialized attachés, has markedly diminished the importance of the ambassadorial role. On the other hand, the difficulties, and even the dangers, of life abroad become greater. The wives of diplomats are obliged to support their husbands in their heavy worldly duties; there are frequent changes of domicile (an average of three years in any one post): there is no true recompense for the expenses of representation, which are only awarded to the head of mission; diplomats' children have considerable difficulties pursuing their studies in foreign countries; there are the rigours of strange climates, the possible lack of comfort during a stay in some developing countries or those that are uncaring or even frankly hostile; and the practice of taking hostages, which has grown increasingly common in the diplomatic service . . . all these reasons mean that more and more diplomats are asking to serve in the central administration rather than in postings overseas. Living at the ends of the world has lost its charm now that journeys to even the most distant countries come within the range of everybody.

The old tendency of most agents to prefer an establishment abroad has perhaps begun to be reversed. But diplomats would be wrong in thinking that they can better influence the course of events from the Quai d'Orsay than from posts where they are merely transmitting agents of Parisian decisions. They know that only their presence and activity on the spot can impose a living image of France abroad, and they understand, by serving in both one and the other, that their functions in the embassies and consulates or in the central administration are essentially complementary.

September 1980

BIBLIOGRAPHY

J. Baillou and P. Pelletier, *Les Affaires Etrangères* (Paris 1962).

A. Baschet, *Histoire du dépôt des Archives des Affaires Etrangères* (Paris 1874).

F. de Callières, *De la manière de négocier avec les souverains* (Paris 1716).

J. Chazelle, *La diplomatie* (Paris 1962).

F. Masson, *Le Département des Affaires Etrangères pendant la Révolution 1787–1804* (Paris 1877).

C. Piccioni, *Les premiers commis des Affaires Etrangères au XVII° et au XVIII° siècles (Paris 1928).*

A. Outrey, *L'administration française des Affaires Etrangères* (extract from the *Revue française de science politique*, 1954).

J. P. Samoyault, *Les bureaux du Secrétariat d'Etat des Affaires Etrangères sous Louis XV* (Paris 1971).

F. Seydoux de Clausonne, *Le métier de diplomate* (Paris 1980).

A 'History of the French Administration of Foreign Affairs' is in preparation under the direction of M. Jean Baillou, and will be the work of a team of diplomats, historians and archivists. The author has been able to consult material already prepared and to make use of it for the present study.

For the more recent period, the following works may be consulted:

H. Alphand, *L'étonnement d'être. Journal 1939–1973* (Paris 1977).

V. Auriol, *Journal du septennat* (in course of publication; Paris, 6 vols since 1970).

J. Chauvel, *Commentaire*, 3 vols (Paris 1971–3).

R. Couve de Murville, *Une politique étrangère 1958–1968* (Paris 1971).

J. Dumaine, *Quai d'Orsay* (Paris 1955).

C. de Gaulle, *Mémoires d'espoir* (Paris 1970).

In addition, there are numerous works published by ambassadors since the last century, of which the most famous is undoubtedly André François-Poncet's *Souvenirs d'une ambassade à Berlin, 1931–1938* (Paris 1946), and the most moving the work by Albert Chambon, *Ce que l'homme a cru voir. De New York à Hanoi* (Paris 1969).

FRANCE – APPENDIX A

MINISTRY OF FOREIGN AFFAIRS
(May 1980)

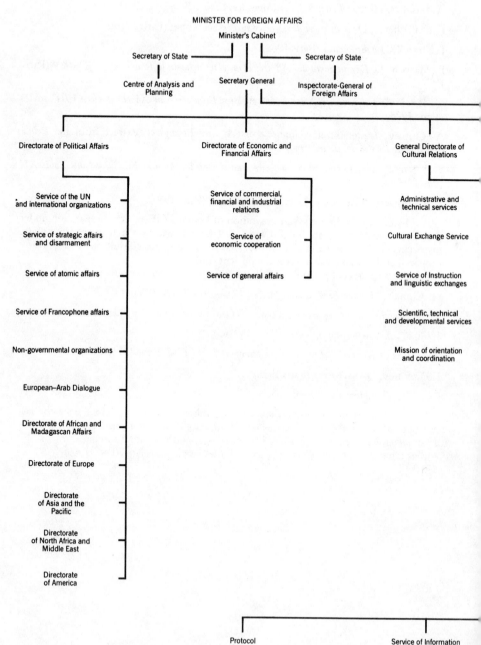

MINISTER FOR FOREIGN AFFAIRS

Minister's Cabinet

Secretary of State

Secretary of State

Centre of Analysis and Planning

Secretary General

Inspectorate-General of Foreign Affairs

Directorate of Political Affairs

Directorate of Economic and Financial Affairs

General Directorate of Cultural Relations

Service of the UN and international organizations

Service of commercial, financial and industrial relations

Administrative and technical services

Service of strategic affairs and disarmament

Service of economic cooperation

Cultural Exchange Service

Service of atomic affairs

Service of general affairs

Service of Instruction and linguistic exchanges

Service of Francophone affairs

Scientific, technical and developmental services

Non-governmental organizations

Mission of orientation and coordination

European–Arab Dialogue

Directorate of African and Madagascan Affairs

Directorate of Europe

Directorate of Asia and the Pacific

Directorate of North Africa and Middle East

Directorate of America

Protocol Service

Service of Information and the Press

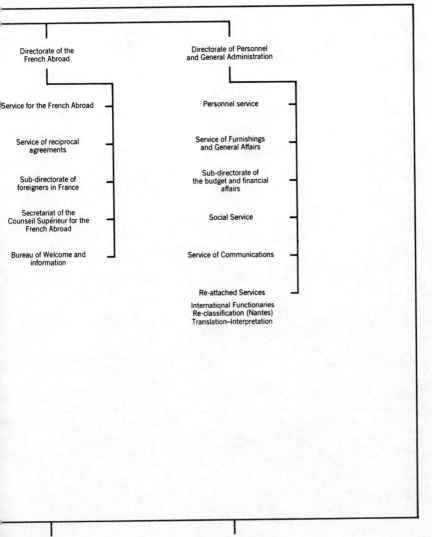

Directorate of the
French Abroad

Directorate of Personnel
and General Administration

Service for the French Abroad

Personnel service

Service of reciprocal
agreements

Service of Furnishings
and General Affairs

Sub-directorate of
foreigners in France

Sub-directorate of
the budget and financial
affairs

Secretariat of the
Counseil Supérieur for the
French Abroad

Social Service

Bureau of Welcome and
information

Service of Communications

Re-attached Services

International Functionaries
Re-classification (Nantes)
Translation–Interpretation

Directorate of
Judicial Affairs

Services of Archives
and Documentation

The History of the
German Foreign Office

KURT DOß

Dr Kurt Doß has published two important books, *Das deutsche
Auswärtiges Amt im Übergang vom Kaiserreich zur Weimarer Republik*
(1977) and *Reichsminister Adolf Köster 1883–1930 – Ein Leben für die
Weimarer Republik* (1978) as well as numerous articles in scholarly
journals Dr Doß was born in Hamburg in 1907, studied at
Tübingen, Berlin and Königsberg. From 1931 to 1972, he worked in
the field of higher education, including posts as head of history in a
teachers' training college, as director of a UNESCO model school
and as school inspector. He also served for some years at the
Pädagogische Hochschule in Hanover.

The history of the German Foreign Office is one year longer than that of the German Empire, established in 1871. The origin and development of this highest office of foreign affairs reflects the complex and sinuous way the German Empire was founded.

With the creation of the North German Federation (Norddeutscher Bund) a new state was established in northern and central Germany under Prussian leadership, in which the national and liberal forces were to be checked by the étatist interests of the individual states. As opposed to the Reichstag, which was constituted in an almost revolutionary manner based on a universal, direct and secret ballot of the citizenry, the Bundesrat, 'in accordance with tradition', represented the individual states. In the Bundesrat, Prussia presided. As the German Empire was still incomplete, the King of Prussia had to be content with a neutral title. His competence was circumscribed as 'President of the Norddeutscher Bund'. Among other things, he had the right to 'represent the Federation in international affairs, to declare war in the name of the Federation and to make peace, to enter into alliances and other treaties with foreign states, to accredit and to receive ambassadors' (Article 11).

Bismarck had wanted through the creation of the Norddeutscher Bund to avoid giving the impression that the sovereignty of individual states was impaired. This prudence was necessary, as the south German states of Bavaria, Baden and Württemberg still had to be won. On the other hand, the new Constitution gave Bismarck a free hand to conduct foreign affairs, which were initiated by him as Chancellor (Bundeskanzler) appointed by the Präsidium.

The Prussian Prime Minister and Foreign Minister, Otto von Bismarck, was appointed Chancellor of the Norddeutscher Bund on 7 July 1867 by decree of the Prussian State Ministry. First of all, the Chancellor's office was the only central office to handle the internal and external affairs of the Federation. Prussia, as a European power, already had a fully developed diplomatic apparatus at home and abroad, but the Norddeutscher Bund was responsible for foreign affairs; this created a dual system, which made it seem obvious that the Prussian Foreign Office should become the central institution of the Federation. The Reichstag voted for this and demanded the creation of other federal ministries for the other federal tasks.

Bismarck was in a difficult position. On the one hand, he recognized that he could not fulfil the external political needs of the Federation without the experienced apparatus of the Prussian Foreign Ministry; on the other hand, he wanted to avoid creating a number of federal ministries between the Bundesrat and the Bundespräsidium. These would not only jeopardize the federal structure of the state by too great a tendency towards centralization, but the ministries could be forced to accept 'ministerial responsibility' towards the parliament.

In the long run, Bismarck was not willing to add departments to the Chancellor's Office, thus creating a large governmental apparatus. The first and very delicate task in the field of foreign affairs, made necessary by the Constitution, was the subordination of the consulates to the direct administration of the Federation. This was done through the Chancellor's Office, not by the Prussian Foreign Ministry, in order to spare possible anti-Prussian feelings. The dissolution of the consulates of the individual states led to some discord, especially in the Hanseatic towns, which already had a widespread and well-functioning system of consulates all over the world. The day (31 March 1868) on which the flags of Hamburg and Bremen were hauled down on commercial ships, the black, white and red flag of the Norddeutscher Bund put up, and the Hanseatic consulates lost their emblems, was regarded as a black day, despite the patriotic feelings towards the Reich in these towns.

A great part of the work of the second (non-political) department of the Prussian Foreign Ministry had been delegated to the Chancellor's Office in order to carry out this reorganization. Three higher officials of the Prussian Foreign Ministry were assigned to the Chancellor's Office. In order to emphasize the federal character of these tasks, a Saxon official from the foreign department joined them. It is interesting to note that this solution did not last long. After the foundation of the Foreign Office (Auswärtiges Amt) these departments were reintegrated into the old diplomatic offices.

Bismarck's skilful tactics succeeded in that the whole Prussian Foreign Ministry was taken over as the supreme federal office and as a part of the state; but it did not gain the status of a ministry, as the majority of the North German Reichstag had wanted, but was merged into the Bund. In his report to the King on 4 January 1870, Bismarck emphasized that this office was subordinate to the Chancellor, and that the head of this office was to bear the title of a state secretary (Staatssekretär), as he permanently represented the Chancellor. Bismarck's proposals were accepted by the King. With the order in cabinet, signed by King William I on 4 January 1870, the Prussian Ministry for Foreign Affairs was given the official title of Foreign Office of the North German Federation (Auswärtiges Amt des Norddeutschen Bundes).

With the foundation of the German Reich in 1871 the name 'Auswärtiges Amt' was transferred to the new Empire simply by omitting the words 'of the North German Federation', and it has kept this name throughout all the changes in Germany until now. What at first sight looked like a degradation of an independent ministry to an office dependent on the Chancellor – and this was Bismarck's intention – became, during the imperial period, a sign of quality. Among the other imperial offices created after the foundation of the Reich, all of which were substitutes for 'imperial ministries', the supremacy of the Foreign Office remained uncontested. The assertiveness of the members of the higher offices – especially of the members of the German diplomatic corps and of the 'councillors' in the central office – in the decisive Department (Abteilung) I, could only be compared to that of the officers of the Prussian guards' regiments. The homogeneity of the German diplomatic corps in imperial Germany was safeguarded through the principle that its members invariably came from the 'right' noble families, that during their student days they had belonged to the 'right' corps, that they were reserve officers in a distinguished cavalry regiment and that they had the necessary financial means to live 'in accordance with one's rank' both at home and abroad, even on the low salary of a young diplomat. The aura that the institution and the name Auswärtiges Amt gave its members was so great that even at a time when the Office became a responsible ministry the first Foreign Minister of the German Republic, Graf Brockdorff-Rantzau, insisted that his ministry alone kept its old name 'Amt'. Indeed, even after the complete military and social catastrophe of 1945, the 'lobby' of the old diplomacy in the Federal

Republic was so strong that the newly created Foreign Ministry of the Federal Republic stuck to its traditional title 'Auswärtiges Amt' (sometimes referred to as the AA) in obvious imitation of the English name 'Foreign Office'.

The Foreign Office that was taken over by the German Empire in 1871 was in its arrangement and work an instrument for the use of the Chancellor, and during the twenty years that Bismarck managed the politics of the Reich he made skilful use of it. The Office was never able to develop its own foreign policy. The ambassadors and state secretaries had to follow the instructions of the Reich Chancellor rather than their own wishes. Those who ignored his warnings had the implacable fury of the Chancellor to fear.

At the very beginning of his Chancellorship Bismarck had made an example of the German ambassador to Paris, von Arnim, a lesson that did not lose its significance for many years. The ambassador was recalled from Paris on Bismarck's instigation in 1874 because he had supported the monarchist movement in France. As von Arnim had taken some official documents with him he was, again at Bismarck's instigation, sentenced to prison in a trial that attracted a good deal of attention. The former ambassador fled to Switzerland and published in 1876 a brochure, *Pro nihilo*, in which he sharply attacked Bismarck. For this he was sentenced in his absence to five years' hard labour. The ambassador, thus *déclassé*, died some years later as an *émigré* in Nice.

The von Arnim case was proof of how hard Bismarck could hit even in the highly privileged circle of the AA should there be any resistance against his policies. It was a fine irony that the diplomat who gave Bismarck the greatest help in the Arnim affair was the only official in the post-Bismarckian period who to some extent, pursued his own policy – Baron von Holstein.

Bismarck insisted on having his own way in foreign policy, but he could be generous where the more social aspects of the diplomacy of the new Empire were concerned. According to the 1871 Constitution foreign policy was the exclusive concern of the Empire, and the federal states, even the large south German states, had to renounce their own separate foreign policies; they were nevertheless able to retain, without any objection from Bismarck, their own foreign ministries and some of their foreign missions. Bismarck, here, was prepared to wait patiently (speech of 9 December 1867) until the missions fell 'like ripe fruit'. In 1872 there were eight embassies of the German states abroad; in 1914 the number was the same. None took any diplomatic initiative on its own – each was more or less a courtly sinecure.

The Chancellor managed to solve the relationship between Prussia and the Empire by uniting the offices of the Reich's Chancellor and that of the Prussian Minister for Foreign Affairs in his own person. In the departments of the AA the foreign affairs of the Reich and of Prussia were kept separate but were handled by the same officials. It was left to the skill and tact of each official (even to the point of selecting the appropriate letterhead) to decide whether the AA was to be the responsible imperial or Prussian Foreign Ministry. An amusing incident from the later period of the Empire illustrates the point. In 1917, when Count Hertling was Chancellor, there was a horrified reaction in the highly conservative Prussian circles because a Bavarian Catholic had become Prussian Prime Minister and Prussian Minister for Foreign Affairs.

When, in 1871, the AA took over the work for the new German Empire, it consisted of two departments, as had the old Prussian Ministry for Foreign Affairs: the Political Department (I) and the Legal and Commercial Department (II). In the course of the next decade, as the amount of diplomatic work increased, the distribution of work became more differentiated. In 1879 the Personnel Department was separated from Department II, and except for the consular service made into an independent department. In 1885 Department II was again divided, into Department II (economic policy including the consular service) and Department III (legal affairs). In 1890 colonial affairs were taken away from Department I and made independent. This department was removed from the AA entirely in 1907 and made into a new imperial office.

In 1895 the personnel department in charge of the diplomatic service was separated from the personnel department and made subordinate to the political department as Department IB. This measure was initiated by Holstein, the longest serving councillor in Department I, the decisive political department. In this way, Holstein considerably strengthened his own position in the Office because there was now no way around him in the distribution of jobs – except for the 'highest' decisions.

The power of Department I was illustrated by the fact that it was directly subordinate to the state secretary, whereas all the other departments were led by 'directors'. It was not too much to say that Political Department I formed a 'ministry' within the Office. At the head of the Office was a state secretary, who was responsible to the Chancellor. In 1881 the post of state under-secretary was created. The new official was supposed to relieve the state secretary of all his non-political responsibilities, but in practice he was almost completely absorbed in the work of the Political Department.

The 'councillors' of Department I all came from the diplomatic career, whereas the other leading officials came from legal–administrative backgrounds. The separate handling of political and economic affairs was already difficult to maintain during Bismarck's day. The gap between the political and other departments increased with the passage of time. 'I find it very good that the important and fine work is transferred to the Political Department and that only the bulk work stays in Department II' (Herbert von Bismarck to Holstein, 8 September 1884). A peak of arrogance was reached, without doubt, when Herbert von Bismarck was state secretary in the AA (1885–90). When Holstein asked him about a question of personnel, he answered: 'I don't know the people from the consular service well enough to make a proposal.'

In spite of the rapidly increasing importance of Germany's overseas relations, the diplomatic and consular careers remained separate until the end of imperial Germany. Changing from one career to the other was almost impossible. In rare cases, the career of an excellent consul-general in South or Central America could end with the post of a German 'minister resident' or an ambassador in a tiny country overseas. But it must be noted that Bismarck did have an eye for economic relations in foreign policy. His interest in consular reports grew with his adoption of the agrarian-centred protective tariff policies of the Empire. He was also less prejudiced about the background of his officials than his son Herbert. The first holder of the office of state under-secretary in 1881 was a consul-general, Dr Busch, a bourgeois coming from the consular career. He was an exception, an example of what was still possible. Bismarck had chosen him because Busch was familiar with commercial policies, 'so that one may hope that he will stand the test also in this field which is so important at this time'. The fruits of this appointment in the field of economic policy would ripen only decades later in the field of German foreign policy.

However privileged the position of the political department in the AA or influential the position of the 'political councillors' inside the Office, it was the post of an ambassador or a minister, not one of even a high official in the central office, that was the apex of one's career. Even the post of state secretary seemed to the grand seigneur type of German ambassador only a temporary substitute for a post abroad. Prince Hohenlohe-Schillingsfürst was happy to give up this undesirable position after a short period to Count Hatzfeldt in order to become ambassador in Paris. His successor annoyed Bismarck by his long deliberation before taking the post. He fulfilled his duty with little enthusiasm, and with the next political redistribution of positions went as ambassador to London, where he excelled. Among the state secretaries who did manage to impose their own personalities on this office were: Bernhard Ernst von Bülow (1873–9), Herbert Graf von Bismarck-Schönhausen (1886–90), Adolf Freiherr Marschall von Bieberstein (1890–7), Bernhard von Bülow (1897–1900), Alfred von Kiderlen-Wächter (1910–12), Richard von Kühlmann (1917–18). Nonetheless, this group remained a minority among the sixteen holders of this position between 1870 and 1918.

The highest rank of the diplomatic hierarchy was the circle of German ministers and ambassadors, not the circle of working officials, who were regarded by the German 'birds of paradise' in their foreign residences more like 'grey workers' *(Zuarbeiter)*, though from the point of view of their work it should have been the other way round. German diplomats abroad were recruited from members of the nobility who had made careers in the civil service, from the financial aristocracy and, in part, from the officer corps. The relations between diplomats and officers were not as good as might have been expected from their common social background. Tensions especially resulted from the direct subordination in 1900 of military attachés to the Kaiser, which allowed them the privilege of reporting directly to the monarch. The diplomats, with their enclosed caste feeling and their claim to be the only ones who could judge matters of foreign policy, always reacted sensitively when outsiders, even of their own social background, intruded into this inner circle or developed and passed on their own rival ideas. One such outsider from the highest circle was Prince Hohenlohe-Schillingsfürst, the former Bavarian Prime Minister and later imperial Chancellor, who became German ambassador to Paris in 1874. He noted in his memoirs: 'I met more and more unfriendly faces among the Prussian aristocracy and the young diplomats, who resented my appointment and who saw their hopes of advancement disturbed.'

The inner circle of the great embassies in Paris, London, Vienna, Rome and St Petersburg was invariably filled by members of the high aristocracy. Only those who were wealthy enough to maintain an appropriate lifestyle were regarded as desirable candidates for these posts. For example, there was Fürst Münster von Derneburg, who had first served the King of Hanover as ambassador in St Petersburg and was then for many years the imperial ambassador in London and Paris. In this group belong Count Monts (Rome), Prince Reuss (Vienna), Fürst Hohenlohe (Paris), Fürst Lichnowsky (London) and others.

The activities of these diplomats were limited to the circles of the court, aristocracy, and the group of leading statesmen of the country to which they were accredited. One should neither over- nor under-estimate the contacts created through the family relationships of the ruling houses as a factor in foreign policy. Here an able ambassador who came from the high aristocracy could perform important work as a mediator. But the trends of the time – nationalism, imperialism and economic rivalry – were by the end of the century already proving to be stronger than mutual monarchic ties. This was an especially disappointing experience for William II after his meeting with Tsar Nicholas II at Björkö in 1904. The private letters that the Kaiser wrote to his Russian cousin, with the full approval of the AA, in order to influence Russian foreign policy, proved ineffectual. The unfortunate family relationship between Edward VII and William II was more a burden for German diplomacy than a means for bettering relations between the two peoples. The age in which monarchs decided the foreign policies of their countries had come to an end. Other powers than those selected from a narrow social circle took their positions in politics and pushed forward.

It has to be asked whether the German AA correctly understood this change in foreign policy, which was common to all Europe, and correctly estimated its importance for the future. The AA was, according to the will of its initiator, Bismarck, and according to its constitutional position in the Reich, incapable of making its own policies but worked for the Chancellor who, as the only 'responsible minister', shaped his own diplomacy. The famous quotation from Bismarck, 'My diplomats must turn about on command like soldiers', was true for much of the long period of his chancellorship, but according to new research must be qualified for its final phase. We know that from 1886 onwards Holstein tried increasingly to have his own way in foreign policy. His participation in the fall of Bismarck cannot be denied; the non-renewal of the Reinsurance Treaty was a part of his new policy. The fact that Bismarck faced difficulties in his own office can be seen from a letter to his official of 30 October 1888, in which he reproaches Holstein for corresponding directly with the Kaiser on official business. Holstein is the best example of an attempt to use the office to gain a decisive influence on high policy without being accountable. With the publication of the 'Holstein Papers' after the Second World War, this German diplomat has been more justly judged. The image of the intriguer and the 'man with the hyena eyes' has somewhat faded. What remains is a portrait of a man in the background who through his industry, his great knowledge of the files and the wide-ranging diplomatic correspondence in which he instructed German ambassadors, but also through his shyness, frustrated nature, distrust and mild inferiority complex, tried to introduce a policy of the 'free hand' to gain for Germany, with the help of England, freedom of movement with regard to Russia and France.

In the post-Bismarckian period from 1890 to 1906, Holstein was the adviser to successive Chancellors, especially to von Bülow, who continued to seek his advice until Holstein's death. Holstein was the central figure in German foreign policy until the unsuccessful conference of Algeciras, which

ended his career. With Holstein's disappearance the most influential figure of
the post-Bismarckian era left the AA. The Office had undoubtedly gained
more freedom of movement after 1890, but its position had also become
more difficult. The public criticism of the Office in newspapers and in the
Reichstag became sharper. The unsatisfactory representation of economic
interests by the AA and the choice of German diplomats according to their
aristocratic backgrounds were especially criticized. At a time when the
director of the Hamburg-America Line, Albert Ballin, and Sir Ernest Cassel,
two leading businessmen of the rival countries, worked semi-officially for an
Anglo-German agreement, the contribution of the AA in this field seemed
rather unpromising. The talks with England in August 1909, which
Bethmann Hollweg had encouraged, came about not through the AA but
through the mediation of private persons.

Attempts to adapt to the new political and world economic problems were
barely seen from outside. They became public only through criticism in the
Reichstag. In 1907, when the French abandoned the old structure of the Quai
d'Orsay (which had been similar to that of the AA) and constructed a modern
Ministry for Foreign Affairs based on regional principles, in which the heads
of department handled politics and economics from a single point of view,
nothing was done in the AA. There was in the latter no balance between
general foreign and trade policy. Furthermore, there was in the AA neither a
department for propaganda abroad nor a real press department that could
have worked together with the press in using its own reports and information
to support German foreign policy through publicity. It was a severe shock
for the AA to see that the Imperial Naval Office under Admiral Tirpitz had
created a public relations department that – very much in opposition to the
position of the AA – publicized the idea of a great German fleet and the
'Risiko-Flotte' policy in circles that had previously not favoured it.

The negative influence of the Imperial Naval Office was to be fatal to that
last attempt at an adjustment with England in 1912, the Haldane Mission.
With the German 'no' to a slower pace of naval building and the passing of a
naval law four weeks after the Haldane visit to Berlin, the last attempt at an
Anglo-German agreement failed. The Naval Office had a powerful modern
lobby, the German Naval League, behind its demand for an accelerated fleet-
building programme, and a press that was supplied with information
supporting its purpose. Recognition of the danger that was threatening led
the AA to press for an agreement with Britain, but its voice was heard only
'officially' and then dismissed. A policy with means other than diplomatic
reports or personal negotiations – i.e. with the help of the press – lay outside
the imagination of the Office. Even the vivacious Swabian, Kiderlen-Wächter,
the state secretary and outspoken critic of German naval policy, had no
chance to make himself heard.

These examples illustrate the fatal traditionalism of the Office, whose
outlook was still grounded in the thinking of the early nineteenth century
that foreign policy could *only* be conducted by a chosen circle of men destined
for this work. This way of thinking was reinforced by the semi-monarchial
and feudal structure of the Constitution and of the society that prevailed until
1918. In the last year of the monarchy the Liberal politician, Friedrich Payer,
who became Vice-Chancellor in 1917, characterized the archaic structure of
the Foreign Office as follows: 'Over the AA prevailed a spirit of exclusiveness;

for outsiders it had the aura of a mystery, impenetrable to laymen. It was an enclosed organism inside the government, into which only selected people were allowed glimpses, and even these reluctantly and not more than was absolutely necessary.'

The Foreign Office during the First World War

With the outbreak of the First World War (especially after the first years of the war, when the consequences of a faulty German foreign policy became publicly known through the enemies' blockade and Germany's isolation from the rest of the world) the number of voices complaining of 'bad German diplomacy' increased. This criticism reached its peak shortly after the declaration of unlimited submarine warfare in 1917 and the entrance of the United States into the war. It was at this time that the AA and the Chancellor lost their last, decisive battle against Ludendorff and the Admiralty in an effort to prevent unrestricted submarine warfare. The strongest criticism came not from the mass of the working population, who did not yet understand the consequences of this turn of the war, but from among the Hanseatic exporters and shipowners. Agriculture and industry had not yet suffered losses because of the war – on the contrary, they experienced a boom in orders – but shippers and overseas traders were excluded from their daily business. Most of the German merchant fleet lay in neutral harbours, and each extension of the war, especially towards the United States and South America, meant further losses of millions of tonnage and an additional cutting off of the commercial connections that needed to be preserved for the post-war period. It was one of the greatest concerns of German overseas companies that connections with the large South American states should not be broken, but each sinking of a South American merchant ship brought a declaration of war by these states a step nearer.

The struggle of the AA against the naval leaders over unrestricted submarine warfare is one of the most honourable chapters in the history of the German Foreign Ministry. Although the AA did not succeed in keeping Brazil out of the war, it did help to keep Argentina, the most important of the South American states, neutral. Argentina was driven close to a declaration of war by the clumsy and arrogant acts of the German ambassador in Buenos Aires, Graf Luxburg, who manoeuvred both governments into an almost impossible political position through his notorious 'Luxburg dispatches', in which he invited the German government to sink Argentinian ships 'without a trace' and called the Argentinian Minister for Foreign Affairs an 'anglophile ass'. When the American secret service deciphered these dispatches and the whole world was informed, there was a storm of indignation against this 'barbaric' German foreign policy.

If it had not been for the clever and farsighted President Yrigoyen of Argentina, and for von Kühlmann, Bussche-Haddenhausen and Haniel von Haimhaussen of the AA, working together with the assistance of the Argentinian ambassador in Berlin to make common sense prevail, German–Argentinian relations would have been shattered by this affair. Both sides managed to moderate their extreme demands. Yrigoyen won over the moderate majority in both houses of parliament, while the AA pushed the blame on to the German envoy and gave a half-promise to spare Argentinian ships. In a tricky game the Admiralty was made to give in on this occasion.

Here, at the time of the dénouement of the First World War in 1917, was a masterpiece of diplomatic action and a showpiece of the old secret diplomacy. In a limited but important field the AA, which was so much slandered, had proved that its leading officials knew their jobs if they were given enough room for action. Both sides agreed that the results of their work should not become public. Only the incomprehensible behaviour of Graf Luxburg was known to the public, and it raised a great scandal that resulted in demands for a thorough reform of the AA. Luxburg was regarded as a typical example of the incompetent but arrogant German diplomat; his blunders became – again and again – the signal for the now increasing demands for reform.

The call for reform of the AA became even stronger during the last decades before the First World War. There was scarcely one annual debate of the budget in the Reichstag in which members of the National Liberal or Centre parties did not complain about the AA, about the aristocratic exclusiveness of its leading officials and the neglect of Germany's commercial interests. One of the strongest demands for reform came from the young National Liberal MP, Dr Gustav Stresemann, who on 15 March 1910 in a speech to parliament severely attacked the personnel policies of von Schoen, at that time state secretary in the AA, because he had dared to declare that he did not differentiate between the nobility and the bourgeoisie. Stresemann's reproach, that the German embassies were in fact exclusively manned by aristocrats and that the same was true for the major consulates, could not be refuted.

More important than his critique of the personnel policies was Stresemann's demand that 'politics and international politics first and foremost, had to be economic politics and that is why the tradition that we still preserve today with regard to the coming generation of diplomats is hardly based on fact'. This question had gradually become so important that Chancellor von Bethmann Hollweg, in addition to being the only responsible 'minister' to be stirred on this subject, promised to do something about the reform plans for the AA.

But these remained only verbal promises. From 1911 onwards the education of attachés was slightly broadened: excursions were organized into areas of industry and trade, leading figures in the economy gave short talks in order to give future diplomats an insight into economic practices. These first small steps into a field previously unknown to diplomats were organized by Schüler, then leader of the consular section in the Personnel Department. He was assisted by the cosmopolitan state secretary, von Kiderlen-Wächter. But on the whole the structure and personnel policies of the AA remained unchanged. It was only the Luxburg Affair that, with one blow, gave impetus to reforms that were almost revolutionary when one thinks of the social structure of the German Empire.

A group of Hamburg overseas merchants formed an action committee, which on 29 November 1917 sent a short complaint with over a hundred signatures from 'first Hamburg addresses' to the Chancellor, Count Hertling. In it they referred to the conduct of Graf Luxburg and heavily attacked 'the great errors of the AA, which became visible through the war . . . and which only partly resulted from the lack of knowledge about the situation abroad'. While this first memorandum still rings with spontaneous annoyance, the second memorandum of the same circle, the so-called 'Hamburg memorandum' ('Hamburg proposal for the reorganization of the German foreign service') of April 1917 offered a well-considered rearrangement of a future German foreign service, in which the structure of the office, its tasks and the choice of its officials were supposed to meet the needs of a modern world economy. In the same spirit as these proposals were the official representations of the Hanseatic overseas merchants, the Chambers of Commerce in Hamburg, Bremen and Lübeck, and that from the leading Hamburg banker, Max Warburg. These plans for reform were approved by the Hamburg citizenry in a resolution passed on 29 May 1918.

This criticism in the fourth year of the war against the thus far 'most noble' Imperial office provoked a notable reaction there. It was not rejected as it would have been by the old authoritarian state; the new state secretary, Richard von Kühlmann, a man who was related through marriage to people in heavy industry and who understood more about economics than his predecessors, was willing to negotiate. One week later, after the German members of the Reichstag had been invited to Hamburg to familiarize themselves with the Hamburg overseas problems, the state secretary came to discuss with both official and unofficial boards the future of his office. This meeting of von Kühlmann on 20 June 1918 with official representatives, especially of the merchants, illustrates how the old power structure in imperial Germany was disintegrating. Kühlmann proved an able tactician who managed to answer polemics by referring to the competent and responsible persons in the Reichstag and to the Chancellor. On some points (i.e. the diplomatic career) he offered the possibility of a compromise, but on the whole he left the really important problem, the relationship between merchants and diplomats, to his aide, Edmund Schüler.

Thus the Hamburg board saw for the first time the man who was to become responsible for the reforms in the AA during the next three years, a man who had an open eye for the significance of economic–political questions but who also clearly saw the limits between the independent activity of the merchant and the official activity of a representative of the Reich.

Edmund Schüler was the councillor of the legation and head of the Consular Department in the AA when he accompanied his state secretary to Hamburg and took the main responsibility for the negotiations with the Hanseatic representatives. Born in 1873, the son of a bourgeois Prussian major-general and director of the Prussian artillery workshops in Spandau, Schüler passed his second legal civil service examinations, travelled through England and Scotland, worked for a time at the Deutsche Bank and started his consular career in 1900. He was highly gifted, had strong artistic talents – he had worked creatively in the office of an architect – and combined an appreciation for all questions of political economy with a clear view of the future shape and working possibilities of a new AA. The extraordinary talent for organization in the young consul was soon discovered by Stemrich, his superior in Constantinople as consul-general, and later state under-secretary. In 1906, after only five years abroad, Schüler was called back to the central office, never again – except for short missions – to leave.

The Schüler reforms

With Edmund Schüler the AA had gained a highly qualified representative, who in the critical transitional period between empire and republic was the only person with a concept of the reorganization that the Office required, in both its personnel and its structure, which despite his sensitive character Schüler had the will-power to enforce. In the history of the Prussian–German civil service it is very rare for a reform to be closely connected with the name of one civil servant; in the history of the AA the 'Schüler reform' has become a fixed expression for the only great attempt at modernization in the first third of the twentieth century, though the personality of this exceptional man remained unknown to the public.

During the last months of the Empire the wish for a reform of the AA became clearly visible. State Secretary Kühlmann asked Schüler and Graf Wedel on 14 May 1918, 'to work on the reorganization of the foreign service', and as early as 30 June Chancellor Hertling reported to the Emperor 'that the preparations for the reorganization of the foreign service have been carried out provisionally'. These hasty activities in the AA were not only the results of Stresemann's new attacks in the Reichstag and the Hamburg initiatives, but also of the unexpected rivalry of a new imperial office. In 1917 the newly founded Imperial Office for Economics (Reichswirtschaftsamt) had claimed rights in the field of foreign trade. Many commercial and industrial groups, especially in central and southern Germany, were sympathetic towards this Office, from which they expected greater advancement of their economic interests than they felt the exclusive AA could provide. The subordination of the whole consular system to the Reichswirtschaftsamt was among the demands voiced. It was only with great difficulty that during the negotiations on the Hanseatic memorandum the Bremen Chamber of Commerce was dissuaded from similar ideas. The struggle over jurisdiction between the offices had already become public with regard to the administration of the Ukraine and other eastern regions. In June 1918 the AA stated unequivocally in a conference of state secretaries: 'After this war economic politics and politics cannot be separated, even less than before, and therefore the AA must insist that representations abroad remain directly dependent on the AA.' This reform of the AA was hastened by the establishment of the new Reichswirtschaftsamt, a powerful and feared rival. Suddenly reformers and conservatives found themselves in the same boat!

A remarkable feature of the Schüler reform is its continuity of work from the autumn of 1918 through 1919; the student of this reform who looks only at the appropriate files scarcely notices that within this period the First World War ended, a revolution took place and a republic was proclaimed. In the last weeks of the Empire, Schüler was made superintendent of the Personnel Department, and in the first year of the Weimar Republic, on 13 August 1919, its director. Numerous journeys of Schüler, conferences both within the Office and outside it with chambers of commerce and with associations of trade and industry, took place in and out of Berlin under extremely difficult circumstances during the revolutionary winter of 1918–19. Only now and then is there a remark in the protocols that some representative could not come because there were no trains, or that Schüler was late for a meeting of south and north German chambers of commerce for the same reason. During these months Schüler worked hard and energetically to the limits of his physical powers.

One of the most important reforms was announced scarcely four weeks after the revolution. On 2 December 1918 the diplomatic and consular careers were merged. This decree was signed by the last imperial and first republican state secretary, Solf. It was, of course, essential to this reform that with the revolution all imperial offices had been transformed into constitutional ministries of the Reich under a Reichsminister who was responsible to parliament (Law of the Provisional Sovereignty of 10 February 1919). Former state secretaries became ministers, state under-secretaries were now to be called state secretaries. All former imperial offices were called Reichsministerium (Ministries of the Reich), only the Foreign Office keeping its old imperial name. The extreme traditionalism of this Office, of its leading officials and of its first Minister, Graf Brockdorff-Rantzau, accounted for this exception, even though constitutionally the word 'office' meant much less than 'ministry'. The name, however, remains until today. The first Foreign Minister of the Republic, Graf Brockdorff-Rantzau (2 February to 21 June 1919), announced these overdue reforms on 10 April 1919 during his speech on the budget. He and his successors, the Social Democratic Foreign Ministers Müller-Franken (21 June 1919 to 27 March 1920) and Dr Adolf Köster (13 April to 25 June 1920), gave Schüler the necessary political backing to carry through his reforms. Only the fourth Foreign Minister of the Republic, the Conservative Dr Walter Simons (25 June 1920 to 10 May 1921), no longer supported Schüler, who consequently left the Office on 31 December 1920 and retired, at the age of forty-eight; from this time he never again took on a public office. He died in Berlin on 20 October 1952, at the age of seventy-nine.

Schüler's reform comprised four major fields that are organizationally separate but have the same origins: (1) The unification of the diplomatic and consular careers; (2) The introduction of a regional system, i.e. the grouping of political and economic questions according to groups of countries, as an administrative reform in the central office; (3) The foundation of a department for foreign trade, which was loosely connected with the Office but mostly independent (later 'Department X'); (4) The opening of the foreign service, especially its leading positions, to men from the world of commerce and industry, and also from politics and science.

From an era in which courtly and social norms in international relations had made possible a certain uniformity in international politics, the AA was to be led towards a time in which international politics were confronted with economic and social questions to a degree hitherto unknown and in which new élites all over the world claimed their rights.

Schüler by no means intended to replace politics by economics. But he regarded the separation of the two fields as one of the 'fundamental errors of the old AA'. In a 'secret circular' of the minister (22 January 1919), Schüler was asked to represent the minister and take the chair in a reform committee, in which officials like Toepffer (second state secretary for economics) and Dr Bosenick (a consul who worked with Schüler) sat together with six representatives called from practical industrial life. Among these were the well-known merchant from Bremen and consul-general to Bulgaria, Ludwig Roselius, who was also a friend of Schüler. Schüler did not think much of committee meetings. In the circular, general meetings were already regarded as exceptions, whereas it was the rule to consult its single members.

The way in which Schüler worked can almost be called hectic. He himself had the feeling that he could not for long keep the power that he held in 1919 and 1920. Thus he wanted at least to tackle the problems that appeared to him to be most important. In the foreground stood the new regulation for the education of recruits. For the first time, attachés were given a salary. Also new was an intensified education in economic questions. A university degree was no longer a necessary precondition for entering the foreign service; work in commerce or banks could also be taken as prerequisites for a career. This rule seemed so outrageous to the conservative permanent staff of old civil servants that after some years it was repealed.

Schüler was mainly interested in the building up of Department X for foreign trade, which was loosely associated with the Office. In the context of the reform, it was supposed to coordinate the demands of the economy with those of the state, and to become, according to Schüler, 'a living connection between the economy and Wilhelmstrasse' to meet the completely new situation created after the lost war. But obviously it was not yet time for such a semi-national enterprise. It was dissolved in October 1921 as one of the cuts in public expenditure, and was replaced by the far more modest 'Branch of the AA for Foreign Trade'. Schüler's idea, however, that there ought to be a connection between overseas trade and export industry on the one hand and the AA on the other, was subsequently maintained and organizationally expanded. Its successor today is the Federal Office for Information on Foreign Trade (Bundesstelle für Aussenhandelsinformation) in Cologne. The reformers in the Office, led by Schüler, and the conservatives agreed on one point: foreign policy, even if based on economics, could be made only in the AA. Only the support, which ministers as different as Brockdorff-Rantzau and Müller-Franken gave to Schüler, enabled him to succeed in his fight about the 'competences of the offices', especially against the Reichswirtschaftsministerium.

In another field, too, Schüler was well supported by his ministers. In spite of the persistent resistance of conservative officials, he united embassies and consulates 'wherever they are in the same place'. On the surface he could argue the case on grounds of economy. But in reality he initiated a diplomatic experiment: embassies abroad were to be given preference where economic policies were an equal or integrated factor of general politics. Conservatives like von Neurath, at one time German minister in Copenhagen and later Foreign Minister under Papen, Schleicher and Hitler, were strongly opposed to the fact that officials in the consular departments of the embassies had gained diplomatic status, 'so that on all official occasions a disproportionately high number of embassy officials comes along'. This quote shows that the old 'thinking in two classes' in the career service had by no means disappeared with the revolution.

Schüler was enough of a realist to know that he could only succeed if the decisive posts in the Office were held by men he trusted. He managed to place his followers as heads of the six newly created regional departments. Schüler's changes in personnel in the central office were of decisive importance. For the first time, the leading officials of the most important departments came mostly from the consular career and had not only a new understanding of economic policies as a part of foreign politics but also a different social background. Certainly one cannot speak of 'leftist' personnel politics in the AA; rather it was representatives of the bourgeoisie who took some of the places of the nobility in the career service. The simple advancement of the 'consulars' into the first rank of the higher offices was a revolutionary act for this Office.

Even more revolutionary was the fact that important posts abroad were given to outsiders, to men who did not come from either the diplomatic or the consular career. This question became especially relevant after the ratification of the peace treaty in 1920, when the crucial posts of ambassadors to the former enemy states had to be filled. Schüler was looking for talent as early as 1919, especially in the Hanseatic trade circles, that he valued so highly. 'I am looking only for "first addresses"', he wrote to a friend; but it was not that easy to find 'first addresses' for work in the AA. The Hamburg shipowner, Woermann, turned his offer down with the argument that he had first of all to rebuild his own shipping company. Other leading businessmen refused on similar grounds. At last Schüler succeeded in winning two senators from Hamburg, Mayor Dr Sthamer, who went as ambassador to London, and the banker Berenberg-Gossler, who became ambassador to Rome. In Paris the Reich was represented by the former MP of the Bavarian People's Party, Mayer-Kaufbeuren, in Brussels by Landsberg, a former member of the Council of the People's Representatives (Rat der Volksbeauftragten) and later Minister of Justice. The former Saxon Minister of the Interior, Dr Walter Koch, a qualified lawyer and financial expert, represented the Republic in Prague. The most senior of the newly invested outsiders was the Social Democrat, Dr Adolf Müller, who was German envoy in Berne until 1933. Shortly after Schüler's retirement two extremely gifted Social Democratic outsiders were given diplomatic posts: the former chief of the press, Rauscher, went in 1922 to the embassy in Warsaw, which he led cleverly and capably until his death in December 1930, and the former Foreign Minister, Dr Adolf Köster, successfully represented the Reich in Riga and Belgrade until his death in March 1930.

On 5 March 1923, two years after Schüler's retirement, a survey made by the AA of twenty-six leading diplomatic posts in Europe showed that sixteen places were taken by 'officials of the AA', eight by 'gentlemen who so far did not belong to the AA', and two posts were vacant (in Copenhagen and Budapest). This ratio of 2:1 of insiders to outsiders in diplomatic posts abroad was the result of Schüler's personnel policies. After Schüler only one more outsider was given a leading post. This was the Krupp director, Dr Wiedfeldt, who represented the Reich in Washington from 1922 to 1925 as its first ambassador after the war.

At least two of these outsiders died too early to reach the highest positions. Stresemann had planned to make Rauscher state secretary, and Köster was supposed to become Sthamer's successor in London. In the last years of the Republic only two outsiders were still ambassadors – Koch in Prague and Müller in Berne – which shows that no new outsiders reached top positions. The corps of career civil servants had throughout the Weimar Republic carried through its claim to be the only source of appropriate candidates for top positions in the diplomatic service. Even an experienced Foreign Minister such as Stresemann, who led the AA very competently for six years, never tried such a spectacular outsider policy, despite the fact that he wanted to make Rauscher state secretary in the last months of his life. Rauscher had been accepted by the insiders, with great difficulty, after ten years of successful activity as ambassador. Only in the first generation after 1918 did outsiders manage to get the leading posts, though this experiment was to be repeated after 1951. In both cases, the *esprit de corps* of the career civil servants proved to be the most conservative element in the Office.

Were the Schüler reforms a failure? In spite of some modifications after his retirement, the Office has kept some of the distinctive features of this period of reform. The separation of the consular and diplomatic careers was never again seriously considered. The idea that economic policies have to be an integral part of all foreign policy, which was Schüler's heritage, was perhaps only understood by the generation of diplomats who tried to create a new foreign policy in the Federal Republic after the complete political breakdown of Germany in 1945. Their policies realized Schüler's ideas far more than was possible in the 1920s.

The balance between regional and central departments shifted towards one or the other side, but the six departments created in the era of reform lasted until 1936 (I) Personnel and Administration; (II) West and South-East Europe; (III) England, America, the Orient; (IV) Eastern Europe, Scandinavia, East Asia; (V) Legal Department; (VI) Department of Culture. The creation of a separate department for culture, which had not existed in the old AA, was also part of Schüler's work. In order to counteract diverging special interests of single departments and sub-departments, Schüler had created the Bureau of the Minister. It became, especially under Stresemann, the central political bureau in which all the foreign political problems came together and where all the foreign political decisions of the Office were made. It was supported by the Bureau of the State Secretary.

In the daily 'conference of directors', held under the chairmanship of the state secretary, all questions of general political importance were discussed. Closely associated with the AA was the Associated Press Department of the Government, founded on 1 October 1919. The director of the Press Department was directly subordinate to the Chancellor, so it was possible for the AA not only to collect and sift news from all over the world but also to distribute its own news via the Press Department. The Referat Deutschland (D) which Schüler had taken out of the Political Department in 1920, was responsible for all questions concerning domestic politics, especially the connections with the Reichstag and Reichsrat. This department gained great importance with the transition to parliamentary government with its system of responsible ministers, though its role was to become perverted and sinister during the Third Reich (see below).

The AA during the Weimar Republic was on the whole an efficient instrument that, while still conservative in its basic attitudes, remained loyal to the Government. It reached its greatest influence in the hands of a politician like Stresemann, who knew how to cooperate with these highly qualified experts to prepare the evacuation of the Rhineland, to conclude the Locarno treaty, to guarantee the Dawes and Young plans in the fields of foreign and domestic politics, to conclude the Treaty of Rapallo with the USSR, and to lead Germany into the League of Nations. All the civil servants who led the Office as state secretaries from 1920 until 1936 came from the old élite of the imperial Office. But all of them were well educated in their fields and all served the Republic unconditionally. They were: Dr Edgar Haniel von Haimhausen (1920–2), from 1923 envoy of the Reich in Munich; Ago Freiherr von Maltzan (1922–4), from 1925 ambassador in Washington; Dr Carl von Schubert (1924–30), from 1930 ambassador in Rome (Quirinal); Dr Bernard Wilhelm von Bülow (1930–6), who died on 21 June 1936.

The Foreign Office under National Socialist rule: Neurath and Ribbentrop

On 30 January 1933 and during the first years after the Nazi seizure of power the AA, unlike other ministries, was treated gently. At the head of the AA since 1932 stood the Foreign Minister, Konstantin Freiherr von Neurath, a conservative, experienced diplomat of the old school and the confidant of Hindenburg. In the Office, the state secretary was Dr Bernard Wilhelm von Bülow, a diplomat by profession, who remained in his post until his death in 1936. The heads of the seven most important departments, who had started their careers before the First World War, also remained, as did the German representatives abroad, apart from one honourable exception, the ambassador to Washington, Friedrich Wilhelm von Prittwitz and Gaffron, who resigned from his post immediately after the Nazi seizure of power. Johann Heinrich Graf von Bernstorff, ambassador to Washington from 1908 to 1917, should also be mentioned; during the First World War he had tried in vain to prevent the declaration of unlimited submarine warfare and to keep the USA out of the war. A convinced democrat, he had been working for international reconciliation as German representative to the Geneva conference for disarmament since 1926. Over seventy years old, he left Germany in 1933 and did not see his homeland again until 1945.

How can the Nazis abstention from a seizure of power in the AA be explained? It might be argued that until Hindenburg's death in the summer of 1934 the Reich President had reserved to himself the right to give positions in the armed forces and in the AA. But even after Hindenburg's death the party leadership continued to refrain from acting against the AA. When, on 4 February 1938, Freiherr von Neurath resigned, the last but one minister of a bourgeois party left Hitler's Cabinet. Neurath had lasted for four or five years longer than his former colleagues. Only in 1938 did Ribbentrop start the party's attack on this last bourgeois citadel. What were the reasons for this initial restraint?

In 1933 the party had few members with diplomatic experience abroad. In the summer of 1933 it soon became obvious that the few National Socialists who were sent abroad by Hitler on goodwill tours or for negotiations suffered miserable defeats. Rosenberg, as 'personal representative of the Führer', had to come back from London in May 1933 because he could not get in touch with official organizations. The same happened to Robert Ley in Geneva in June 1933, when at the conference of the International Workers' Association his credentials as 'representative of the German employees' were not acknowledged. When Reinhard Heydrich, later head of the Main Office for Security of the Reich (chef des Reichssicherheitshauptamts), was in Geneva as a member of the German commission for disarmament, he made a fool of himself when he personally took down the – then still official – black, red and gold German flag and put up the swastika flag in the hotel where his delegation was staying.

In the first years after 1933, Hitler had to go through the dangerous period of a vacuum in power politics and was at the time still forced to hide the final goals of his ruthless expansionary and racial politics. He very quickly realized that German diplomacy was for the moment only possible with the help of the AA as an international cover. Although he despised careful diplomats, whom he used to call 'Santa Clauses', good for 'quiet times', he was clever enough to make use of their work and their international success whenever he needed diplomatic backing for his surprise coups. He could be sure of the willing help of the Office, where it was believed that Hitler wanted to abolish the remnants of the Treaty of Versailles. In addition, many leading officials in the AA thought – though they were soon proved wrong – that it would be far more useful to the Reich if they stayed in office rather than leaving this difficult apparatus in the coarse hands of the 'old fighters'. Even Brüning admitted many years later that he had advised State Secretary Bülow 'to remain in office and also to urge his colleagues to do so . . . in order to thwart Hitler's aggressive military and foreign politics'.

Although Hitler despised professional diplomats as a class, these qualified personnel proved to be an important factor in German diplomacy. The Office collected material on domestic and foreign events in all important states of the world, and worked out foreign policy recommendations. The German 'politics of revision' from 1933 to 1938 was only technically prepared in the AA, but its leading officials also agreed with it. This applies to the withdrawal of Germany from the League of Nations, to the notice of withdrawal from the disarmament clauses of the Treaty of Versailles, and to the military reoccupation of the Rhineland. Other major problems on which the German diplomats agreed with Hitler, and which were in accordance with the general ideas of German diplomacy, were the annexation of Austria and the 'settlement of the question of the corridor' with Poland. The Anglo-German naval agreement of 1935 was seen as part of a Bismarckian foreign policy.

So the officials of the German Foreign Office who were not Nazis were able to cooperate to a considerable degree with the new government. The remaining two élites in Germany that were as yet influential and not at all 'brought into line', the diplomats and the high officers, were during the first six years of Nazi government alarmed only that revision was being carried out too hastily. They feared that this might lead to war at a moment when Germany was not yet militarily prepared far more than they feared that Hitler's foreign policy as a whole, with its breaches of law, could become such a risk for Europe that it might ultimately lead to war and the destruction of the Reich.

The last 'reform' in the structure of the Office was carried out in 1936. Faced with the world economic crisis, the Reichstag had already demanded cuts in expenditure in the early 1930s. These cuts were continued during the first years of National Socialist government. The last remnants of Schüler's plan of reorganization were abolished, and the Office was organized on pre-war lines. The regional departments disappeared in favour of the old departments according to theoretical divisions. The Office had five of these: (I) Department of Personnel and Budget (Pes); (II) Political Department (Pol); (III) Department of Commercial Politics (W, from 1 January 1941 known as HaPol, probably as a result of the feeling that commerce and politics could not be separated after all); (IV) Legal Department (R); (V) Department of Cultural Politics (Kult).

It cannot be proved that this reorganization was to be blamed on the Nazis. It is more likely that, for the last time, the old conservative powers in the Office managed to have their way, in order to emphasize the precedence of foreign politics *proper* in the affairs of an expansive world power.

The 'closed section' for the bourgeois and conservative German Foreign Office came to an end in 1938. Until then Hitler had scarcely intervened in the personnel policies of the Office, despite his disdain for diplomats. Only a few of the outsiders who were accepted for the diplomatic service at that time were Nazis. In 1933 Hitler made the former Reich Chancellor, Martin Luther, who did not belong to any party, ambassador to Washington. Franz von Papen, who had just resigned as Vice-Chancellor of the Cabinet, went to Vienna at the end of July 1934, on Hitler's orders, as an 'appeasing' ambassador after the Austrian Chancellor Dollfuss had been assassinated by the Nazis. The former lord mayor of Berlin, Dr Sahm, became German ambassador in Oslo after struggles with Goebbels' supporters. One of the few National Socialists was General Faupel. He was sent by Hitler as ambassador to General Franco, but he had to be recalled after only one year, in 1937, because his peculiar ideas about his role in Spain were disliked. Lieutenant-Colonel Hermann Kriebel, an old comrade in arms of Hitler in 1923, was made consul-general in Shanghai on special orders from Hitler in 1934 after having been military adviser to Chiang Kai-shek for several years. Among the career officials of the higher ranks there were scarcely any old party members. There were only two exceptions: Prince zu Wied, who had become a party member in 1932 but had been made to resign in March 1933, was reactivated in the autumn of 1933 and made ambassador to Stockholm. Freiherr von Thermann in Danzig, consul-general of the first class and an old party member, was given the post of an envoy, first class, in Buenos Aires at the end of 1933.

The most prominent representative of the Nazis in the AA was, of course, Joachim von Ribbentrop, who had been government deputy for security questions since 1934, and who concluded the Anglo-German naval agreement as a 'special ambassador' in 1935. In 1936 he was appointed ambassador to London, only because of the sudden death of the experienced ambassador, Leopold von Hoesch, who was highly esteemed in England and France.

Although few Nazis infiltrated the Office itself, there were groups outside the AA during the first years of Hitler's government who basically did nothing but await their entry into it. The Foreign Political Office of the NSDAP (Aussenpolitisches Amt der NSDAP) was the oldest enterprise to compete with the AA. It was founded on 1 April 1933 under Reichsleiter Alfred Rosenberg. This office was supposed to represent the proper foreign policy of the Nazis and to educate diplomatic recruits. This programme was announced with grandeur but soon became futile. Rosenberg's failure in England in 1933, and Hitler's favouritism towards Ribbentrop, made Rosenberg's influence in foreign policy disappear almost completely.

Numerically most important was the Organization of the NSDAP outside Germany (Auslandsorganisation der NSDAP). From the autumn of 1933 it was led by Rudolf Hess. The leader of the Auslandsorganisation, Ernst Wilhelm Bohle, was appointed Gauleiter of the party. He was an able organizer and could mobilize many groups of the NSDAP abroad, but he did not succeed in forming a ministry for Germans abroad in competition with the AA. Hitler was so impressed by the Nazis' work abroad that he appointed Gauleiter Böhle on 30 January 1937 as head of organizations abroad in the AA. On 27 December 1937 Hitler appointed him state secretary in the AA. This appointment was the decisive breakthrough of the party into the inner circle of the AA. The party's influence was even more important, as all officials in the AA both in Berlin and abroad were now directly subordinated to the Gauleitung Ausland. Influence over all promotion and transfers was now guaranteed to the party. The officials in the AA were now more than ever under pressure to join the party.

The Ribbentrop Office, founded in 1934, became the most dangerous Nazi rival to the AA. Neither Rosenberg nor Hess nor Bohle had a comparable influence on Hitler's foreign policies. Ribbentrop's experience abroad, his elegant behaviour, his good knowledge of English and French and his assiduity in proclaiming Hitler's ideas quickly won him Hitler's confidence. He was especially close to Hitler in their common antipathy to traditional and professional diplomacy. The Ribbentrop Office soon became a rival enterprise to the AA, as was shown in certain actions in which both were involved but did not cooperate (e.g. in the preparation of the anti-comintern pacts with Japan and Italy in 1936–7 and in German activities in the Spanish Civil War). In 1936 the office already had 160 members, some of whom were members of the AA on leave but who increasingly belonged to the SS or SA.

Ribbentrop's advancement from 'the Führer's adviser on foreign politics' to a minister was deliberate; it took four years, which demanded much patience from the ambitious careerist. Hitler gave this post to his protégé only after the retirement of Neurath in the spring of 1938, at a time when he thought he could occupy the last two strongholds of the bourgeois élite, the army and the diplomatic corps. The occasion for this was provided in the army by the dramatic Blomberg-Fritsch crisis and in the Foreign Office by the honourable, but completely surprising, retirement of the Foreign Minister, Freiherr von Neurath, after he had reached e age of sixty-five. Hitler was convinced that the really dangerous initi. phase of German foreign politics, when it was necessary to be careful in relations with the great powers, had been overcome. He believed that he could go through the next phase, the rise of Germany to the level of a world power once again, without being hindered by anxious generals and diplomats. The prestige of the new Foreign Minister, von Ribbentrop, reached its peak in August 1939 with the conclusion of the German-Soviet non-aggression pact. It received its first heavy shock with the declaration of war by England and France (3 September 1939), which Ribbentrop had always thought impossible. Ribbentrop never recovered from this misjudgement of the foreign political situation, especially with respect to England. He remained an unconditionally devoted follower of Hitler until the last hour, but Hitler needed his faithful vassal less and less.

This first and last National Socialist Foreign Minister, Joachim von Ribbentrop, started to assume power over the AA in 1938. He did not attempt to inundate the AA with associates from the Ribbentrop Office, taking only a minority of reliable colleagues over into the AA with him. The majority of the more dubious figures remained in the Ribbentrop Office, which was never dissolved and led a shadowy existence. One cannot say that Ribbentrop corrupted the diplomatic apparatus with a clumsy hand. From his old office he brought with him M. Luther, head of the soon notorious department 'D' and later a junior state secretary. Moreover, he appointed Dr Ernst Woermann, his old embassy adviser in London, junior state secretary and head of the department Pol. Both of them were old party members.

Ribbentrop had realized that a forced 'nazification', filling all relevant posts with National Socialists who were not experts, would diminish the ability of the Office to fulfil its functions, and his ambition forced him to offer the Führer an office that was technically perfect; the desire for technical perfection and the desire to build up a strictly National Socialist Office were often in direct opposition.

Ribbentrop's attempt to 'nazify' the Office had two aspects. On the one hand it was necessary to bind the old officials to the party, if only superficially. Thanks to 'suggestions' by the Minister, the majority of officials joined the NSDAP from 1938 to 1940. By 1940, of 120 higher officials 71 were party members, and 11 tried to gain membership but had been refused. All the heads of departments (Woermann, Wiehl, Kriebel, Twardowski, Altenburg, Schmidt, Dörnberg) had joined the party with the exception of Gaus, an indispensable legal expert who served both the Weimar Republic and the Nazi state to the best of his ability.

The infiltration of the party into the AA was by no means an exception to the 'nazification' of German state offices; indeed, it was less complete than in other ministries. It became conspicuous because after Neurath's resignation five years after the Nazi seizure of power changes that had long since occurred elsewhere had to be made. The figures say nothing about a massive change of opinion among the old officials who belatedly entered the party. Fear for one's own position, the consciousness of not being promoted if one was not a party member, and during the war the possibility of being 'set free' for service at the front, may all have been reasons for party entry, and can be understood if not excused. One can say, however, that the AA was neither a retreat for resistance against the Nazis nor a place where criminal National Socialist ideas could be realized. A part of the AA was misused for these latter pursuits during the last years of the Nazi regime. This was connected to the last structural changes in wartime, which opened the way for many members of the party – and especially of the SS – to penetrate the inner circle of the Office. This makes one more readily appreciate the courage and the preparation for death of the few diplomats who did not keep quiet but were prepared for counter-action.

Adam von Trott zu Solz declared, even in front of the notorious People's Court and its president, Freisler, that it would be easier to enumerate the 'reliable' elements supporting the Nazi regime in the AA than the 'unreliable' ones; and he paid for his own opposition with his life. So did his friend Hans-Bernd von Haeften, a counsellor of legation, with death by the rope. The same fate befell the conservative former ambassadors, Ulrich von Hassell and Friedrich Werner Graf von der Schulenburg, who had become bitter enemies of Hitler; and a similar fate faced a disloyal protégé of Ribbentrop, Eduard Brücklmeier who, disillusioned by Nazi crimes, had contacted the resistance movement and was executed on 20 October 1944.

The Nazi reforms already mentioned included the foundation of a 'Deutschlandabteilung' from the former Deutschlandreferat and the Referat 'Partei' in 1940. Its head was the state under-secretary, Martin Luther, a protégé of Ribbentrop. He had become acquainted with Ribbentrop in 1932, when they worked together in the party in the area of Berlin where Ribbentrop lived. He was an obscure gentleman with financial contacts, but who was patronized by Ribbentrop in his office and brought into the AA as a confidant. Under Luther's leadership the department 'Deutschland' soon became the most important and least transparent department in the AA. It included work in the following fields: cooperation with the Reichssicher-heitshauptamt (RSHA) of Heydrich and the Gestapo; organization of diplomatic journeys abroad; surveillance of political enemies including Jewish affairs, which were brought into the responsibility of the ministry insofar as they were concerned with the AA. In a perverted form the AA thus kept its old right to consultation by every other office of the Reich where questions of the Reich's foreign relations were concerned. Himmler's RSHA kept in close contact with Luther and his colleagues over questions of the deportation of political prisoners from the occupied areas to Germany, when hostages and prisoners of war were supposed to be shot, or when 'volunteers' of the Waffen-SS were supposed to be recruited in the occupied areas. The AA was also involved in the distribution of forced labour.

The more Ribbentrop's political prestige sank, the more he struggled not to lose control over the Office; a great deal of his time was spent in trying to maintain his position. The newly created Ministry for the East (Ostministerium) under the leadership of Rosenberg, once again powerful, prevented Ribbentrop from having any influence over the Ukraine and the fringe states. Goebbels tried to impede the work of the AA information, press and radio departments. Ribbentrop's relations with the higher ranks of the SS, to which he himself belonged, was ambivalent. He almost became the victim of an intrigue of his former protégé Luther, who in 1943 wanted to declare him 'unaccountable' and to have him dismissed with the help of the SS. Luther seems to have had some support from Himmler and from Schellenberg, head of the 'Auslandsreferat' of the SD, but he had overestimated his position. Himmler was not prepared to risk anything for the former SA-Obersturmbannführer, and the SS dropped him. Luther was arrested in February 1943, but he was not sentenced to death as Ribbentrop had wanted. He was sent to the concentration camp of Oranienburg as an 'honourable prisoner'. Apparently this was the hidden response of the SS to Himmler's real opinion of Ribbentrop. Luther was freed from Oranienburg by the Russians in 1945, but he is said to have been shot shortly afterwards in a quarrel with Russian guards. This example shows how dubious were some of the leading figures of the AA, and also demonstrates that the struggle between competing groups was just as inexorable inside the party as it was between the party and other groups.

During the war years the AA increasingly lost its proper diplomatic tasks in foreign policy and became more and more an executive assistant in the politics of occupying and observing the smaller allies of Germany in Europe. The number of independent states with which Germany had diplomatic contacts decreased rapidly. In 1940 there were forty states left, in 1942 only twenty-two, of which nine were dependent (Vichy France, Greece, Croatia, Serbia, Slovakia, Hungary, Romania, Finland, Denmark). Only ten German representations abroad still existed in neutral states; in Europe these were Sweden, Switzerland, Spain, Portugal and Iceland. But in inverse proportion to the decrease in foreign political tasks, the number of officials in the Office increased during the years 1938 to 1945 from 2665 to 6458 persons, a growth of 143 per cent.

The Foreign Minister, with a small group of colleagues in a special train, nearly always accompanied the Führer's headquarters after the first day of the war. This was probably not so much to give Hitler advice on foreign affairs as the constant fear that a rival might become the favourite of his master, who took no advice in any case. Ribbentrop was present at the attempted murder in the 'Wolfsschanze' near Rastenburg on 20 July 1944, and also when Hitler began Germany's last active part in the war, the offensive of the Ardennes in December 1944. The Foreign Minister stayed with Hitler in Berlin during the last months of the Third Reich. During the last days of February 1945 he had an uncanny talk with Count Folke Bernadotte, representative of the Swedish Red Cross, in the AA, the greater part of which had already been destroyed by bombs. The Minister's office was still undestroyed, 'miraculously'. The last order Ribbentrop gave to his head of bureau, Reichsaussenminister (RAM), was to transfer the bureau to Garmisch, the 'new seat of government'. This happened on 14 April 1945. The Minister himself disappeared towards the west. He was arrested on 16 June 1945 by English soldiers in Hamburg in a friend's flat. He had followed his Führer only to the penultimate hour, not to the end in the bunker of death, which was situated next to his office in Berlin.

The Office itself had not seen much of its Minister during the war. The state secretary, Dr Ernst Freiherr von Weizsäcker, had administered it conscientiously until 31 January 1943. Weizsäcker was a conservative, able and cautious official of the old school. His statement that he had fulfilled his task with distress, in order 'to prevent worse things', cannot be rejected out of hand. When he was appointed German ambassador to the Vatican he felt greatly relieved. Weizsäcker's leaving was connected with Luther's arrest: Ribbentrop now wanted someone in the highest diplomatic post at home who was loyal to him personally as well as a reliable party member.

At the same time Department Germany, which had become too powerful, was dissolved into two groups, Inland I and Inland II, both of which were directly subordinate to the Minister. The anti-Semitic propaganda was supposed to be reinforced, as was cooperation with Himmler's RSHA, but all these measures were only half carried out. The new state secretary, Dr Gustav Adolf Baron Steengracht von Moyland, came from Ribbentrop's bureau and had been agricultural attaché when Ribbentrop was ambassador in London. Apart from 'amiable manners' he did not possess any qualifications for his new office. His only merit was that he – together with the head of the Personnel Department, Hans Schröder – managed to enforce the 60 per cent cutback in personnel in the AA, which had been ordered by Hitler after 20 July 1944. The Office was in any case in a state of dissolution. On 23 November 1943 the buildings in the Wilhelmstrasse were heavily hit in an air attack. Among other things nearly all the personnel files were lost. The officials had to make new files on themselves with sworn statements in lieu of an oath that these were true. For someone who looks at these files today it is quite surprising that probably no one 'forgot' anything in 1944: the officials faithfully filled in for the second time all the positions they had held in the party and its subdivisions. The Office was evacuated and dispersed to several places in the Riesengebirge, in Thuringia, and on Lake Constance. In January 1945 only a small group remained in Berlin with Ribbentrop and the state secretary, but they fled to the south in April 1945 without their Minister. The German Foreign Office in Berlin had ceased to exist. The Wilhelmstrasse was a heap of ruins.

The 'Geschäftsführende Reichsregierung' was formed according to Hitler's last will on 1 May 1945 by Grossadmiral Dönitz in Flensburg. The admiral remained in office for twenty-three days, until arrested by the English. In this government the former Minister of Finance, Graf Schwerin-Krosigk, had taken the post of Foreign Minister only reluctantly, not being an expert. One of his few activities in office was to ask the last German missions abroad to tell the governments of their host countries on 4 May 1945 that 'the Führer of the Great German Reich, Adolf Hitler, died as a hero on 1 May 1945. His successor according to German constitutional law in force is Herr Karl Dönitz.' With this last lie the AA of the Great German Reich took leave of the world. Hitler had not died 'as a hero' but had committed suicide, on 30 April not on 1 May. A general tendency to retreat now began among the few remaining foreign diplomats in Germany. The ambassadors of the fascist governments of Mussolini and Japan left 'the southern area' with their personnel. The few neutral states with which Germany still had diplomatic relations – the Reich was in the meantime at war with fifty-five states – broke off their relations: Portugal on 6 May, Sweden on 7 May, Switzerland on 8 May and, after the capitulation, Spain and Iceland. The last attempts of the 'managing government' to develop initiatives with Denmark and Sweden were made impossible by the general capitulation on 9 May 1945. What was finally recorded in Proclamation No. 2 of the Allied Control Council of 2 September 1945 was valid *de facto* since the day of the capitulation: 'By virtue of the unconditional surrender . . . the diplomatic, consular, commercial and other relations of the German state to other states have ceased to exist. All German diplomatic, consular, commercial and other officials or members of military missions abroad are herewith recalled.'

With this a vacuum was created in the field of German foreign relations that was to last for five years, an unprecedented occurrence in the history of the European powers. When it ended, the face not only of world politics but also of Germany had significantly changed. There was and is no more a Deutsches Reich, but only a Federal Republic of Germany and a German Democratic Republic, two states occupying the soil of the old Weimar Republic, which had shrunk to about three-quarters of its former size. There were now two states, with different social structures, different foreign policies and two different Foreign Ministries.

The period of stateless existence
During the years of Germany's 'stateless existence' from 1945 to 1949, it quickly became evident that a large country cannot live without foreign relations, even if it is ruled under an occupation statute. From 1945 until the spring of 1947 it still seemed possible to negotiate a peace treaty for the whole of Germany. This possibility encouraged a number of old diplomats to attempt to unite initiating groups for the preparation of a peace treaty in the northern and southern German states of the Western Occupation Zones. Among the first initiators were such distinguished diplomats of the Weimar Republic as the former ambassadors Herbert von Dirksen and Rudolf Nadolny, and also Eugen Budde, who had been legation councillor under Stresemann and Brüning and had worked on internal preparations for European peace politics, but had been dismissed from the AA in 1933 by the Nazis. In both the north and south discussion groups on the future peace

treaty were formed. The true founder of some sort of 'bureau' to unite these discussion groups was Erich Rossmann, secretary-general of the South German Länderrat. On 11 December 1946 he proposed 'the foundation of an official bureau to prepare a German peace treaty'. This was discussed inside the parties. Rossmann, a Social Democrat, was opposed to the leader of his own party, Kurt Schumacher, who wanted to wait until the occupying authorities had decided their own policies. But Rossmann's initiative gained support, especially in the southern German Länder. On 25 January and 17 February 1947 the prime ministers of the Länder of the American and British Occupation Zones decided that the foundation of a 'bureau for peace questions' was necessary. Their model was the so-called 'Pax conference', which had been created in the winter of 1918–19 by the AA under the leadership of a former ambassador, Graf Bernstorff, in order to formulate German ideas on peace to be heard at Versailles. This first German 'peace bureau' had been unsuccessful, as despite its considerable work there were no peace negotiations at Versailles.

The second 'peace bureau' in the history of German foreign relations was doomed to a similar fate. With the tacit approval of General Clay, the prime ministers in the American Occupation Zone agreed on 15 April 1947 to found a German Bureau for Peace Questions. But Clay had declared explicitly that the foundation of a bizonal peace bureau was not opportune. The Moscow conference of Foreign Ministers in March and April 1947 and the Munich conference of Prime Ministers – the only 'all-German conference' of East and West German Prime Ministers – in June 1947 failed. Their failure showed that on the side of the victorious powers, as well as on that of the Germans concerned, the fact of the separation of Germany was becoming apparent. The tasks for a German Peace Bureau became just as utopian as the tasks for the Pax conference had been nearly thirty years earlier. Nevertheless, the Bureau became a meeting place for former diplomats, who now cooperated closely with the administration of the United Economic Area in Frankfurt am Main and with the German Länder of the Western Zones. They helped with advice on questions concerning foreign policy such as the occupation statute, the Ruhr statute, etc.

The step-by-step reclamation of German sovereignty from 1949 onwards strengthened the importance of the institutions that had been concerned with foreign policy before the foundation of the Federal Republic, especially the German Peace Bureau in Stuttgart and the Main Department V of the United Economic Area (Hauptabteilung V des Vereinigten Wirtschaftsgebiets) in Hoechst near Frankfurt (founded in 1947). This department had been asked to prepare an economics department for a new Foreign Ministry by Dr Hermann Pünder, a well-known German politician, who succeeded Adenauer as Lord Mayor of Cologne (1945–9), and later became Director of the Administration Council of the United Economic Area. Moreover, in spring 1949 the Western Allies had created a link between the Allied High Commission and the slowly evolving future Federal Government in which the political questions of the occupation powers were supposed to be discussed with West Germany. The former secretary-general of the Advisory Council of the British Zone, Herbert Blankenhorn, became head of this department on the German side. Blankenhorn had been in the diplomatic service since 1929. After several posts abroad he worked in the AA in Berlin from 1943 to 1945. In the British

Zone he became one of the co-founders of the CDU. In 1948, as secretary-general of the CDU, he was one of Adenauer's closest colleagues and confidantes. Blankenhorn had the most decisive part in the reconstruction of the AA in Bonn. The first visible step towards state sovereignty was taken with the founding of the Government of the Federal Republic of Germany on 20 September 1949, which reopened the door to an autonomous foreign policy. The Petersberg agreement of 22 November 1949 allowed the resumption of 'consular and commercial relations'. Then, on 1 April 1950, an Office for Foreign Affairs, directly subordinate to the Federal Chancellery, was founded in Bonn. Dr Wilhelm Haas, Staatsrat in Bremen, had in the meantime prepared an outline plan for a future Foreign Ministry, which united all the working groups in the Chancellor's office concerned with foreign politics. On 16 June 1950 the consulate-general in London was established as the first foreign service office abroad. In the same year, German consulates in Amsterdam, Brussels, Rome and Athens followed.

The new Foreign Office, 1951 to the present

The new Foreign Office of the Federal Republic of Germany was born on 15 March 1951. On that day the first President of the Federal Republic, Heuss, appointed the first Chancellor, Adenauer, as Minister for Foreign Affairs. On the same day the new office was founded with its old name: the 'Foreign Office' of the Federal Republic. The above-mentioned bureaux in the Chancellor's Office became the nucleus of the new Office. They were joined by Main Department V in Frankfurt, and the German Bureau for Peace Questions, most of whose personnel had already been appointed by Adenauer for the Dienststelle für Auswärtige Angelegenheiten in the Chancellor's Office.

In a dry, official declaration to the press on 14 March 1951 it was announced that Federal Chancellor Adenauer would also take charge of the new Foreign Ministry. The FDP and SDP protested strongly but in vain against this decision. Later, the Chancellor gave as his reason for this decision the view that it would be useful to unite both offices in one person as long as he, the Chancellor, would have to negotiate constantly with the High Commissions of the Western Allies. Adenauer himself negotiated all the treaties, from the treaty for the Marshall Plan (January 1950), the General Treaty (26 May 1952), to the day when the Paris Treaties came into force (5 May 1955), which fully involved the Federal Republic in the defence system of the West. Once again the Bismarckian situation had been repeated, albeit under completely different circumstances: the Chancellor was his own Foreign Minister. He not only laid down the general policy, according to the Constitution, but as his own Minister also carried this policy out. This exceptional situation was only abandoned after strong pressure from all parties, including his own, after the most important bases of the foreign policy of the independent Federal Republic had been laid.

On his visit to Moscow (9 to 13 September 1955), where diplomatic relations between the USSR and the Federal Republic were established and when the Soviet Union agreed to free the last German prisoners of war, Adenauer was accompanied by the new Foreign Minister, Heinrich von Brentano, who had started work on 7 June 1955. The era of Adenauer's 'Chancellor's democracy', during which foreign policy was made in the

Chancellor's Office and the AA did nothing but prepare the Chancellor's work, was slowly coming to an end.

One of the greatest difficulties was the coordination of personnel in the new Office. To supervise the training of a new generation of diplomats Adenauer selected Consul-General Peter Pfeiffer, brother of the Bavarian minister and former German envoy Arnold Pfeiffer, who had already worked out a general plan for the organization of the future Foreign Ministry. Peter Pfeiffer became the founder and leader of the first training centre for future German diplomats in Speyer. At first courses were short to meet the immediate demand for diplomats, but later training took two years. Applicants for the higher diplomatic service had to have a university degree and a good knowledge of English and French, and were then introduced to the practical and theoretical tasks of their profession. The 'school for diplomats' in Speyer had in a short time become so good that the institution was transferred to Bonn in 1955 in order to establish closer relations with its future practical field of activity. Each year the 'crew' was accommodated in boarding schools, and this seemed to have a good influence on the self-confidence and sense of responsibility of the young German diplomats. Most of the candidates to this day make use of the offer to live and work under the same roof, an opportunity also extended to candidates of the middle-rank service. Obviously Pfeiffer was very fortunate in his choice of trainees and in the arrangement of their education. Karl-Günther Hase, then state secretary and later head of the Federal Department for Press and Information, wrote in 1965 on the occasion of Pfeiffer's sixty-fifth birthday: 'Many more than half the higher officials of the Foreign Service of today went through the education created by Peter Pfeiffer. One is justified in saying that in the whole history of the foreign service no one has had a more impressive and extensive effect than Peter Pfeiffer.'

The entrance examination for candidates was and still is very exacting. Of the 218 applicants to the higher civil service in 1976 only 36 were accepted for training; in 1977 it was only 42 out of a total of 283 applicants. The successful candidates then become attachés and serve their preparatory period in the central office in Bonn and in German offices abroad. After finishing his training with a further examination, the attaché is as a civil servant only available to the Foreign Office; he can be deployed in a consulate or embassy or in the central office.

Good though the education was of the rising generation of diplomats, despite the initial improvisations, the distribution of top diplomatic posts, especially abroad, proved to be extremely difficult given the lack of representatives with both expert knowledge and an acceptable political past. In the initial phase of reconstruction (even before the official foundation of the AA thirty-two German diplomatic missions had already been planned) the number of officials and employees of the higher service who had been members of the NSDAP was relatively high. All went through the denazification process, but the actual percentage still shocked the public: On 1 October 1950 there were some 120 higher officials; 44.5 per cent of them came from the old AA, and 42.3 per cent were former party members. By 1 April 1952 there were approximately 469 higher officials; 30.3 per cent had been in the old AA, and 33 per cent were former party members.

In the 'Frankfurter Rundschau' of September 1951 twenty-eight-year-old journalist Heinze-Mansfield published a series of five articles with the title 'You come again . . .', in which he looked into the *curricula vitae* of twenty-one readmitted officials of the old AA. Mansfield wished to prove that the higher service of the new AA, which was in the process of being rebuilt, was nothing but a restoration of the Nazi AA. The Bundestag appointed a commission that between September 1951 and June 1952 very carefully investigated his accusations. As a result, four cases out of twenty-one were denied suitability for further employment in the foreign service, and in seven cases further employment was recommended only in limited areas.

This first and only 'scandal' in the reconstruction of the new AA was an early and useful warning that the young parliamentary democracy placed before the once all-powerful Office. The choice of employees from old officials became more careful and the number of only 'nominal' party members decreased rapidly. Such a strong reproach against the AA as that of 1951 was never repeated. By 1974 the group of former Nazi party members among the 1299 officials and employees of the higher service represented an unimportant minority, simply on grounds of age.

As after the First World War, so after the Second World War outsiders were used for leading positions abroad. The prestige of German diplomacy, which had suffered from the Nazi diplomats under Ribbentrop and from the Nuremberg trials, was supposed to be corrected by heads of missions with clear records. Among the best-known ambassadors sent abroad by the Federal Republic during its first period of independence were Prinz Adalbert von Bayern to Madrid, Wilhelm Hausenstein to Paris, Hans Schlange-Schöningen to London, Wilhelm Grewe to Washington, and Heinz Krekeler to New York and Washington. After the first wave of outside diplomats, no more followed; the traditions not only of the Office but also of the German professional civil service as a whole obviously admitted only under exceptional circumstances that a non-career civil servant could represent his government abroad.

The new AA was, and is, confronted with a world in which foreign politics are made according to different standards and forms from those of the 1930s. The flood of information with which the Ministry has to cope demands new types of organization similar to those of industrial management, and far more personnel. This situation can be illustrated by a simple example. The number of telegrams sent out and received annually was 786 in 1874, 2190 in 1923, 12829 in 1952 (and from now on telegrams and teletyped messages), 65553 in 1960, and 202361 in 1970.

The old and persistently defended claims of the AA to take part in all affairs that involve negotiations with other countries is still laid down today in §11 of the Federal Standing Orders. The degree to which the Chancellor can interfere with the independent work of the Foreign Minister depends mainly on the willingness of the Chancellor concerned to cooperate. In this respect the second Foreign Minister of the Federal Republic, Heinrich von Brentano (1955–61) certainly had the most difficult position with regard to his predecessor, Chancellor Adenauer. But his successors, Gerhard Schröder, Willy Brandt, Walter Scheel and Hans-Dietrich Genscher, also had to continue this fight against the 'excavation' of the Office. It is weakened not only by the Chancellor's Office and by its old rivals, the Ministries for Economics and for Defence, but by nearly every Federal ministry that demands to have a say simply on the grounds of its expert knowledge in the international organization to which the Federal Republic belongs. A few examples may illustrate the general situation. The European Community's Ministers' Council in Brussels often consists of Ministers for Agriculture, Finance and Economics. The same applies to NATO in Brussels. Here the tendency towards independence is perhaps pushed furthest because the Federal Ministry for Defence supports branch offices in several member states of NATO that are not affiliated to the embassies. There are also several other international organizations in which Federal ministries are directly represented.

In the second half of the twentieth century political, economic and cultural affairs have become so closely interwoven that they can no longer be managed by one Ministry. In theory, as before, the Foreign Office still claims to decide all questions of foreign policy. In practice, this claim is very often reduced to a 'right to be heard' on all such questions. Although its influence may be diminished, the Foreign Office keeps its influence in all questions of international politics where other ministries need the help of German missions abroad to carry out their plans, be they questions of humanitarian help, development work, science and education, or others. Here the expert opinion of the diplomats, their knowledge about the economic, social and cultural problems of the country in question, and their official and personal relations with its ruling élites, are indispensable.

Closely connected with these problems is the question of how to organize the Office and to train its civil servants properly. Even today the old struggle about the most suitable form of organization has not been decided. Should the Office for the most part be divided regionally, i.e. according to groups of countries, in which *all* the questions concerning one country should be tackled? This was the ideal of the great reformer Edmund Schüler. The alternative is: should the Office be divided according to sections, as under the old Imperial Office, i.e. should questions of commercial policy, development politics, culture or international character be tackled in special divisions, with a view to the totality of the problems to be handled?

More and more people have defended this latter system during the last twenty-five years, as the prestigious thinking of the old Office, which separated the 'noble' department (questions of pure foreign affairs) from the 'less noble' departments (economics, culture, law), has become obsolete. The AA of today has followed neither one form nor the other in its entirety, though the Reform Commission of 1971 had advocated a regional structure. In practice, experience has shown that the mixed form is most useful (see Appendix A).

As far as the staff is concerned, there is no specialist training directed primarily towards consular or embassy duties. The principle that the young civil servant should be trained as broadly as possible so that he can serve in a wide area is still upheld. However, the last Reform Commission of the Foreign Office found that 'the demand for specialists will increase heavily in the future'. It is proposed to employ a specialist from outside 'for a time' in the foreign service. It is questionable whether this practice can be implemented in the long term in view of the ever-increasing need for specialization, which does not stop short even of this profession.

The proper art of administration in the central office consists in evaluating for the Federal Chancellor and various committees all the regional impulses and information that arrive daily from all over the world – not only regional but also sectional – at the top and for the top of the Office, and occasionally to transform this material into decisions or recommendations. The enlarged workload thus created for the senior staff of the Office results in an increase of senior personnel.

Apart from the considerable growth of the Bureau of the Minister, the state secretary *of* the Foreign Office has the assistance of a second civil servant, the state secretary *in* the Foreign Office, who deals mainly with questions of economic and cultural politics. Two parliamentary ministers of state, with changing functions, have also been appointed.

The unique position of the German AA is to be seen in its function as the 'most noble servant' of the Bund rather than as its 'noblest office'. The Office is supposed to serve the Chancellor in expanding his competence to set a general political line. But it is also supposed to assist each Minister with its advice and experience whenever bilateral or multilateral questions touch this Ministry's special field. The AA is not a collection of specialists for the different technical, economic, social or cultural sections in the field of international relations. The Office until now has successfully maintained the generalist principle. The attachés are trained according to the following principles: 'The official is not appointed for specialized work, for instance in the cultural, economic or legal department, nor for work in a specific country, but independent of his preparatory training, for the whole field of activities of the higher foreign service' (instruction sheet, 1973).

It is doubtful whether this principle can be maintained. It has already proved necessary in economic relations, social politics, science and education to send specialists from universities to the larger embassies, and especially to permanent delegations at the UN, EEC and OECD. The profession of diplomacy has lost its old glamour. At a time when diplomacy is made in conferences at the level of heads of state, Foreign Ministers, heads of international banks or industrial groups or other communities with special interests, the decision-making roles of independent diplomats are reduced in importance. Ambassadors who can be allowed to make their own policies, like Graf Brockdorff-Rantzau, the ambassador in Moscow, no longer exist.

The elitist character of the diplomatic profession can still be observed in the social backgrounds of the new generation of applicants. It is no longer the old families of the aristocracy and middle classes that supply the majority of applicants. Those times are over for both the officer and the diplomatic corps. The majority of candidates now come from the upper middle class, the judiciary and the officer class. Approximately 50 per cent of the applicants in 1969 came from this group, while the group of artisans' and labourers' sons, as well as sons of fathers in the 'free occupations' (doctors, independent farmers, lawyers, etc.), is declining. The profession of diplomat is more and more one for the upper middle classes, not one for social advancement.

The ideal type of young German diplomat – and in this he resembles his colleagues in other countries – is a man who can listen but also act, who removes difficulties unobtrusively but who at his best does not allow difficulties to develop, and who above all has a secure feeling for what he represents: a country whose economic power easily leads one to forget its endangered foreign political situation. Prudence, consistency and reliability are supposed to mark the acts of a German 'generalist' as long as he still exists in foreign politics.

The 198 external legations (their number on 31 December 1979) of the Federal Republic of Germany form a widely spread net that stretches across the world. It consists of 124 embassies, 59 consulates-general, seven consulates and eight delegations with international organizations. As the Federal Republic's latest annual report states, developments in the training and advanced training centres of the AA for the senior, high-ranking and middle-ranking services continue. In 1979, 42 attachés in the senior service, 41 candidates for consular secretaryships in the higher service and 24 candidates for governmental assistantships in the middle-ranking service took the professional examinations. Since 1 October 1979 candidates for higher ranking external services have been trained on a course in public administration at the Federal Technical College.

With regard to German cultural policy, the AA's efforts increase from year to year. In 1979 the cultural budget of the AA was 596.5 million marks, an increase of 6.3 per cent over the 1978 figure. Above all, strenuous efforts were made to promote the German language in the world. The most recent assessment of the situation gave the following picture: in 61 countries, there were between 16 and 17 million students of German in foreign schools (over 12 million of them in East European countries), 1.2 million students of German in schools of further education, and 3 to 4 million people learning German in adult education courses. The AA supports this cultural work with, among other things, 509 German schools abroad, 113 Goethe Institutes, 52 technical advisers and 350 university lecturers.

Despite the many fundamental changes – political, social, economic and cultural – that our world has undergone, it will remain the highest goal of the diplomatic work of the German AA in the future to so shape relationships with individuals, with peoples and with nations that the work will serve the cause of world peace.

BIBLIOGRAPHY

Die Auswärtige Politik der Bundesrepublik Deutschland edited by the AA with the cooperation of a scientific consultant (Cologne 1972).

Der auswärtige Dienst des Deutschen Reiches (Diplomatie und Konsularwesen) edited by H. Kraus (Berlin 1929).

Aus der Schule der Diplomatie. Festschrift zum 70. Geburtstag von Peter Pfeiffer (Düsseldorf, Vienna 1965).

Handbuck der deutschen Aussenpolitik edited by Hans-Peter Schwarz (Munich, Zurich 1975).

100 Jahre Auswärtiges Amt 1870–1970 edited by the AA (compiled from the Political Archives of the AA under the editorship of Dr Heinz Günther Sasse in collaboration with Dr Ekkehard Eickhoff) (Bonn 1970).

Auswärtiges Amt Special edition from the 1979 Annual Report of the Federal Government edited by the AA (Bonn 1979).

Lamar Cecil, *The German Diplomatic Service 1871–1914* (Princeton 1976).

Klaus Curtius and Gerrit von Haeften, *Die Nachwuchsausbildung für den höheren Auswärtigen Dienst der Bundesrepublik Deutschland und der Vereinigten Staaten von Amerika* (Frankfurt am Main 1974).

Kurt Doß, *Das deutsche Auswärtige Amt im Übergang vom Kaiserreich zur Weimarer Republik – Die Schülersche Reform* (Düsseldorf 1977).

Heinrich End, *Erneuerung der Diplomatie. Der Auswärtige Dienst der Bundesrepublik Deutschland – Fossil oder Instrument?* (Neuwied and Berlin 1969).

Wilhelm Grewe, *Deutsche Aussenpolitik der Nachkriegszeit* (Stuttgart 1960).

Wilhelm Haas, *Beiträge zur Geschichte der Entstehung des Auswärtigen Amtes der Bundesrepublik Deutschland* (Bremen 1969).

Hans Adolf Jacobsen, *Nationalsozialistische Aussenpolitik 1933–1938* (Frankfurt/M. and Berlin 1968).

Winfried Kasulke, *Die Bundesstelle für Aussenhandelsinformation* (Bonn 1971).

Erich Kordt, *Nicht aus den Akten Die Wilhelmstrasse in Frieden und Krieg. Erlebnisse, Begegnungen, Eindrücke 1928–1945* (Stuttgart 1950).

P. G. Lauren, *Diplomats and Bureaucrats: The First Institutional Responses to Twentieth-Century Diplomacy in France and Germany* (Stanford, Calif. 1976).

Albrecht Lohmann, *Das Auswärtige Amt 2. überarbeitete und ergänzte Auflage* (Düsseldorf 1973).

Rudolf Morsey, *Die oberste Reichsverwaltung unter Bismarck 1867–1890* (Münster 1957).

Manfred Overesch, *Gesamtdeutsche Illusion und westdeutsche Realität. Von den Vorbereitungen für einen deutschen Friedensvertrag zur Gründung des Auswärtigen Amts der Bundesrepublik Deutschland 1946–1949/51* (Düsseldorf 1978).

Heribert Pionkowitz, *Das deutsche Büro für Friedensfragen 1947–1949. Ein Vorläufer des Auswärtigen Amts im Widerspiel der Kräfte* (Göttingen 1977).

Otto Reinfried Schifferdecker, *Die Organisation des auswärtigen Dienstes im alten und neuen Reich* (Heidelberg 1931).

Paul Seabury, *The Wilhelmstrasse: A study of German diplomats under the Nazi Regime* (Berkeley, Los Angeles 1954).

APPENDIX A: THE GERMAN FOREIGN OFFICE (1980)

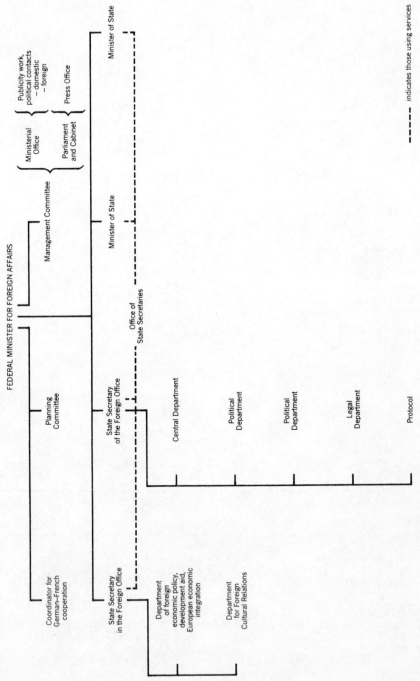

FEDERAL MINISTER FOR FOREIGN AFFAIRS

Coordinator for German–French cooperation

Planning Committee

Management Committee

Publicity work, political contacts
– domestic
– foreign

Ministerial Office

Parliament and Cabinet

Press Office

Minister of State

Minister of State

State Secretary of the Foreign Office

Office of State Secretaries

State Secretary in the Foreign Office

Department of foreign economic policy, development aid, European economic integration

Department for Foreign Cultural Relations

Central Department

Political Department

Political Department

Legal Department

Protocol

- - - - - indicates those using services

Greece

The Greek Foreign Ministry

DOMNA DONTAS

Dr Domna Dontas is the Director of the Archives of the Greek Foreign Ministry. She studied in Athens and at the University of London where she took her Ph.D. She was the Greek Deputy Permanent Delegate to UNESCO in Paris until the autumn of 1981. Dr Dontas has published several articles and books including *The Last Phase of the War of Independence in Western Greece* (1966), *Greece and the Great Powers 1863–1875* (1966) and, in Greek, *The History of the Post-War World 1945–1970* (1973).

From Greece's beginnings as a nation state in the early nineteenth century its rulers developed a foreign policy and a rudimentary organization to formulate and conduct it. A few months after the outbreak of the Greek War of Independence of 1821 the first so-called National Assembly appointed a five-member provisional administration for the prosecution of the war – a task that involved appeals to foreigners for help. In this administration there was no separate foreign department: the head of the Government acted as secretary for foreign affairs but his scope was very limited, as Greece was entirely devoid of an official diplomatic representation abroad and there were no Europeans in any official political capacity within insurgent Greece.

In January 1822, when the first Greek Constitution was promulgated, a Ministry of Foreign Affairs was instituted, its first Minister being Theodore Negris, a Greek who came from the Greek community in Venice. This Ministry was abolished by the second so-called National Assembly, which met at Astros in March 1823; its duties were allocated to the secretary-general of the executive, Alexander Mavrokordatos. Already Mavrokordatos' close friend, John Louriottis, after abortive missions to Spain and Portugal, had arrived in London to raise a loan, which had been sanctioned by the National Assembly. His business in London was, however, conducted not with the government but with the London Greek Committee, a purely private concern. Greece was not yet formally recognized, and Greek foreign relations had necessarily to be conducted either with unofficial persons in foreign lands or with unofficial European agents on Greek soil. In August 1822 Negris had sent to the Christian powers, who were assembled for the Congress of Verona, a letter stating the Greek case. This letter was carried by two 'ambassadors', Count Andreas Metaxas and the French Philhellene Count Philippe Jourdain, who hoped to gain permission to address the Congress. The two 'ambassadors' were, however, turned away and expelled for being representatives of an illegal state. Nevertheless, Greece was not entirely without official contact with the foreign powers: the Greek government received complaints from European naval commanders of breaches of inter-national maritime law, and the Greek government, wishing to assume the responsibilities of a modern state, announced in a declaration of 13/25 March 1822 (the first recorded Greek diplomatic act) – a declaration communicated to consuls of the foreign powers and to the British High Commissioner of the Ionian Islands – that all Greek ports still occupied by enemy garrisons were blockaded. In March 1823 the British Foreign Minister, George Canning, recognized Greek blockades.

Although, in December 1824, Canning rejected a Greek appeal (of 4 August) for intervention, and left unanswered a Greek petition (the so-called Act of Submission of 1825) for the sole protection of Great Britain, his cousin, Stratford Canning, ambassador to the Porte, held unofficial discussions with Mavrokordatos, the outcome of which encouraged George Canning to negotiate a solution of the Greek question in company with Russia. The following year the Greeks, sensing that the powers were on the point of beginning negotiations, appointed (in their Third National Assembly, at Trizene) a committee to conduct talks with Great Britain. Nothing came of these labours: negotiations between the powers were not completed until July 1827, and the Greeks themselves were in a state of disorder until, in April 1827, the warring parties united at Damala and elected Count John

Capodistrias as President of Greece. He had remained outside Greece during the war of liberation and had taken no active part in Greek party conflicts. He also had the advantage of having vast experience as Foreign Minister of the Tsar of Russia, in whose service he had remained until 1822.

On arriving in Greece in January 1828 Capodistrias appointed among other Ministers, a Secretary of State for Foreign Affairs and the Marine. Capodistrias himself, however, conducted all negotiations with the agents ('Residents') whom Great Britain, France and Russia had accredited to Greece following the signing of the Tripartite Treaty of 7 July 1827. He signed all communications addressed to those Residents, the signature of the Secretary of State being added merely as a matter of form.

As a result of these negotiations (which were protracted because of Turkish intransigence, rivalry between the Three Protecting Powers, civil strife in Greece and the assassination of Capodistrias in October 1831) Greece emerged (treaty of 7 May 1832) as a kingdom, its ruler-designate being Prince Otho of Bavaria, who arrived in Greece early in 1833. Still a minor, Otho was accompanied by a three-member Bavarian regency, which established seven departments of government, each under a Secretary of State, the head of the government being the Secretary-General of State. One of the secretaries was described as Secretary for the Royal House and for Foreign Affairs. By a royal decree of 3/15 April 1833 his staff was established as one counsellor, three secretaries, a copyist and a messenger. His duties were: (a) political affairs, relations with foreign states and maintenance of treaty obligations; (b) correspondence of the King with foreign sovereigns and governments; (c) administration and protection of the rights of the Royal House; (d) protection of Greek nationals abroad; (e) correspondence with the Holy See of Rome and the Roman Catholic Church in Greece; (f) issue of passports; (g) issue to Greek nationals of permits to enter foreign military service and to accept foreign decorations; (h) emigration: export of private movable property; (i) conferment of Greek nationality; (j) decorations; (k) maintenance of the Royal and State archives.

All appointments of diplomats and diplomatic agents (later called consuls) and of commercial agents were made by the King. Politicians with a 'European' education, or those who had read law or were well versed in foreign languages (particularly French) were usually appointed to high ranking diplomatic posts. Until the 1850s these politicians were immigrant Greeks (many of whom had arrived with Otho), for graduates of the University of Athens, which had been founded in 1837, were not yet of sufficient seniority for such appointments.

Documents embodying policy decisions of the Secretariat of the Royal House and Foreign Affairs were signed by the King; those issued in execution of the King's decisions were signed by the Secretary of State, drafts having been previously submitted to the King for his approval. From 1833 to 1835 drafts of important documents were accompanied by a German translation for the benefit of the young sovereign and the Bavarian members of the regency. From 1835, when Otho attained his majority, all documents were drawn up solely in Greek. All correspondence with foreign envoys in Athens was conducted in French. It was, moreover, not unusual for Greek representatives abroad to write their dispatches to the Ministry in French, a practice followed by the Russian, Austrian, Turkish and other diplomatic services, and continued by the Greeks until the 1880s. For technical reasons Greek telegrams were always transmitted in French until the 1920s. In 1834 King Otho appointed ministers to the courts of the Three Protecting Powers and to certain other capitals. To London he sent Spiridon Trikoupis, whose many qualifications included his excellent knowledge of the English language and culture, his Anglophilism, and the great respect he commanded in English society. To Vienna and Munich he sent Alexander Mavrokordatos. This appointment was made largely for internal political reasons: Otho and his entourage considered that Mavrokordatos was too much under the influence of Dawkins, the British Minister in Athens, and too likely to rally certain factions against the government. To Constantinople Otho sent Constantine Zographos, who was well acquainted with Turkish affairs; to Paris he appointed Constantine Karadja; and to St Petersburg he sent Michael Soutzos. All these ministers, who were given opportunities to visit certain other capitals, possessed not only the necessary educational background but also substantial private incomes. Members either of the Phanariot families of Constantinople or of wealthy Greek families in Europe, they had a familiarity with international affairs and the manners to conduct themselves with dignity in society.

By a royal decree of 20 August 1834 Otho created a consular body, which represented Greece in the more important ports in the Black and Mediterranean Seas, in India and America, and also in numerous European cities where Greek communities had flourished for over two centuries. Usually the consuls were drawn from well-known and wealthy Greek families – as, for example, the Rodocanachi family in Geneva or the Ionidis family in Manchester. Almost everywhere they were concerned with large Greek communities (especially in the confines of the Ottoman Empire). Their duties were not restricted to routine consular business; indeed, their extensive role finds no parallel in the diplomatic history of other nations. As E. Driault and M. Lhéritier have written: 'All the Greeks living in Turkey enjoy the same municipal freedoms as in the Kingdom. All those over twenty-five years of age make up the national assemblies, which elect two deputies, a municipal council and two treasurers. The revenues are assured by a duty of 1 per cent on merchandise imported or exported through the ports of the department. The assembly has the right to vote, in addition, special taxes.

'This "body of the nation", continuing the most ancient traditions in memory of the "colonies" of Athens, organizes, from generation to generation, the renewal of all the economic, political and social activity in the Turkish empire, and by doing this dissolves the empire. Such are the living cells, which in the midst of tardiness and diplomatic obstacles, invincibly recreate the Greek nation.' (Translated from *Histoire diplomatique de la Grèce de 1821 à nos jours,* Paris 1925, 1926, vol. ii, p. 112.)

These 'living cells' were of paramount importance to all political men of Athens. To them the new kingdom was far too small in comparison with the extent of territories that were traditionally Greek, and from the outset they aimed to achieve the 'Great Idea', that is to say the redemption of all Greeks still remaining under Turkish rule. Of necessity, this aim could be achieved only within the framework of European politics, concerning which every Greek had his own ideas. Hence Greek foreign affairs were bedevilled by pro-Russian, pro-English and pro-French orientations, and it was only natural that the Greeks should encourage the Protecting Powers to interfere in their internal politics, just as they had done during the War of Independence.

In the first ten years of Otho's reign foreign affairs were conducted by the Palace, the Foreign Secretary acting merely as an adviser or simply as an assistant to the King. On matters of substance Otho himself received ministers, only the less important business being delegated to the Foreign Secretariat. But after the Revolution of 1843, which forced the King to give Greece a parliamentary regime, the Foreign Secretariat assumed a greater responsibility. According to a law of 3/15 June 1846, which renamed the Foreign Secretariat 'Ministry of the Royal House and Foreign Affairs' and placed it under a Foreign Minister, the diplomatic personnel was nearly doubled (from six to eleven). Some seven years later a law of 25 October/6 November 1853 empowered the government to create, as required, new diplomatic missions abroad though it was stipulated that no mission should have more than two paid persons – the minister and a secretary. By a royal decree of 21 February/5 March 1856 a secretary-general was appointed to assist the Foreign Minister, his task being to direct and control the administration of the Ministry. That same year a royal decree of 19 June/1 July instituted a council to give rulings on questions of international law. It consisted of five members – a Member of Parliament, the Crown Prosecutor in the Supreme Court, the Dean of the Faculty of Law in the University of Athens, a distinguished lawyer and a Counsellor of the Ministry.

Although deprived by a law of 3/15 June 1846 of the right to formulate foreign policy or to issue documents pertaining to Foreign Ministry business without the signature of the Minister, the King continued to appoint the Minister for Foreign Affairs and the ministers. He was, therefore, still able to play a major role in foreign affairs and to continue the old practice of 'exiling' unwanted politicians to diplomatic posts abroad. During the Crimean War (1854–6), Otho and his entourage conducted an aggressive foreign policy, hoping to turn the conflicts of the Protecting Powers and the difficulties of the Ottoman Empire to his advantage. His policy failed, and it was this failure that greatly contributed to his downfall in the next decade.

As a result of yet another revolution, in 1863, Otho went into exile and the powers, after protracted negotiations, agreed on a new dynasty for Greece, the new king being George I of the House of Glücksburg. By that time the generation of the War of Independence had almost completely passed away. The new politicians were generally better educated, more enlightened and more liberal than their predecessors. Like them, however, they hoped to realize the 'Great Idea', but the means contemplated were primarily diplomatic and less warlike. They formed political parties that were no longer so orientated towards the Protecting Powers, and they tended to stress internal issues. Nevertheless, foreign policy remained a highly contentious element in the party struggle. Although there was general agreement on the need to fulfil the 'Great Idea', there was endless dispute on how this should be done and who should do it.

By a decision of a Greek National Assembly, which had been convened following the Revolution of 1862, the former department dealing with foreign matters had been renamed the Ministry of Foreign Affairs. In 1864, after protracted debates and negotiations, the Assembly approved a new

Constitution, which George I accepted. This Constitution was based on the Belgian Constitution of 7 February 1831, which had in turn been modelled on the French Constitution of 3 September 1791. In theory the King had no powers other than those specifically bestowed upon him by the Constitution; he had, for instance, no powers of constitutional revision or of veto. But – and here the Greek Constitution differed from the French Constitution of 1791 – he had the right to appoint and dismiss ministers and to dissolve parliament. This gave him considerable power and influence, especially as most Greek governments were unstable coalitions based on shifting parliamentary factions and as no Greek politician was averse to using royal influence when it suited him to do so. Where foreign policy was concerned the King, especially when he became more experienced, though he was constantly obstructed, usually had the last word; as time went on, he came to have a better understanding of international politics than his Ministers and, for a variety of reasons, was better able to wring concessions from the European powers.

The Foreign Ministry bequeathed by the previous dynasty soon proved to be inadequate, and in 1868, by a royal decree of 1/13 March, it was divided into three departments: the first was responsible for political and ecclesiastical affairs, treaties, and relations with foreign courts; the second dealt with consular and administrative matters, commercial conventions, decorations, archaeological excavations, exhibitions, Greek students abroad and questions of protocol; the third was in charge of the establishment of new consulates, legal matters, postal and telegraphic conventions, bequests, commercial fairs and maritime questions. By that same decree, a special competitive examination was established for entry to the diplomatic service: candidates (who were required to hold a degree in law) were examined in international, maritime and commercial law, and in French, geography and general history (emphasis being placed on important treaties). It was hoped that this new personnel would raise Greek prestige and show to the world that Greece was governed constitutionally. Nevertheless, despite this move to create a diplomatic service based on merit, in the appointments of ministers and of the heads of departments in the Foreign Ministry, political affiliations continued to play a dominating role.

In 1877 Greece reorganized its consular service. The former consular agencies became consulates-general, consulates or vice-consulates. Career diplomats were appointed to the new posts in the Balkan consulates, for in view of the possibility of a Russo-Turkish war the Greek government considered it essential to compete with its northern neighbours for supremacy in regions that might succeed in throwing off Turkish rule. Fortunately for Greece, the terms of the Treaty of San Stefano (March 1878), which followed the Russo-Turkish war, were not to the liking of Great Britain, Austria and Germany, who drastically revised them in the Congress of Berlin (June–July 1878). Although Greece gained nothing (despite the efforts of Greek consuls and other agents to foment rebellions in various regions of European Turkey) it had the satisfaction of knowing that Russia had failed to establish a Greater Bulgaria, which would have extended from the Danube to the Aegean and from the Black Sea to Lake Ochrid, and that at some future date Greece itself might make gains in Thessaly and Epiros. Greece did not have long to wait for these gains: in 1881, she obtained Thessaly and the province of Arta.

The Greek acquisition of Thessaly and the reduction in size of the newly established Bulgarian principality meant that the region known as Macedonia would be fiercely contested by Bulgarians, Serbs and Greeks. In this region, as indeed in Crete, where the Greeks were engaged in another war of liberation, the Greek consulates had a major role to play. At first their main task was to encourage local Greek organizations to resist the expansion of the Bulgarian exarchate and the spread of Bulgarian propaganda. Later, when the Bulgarians and their supporters in Macedonia had intensified band warfare, they were called upon to devise means for the protection of the Greek Orthodox population. In 1904 the Greek government, after years of hesitation during which Greek irredentism had been left largely to private enterprise, decided to intervene actively in the Macedonian armed struggle while adopting, on the diplomatic front, a pose of neutrality. Towards this end they attached to the consulates of Monastir and Thessaloniki, under various guises, army personnel to organize operations; they made funds available; they supplied arms and ammunition; and they sent a steady stream of bands across the frontier.

During the decade of the Macedonian struggle, Greece made considerable economic progress and, like its Balkan neighbours, increased, reorganized and rearmed the military forces. From 1896 Greece began to send military and naval attachés to certain of the missions abroad; one of their tasks was to observe and report on European military developments and available equipment and to arrange further training of Greek personnel. By 1910 Greece was a power of some military importance, and it was only natural that its diplomatic relations should have become more complicated. In that year (the year that Elefterios Venizelos appeared on the vastly changed political scene of Greece) the Ministry of Foreign Affairs was reorganized. As a result of a law of 31 March/12 April, the establishments of the political, legal and consular directorates were increased and various auxiliary services were added. As reorganized, the Ministry of Foreign Affairs consisted of: the Directorate-General of Political Affairs, divided into four directorates; the Directorate-General of Treaties and Consular Affairs; the Accountancy Department; the General Archives (provision being made for the development of a library).

The new law provided for twelve missions (Belgrade, Berlin, Vienna, Bucharest, Cettigne, Constantinople, London, Washington, Paris, St Petersburg, Rome and Sofia) and for a diplomatic agency in Cairo. It established the consular service as seventy-five consulates and vice-consulates, twenty-two being in the Ottoman Empire and the remaining fifty-three in the ports of the Black Sea, the Middle East, North America, the Balkan states, Western Europe and Great Britain. It provided, moreover, for some 300 honorary consular officers: these were to be found in most parts of the world (in North and South America, central and northern Europe, the British colonies and Asia).

The directors-general of the Ministry were ministers plenipotentiary or legal specialists, usually professors of law; they were given greater powers to make decisions. The old Legal Council (first established in 1856) was expanded and staffed with persons of high diplomatic status. For the first time, a chief archivist was appointed with responsibility for all the papers of the Ministry except for those in current use.

Admission to the diplomatic service continued to depend upon the results of a competitive examination. Candidates were required to have a degree in law (which was awarded on a successful short thesis, somewhat like the present French *maîtrise*). Preference was given to candidates well versed not only in French but also in a second foreign language. Promotions (as in the administrative civil service) depended on length of service and proof of capability. Salaries were fixed according to grade. For promotion to the rank of minister a diplomat needed about twenty years of successful service. No minister was allowed to remain in a post abroad for more than five years or for less than two. The same rule applied to those of lower grades, but it was not always strictly enforced.

By 1911 the number of diplomatic personnel had risen to 132; the number of administrative staff (secretaries, archivists, typists and others) had risen proportionately. All employees, both in the diplomatic and the administrative grades, were men. Women were not admitted until the inter-war period, and then only as typists and clerks.

As a result of the reorganization of 1910, the Greek diplomatic service lost much of its former exclusive character. Recruitment had been widened and improved, partly because of better salaries and partly because of the realization of the need to meet the demands of the increasing complexity of international relations. In this, Greece was merely following a trend common to the services of all European powers. In the Greek diplomatic records, which are housed in the central building of the Ministry in Athens, there exists from 1910 onwards an extraordinary wealth of dispatches, both embassy and consular, which are highly informative and politically perceptive.

In the period 1911–23 the main aim of Greek foreign policy continued to be the fulfilment of the Great Idea. During those years Greece was sometimes a participant in, sometimes a witness of, the events that led to the disintegration of the old Europe and to the demise of the Ottoman Empire, of which it claimed certain parts. In the Balkan Wars (1912–13), owing to a vigorous foreign policy and military exertions, and also to a fortunate turn of events, Greece increased its territory at the expense of Turkey by 68 per cent and its population from 2.7 to 4.8 millions. During the 1914–18 war those gains were placed in jeopardy. Greece had to choose between two, if not three, precarious courses of action – to join the Western powers, to remain neutral or to join the Central powers. Venizelos, the Prime Minister, opted for the first: Constantine, who had become king in 1913, opted for the second and would probably have considered the third had the Germans broken through at Verdun. The amended Constitution of 1911 had given the King a strong claim to control foreign policy, but (and this is a well-known story) Venizelos won the day in Greece and his allies won the war. This meant that at the Paris Peace Conference of 1919 Venizelos was able to put forward extensive Greek claims. Like prime ministers of other states, he personally conducted all important negotiations pertaining to his country. He was, however, willing to listen to the advice of his Minister and of the diplomatic service, which furnished the information necessary in putting forward Greek claims. In the course of those negotiations in Paris, he accepted a mandate from France, Great Britain and the United States to employ Greek forces in Asia Minor, and for these services Greece was given extensive gains in what later proved to be the abortive Treaty of Sèvres.

Despite his great triumph, Venizelos was defeated in the Greek elections of November 1920. The following month, as a result of a plebiscite, Constantine, who had been in exile since 1917, returned to Greece. Although he opted to continue the foreign policy of his deposed Minister, he replaced the personnel of the Venizelist regime by Constantinists. Following the Greek defeat in Asia Minor, however, and Constantine's second exile, Venizelos, who refused to return to the political scene in Athens, consented to represent Greece at the Conference of Lausanne (November 1922–July 1923) where, having what was virtually a free hand, he managed to salvage the greater part of Greece's gains and to obtain the frontiers that are those of Greece today (less the Dodecanese, which were not obtained until 1947).

After the signing of the Treaty of Lausanne (in July 1923) the Foreign Ministry, not without political difficulties, again took charge of foreign policy. It had to deal with many problems left over by the peace treaties. These problems were difficult, and when Venizelos returned to power in 1928 little had been done to solve them. By that time the Ministry had become involved in the European movement for the maintenance of peace and security. Greece was a member of the League of Nations, to which it sometimes referred minority problems and other matters concerning its neighbours. Greece had established commercial relations with the Serb–Croat–Slovene state (later renamed Yugoslavia) and friendly relations with Romania and (after the Corfu incident) with Italy. Relations with Turkey, however, remained as they had been left at Lausanne. On returning to power, Venizelos saw the need for a united Balkan front, of which friendly Greco-Turkish relations had to be the cornerstone. With Kemal Atatürk, he negotiated the Convention of 10 June 1930 and a Treaty of Neutrality, Conciliation and Arbitration (30 October 1930), which put an end to over a century of Greco-Turkish antagonism.

The cornerstone thus laid, Venizelos and his Foreign Minister embarked on the difficult task of creating a Balkan front covering economic, social, cultural and political affairs. Between October 1930 and November 1933 four 'unofficial' conferences were held (respectively in Athens, Ankara, Bucharest and Thessaloniki). To meet the demands and to cope with the ever-increasing complexity of international affairs, Venizelos carried out a general overhaul of the Greek diplomatic service. This was effected by Law 4952 (1931), which consolidated and revised piecemeal changes made since 1910 and increased once more the establishment of the Ministry and of missions abroad. Backed by an improved diplomatic service, on 9 February 1934 Greece signed in Athens with Turkey, Yugoslavia and Romania a pact of mutual guarantee. In the autumn of that year these four powers met at Ankara and adopted statutes modelled on those of the Little Entente (Czechoslovakia, Yugoslavia and Romania) a regional combination opposed to revision of the Versailles settlement. Bulgaria did not enter into these arrangements, and the pact (known as the Balkan Entente) was further weakened by certain reservations made by Greece and Turkey.

By that time Venizelos was out of office; his successor Tsaldaris (March 1933–October 1935) prepared the way for the return of the dynasty, George II having succeeded Constantine. The change of government led once more to sweeping changes in the personnel of the various ministries. Elections held in January 1936 produced political instability, which was brought to an end by the dictatorship of General Metaxas (August 1936–1941). Already the European scene was changing fast, and the days of the Little and Balkan Ententes were numbered. By the end of 1939 Greece was to find itself in almost the same predicament as in 1914. This time, however, the Greek King and his Prime Minister chose to side with the Western powers.

Following the Axis invasion of Greece in 1941, part of the Foreign Ministry went into exile in London and Cairo. The part that remained in Athens was disbanded by the 'Greek government of occupation', and the Foreign Ministry building was commandeered by the Italians. When, at the end of 1944, the Greek government returned to Greece it faced, among countless other difficulties, the task of reconstructing its various ministries. Where the Foreign Ministry was concerned, there was the necessity to reassemble what remained of the old diplomatic staff, to man the vacant posts abroad and to resume recruitment. In March 1945 entrance examinations were held, in which the English language was a compulsory subject. Not only was there a considerable wastage of personnel to make good, but there were many posts to fill in the various newly created international organizations. In 1946 Greece joined the United Nations and UNESCO, in 1948 the Organization for European Cooperation and Development, in 1950 the Council of Europe, and in 1952 the North Atlantic Treaty Organization (NATO). All this meant that the work of the Foreign Ministry was increasing. Moreover, there were many special problems to be dealt with, among them war reparations from Italy, Germany and Bulgaria – a problem that along with those arising from participation in economic international organizations, demonstrated the need for a Department of Economic Affairs, which was duly created in 1948. This development, despite the existence of a Ministry of Coordination, gave rise to demarcation disputes between the Foreign Ministry and the Ministries of Commerce, Agriculture and Industrial Development. These disputes were ended when it was generally agreed that the Foreign Ministry should participate in all international conferences and make decisions on all political matters involved. All this increased the workload of the Foreign Ministry; and yet more work arose from a government decision to obtain help from wealthy Greeks abroad, particularly from those in the USA and Australia. Part of this work fell upon the Department of Ecclesiastical Affairs, as it had been decided to involve the higher Greek clergy as well as the foreign missions in this important venture.

By 1951 there were 117 Greek diplomats at home or abroad; many of them were relatively young, yet highly experienced for their age. The number of administrative personnel was 236. In that year it was decided to appoint a permanent under-secretary of state for foreign affairs, mainly because the Foreign Minister (who sometimes also held the post of Prime Minister) was frequently engrossed in other matters or attending conferences abroad. This new official was selected from among diplomats of ambassadorial status. His chief duty was to supervise and coordinate the work of the different departments. He was, moreover, called upon to preside over the Council for Political Affairs, first established, as we have seen, in 1910. This Council had grown in importance. Parallel to it was an Administrative Council, which included among its general administrative duties promotions and appointments abroad, except those of ambassadors, which were made by the Cabinet.

As in the past, important posts tended to be filled by men who supported the government in power. Under the rule of the colonels, for instance, retired generals were placed in such important embassies as London, Paris, Bonn and Washington and were also given key posts in the Ministry itself. As soon as the regime fell in 1974, these men were replaced by career diplomats. It is true, moreover, that throughout the history of the Ministry unwanted political figures in Athens have been sent abroad as ambassadors.

Since 1951 the work of the Greek Foreign Ministry has been further increased. A notable development has been in cultural relations, which are often a prelude to closer political relations. Greece has established many contacts with countries of the Third World: Tunisians have studied in the Greek Naval Academy and Libyans in the Greek Air Force Academy; Ethiopians have become graduates in theology of the Universities of Athens or Thessaloniki; Pakistanis have been trained in various Greek technical schools. Through UNESCO, Greek specialists have also participated in programmes for assistance to developing countries. As a result the Ministry's Directorate of Cultural Relations has become an establishment of considerable dimensions. Yet another development that has increased the workload of the Ministry is that of tourism, not to mention the many problems raised by Greek migrant workers (whose remittances to Greece represent one-third of the imported income). At the same time, the work of the Legal Department has greatly expanded, mainly because of the reference of important legal questions to the United Nations or to the International Court at The Hague.

In 1976 a thorough survey was made of the Foreign Ministry's duties and structure. The outcome was Law 419 (20 August 1976). This enlarged the establishment of the Legal Service and placed at its head, instead of a professor, a full-time specialist who is assisted by full-time legal specialists in the different fields of international law. This same law also provided for specialists to be attached, on either a permanent or a temporary basis, to other departments, their chief task being to prepare reports and memoranda. Yet another innovation (which had long been under discussion) has been the creation of a Centre for Diplomatic Studies, which is attended by new recruits who improve their knowledge of foreign languages and world politics, and become acquainted with problems of special interest to Greece.

The Foreign Minister, who is responsible for the formulation of foreign policy, is assisted by two Deputy Ministers who, like the Minister, are as a rule members of parliament. The Ministry has a secretary-general of ambassadorial rank, who supervises all departments and coordinates their activities. There are eight councils or committees. These are: the Supreme Council of the diplomatic service, dealing with all important service questions; the Administration Board, dealing with less important matters concerning personnel; the Council of Political Affairs; the Council of Decorations; the Budget Committee; the Bequests Committee; the International Conferences and Assemblies Committee, which is an interministerial committee; and the Headquarters Committee. The establishment of the diplomatic service is as follows:

ambassadors 8, ministers plenipotentiary'(I) 33, ministers plenipotentiary (II) 50, counsellors of embassy (I) 50, counsellors of embassy (II) 61, secretaries of embassy (I) 60, secretaries of embassy (II) 78, secretaries of embassy (III) and attachés of embassy 146, administrative personnel (I) (university graduates or equivalents) 210, administrative personnel (II) (clerks, etc.) 602.

Today candidature for the competitive entrance examination is open to all who hold a university degree – it is no longer confined to those who hold a degree in law. The subjects examined, however, remain the same: diplomatic history; international, private, public and maritime law; economics; geography; Greek cultural and literary history; French and English language.

Recruits, both men and women, come from many different socio-economic strata. There are families in Greece who have traditionally served in the diplomatic and consular services (the two have never been separate) for two and even three generations. But now, as in other countries, the influx of new blood into a career becoming ever more demanding has necessitated the establishment of a Centre for Diplomatic Studies.

At the present time, there are sixty Greek embassies and legations and eight permanent delegations to international organizations. There are 32 consulates-general, 21 consulates and four vice-consulates. The Ministry is also responsible for two research centres abroad: the Institute of Byzantine and Post-Byzantine Studies in Venice and the Centre for Greek Studies in Alexandria. Since 1976 a new directorate-general has been added to the Ministry – that of European Economic Community Affairs. Negotiations for the entry of Greece into the EEC began as early as 1959, but were interrupted between 1967 and 1974 during the regime of the military junta. After 1974 negotiations were resumed and eventually the Ministry of Foreign Affairs prepared a draft treaty, which was signed in Athens on 28 May 1979. Greece has thus secured its place in the European family of nations, and continues to contribute to all efforts for international cooperation and security.

The Greek Foreign Ministry is housed in a building situated opposite Parliament House, in the very centre of Athens. The original part of this building, formerly the residence of a wealthy Greek called Andreas Syngros, was bequeathed to the state by his wife in May 1921, to be used as a Foreign Ministry but only in its original form. There was not enough space to house all the departments of the Ministry. Another building had to be erected on part of its grounds behind it; this was completed in 1933 and occupied by all the departments of the foreign service. Before that date the Ministry was housed in a government building on Philhellinon Street, also in the centre of the city, which became the Ministry of Agriculture after the foreign services left in 1933.

After the last war, more space was needed to house additional departments. On the remaining land of the original Syngros estate another wing was built; consisting of seven floors, it was completed in 1979. The former residence of the donor has been kept intact, according to her will, and is used as the office of the Minister and his cabinet as well as that of the under-secretary of state and his cabinet. One small part of it is occupied by the Directorate of Protocol. In this same former residence the Minister holds official dinners and receptions. And there is a conference room where bilateral conventions are usually signed.

The architectural style of the Syngros residence is neo-classic, as is the wing built in 1933, but the new wing of 1979 is an ultra-modern building – a fact that raised a lot of criticism. The expansion and the style may be seen as a partial commentary on Greece's enhanced international position.

The editor and author wish to thank Professor Douglas Dakin for his assistance in the preparation of this chapter.

BIBLIOGRAPHY

The main source for the history of the Greek Foreign Ministry is the *Government Gazette* from 1833 to 1980. Documents on the subject in the archives of the Ministry are scattered in different files and are not easy to find. Other important sources are: B. C. Colocotronis, *Diplomatic and Consular Guide of the Ministry of Foreign Affairs* (Athens 1911); The *Yearbooks* of the Ministry from 1878 to 1951, when publication ceased; *The Statute of the Ministry of Foreign Affairs*, edited by the Director of Personnel (Athens 1956). It is a valuable work, for it includes a list of all relevant laws from 1931 to 1956.

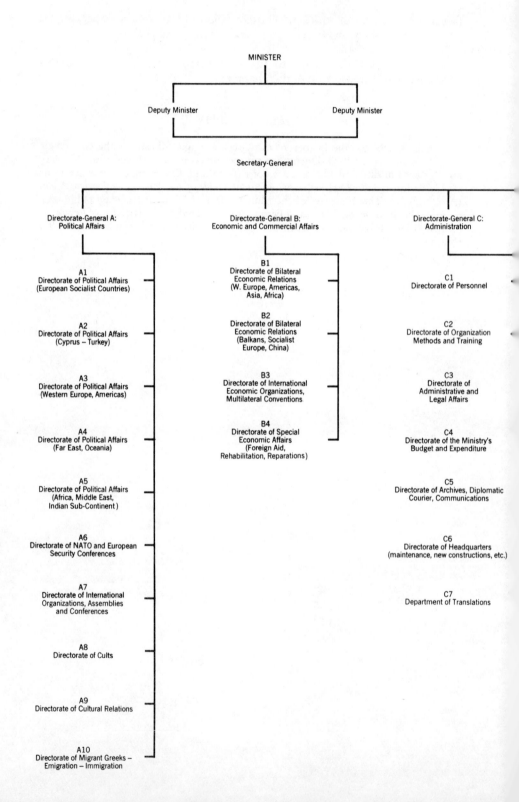

APPENDIX A: THE GREEK FOREIGN MINISTRY

MINISTER

Deputy Minister

Deputy Minister

Secretary-General

Directorate-General A:
Political Affairs

Directorate-General B:
Economic and Commercial Affairs

Directorate-General C:
Administration

A1
Directorate of Political Affairs
(European Socialist Countries)

A2
Directorate of Political Affairs
(Cyprus – Turkey)

A3
Directorate of Political Affairs
(Western Europe, Americas)

A4
Directorate of Political Affairs
(Far East, Oceania)

A5
Directorate of Political Affairs
(Africa, Middle East,
Indian Sub-Continent)

A6
Directorate of NATO and European
Security Conferences

A7
Directorate of International
Organizations, Assemblies
and Conferences

A8
Directorate of Cults

A9
Directorate of Cultural Relations

A10
Directorate of Migrant Greeks –
Emigration – Immigration

B1
Directorate of Bilateral
Economic Relations
(W. Europe, Americas,
Asia, Africa)

B2
Directorate of Bilateral
Economic Relations
(Balkans, Socialist
Europe, China)

B3
Directorate of International
Economic Organizations,
Multilateral Conventions

B4
Directorate of Special
Economic Affairs
(Foreign Aid,
Rehabilitation, Reparations)

C1
Directorate of Personnel

C2
Directorate of Organization
Methods and Training

C3
Directorate of
Administrative and
Legal Affairs

C4
Directorate of the Ministry's
Budget and Expenditure

C5
Directorate of Archives, Diplomatic
Courier, Communications

C6
Directorate of Headquarters
(maintenance, new constructions, etc.)

C7
Department of Translations

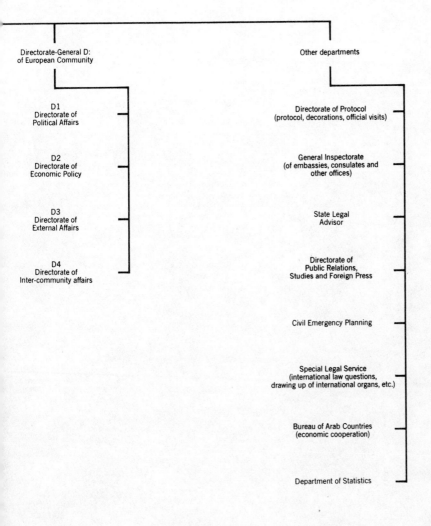

Directorate-General D:
of European Community

Other departments

D1
Directorate of
Political Affairs

D2
Directorate of
Economic Policy

D3
Directorate of
External Affairs

D4
Directorate of
Inter-community affairs

Directorate of Protocol
(protocol, decorations, official visits)

General Inspectorate
(of embassies, consulates and
other offices)

State Legal
Advisor

Directorate of
Public Relations,
Studies and Foreign Press

Civil Emergency Planning

Special Legal Service
(international law questions,
drawing up of international organs, etc.)

Bureau of Arab Countries
(economic cooperation)

Department of Statistics

Ireland

The Department of Foreign Affairs

DERMOT KEOGH

Dr Dermot Keogh is Lecturer in the Department of Modern
History, University College, Cork. He studied at University College,
Dublin and the European University Institute, Florence, where he
was awarded a doctorate in 1980. Dr Keogh has published a study on
Archbishop Romero: El Salvador's martyr and is completing a survey on
'Ireland and the rise of Catholic nationalism'.

Propaganda before diplomacy

The Irish Department of Foreign Affairs was born in troubled times.[1] It first came into existence principally as a Propaganda Department during the violence of 1919–21, the period known euphemistically as 'the Troubles'. A clandestine government had been set up in Dublin in 1919 with a series of conventional departments that were later, after Independence, merged with Dublin Castle sections. Foreign Affairs had to restart in 1922, with the nucleus of the personnel who served in the Sinn Féin 'diplomatic service' and who remained loyal to the Treaty side.[2]

The Propaganda Department took over the small Sinn Féin publicity unit (set up in 1917) after the first Dáil sat in 1919. Desmond FitzGerald headed the bureau. He was a journalist well known in Fleet Street, where he had worked for a number of years. FitzGerald made five visits to London up to June 1920 and made contact with many leading newspaper correspondents – a step approved by a Sinn Féin committee 'dealing with foreign relations'.[3]

The main Sinn Féin propaganda weapon was the *Irish Bulletin* – a clandestine paper – which appeared for the first time on 11 November 1919 and did not miss an issue despite having to move 'office' rather hurriedly thirteen times in order to avoid discovery by the troops. It carried on until the Truce of 11 July 1921.[4] FitzGerald was the first editor of the paper, which was distributed widely abroad through Sinn Féin 'envoys'. It was designed to provide a nationalist view of the violence in Ireland and to act as an alternative news source for the international media. Sinn Féin felt that the main press agencies were pro-British. It was something of a tribute to the effectiveness of the *Bulletin* that Dublin Castle, the centre of British administration in Ireland, started a bogus *Irish Bulletin* using captured typewriters. But it folded after only a few issues. Sinn Féin also used the wires of the *Freeman's Journal* to send reports abroad to agents and correspondents.

After FitzGerald's capture and imprisonment, Erskine Childers took over as editor of the *Bulletin*. Frank Gallagher, who later became editor of the *Irish Press* and also chief of the Government Information Service, did most of the actual writing and sub-editing. Robert Brennan also helped to produce some of the early editions before he was made Minister for Fine Arts.

From the outset of the political and military agitation in 1919 Sinn Féin was very conscious of the fact that victory depended upon the mobilization of public opinion abroad. America, with a large immigrant Irish population, was the most important target for Sinn Féin propaganda. Éamon de Valéra took personal responsibility for that task and spent over a year lecturing and politicking in the United States.[5] Seán T. O'Kelly was sent to Paris in 1919 with the heady task of winning international recognition for Ireland at the Peace Conference.[6] Of course, Sinn Féin had received no official invitation. Before leaving Dublin, O'Kelly enlisted the support of Michael MacWhite – a nationalist sympathizer who had fought in the war as a member of the French Foreign Legion and had been awarded the *croix de guerre*. MacWhite who was a friend of Arthur Griffith from the early days of Sinn Féin, was at home on leave when he met O'Kelly. He was persuaded to join the 'diplomatic' team and he agreed to smuggle nationalist documents to Paris. The documents were concealed in his puttees. Eventually he got some of the propaganda published.[7] There was very little sympathy in France for Sinn Féin and the first Dáil. The 1916 Proclamation had spoken of the Germans as 'our gallant allies in Europe'. But despite the popular hostility towards Ireland, O'Kelly, with the help of MacWhite, soon built up a good range of useful journalistic contacts. The little Paris 'office' was joined by an ex-Jesuit scholastic, Joseph Walshe, in late 1919; another student, Seán Murphy, also joined the staff at about the same time. Both men were to play central roles in the building up of the Department of External Affairs (as it was known until 1971).

O'Kelly played the role of the diplomat with limited success in Paris. In 1920 he spent over six months in Rome, where he successfully discouraged the Vatican, with a little help from clerical friends, from issuing a condemnation of Sinn Féin violence. He established strong contacts with a section of the *Partito Popolare*, and visited Mussolini in Milan, where he won his support for Irish nationalism. He also made contact with the poet-adventurer, Gabriele D'Annunzio. The latter wanted to lead an expedition to Dublin and became all the more vigorous in his determination to fight for Irish freedom when it became apparent that the mission could never take place. The British navy was ready to prevent the poet sailing to Dublin.

The Sinn Féin 'diplomatic' and propaganda network was surprisingly widespread. John Charters was appointed envoy to Berlin with Dr Nancy Wyse Power as his chief assistant. Máire O'Brien set up office in Madrid. Brussels and Bern were covered from Paris. At one point MacWhite moved to Switzerland, where he replaced the Italian writer, Annie Vivanti, who had helped to strengthen Sinn Féin ties with her close friend, Mussolini. George Gavan Duffy had a roving brief. He visited France, the Low Countries, Scandinavia, Spain and Italy. In 1920 he was appointed to Rome and was succeeded there by his wife when he was recalled to participate in the Treaty negotiations.

It was not until early 1921 that really successful efforts were made to coordinate the work of representatives abroad. Pride of place was given to propaganda 'but since the new office was opened a good deal of work has been done in the matter of coordinating the work of our foreign representatives and of keeping them closely informed of the news at home'. Special envoys had by that time been sent to 'Germany, Russia, South America, South Africa, and an accredited representative had been appointed in Germany, press bureaux had been established in Germany, Switzerland, Spain and Rome and the organization of similar bureaux in South Africa, Australia, Chile and Argentina was under way'.[8] The organization looked far more efficient on paper than it was in reality.

A certain air of infectious optimism seems to have characterized the reports from abroad. Yet Sinn Féin envoys could not influence governments, as could British diplomatic representatives with comparative ease. For example, Eamonn Bulfin, who reported from Argentina, found the situation there 'affords great encouragement' while the same was also alleged to be the case in Chile, where Fran W. E. Egan was the honorary representative.[9]

The British secret service kept the Irish propaganda and diplomatic network under very close surveillance. It is likely that most dispatches, other than those carried by hand, were intercepted by London. Sinn Féin seems to have used no cipher. Correspondents attempted to disguise their messages by dropping a surname or using initials. For example, when Michael Collins wrote to Donal Hales in Genoa about buying arms, he encoded his message in the following way: 'You will remember the friend who called on you some time ago – the man who was working up agencies as between Italian and Irish houses. His reports were so satisfactory that the Trade Department say they are sending another friend of ours shortly who is interested in the *same business*' (underlined in pen by Hales and 'the arms' written in the margin in his hand). Collins was using the ordinary postal service to communicate such a sensitive message. What was not intercepted by the British was probably made up for in the huge collections of Dáil documents captured in military raids on ministers' houses. The British were very well informed about the 'diplomatic' activities of the clandestine government.

A bizarre 'diplomatic' escapade occurred in New York when de Valéra and Harry Boland were introduced to the representatives of the Union of Socialist Soviet Republics, Ludwig Martens and Nuorteva, who were, like Sinn Féin, seeking American recognition. Although 'the Chief' was a naturally cautious man, he agreed to advance $20 000 from Sinn Féin funds in exchange for certain precious pieces that were reputed to have been part of the Russian crown jewels. A draft treaty between the two countries was drawn up with Dr Patrick McCartan as the go-between. The article on religion read:

> 'The government of the Russian socialist Federal Soviet Republic accords to all religious denominations represented in the republic of Ireland every right accorded to religious sects by the Russian constitution and entrusts to the accredited representatives of the Republic of Ireland and in Russia the interest of the Roman Catholic Church within the territory of the Russian republic.'

In his notes a sanguine McCartan wrote: 'this clause gives us a good grip on the Vatican and makes them less impressionable by British agents'. The paragraph is almost like a section from Lewis Carroll. Although McCartan went to Moscow, no treaty was signed. Sinn Féin did not get recognition from Moscow, largely because de Valéra was reluctant to pursue the possibility seriously.

Whatever the bizarre flirtations with Moscow, the real test for the fledgling diplomatic service followed the Truce, when bilateral discussions to find a negotiated settlement took place in late 1921. Gavan Duffy, with his legal training, was included in the team, as was the able Erskine Childers.

But the diplomatic resources available to Whitehall were far greater than those at Dublin's disposal. The Irish plenipotentiaries were inexperienced in high level negotiations, and, moreover, they had neither the diplomatic nor the administrative backup required to counter-balance that lack of expertise. De Valera seemed to entertain a US presidential style concept of his own role in foreign policy formulation while the plenipotentiaries held a diametrically opposed view.

The Department of Foreign Affairs was very seriously weakened by the split over the Treaty. Seán T. O'Kelly resigned in protest. Art O'Brien in London was not prepared to serve either. The implacable Donal Hales in Genoa was even more hostile than the other two to the Provisional Government. Seán Noonan, Bob Brennan and Leopold Kearney were also disaffected. The quite considerable Sinn Féin funds, lodged in Paris during the O'Kelly period, were quickly acquired by the 'republican side' before the Provisional

Government could stake a claim. Donal Hales continued his 'consular' activities in Genoa for the anti-Treaty side. With the threat of civil war there emerged a parallel 'diplomatic' and propaganda service. But the thrust of the publicity was no longer against the British. Pro- and anti-Treaty factions vied for funds and the loyalty of the Irish abroad.

Gavan Duffy had lost many of his 'republican' friends by taking over as Foreign Minister in the Provisional Government. Before he resigned his post in protest in June 1922, he outlined his thinking on the future of the Irish 'Foreign Office', as he chose to term it.[10] His optimism, given the circumstances in which his memorandum was written, was admirable if not a little unrealistic:

> '. . . we are still beyond question, in high favour among influential people on the continent and our Envoys will be much sought after. The reasons are: first, that Ireland is a world-race with great possibilities; secondly, that we are supposed to have great influence upon American politics and policy; thirdly, that we know England better than the continental peoples and that the friendship of an Ireland lying on England's flank may at any moment be very useful. Moreover, we have a reputation for frankness and fearlessness which stands us in good stead, and it has often been said that Ireland in the League of Nations will be invaluable, because she may be expected to say plainly the things that everyone is thinking and that other Powers are too cowardly to be the first to say.'[11]

The smaller countries particularly would want closer connections with Ireland because it stood for 'democratic principles, against Imperialism and upon the side of liberty throughout the world'. Ireland's geographic position would also provide a bridge between the Old World and the New, and that would be facilitated by the development of air transport. Gavan Duffy felt that if the question of changing the seat of the League of Nations was ever raised, Ireland's geographic position would 'give her a claim to serious consideration as against Switzerland'.

He wanted Ireland to apply for League membership as soon as possible, and he outlined his priorities for representation abroad. The principal posts were to be Washington, Berlin and Geneva. Next in line were Paris, Rome and Ottawa. Washington was the main target for diplomatic assault because it was felt that in America Ireland could best counter British influence and press a great power into the services of a small nation. He saw Berlin superseding Paris as the most active centre in Europe. But Geneva was to be 'our best centre in Europe' because no other city would 'furnish the same opportunities for making contact and creating friendly relations'. The home of the League of Nations was the real centre of 'convergence of international democratic effort, overt and concealed'.

Gavan Duffy saw Ottawa also as of importance because Canada provided Ireland with a lively constitutional parallel, which would stimulate Dublin. He wanted to keep close ties with the Dominions.

What the outgoing Minister was stating actually became reality in the years that followed. The European side of the Irish diplomatic service had a secondary significance as the country was still wed, both constitutionally and economically, to Britain and the Commonwealth. History triumphed over geography.

Gavin Duffy emphasized the particularly difficult job of trying to find suitable personnel to fill diplomatic posts in Europe:

> 'Our representation abroad is going to be a very delicate and difficult matter, because we have not suitable people to fill the posts that we have created. Even the existing posts are not properly filled; our representative in Berlin knows little German, our representative in Madrid is only learning Spanish, and our Rome representative does not know Italian. It is idle to expect that anyone representing Ireland in a foreign country can ever get into very intimate contact with the people behind the scenes in the country to which he is sent, unless he knows the language thoroughly well.'

In Paris, Rome and Madrid, Gavan Duffy thought it necessary to bear in mind the undoubted fact that tradition was still very strong and that any nominee to those capitals should either be 'a person of aristocratic descent or known to have been trained from youth for the diplomatic service'. That was a rather quaint view for a republican to hold, but it was certainly true that representatives needed training and could not simply be sent out because of their fervent political commitment or loyalty of service.

Ministry 'for finding jobs'

There was often little sympathy or understanding for foreign policy issues in the Dáil. It did not take long for that particular trend to assert itself. On 16 November 1923 a deputy, Gorey, suggested that the department should be scrapped:

> 'The Ministry of External Affairs has been referred to – Foreign Affairs I believe Mr Gavan Duffy called it. That was a phrase he used to revel in. I do not see why we want a Minister for External or Foreign Affairs. We have no colonies and have no interest to clash with any other nation. I think it is ridiculous to be playing with theatricals *(sic)* like this. This Ministry of Foreign Affairs ought to be scrapped and let the Executive Council deal with any foreign matters that have to be dealt with. To my mind, and to the mind of the average man in the country, the Ministry of Foreign Affairs or External Affairs, or whatever you like to call it, will be known as a Ministry for finding a job for somebody.'

This lamentable cry was taken up by others, no doubt speaking for 'Seán citizen'. Darrel Figgis, in the same debate, felt that 'this Department could be dispensed with at the present time'. He argued further that it was 'much less a Department of External Affairs than a department of publicity' which was 'not always calculated to assuage some of the national wounds'. Many deputies would have been quite content to place the portfolio under the responsibility of the President's own department.

The raw edge of Irish nationalism, as represented by Darrel Figgis and Gorey, was never quite convinced of the usefulness of such an 'expensive' service manned by men of high culture – some distinguished by social background – and academic achievement. 'Iveagh House types' were to become a source of envy in the general civil service and the target of opprobrium in the Dáil from backbenchers like Martin Corry who complained, in 1928, that salaries of £1500 had to be paid to representatives abroad so that they 'might squat like the nigger when he put on the black silk hat and the swallow-tail coat and went out and said he was an English gentleman'. Conor Cruise O'Brien also recalls how – as late as 1943 – an elderly official of the Department of Finance used to mutter '*mothor*-car allowances' – and spit whenever he encountered the words 'External Affairs' on a file.

One of the country's best known satirists, Myles na Gopaleen, once argued that the real place for ambassadors was at home, as their main function was to help stranded Irish drunks – they could therefore best serve their country in Dublin, where it was impossible for an inebriated citizen to get diplomatic help on a Saturday night. Popular prejudice would probably have been less charitable than even Myles na Gopaleen.

Recruiting the elite

In the post-civil war climate of popular hostility and backbench sniping, it was not easy to build a Department, as Gavan Duffy's successor, Desmond FitzGerald (1922–7), quickly discovered. He was, however, a particularly talented Minister. It was also very fortunate for the service that he was quickly followed by an equally gifted administrator with a determination to build up the diplomatic service and strengthen the administration in Dublin.

One of the earliest and most important administrative decisions made by FitzGerald was to fuse the Publicity Department with External Affairs, bringing the nationalist propaganda machine under diplomatic control. The effects on the Department of ingesting a wartime publicity instrument were to remain a source of tension within the service. The determination of some politicians to keep the embers of nationalism aglow in Irish America was to impose a major burden on External Affairs and engage overworked envoys in a thankless task of 'green' diplomacy. The 'ungreening' of the nationalistic diplomacy of illusion was a very slow process – the residue of which still remains in 1981.

The administrative shape of the Department was very much determined by the pattern of diplomatic expansion. FitzGerald, perhaps unknowingly, followed the Gavan Duffy blueprint of priorities. The Free State joined the League of Nations in September 1923. Entry was negotiated by Michael MacWhite. As the new delegation took their seats 'members rose to their feet and cheered enthusiastically'. De Valéra lodged a formal objection with Geneva, protesting against Article 10 of the Covenant, which recognized existing European frontiers, and he felt that had direct bearing on the Irish border question. Considerable diplomatic attention was also devoted to Commonwealth conferences. In London, John Dulanty became high commissioner. But as Gavan Duffy had indicated, there was a need to develop strong links with America. In 1926, the Free State became the first Commonwealth country to open a legation in Washington. Professor T. A. Smiddy, who had been economic adviser to Michael Collins at the Treaty negotiations and had undertaken a number of trade missions to the United States, was given the post.

Within two years of Patrick McGilligan taking over in 1927, the Department had to recruit at envoy level to fill new posts in Berlin, Paris and the Vatican. Charles Bewley was appointed to the Holy See. He was Oxford-educated, a convert to Catholicism and a distinguished solicitor who had defended many republican prisoners during the 'Troubles'. Count O'Kelly, who had been associated with External Affairs in its early days, went to Paris, while Dr Daniel Binchy was assigned to Berlin – making the latter the country's youngest envoy at 29.

An eminent jurist and Celtic scholar, Dr Binchy remained at his post for nearly three years, but chose not to continue in the service when de Valéra came to power in 1932.[12] He revealed some of the frustration he felt with the Cosgrave government during his time in Berlin when he wrote – in 1935 – to a friend who was resigning over the Fine Gael 'stand' on Abyssinia:

> 'It must be some consolation to you to feel that every word uttered by you in the course of this controversy will be heartily endorsed by decent people of all parties. Your action was just what I would have expected from you. Neither was I surprised at the reaction of your colleagues. I have had more first-hand experience than most people of their 'international' *(sic)* policy when they were in government, and accordingly I know that in the present case they are merely running true to type. The loss is their own.'[13]

The Department was a little disappointed in his successor. Charles Bewley was moved from Rome largely because of his knowledge of German – a rare talent in the Irish diplomatic service at that stage. Unfortunately, he exhibited a strong liking for the Axis and was somewhat uncritical of the official political philosophy in Berlin. Bewley's enthusiasm for National Socialism exceeded all bounds of diplomatic discretion when he said:

> 'My government will always do everything to promote the old friendship between Ireland and Germany. Undoubtedly our growing patriotism helps us to find recognition especially in countries where people are willing to stake their lives for liberty and honour. That your Reich and its leaders has many admirers among our youth is a well known fact.'[14]

If there were many admirers in Ireland for the Reich and its leaders, and that is very doubtful, few were to be found in the Department of External Affairs, and Joseph Walshe was certainly not counted among them. It is very doubtful if Bewley's credibility ever recovered from that indiscretion. He quit the service in the late 1930s and spent most of the war in Rome working as a pro-Axis journalist.

The quality of the first selection of envoys was very high. They were men who had given distinguished service to Sinn Féin, like Michael MacWhite and Professor Smiddy, Count O'Kelly, John Dulanty (high commissioner in London), and Charles Bewley. Dr Binchy was appointed because of his outstanding linguistic and scholarly achievements.

An ambassador is given a letter of credence signed by the President and addressed to the head of the receiving state. Up to the time that Ireland left the British Commonwealth in 1949 the letter of credence was signed by the British monarch. That practice was a source of some contention between

Dublin and London in 1947 and 1948, when the Irish government insisted on the President signing the letters of credence.

Recruitment and organization

The personnel problems caused by the civil war made it both more difficult and more urgent for the Department to set up a career service. There was continuity between the Sinn Féin Publicity Department and the Free State Department of External Affairs. In 1922, Joseph Walshe was acting secretary of the Department and Seán Murphy was assistant secretary; both had originally joined O'Kelly as enthusiastic recruits in Paris. They had remained to help run the office.

The Minister and Secretaries Act (1924) governed the permanent appointment of Walshe and his successors: 'The Executive Council shall, on the recommendation of the Minister, appoint the principal officer of each of the said Departments' (section 2, subsection 2). Throughout the civil service it became the practice to appoint secretaries on the basis of seniority. The Department of External Affairs has proved an exception. Walshe remained secretary until 1946 but after that Ministers have tended to ignore general practice on occasions and to choose the person they felt best suited for the rigours of the post.

In the early days of the Department prospective cadets were expected to take a written examination in Irish and then sit an interview that involved questions on general knowledge, politics and history. The candidate would also be expected to answer in Irish and the continental language or languages chosen. There was a public examination in 1935 and 1938, when three cadets were taken on each occasion. It was also possible, although not very usual, for cadets to be recruited from other branches of the civil service. Frederick Boland had spent some time in the Department of Industry and Commerce before joining External Affairs. Competition for the coveted posts was very stiff, and the calibre of the early cadets was remarkably high.

Today the channel of entry into the diplomatic and consular service is the third secretary competition conducted by the Civil Service Commissioners. The competition consists of a qualifying written test and a competitive interview for candidates who have the necessary educational and other qualifications.

The minimum academic qualification required (except for certain classes of civil servants) is a first or second class honours university degree in any faculty or an equivalent qualification. Persons completing the final year of a course are eligible to compete for posts of third secretary, but their appointment depends on their obtaining the necessary qualifications. Candidates are expected to have a good general knowledge, and a high degree of intelligence and reasoning power. They must be Irish citizens and under 30 years of age. This includes Irish passport holders from Northern Ireland and those born of Irish parents in Britain. The proportion of officers from Northern Ireland in the Department rose considerably in the 1970s. According to one source, there was a policy of positive discrimination practised in their favour, though this seems somewhat unlikely. The relaxing of the Irish language qualification, however, allowed the Department to recruit from a wider constituency. As a result of that change, Irish citizens educated outside the home system were at less of a disadvantage. So, too, were many potential recruits from north and south of the border who enjoyed an education more attuned to the British system.

Serving civil servants with at least two years' established service and who have passed an examination of at least the standard of Leaving Certificate, are also eligible to compete in the competition. The grade of third secretary is essentially a training grade both at home and abroad. Following appointment, they may be expected to stay for two or three years at Iveagh House, where they have an opportunity to work in various divisions of the Department.

A third secretary is then sent abroad at the same grade to a post in an embassy or as a vice-consul to a consulate-general. Within two to three years they are recalled to Iveagh House and can expect to be promoted to the grade of first secretary within five years of entering the service. The higher grades of counsellor, chargé d'affaires and ambassador provide opportunities for further promotion. But in the late 1920s it was quite inappropriate to speak of sections within the Department so much as individuals with specific briefs. Membership of the League of Nations provided a lot of additional work for the 'political section', which also had to cope with Commonwealth affairs. Trade was another important area. Consular work was very time-consuming.

The main functions of the Department were set out as:

> Advising the Government on the conduct of relations with foreign governments and international organizations, and collecting and assessing the information necessary for that purpose.
>
> Coordinating the policies and activities of all branches of government in respect of relations with foreign governments and international organizations having regard to the overall national interest.
>
> Diplomatic and consular representation in foreign countries, at the League of Nations and other international organizations and conferences.
>
> Negotiation and ratification of international treaties and conventions.
>
> Activities directed toward the expansion of foreign trade and other foreign earnings.
>
> Dissemination abroad of information on Ireland and Irish affairs and the development of cultural relations with other countries.
>
> Granting of passports and visas, notarial services and protection of the interests of Irish citizens abroad.
>
> Matters of protocol, including state and official visits to and from other countries.

The onerous burden of running the 'Cinderella' department of government in the late 1920s was the task of a small home-based staff who had to cope with all the demands of External Affairs, housed in a corridor of the Department of Agriculture, and under the ever watchful eye of the Department of the President.

Yet despite the nationalist hostility to expensive 'diplomacy', despite the lack of resources and personnel, despite the fact that the Department lacked even a full-time Minister (McGilligan also had the Industry and Commerce portfolio), the achievements of the Department of External Affairs were considerable. Not the least of these achievements was the fact that External Affairs had survived as an independent Department.

Tranquil transition

The foundation of Fianna Fáil and the entry of de Valéra and his new party into the Dáil in 1927 completely changed the balance of Irish politics. The Soldiers of Destiny (Fianna Fáil) continued to make strides, much to the consternation of the governing Cumann na nGaedheal. Éamon de Valéra took office in March 1932, amid wild rumours and fears of a *coup d'état*. His own party, Fianna Fáil, revered him as the 'chief'. The main opposition party, Cumann na nGaedheal, saw him as a dangerous revolutionary nationalist, the dupe of the IRA, a Kerensky at best, who would be toppled rapidly by the republican extremists.

There was certainly cause for apprehension in London – Anglo-Irish relations were liable to become much more fraught with de Valéra in office. Despite the strident rhetoric of the hustings, the new President was no revolutionary. His somewhat political character had been as misunderstood in official circles at home as it was abroad. He was a conservative. Compared with Cosgrave, de Valéra's public style was more demonstrative and theatrical. A number of de Valéra's colleagues were less forgiving and entertained lasting suspicions towards certain prominent civil servants who, in turn, did nothing to conceal their personal hostility towards the new order. At the same time, de Valéra did not neglect to 'reinstate' some of his followers in the Department. Leopold Kearney, who had remained a 'republican representative' in Paris after the civil war, became ambassador to Spain in the mid-1930s. Robert Brennan, who had been Sinn Féin Minister of Fine Arts, went to Washington. Seán Noonan, another de Valéra supporter, was also reinstated, as was Art O'Brien, who had been the London envoy of Sinn Féin. Donal Hales in Genoa refused the opportunity to be 'reinstated', so bitterly did he disagree with the creation of Fianna Fáil. Paradoxically, the reinstatement of the loyal republican envoys was received with equanimity by members of the Department. It seems that officials had been given assurances by de Valéra that there would be no victimization. A good example of de Valéra's non-vindictive, businesslike approach was reflected in the relationship between Walshe and his new boss. They worked well as a team. Whatever initial awkwardness there might have been was smoothed over by the friendship between Seán T. O'Kelly and Walshe, which had survived the Civil War. But the secretary for the Department of External Affairs was confronted with problems from the very outset of Fianna Fáil's arrival in power.

The uncontentious area of protocol suddenly became a matter of considerable importance due to the temporary aversion of de Valéra and his Cabinet to the wearing of formal dress. For the 'republicans' the top hat was a dreaded symbol of British imperialism. One Dublin wag asked how one would know a Minister at an official function – he would be the one wearing the bicycle clips.

The Eucharistic Congress, which was held in June, provided Walshe with a number of protocol headaches. The government would not wear formal dress while the opposition did so. There was one potentially rather embarrassing moment when the Papal legate arrived at Dun Laoghaire and thought as he was walking down the gangplank that he was being surrounded by the Special Branch, only to discover that the plainly dressed gentlemen were in fact the Executive Council led by de Valéra.

It was not the plain clothes image de Valéra cultivated when he travelled abroad. He addressed the League Council as President in 1932 and delivered a sharp rebuke to delegates for the unwarranted sense of self-satisfaction and complacency he seemed to detect at Geneva. He hinted, on that occasion, at the 'guilty men' of Europe who only paid lip-service to the spirit of the covenant. Under Walshe's and other well-informed counsel, de Valéra continued to adopt a vigorous pro-League stance. He took a strong pro-sanctions line in the Abyssinian crisis of 1935 and for a time advocated a League war against Italy. He supported non-intervention in the Spanish Civil War and maintained a minister accredited to the Republican Government up to 1939 despite the chorus of protests from the opposition, who wanted Dublin to recognize Franco.

In view of the fact that the Department archives are not open to researchers, it can only be postulated that Walshe ran his office in a strongly hierarchical way. According to one source, he carried a large notebook around into which he transcribed minutes of key meetings between de Valéra and foreign envoys. In the normal course of events, memoranda itemizing the central points of discussion ought to have been drafted and circulated to senior members of the Department. That was not the practice in External Affairs, and during the Second World War Walshe became even more tight-lipped than before. It is probable that Walshe, with his complex, ponderous approach, was far less influential in the final formulation of foreign policy than he himself believed was the case. He felt he knew 'everything'. But knowledge and influence were not synonymous.

The 'old diplomacy'

In political style, de Valéra was extraordinarily possessive about diplomatic knowledge and hypersecretive in his handling of high state affairs. During the Spanish Civil War, Cosgrave complained in the Dáil that:

> 'Unfortunately, the President has adhered to his deliberate plan of keeping the leaders of political parties in opposition to him completely in the dark with regard to the facts or reports upon which decisions with regard to foreign policy are based. This is an undesirable state of affairs, and it has been repeatedly urged from these benches that political leaders should receive such information, in absolute confidence if need be, so that as far as possible there may be agreement on vital matters of foreign policy. Our representations have been ignored.'[15]

De Valéra's concern with secrecy was not directed solely at the opposition. Within the government there were many Ministers who regarded foreign policy – like the theory of relativity – as a discipline for superior beings, accessible only to great minds like that of 'the Chief'. A more lively interest was maintained in Anglo-Irish affairs by Ministers generally. It is doubtful whether the envoys' 'confidential reports', or even extracts from them, were ever circulated to the majority of Ministers. Foreign policy was formulated by de Valéra with the help of a small 'inner cabinet' in collaboration with Walshe, and other senior members of the Department of External Affairs. But Walshe was never the key figure in the process. Final decisions were taken at a higher level.

Irish diplomacy: a British view

The relationship between Walshe and de Valéra is central to an understanding of the Irish foreign policy process in the 1930s and 1940s. Walshe would not have been regarded by the Taoiseach as his closest and most perceptive civil servant. That position was reserved for the Moynihan brothers, Seán and Maurice. The former had served simultaneously as secretary to the Executive Council, secretary to the Department of the President and private secretary to the President, before being transferred to the Department of Finance. His brother, Maurice, who was an assistant principal officer in the Department of Finance, replaced him in March 1937 in the single most important combined post in the civil service. There was a strong contrast in the administrative styles of Walshe and the Moynihan brothers.

Walshe was a man of strong views. For example, he was strangely preoccupied with the advance of Communism, and was so alarmed by the situation in Ireland at one stage that, according to Mr Seán MacEntee, he prepared a memorandum setting out the case for establishing a single-party state.[16] But such strong feelings in one area did not negate the impact of his counsel in others. As de Valéra remained his own Minister of External Affairs from 1932 until his electoral defeat in 1948, the relationship was a formidable one and offers the key to an understanding of many of Irish diplomacy's unspoken assumptions. The volume of work carried by de Valéra, coupled with the fact that he was having considerable difficulty with his eyesight, indicates that the influence of Walshe was quite significant in specific areas. Walshe was well read and a good linguist. He was one of the few who had studied diplomacy and was an able practitioner of that art. But he suffered all the disadvantages of the man who could not draw upon a ready-made domestic diplomatic tradition. He was self-taught, yet he was not innovatory. He read the diplomatic texts and practised the art accordingly. But he was not open to the promptings of the 'new diplomacy'. He was bookish rather than creative. Walshe shared de Valéra's religious interests. More importantly, he shared his antipathy to 'open government': he reinforced de Valéra's secretive approach to diplomacy. Walshe was highly successful to the extent that he was a mirror image of the Taoiseach. He was polite, cultured, deeply religious and a very hard worker. Diplomacy was part of the inner workings of the state about which neither the opposition nor the public had any right to know. Whatever his considerable prestige, Walshe was reportedly not popular in government circles. He was regarded 'as too much of a trimmer'. From being pro-Cosgrave and bitterly 'anti-Dev' he changed with the turning tide, according to the British Minister Sir John Maffey (1939–49), and became anti-Cosgrave and hotly 'pro-Dev'.[17] Maffey also claimed that in a small country like Ireland the civil servant was not a 'detached and anonymous figure'.

Maffey, in a critical but penetrating profile of Walshe, claimed it was impossible to avoid using the 'hackneyed expression inferiority complex' in speaking of him as a clue to his moods and to his character: 'This complex indeed is an ingredient in the whole Anglo-Irish problem. In some individual cases, and this is one, it is the key to all thought and action. There is the ever present query "does London take our Department of External Affairs seriously? Am I not the equal in stature to the top rank of their Foreign Office?".'

Walshe had no real reason to feel inferior. Achievements in the field of Anglo-Irish relations, the new Constitution of 1937, the agreement with London in 1938 that ended the 'economic war' and returned the Treaty Ports, together with the successful government policy of neutrality during the Second World War, helped considerably to build political and diplomatic self-confidence in Dublin.[18] The conciliatory diplomatic line adopted by Maffey – often to the annoyance of London – helped reinforce the good working relations that developed between the British Minister, de Valéra and Walshe. Considerable credit, therefore, must go to Maffey for the positive way in which Anglo-Irish relations developed through the war years.

The emphasis on Anglo-Irish diplomacy in the 1930s accentuated the subordinate position of External Affairs to the Taoiseach's Department. The move to Iveagh House in 1940 did not immediately signal greater administrative autonomy for External Affairs. The eighteenth-century splendour of their new surroundings, once the residence of the Guinness family, did give Walshe and his team room to expand. Iveagh House, with its beautiful ballroom, continues today to serve as an ideal centre for entertaining foreign dignitaries. But the servants' quarters do not provide ideal working accommodation for senior civil servants. The Department has had to spill over into adjoining buildings. The result is that the present overcrowding makes organization extremely difficult for an expanding Department.

Diplomacy in the ascendant

Walshe did not have the luxury of facing such problems in the post-war period. There had been no examination held since 1938. A small number of new staff had been recruited from other sections of the service. His Department was seriously understaffed, and but for the energy of a few senior officials Iveagh House would not have been able to cope with the additional work imposed by the implementation of the controversial policy of neutrality. London and Dublin had to work closely on a number of different occasions during the war, and despite the occasional clash at governmental level good relations were sustained between the Departments of Defence, Finance, and External Affairs and their British counterparts. The strident tone of Anglo-Irish relations in the 1930s virtually disappeared towards the end of the war. Just as the time of maximum danger had passed, there was a momentary lapse on de Valéra's part. He showed unusually bad judgement and taste when he visited the German legation on 2 May 1945, accompanied by Joseph Walshe, to offer condolences on the death of Hitler. Diplomatic protocol dictated that this should be done. An exception might have been made in such a case, and the Department strongly advised against the visit. Unusually, de Valéra ignored the recommendations of the Department on that crucial occasion.[19]

The highly publicized visit to the German legation earned the Taoiseach a very bad international press and a stern rebuke from Churchill. The speech by the British Prime Minister gave de Valéra an opportunity to recoup lost ground at home, and his reply made him, according to Maffey, 'as great a hero as is the Irishman who scores the winning try at Twickenham'.[20]

Maffey was confident, despite the controversy, that the end of the war had seen a qualitative change in the relations between the two countries, although at first sight Anglo-Irish relations suggested 'nothing but regret and pessimism'. For many generations the slogan of Irish patriotism had been 'England's difficulty is Ireland's opportunity'. During the war that had changed, according to Maffey, to the milder version 'England's difficulty is none of Ireland's business'. If the question of the ports was left aside – 'a difficulty which we created ourselves and which at once threatened disaster' – the history of Irish neutrality was 'far from being a black record'.

> 'For the first time in history the British Cabinet have been able to conduct a long war without any anxiety about Ireland. Compare the war of 1914–18 when Ireland was still in the United Kingdom. We had to keep a big garrison in Ireland. We had to suppress a rebellion. We suffered deep humiliation. German intrigue was rampant. Roger Casement was landed by a German submarine. The full story of espionage and submarine links has never been fully told.'

The picture during the Second World War was much changed, not because the Irish government was friendly but because, said Maffey, Ireland was neutral and was never allowed to forget for one instant that its immunity could not last a day if it became a base for German intrigue. After the war there was the 'quiet hope' that Eire would 'quietly discard' the bitter dictum of Arthur Griffith, who when asked to define the foreign policy of his country said: 'Find out on which side the English stand. Ireland will be found on the other side.'

While all tension had by no means been taken out of the relationship between Dublin and London, the crudity of Griffith's oft-quoted remark no longer represented the reality. Rhetoric had, at least at the diplomatic level, given way to reason, and even the most sensitive of outstanding issues between the two countries (excluding the question of partition) were treated at government level in a moderate and restrained way. Maffey spoke of the need for 'a policy of forbearance', a patient, consistent policy, and a policy described as 'absent treatment'. It was Maffey's unenviable task to coax de Valéra to 'normalize' relations with Britain. The latter had moved forward rapidly towards the close of the war in a way that local public opinion at the time often failed to perceive.

The Boland period

Joseph Walshe left the secretaryship of the Department in 1946 to become the first Irish envoy to the Vatican to hold the rank of ambassador. His successor, Mr Frederick H. Boland, had first come into the Department in the late 1920s as one of the earliest young recruits. His poise and professionalism helped remove the element of 'inferiority complex' that Maffey had said characterized Irish diplomacy for over twenty years. His working relationship with de Valéra was excellent.

It seemed that the path of diplomacy was at least destined to take precedence over the strident rhetoric of anti-partitionist propaganda when de Valéra lost the 1948 general election. The country had its first change of government in sixteen years. The national question once again found itself at the centre of Irish politics. De Valéra as Taoiseach had learned the lessons of diplomacy. De Valéra as leader of the opposition was forced into a more traditional nationalist role where he could not be seen to be outflanked by the irredentist rhetoric of the new government. Partition became a central issue of politics as the government set out to solve 'the problem' and to pillory de Valéra for not having done so after sixteen years in power.

De Valéra set out on a round-the-world tour to highlight the 'injustices of partition'. Meanwhile, the scarce resources of the Department were mobilized and concentrated on propaganda. Mr Seán MacBride, the new Minister of External Affairs, felt that the reactivating of public opinion abroad would help bring about the unity of the two Irish states. That was to be backed up by a strong diplomatic offensive. The culmination of the campaign came with the refusal to join NATO because MacBride could not work out a deal to enlist American support against the British with regard to partition. At that point, there did not appear to be anything other than a highly pragmatic approach to neutrality. It could be bartered for a deal on partition.

But if the role of diplomacy was down-graded in that area, there were strong demands made on the Department in the period of post-war European reconstruction, due to Ireland's participation in OEEC and the Council of Europe. This indicated a shift in emphasis away from the diaspora to Europe – a triumph of geography over history, as Professor T. Desmond Williams has phrased it.

During another three-year Inter-Party government from 1954 to 1957, William T. Cosgrave's son, Liam, held the External Affairs portfolio. He negotiated Ireland's entry to the United Nations. After Fianna Fáil's return to office, Mr Frank Aiken took over the portfolio again and remained at Iveagh House until his retirement from politics in 1969. Mr Aiken, who was perhaps the closest person to de Valéra in the Cabinet, conducted an Atlantic-orientated foreign policy which showed itself to be strongly independent of American influence. Despite the protestations of church and state in America, Aiken voted against Washington on the 'China question' in 1961.[21]

Departmental expansion

By the mid-1960s the Department had expanded considerably. In 1966 there were 78 in the service with ranks above higher executive officer level. There were three assistant secretaries over nine sections: Political and United Nations; International Organizations; Information; Cultural Relations; Economic; Legal; Consular; Protocol and Administration.

By 1970 the Economic Section had been divided into General Foreign Trade and EEC, GATT and EFTA. (This became the European Communities Division in 1973.) An Anglo-Irish section was formed in 1971, reflecting the growing concern in Dublin provoked by the recent explosion of violence in the North. Ireland's admission to the EEC in 1972 helped to consolidate the dramatic expansion of the Department of Foreign Affairs, which had been going on since the late 1960s.

The English name of the Department was changed in 1971 to Foreign Affairs. A note from the Legal Section of the Department indicated that the use of the term External Affairs was of British Commonwealth origin and had already been dropped by a number of Commonwealth countries. 'Foreign Affairs was now the more usual and appropriate term,' it added. In the Dáil, the Minister, Dr Hillery, explained that the change would bring the name of his Department into line with common usage. The term External Affairs was, he said, a legacy of the British Empire when foreign affairs were controlled from London and the 'satellites' of the Empire dealt among themselves in external affairs. It is of interest to note that the title remained unchanged in Irish, An Roinn Gnóthaí Eachtracha. This title had been amended in 1939 by the Ministers and Secretaries (Amendment) Act. It had been called Roinn Gnóthaí Coigríche since 1924.

In 1973 Mr Liam Cosgrave became Taoiseach of a Fine Gael–Labour Party Coalition. Dr Garret FitzGerald took over the same portfolio held by his father, Desmond, in the mid-1920s, and remained Minister of Foreign Affairs until 1977. He brought a new dynamism to the post, which was greatly appreciated in Iveagh House. In Brussels, he enjoyed a reputation for clarity of thought and high administrative competence unequalled by any other Irish politician in Europe. During his ministry the Overseas Development Assistance Division was set up to coordinate aid to the Third World.

Dr FitzGerald's 'whirlwind' style gave a new vitality to the service. One of his first moves on taking up the portfolio was to recall all ambassadors home for personal briefings and a general conference. Normally, ambassadors report to the Department personally when on annual leave. There are a number of foreign assignments, known popularly in the Department as 'hardship' posts, where ambassadors and staff are given leave every six months. But an envoy will not necessarily return to Dublin each holiday, unless specifically requested to do so.

The growth of the Department of Foreign Affairs has been rapid in recent years. In 1934, Joseph Walshe had a staff of less than 15, with offices in a corridor of the Department of Agriculture. By 1981, Ireland had 31 serving ambassadors. There were two ministers plenipotentiary, 41 councillors, 103 first secretaries, two second secretaries and 63 third secretaries. Despite the expansion, the cramped though elegant surroundings of Iveagh House continue to house the Department, which has been forced to take offices in the Department of Justice and premises behind Foreign Affairs. There are very few in the Department who would not readily trade the 'splendour' of their present surroundings for more modern, roomy accommodation.

Although women played a very active part in the revolutionary phase of the Department of Publicity's existence from 1919 to 1921, they failed to hold senior posts after the civil war largely because of the 'marriage bar'. There was one notable exception. Miss Sheila Geraldine Murphy, who was in the Department since 1921, was appointed assistant secretary in 1962 and held that post until her retirement in 1964. But on 31 July 1973 the practice of preventing women who had married from maintaining their posts in the civil service ended. In 1981, there was one woman legal adviser with the rank of assistant secretary, a deputy with the grade of counsellor, 19 first secretaries and 16 third secretaries. Miss M. Tinney was the only woman serving as an ambassador in 1981.

The threefold role of the Department – cultural, political and economic – has weighted the ambassadorial role in the past heavily in favour of the first two areas, very much on the lines of British diplomacy. But since the return of Fianna Fáil in 1977, the brief has laid increasing stress on the commercial and economic function of the envoy and of embassy staff. Some difficulty had been encountered adapting to the newly defined role, resulting in a series of reshuffles that have tended to bring younger men to ambassadorial posts.

It is very fortunate that, facing the 1980s, Ireland has such an outstanding diplomatic service. The next decade confronts most European countries with a series of major foreign policy options that could have enormous domestic political repercussions. In the case of Ireland, the future of its policy of neutrality is of paramount importance. Ireland is neutral by accident, not by conviction. That was evident during the Second World War, and more blatantly obvious in 1949 over proposed membership of NATO. Successive Dublin governments have adhered to a *tactical neutrality* with no obvious enthusiasm. There is a growing lobby among the politicians and the military who would favour membership of NATO. An even larger number would support the idea of a European Defence Community. In itself, that is not likely to result in a major policy change. The island has limited strategic importance. The existence of Northern Ireland further undermines NATO's interest in the Irish Republic. That presupposes, however, the continued dependability of Britain as a loyal member of the Alliance. With the growth of unilateralism and the strong anti-nuclear feelings there, it is objectively the case that such unpredictability must increase the desirability of establishing NATO bases in the Irish Republic.

In such a climate of uncertainty and pressure from international organizations, the onus on the Department of Foreign Affairs to provide clear analyses and solid advice is greater than ever before. The need to set out the national benefits of a positive neutrality is pressing. The history of Irish diplomacy would indicate that there is some reason for confidence. The 'good faith and integrity' of officials should continue the tradition of providing recommendations even if they do not 'coincide with what happens to be politically expedient'.

NOTES

[1] By comparison with our EEC partners and British Commonwealth countries, very little has been written on either the Department of Foreign Affairs or Irish Foreign Policy.

[2] The Irish Department of External Affairs did not move to Iveagh House until 1940. For convenience, I have chosen to use Iveagh House throughout the article as one might use Chigi, Quai d'Orsay, etc.

[3] Desmond FitzGerald, *Report on Propaganda Department*, June 1920, No. 12 (in possession of Mrs Napoli McKenna, Rome).

[4] See Napoli McKenna manuscript history of the *Irish Bulletin*.

[5] See Patrick McCarton, *With de Valéra in America* (Dublin 1932). Donal McCartney, 'De Valéra's mission to the United States, 1919–1920' in Art Cosgrove and Donal McCartney (eds), *Studies in Irish History* (presented to R. Dudley Edwards) (Dublin 1979).

[6] Seán T. O'Kelly manuscript, in possession of his wife, Phyllis. Much of the material has been published in his memoirs: Pádraig Ó Fiannachta (ed.), *Seán T. Scéal a bheatha ó 1916–1923* (Dublin 1972).

[7] Michael MacWhite profile, *Irish Times*, 26 November 1949.

[8] See author's thesis, *Ireland, the Vatican and Catholic Europe, 1919–39* (European University Institute, Florence 1980), 60–80.

[9] The report cited was taken in a raid on de Valéra's house in Dublin (FO 371 C4452/272/47). It was signed, according to A. F. Hemming of the Foreign Office, by Robert Brennan, 'the under-secretary for foreign affairs in the Sinn Féin Government'.

[10] Gavan Duffy resigned mainly because he felt that the Provisional Government had mishandled the constitutional negotiations.

[11] Confidential memorandum by outgoing Minister of Foreign Affairs on 'The position of Ireland's "foreign affairs" at date of general election, 1922'. Foreign Office is the term used to describe the department that is more usually described as foreign affairs, p. 1, No. 66 (FitzGerald papers). Gavan Duffy retained the British terms for his department: Foreign Affairs and Dáil documents often refer to the Under-Secretary for Foreign Affairs. The committee system was introduced by FitzGerald in late 1919: the members were Alistair McCabe, Liam de Róiste, J. McBride, J. A. Burke, J. MacSuibhne, M. MacStain and D. FitzGerald; but it did not meet regularly or operate very effectively; see D 21269 SPO (Dublin).

[12] Professor Binchy is the author of the classic work, *Church and State in Fascist Italy* (Oxford 1941). His essay on Adolf Hitler is also worth noting, see *Studies*, Vol. XXII, March 1933, 29–47.

[13] Binchy to MacDermot, 3 November 1935, Frank MacDermot papers, 1065/114/5, PRO Dublin.

[14] *Irish Times*, 6 April 1937.

[15] *Dáil Debates*, Vol. LXIV. Cols 1194–1219, 27 November 1936.

[16] Interview with Mr Seán MacEntee.

[17] The profile was composed for Sir D'arcy Osborne of the British Legation to the Holy See, who had written to the Foreign Secretary, Ernest Bevin, on 5 February 1946 regretting that Tom Kiernan and his wife were being replaced by Walshe, who he had heard was 'anti-British'. He had heard the same about Kiernan when he arrived but had seen no evidence of it.

[18] O'Neill and Longford, op. cit., 313–26.

[19] *Irish Times*, 12 May 1945.

[20] Sir John Maffey annual report on Ireland for 1945–6. The Dominions Office did not share Maffey's feelings.

[21] Conor Cruise O'Brien, 'Ireland in International Affairs', Owen Dudley Edwards (ed.), *Conor Cruise O'Brien introduces Ireland* (London 1969), 104–34; see also *To Katanga and Back* (London 1962).

Since the completion of this chapter, the Fianna Fáil government was defeated in mid-1981 and Dr FitzGerald was returned as head of a Fine Gael–Labour coalition. Two key foreign policy appointments – one concerning Northern Ireland – were made to the Department of the Taoiseach. The post of Foreign Minister was filled by a non-Dáil member who was a Taoiseach's nominee to the Senate. The Iveagh House hierarchy underwent a significant reshuffle. A most important development was Dr FitzGerald's decision to appoint a Minister of State at the Department of Foreign Affairs with special responsibility for Development Cooperation. The Minister of State also has responsibility for the legal section. He deputizes for the Minister in his absence.

BIBLIOGRAPHY

Archival note
The study of the foreign policy process and the workings of the Department over the past 50 years is made very difficult by the total closure of archives. Organizational files may not even be consulted. Many important files may not have survived. In 1940, fearing invasion, the secretary of the Taoiseach's office is believed to have given the instruction to destroy all sensitive material in External Affairs. A former Irish ambassador, John A. Belton, who began to write a history of the Department at one stage, estimated that as much as 50 per cent of the files have been destroyed.

The register to the Department's D files, which is under lock and key in the PRO, would indicate that the 'confidential reports' from envoys would be the category of most interest to researchers. There is another category of file, referred to in the Department as the secretary's files, which no doubt would contain material most valuable to researchers. The records from Irish embassies in Paris, Bonn, Madrid and Washington have been transferred back to Dublin and are lodged in the Public Records Office, together with a large collection of the D files already mentioned.

The following works are among the most important published in the field. The Royal Irish Academy has prepared an extensive list of works on Irish foreign policy.

Joseph Carroll, *Ireland in the War Years, 1939–1945* (London 1973).

Conor Cruise O'Brien, 'Ireland in International Affairs' in Owen Dudley Edwards (ed.), *Conor Cruise O'Brien introduces Ireland* (London 1969), 104–34, provides an interesting survey by a former Irish diplomat.

Basil Chubb, *The Government and Politics of Ireland* (London 1970).

Brian Farrell, *Chairman or Chief? The role of the Taoiseach in Irish Government* (Dublin 1971).

Patrick Keatinge, *The Formation of Irish Foreign Policy* (Dublin 1973).

——, *A Place among the Nations* (Dublin 1978).

——, 'Odd man out: Ireland's neutrality and European Security' in *International Affairs*, Vol. 48, no. 3, July 1972, 438–45.

Robert Kee, *The Green Flag* (London 1971).

Earl of Longford and T. P. O'Neill, *Eamon de Valéra* (London 1970); an expanded two-volume version in Irish: Tomás O'Neill and Pádraig Ó Fiannachta, *de Valéra* (Dublin 1968); Maurice Moynihan, *Speeches of de Valéra* (Dublin 1980). The de Valéra papers are lodged with the Franciscans in Killiney, Co. Dublin.

John A. Murphy, *Ireland in the Twentieth Century* (Dublin 1975).

T. Ryle Dwyer, *Irish Neutrality and the USA, 1939–1947* (Dublin 1977).

E. Rumpf and A. C. Hepburn, *Nationalism and Socialism in twentieth-century Ireland* (Liverpool 1977).

John H. Whyte, *Church and State in modern Ireland* (Dublin 1975).

T. Desmond Williams, 'A Study of Neutrality', *The Leader*, January, April 1953.

——, 'de Valéra in Power', in Francis MacManus (ed.), *The Years of the Great Test, 1926–1939*, 30–42, 173–83.

——, 'From the Treaty to the Civil War', in T. Desmond Williams (ed.), *The Irish Struggle*, 117–28, 183–93.

——, 'Ireland and the War', in T. Desmond Williams (ed.), *Ireland in the War Years and after, 1939–1951*, 14–27, 201–12.

——, *Irish Foreign Policy, 1949–1969* in J. J. Lee (ed.), *Ireland, 1945–1970*, 136–50.

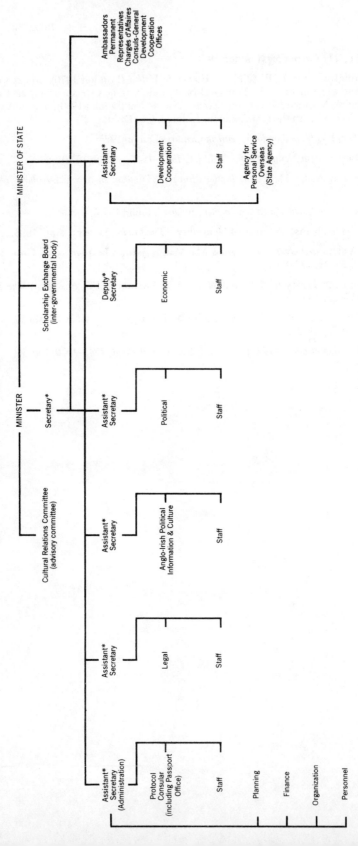

IRELAND – APPENDIX A

DEPARTMENT OF FOREIGN AFFAIRS (1981)

MINISTER — MINISTER OF STATE

Secretary*

Cultural Relations Committee (advisory committee)

Scholarship Exchange Board (inter-governmental body)

Ambassadors
Permanent Representatives
Chargés d'Affaires
Consuls-General
Development Cooperation Offices

Assistant* Secretary (Administration)
- Protocol
- Consular (including Passport Office)
- Staff
- Planning
- Finance
- Organization
- Personnel

Assistant* Secretary
- Legal
- Staff

Assistant* Secretary
- Anglo-Irish Political Information & Culture
- Staff

Assistant* Secretary
- Political
- Staff

Deputy* Secretary
- Economic
- Staff

Assistant* Secretary
- Development Cooperation
- Staff
- Agency for Personal Service Overseas (State Agency)

* members of Management Advisory Committee

Italy

The Ministry for Foreign Affairs

ENRICO SERRA

Professor Enrico Serra is head of the Historical and Documentation Service of the Italian Ministry for Foreign Affairs and is Professor of the History of Treaties and International Relations at the University of Bologna. He was a student of Federico Chabod and Luigi Salvatorelli and studied at the Institute of Historical Research and at the Sorbonne. He is a member of the Executive Committees of the Institute for the Study of International Relations in Milan and the Diplomatic Institute of the Ministry for Foreign Affairs. His numerous publications include *L'Intesa Mediterranea del 1902* (1957), *La questione Tunisina da Crispi a Rudinì* (1967), *Manuale di Storia dei trattati e di diplomazia* (1980) and with J.-B. Duroselle, *L'emigrazione italiana in Francia prima del 1914* (1978), *Italia e Francia: 1919–1939* (1981).

The Kingdom of Italy was created on 17 March 1861, as was the Ministry for Foreign Affairs, whose first head was the Prime Minister himself, Camille Benso di Cavour. He held the two posts from 20 January 1860, in other words under the preceding regime as well.

At that time, and in the following years, there was a lively controversy over the constitution of the Kingdom of Italy, a controversy that soon became formal and academic. Should it consider itself a completely new state, born from the fusion of the previously existing Italian states; or should it rather be a continuation under another name of the Kingdom of Sardinia, having grown through the addition of other states or their provinces?

From a pragmatic point of view, this question is of minor importance. The new Ministry for Foreign Affairs was in fact structured and organized according to the rules and regulations in practice in the Kingdom of Sardinia, which bore the mark of Cavour himself.

For example, one rule that remained in practice (and was reconfirmed in January 1864) was that of 22 December 1856 on the 'admission, exams and voluntary corps'. The careers within the Ministry remained the same as before, in three divisions of internal administration, legations and consulates respectively. The candidate had to be 'possessed of sufficient financial means to maintain the volunteer in the Italian consulates abroad and, for a diplomatic career, a compulsory income of 6000 lire'; this last figure was fairly high so as to ensure that the number of candidates was limited. After a short time the sum was reduced to 3000 lire for a career in the consulate alone. A candidate was dubbed 'voluntary' if he had passed the exams of civil, penal, commercial, constitutional and international law, of political economy, ancient, modern and medieval history, and geography. There were three written exams, to be taken in Italian with at least one in French, and the same number of oral exams. The successful candidate had to lend his services, unpaid, for two years as a volunteer. Then, once he passed further exams, he was admitted for a career in the Ministry.

The rules for a career in 'internal administration' were still those laid down on 23 October 1853. The scale in descending order was: secretary-general of the Ministry for Foreign Affairs (Ministero degli Affari Esteri, MAE); director-general; head of division; acting head *(capo servizio)*; secretary first and second class; under-secretary *(applicato)* first, second, third and fourth class; clerks.

The first secretary-general of the Ministry for Foreign Affairs of the Kingdom of Italy, who also held that post for the Kingdom of Sardinia, was Domenico Carutti di Cantogno, who had been nominated to the post in October 1859. He was followed in March 1862 by Luigi Amedeo Melegari.

While the consular career continued to be governed by the consulate laws of 1858 and 1859,[1*] the diplomatic regulation was modified in the Royal Decree of 9 November 1862 which was approved by General Peppino Durando, the third Foreign Minister since the death of Cavour (after Bettino Ricasoli and Urbano Rattazzi) simultaneously to hold the post of Prime Minister.

The new regulation divided the diplomatic career into envoys extraordinary and ministers plenipotentiary, resident ministers, and chargés d'affaires; the last was abolished as a separate grade in 1864.[2*] They were assisted by councillors of legation and by secretaries, first and second class. The number of envoys extraordinary and resident ministers 'will be regulated on the basis of the law of budget'. The number of councillors of legation was fixed at five, the secretaries first class at ten and second class at twelve. The salaries of the diplomatic corps would remain as laid down in the Royal Decree of 1859.

Regulations for Interpreters assigned to the legations and consulates in the East were confirmed in 1862.[3]* They were divided into two categories, each of which was subdivided into three classes. Those interpreters belonging to the first category were nominated by the king on the advice of the Ministry for Foreign Affairs, and followed a real career. Those in the second were nominated by the consuls on previous authorization of the MAE. In October 1862 the staff of the MAE was increased as a result of growing pressure; even diplomats coming from other states united in the Kingdom of Italy were admitted.[1]

At the end of 1865, when the Prime Minister and Foreign Minister was General Alfonso La Marmora, the internal structure of the MAE was as follows. It was headed by the secretary-general (Marcello Cerruti, career diplomat, who in March 1863 had succeeded Emilio Visconti Venosta). The cabinet was entrusted to Alberto Blanc, legation secretary, and consisted of two offices: the first dealt with restricted and confidential political correspondence, with the private correspondence of the Minister and also with the reading and annotation of newspapers; the second with coded and telegraphic correspondence, the orders of the day and the audiences held by the Minister. The courier service was also dependent on the cabinet. There were three divisions of the legations, which were geographically subdivided (the third also dealt with legal matters). The consular division (headed by Professor Cristoforo Negri), was subdivided into two sections, one for the consulates proper and the other for negotiations and commerce, including commercial publications and the *Consular Bulletin*. The administrative division was in two sections; the first handled the archives, protocol, ceremonies, personnel and the library, and the second handled book-keeping and passports. The central administration also made use of diplomatic and consulate staff. There were 23 heads of foreign missions in service; about ten of these were already established in the same office before the Kingdom of Italy had been constituted. The legation at Vienna was still vacant.

The basic administrative body of the internal administrative career, halfway through 1865, included: three heads of division first class; one head of division second class; 7 heads of section, 9 secretaries second class; 5 under-secretaries first class; 5 under-secretaries second class; 5 under-secretaries third class; 6 under-secretaries fourth class; 5 couriers of the cabinet. At the same time, the diplomatic corps was composed of: 10 envoys extraordinary and ministers plenipotentiary; 10 resident ministers; 5 councillors; 10 secretaries first class, 12 secretaries second class. The consular corps, first category, included: 7 consuls-general first class, 10 consuls-general second class, 12 consuls first class, 14 consuls second class, 14 vice-consuls second class, 18 vice-consuls third class, 12 voluntary officers, and 3 justice consuls *(consoli giudici)* assigned to the eastern consulates. The roll of the interpreters and harbour-masters included 1 interpreter first class, 3 interpreters second class 2 interpreters third class, 2 pupil interpreters, and 1 harbour-master (Constantinople).[2]

Emilio Visconti Venosta, who was already a collaborator of Cavour, was secretary-general of the Ministry from December 1862 to March 1863, the date on which he became Foreign Minister. He returned to the post of Foreign Minister from June 1866 until April 1867 and again from December 1869 until March 1876, and twice more after that. He left a strong personal mark on Italian foreign politics and on the structure of the Ministry. Visconti Venosta had a new order for the Ministry approved,[4*] which retained the post of secretary-general but abolished that of head of cabinet. The central administration as subdivided into the Political Department, the Commercial Department, and the Department for Private and Legal Affairs.

A circular of 9 February 1867 specified the responsibilities of these departments and made arrangements for the dispatch and retention of correspondence on the part of the foreign offices. Among other things it gave the order that all documents must discuss one topic and one only.

Not long before this, when Luigi Amedeo Melegari was Foreign Minister, a new consular regulation had been approved.[5*] The consular staff was divided into two categories, envoy agents and those resident locally. The first, by royal appointment, comprised consuls-general first and second class, consuls first and second class, vice-consuls first, second and third class. The composition of the consular staff was modified further in subsequent years.[6*] At the end of 1886 it was made up of 148 units, comprising 8 consuls-general first class, 9 second class, 18 consuls first class, and 20 consuls second class. In the same decrees the overall list of diplomatic personnel was extended, bringing it to a total of 59, including 10 extraordinary envoys and ministers plenipotentiary first class.

With the royal decree of 29 November 1870,[7*] which carried the seal of Visconti Venosta, measures were taken to establish the first ordering (since unification) of the staff of the diplomatic corps, with particular attention to its career structure, duties and responsibilities, salaries and allowances, diplomas, dismissals and correspondence. Article 57 bound the diplomats officially to correspond *solely* with the Ministry for Foreign Affairs; and Article 65 to request the anticipatory authorization of the Government in order to receive honours and gifts from foreign countries. Article 3 laid down that legation attachés were part of the diplomatic corps, but that their number could not 'exceed a quarter of the body of salaried diplomatic officials'. Article 67 took into consideration the recognition of the title of military attaché for the general or superior officials of the three branches, an agreement reached earlier between the Ministry for Foreign Affairs and the War and Naval Ministries. From 1882 four military attachés were appointed (Vienna, Paris, St Petersburg and Berlin), and two naval attachés (London and Paris).

In 1885,[8*] the structure of Ministry staff was amended. The staff were divided into three categories. The first comprised 41 individuals, including two directors-general, three heads of division, seven heads of section (among whom was a director of the archives), 19 secretaries, and so on. A ministerial decree dated 15 May 1869 laid down new standards (not in fact greatly dissimilar from the preceding ones) for the admission to the three careers of the Ministry for Foreign Affairs. Any young person between the ages of twenty and thirty could apply if in possession of 'any kind of degree', and if (here the Piedmont tradition still survives) he had passed the exams of the High School of War and those of the application courses for the branches of the engineers, artillery, marine corps, and general staff. The examination qualifications stayed the same as those laid down in Cavour's time.

The reorganization of the Ministry for Foreign Affairs after unification, while retaining the essential nucleus of the Sardo-Piedmont order (for example, the 'Regulation on the order of the central administration' continued to be the one passed on 23 October 1853) continued until 1885.[9]* The Council of Legal Diplomatic Questions was reformed, with some modification of the earlier dispositions.[10]* Other legislative dispositions laid down between 1863 and 1864 controlled vacancies, leave, temporary retirements, dismissals and pension rights. In 1868 a new order of precedence was established for the various offices and ranks at court and at public functions.[11]*

The decree of 5 July 1882 deserves to be noted, for it established 'an Italian colony in the territory of Assab on the west coast of the Red Sea', directly dependent on the Ministry for Foreign Affairs.

If we compare the central organization of the MAE in 1870 with that in 1886, we can see that the basic inspiration was still that of the reforms carried out by Cavour for the Kingdom of Sardinia in 1856, and then adapted by Visconti Venosta to meet the wider needs of post-unification Italy. In effect, in 1870, when Visconti Venosta was Foreign Minister and Alberto Blanc secretary-general, the central administration of the MAE was as follows. The Political Division comprised two branches. The first dealt with political and special correspondence, negotiations, diplomatic publications, and codes. The second dealt with personnel, protocol, legal documents, orders of knighthood, archives of the division. The Accounts and Archives Division also had two branches. The first dealt with the accounts, the second with the library and the keeping of the ministerial archives. The Directorate-General of Consulates and Commerce was divided into two departments and five offices. It also dealt with the *Consular Bulletin*. This first appeared in January 1862, accompanied by a circular dated 15 January 1862 signed by Emilio Visconti Venosta, in which he warned that: 'In order that the useful results which is hoped for are obtained from this publication, it is deemed opportune that the Royal Consuls should compete in conveying to the Ministry timely and trustworthy information, both about the conditions of the commercial relations existing between Italy and the other states where they are residing, and about suitable means of improving and documenting them . . .' Emilio Visconti Venosta returned to the subject of the importance of the *Consular Bulletin*, this time in the capacity of Foreign Minister, in a long circular dated 6 April 1863.[3]

The Ministry for Foreign Affairs, along with other government offices, had been transferred from Florence to Rome in February 1871, and had begun to function from 1 July of that year in the Palazzo della Consulta (from which the MAE took its colloquial name).

In 1886, when the Minister was Carlo Felice Nicolis di Robilant, the MAE was headed by the secretary-general (Raffaele Cappelli) and had two main divisions. The Directorate-General of Political Affairs and Administrative Offices (Director Giacomo Malvano) included the Political Division, consisting of two offices, the archives, library, accounts, cabinet couriers, bursary and dispatches. The Directorate-General of Consulates and Commerce (Director Augusto Peiroleri) included the personnel office and two divisions, each consisting of two offices. There existed also the post of honorary inspector-general of the consulates, an *ad hoc* title for Professor Cristoforo Negri, consul-general first class.

Of the nine envoys extraordinary and ministers plenipotentiary first class in office in 1886, five had credentials as ambassador – to Berlin (De Launay), Vienna (Nigra), Paris (Menabrea), London (Corti), St Petersburg (Greppi). The other headquarters occupied were Monaco, Bern, Lisbon and The Hague.

The headquarters occupied by ministers plenipotentiary second class were: Madrid, Stockholm, Brussels, Bucharest, Washington, Athens, Buenos Aires, Tangiers, Montevideo, Peking, Copenhagen and Rio de Janeiro. Those staffed by councillors of legation or secretaries of legation second class were: Tokyo, Sofia, Belgrade, Constantinople, Budapest and Lisbon.

The Left had come to power in 1876, but Depretis was forced to resort to the famous *connubio* (marriage) in order to enlist the aid of the politicians *(statisti)* of the Right. The Foreign Ministry was perhaps the least affected by the reform. The situation changed in 1887 when Francesco Crispi became Prime Minister, Minister for Home Affairs and Foreign Minister *ad interim*. For his head of cabinet for the MAE he nominated a trusted collaborator, the diplomat Alberto Pisani Dossi, a Lombard nobleman. The latter had made a name for himself as a writer and exponent of the Scapigliatura movement, which advocated a break with tradition in the field of literature and the arts.

Crispi introduced for the first time into the Ministries (and therefore also into the MAE) the post of Under-Secretary of State, a position given to a Member of Parliament who had to represent the Minister, both before the Chamber and in relations with the public, if he should be prevented from attending.[12*] The Under-Secretary of State for Foreign Affairs (the Hon. Abele Damiani) for a brief period (from 2 January to 4 March 1888) also took on the duties of secretary-general of the Ministry. Later this appointment was left vacant, then shelved, and finally abolished.

The central administration of the MAE was restructured in 1887[13*] by decrees that carry the imprint of Pisani Dossi, who had concerned himself with these problems before.

The functions of secretary-general were divided in such a way as to assign the personnel and administrative duties to Damiani (as Under-Secretary), and the political and diplomatic side to the head of cabinet. In this way it was made possible for the political power, i.e. Crispi, to exercise more direct and incisive influence on diplomats and diplomacy, since it was no longer necessary to pass through the secretary-general. This precedent was later imitated by Mussolini. The posts of director-general of political affairs and legislative offices, and director-general of the consulates and commerce were also abolished.

The central administration of the Ministry was reorganized into five divisions (each one of which was then further divided into sections), and at their heads Crispi and Pisani Dossi placed persons they trusted. These divisions were: Division I Political Affairs, which included a colonial section; Division II Private Affairs; Division III Personnel; Division IV Archives and General Registry (in fact directed by Prof. Giacomo Gorrini, director of archives); Division V Accounts.

It might be interesting to know how the five divisions were subdivided. The Political Affairs Division had the following departments: (1) general politics, (2) commercial politics, (3) Italian colonies. The Private Affairs

Division comprised: (1) Europe and European colonies, (2) America, (3) Asia, Africa, Oceania. The Personnel Division contained (1) personnel, (2) ceremonial passport office. The Archives and General Registry Division consisted of: (1) archives, (2) library, registration office, copyist's office, office for consignments and dispatches. The Accounts Division was divided into (1) balance and accounting, (2) cash till and current accounts, (3) bursar's office.

The bulk of the duties left to the discretion of the Under-Secretary were concerned with administration, which he controlled, and the inspection of Italian offices and institutes abroad. Moreover, he had the right to preside over the Council of the Foreign Office, another novelty introduced by Crispi[14*] with the principal aim of linking the various services and the offices of the Ministry. It operated like an administrative council, as it was composed of five heads of divisions and their deputies, and it expressed its collective opinion on arrangements concerning internal rules, personnel and disciplinary measures.

The predominating importance that Pisani Dossi was gradually assuming became obvious. He was also favoured by another technical factor, which was that the cabinet was one and the same for the Minister and the Under-Secretary. He therefore came to control all business, whether political or administrative.

To realize this, one only has to glance at the Order of the Ministry.[15*] The following functions were attributed to the Minister's cabinet: 'Opening of the Minister's correspondence. Restricted political affairs. Confidential affairs. Personal correspondence of the Minister. The Minister's relations with Parliament and the Diplomatic Corps. Audiences. Diplomatic tribunal. Order of the day. Last revisions of ministerial publications. Communications to the newspapers and telegraph agencies. Ciphers of royal officials abroad. Telegraphs and codes. Minister's portfolio.' And again: 'Archives and special copy for restricted business. Printing house of the Cabinet.'[4] In fact Pisani gathered into his own hands the private secretarial office of the Minister, and also what we might call today the press office and coding office. Later, Crispi incorporated the 'colonial office' as a section of the cabinet, which therefore became directly responsible to Pisani.[5]

One can truly say that there was not one field or sector of the Ministry that Crispi did not reform, evidently under the auspices of Pisani Dossi, who was the only one fully to understand its functions and administrative structure. His influence was felt from the initial entry examinations to the various careers in the Ministry (including the diplomatic ones, of course)[16*] right up to the discipline of employees of the central administration and of the legations and consulates.[17*] Among the measures taken at that time some should be mentioned for their characteristic quality: the institution of a regular career in the diplomatic and consular chancelleries,[18*] the adjustments to the rules on vacancies, temporary leaves and retirements, dismissals, and retirement classifications[19*] not to speak of the regulation for the execution of this law, which is even more relevant.[20*]

The aim was to modernize the service, to stamp it with greater efficiency and discipline, to make the MAE a valuable instrument of foreign and colonial politics in an Italy that was at last active and ambitious. Crispi and Pisani did not hesitate to make victims even out of illustrious figures, beginning with the secretary-general, Malvano, who resigned from the profession. Between 1 July 1887 and 1 May 1890, 31 functionaries were sent into full or temporary retirement. At the time it was said that Crispi's aim was to dismantle the Piedmont framework of diplomacy.

The activity of Crispi and Pisani, which seemed to have no limits, was disseminated by circulars, orders of service, advice often drawn up in imperious tones; the purpose was to encourage diplomats to use less conventional tones in their correspondence, to study to the full the country in question, to carry out their representative duties better, to abolish consulates wherever possible, transferring their duties to the embassies and legations; in a word, to make the diplomats work harder. And it certainly cannot have given much pleasure to the diplomats to see the assignments of the principal representatives reduced. Among other things, the 12 per cent commission for diplomatic agents on payments and cash collected was abolished in 1888.[6]

One can understand that Crispi emphasized certain causes dear to his heart – for example, that of raising the prestige of Italians abroad; keeping the Italian colonies united and encouraging their sense of being Italian; ensuring the spread of Italian schools and language abroad. Also, there was his other fixed idea – the statistical data, which diplomats should relay to the Ministry, on the economic situation of their respective countries, of movement in and out of harbours and on railways, on foreign commerce and, obviously, on emigration. The organization and interpretation of these data was undertaken by a famous personage, Luigi Bodio, whom Crispi had promoted to the post of director-general of statistics and whose offices were in Via della Stamperia.

A circular of 14 November 1887 informed royal diplomatic agents that they should suppress the forms of courtesy, 'always superfluous and often unbecoming', in their official correspondence. 'I hope', concluded Crispi, 'that each man will understand the aim of this circular, which is to bring back consciousness and simplicity as far as possible into the official style, which best responds to the great traditions of the Italian language and to modern handling of business, more candid and more rapid than the ancient.'

It was, however, necessary to find a way to publicize all this material if it was to be useful to all diplomats. The Ministry already published a modest *Consular Bulletin*, which had been started in December 1861 by Ricasoli, and which appeared without any real regularity in rather thin issues. A restructuring was immediately planned to render it more useful and better known. This idea was typical of Dossi. There is no need to underline the large part that Pisani Dossi played in its transformation – it was planned by him in all its details.

From 1 January 1888[21*] the publication took the name of the *Bulletin of the Ministry for Foreign Affairs*, and a regulation was passed that is indicative of the stimulus that Crispi intended to give it. Henceforward, it would no longer contain merely consular information but all principal news regarding the Ministry: decrees about rules and standards, promotions, transfers, honours given to officials and dependants, ministerial circulars, international acts and agreements, principles of law, questions of international law, and so on.

The newest and most important part was that which condensed the consular and diplomatic reports complete or summarized. In addition, there was all the administrative information that might interest the profession. Particular attention was given to statistical, commercial, agricultural and maritime information. The impetus provided by Crispi bore fruit: by 1888 the *Bulletin* already had over two thousand pages. After Crispi, it would never again be so rich, precise and methodical. From 1888 another novelty was instituted: a special printing works of the Ministry for Foreign Affairs, employed by the head of cabinet, which printed diplomatic reports, circulars, Green Books (a collection of diplomatic documents on a question), and, for a limited period, the *Bulletin* itself.

The *Diplomatic Yearbook of the Kingdom of Italy* also came out in 1890, having almost doubled its number of pages and quantity of information, with an appendix dedicated to the Eritrean colony, and included a list of Green Books published by the Government from the unification of Italy onwards.

For all this activity, Crispi and Pisani employed the services of Prof. Giacomo Gorrini, who had been director of the MAE archives since 1886 but who also fulfilled the function of a proper head of the Studies Office. If it is possible today to reconstruct in detail the history of the Ministry, we owe it entirely to him and to his diligence in reorganizing the archives, and in collecting and publishing the principal circulars and instructions relating to it.[7]

One of the greatest preoccupations of Italian diplomacy was with the Italian colonies abroad, as the places for Italian emigration were then called. Initially emigration was directed towards Europe (France, Switzerland, Austria–Hungary, Germany) and was a phenomenon mainly restricted to northern Italy. Only towards the end of the century did it begin to extend to the population of central and southern Italy and the islands, and become transatlantic.[8]

Crispi, who had at first thought about arresting Italian emigration or directing it towards Sardinia or Africa, surrendered to the arguments of Luigi Bodio, and instead of opposing it tried to regulate it. According to Crispi, Italy had a duty not only to protect and defend the emigrants but also to keep them tied to the fatherland; in other words, to make emigration an element of Italian foreign politics – a programme that would later be imitated to far too great an extent by Mussolini.

However, it is to Crispi that we owe the first Italian law on emigration, passed on 30 December 1888; it was followed by the regulation of 10 January 1889, which fixed methods of application and protected the emigrant against too much abuse at the hands of the organizers and the transporters. In addition the Foreign Minister compelled diplomats and consuls to send back periodic reports on the state of Italian emigration, on the problems of relations with the authorities and local population, and on everything that could be of possible relevance.[9]

Crispi's interests were obviously turned also towards Italian associations abroad, some of which had originally arisen before the Unification of Italy, notably the Italian hospital in Buenos Aires, and the Union and Goodwill foundation, also of Buenos Aires. He ordered the consuls to take a census, which resulted in the information that in 1889 there were 352 of these associations, mainly benefit societies (in case of illness or accidents at work), and charitable or teaching foundations. About twenty received subsidies from the Government. These associations often published newspapers, weekly, fortnightly or monthly, whose significance did not escape Crispi's notice, especially since some of them, with socialist or anarchical origins, had a markedly anti-Crispi tone. Indeed, it is under the rule of this Sicilian statesman, who became increasingly authoritarian, that the long history of the political outlaws (the socialists and anarchists) began which was to gain importance only under the regime of Mussolini. Crispi intervened in order to deal with certain of these newspaper mouthpieces, but above all to give financial support to those favourable to him or to create new ones.

Particular impetus was given by Crispi to Italian schools abroad, which, apart from teaching the language, had the purpose of keeping Italian feeling alive. In the decree of 8 December 1889, and with the approval of the Minister of Public Instruction (Boselli), Crispi had the first regulations passed on Italian schools abroad. These were composed of as many as 180 articles; they entrusted the superintendence of the schools to consuls, as is still the case today. There were two kinds of schools: state and subsidized. Of the former there were 92 in 1889, of which 37 were in Turkey and 13 in Tunisia. There were about 12 000 pupils registered, half of whom were not Italian. There were 35 subsidized schools, mostly situated in Latin America, France, the United States and England, with about 9000 pupils.[10]

Crispi and Pisani Dossi paid particular attention to the press. The Sicilian statesman had reopened publication of the daily newspaper *La Riforma*, making use of the aid of Lombard friends. Among these were the 'Three Ps' of the Scapigliatura movement: Pisani Dossi, collaborator for foreign politics, Luigi Perelli, manager of the newspaper, and Primo Levi, editor-in-chief, then director, and finally collaborator with Pisani Dossi at the Ministry for Foreign Affairs. The foreign news published in Italian newspapers came from the French agency Havas, even the news sent to Paris by Reuters. In Italy, the news from Havas was distributed by the Stefani news agency, founded in the time of Cavour.

Crispi and Pisani Dossi wanted to modify this flow of news, which, in passing through Paris, was often coloured by feeling against Crispi and the Triple Alliance. After difficult negotiations Crispi succeeded in concluding an agreement between Stefani, the German agency Wolff Bureau and the Austrian Correspondenz, as well as one between the Stefani and Reuters, thus removing Italy from the influence of French information.[11]

In order to confront foreign public opinion, Crispi also made use of a newspaper published (in French) in Rome, *L'Italie*, which was subsidized by the Consulta (as the MAE was often called). He could count on the friendship of *The Times* correspondent, W. Stillman, who published in London a favourable biography of the Sicilian statesman.

It should be added that a scholar from Trieste, Giacomo Venezian, founded the Dante Alighieri association in 1889, with the aim of helping the spread of Italian language and culture abroad. In reality, the association was attempting to keep alive the irredentism among the Italian populations still under the rule of the Austro-Hungarian Empire. This did not meet the requirements of Crispi. The association later took on the more politically biased duty of defending Italian sentiments abroad, and was divided into about 500 committees that maintained fairly close links with the Consulta.

If the description of the actions taken by Crispi in the restructuring of the MAE has been rather prolonged, it is because such actions were more profound, radical and energetic than anything previously undertaken. This does not necessarily mean they were better than any other, but that many of the innovations remained in force, despite the fact that as his successor the King called upon a resolute adversary of Crispi's, the Marquis of Rudinì.[12]

The Marquis hastened to re-establish the post of secretary-general of the Ministry, calling back Giacomo Malvano to fill the post. He also abolished the position of head of cabinet, but at the same time kept that of Under-Secretary of State. The central administration comprised five divisions. Division I, Political Affairs, in three sections: Europe and the colonies, Africa, Asia and Oceania; America; Eritrea and its protectorates. Division II, Commercial Affairs, Emigration and Schools: commercial affairs; emigration; schools. Division III, Private Affairs: Europe, Africa, Asia and Oceania; America. Division IV, Personnel: personnel; ceremonies and protocol; legalizations. Division V, Accounts: accounting; balance of expenditure; archives; library; bursar; dispatches; printing-press.

The insertion of the colonial office as the third section of the Political Affairs Division signified the diminishing importance that the colonies held for Italy. Indeed, one of the reasons for the resignation of Duke Caetani di Sermoneta from the Ministry a few months after his nomination seems to lie in the non-acceptance of his proposal to renounce *all* colonies.

Emilio Visconti Venosta was called upon to take Caetani's place. Venosta managed to deal Italian foreign politics the famous 'blow to the helm', disposing of the Tunisia question and approaching closer to France.[13] This move was followed up and further accentuated by Visconti Venosta's successor, Giulio Prinetti, a Lombard industrialist who had made a name for himself as Minister for Public Works. Prinetti undertook to give an unusual ordering to the central administration of the MAE.[22*] He restructured it into five autonomous offices and five divisions. The autonomous offices were: the Diplomatic Office (which took the place of the Political Affairs Division); the Codes and Telegraph Office; the Colonial Office; the Emigration Commissariat; and the Inspectorate-General of Schools Abroad. The five divisions were: the Commercial Affairs Division, the Private and Legal Affairs Division, the Personnel Division, the Library, Registration and Dispatches, Bursary Legalizations Division; Accounts Division. While the historical archives formed part of this last division, ceremonial was part of the Personnel Division.

Prinetti's aim was, without doubt, to create an instrument that would be beneficial to an active foreign policy but that he would control himself. And indeed, in his two years in the Consulta before he became stricken with paralysis, Prinetti reached an agreement with France and another with England, renewed the Triple Alliance, and tried to obtain a joint government over Tripolitania with Turkey.

Another fairly important deed from the political point of view was the institution of the Emigration Commissariat[23*] in 1901, which had its own rules and regulations. An excellent man, Luigi Bodio, was called upon to head it.[14]

Under Prinetti, too, a new ruling was passed for admission into the diplomatic profession. Admission remained based on wealth, written examinations (international law, civil law, modern history, French, another foreign language), and oral exams.[24*]

After Prinetti we enter the so-called 'Giolittian decade' (1904–14), dominated by the personality of Giolitti. This was a period of reform for

Italy, of economic and social conquests and of achievements at home and abroad. Unusually, there were only four Foreign Ministers during this time: Tittoni and San Giuliano four times each and Guicciardini twice. Tittoni held the post without a break from November 1903 to December 1905, and again from May 1906 to December 1909. There was sufficient time for him to leave his imprint on the mechanism of the MAE, all the more so since he was, like Giolitti, a profound expert on bureaucratic structures.

If we look at the internal organization of the MAE in 1908,[25*] it is easy to realize this. The Minister retained the posts of Under-Secretary of State and secretary-general (plenipotentiary minister Riccardo Bollati, who followed Giacomo Malvano in September 1907), but in addition reinstated the post of head of cabinet in 1906.[26*]

Under the direct supervision of the secretary-general were the Codes, Printing and Translations Office and the Office for Correspondence and Dispatches. Then followed the Directorate-General of General Affairs, which supervised Division I, Personnel and Ceremonial; Division II, Accounts and Bursary; Historical Archives and Library; Passports; Printing press. The Directorate-General of Political Affairs was in three divisions, geographically subdivided, plus the Legal Office and the Legislation Office. The Directorate-General of Commercial and Private Affairs and of the Royal Schools Abroad was split into three divisions, plus the Inspectorate of Schools Abroad. The Central Directorate of Colonial Affairs had two offices. Finally, there was the Emigration Commissariat.

The fact that the Colonial Office had been raised to the rank of Central Directorate shows the importance that African topics had resumed, about ten years after the Battle of Adowa.

Tittoni reordered the career structure of the MAE,[27*] dividing it into two main lists, the diplomatic and the consular, thus abolishing the internal administrative career service (except for the nominal lists of accounting and regulations) and dividing out the staff so that two-fifths went onto the diplomatic list and the rest to the consular ones. For the central administration the Minister could draw indiscriminately from the staff of the two lists. Certain regulations for admission into the diplomatic and consular professions were also abolished. There remained among the requirements the possession of an annual income of 8000 lire for the diplomatic profession and 3000 lire for the consular. This requirement was abolished only in 1923.

In 1909 the nominal lists of the diplomatic personnel included 10 ministers first class; 19 ministers second class; 11 councillors of legation first class; 10 councillors of legation second class; 22 secretaries of legation first class; 16 secretaries of legation second class; 19 secretaries of legation third class; 12 attachés of legation.

The nominal list of the consular personnel included 16 consuls-general first class; 30 consuls-general second class, 35 consuls first class, 28 consuls second class, 28 vice-consuls first class, 36 vice-consuls second class, 12 consular attachés.

Foreign Minister Antonio di San Giuliano, who was to head the MAE from March 1910 until October 1914, was a Sicilian, like Crispi. Like Crispi, too, he favoured the 'Mediterranean' direction of Italian politics, rather than the 'continental' one. Naturally he also wanted to provide himself with a suitable instrument of control, so he introduced some modifications in the organization of the central administration,[28*] which emerged with the following composition: Minister's cabinet, cabinet of the Under-Secretary of State, secretary-general, who supervised Division I: Accounts and Bursary; Codes, Press and Translation; Correspondence.

There then followed the Directorate-General of General Affairs, which included Division II, Personnel and Ceremonial, Historical Archives and Library, Printing press; the Directorate-General of Political Affairs, in two divisions (III and IV) and five offices; the Directorate-General of Commercial Affairs and Schools Abroad, in two divisions (V and VI) and the Inspectorate of Schools Abroad; the Directorate-General of Private Affairs in two divisions (VII and VIII) and an Office for Disputes and Legislation: the Central Directorate for Colonial Affairs. This last, after the victory over Tripolitania Cirenaica, became the nucleus of the Colonial Ministry, instituted with the law of 6 July 1912.

San Giuliano died on 16 October 1914. His place in the MAE was taken by Sidney Sonnino, who remained there throughout the First World War, until the forming of the Nitti-Tittoni government in June 1919. At the time that Italy entered the war, the central administration of the MAE remained the same as that of 1910, except for a few small modifications. In the Directorate-General of Political Affairs a fourth division had been introduced to deal with matters relating to colonial politics, while the Inspectorate of Italian Schools Abroad had been elevated to the level of a directorate-general, independent of the Directorate-General of Commercial Affairs. The Italian embassies and legations abroad were 49 in number, while there were 38 foreign ones in Italy.

This situation remained the same until Carlo Sforza, a diplomat who had come to the forefront during the time of Nitti, who had given him the post of Under-Secretary of State, was called upon by Giolitti to head the 'Consulta' (from 15 June 1920 to 4 July 1921).

He revolutionized the Ministry for Foreign Affairs,[29*] substituting the 'functional' criterion previously adhered to with a 'geographic' one. The main pillars of the MAE became the Directorate-General of Political, Commercial and Private Affairs of Europe and the East and the Directorate-General of Political, Commercial and Private Affairs of Africa, America, Asia and Australia. These directorates were subdivided, often according to a geographic criterion, into five offices for the first and four for the second. Besides these there were the Directorate-General of General Affairs, whose competence extended to the Personnel Office, the Ceremonial Office, Administrative Office, the Legalizations and Passports Office, the historical archives and the library; and also the Directorate-General of Schools Abroad and the General Commissariat for Emigration.

Below the Minister, there was still the Under-Secretary of State, followed by the head of the Minister's cabinet, supported by the secretary to the Minister himself. The range of the secretary-general of the MAE had been considerably widened. It now included the Press Office, Codes Office, Correspondence Office, the Economic Coordination Office (an innovation with the job of co-ordinating the economic and commercial activity of the directorates-general of the MAE and of the technical Ministries); the Office of the Secretariat for Diplomatic Disputes, the Disputes and Legislation Office, the Treaties Office, the Office of the League of Nations, and the Central Accounts.

This growth in the secretary-general's functions can be better understood if it is remembered that from 31 December 1919 the post was filled by an ex-collaborator of Crispi, Salvatore Contarini, an outstanding person whose reputation has recently been somewhat diminished, above all for his so-called 'opposition' to Mussolini, who liquidated him in April 1926.

Immediately after the conclusion of the peace treaties following the First World War, the number of Italian embassies and legations rose to 60, and the number of foreign ones in Italy to 51.

Besides the post of Prime Minister and Minister for Home Affairs, Mussolini, like Crispi, also kept for himself the headship of the MAE, from 1922 to 1929. Like Crispi, too, he left a personal mark on diplomatic action. The coexistence between the head of the cabinet and the secretary-general is never easy – the first represents political power and the second administrative power. Even though a decree of 1924[30*] forbade the cabinets and the particular private secretaries to 'impede the normal action of the administrative offices and to substitute themselves for them',[15] Mussolini (again like Crispi) preferred the direct action of his cabinet to the filtered one of the secretary-general of the MAE. When Contarini was forced to resign, his post at first remained vacant, and was then definitely abolished in August 1932.[31*] The functions of coordination and control were taken on by a Coordination and Secretarial Office, which was part of the cabinet. In 1924,[32*] a General Coordination Office was instituted with the task of collecting, coordinating and systematically evaluating the information drawn from the correspondence of representatives abroad, as well as preparing political and economic studies. It was placed under the control of the Directorate-General of General Affairs, as was the newly instituted Historical Diplomatic Office. This last was a kind of office for studies and documentation, which should not be confused with the Archives and Correspondence Office, nor with the Historical Archives. A decree of 1927[33*] abolished the Emigration Commissariat, and in its place the Directorate-General of the Italians Abroad was set up; in this Mussolini was once again taking up Crispi's policies:[16] Italian emigrants ought to feel sheltered, protected and guided just like citizens abroad. Moreover, they were supported by a suitable organization in the National Fascist Party; which in the future was to serve the emigrants badly, separating them one from the other and making them unpopular with the local people. Soon afterwards the Office of the League of Nations became autonomous, and underwent a new development when Dino Grandi was Foreign Minister. He elevated it to the Directorate-General for League of Nations Affairs, dividing it into three offices. This too was an indication of a policy in favour of the League and of France and England, which Mussolini reversed when he 'dismissed' Grandi on 20 July 1932.

The organization of the central administration of the MAE in 1932[34*] consisted of the Minister's cabinet, the Press Office, six directorates-general divided into offices, offices directly dependent upon the Minister and other offices grouped into services.

As can be seen, the Foreign Minister was definitely accentuating his control over the administration. This was confirmed by article 2 of the 1932 decree, in which he took up powers that had previously been entrusted to a normal legislative process, which effectively divided the services according to the exigencies of the international situation as it developed. Not only this, but the

Minister also had the authority to alter 'the responsibilities of the individual directorates-general, services and offices, as well as modifying the grouping of the offices in the directorates-general and the services.'[17]

In other words, the Foreign Minister could change the basic structure of the MAE by his own autonomous decision and by means of simple orders of service. Even though the Minister was Mussolini himself, this nevertheless represented a tremendous administrative change, which can be explained by his intention to 'fascistize' diplomacy.

This reform reintroduced the functional system instead of the geographic one that had been introduced by Sforza in 1920. The basic structure of the central administration at the end of 1932 was as follows: Cabinet; Press Office; Ceremonial Office; Service for International Institutions; Directorate-General of Political Affairs, in six offices geographically subdivided; Directorate-General of Economic Affairs, in four offices; Directorate-General of Treaties, Acts, Affairs concerning the Holy See and Private Affairs, in four offices; Directorate-General of Personnel, in four offices; Directorate-General of Italians and Schools Abroad, in three offices; Historical and Diplomatic Services, in two offices; Correspondence Services; Central Accounts.[18]

The growing importance of the Press Office mainly due to the fact that Mussolini was a journalist, must be pointed out at this juncture. The Press Office of the MAE absorbed in 1924 that of the Interior (home) Ministry; then in 1928 it became the Press Office of the Prime Minister with two branches, home and abroad. In 1933 it became the Press and Propaganda Office, autonomous from the Foreign Ministry, with a separate seat in Via Veneto. In 1934 it was elevated to an Undersecretariat of State for Press and Propaganda, under the lead of Galeazzo Ciano. In June 1935 it was transformed into the Press and Propaganda Ministry,[35*] which in June 1937 changed its name to the Ministry for Popular Culture.

Galeazzo Ciano, called up to head the MAE on 11 June 1936, hastened to reintroduce (at least in part) the geographic criterion into the reform of the central administration.[36*] The cabinet continued to be the immediate mouthpiece of the Minister and the most important organ in the administration. There followed the Ceremonial Office, and a newly instituted Superintendence Office (a military term) whose control extended over the Historical Archives, the Library, publications of an administrative character, automobile and telephone services, and personnel discipline in the service.

The Directorate-General of European and Mediterranean Affairs took over the greater part of the control previously exercised by the Directorate-General of Political Affairs. This was geographically subdivided into five offices, the fourth concerned with Albania and the last with the Holy See. The Directorate-General of Transoceanic Affairs consisted of four offices. The Directorate-General of General Affairs was divided into five offices; the first was concerned with the League of Nations; the fourth covered military, naval and aeronautic coordination; and the fifth was concerned with the study of historical matters and international questions. The League of Nations Office was then suppressed in anticipation of Italy's retirement from the League (11 December 1937).

The Directorate-General of Commercial Affairs had three offices. The Directorate-General of Italians Abroad was divided into four offices; the first was concerned with Fascist organizations and cultural institutions, the third with schools abroad and the fourth with Italian work abroad. As for the attempts to 'fascistize' the organizations of Italians abroad, the decree of 20 September 1937 must be cited: it put under the direct control of the Under-Secretary of State (Bastianini) all the services concerning the Fascists, as well as all the Fascist organizations, cultural institutions, schools and work abroad, Italian houses, spare-time activities *(dopolavoro)*, etc.

The Directorate-General of Personnel and Internal Administration comprised six offices. Finally, Central Accounts consisted of three departments.

After the conquest of Albania in April 1938[37*] the Under-Secretariat of State for Albanian Affairs was introduced into the framework of the MAE, organized in five departments.[19]

This structure remained substantially the same until 1943. As happens with a concern under continual development certain measures were taken, of which we will mention the creation on 7 May 1940 of a Germany Co-ordination Office within the Minister's cabinet. A short while afterwards, in 1941, also within the cabinet, an Armistice-Peace Office was instituted.[38*]

The Under-Secretariat for Albanian Affairs was dissolved in favour of an Albanian Office, which in 1942 became the Clearing Office of the ex Under-Secretariat of State for Albanian Affairs, and later simply Administrative Clearing Office SSAA (Under-Secretariat of State for Albanian Affairs). At the end of 1941 a Directorate-General of Affairs for Greece, Montenegro, Dalmatia, Slovenia, Croatia, Armistice and Boundaries was added.

A note regarding the personnel of the MAE. The 'carriera' was reordered in 1927,[39*] into a single diplomatic-consular listing. Entry was by way of competitive examinations, no longer with the income requirements, but it was necessary 'to have maintained regular civilized moral and political conduct'. Nevertheless the possession of the requirements 'does not bind the Ministry to accept the requests for admission to the exams. The administration's judgement in this regard is final.' It is clear that this clause was also a means of eliminating from the examinations persons regarded as anti-Fascist, and of trying to favour those considered Fascist or Nationalist-Fascist, a small number of whom were in fact admitted into the profession during that year. The law specified promotion and advancement requirements as well as the various indemnities.

A decree of 1931,[40*] fixed the basic staff lists of the MAE. There were: 16 ambassadors, 20 ministers plenipotentiary first class, 31 ministers plenipotentiary second class, 24 legation councillors, 32 first secretaries of legation first class, 30 first secretaries of legation second class; also: 26 consuls-general first class, 26 consuls-general second class, 42 consuls first class, 64 consuls second class, 54 consuls third class, 50 vice-consuls first class, 37 vice-consuls second class, 40 consular attachés.

In 1923[41*] a regular staff of Consular Delegates (Commissari) was instituted; they had an administrative function in Italy and abroad, and their specific functions were outlined one year later.[42*] The staff list of the Interpreters remained substantially the one fixed in 1862,[43*] with subsequent modifications regarding their qualifications and promotions. In 1940 the title changed to Staff list of the Technical Delegates for the Orient. Separate examinations were set for the personnel of the historical–diplomatic archives, the library, and the reserved printing press. Alongside the Council of the Ministry for Foreign Affairs founded by Crispi in 1888 an Administrative Council was created.[44*] This handled personnel affairs, while the Council of Diplomatic Disputes[45*] was called upon to express its views (advisory) on questions of jurisdiction that might arise in international relations.[20]

In 1940, at the beginning of the Second World War, 53 foreign countries were accredited in Rome, while there were 58 Italian representatives abroad. There were 16 Italian military attachés, 17 naval and 17 air attachés, some of whom were accredited to more than one country.

When Mussolini was dismissed on 25 July 1943 the new Prime Minister, General Pietro Badoglio, entrusted the portfolio of the MAE to a professional diplomat, Raffaele Guariglia. The only administrative measure taken during that time seems to have been the restoration of the post of secretary-general on 1 August 1943, filled by the ex-ambassador to Washington and Moscow, Augusto Rosso.

The armistice of 1943 prefaced the total occupation of Rome by German armed forces. While Guariglia and Rosso went into hiding, along with many other diplomats, a small group (about a dozen) of career officials gathered at Brindisi and then at Salerno, where Vittorio Emanuele III, Badoglio, and other ministers had taken refuge.[21] Meanwhile, since Mussolini had formed his own 'republican' government at the end of September, and had included in it the Ministry for Foreign Affairs, Serafino Mazzolini was nominated its secretary-general. Only a very few of the officials accepted collaboration with the republican MAE, which the events of war soon forced to be transferred to Salò and other locations, including Venice.

Meanwhile Badoglio had undertaken the interim legitimate MAE, and at the beginning of November he nominated the minister Renato Prunas as secretary-general. Prunas had the difficult task of reconstructing the administration, which for a certain time operated as a department of the Prime Minister's Council (Presidenza del Consiglio). It was only in July 1944, after the liberation of Rome, that Prunas and his associates, whose numbers had grown to over a hundred, were able to return to the Chigi Palace.[22]

Only then was it possible to rebuild the basic structure of the central administration. Bonomi set this out in 1944[46*] as follows. The *General Secretariat* coordinated five offices (Coordination, Diplomatic Disputes, Liaison with the Allies, Ceremonial, Foreign Press). The *Directorate-General of Political Affairs* had nine offices: (1) British Empire and the Middle East; (2) France and its Colonies; (3) Iberian peninsula and its Colonies; (4) USSR, Turkey, Danubian and Balkan; (5) Europe; (6) America and the Far East; (7) the Holy See; (8) Albania; (9) prisoners of war and civil prisoners. The *Directorate-General of Economic Affairs* had four offices, covering respectively (1) general questions and America; (2) Western Europe, Morocco and South Africa; (3) Eastern Europe and Asia; (4) Armistice and peace treaties. This directorate took some time to be organized. The *Directorate-General of Personnel* comprised four offices of which the last was concered with codes. The *Service of General Affairs* consisted of three offices: (1) International Conferences and Cultural Relations; (2) Treaties and Acts; (3) Historical-Diplomatic. Finally there were the *Historical Archives and Library*.

The attitude of Renato Prunas and his collaborators was necessarily pragmatic: the orders of service created or eliminated offices according to need (for example, the Clearance Office for Rhodes, the Boundaries Office, etc.). In 1945, under Foreign Minister Alcide De Gasperi the *Directorate-General of Italians Abroad* and the *Service for Private Affairs* were reinstated. In December 1946[47*] Foreign Minister Pietro Nenni suppressed the Directorate-General of Italians Abroad, substituting for it the *Directorate-General of Emigration* (indicating a significant political change), and introduced the *Directorate-General of Cultural Relations*.

On 2 February 1947, after a little less than thirty years, Carlo Sforza returned to the head of the MAE, a post he held until 16 July 1951. The conclusion of the peace treaty (19 February 1947), the new situation in Italy, the tension between the USSR and the Western powers, the German problem, the decolonization process, etc., all gave new scope for Italian diplomatic action.

It was therefore logical that Carlo Sforza should undertake a reorganization of the MAE, studies for which had been carried on for some time under the guidance of the new secretary-general, Francesco Fransoni. The interesting point in the Order of Service of 5 July 1947 is that Sforza had not thought to reintroduce the geographic criterion (as he had done in the reform of 1920), but kept the already existing functional one, with a few modifications. Essentially the order was as follows. Cabinet, with private secretaries of the Minister and under-secretaries of state. The General Secretariat had the following offices: Coordination; Boundaries and Colonies, Ceremonial, Foreign Press; Studies, Documentation, Historical Archives and Library; Diplomatic Disputes. The Service of General Affairs (instituted in 1948) was in two offices: (1) Treaties and Acts; (2) International Organizations. The Directorate-General of Political Affairs had eight offices, divided on a geographic basis, more or less as they had been previously. This directorate also controlled the Rhodes Office, the Italian Delegation Office for the International Refugee Organization (IRO) and the Liaison Office with the IRO. The Directorate-General of Economic Affairs, in five offices, was geographically divided, except for the office that dealt with questions on the peace treaty (which was later transformed into the Economic Treaties Service (SET), for all interministerial questions referring to the peace treaty). The Directorate-General of Emigration, in four offices, was also divided geographically, plus various autonomous sections such as studies, transport, inspectorates and frontier offices. The Directorate-General of Cultural Relations Abroad divided into three offices one for general affairs, the second for cultural action abroad and the third for Italian schools abroad. The Directorate-General of Personnel and Internal Administration, in six offices, dealt with questions concerning diplomatic personnel and non-diplomatic administration and accounting, courier headquarters abroad, codes, and the reserve printing press. The Service of Private Affairs, in three offices, was divided according to subject, and included a war damages section and a legalizations department. The Service of International Institutions comprised two offices: (1) United Nations; (2) International Conferences and Congresses. (This service was suppressed in 1948.) Lastly, Central Accounts had three departments.[23]

Small administrative adjustments followed, leading to a structure that was in continual movement, but they did not change the basic organization.

The staff list of the diplomatic–consular career was fixed, with a decree of the provisional head of state, on 2 July 1947[48*] as: 8 ambassadors; 30 ministers plenipotentiary first class; 32 ministers plenipotentiary second class; 33 first secretaries of legation first class; 32 first secretaries of legation second class; 26 consuls-general first class; 26 consuls-general second class; 42 consuls first class; 64 consuls second class; 57 consuls third class; 53 vice-consuls first class; 41 vice-consuls second class; 45 consular attachés.

A decree of October 1944,[49*] had brought into the pattern of the MAE the staff list of the Commercial Offices Abroad, absorbing the officials of the Ministry of Exchange and Prices. The list was composed of 49 units: two commercial councillors first class; seven commercial councillors second class; eight commercial attachés first class; 10 commercial attachés second class; 10 commercial assistants first class; 12 commercial assistants second class and third class. The list of the commercial secretaries consisted of five first commercial secretaries and 18 other persons ranging between commercial secretaries and supplementary commercial secretaries.

In 1948[50*] the MAE also absorbed the list of personnel attached to the foreign press, established in 1936,[51*] taking the title of the Ministry of Press and Propaganda. The staff was initially composed of three press attachés first class, four press attachés second class and eight press attachés third class.

Staff of the technical services continued to be part of the personnel of the MAE, as did the consular commissars and the technical commissars for the Orient; so did the personnel for Albanian affairs (suppressed in November 1944[52*] and reduced to two units only), and personnel with 'special duties' (historical archives, library, printing press, etc.), as well as the list of the registrars, both personnel of rank and subordinates.

Decrees of 1948 and 1951,[53*] also created a 'special transitory staff list' in the MAE for state employees not on the regular staff, who were admitted to take part in exams for promotion up to the eighth grade of the higher ranking officials.

Finally, a decree of 1954[54*] arranged the transfer of the personnel of the suppressed Ministry of Italian Africa to the other state administrations, including the Ministry for Foreign Affairs, which accepted about a hundred officials into the different staff lists, diplomatic and consular.[24]

The archives of the former Ministry of Italian Africa were also assimilated almost in their entirety into the historical–diplomatic archives of the MAE.

The first headquarters of the MAE after the Unification of Italy (March 1861) was the Palazzo delle Segreterie, in the Piazza Castello in Turin, where the Ministry for Foreign Affairs of the Kingdom of Sardinia was already situated. After the famous Italian-French Convention of September 1864, the capital of the Kingdom of Italy was transferred from Turin to Florence, where in May 1865 the MAE was established in the Palazzo della Signoria, better known as the Palazzo Vecchio. After the occupation of Rome by Italian troops in September 1870, the government decided to transfer the capital of the Kingdom there. Thus in July 1871 the MAE was installed in the Palazzo della Consulta, in the Piazza del Quirinale, which was already the headquarters of the judiciary and the administrative organizations of the Holy See. At the end of 1922 the MAE exchanged sites with the Colonial Ministry: the latter went to the Palazzo della Consulta, and the former to the Palazzo Chigi, at the corner of Piazza Colonna and the Via del Corso. It was a magnificent site, artistically and historically unrivalled, but it soon proved insufficient to house the expanding offices of the MAE, some of which had to find a place in other Roman palaces. After the Second World War the problem of a new and more spacious site arose. In 1960 it found its present site, called 'la Farnesina' after the area in which it is situated.[25] The Prime Minister's residence was transferred to the Palazzo Chigi.

During the post-Fascist period, when the principal legislative activity was aimed at eliminating totalitarian administrative regulations, or at least those contrary to the spirit of the newly constituted Italian Republic (1947), a debate developed in Italy, as in other countries, about how to structure the diplomatic service. The ideas and observations contained in Anthony Eden's famous White Paper certainly did not escape the attention of the specialists.[26] In Rome the Institute for Documentation and Legislative Studies entrusted the burden of studying the problem of the reorganization of the diplomatic service in 1962 to a mixed commission of diplomatic scholars and experts, under the leadership of the ex-minister, the Hon. Dino Del Bo. The results of the commission's work (in which the present writer also participated) have been published in the volume *Investigation into Italian diplomacy: Problems and Views* published in 1964, with an appendix of the principal legislative texts and an introduction by the Hon. Giuseppe Vedovato.

This text contributed greatly to the reorganization of the MAE, brought about by a decree of the President of the Republic on 5 January 1967[55*] which had as its title *Order for the Administration of the Foreign Office*.[27] This decree carried through the fusion of the various professions of the MAE, press, commerce and emigration, into a single diplomatic one. Other innovations have included the institution, in each directorate-general, of a Research Studies and Programming Office, which studies how the directorate's work is functioning, and is responsible for the simplification and mechanization of services, interpretation of statistical data, superintending the confidential printing press, the automatic documentation systems, the xeroxing centre, etc. Although it has been updated, modified and integrated by successive legislative regulations, this decree remains the basis of the present structure of the Ministry for Foreign Affairs, which is given in Appendix A.[28] The 1967 decree and successive modifications to it have fixed the basic structure of the diplomatic profession at 1041 members of staff, including: 18 ambassadors, 50 envoys extraordinary and ministers plenipotentiary first class, 80 envoys extraordinary and ministers plenipotentiary second class, 160 embassy counsellors, 223 legation counsellors, 510 first legation secretaries and legation secretaries.[29] At the beginning of 1981 there were about 800 diplomats in service, of whom about 40 were women.

A diplomatic structure needs above all to be flexible and responsive to society's changes.[30] The Foreign Minister has the power to introduce regulations, integrations and modifications within the framework of the 1967 decree, which remains the basis of the Ministry's present organization. Some recent regulations should be mentioned. The Ceremonial of the Republic follows an order of precedence of 26 December 1950, fixed by the Presidency of the Ministers, while a circular of the MAE dated 12 July 1979 regulates protocol for visits by foreign VIPs. If these regulations are compared to those of 1945, the extent of the political, social and cultural changes in the country will be evident.

These changes are also reflected in the field of emigration. From being a country that exported manual labour, Italy has become an importer: at least half a million foreigners now work in Italy. This has altered the scope and duties of the Directorate-General of Emigration and Social Affairs, stressing the social aspects of its work.

The Directorate-General for Cultural Relations changed its name in 1971[56*] to Cultural, Scientific and Technical Cooperation, when a Service for Technical Cooperation with Developing Countries was created within it. In 1979 this service became an autonomous department,[57*] equivalent to a directorate-general; two years later the Directorate-General for Cultural, Scientific and Technical Cooperation reverted to its earlier name.

At a time when the professionalization of the diplomat is more and more necessary, the importance of the Diplomatic Institute is increasing. The Institute has the duty of preparing young people for entrance examinations to the diplomatic service, of training new diplomats and of bringing middle and advanced grade diplomats up to date. A change in the recruitment of new diplomats is under consideration: from the current system based on examinations to one based on a college or diplomatic academy that would provide a more general educational framework for young people.

A rule of the 1967 decree provides for the utilization by the MAE of specialists already belonging to the state administration. As a result, the Historical and Documentation Service and the Service for Diplomatic Disputes, Treaties and Legislative Affairs are now entrusted to a professor of the history of treaties and international relations and to a state councillor respectively.

Does the actual structure of the Foreign Office respond to Italy's needs in the world at the present time? This is not an easy question to answer. Italy's membership of the United Nations, the European Community and the North Atlantic Alliance has conditioned its diplomatic activity, and particularly its multilateral role. At the same time, other Ministries (Defence, Treasury, Agriculture, Navy, etc.) have become increasingly interested in foreign activities. The Consultative Coordination Committees instituted[58*] by the President of the Council of Ministers and promoted by the Foreign Minister could provide the right answer for handling these areas of common interest, as they do in the field of technical cooperation. Other means have been suggested: for instance, the reorganization of the Ministry on a geographic basis instead of the functional one in use today. Some changes probably will be made sooner or later. Reformers need to adopt a pragmatic approach and to bear in mind that the most important, and also the most difficult, task is to induce the various departments and offices themselves to coordinate their work.

Finally, in Italy, perhaps even more than in other countries, the men are more important than their position in the bureaucratic hierarchy. The diplomats, coming mainly from the upper classes, are in general professionally very good, though there is perhaps a tendency to undervalue the real situation of the country. Diplomatic archives show that Mussolini was always well informed and well advised by the staff, even if eventually he did not care to listen.

The Italian diplomatic bureaucracy is well structured. Its ability to cope with the future of international relations largely depends on its flexibility, pragmatism and the quality of its coordination.

NOTES: REFERENCES

[1] Rodolfo Mosca, 'Das italienische Aussenministerium', in *Berliner Monatshefte*, 1938, May, 387–413; Luigi Vittorio Ferraris, *L'Amministrazione centrale del Ministero degli Esteri Italiano nel suo sviluppo storico (1848–1954)* (Florence 1955); Ruggero Moscati, *Le scritture della Segreteria di Stato degli Affari Esteri del Regno di Sardegna* (Rome 1954); *idem, Le scritture del Ministero degli Affari Esteri del Regno d'Italia dal 1861 al 1887* (Rome 1953); AAVV, *Indagine sulla diplomazia italiana* (edited by the ISLE) (Milan 1964); Enrico Serra, *Manuale di storia dei trattati e di diplomazia* (Milan 1980). The series *Documenti Diplomatici italiani* (1861–1943) edited by the Ministry for Foreign Affairs is also very useful because in each volume there is a diplomatic outline of the time.

[2] *Annuario Diplomatico del Regno d'Italia* (Diplomatic annual for the Kingdom of Italy) for 1865, compiled and edited by the Ministry for Foreign Affairs (the first to come out after the Unification) (Turin 1865). The annual was then published only for the years 1886, 1887, 1890 and 1902. It was Visconti Venosta as Minister who sent out instructions in a circular of 4 October 1863 that a diplomatic annual was to be published 'following the example practised annually by the governments of France and England . . .'.

[3] Cf. the extremely useful *Raccolta delle circolari e istruzioni ministeriali* (Collection of ministerial circulars and instructions) of the Ministry, edited by Giacomo Gorrini, Vol. 1, 1 January 1861–31 December 1887 (Rome 1904).

[4] *Annuario Diplomatico*, 1887 and 1890; *Bulletin of the Foreign Ministry*, 1888. Archives of Pisani Dossi, *passim*.

[5] Enrico Serra, 'Eritrea, Crispi e l'Ufficio Coloniale', in *Affari Esteri*, October 1978, 709–16. The Colonial Office was made autonomous in the set-up of the Ministry under Crispi, with the Royal Decree of 5 May 1895, No. 251.

[6] *Raccolta delle circolari e istruzioni ministeriali*, Giacomo Gorrini (ed.), Vol. II, 1 January 1888–30 September 1904 (Rome 1904).

[7] Giacomo Gorrini left the profession on request in 1923, after having held a consulate post and having been elected minister plenipotentiary. Gorrini's private papers can be found in the Central State Archives in Rome.

[8] There is plentiful literature on the subject. Cf. *L'Emigrazione italiana in Francia prima del 1914*, J.-B. Duroselle and Enrico Serra (eds) (Milan 1978).

[9] These reports were published later in *M.A.E., Emigrazione e Colonie. Rapporti dei rr. Agenti diplomatici e consolari* (Rome 1893).

[10] MAE, *Annuario delle Scuole coloniali* for the year 1889–90 (Rome 1890).

[11] Enrico Serra, 'Crispi, Pisani Dossi e le Agenzie di Stampa' in *Storia Contemporanea* 1978, 477–82.

[12] Rudinì replaced Crispi twice: when the Government fell the first time in 1891, to return later at the end of 1893, and when it fell definitively in 1896 after Adua's defeat. The Ministry for Foreign Affairs also changed its structure twice: Rudinì had immediately modified Crispi's work (decree of 9 February 1891 and 19 February 1891), and Crispi had abolished this decree to reinstate the previous one (decree of 28 December 1893); and finally Rudinì, with Caetani di Sermoneta as Foreign Minister, restored the 1891 structure with the decree of 15 March 1896.

[13] Cf. Enrico Serra, *La questione tunisina da Crispi a Rudinì ed il 'Colpo di timone' alla politica estera dell'Italia* (Milan 1967); and *idem, Camille Barrère e l'intesa italo-francese* (Milan 1950).

[14] Luigi Bodio (1840–1920), born in Milan; graduated from Pisa University and studied in Paris. Professor of economics and statistics, he was head of the Directorate-General of Statistics at the Ministry of Agriculture. In 1885 he was among the founders of the International Institute of Statistics in Paris, and was the first secretary-general of that foundation. Councillor of state and senator, he left numerous studies on emigration, statistics and economics.

[15] *Annuario diplomatico* for 1909, 45ff.

[16] A Committee for the expansion of Italian Culture abroad was even created for this purpose (decree of 10 February 1928 and 23 September 1929).

[17] MAE, *Norme Generali. Organizzazione e Servizi*, A. Toscani (ed.) (Rome 1938), 63ff.

[18] L. V. Ferraris, *L'Amministrazione Centrale del MAE . . .*, op. cit., 82.

[19] The rise in the number of offices was sanctioned with the royal decree of 5 October 1939, No. 1746 and the decree of 19 May 1941, No. 639.

[20] MAE. *Nome Generali* (cf. note 17), 87ff.

[21] Agostino Degli Espinosa, *Il Regno del Sud: 8 settembre 1943–4 giugno 1944* (Rome 1946).

[22] *Il Ministero degli Affari Esteri al servizio del popolo italiano* (1943–9), Giuseppe Brusasca (ed.) (Rome 1949), 2nd edn, 41ff; L. V. Ferraris, *L'Amministrazione Centrale del MAE . . .*, op. cit., 86ff.

[23] *Il Ministero degli Affari Esteri al Servizio del popolo italiano*, 253ff. This basic organization then underwent several modifications, which deserve to be mentioned. According to the *Annuario Diplomatico 1963* (the first to be published after the war), the Passports Office passed under the control of the Cabinet. The Ceremonial (four offices) was removed from the General Secretariat to become autonomous. The Foreign Press Office became the Press Service, still under the control of the General Secretariat, as was the newly instituted Studies Service, which was formed from the Office for Studies and Documentation, the Historical Archives, the Library, and the General Archives. The Diplomatic Disputes Office also became a service, under the control of the General Secretariat, as was the Service of Codes and Cryptographs. The Service for General Affairs was transformed into a Treaties Service. An Office of the Inspector-General of the Ministry and Diplomatic and Consular Representatives Abroad was created. Other institutions within the Directorate-General for Political Affairs were: the NATO Service, the UNO Service, the Service for Foreigners, and the Office of European Co-operation. More were created to take on autonomous forms: the Italian Delegation for European Economic Cooperation, the Italian Delegation for European Space Cooperation, and other offices.

[24] MAE, *Norme generali*, op. cit., 166, 178–82, 223–4, 395.

[25] This note of the different headquarters of the MAE has been made so as to prevent scholars from making erroneous statements, as has sometimes happened – for example, to speak of the 'Chigi Palace' as synonymous with the MAE, when the latter was in fact still in the Palazzo della Consulta or had already been transferred to the Farnesina. The MAE's present headquarters are the work of the architects Foschini, del Debbio and Ballio Morpurgo.

[26] E. Serra, 'La crisi della diplomazia', in *Rassegna d'Italia*, 1949, 1025–35. E. Serra, 'Una nuova diplomazia per una nuova problematica', in *Studi in onore di G. Zingali* (Milan 1965), II, 569–85.

[27] It should be remembered that two other decrees came out at the same time: that of 5 January 1967, No. 200 'Disposition on the functions and consular powers', and that of 23 January 1967, No. 215 'Personnel in service in scholastic cultural institutions abroad'. The texts are in MAE, *Ordinamento della Amministrazione degli Affari Esteri* (Rome 1967).

[28] Decree of 9 February 1978, No. 235, and 26 March 1979, No. 1083.

[29] The decree of the President of the Republic of 28 December 1970, No. 1077 (art. 47) has brought together the first three grades of the profession (legation attaché, legation secretary second and legation secretary third class) into the one grade of 'legation secretary'.

[30] The MAE has several liaison bodies including the Council of Administration, the Council for Diplomatic Disputes and the Committee for Italians Abroad. There is also a mixed Consultative Committee for the co-ordination of activity in the field of technical co-operation. The President of the Council of Ministers (following proposals by the Foreign Minister) can institute mixed Consultative Committees in the MAE for activity undertaken abroad or in international organisations by other Administrations of the State or by public bodies.

NOTES: LAWS AND DECREES

[1*] Consular laws of 15 August 1858 and Consular Regulation 16 February 1859.

[2*] RD (royal decree) 10 January 1864.

[3*] RD 18 September 1862.

[4*] RD 23 December 1866.

[5*] Law 28 January 1866, no. 2804.

[6*] RD 1879, 1882, 1884, 1885.

[7*] RD 29 November 1870, no. 6090.

[8*] RD 25 September 1885.

[9*] RD 17 February 1885, no. 1236.

[10*] RD 29 November 1857, slightly modified.

[11*] RD 19 April 1868, no. 4349.

[12*] Law 12 February 1888.

[13*] RD 25 December, 29 December 1887.

[14*] RD 8 March 1888.

[15*] RD 25 December 1887.

[16*] RD 27 February 1890.

[17*] RD 24 June 1888, no. 5503.

[18*] RD 6 August 1889, no. 6347.

[19*] Law 11 July 1889, no. 6233.

[20*] RD 28 November 1889, no. 6581.

[21*] RD 4 December 1887.

[22*] RD 2 January 1902, no. 2.

[23]* Law 21 January 1901.

[24]* RD 9 September 1902, no. 415.

[25]* RD 9 April 1908.

[26]* Law 8 April 1906, no. 109.

[27]* Law 9 June 1907, no. 298.

[28]* RD 1 August 1910, no. 607.

[29]* RD 19 September 1920, no. 1468.

[30]* RD 10 July 1924, no. 1100.

[31]* RD 25 August 1932, no. 1086.

[32]* RD 20 March 1924.

[33]* RD 29 April 1927.

[34]* RD 25 August 1932.

[35]* Royal law 24 June 1935.

[36]* RD 18 July 1936 and Order of Service 1 August 1936.

[37]* RD 18 April 1938, no. 624.

[38]* RD 3 August 1941, no. 1048.

[39]* Law 2 June 1927, no. 862.

[40]* RD 14 August 1931, no. 1354.

[41]* RD 4 March 1923, no. 500.

[42]* RD 20 March 1924, no. 385.

[43]* RD 18 September 1862, no. 1064.

[44]* RD 30 December 1923, no. 2960.

[45]* RD 3 January 1924, no. 3, and successive modifications.

[46]* DM (Decree of the Minister) 15 July 1944.

[47]* DM 20 December 1946.

[48]* Decree 2 July 1947, no. 775.

[49]* DL Lgt (decree of the Royal Lieutenant) 5 October 1944, no. 310.

[50]* DL 8 April 1948, no. 274.

[51]* Decree 3 February 1936, no. 447.

[52]* DL Lgt 30 November 1944, no. 427.

[53]* DL 7 April 1948, no. 262; 5 June 1951, no. 376.

[54]* DPR (Decree of the President of the Republic) 30 November 1954, no. 1496.

[55]* DPR 5 January 1967, no. 18 (Official Gazette no. 44, 18 February 1967).

[56]* Law 15 December 1971, no. 1222, art. 7.

[57]* Decree 26 March 1979, no. 1083.

[58]* Law 15 December 1971, no. 1222.

BIBLIOGRAPHY

Luigi Albertini, *Le origini della guerra del 1914*, 3 vols (Milan, 1943).

Luigi Aldrovandi Marescotti, *Guerra diplomatica: ricordi e frammenti di diario: 1914–1919* (Milan 1936).

——, *Nuovi ricordi e frammenti di diario* (Milan 1938).

W. C. Askew, *Europe and Italy's Acquisition of Libya, 1911–1912* (Durham 1942).

R. J. B. Bosworth, *Italy. The least of the Great Powers* (London 1979).

B. H. Bülow, *Memoirs*, 4 vols (London 1930–32).

Roberto Cantalupo (Legatus), *Vita diplomatica di S. Contarini* (Rome 1947).

——, *Ritratto di Pietro Lanza di Scalea* (Rome 1939).

Francesco Cataluccio, *Antonio di San Giuliano e la politica estera italiana dal 1900 al 1914* (Florence 1937).

Elisabetta Cerruti, *Visti da vicino. Memorie di un ambasciatrice* (Milan 1951).

Federico Chabod, *Storia della politica estera italiana dal 1870 al 1896*. Vol. I, *Le Premesse* (Bari 1965).

Renzo De Felice, *Mussolini: gli anni del consenso, 1929–1936* (Turin 1974).

——, *Mussolini il Duce* (Turin 1981).

Domenico Farini, *Diario di fine secolo*, 2 vols (Rome 1961).

Luigi Federzoni, *L'Italia di ieri per la storia di domani* (Milan 1967).

Franco Gaeta, *Nazionalismo italiano* (Naples 1965).

Carlo Galli, *Diarii e lettere* (Florence 1951).

Raffaele Guariglia, *Ricordi 1922–1946* (Naples 1950).

Francesco Guicciardini, *Cento giorni alla Consulta: diario e ricordi* (Florence 1943).

Mario Luciolli, *Palazzo Chigi: anni roventi* (Milan 1976).

Ferdinando Martini, *Diario, 1914–18* (Milan 1966).

D. Mack Smith, *Italy. A Modern History* (London 1959).

A. A. Mola, *Storia della Massoneria italiana dell'Unità alla repubblica* (Milan 1976).

Maria Pansa, *Ricordi di vita diplomatica (1884–1914)* edited by E. Serra (Rome, new anthology 1961).

Pietro Quaroni, *Valigia Diplomatica* (Milan 1956).

——, *Il mondo di un ambasciatore* (Milan 1965).

J. R. Rodd, *Social and Diplomatic Memoirs*, 3 vols (London 1922–5).

Giuseppe Salvago Raggi, 'Memorie' in C. Licata, *Notabili della Terza Italia* (Rome 1968).

Luigi Salvatorelli, *La Triplice Alleanza* (Milan 1939).

Gaetano Salvemini, *La politica estera dell'Italia (1871–1914)* (Florence 1944).

Christopher Seton-Watson, *Italy from Liberalism to Fascism* (London 1967).

Carlo Sforza, *L'Italia dal 1914 al 1944 quale io la vidi* (Milan 1944).

Sidney Sonnino, *Diario*, 3 vols (Bari 1972).

Giovanni Spadolini, *Il mondo di Giolitti* (Florence 1970).

Zara Steiner, *The Foreign Office and Foreign Policy 1898–1914* (Cambridge 1969).

Francesco Tomasini, *L'Italia alla vigilia della guerra (1934–41)*, 5 vols (Bologna 1934–41).

Daniele Varé, *Il diplomatico sorridente* (Milan 1941).

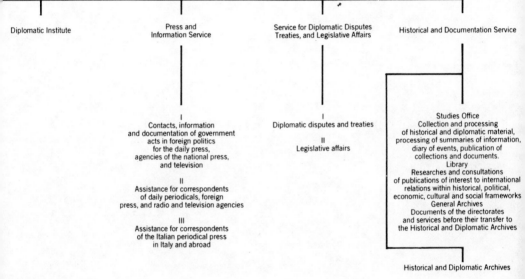

Diplomatic Institute

Press and
Information Service

Service for Diplomatic Disputes
Treaties, and Legislative Affairs

Historical and Documentation Service

I
Contacts, information
and documentation of government
acts in foreign politics
for the daily press,
agencies of the national press,
and television

II
Assistance for correspondents
of daily periodicals, foreign
press, and radio and television agencies

III
Assistance for correspondents
of the Italian periodical press
in Italy and abroad

I
Diplomatic disputes and treaties

II
Legislative affairs

Studies Office
Collection and processing
of historical and diplomatic material,
processing of summaries of information,
diary of events, publication of
collections and documents.
Library
Researches and consultations
of publications of interest to international
relations within historical, political,
economic, cultural and social frameworks
General Archives
Documents of the directorates
and services before their transfer to
the Historical and Diplomatic Archives

Historical and Diplomatic Archives

THE MINISTRY FOR FOREIGN AFFAIRS
(March 1981)

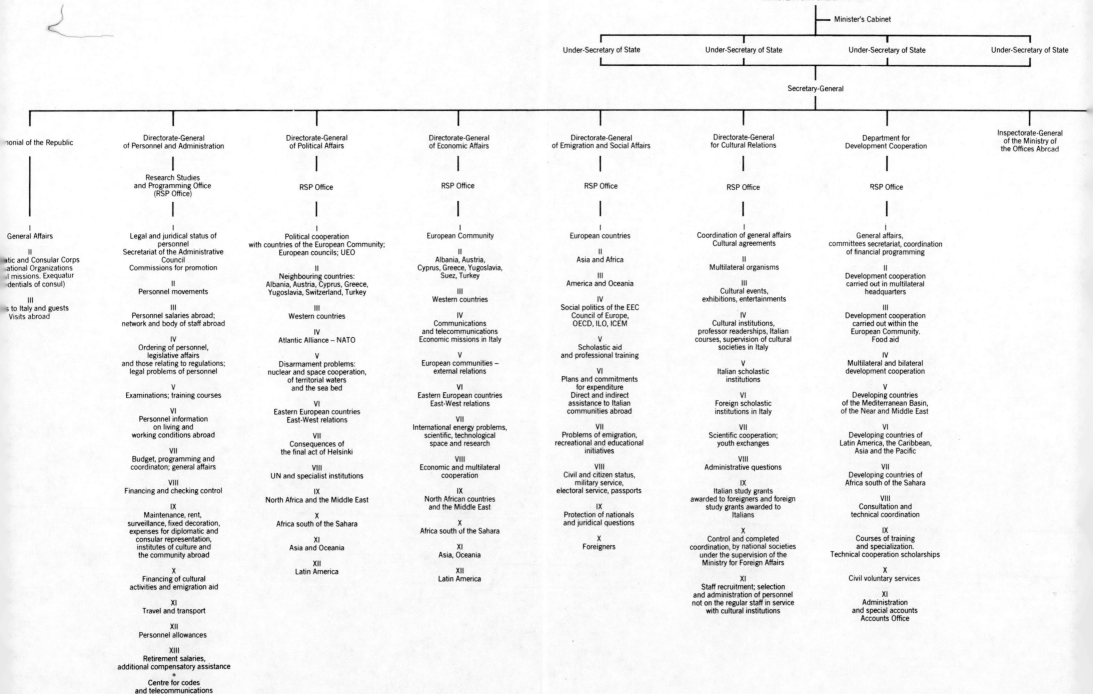

MINISTER FOR FOREIGN AFFAIRS

— Minister's Cabinet

Under-Secretary of State   Under-Secretary of State   Under-Secretary of State   Under-Secretary of State

Secretary-General

| ...monial of the Republic | Directorate-General of Personnel and Administration | Directorate-General of Political Affairs | Directorate-General of Economic Affairs | Directorate-General of Emigration and Social Affairs | Directorate-General for Cultural Relations | Department for Development Cooperation | Inspectorate-General of the Ministry of the Offices Abroad |

Research Studies and Programming Office (RSP Office)   RSP Office   RSP Office   RSP Office   RSP Office   RSP Office

...monial of the Republic

I
General Affairs

II
...atic and Consular Corps
...national Organizations
...al missions. Exequatur
...dentials of consul)

III
...s to Italy and guests
Visits abroad

Directorate-General of Personnel and Administration

I
Legal and juridical status of personnel
Secretariat of the Administrative Council
Commissions for promotion

II
Personnel movements

III
Personnel salaries abroad;
network and body of staff abroad

IV
Ordering of personnel,
legislative affairs
and those relating to regulations;
legal problems of personnel

V
Examinations; training courses

VI
Personnel information
on living and
working conditions abroad

VII
Budget, programming and
coordinaton; general affairs

VIII
Financing and checking control

IX
Maintenance, rent,
surveillance, fixed decoration,
expenses for diplomatic and
consular representation,
institutes of culture and
the community abroad

X
Financing of cultural
activities and emigration aid

XI
Travel and transport

XII
Personnel allowances

XIII
Retirement salaries,
additional compensatory assistance

*
Centre for codes
and telecommunications

*
Office of correspondence
and transports

*
Office of translating
and interpreting

Directorate-General of Political Affairs

I
Political cooperation
with countries of the European Community;
European councils; UEO

II
Neighbouring countries:
Albania, Austria, Cyprus, Greece,
Yugoslavia, Switzerland, Turkey

III
Western countries

IV
Atlantic Alliance – NATO

V
Disarmament problems:
nuclear and space cooperation,
of territorial waters
and the sea bed

VI
Eastern European countries
East-West relations

VII
Consequences of
the final act of Helsinki

VIII
UN and specialist institutions

IX
North Africa and the Middle East

X
Africa south of the Sahara

XI
Asia and Oceania

XII
Latin America

Directorate-General of Economic Affairs

I
European Community

II
Albania, Austria,
Cyprus, Greece, Yugoslavia,
Suez, Turkey

III
Western countries

IV
Communications
and telecommunications
Economic missions in Italy

V
European communities –
external relations

VI
Eastern European countries
East-West relations

VII
International energy problems,
scientific, technological
space and research

VIII
Economic and multilateral
cooperation

IX
North African countries
and the Middle East

X
Africa south of the Sahara

XI
Asia, Oceania

XII
Latin America

Directorate-General of Emigration and Social Affairs

I
European countries

II
Asia and Africa

III
America and Oceania

IV
Social politics of the EEC
Council of Europe,
OECD, ILO, ICEM

V
Scholastic aid
and professional training

VI
Plans and commitments
for expenditure
Direct and indirect
assistance to Italian
communities abroad

VII
Problems of emigration,
recreational and educational
initiatives

VIII
Civil and citizen status,
military service,
electoral service, passports

IX
Protection of nationals
and juridical questions

X
Foreigners

Directorate-General for Cultural Relations

I
Coordination of general affairs
Cultural agreements

II
Multilateral organisms

III
Cultural events,
exhibitions, entertainments

IV
Cultural institutions,
professor readerships, Italian
courses, supervision of cultural
societies in Italy

V
Italian scholastic
institutions

VI
Foreign scholastic
institutions in Italy

VII
Scientific cooperation;
youth exchanges

VIII
Administrative questions

IX
Italian study grants
awarded to foreigners and foreign
study grants awarded to
Italians

X
Control and completed
coordination, by national societies
under the supervision of the
Ministry for Foreign Affairs

XI
Staff recruitment; selection
and administration of personnel
not on the regular staff in service
with cultural institutions

Department for Development Cooperation

I
General affairs,
committees secretariat, coordination
of financial programming

II
Development cooperation
carried out in multilateral
headquarters

III
Development cooperation
carried out within the
European Community.
Food aid

IV
Multilateral and bilateral
development cooperation

V
Developing countries
of the Mediterranean Basin,
of the Near and Middle East

VI
Developing countries of
Latin America, the Caribbean,
Asia and the Pacific

VII
Developing countries of
Africa south of the Sahara

VIII
Consultation and
technical coordination

IX
Courses of training
and specialization.
Technical cooperation scholarships

X
Civil voluntary services

XI
Administration
and special accounts
Accounts Office

The Foreign Ministry

IAN NISH

Ian Nish is Professor of International History at the London School
of Economics and Political Science. He was educated at the
Universities of Edinburgh and London, and has taught at the
University of Sydney. His principal publications include *The Anglo-
Japanese Alliance 1894–1907* (1966), *Alliance in Decline 1908–1923*
(1972) and *Japanese Foreign Policy, 1869–1942* (1977).

Japan's history over the last century has been a dramatic one with many dramatic changes in direction. The Japanese Foreign Ministry (Gaimushō), which has been an important factor throughout this period, reflects these changes in direction and mood in its own history. Japan's story has several well-defined phases, which are cut by the traumatic experience of the wars of 1937–45. The hallmark of these successive phases might be described as modernization (1868–90), wars (1890–1918), international cooperation (1918–30) and international isolation (1931–45). And then, after the great divide of the war years, follow the phases of occupation (1945–52), reconstruction (1952–65) and prosperity and world status. Clearly there are continuities and discontinuities in the history of the Japanese Foreign Ministry. In looking at the evolution of the Ministry, we have to study separately the characteristics of each phase in the context of Japan's national development.

Our starting-point will be 1869, the year chosen by the Japanese Foreign Ministry as the one from which to trace its centenary. It decided to celebrate its first hundred years in 1969 and to issue a celebratory history of 1669 pages. There had of course been foreign relations for many centuries before this; then a period of enforced isolation (sakoku) when foreign contacts were minimal; then the opening of Japan under the threat from Commodore Perry in 1853, which led to the signature of treaties with many foreign countries. But our concern is with the founding of something resembling the Foreign Ministry in embryo under the authority of the Emperor, who was restored to power in Tokyo in 1868.

1869 to 1894

The Dajōkan (or Supreme Council of State) presided over government institutions from the Meiji restoration until the formation of a Cabinet-type government in 1885. The ordinance governing the Foreign Ministry was first issued in 1868 and was revised every year in the early post-Restoration period. From that time Japan had a Gaimukyo (Foreign Minister). Only in 1885 did the present titles of Gaimushō (Foreign Ministry) and Gaimu Daijin (Foreign Minister) come into use. In this period of a quarter-century the Foreign Ministers enjoyed high status, since they had generally played some role in the civil war or the imperial restoration that followed it. In a way, many of them were statesmen and enjoyed a prestige second only to the Prime Ministers of the day. In some cases they possessed an exceptional knowledge of foreign countries by virtue of having travelled abroad. Of the early Foreign Ministers the following had visited overseas before taking up office: Inoue Kaoru; Saionji Kimmochi; Mutsu Munemitsu; Enomoto Takeaki; and Aoki Shūzō. Certainly the Ministry had prestige, and it attracted men of drive, ambition and talent, many of whom were to become Prime Ministers later in their careers – like Katō Takaaki, Prime Minister from 1924 to 1926, and Hara Takashi (Kei), Prime Minister from 1917 to 1921.

Under the Meiji constitution of 1889 the authority for foreign affairs was designated as one of the supreme powers of the Emperor. This gave the Foreign Minister a relatively independent position. In practice, however, he acted in consultation with the Cabinets of the day who accepted joint responsibility for foreign policy.

The organization in Tokyo was on a small scale at this stage. But business was still limited and depended on the personal wishes of the Minister. By

1873 there were nine overseas legations in existence. They were located in Great Britain, the United States, France, Germany, Austria, Holland, Russia, China and Korea. There was a shortage of qualified people to fill these posts and the incumbents were sometimes very young. Thus, in 1879 Mori Arinori was appointed minister in London at the age of thirty-two, having previously held the post of envoy in Washington at the age of twenty-three.

Recruitment to the Foreign Ministry seems to have been haphazard and personal. Much depended on the patronage of the Meiji oligarchs who were the rulers of the country. They would take on, or recommend, a promising youngster as an official; and he would tend to move round the ministries following his master. Part of that patronage depended on clan influence; and some former *daimyō* were appointed as diplomats overseas. But it was also possible for young aspirants to enter the school set up by the Foreign Ministry; and entry to the profession was by no means confined to those from aristocratic families. There are cases also of older persons entering the foreign service from the ranks of journalists and merchants.

Japan was ready to learn what it could from foreign advisers. The Foreign Ministry was no exception to this. The earliest of its advisers (from 1871 to 1880) was E. P. Smith, a graduate of Columbia and Harvard. The next was Henry Willard Denison (from 1880 to 1914). Born in Vermont in 1846, he became legal adviser to the Foreign Ministry at the comparatively early age of thirty-four. He continued in the service of the Ministry until his death at the age of sixty-eight and received the highest Japanese honours for his service. He had an influence on two young officials in particular: Ishii Kikujirō and Shidehara Kijūrō. The latter was particularly close to Denison who taught him English style as well as diplomatic method and practice. Denison so effectively won the confidence of the Japanese diplomats that they allowed him a major role in the drawing up of documents and sometimes a voice in negotiations, as is alleged to have happened during the Portsmouth peace negotiations in 1905.

Among foreign employees in Japanese government service *(o-yatoi-gaijin)* Denison was not unique. Especially at the time when the law codes were being modernized in preparation for the revision of the treaties there were many legal advisers around, such as Gustave Boissonade and Sir Francis Piggott. But Denison out-served them all, and had special qualities that endeared him to the Japanese. He influenced a generation of officials and had a hand in drawing up most of Japan's treaties in these times. In an age when the language of diplomacy was increasingly becoming the language of the telegraph – English – Denison was an invaluable expert to have attached to the Ministry.

The policies in the early Meiji period, though important enough, were on a modest scale. Important business tended to be conducted in Tokyo rather than in legations abroad. The most conspicuous issue was that of Treaty Revision, which was initially settled with the signing of the Anglo-Japanese commercial treaty of 1894. In general, the spirit of the day that was reflected in the Foreign Ministry was that of 'Datsu-A nyū-Ō', an expression that implies turning the back on things Asian and welcoming things European or Western. This goes some way towards accounting for the remarkably inter-nationalist attitude adopted by most Japanese leaders very soon after they had taken their country into the modern world.

1894 to 1913

Great strides were taken during this period towards the modernization and rationalization of the Foreign Ministry. Its buildings were improved, though they were not reconstructed until after the damage sustained in the Great Kantō Earthquake of 1923. The Foreign Ministers tended to be drawn from among professional diplomats. As the Diet had come into being under the constitution, politicians lacked the foreign experience of their predecessors and were less well qualified to act. The Prime Ministers on election called on one of their representatives overseas to become Foreign Minister. This meant that there was little doubt about his subordination to the Premier and the Cabinet when it came to policy-making. On the other hand, policies were often influenced by and sometimes altered by the elder statesmen (genrō) – a group that had guided the nation's affairs in the 1870s and whose members were able, by virtue of being consulted by the emperor on an extra-constitutional basis, to express their views and often to carry the day. Important instances of their interventions are to be found in the negotiation of the British alliance in 1901 and in the run-up to the outbreak of the Russo–Japanese war in 1904.

Within the Gaimushō a political affairs bureau and commercial affairs bureau were created to cope with the increasing flow of business. The vital change abroad came in 1906 at the end of the successful Russo–Japanese war, when Japanese legations were raised to embassies in London, Washington, Paris, Berlin, Vienna, Rome and St Petersburg. The appointment of ambassadors was important to the Japanese for prestige reasons and had been considered so for many years. Minister Aoki proposed as early as 1893 that Japan should start appointing ambassadors to European courts. When he again became Foreign Minister, he proposed in 1898 the appointment of six ambassadors to coincide with the settlement of Treaty Revision, arguing that 'The prestige of our country is somewhat lessened as a great power in diplomacy. In other words, Japan is regarded in diplomacy as a second-rate country among the powers. Among countries with populations of more than thirty millions, only Japan and China do not yet exchange ambassadors.' But for technical reasons the matter was allowed by his Cabinet colleagues to rest.

With the greater role, both political and commercial, that Japan was playing in the world, it was necessary for the Foreign Ministry in 1894 to begin special training arrangements for both diplomatic and consular recruits. Until then appointments had been in the main personal. The Japanese had introduced qualifying entrance examinations for the civil service in the 1880s. In 1894 the same principle was extended to the foreign service. The intake was initially small but included some of the great names in the service later on. Thus Shidehara Kijūrō passed the examinations in 1896, Matsuoka Yōsuke in 1904 and Satō Naotake in the following year, Hirota Kōki and Yoshida Shigeru passed together in 1906 and Arita Hachirō in 1909. All of these were to become Foreign Ministers in the critical decade after the Manchurian crisis, except Yoshida, who became Foreign Minister only in 1945 and Prime Minister in later years. There seems to be little doubt that the examination system and the testing methods worked well and ensured an intake of high calibre.

Great pains were taken over the systematic admission and training of the new officials for the foreign service. The prime object was to create one service covering both bureaucrats in the Tokyo office itself and diplomats overseas, who were to become naturally interchangeable. The scheme for legation and consular officials laid down that recruitment should be by special examination, which should be separate from the ordinary civil service examination. These examinations should test the candidates' knowledge of foreign languages, especially English, French and German, and of such academic subjects as the constitution, administrative and international law, economics, finance and diplomatic history. Examinations of a lower standard would be set for those wishing to qualify for special language training as translators and interpreters and for clerkships. The intention underlying this system of recruitment was to prevent the country's diplomacy being monopolized by clan influences on the one hand and by the new academic influences *(gakubatsu)* of Tokyo Imperial University, founded in 1886, on the other. In general, it succeeded in the first of these objectives but failed to exclude the influence of Tokyo University. At a personal level, the Foreign Ministry hoped that the examination system would ignore the native place and the *alma mater* of the applicant but insisted that he should possess above average intelligence and knowledge of foreign languages.

These reforms of 1894 have held good ever since. There have of course been changes of procedure. Thus in 1918, at a time of large-scale recruitment into the foreign service, the special examinations for diplomatic and consular officers were absorbed into the general structure and it became necessary for candidates for the foreign service to take the ordinary higher civil service examinations, together with special tests to meet the needs of the Ministry. But the spirit of the reforms has been accepted. Under them, fifty-three candidates entered the Ministry between 1894 and 1903, seventy-four between 1903 and 1917, and 121 between 1918 and 1921.

In later life it was the year in which he passed the examination that was critical for the diplomat. It was this that determined his seniority; and this was important because of the strong hierarchical sense within the Japanese bureaucracy. An entrant from the class of 1906 expected to reach higher office before one from the class of 1907. They were also very conscious of their contemporaries. Thus Hirota and Yoshida, who came out of the class of 1906, remained close for the rest of their careers.

Other factors that affected the careers of those who entered the Ministry were linguistic skills, marriage, family wealth and connections, and luck. From the earliest times it was English that was the key language; recruits tended to be posted to an English-speaking post, generally the London embassy, for a spell spent on language study. Some, such as Shidehara, became specially adept and owed their advancement to language ability. A good marriage, too, was an advantage. Katō Takaaki and Shidehara married daughters from the Mitsubishi family; and the question is often asked how far their attitudes and policies were moulded by this. Yoshida came from a wealthy shipping family and married the daughter of Count Makino, who was from 1925 to 1934 an important official at Court, the Lord Keeper of the Privy Seal. Regarding connections, there were, of course, those from noble families such as Tokugawa Iyemasa and Matsudaira Tsuneo. Less important in Foreign Ministry circles was the influence of clans, which was still an important factor in the army and navy elites. But diplomats seem to have come in the main from former samurai families.

For aspiring diplomats, the summit of their ambition was the posts of vice-minister and minister, which were normally bureaucratic appointments. Even in the case of a political party Cabinet, the appointee was not a party man. He was generally drawn from an embassy overseas so that, when he returned to Tokyo, he was in the main out of the political hurly-burly. He was not generally around pulling strings for his own preferment. The post of vice-minister was generally an administrative office, the head of the office who kept the machine running, a sort of permanent under-secretary.

1914 to 1931

The Foreign Ministry reached its highest peak after the First World War, when its staff was increased in numbers and improved in training. Japan had been recognized at the Paris Peace Conference as one of the 'big five' and had a competent, professionalized delegation of sixty members. In the years that followed Japan was pushed into world affairs and had, among other things, to take an interest in Europe. The pattern of diplomacy of the time was that of high-level conferences and Japan, by virtue of being a world power, had perforce to be represented, even if its own interests were not at issue.

It was a period also of 'Kasumigaseki autonomy', that is, a time when Kasumigaseki, the place where the Foreign Ministry was located, was able to formulate policy without too much overt outside interference. The influence of the elder statesmen was on the wane as they became older or died. Thus Yamagata died in 1922, leaving as sole survivor of the Genrō Saionji who, while he had the task of advising the Emperor on the choice of Prime Minister, rarely interfered with the formulation of individual policies. This left the Foreign Ministry with greater freedom of action than it had either before or after.

'Kasumigaseki autonomy' also applied to the appointment of Foreign Minister. Except for the brief period when Tanaka Giichi, the Prime Minister, acted as his own Foreign Minister, the position of Foreign Minister was always held by an ex-diplomat. From 1919 this office was held by a product of the 1894 examination system. He was competent, reliable, efficient; but he was not a world leader, lacking in political muscle in Japan itself, retiring rather than a demagogue who was used to making popular public speeches.

There were important reforms to improve the efficiency of the office. In 1920 the Political Affairs Bureau was divided and the Bureaux of Asian Affairs and of European-American Affairs were set up. This was a sign of the shift of emphasis that was taking place in Japanese thinking over foreign policy and the vital needs of the nation. Later, in May 1934, the Bureau of European-American Affairs was broken up into its constituents: the Bureau of American Affairs and the Bureau of European and Asiatic (later East Asian) Affairs. A new specialized agency was the Cultural Work Division, created in 1923, which became an independent bureau in 1927.

With the Paris Peace Conference in 1919 the Japanese set up a temporary peace treaty office to deal with matters relating to the German and other peace treaties, the League of Nations, and other international agencies such as the International Court. These affairs were transferred *en bloc* to the Treaties Bureau in 1924. Even after Japan announced its secession from the League in

1933, the Bureau still continued to cooperate technically with the League until the League declared sanctions against Japan in 1938.

A change of emphasis was to be noted in the overseas postings of young diplomats. In the 1910s a budding recruit would commonly be posted to London, Washington or some European capital. In the 1920s it became increasingly common for him to go instead to one of the numerous consular postings in China. The balance of the service was gradually being redressed from the days of *Datsu-A nyū-Ō*.

Such was the Kasumigaseki establishment. It had *esprit de corps* and high bureaucratic standards, operating in the twenties in a basically political party atmosphere. The phrase 'Kasumigaseki orthodoxy' means the liberal internationalist attitude that tended to be adopted during the 1920s by the officials and diplomats trained by the Foreign Ministry. It came to an end with the Manchurian incident.

The Foreign Ministry was responsive to the opinions of outside academic advisers in the field of international law. Since most recruitment was from the Faculty of Laws at Tokyo Imperial University and since diplomatic history and international law were firmly rooted there as academic disciplines, it is reasonable to assume that much of the legal advice would come from that quarter also. The law professors who appear to have exerted some influence by giving advice on legal problems were Dr Suehiro Shigeo, Dr Shinobu Jumpei, himself a former diplomat, Dr Tamura Kōsaku, another diplomat of some standing, Dr Yano Jinichi, Dr Ariga Nagao, who served as legal adviser to President Yuan Shih-k'ai of China, and Dr Tachi Sakutarō, perhaps the most influential of all. The diplomats came under both the general intellectual influence of the books and articles written by these scholars and the specific advice of consultants preparing position papers for the Ministry. One has the feeling that the Japanese Foreign Ministry was greatly under the influence of experts in international law; and this may account for the slightly legalistic approach that Japanese officials were inclined to take on many problems, such as the Sino-Japanese treaties of 1915 and 1918.

A word should also be said about academic journals specializing in the study of diplomacy. The most prominent was *Kokusaihō Gaikō Zasshi*, published by Tokyo University, which was the academic medium for the professors mentioned above. A more popular journal dealing with all varieties of diplomatic issues was *Gaikō Jihō*. It was thought to have been a kind of forum for the ideas of the Foreign Ministry and the War Ministry at different times. It moved during the 1920s from an emphasis on Japan's need for international cooperation to an emphasis on Japan's need for 'autonomous diplomacy' *(jishū gaikō)*. This was to take sides on one of the great debates of the day, and was equivalent to an attack on Kasumigaseki orthodoxy.

The Foreign Ministry sought a foreign adviser as a successor for Denison, who had died in 1914. Eventually Dr Thomas Baty (1871–1954) was chosen. He was a native of Cumbria, England and a graduate in law from both Oxford and Cambridge universities. He was a prodigious author of studies in the field of international law and a highly qualified barrister. He took up his appointment as legal adviser *(hōritsu kōmon)* in 1916. After a career spanning almost forty years he died in Japan in 1954. He was the author of an autobiography in English entitled *Alone in Japan: The reminiscences of an international jurist in Japan* and published posthumously in Tokyo in 1959, and wrote another reflective volume *International Law in Twilight* (Tokyo, 1954).

In describing the evolution of the Foreign Ministry, it is appropriate to record some of the criticisms that were made overseas about Japanese diplomatic methods and competence. In the twenties there was still assumed to be goodwill on both sides; but there was generally a feeling abroad that the Japanese were extremely hard to tie down. One frequent complaint was the difficulty of getting to grips with the Japanese government itself through discussions with an official overseas, because of the subordination of its foreign representatives to Tokyo head office. Even when approaches were made to Tokyo, decisions were often long delayed. Japan had the reputation of vagueness and avoidance of commitment: the ordinary response was one of the need to refer to higher authority or being without instructions. Part of the vagueness may justly be blamed on the Japanese language, and there were also problems connected with the knowledge of English. In diplomatic parleys faulty interpretations were often a source of much trouble, while progress could be slow if no interpreters were present. It was still true that Japanese diplomats were slow in conversation as a general rule, though they were often highly competent at reading English; there were of course distinguished exceptions. The Foreign Ministry was itself not immune from language problems: in an age when messages between embassies and Tokyo took the form of telegrams in English, they often arrived in badly garbled form and served as yet another obstacle to communication.

1932 to 1945

This was a time of collision between the Foreign Ministry and the military. They pursued a foreign policy in parallel, though with connections. The main disagreements were over policy towards China, Germany and the United States. There were even differences between the foreign policy standpoints of the army and navy. The Foreign Ministry was not the only westernized section of Japanese government, but was probably more so than any other department of state.

Kasumigaseki orthodoxy and Kasumigaseki autonomy were brought to an end after the crisis over the London Naval Treaty and the Manchurian incident. From 1932 the Foreign Ministry assumed the role of international defender of Japanese policies, which were often not of its own making. Indeed, it sometimes defended in public courses that it fought against in private. From 1936 onwards it lost out further; a struggle between Ministry and military became a normal factor of policy-making.

This tension led to the growth of factions within the Foreign Ministry itself. Some diplomats, such as Yoshida, deliberately antagonized the army, both at overseas stations and in the Ministry. This was their privilege. Others found that a more cautious stance was more opportune, in view of the increasing power of the armed services in the state. In the background there was always the threat, or blackmail, held out by the cases of assassination of important political figures that occurred in Japan with increasing frequency from 1931 onwards.

The consequence of this was that from 1938 onwards the Foreign Minister increasingly came to be chosen from the ranks of the services. Examples of this were the selection in May 1938 of General Ugaki Kazushige (Konoe

Cabinet), in September 1939 of Admiral Nomura Kichisaburō (Abe Cabinet), and in 1941 of Admiral Toyoda Teijirō (Konoe Cabinet). These men were not in any sense nominees of their service. They were just exceptional outside appointments, showing that the civilians were not too ill-disposed towards appointing moderate service leaders. These appointments were, however, resented by the Foreign Ministry bureaucracy – as was the appointment of Nomura in 1940 to the then senior diplomatic post of ambassador to Washington. But the Ministry did not carry enough weight to prevent such appointments; indeed, their protests only emphasized their weakness.

It is difficult to be specific about the factions that operated. At one level, it was a question of renovation against conservatism. At another, it was a question of affiliation: with which country or group of countries should Japan cultivate relations? Thus there was the Anglo-American faction (sometimes described as the European-American faction), opposed to the China faction and, later in the 1930s, to the Axis faction. The existence of these factions affected both the Ministry itself and the embassies abroad. In the Ministry there was immense in-fighting (and bitterness) over appointments to key posts. In embassies abroad there was also some impact. Thus the military attaché in London, at the request of other military attachés in Europe, tried to convince Ambassador Yoshida in 1937 that there was merit in Japan's anti-Comintern pact with Germany. Later, by prior arrangement as members of the Axis faction, Ambassador Ōshima in Berlin and Ambassador Shiratori in Rome gave to governments to which they were accredited undertakings that were not authorized by the Foreign Ministry. This was gross defiance, and the Emperor had to step in and administer a reprimand.

This faction-fighting resulted in gradual encroachment on the Foreign Ministry monopoly of overseas affairs. It took the form of a whittling away of the responsibility of the Ministry in various areas. The first of these was the new state of Manchukuo. It was laid down that a single person would hold the positions of ambassador to Manchukuo, governor of the Kwantung leased territory and commander of the Kwantung army. The Ministry's control over the ambassador became very restricted. In December 1934 a Manchukuoan Affairs Board was established under the Prime Minister, but it seemed to be an offshoot of the War Ministry. The next instance was the creation of the Kō-A-in (Asian Development Board or China Board). The army followed up its Manchukuo success by urging the necessity for something along the same lines to cover Chinese affairs and the China Board was set up in December 1938, despite the opposition of the Foreign Ministry. Since the Nationalist Government was not officially recognized by Japan, the Ministry had only minimal responsibility for Chinese affairs. In September of the following year there was a proposal to set up a Ministry of Trade (Boeki-shō) that would combine the commercial sections of the Foreign Ministry with those of other ministries. The Foreign Ministry officials rallied round and with a great show of solidarity offered their resignations – a keynote of Kasumigaseki orthodoxy was that commercial relations were an essential part of the diplomat's duties. Faced by this mutiny, the Cabinet had no alternative but to withdraw its proposal. But this was a hollow victory. In August 1942 the Tōjō Ministry wished to establish the new Great East Asian Ministry in order to take over dealings with the various territories occupied by the Japanese armed forces. The Foreign Ministry argued that to deal with East Asian countries through a ministry different from that which handled the rest of Japan's diplomacy would be to place on these countries a stigma that they would resent. Prime Minister Tōjō was not prepared to tolerate rebellion, and in any case met with less solidarity over this issue. Accordingly, he called for the resignation of the Foreign Minister, who had been impeding his schemes, and after the appointment of a more amenable successor instituted the new ministry.

This protracted campaign of 'wing-clipping' left the Foreign Ministry demoralized. Yet it was a sign of the supremacy of the army in the Japanese state. There were none more critical of Kasumigaseki orthodoxy than Matsuoka, the wayward Foreign Minister of 1940–41, who dismissed any trusted retainers of the Ministry who disagreed with him, and, more importantly, General Tōjō, who had much of the simple soldier's prejudice towards the diplomats whom he regarded as far too clever. Thus Tōjō wanted the Foreign Ministry to confine itself to 'pure diplomacy', which he defined as the reception of envoys and the signing of treaties; he described the Foreign Minister as 'the mouthpiece of the national will as decided upon by the Cabinet'; he had a low opinion of diplomats, taking the view that what the soldiers had acquired for the nation was generally lost by weak diplomacy.

Even if the Foreign Ministry was sunk low, it could claim to have mounted high towards the end of the war. Though the diplomatic service overseas was on a limited scale during the war, and existed only in friendly and neutral capitals, it was an essential factor in the search for a peace settlement. The endeavours of Satō Naotake, ambassador to the Soviet Union, to find a peace formula through Moscow were one of the highlights, while the Ministry came back into its own in dealing with the situation created by the Allied conference at Potsdam. Many of its officials were reserved from military service, though older diplomats also helped out.

1945 to 1952

These years of occupation were a unique part of Japan's experience. Embassies and consulates overseas were closed and the diplomatic staff repatriated; foreign policy was conducted on Japan's behalf by the Supreme Commander Allied Powers (SCAP), General Douglas Macarthur; the purge of those ministers and officials who had had special responsibility for the war applied to the Foreign Ministry and reduced its ranks for the period of the occupation. The International Military Tribunal for the Far East (IMTFE) charged several Foreign Ministers, especially Hirota (who was condemned to death), Shigemitsu, Matsuoka and Tōgō. While all this might suggest that the Foreign Ministry would have only a diminished role, this would be a misapprehension. It was in a position to control what became an essential part of occupation bureaucracy, the Central Liaison Office.

The Liaison Office dealt with negotiations for terminating the war and was responsible for direct negotiations with SCAP at a time when there was a genuine shortage of those with a knowledge of English – a skill that was in particularly short supply and belonged especially to the diplomats. It was therefore the Foreign Ministry that was closest to the United States. The fact that a former diplomat, Yoshida Shigeru, was Prime Minister from 1947 to

1954 and Foreign Minister from 1945 to 1947, gave a certain additional cachet to the Foreign Ministry.

As the occupation ran its course and peace was being negotiated by John Foster Dulles, public opinion felt that the Foreign Ministry was too close to the Americans and was lacking in a spirit of independence. Some of the unpopularity of the Americans was inevitably reflected onto the Ministry, especially when the problems of China, the peace conference, and the security arrangements associated with the peace treaty threw up many issues that became subjects of sharp public controversy.

There were few structural changes of note in the Ministry during this period. As diplomatic activities were suspended after 1945, there was no need to divide the work by regions; it was divided instead into general, political and economic affairs. A more important change was in the legal status of the Ministry, when the Meiji constitution of 1889 was replaced. By Article 78 of the new constitution of 1947, diplomatic affairs were placed in the hands of, and under the responsibility of, the Cabinet rather than the Emperor; and the Foreign Minister had to acknowledge the authority of the Prime Minister. The constitution does not, however, require that every minister of state has to be a representative in either house of the Diet.

1952 to the present

Since the San Francisco peace treaty Japan has operated within a democratic system of political parties. The Foreign Ministry has been influenced in the following ways: the Foreign Minister and the parliamentary vice-minister and ministers of state have generally been party politicians and members of the Diet; foreign policy has had to be argued before the relevant party committees and justified in debates in the Diet that have often been acrimonious, which has meant that bureaucratically arranged policies of pre-war days are subject to new checks. One result of this is that much more information has been published about foreign policy than was the case before the war, though even then it was not inconsiderable. A genuine attempt has been made to follow an open diplomacy with due process of consultation. Clearly the new system has had its critics. Within the Ministry there are those who claim that politicians are amateurs, not widely travelled enough and not experienced in overseas affairs; that party influence has been detrimental and unduly influenced by lobbies; and that debates in the Diet have contributed little but steam. Similar views have also been expressed in academic circles. Nevertheless, democratic control of foreign policy has been accepted.

From the time that Ishibashi became Prime Minister in 1956 there has been political party diplomacy. The Foreign Ministers of the period have been politicians rather than bureaucrats and have generally been household names. Many Prime Ministers since 1952 have served for some time as Foreign Minister as part of a Liberal-Democratic party strategy of circulating the ministers around the various departments of state in order to give them breadth of experience. Kishi, Miki, Fukuda and Ōhira have all acted as Foreign Minister. Clearly this is a healthy convention in circumstances where so much of foreign relations is now closely related to summit meetings, where the Prime Minister is inevitably involved. It has the disadvantage that the Foreign Minister tends to be a bird of passage who is merely flying around in order to get a broader vision, and his stay in the Ministry is inevitably short. Since 1956 Japan has not had any Foreign Ministers who have spent the greater part of their lives as career diplomats. Yoshida and Shigemitsu were virtually the last of the old-style bureaucratic Foreign Ministers who came to office after a long diplomatic career.

Accompanying the new-style political Foreign Ministers, there were the parliamentary or political vice-ministers *(seimu jikan)*, generally one for each house of the Diet. These men were required to answer questions on the floor of the house or in committees. They were therefore go-betweens between the politicians and the Minister and his officials. The administration of the office was handled by career diplomats as administrative vice-ministers *(jimu jikan)*. Alongside them were the officials known in official translation as deputy vice-ministers *(gaimu shingi kan)*, who are in effect consultative officials. The Foreign Minister's personal staff, led by his private secretary, completes his headquarters.

The technical interruption in the activities of the Foreign Ministry during the occupation period necessitated the adoption of new recruitment policies. The Foreign Service Training Institute (Kenshūjo) was set up after the war to test entrants to the profession. It has greatly extended the range of universities from which entrants are drawn. In pre-war days four-fifths of recruits came from Tokyo Imperial University; entrants now come not only from national but also from private universities, not only from metropolitan but also from provincial universities. They have studied many disciplines, but the majority have specialized in the core subjects of law, politics and economics. The Foreign Ministry also encourages those recruited to spend time overseas by studying at a foreign university before their first posting. Between 1940 and 1950 most career diplomats were not able to avail themselves of the opportunity to go overseas as part of their training in the way their predecessors had done, but this shortcoming has now been overcome. The kinds of families from which foreign service recruits are drawn have again been widened, though there still seem to be 'Foreign Ministry dynasties' – that is, names in the lists of the 1970s that echo those familiar in pre-war days. But perhaps this is not unexpected in a department that has in recent years gradually increased the number of its employees to over 3300 (1978 figures). Yet it is a specialized service, and its numbers are smaller than those of government departments concerned with internal affairs, such as finance, agriculture, commerce and industry.

The Foreign Ministry has retained basically the same shape as it has had over the years. But the complexity of the organization has increased with the complexity of international affairs. It has been moulded and remoulded on about twenty occasions in the post-war years in order to meet the prevailing needs of foreign relations, the most radical attempt having taken place in the centenary year of 1969. At this time the Ministry was divided into regional and functional sections. The first of these was represented by the bureaux for Asia, America, Europe and Oceania and the Middle East and Africa; the second by the Bureaux for Economic Affairs, Economic Cooperation, Treaties, United Nations, Information and Culture (with a sub-department for culture). Political and economic affairs were to be combined within regional bureaux (except for the Americas). In the fifties the dominant department was perhaps the Treaties Bureau, with its strong staff well versed in the law, which had to deal with the protracted agenda of reparations treaties in the aftermath of war and of the new treaties of commerce and friendship that have been entered into as Japan reestablished itself as an international trading power. At other times the dominant bureau has been a regional one, when the United States, Korea or China has been the focus of Japan's diplomatic initiatives.

As one looks at the diplomatic establishments overseas one marvels at its post-war expansion, largely created by the decolonization of the world and the growth of Japan's commercial interests in all parts of the globe. Japan's diplomats are more numerous: the number of ambassadors has shot up to 116, many accredited to Third World countries. The size of embassy and consulate staffs has also increased. In the 1970s there was a considerable increase in educational and cultural activities, most conspicuously in the United States and the countries of South-East Asia. The expanding size of this overseas representation is partly due to the growing number of developing countries in which Japan has wanted to be represented because of trade. It is not so much due to Foreign Ministry representation as to the other ministries laying claim to send representatives to agencies around the world to observe at first hand labour, commercial or financial conditions at world centres. The impression of an embassy is therefore much less homogeneous than the almost paternalistic grouping found before the war. Ambassadors who at home cannot interfere with the work or thinking of other ministries are now responsible abroad for all Government officials. But they are not his own men.

Allowing for the fact that Japan's growth to post-war stardom has been as an economic power, how has this affected the Foreign Ministry? On the one hand, the Foreign Ministry orthodoxy never felt a great aversion to commercialism in the past – indeed, always considered trade relations to be one of the functions of an overseas legation. Even at head office, as we saw over the Boekishō crisis of 1939, the Ministry held that it had an important role to play. On the other hand, Japanese diplomats have always resented the suggestion that their country pursued an 'economic diplomacy' – or even that a large part of their diplomacy was economic in orientation. Be that as it may, it seems that the economic ingredient in Japan's post-war foreign policy decision-making has far exceeded that of pre-war Japan.

In economic terms Japan pursued bilateral trade agreements in the 1950s in order to re-establish its pre-war trade relations. The first success was when Japan joined GATT in 1955, though many countries continued to reserve their position over 'most favoured nation status'. That hurdle was passed with the signing of the Anglo-Japanese treaty of commerce and navigation in November 1962. It was a natural consequence that Japan joined the OECD in 1964. Its successful trade promotion reached a symbolic climax with the International EXPO at Osaka in 1970. This process of integrating Japan into the world economic community, which culminated in the presence of her Prime Minister at summits at Puerto Rico (1976), London (1977) and Bonn (1978), has clearly taxed the resources of the Foreign Ministry. Naturally the Ministry has shared these negotiations with other ministries; but it still places a premium on those diplomats who studied economics or have specialized in economic questions.

Such a process can only be achieved by cooperation between the various agencies, and one of the post-war trends has been the rapprochement between the diplomatic and the economic and financial aspects of government. This has been particularly noticeable in the relationship between the Foreign and the giant Ministry of International Trade and Industry (MITI: Tsūsanshō), which tries to integrate the needs of the industrial and the trading sectors – no mean task. It goes without saying that there have been major disputes between the two ministries, notably the Foreign Ministry's coolness towards MITI's desire for increased trade with mainland China and the Soviet Union in the 1960s. There has also been collaboration. Indeed, it can be said that when MITI was set up in 1949 it included large numbers of officials from the Foreign Ministry whose expertise in English was thought to be indispensable in restoring Japan's seaborne trade. Since then there have been large-scale exchanges of officials at the higher levels, and those who have gone on secondment to an economic ministry have tended to benefit from the experience by promotion later in their careers. Even then, however, there are major difficulties in harmonizing policies by an intricate network of inter-ministerial committees under the wider supervision of the Cabinet.

Equally there is the pressure exercised on the Ministry from commercial lobbies. While there has to be differentiation between *zaikai, gyōkai* and *kigyō* and these do not offer identical policy recommendations, the influence of the 'big business' lobby on officials is now less than was once generally assumed. Indirectly, through public opinion and the mass media, they make their impact on the minds of politicians and thus on the evolution of policy. A Japanese politician has to react to the views of those he is wooing. But the party organization itself appears to be assuming an even more important role. The Liberal-Democratic party's political affairs research group acts as an instrument for harmonizing the plans of the Foreign Ministry officials and the often hostile views of outside pressure groups. The politicians of the Liberal-Democratic party and behind them the pressure of business opinion play their part as constraining influences on foreign policy-making.

Is the Foreign Ministry more or less important than in the pre-war period? Some are inclined to say that Japan has had no foreign policy of its own in the post-war period; that this is disgraceful considering its standing in the world; and that it has followed too much an American line and has not cultivated a diversified policy that would aim at an independent, neutral status in the world. This is a widespread criticism of the post-war Foreign Ministry. Since the Ministry has relaxed its attitude towards publication by its employees some of these criticisms have come from prominent diplomats: witness the outspoken writings of Nishi Haruhiko and Kawasaki Ichirō. It must, however, be said that during the 1970s it increasingly sought a diversified foreign policy, so that part of the criticism has lapsed. Moreover, it can be argued that the low posture of the Foreign Ministry in the fifties and sixties suited the country well; it would have been out of place for Japan to be too intrusive. Indeed, it can be argued not that the post-war Foreign Ministry is especially weak, but that like similar institutions the world over it is different. In a period when high policy has more and more been devised and negotiated at summit conferences, the Foreign Minister has had to yield something to the Prime Minister and his other colleagues; in a world where the main issues are related to trade, and where the policies of all countries are in flux in view of the international economic and financial considerations, the Foreign Ministry has had no choice but to give up part of its autonomy.

The Japanese Foreign Ministry, like the country itself, has had a variegated experience over the past century and more. It has built up a modernized, professional service with great shrewdness and skill. By the 1920s that service had acquired traditions and could look with some pride at its Kasumigaseki autonomy. In the 1930s the autonomy and independent position of the Ministry were challenged by the armed services. It was not the case that the Foreign Ministry sold itself out to the army, rather that the army pursued an independent foreign policy, using loopholes in the constitution and in the administrative system, which had seriously broken down. There was a hiatus from 1937 to 1952, during which Foreign Ministry officials were often assigned to other duties. In the post-war period it is still the bureaucracy that has a major steering role in foreign policy-making; and, provided that they make accommodations with business groups and politicians of the governing party, they will not be challenged unduly. But issues have arisen where politicians have been stealing the initiative; and from time to time these three forces fail to harmonize their views and come in for public censure. It is sometimes said that big business is taking the role of the army in pre-war policy-making, but the degree of direct business interference seems to be very small by comparison with the army in its days of dominance. In fact, when one is pursuing an economic diplomacy harmonization between the three forces has some things to commend it.

The Japanese Foreign Ministry has developed proud traditions over the years. There is among its diplomatic representatives overseas a strong tradition of observation and reporting, of loyalty to Tokyo and of conscientious service. Because of the turbulent history of Japan over the past century, the diplomats have had a changing and subtle role to play abroad. Because of the unstable domestic background within Japan itself, the careers and prospects of diplomats have been more than normally subject to difficulties and anxieties. Now that Japan has greater stability than it has enjoyed since the Meiji restoration, it has the unusual status of a great economic power with little military muscle. It is no mean task to be the guardian of foreign affairs of such a country.

BIBLIOGRAPHY

[Throughout this article I have treated Japanese names according to Japanese convention by placing the family name before the given name.]

Banno Masataka, *Gendai gaikō no bunseki* (Tokyo 1971).

M. Blaker, *Japanese International Negotiating Style* (New York 1977).

Gaimushō no 100-nen, 2 vols (Tokyo 1969).

Kawasaki Ichirō, *The Japanese are like that* (Tokyo 1955).

Kawasaki Ichirō, *Japan unmasked* (Tokyo 1969).

Nihon gaikō 100-nen shoshi (Tokyo 1954).

I. H. Nish, *Japanese foreign policy, 1869–1942: From Kasumigaseki to Miyakezaka* (London 1977).

Ōno Katsumi, *Kasumigaseki gaikō* (Tokyo 1978).

R. A. Scalapino (ed.), *The foreign policy of modern Japan* (Berkeley 1977) (especially the essays by Fukui Haruhiko and C. Johnson).

Shigemitsu Mamoru, *Japan and her destiny: My struggle for peace* (London 1958).

Shiroyama Saburō, *War criminal: The life and death of Hirota Kōki* (Tokyo 1977).

A. Stead (ed.), *Japan by the Japanese* (London 1904).

Uchiyama Masakuma, 'The Foreign Office of Japan: Past and present' in *Keio Journal of Politics*, 1976, 1–21.

Yoshida Kenichi, *The Yoshida memoirs: The story of Japan in crisis* (London 1962).

JAPAN – APPENDIX A

EXPANSION OF STAFF OF THE JAPANESE FOREIGN MINISTRY

Year	1886	1904	1921	1931	1942	1951	1969
Head Office Staff	133 plus 21 under training	123	288	302	920	1419	1584
Overseas Staff	115	263	585	865	994 403 non-permanent	85	1351
Selected Posts Overseas Status of Posts	Legations			Embassies (E) Legations (L)		Offices	Embassies
Britain	6	10	E 19	E 24	E 22	6	52
France	6	7	E 22	E 25	E 21	6	43
United States	9	29	E 18	E 22	E 26	25	134
Germany	9	7	E 8	E 24	E 35	—	39
Holland	1	3	L 5	L 7	—	4	8
Italy	6	4	E 10	E 9	E 18	—	23
Russia	8	—	[E 3]	E 16	E 14	—	39
Austria	4	6	L 1	L 6	—	—	12
China	19	23	L 24	L 33	E 91 Manchukuo 34	—	20 (Taiwan)
Korea	42	51	—	—	—	—	29
Mexico	—	7	L 3	L 6	E14	—	12
Brazil	—	3	L 5	E 11	E 19	6	38
Belgium	—	4	L 6	E 25	—	4	19
Spain	—	3	L 5	L 6	L 8	—	11
Sweden	—	5	L 9	L 8	L 8	4	6
Thailand	—	9	L 5	L 5	E 50	4	28
Chile	—	—	L 2	L 7	—	—	6

APPENDIX B

JAPANESE FOREIGN MINISTRY ESTABLISHMENT (1979)

FOREIGN MINISTER

Private Secretary

Vice-Minister
(Gaimu jimu jikan)

Parliamentary Vice-Minister
(Gaimu seimu jikan)

Secretariat
(Daijin kambo)

Deputy ministers 6
(Shingikan)

Assistant vice-minister 1

Special assistants 3
(Chosa kan)

General Affairs division
(Somuka)

Personnel division
(Jinjika)

Archives division
(Bunshoka)

Telecommunications division
(Denshinka)

Finance division
(Kaikeika)

Overseas Establishments division
(Zaigai kokanka)

Chiefs of protocol 2
(Gitenkan)

Welfare superintendent
(Kosei kanrikan)

Research department
(Chosabu)

Planning division
(Kikaku ka)

Analysis division
(Bunseki ka)

Consular and Emigration Affairs
Department (Ryoji ijubu)

Consular divisions
(Ryojika)

Passport division
(Ryokenka)

Visa room
(Sashoshitsu)

Emigration Affairs Division
(Ijuka)

Asian Affairs Bureau

North American Bureau

Central and
South American Bureau

Europe and
Oceanic Affairs Bureau

Middle Eastern
and African Affairs Bureau

Economic Affairs Bureau

Economic Cooperation Bureau

Treaties Bureau

United Nations Bureau

Public Information Bureau
(Joho bunkakyoku)

Miscellaneous agencies

Personnel review body
(Gaimu jinji shingikai)

Foreign service training centre
(Gaimusho kenshujo)

Establishments overseas

Embassies 139

Consulates-general 52

Consulates 7

Government representatives 5

Luxembourg

The Ministry of Foreign Affairs in the Grand Duchy

GILBERT TRAUSCH

Gilbert Trausch is Director of the Bibliothèque nationale de Luxembourg. He was born in 1931 in Luxembourg and studied history at the Sorbonne and at the University of Exeter. For some years he taught at the Lycée de Garçons de Luxembourg. Since 1968, he has been Professor at the Centre universitaire de Luxembourg and since 1970, Lecturer at the Université de Liège. He was appointed to his present position at the Bibliothèque nationale in 1972. His fields of research and publication include the French Revolution, modern agricultural history and international relations (nineteenth and twentieth centuries).

Writing the history of the Ministry of Foreign Affairs of a small country –
indeed the smallest European state – poses difficult problems, of which some
are *sui generis*. In fact, of the present EEC members Luxembourg is the last to
have acquired the status of a sovereign country.

In 1815 the Congress of Vienna created the Grand Duchy of Luxembourg[1]
as an independent and sovereign state, and in accordance with the principle of
compensation, granted it to William I, King of the Netherlands (that is,
present-day Netherlands and Belgium), as his own personal property. The
Netherlands and the Grand Duchy were thus linked by a personal bond. At
the same time, Luxembourg was made part of the new German Confederation.
What scope could there be in the field of foreign affairs for a small state
hampered by such exacting restraints? The question did not arise in concrete
terms, since William I, sweeping aside the stipulations laid down by the
Congress of Vienna, simply treated the Grand Duchy as the eighteenth
province of his realm of the Netherlands. At the time no one protested,
neither the signatories of the Treaty of Vienna nor the Luxembourgers,
which clearly shows that they had as yet no sense of a national identity. In
these circumstances, Luxembourg had no foreign policy and no need for an
ad hoc administration.

In 1830 the Belgian Revolution broke out in Brussels. Quite logically, the
Luxembourgers took part in it, though their reasons were not quite those of
the Belgians. The King and Grand Duke was too late in granting the essential
concessions: the suppression of the most unpopular taxes and the separation
for administrative purposes of Luxembourg from the Netherlands.[2] The
whole country – with the exception of the capital, which was forced into
obedience by the Prussian garrison of the German Confederation – rallied to
the new Belgian state. The combination of the two powers lasted until 1839,
when William I at last accepted the Treaty of the XXIV Articles, that is, the
division of the Grand Duchy. The Treaty of London (19 April 1839) drew up
the practical details of the separation. The entire western section of
Luxembourg (mainly French-speaking, apart from a small section of German-
speakers) was assigned to Belgium, forming the province of Luxembourg
with Arlon as its capital. The eastern part (entirely German-Luxembourg-
speaking) formed the Grand Duchy (2586 square kilometres, population
175 000). Henceforth separated from the Netherlands and governed by its
own citizens, this Grand Duchy, now reduced to its smallest viable part, had
to establish those structures (political organs as well as administrative bodies)
essential to a truly independent state. National feeling, still weak during the
years 1830 to 1839, grew rapidly. As early as 1859 an occasional song with
the significant refrain *Mir welle bleiwen wat mir sin* ('We want to stay what we
are') rapidly became the national anthem. The Luxembourgers, therefore,
consider the year 1839 as the true birth-date of an independent Luxembourg.
Luxembourg, late in joining the community of sovereign states in Western
Europe, offers the peculiarity of a political and administrative framework
that preceded the birth of national feeling.

The beginnings of the Ministry of Foreign Affairs
The problems of foreign policies could now be approached in a new light.
The royal decree of 31 December 1830, which established the administrative
separation of Luxembourg and the Netherlands, had, by special dispensation,

left foreign and military affairs in the hands of a Dutch minister.[3] It was not until 1841 that William II, entrammelled in difficult negotiations with Prussia regarding the possible entry of Luxembourg into the Zollverein, transferred responsibility for these two fields to a 'Royal and Grand Ducal Chancellery for the Affairs of Luxembourg'. This was situated at The Hague[4] and run by a German civil servant, C. E. Stifft. In a certain sense one can regard this German as the Grand Duchy's first Minister of Foreign Affairs.[5] Stifft resigned on 4 November 1841 and was replaced by a Luxembourger, Baron Frederick Blochausen. His brief was to 'maintain diplomatic relations with the foreign ministers residing in The Hague, and with the German parliament'.[6] Luxembourg's interests abroad were represented by the ministers of the Dutch king.

In spite of some progress it is not possible to speak of a true Luxembourg foreign policy at this stage. William I used three German civil servants to negotiate Luxembourg's treaty of accession into the Zollverein (1840); William II brought in Luxembourgers when he resumed the negotiations in 1841–2, but when he came to choose a representative for Luxembourg at Frankfurt, the seat of the German Confederation, he nominated a German, Frederic von Scherff.

The 'Luxembourg question' arose in 1866 when, following the Austro-Prussian war, the German Confederation was dissolved. William III tried to sell his Grand Duchy to Napoleon III in 1867. The negotiations were carried out without reference to the Luxembourgers, and the Luxembourg government, conscious of its weakness, made no attempt to intercede. If annexation was prevented, Luxembourg owed this more to Franco-Prussian rivalry and Bismarck's opposition than to its own efforts.[7] The 1867 crisis at least had the merit of highlighting the diplomatic deficiencies of the Grand Duchy. Stripped of representation outside its border the country was, in a manner of speaking, blind. The Dutch government, aware of the conflict between its own interests and those of Luxembourg in 1867, and afraid that the Grand Duchy would drag it into international complications, resolved in April 1867 to renounce its right to represent Luxembourg's interests abroad. Through the intermediary of William's brother Prince Henry, who was Lieutenant of the Grand Duchy, Russia undertook the representation and protection of Luxembourg's interests from 1867 to 1873. In 1867 the Luxembourg government, 'drawing the lesson of events', with the successful conclusion of the crisis created two diplomatic posts, one in Paris, the other in Berlin; soon after, a third was opened in Brussels.

When, in 1873, Russia renounced its representation of Luxembourg's interests, the country spent seven years without diplomatic representation, except in the three neighbouring countries (Belgium, France and Germany), where it had its own agents. It was not until 1880 that the Netherlands undertook to represent Luxembourg, and then it stipulated as a cautionary measure that this representation could under no circumstances apply to the Grand Duchy's three neighbours. The representation applied to both political and economic questions (through legations), and to the material interests of individuals (through consulates).[8]

At the same time there grew up a small consular network. As early as 1841, William II, on his own initiative and without consulting the Luxembourg government, had appointed as the consul of the Grand Duchy in Amsterdam a Jew of Luxembourg extraction who was resident in the Netherlands.[9] This was an isolated act, which came about through the request of the individual concerned; it had no political import and led to no further developments. It was in 1869 that Luxembourg consuls were appointed at Brussels and at Vienna, in 1874 a third was appointed to Paris, and in 1880 a fourth at New York.[10] Including the consul appointed at Amsterdam (who was to die in 1883), Luxembourg thus had five consuls in 1880. This was a start, but the logical development was slow in coming. On the eve of the First World War, Luxembourg still had three chargés d'affaires (Paris, Brussels and Berlin), but only two consuls (Paris and New York).

The death of the King and Grand Duke William III in 1890 represents an important step in the political emancipation of the country. As there was no male heir, the crown of the Grand Duchy passed to the elder branch of the Nassaus, of whom Duke Adolphe,[11] stripped in 1866 of his duchy by Bismarck, was the claimant. This cut the umbilical cord that had linked Luxembourg to the Netherlands since 1815.

The consequences on the diplomatic level are obvious. The three neighbouring countries, until now accredited at The Hague to the King and Grand Duke, were henceforth accredited to Grand Duke Adolphe (1817–1905). Quite logically Germany (1890), France (1890) and Belgium (1892) opened legations in Luxembourg, where they were represented by a minister plenipotentiary and an envoy extraordinary. Italy was to do likewise in 1912.[12]

Yet it was not Grand Duke Adolphe, who was already seventy-three years old at the time of his accession and almost always absent from the country during his reign, nor his son and successor William (who reigned from 1905 to 1912), who was gravely ill for most of his reign, but the Minister of State and President of the Government, Paul Eyschen (1841–1915) who was to control the country's foreign policy.

The era of Paul Eyschen

A member of the government since 1876, Eyschen was its President from 1888 and the Department of Foreign Affairs therefore came under his control. For a quarter of a century he made it his private domain, carefully avoiding any sharing of responsibility and even of the experience acquired. He himself had been Luxembourg's chargé d'affaires in Berlin from 1875 to 1888 and had developed a decided taste for diplomacy. The ascendency of this man explains why we can speak of a veritable Eyschen era in foreign policy.

He operated with the most reduced of administrative systems. In Luxembourg he drew on the services of a government adviser and an office head whose duties also involved other ministries.

Abroad there were still the three chargés d'affaires. According to tradition they were not called 'ministers' because Eyschen wanted to be the only one to have that kind of title;[13] the real reason was that the more modest title was more suitable for men who were only intermittently resident in their foreign posts, generally staying there for no more than a few weeks each year. There was no need for a legation building – the chargés d'affaires stayed at hotels – and thus no need for counsellors or even for secretaries and typists. The very fact that Eyschen could, for thirteen years, hold concurrently and without any problems his post as chargé d'affaires in Berlin and his ministerial mandate as director-general in Luxembourg is revealing. As far as diplomatic and consular representation was concerned, the arrangement concluded in 1880 with the Netherlands still held good.

Two reasons explain the slow development of the Luxembourg diplomatic service. First, the tenacious desire to keep spending to a minimum in an area that aroused little public interest. This concern for economy is also justified by the very small scope of Luxembourg's diplomacy. Three treaties in fact placed very strict limits on the means at its disposal. Since 1842 Luxembourg had had an economic alliance with Prussia, and since 1871 with the German empire. In 1872, the empire took control of the principal rail network in Luxembourg, and in 1902 the economic association with Germany was renewed, in advance, until 1959. The inequality between the two partners explains why it was a case of economic annexation rather than a customs union. In matters concerning customs Luxembourg had no say in the matter, either in the customs parliament or in the Bundesrat. The 1867 Treaty of London, by imposing on Luxembourg a permanent, obligatory and unarmed neutrality, also considerably limited its freedom of action in the field of foreign affairs. It is not far from the truth to assert that, faced with these severe restrictions, the country's real foreign policy consisted precisely in not having one.

In fact, Paul Eyschen relied on two guiding principles:[14] a scrupulous respect for the duties of neutrality, and strict abstinence from any initiative likely to be misinterpreted by the powers guaranteeing the neutrality of the Grand Duchy. This concern was coupled to that of doing nothing that could displease the powerful neighbour to the east. Sheltered by the Zollverein, Luxembourg spent the years 1870 to 1914 putting into effect its 'industrial revolution' on the German model.

This policy of prudence and abstention did not prevent Paul Eyschen from seizing opportunities – particularly during the increase in international tensions at the beginning of the present century – that allowed special emphasis to be placed on the country's unique international situation. On the national commemoration day (the sovereign's birthday) he regularly summoned the diplomats (all, except for those of the three neighbouring countries, resident at The Hague or Brussels but also accredited to Luxembourg) and gave them a short talk on international law and foreign policy.

Eyschen drew particular profit from the peace conferences at The Hague (1899 and 1907), using them to remind the world of Luxembourg's existence and to define the rights and duties of neutrality. He tried to emerge as an international figure, and to a certain extent he succeeded. On the eve of the First World War he was the only Luxembourg statesman known outside the country – and even then only to Germany, Belgium and France. In their reports the ministers of Germany and France recognized his diplomatic skill. When, in 1913, he celebrated his twenty-five years as President of the government, the main newspapers of the neighbouring countries *(Le Temps, Kölnische Zeitung, Kölnische Volkszeitung)* devoted articles to him. The *Gazette de Bruxelles* wrote that Paul Eyschen 'is considered by all statesmen of Western Europe as one of the great political figures of the age'.[15] Eyschen clearly believed this to be so, overestimating his influence and thereby exposing himself to bitter disappointments at the hour of truth. It is a temptation to which the star performers of small countries succumb only too readily.

Eyschen ruled as master over Luxembourg's diplomacy, and he ruled it alone. The trouble was that, at the approach of that great testing time for Luxembourg, the First World War, Eyschen was seventy-five years old and no successor had been groomed for office. 'Since Mr Eyschen has been in power, he has sought to control alone and unaided the Grand Duchy's foreign affairs. He would not tolerate any assistant at his side. He prevented anyone wanting to enter the Department of External Relations from gaining a foothold. He was afraid to allow anyone but himself to take an active interest in these great questions.'[16] Particular notice should be taken of the fact that this attack dates from 1917, two years after Eyschen's death; until 1914 his actions were constantly sheltered from criticism. The reason is that from the beginning there was a broad consensus about foreign affairs among the population. No alternative was developed, either in what was done or in the way in which it was done. Public opinion was entirely devoted to disarmed neutrality, which freed the country from the need for military service, and to the Zollverein, which brought prosperity. Apart from the anticipatory renewal of the Zollverein in 1902, there was not a single debate about foreign affairs in parliament in the twenty-five years before the First World War. Running through the index of the numerous volumes of the *Account of Debates in the Chamber of Deputies*, one finds only rarely the words 'legations', or 'external relations' or even 'diplomatic representation'. One has to look to the war years before they begin to appear with any regularity. The budget for external relations was voted for with monotonous regularity, without the slightest debate. 'Admitted without discussion' was the ritual formula. Moreover the budget was very modest: 40 800 francs in 1913 to cover legations, consulates, extraordinary expenses and foreign travel, as well as Luxembourg's share in the functioning of the Permanent Court of Arbitration at The Hague.

This broad consensus among the Luxembourgers on the conduct of foreign affairs was, therefore, based to a large extent on the indifference of public opinion, but also on the trust it placed, with a great deal of naivety, on international guarantees. The increasing hostilities after 1911, the discussions in the French and German press on the 'breach of Luxembourg' (1913–14), obviously opened the eyes of the best informed, and first and foremost those of Eyschen, but it was too late to react, even had that been possible and Eyschen been willing, which is more than doubtful. The German invasion on 2 August 1914 was therefore a rude awakening for the people and the diplomats of Luxembourg.

The impact of the First World War

The violation of the Grand Duchy's neutrality and its occupation by German troops threw into harsh relief the inadequacy of Luxembourg diplomacy. The regime of occupation was not without originality. The Reich recognized that it had acted wrongly, justified itself by alleging imperious military necessity and promised to respect Luxembourg's sovereignty in other matters: the government, the ministers, the civil services, the Chamber of Deputies, the tribunals could all continue under the watchful eye of the occupying forces. It was an occupation, but it was not an enemy occupation as in Belgium and the northern departments of France. The Luxembourg state and all its machinery carried on, there was no military governor, and the commander of the German troops, which were in any case not very numerous, was instructed not to intervene in the internal affairs of the country as long as the army's own interests were not placed in jeopardy. One is tempted to talk of a gentle occupation.[17]

How did the Luxembourg government react to these events? It formally protested at Berlin against the violation of its neutrality and went on to reiterate its objections repeatedly during the course of the war. The occupying forces permitted these protests to be made and even allowed them a degree of publicity, though the tone was too measured to please the Allies. Eyschen decided to stick to his traditional policy of neutrality, thus also upholding his principle of not offending Germany. The Grand Duchy maintained all its diplomatic relations: it did not break with Germany and it attempted to continue its relations with the Allies. The occupying forces maintained a finely balanced attitude; they insisted that the ministers of France and Belgium – and later of Italy – should leave Luxembourg, but did not prevent Luxembourg itself from maintaining its chargés d'affaires in Paris and Brussels. Certainly the Government experienced great difficulties in maintaining these contacts. Travel had to be through Switzerland, special authorizations were needed, the conveying of diplomatic mail functioned badly, and some German civil servants were over-zealous.

Other difficulties were caused above all by the Luxembourgers themselves. The chargé d'affaires in Brussels chose for personal reasons not to follow the Belgian government into exile at Le Havre. He remained in Brussels, where he could indeed concern himself with Luxembourgers living in Belgium but where he was of no political use whatsoever. More serious still, the Government sent no one to Le Havre, so that for the duration of the war it had no real contact with the Belgian authorities. The chargé d'affaires in Paris was a man of the highest calibre. President of the Council of State, a former minister, H. Vannérus had been accredited to Paris for thirty years and was highly valued at the Quai d'Orsay. Alas, he was an old man of eighty-one at the time of the invasion. As the Luxembourg chargés d'affaires did not reside permanently abroad, this noble old man was forced to make tiring journeys to Paris via Switzerland, journeys whose number it was out of the question to increase.

An octogenarian diplomat the sole link between Luxembourg and the Allies! And that at a time when the country's very future was at stake. For the war brought the Luxembourg dossier back to chancellery desks. The Luxembourg question arose spontaneously and immediately, since each of the three neighbouring countries believed, for varying reasons, that it had a claim to the Grand Duchy. Moreover the doubt cast over their future communicated itself to the Luxembourgers themselves, although the majority of them remained faithful to their independence.[18]

Little by little, the Government became aware of manoeuvres beginning to take shape around them. But reactions were slow and timid, because the Government was in the grip of difficult internal problems (food supplies, varying interpretations of the constitution, fierce partisan struggles). Realizing in 1915 that a German victory was only one of several possibilities, Eyschen attempted, but in vain, to regain contact with the Allies through visits to Bern and The Hague. His sudden death on 12 October 1915 left a void in foreign affairs. None of his successors as President of Council and

Minister of Foreign Affairs was known outside Luxembourg. They lacked the political longevity to become international figures.[19] But all of them understood the deficiencies of Luxembourg's diplomatic service. A former Minister, E. Leclère, was appointed as Vannérus' second in command in Paris. The drawbacks inherent in Luxembourg's pre-war diplomatic service became clearly visible in the consular organization in Paris. As an economy measure the Belgian consul-general had also been appointed as consul by Luxembourg. Yet during the years 1914–19 the interests of the two countries were fundamentally opposed, with Belgium seeking the annexation of the Grand Duchy. The Luxembourg chargé d'affaires in Paris was thus obliged to play hide and seek with his own consul.

Lengthy efforts, slowed down by a lack of boldness, were undertaken to increase diplomatic representation abroad. Overtures made to the British Foreign Office met with no success; London did not want a chargé d'affaires from Luxembourg. In 1917 chargés d'affaires were appointed to Bern and The Hague, where, however, they resided only intermittently. The first of these was also Minister of Public Works, while the second was secretary to the Grand Duchess. The 1917 initiative, however limited in appearance, nonetheless represents a turning point. The cardinal importance of foreign affairs to a small state was at last understood. Henceforth the Grand Duchy was to develop its network of external relations and to formulate, little by little, the principles of a true foreign policy. Towards the end of the war, the Luxembourg diplomatic service redoubled its efforts. It installed a press office in Bern, which was to refute the words of 'certain journalists who have felt that they should raise their voices in favour of the annexation of the Grand Duchy by one or other of the neighbouring powers'.[20]

In those difficult months from the Armistice on 11 November 1918 to the signing of peace on 28 June 1919, the country's survival was assured only with difficulty. By instituting a referendum, the Luxembourg diplomatic service invoked in its favour the free right of the people to dispose of themselves, thus throwing into disarray the various moves for annexation by neighbouring states. At the same time, it benefited from Franco-Belgian rivalry by playing its neighbours off against each other, a game to which minor states gladly have recourse, but which is decidedly dangerous as it irritates the major powers. Foreign affairs in those critical post-war years were handled most competently by Emile Reuter, who as Minister of State was in charge of foreign affairs.

At length, the Grand Duchy was strengthened by the testing period of the First World War. It left the Zollverein and formed an economic union with Belgium (25 July 1921), a less dangerous, because weaker, partner. It reinforced its status as an independent state through its acceptance into the League of Nations (16 December 1920).[21] The war had revealed the power of the Anglo-Saxon countries. Thus it was a perfectly logical step for Luxembourg to open legations in London in 1920 and in Washington the same year, still using chargés d'affaires who resided there only intermittently.

Luxembourg diplomacy during the inter-war period
Once the 1914–18 crisis was over, the first concern of the Luxembourg diplomatic service was to consolidate the country's position on the international front. The first point won was that despite its membership of the

League of Nations, the Grand Duchy could maintain its neutrality status, as defined in 1867. The country thus escaped military obligations and the need to contract alliances.

In 1926 there arrived as President of the Government the man who was to remain for thirty-three years, without interruption, as head of the Ministry of Foreign Affairs, Joseph Bech.[22] He can be seen as the true founder of Luxembourg's foreign policy. When, in November 1937, reasons of internal politics forced him to abandon the presidency of the Council, he still remained at the head of Foreign Affairs. This was the first time since 1848 that Foreign Affairs was not linked to the presidency. This was yet another step towards the emancipation of the Ministry, which was moreover physically separated from the presidency from 1937 onwards: at that date the Ministry of Foreign Affairs became the sole occupant of the Hotel du Gouvernement, which in the eighteenth century had been a refuge of the abbey of Saint-Maximin of Trèves. It is still there, but in the meantime has annexed the neighbouring building. The growing importance of international relations is clearly reflected in the extension of its buildings. Just as the Quai d'Orsay has become a synonym in France, so, at a more modest level, the 'Sankt Maximein' has become the symbol of foreign affairs in the Grand Duchy.

Joseph Bech was able to profit from the annual meetings of the League of Nations in Geneva to acquire an international reputation. He had the luck, as representative of a small country, to stay in power long enough to make his name known.

On an administrative level, the volume of work carried out by Foreign Affairs had grown continuously. First there were the problems resulting from the economic union between Belgium and Luxembourg (UEBL); this functioned badly in its early stages (1921–30), causing some friction. Continual adjustments were necessary, which demanded gruelling negotiations with Belgian delegates. The truth is that the Luxembourgers knew how to analyze and plead their dossiers. Eighty years of Zollverein had given them a solid grounding.

The problems of the UEBL and the general intensification of international relations (the League of Nations, Locarno, pacts of arbitration, etc.) did not, however, produce a visible increase in the managerial staff of the Department. Emile Reuter (1918–25) and Joseph Bech (from 1926) worked with the smallest of teams, Reuter and A. Funck, a man drawn from the ranks, and Bech with A. Wehrer, a lawyer. Both were Government counsellors, a title given to high officials sparsely scattered through the different ministries. (There were six of them altogether in 1930 and nine in 1940.) Foreign Affairs was still not distinguished from the other ministries by a special nomenclature. Altogether the structure was ultra-light. On the eve of the Second World War, the Ministry of Foreign Affairs functioned with eight officials, of whom three had a university training. An embryonic structure began to appear. Wehrer was in charge of the running of the service, thus fulfilling, before the letter, the role of secretary-general. This can be seen as a first stage in the division into an administrative and a commercial sector. But all this came about empirically, without any legislative initiative.

How was the Luxembourg diplomatic service able to get by in the inter-war period with such a tiny staff? For questions demanding varied expertise not only were other ministers consulted, as is also the rule elsewhere, but the service also had recourse to experts in private enterprise, such as Albert Calmes, a director of ARBED (an important steel producer with its main base in Luxembourg). Suppleness in the use of manpower has been and remains one of the striking characteristics of small countries.

Some timid progress can be seen in the country's representation abroad. Legation buildings were rented in Brussels, Berlin and Paris. The time had passed when Luxembourg's chargés d'affaires had to use hotels, which were not even of the first category (the 'Bristol' in Berlin, the 'Capucines' in Paris). The newly created legations had a less than enviable fate. The legation in Bern was soon suppressed, that in London was to remain without a head for most of the time. The chargés d'affaires were still itinerant or occasional representatives of the 'Missi dominici' type. On the eve of war, A. Wehrer was both secretary-general to the Government, and as such responsible for the running of the Ministry of Foreign Affairs, and chargé d'affaires in Berlin. One can hardly speak of a homogenous body. If Wehrer and Funck (Paris) had come up through the hierarchy, A. Collart (The Hague), R. de Waha (Washington), A. Pescatore (London), E. Leclère (Paris) were former ministers, while Kirsch-Puricelli (Berlin) and A. Nickels (Berlin) were businessmen, the last mentioned being a director of ARBED. Of course, to sell steel . . .

Apart from the six countries (Germany, Belgium, the United States, France, Great Britain and Holland) where it was directly represented, Luxembourg continued to use the services of the Netherlands. At the time of the negotiations (1919–21) to conclude an economic union, Belgium claimed the right to represent the Grand Duchy. Luxembourg refused, preferring to rely on the Dutch tradition. However, it gave over to Belgium its consular interests in all those places where it had no consuls of its own.[23] This dual system of external representation persists to the present day. In 1940, Luxembourg drew on a network of 52 honorary consuls and vice-consuls.

Conversely, here is the evolution of representation of foreign countries in Luxembourg: in 1920, 14 countries had representatives in Luxembourg, in 1930 there were 21, and in 1940, 30, five of which had a resident minister or chargé d'affaires (Germany, France, Belgium, Italy, USA). The rest were represented by their officials in Brussels. On the consular level, 21 countries were represented in Luxembourg (1930 and 1940).

The shock of the Second World War

The German invasion on 10 May 1940, the hurried departure of the Government into exile and the collapse of France, revealed the full extent of the deficiencies in diplomatic representation. The government in exile had no infrastructure: the legations in London and Washington existed only on paper. Montreal was chosen as the seat of the government in exile (consisting of the sovereign and the Prime Minister), but part of the government established itself in London. Legations were created in Washington and London, and after 1941 in Moscow. Joseph Bech, using whatever means he could and with financial aid from Belgium, initiated considerable diplomatic activity. Well served by the numerous diplomatic contacts he had made before the war, he succeeded in making Luxembourg's voice heard in the concert of Allied nations. Luxembourg signed the Charter of San Francisco;

in 1944, still in exile, it, together with Belgium and the Netherlands, created the union of Benelux. During the war it officially renounced its neutral status. After seventy-three years of an international status imposed by the European powers in 1867, the country recovered its freedom of action and with it a greater scope for diplomatic activity.

The rise of the Luxembourg diplomatic service after 1945

The war served as a lesson. Both the Government and public opinion realized that the country needed a real diplomatic service and that it would be necessary to abandon makeshift solutions and the service of amateurs. Of course the country, with its 220000 inhabitants in 1947 (which had risen to 360000 by 1980), was small and was not able to launch out in imitation of the great powers, but it had to use the means at its disposal. Everything, moreover, pointed to an intensification of international relations; a defence organization among the Western powers and a movement towards European unification. Luxembourg would have its place in these movements, it would have a role to play and it possessed a politician of international stature, Joseph Bech, who was fully competent to assume this role. It is enough to mention, by way of example, the Charter of the United Nations (1945), the Pact of Brussels (1948), the North Atlantic Treaty (1949); the Council of Europe (1949), the European Coal and Steel Community (ECSC, 1951).

The only way in which Luxembourg could fulfil its new obligations was by developing its Ministry of Foreign Affairs. On 11 June 1947 the Chamber of Deputies unanimously adopted a bill 'leading to the organization of the diplomatic corps'.[24] This is the first legal text controlling the status of diplomatic staff; at last one was leaving the stage of improvisation to move into that of established structures – more than a century after the country became independent (1839). The law of 1947 created the following hierarchy, which still exists: extraordinary envoys and plenipotentiary ministers, legation counsellors, legation secretaries, legation attachés. Henceforth the Luxembourg representatives abroad were to be professional diplomats, men educated for that task and devoting themselves to it full-time. This brought to an end the era of enlightened amateurs who, as well as pursuing their other occupations, occasionally ventured onto the diplomatic stage. Little by little, thanks to internal reorganizations, an authentic *esprit de corps* was created. At the time of the elaboration of the 1947 law some timorous spirits had thought of limiting the number of posts abroad. The government succeeded in setting aside the suggestion, thus keeping its freedom to create new posts as the need arose, subject to the necessary finance being raised in the vote on the annual budget. In 1948 a grand-ducal decree regulated precisely the status of diplomatic agents and chancellery agents.[25]

There are other signs of a change of attitude. When the Government of National Union came to an end (March 1947), the Ministry took the title of Ministry of Foreign Affairs and External Commerce (and since 1972, of International Cooperation). At the same time the government bought buildings in Brussels, London and Paris to house its legations. Other purchases followed. The openness of mind clearly stems from the intensification of international relations. It is also the result of a new desire: the country's wish to accept fully its responsibilities at an international level and no longer to be remarkable by its absence. To this was added the desire to play a role in the European movement.

In the evolution of the Luxembourg diplomatic service after the war two stages can be discerned. These are complementary and are both linked to two prestigious personalities of Luxembourg's political life. The first stage corresponds to the work of European unification and is linked to the personality of Joseph Bech. Sole survivor of the pre-war diplomatic service, he succeeded, thanks to his firm belief in Europe and his diplomatic *savoir faire*, as well as his personal friendships with Adenauer, R. Schuman and Spaak, to lift Luxembourg diplomacy to new heights. The city of Luxembourg developed, provisionally, into the capital of the ECSC (1952). Luxembourg watched, regretfully, the failure of the European Defence Committee (1954), but L. Schaus played an active role in the European revival at the Messina Conference of 1956.[26] But at the crucial moment, when in 1958 it came to choosing the definitive site for the European Institutions, the Luxembourg diplomats hesitated, took fright at their own audacity and withdrew. Brussels was chosen, though some services were maintained in Luxembourg, which remains one of the capitals of the Common Market.

At the end of the sixties Luxembourg's international horizons were widened. This was due in part to the arrival of Gaston Thorn in the Ministry of Foreign Affairs in 1969, and in part to the slowing down of European unification and the growing economic difficulties faced since 1973. Thus both subjective factors, the personality of a man and external causes, have pushed Luxembourg towards the open sea. Assuming responsibilities on behalf both of Luxembourg and of the wider international community, Thorn gave an extraordinary boost to the Luxembourg diplomatic service. He inaugurated the era of all-out diplomacy.

And the management side of all this? The law of 1947 created a diplomatic career but it did not establish the structure of the Ministry. An embryonic form dates from before the war and Ministers like Joseph Bech did little to develop it. Of a pronounced empirical nature, Bech preferred to work with men rather than structures. The prerogatives remained only loosely designated, changing with the needs of the moment and ministerial directives. It was just after the war that a group of young men entered the Ministry, and shaped it during the 1950s and 60s before going elsewhere, some to international organizations (C. Calmes, P. Pescatore, A. Borschette, N. Hommel, C. Reichling), others to legations where they represent their country (G. Heisburg, C. Dumont, P. Reuter, P. Wurth). It is as a result of their influence that the necessary structures were formed. One sees appearing at the beginning of the fifties the division of the Ministry into three sections that still correspond to today's three directorates (Political and Cultural Affairs; International Economic Relations and Cooperation; Protocol, Administration and Legal Matters).[27] The early sixties saw the inauguration of the post of secretary-general, held for the first time by P. Pescatore, then by N. Hommel, C. Dumont, P. Wurth, C. Reichling, and at the present time by J. Wagner. Gaston Thorn introduced, in the early seventies, the post of principal private secretary (chef de cabinet). With the formation of the new government in June 1979 there appeared for the first time a Secretary of State for Foreign Affairs (Paul Helminger, former legation counsellor and Thorn's principal private secretary). At the end of 1980, with the departure of Gaston Thorn to assume the responsibilities of President of the EEC Commission in

Brussels, a woman for the first time took up the portfolio of Foreign Affairs: Colette Flesch, former mayor of the city of Luxembourg.

At the present time (1981), the Ministry of Foreign Affairs consists of 31 people (ministers plenipotentiary, counsellors, secretaries, legation attachés and heads of chancellery) posted abroad, and 45 people (of whom 15 have a university training), occupying the Ministry of Foreign Affairs in Luxembourg.

Parallel with the rise of the Ministry has been an extension of diplomatic representations. In 1946, 25 countries were represented in Luxembourg, of which five (Belgium, USA, France, Great Britain and Italy) were directly represented with residences in Luxembourg, and the others through the intermediary of their representative in Brussels. In 1967, 70 countries were represented, of which 10 had direct representation, while in 1981 these figures had risen to 124 and 21 respectively. The countries directly represented in Luxembourg by a minister plenipotentiary are: Austria, Belgium, Bulgaria, Spain, USA, France, Germany (Bonn), Great Britain, Ireland, Italy, Netherlands, Portugal, Soviet Union, Switzerland. Seven countries are represented by a chargé d'affaires: China (Peking), Denmark, Greece, Romania, Turkey, Yugoslavia and Zaire.

Luxembourg has also increased its representations abroad. In 1946 it had eight legations, in 1981 it has twelve. It is represented by a resident ambassador in Germany (Bonn), Austria, Belgium, USA, France, Great Britain, Italy, the Netherlands, Switzerland, Spain and the Soviet Union; in China it has a chargé d'affaires. There are seven permanent representations to international organizations (OECD, NATO, the European Council, EEC, the United Nations, GATT, UEO) but five are carried out by an ambassador already based in the capital in question. Certain ambassadors carry out several functions: the ambassador in residence in Washington is also accredited to Ottawa and Mexico, that in Moscow is accredited to Warsaw and Helsinki. All in all, Luxembourg has direct representation in 26 countries – that is, in those countries it does not use the services of the Netherlands. A little country like Luxembourg cannot be omnipresent. It is for this reason that the 1880 agreement with the Netherlands has lost none of its value.[28]

Final reflections
This contribution has tried above all to emphasize the difficulties a small country has experienced, less perhaps in creating foreign policies than in putting them to work. The obstacles are obviously numerous. When all is taken into account, however, they can be seen to stem from the same source, the smallness of the country. In the nineteenth century and in the first half of the twentieth, Luxembourg had to struggle to gain acceptance by the international community, which for its purposes was still by and large the European community. At the time of the debates concerning the Grand Duchy's membership of the League of Nations, the British delegate cast doubts on the viability of so small a country and on its ability to fulfil international obligations.[29] It is true that since that time even smaller countries have been accepted by the United Nations, as have larger states that lack the moral cohesion, the cultural traditions and the economic means essential to the formation of a nation, which Luxembourg has so often proved it possesses.

The Luxembourg of the second half of the twentieth century has made notable efforts to fulfil its international obligations and to play an honourable role in the concert of nations. A 'Classification according to participation in international organizations' of the various nations (1965) places Luxembourg twelfth, just below the USA and Spain but above Sweden and Brazil. In 1977–8 Gaston Thorn was President of the General Assembly of the United Nations. In January 1981 he took up the duties of President of the EEC Commission. That is an international scope of action closely linked to personal factors. From this can be concluded that Luxembourg must always have at its disposition one or two first-rate individuals. It has had such personalities during the course of the last generations with J. Bech, Pierre Werner (better known in the world of international finance), Gaston Thorn and C. Flesch. Fortunately the country has assured them the political longevity necessary for the outside world to associate their names with the Grand Duchy. But beyond what may after all seem a single, individual exploit, there is the effort of the whole staff (the Ministry of Foreign Affairs and the other ministries concerned). In turn, each member nation of the EEC assumes for six months the Presidency of the Council of Ministers (for example, Luxembourg held this post from July to December 1980). This means an enormous multiplication of duties which the large countries can assume without difficulty thanks to a plethora of diplomats and experts, and which Luxembourg has fulfilled most honourably with a mere handful of civil servants bearing a wide range of responsibilities.

Public opinion has taken its time to understand the problems of external politics and to accept the financial consequences. Not so long ago, the Minister of Foreign Affairs was accused of travelling too much. Since then, the economic crisis, which has struck the Luxembourg iron and steel industry such heavy blows, has opened the eyes of many Luxembourgers to the close relationship between foreign policies and external commerce. It is more important than ever for the Ministry of Foreign Affairs to assert the 'presence' of Luxembourg, for the small powers are more easily forgotten than the great.

NOTES

[1] On the basis of the old Duchy of Luxembourg, without the territories situated to the east of the Moselle, the Sûre and the Our but with the addition of the dukedom of Bouillon, 7077 sq. km. and 213 000 inhabitants.

[2] Royal decree of 31 December 1830, in *Mémorial administratif du Grand-Duché de Luxembourg*, 1831, 2–4.

[3] Article 6 of the royal decree of 31 December 1830.

[4] Royal decree of the Grand Duchy of 13 September 1841, in *Mémorial . . .*, 1841, 321–2.

[5] See A. Calmes, *La création d'un Etat (1841–1847), Histoire contemporaine du Grand-Duché de Luxembourg*, 4 (Luxembourg 1954), 80.

[6] Notice of 9 November 1941 published in *Mémorial . . .*, 1841, 453–4.

[7] Ch. Calmes, *1867. L'affaire du Luxembourg* (Luxembourg 1967).

[8] A. Calmes, 'Des conseillers de légation aux ambassadeurs' in *Au fil de l'histoire*, 2 (Luxembourg 1971), 77–86.

[9] A Calmes, *Le premier consul du Grand-Duché*, ibid., 206–11.

[10] In relation to the important immigration from Luxembourg to the United States.

[11] Family pact concluded between the Nassau branches in 1783.

[12] See *Annuaire officiel du Grand-Duché de Luxembourg pour 1911*. The establishment of a Minister for Italy is a consequence of the important immigration of Italians to Luxembourg. See also G. Trausch, 'L'immigration italienne au Luxembourg des origines (1890) à la grande crise de 1929' in *Risorgimento*, 1980, No. 1, 7–31.

[13] The head of the government had the title of state minister, while the other members of the Cabinet were called simply director-general.

[14] See his *Das Staatsrecht des Grossherzogtums Luxemburg* (Tübingen 1910).

[15] *La Meuse*, 29 March 1912.

[16] *Escher Tageblatt*, 9 February 1917.

[17] See G. Trausch, 'Contributions à l'histoire sociale de la question du Luxembourg' in *Hemecht. Revue d'histoire luxembourgeoise*, 1974, 5–118.

[18] See G. Trausch, 'Les relations franco–belges à propos de la question luxembourgeoise (1914–1922)' in *Les relations franco-belges de 1830 à 1934. Actes du Colloque de Metz 15–16 novembre 1974* (Metz 1975), 275–93. See also Ch. Calmes, *Le Luxembourg au centre de l'annexionnisme belge* (Luxembourg 1976).

[19] H. Loutsch, 6 November 1915–24 February 1916; V. Thorn, 24 February 1916–19 June 1917; L. Kauffman, 19 June 1917–28 September 1918; E. Reuter, 28 September 1918–20 March 1925.

[20] *La question du Luxembourg* (Bern 1918), 1.

[21] See on this subject A. Wehrer, 'L'histoire du Luxembourg dans une Europe divisée 963–1945. Notre politique étrangère d'une guerre mondiale à l'autre', in *Le Conseil d'Etat du Grand-Duché de Luxembourg. Livre jubilaire* (Luxembourg 1957), 195–239.

[22] Joseph Bech, head of the government from 1926 to 1937 and from 1953 to 1958, Minister of Foreign Affairs from 1926 to 1959. On his foreign policy, see G. Trausch, *Joseph Bech. Un homme dans son siècle* (Luxembourg 1978).

[23] Article 26 of the convention held on 25 July 1921, which created an economic union between Belgium and Luxembourg.

[24] *Compte rendu des séances de la Chambre des députés 1946–1947*, col. 1377–1387, see annex, 490–2, and *Mémorial . . . 1947*, 697.

[25] Decree of the Grand Duchy of 28 May 1948 concerning the organization of the external services of the Ministry of Foreign Affairs, *Mémorial . . . 1948*, 805–7.

[26] See the book *Lambert Schaus, Luxembourg. Belgique. Europe* (Luxembourg 1977).

[27] See the *Guide du Ministère des Affaires étrangères et du Commerce extérieur* (Luxembourg).

[28] Treaty between Luxembourg and the Netherlands relating to cooperation in the domain of economic representation, signed 24 March 1964. See *Mémorial . . . 1965*, 1003–6 and *Compte rendu des séances de la Chambre des députés 1964–1965*, 1, col. 2756–2760 and 1963–1964, and 2,2026–35. For the arrangement of 1880, based on a simple exchange of letters, see *Compte rendu*, op. cit., 1879–80, 1, 724–32, 821–61, 864–921.

[29] O. Griessinger, *Die volkerrechtliche Stellung Luxemburgs nach dem Versailles Vertrag* (Würzburg 1927).

BIBLIOGRAPHY

See the series of *Compte rendu des débats de la Chambre des députés*, since 1842; the *Mémorial of the Grand-Duché de Luxembourg* (official journal) since 1815. The *Annuaire officiel*, which has appeared since 1910 (with the exception of the war years) is very useful. For the post Second World War period see the *Bulletin de documentation*, edited since 1945 by the Ministry of State. For a general view see G. Trausch, *Le Luxembourg à l'époque contemporaine. Du partage de 1839 à nos jours*, 2nd edn (Luxembourg 1981).

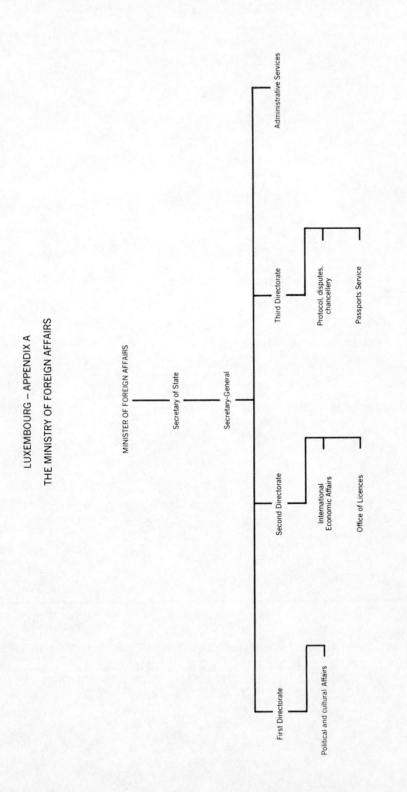

LUXEMBOURG – APPENDIX A

THE MINISTRY OF FOREIGN AFFAIRS

MINISTER OF FOREIGN AFFAIRS

Secretary of State

Secretary-General

First Directorate

Political and cultural Affairs

Second Directorate

International Economic Affairs

Office of Licences

Third Directorate

Protocol, disputes, chancellery

Passports Service

Administrative Services

Netherlands

The Foreign
Policy Institutions in the
Dutch Republic
and the
Kingdom of the Netherlands
1579 to 1980

C. B. WELS

Dr Cornelis Wels is senior lecturer in modern history at the University of Utrecht. He is editor of *Bescheiden betreffende de buitenlandse politiek van Nederland, 1848–1870* (1972), a collection of foreign policy documents of the Netherlands prepared for the State Committee on Dutch history. He is also the author of several publications on Dutch foreign policy and on the development of the representative system in the Netherlands during the nineteenth century.

The Kingdom of the Netherlands dates from 1813, and the present Ministry of Foreign Affairs from 1814. The Netherlands has, however, existed as an independent state since 1579. In the first century of its existence, or 'Golden Age' as it is often called, the Republic of the United Netherlands was a power of the first rank. Its constitution made it unique in Europe and the way in which foreign policy was established differed greatly from practices elsewhere. The officials and institutions involved in policy-making were forerunners of the Ministry founded in 1814. In four centuries of independence, traditions have grown up that survive to this day and that influenced the establishment and working of the institutions that served first the Republic and then the Kingdom in their relations with the rest of the world. The development of these institutions is therefore sketched against the background of international relations.

The office of the greffier of the States General and the chancellery of the grand pensionary of Holland (1579–1795)

There are three periods to be discerned in the foreign policy of the Republic of the United Provinces. The first began in 1579, the year in which the seven provinces united in the Union of Utrecht to continue the struggle against Spain, and ended with the Treaty of Westphalia in 1648, which affirmed the Republic's independence in international law. During these years of conflict with Spain, Dutch foreign policy was inspired mainly by religious motives. The Republic was concerned to form a Protestant front against the Catholic Habsburgs of Spain and Austria.

After 1648 the Republic took its place among the great powers and pursued a more pragmatic policy in which the commercial interests of the influential Province of Holland were the dominant factor. Foreign policy was primarily directed towards remaining aloof from European conflicts to prevent the disruption of Dutch trade and shipping. Only when its commercial interests were threatened or the balance of power was in danger did the Republic resort to action. Such was the case when Danish supremacy in the Baltic was brought to an end in about 1650 and when alliances were formed against Louis XIV. While the Province of Holland was trying to keep the Republic free of international entanglements in Europe, the stadtholders of the House of Orange thought in more continental terms. Their dynastic interests and their position as commanders-in-chief of the army of the Republic (the fleet was primarily the concern of the Province of Holland), played a part in their aspirations. In consequence, the international tensions in Europe affected the position of the princes of Orange as stadtholders. The foreign policy pursued by the Republic thus readily became an issue in internal political conflicts.

The end of the War of the Spanish Succession (Treaty of Utrecht, 1713) marked the beginning of the third period. As a consequence of the debilitating wars with France and economic stagnation, the Republic lacked the financial means needed to play a significant role in Europe. The policy of non-involvement, which had been of particular advantage to France in the second half of the eighteenth century, now became a permanent feature. Even before the Republic had attained independence Hugo Grotius had laid the basis for the international law that was to occupy a central position in Dutch foreign policy. Both respect for international law, which implied stabilization of the existing relations between countries, and protection of the freedom of the seas accorded perfectly with the interests of the Republic.

The seven provinces that formed the Republic of the United Provinces of the Netherlands from 1579 to 1795 were more or less autonomous in terms of their internal affairs. Only in matters pertaining to military organization and foreign policy did they take united action. The Council of State was entrusted with the task of maintaining relations with foreign powers. Before the revolt the Council had acted as an advisory body to the sovereign. After the renunciation of allegiance to Philip II of Spain the Council of State became the executive body representing the whole of the Republic. The States General charged the Council of State with the following responsibility: 'To preserve good correspondence, friendship and neighbourly relations with foreign princes and lords, neighbouring republics, countries and towns by the means which they shall deem the most fitting for the advancement of the industry and trade of these lands.'

The Council of State was chaired by the stadtholder and took decisions on the basis of a majority vote. By the middle of the seventeenth century, however, the Council had largely lost its control of foreign policy, as two factors had eroded its authority. First, the Council had no financial resources of its own: the financial contributions of the provinces for their common foreign policy and joint military operations were fixed by the States General, which also took a hand in the allocation of the money. Furthermore, Holland, the most powerful of the provinces, which also provided the most money, was disinclined to entrust its interests to a body in which it could be outvoted. In addition to that, under the terms of an alliance with England the Council had two English members for a number of years, which effectively ruled out confidential discussions. As a result of these factors, the administration of foreign affairs shifted in the first half of the seventeenth century to the States General, which was a permanent assembly of representatives of the provinces, in which decisions could only be taken on the basis of unanimity. The Council of State began to focus its attention on military matters, which in times of tense international relations or of war naturally had many points of convergence with foreign policy.

Such an unwieldy body as the States General was, however, unable to provide the dynamic leadership required by the Republic as a major power in the seventeenth century. Not only were the members constantly compelled to refer back to their principals, the provinces that had delegated them, but the conditions of secrecy also left much to be desired. On controversial issues particularly, members of the States General often yielded to the temptation to influence decisions by indiscretion, even in their conversations with foreign diplomats. A secret committee of the States General was for a time entrusted with negotiations in 1585; after that it gradually became normal practice in the first half of the seventeenth century to delegate the administration of foreign affairs to a permanent secret committee (secreet besogne) in which all the provinces were represented. The stadtholder, who through lacking sovereign powers nevertheless possessed considerable authority, usually took part in their deliberations.

After the death of Frederik Hendrik in 1647, the influence of the stadtholder was diminished and the secret committee fell into disuse. Instead, the States General apportioned responsibility for foreign affairs among various committees *(gecommitteerde raden)*, formed from its members, which were charged with the task of maintaining relations with one particular country or of arranging negotiations. Every province was represented in these committees, several of which might be active at any one time. In addition, Holland was represented on all the committees by its grand pensionary, the highest-ranking dignitary of the province. By this means the grand pensionary became a key figure in the foreign policy of the Republic. He was the only one who could command a comprehensive view of the various committees, with their often vaguely defined areas of competence, and coordinate their activities. Formally, however, foreign envoys were accredited to the States General and they maintained official relations with the greffier of the States General. The States General also appointed diplomats, though the grand pensionary had considerable influence in their selection. In addition to approximately ten clerks, both the greffier and the grand pensionary of Holland had two or three secretaries in their service. Their duties, however, were only partly concerned with foreign affairs.

Netherlands' envoys maintained three types of correspondence with the authorities in the Republic. First, they wrote public missives *(publieke missieven)* that were read out in the States General and contained no information that required secrecy. Second, they directed secret missives *(geheime missieven)* to the greffier of the States General. However, since these could be read by the secret committees, secrecy could not be guaranteed in this case either. Third, there were the private letters *(particuliere missieven)* to the chancellery of the grand pensionary: matters of importance were dealt with in this private correspondence, particularly in the days when the grand pensionary could still exert great political influence.

To sum up, it may be said that the guidelines for the Republic's foreign policy were laid down by the grand pensionary in consultation with the greffier and the committees. Sometimes the Council of State was also involved in the preparation of foreign policy. Much depended on the capacities of the various people concerned and their interrelationship; sometimes the grand pensionaries (Johan van Oldenbarnevelt and Johan de Witt) or the stadtholders (Frederik Hendrik and William III) predominated, and sometimes the greffier (François Fagel) exerted the greatest influence on foreign policy. It was, however, the greffier who was charged with the practical administration of foreign policy: his office took care of the official correspondence, was responsible for personnel and finances, and attended to matters of protocol. It may thus be regarded as the forerunner of the present Ministry of Foreign Affairs.

The Bureau of the Agent for Foreign Affairs established in 1798

With the arrival of the French in 1795 the Republic of the United Provinces succumbed to its internal weaknesses. It was replaced first by the Batavian Republic (1795–1806) and then by the Kingdom of Holland under the rule of Napoleon's brother (1806–10). Both were in fact vassal states of France. There was no question of their pursuing an independent foreign policy. The offices of stadtholder, grand pensionary and greffier, which had been concerned with foreign policy in the old Republic, were abolished. However, the most important committee for foreign affairs continued to exist, under a new name and with different officials, and even acquired the powers that had once belonged to the grand pensionary. Working on a committee basis, as had been usual under the former Republic, harmonized perfectly with the revolutionary practice of forming committees to handle the most diverse affairs of state. In 1798 the first constitution of the Batavian Republic came into force. Executive powers were now vested in a directory, which delegated foreign affairs to an 'agent'. He had a permanent bureau at his disposal, which may be regarded as the first Ministry of Foreign Affairs. The title of the agent was changed in 1801 to secretary of state, and in 1806 to Minister for Foreign Affairs. Although the duties of these functionaries were constantly changed, the Ministry, which employed about twelve officials, continued in existence until 1810, when the Netherlands was annexed by France.

Diminishing significance of foreign policy – impact on the Ministry (1813–1848)

When, in the autumn of 1813, the French armies were defeated by the Allies, two Orangist aristocrats proclaimed the independence of the Netherlands at The Hague. William of Orange, son of the last stadtholder, became sovereign prince. In 1814 he and his secretary of state for foreign affairs, Van Hogendorp, gave priority to restoring foreign relations so as to be in a favourable position in the peace negotiations. Mainly at the instigation of Great Britain, the great powers decided at the Congress of Vienna to enlarge the Dutch state by combining with it the former Austrian Netherlands. The new kingdom, together with the German Confederation, was to form a buffer zone around France. This extension of its territory meant that the Netherlands became directly involved in maintaining the balance of power in Europe, a change of course from the traditional attitude of the Republic, when foreign policy was directed towards keeping clear of continental conflicts.

The wide differences in their economy, religion and mentality stood in the way of the integration of the northern and southern Netherlands, and the great powers were concerned about the viability of the new state. The Kingdom's close relations with Britain formed the basis for Dutch foreign policy after 1813. From 1820 onwards, however, London's interest in the Continent gradually waned, enabling William I to concentrate on implementing his policy of independence, which gave priority to promoting prosperity.

In the period 1823–8, despite the continuing rivalry between north and south, the Kingdom moved towards unification. The King, who had felt patronized by the great powers and their congress policy, felt that the time was ripe to improve the position of the Netherlands in Europe. In 1829, however, opposition to his rule grew rapidly in the south, and the following year the rebellion broke out that was to lead to the independence of Belgium. William turned for support to the powers that had created his kingdom in 1814. Because of the changing international situation, however, the great powers, and particularly Great Britain, had less to gain than in 1814 from the union of the northern and southern Netherlands, and were prepared to do no more than supervise the process of partition. For years William kept a large army in readiness in the hope that there would be a clash between the Holy Alliance and the Western powers that would furnish him with the opportunity to regain Belgium, though he was not supported in his aspiration by public opinion in the north.

Belgium's status as an independent kingdom was finally affirmed in 1839 by the Treaty of London. The House of Orange nevertheless clung to its claim, thus complicating the country's foreign policy. Since 1830 the Netherlands had regressed to the position of a third-rate state and had lost all confidence in the great powers, particularly Britain. For a time the country managed to maintain its former status in its dealings with other countries, but it gradually lost ground, especially in the commercial sector, where it was forced to yield some of its former advantages and relinquish monopolies with every commercial transaction. The uncertainty concerning its position in the community of European states led some Dutchmen to lose faith in their national identity.

In the 1815 Constitution sole responsibility for the conduct of foreign affairs was vested in the King (William I 1813–40, William II 1840–49), probably as a reaction to the system that had prevailed in the Republic, when it was not unusual for dispatches and instructions to be passed on from one dignitary to another. Agreements with foreign powers did not have to be communicated to the States General, whose approval was required only in cases involving the exchange or surrender of territories in peacetime. Budgets were fixed by the States General for ten-year periods until 1840, and after that for two years. There were seven or eight state departments.

From 1815 onwards the head of the Department of Foreign Affairs had the rank of Minister. Until 1848 ministers were servants of the King and could not be called to account by the States General. The activities of the various departments or ministries were coordinated by the general secretary of state, whose office functioned as a super-ministry. William I delegated very little work to his ministers. His own boundless energy enabled him to keep a firm grip on even the most intricate details in the implementation of his policies, with the aid of the Secretariat of the King and the office of the general state secretary. The King devoted a great deal of his energies to foreign affairs, and his efforts in this field were only limited by the physical impossibility of his dealing with all the documents singlehanded. It was not unusual for the King to correspond with envoys without the mediation of his Minister. Furthermore, it was a regular occurrence for the Minister to be presented with outgoing documents to sign that had been drafted by the King. The way in which the King viewed his role in government activities was expressed in the royal decree of 1814, in which he ordered the envoys to send a copy of all documents intended for the Minister for Foreign Affairs to the Secretariat of the King. In the decree, William I made reference to the practices of the Prussian court on this point during the reign of Frederick the Great.

Early in 1814 Van Hogendorp, the Secretary of State for Foreign Affairs, vigorously set about devising an organizational structure for his Department, including instructions for the individual civil servants and regulations for the foreign service. In an accompanying memorandum to the King dated 25 February 1814 he observed that the Netherlands' new role in Europe 'requires once and for all, diligence and an arrangement of the Ministry such as have never existed before'. Van Hogendorp did not, however, wish to have a cumbersome organization, as had been the case under previous governments, with a 'multitude of divisions and of bureaux within each division'. Two departments should, he believed, be sufficient: one for political and secret affairs, which would be responsible for correspondence with the diplomats;

and one for commercial affairs, correspondence with consuls, financial administration and dispatch. Each department would have its own work schedules and archives.

The Ministry was headed by a Secretary of State, and after 1815 by a Minister. His deputy was the secretary of the Ministry, who in addition to his work in the first of the two departments was responsible for the day-to-day supervision of the Ministry as a whole. The secretary had separate responsibility for keeping a journal that, in addition to reports on current events in the Netherlands, contained news taken from incoming dispatches from Dutch envoys. On the basis of the journal, regular news reports were compiled for diplomatic posts abroad. This information system quickly fell into disuse after 1815, however.

A secretary for secret affairs, whose job it was to edit outgoing documents, was attached to the first department; there was also a senior clerk *(eerste commies)* who was responsible for the work schedule and archives, and a secretary in charge of codes. The second department was headed by a commissioner *(commissaris)* who dealt with the correspondence; he was assisted by a senior clerk *(eerste commies)* for dispatch. The two departments also employed five clerks, two messengers and two porters. There was in addition a *solliciteur* whose duties involved maintaining relations with other ministries, scanning newspapers and pamphlets for information of use to the Minister, and translating documents into English. Moreover, the *solliciteur,* for a consideration, looked after the private interests of diplomats stationed abroad. Between 1816 and 1830 the Ministry, together with all the other ministries and the diplomatic corps, travelled with the court between The Hague and Brussels, where it spent alternate years.

The entire machinery for the maintenance of foreign relations was ambitious, and reflected the view of William I that the Netherlands, compared for example with Prussia, that upstart among the great powers, was underestimated in Europe. This was clear from the structure of the diplomatic service, which closely resembled the system followed by the Republic. In the 1820s the Netherlands had ambassadors in Great Britain and Turkey, envoys or resident ministers in the United States, Bavaria, Denmark, France, Hannover/Saxony, Austria, Portugal, Prussia, Russia, Spain, Switzerland and the German Confederation, and chargés d'affaires in Baden, Brazil, the towns of the Hanseatic League, Naples, Rome/Tuscany and Württemberg. The salaries of these diplomats were such that they could represent their king and country in a manner in keeping with the country's pretensions. During the same period the consular service employed ten consuls-general, 140 consuls and four vice-consuls.

Starting in 1824 all ministries were reorganized. Ranks and salaries were made uniform and general guidelines were drawn up for the keeping of the archives and the internal division of labour. For the Ministry of Foreign Affairs this reorganization entailed the following changes: the secretary received the title of secretary-general and was entrusted with the running of all Ministry affairs. He drew up a work schedule and apportioned tasks among the officials. The two separate departments were abolished and replaced by central archives and one bureau for clerical work. The former secretary for secret affairs, whose most important duty had been to check the style and grammar of documents composed in French, was permitted to retain his title for as long as he remained in Ministry service. The commissioner was given the personal title of chief clerk *(referendaris)* and became deputy to the secretary-general. One clerk *(commies)* was responsible for allocating clerical work, and another for protocol and the archives. In addition there were six junior clerks *(adjunct-commies)*: one for dispatch, one for accounting and the rest for editing and clerical activities. The secretary concerned with codes was difficult to accommodate in the new hierarchical structure and retained his original title, to which the salary of a *referendaris* was attached. The *solliciteur,* whose duties had gradually dwindled to translation into English, ranked as a junior clerk.

As a result of the reorganization, most civil servants had to take a cut in pay. In many cases, however, the King provided compensation in the form of a personal allowance, drawn from the fund for secret expenses. After the previous system of functional organization had been abolished in 1824 there continued to be a certain division of labour that largely corresponded with the civil servants' knowledge of foreign languages. At the same time coding and accounting retained their independence from other duties.

Foreign economic policy was only partly under the control of the Ministry of Foreign Affairs during this period. Until 1834 the promotion of foreign trade and consular reports fell partly within the competence of the Minister of Colonies and National Industry. When this last Ministry was split, for political reasons the National Industry section, with some of its staff, was attached to the Ministry of Foreign Affairs. In 1841 the duties of this department pertaining to the promotion of domestic trade and commerce were divided among other ministries; only foreign economic policy remained permanently in the hands of the Ministry of Foreign Affairs.

The body of civil servants employed at the Ministry and the members of the diplomatic service were entirely separate from each other, though it was usual to place aspirant attachés in temporary positions at the Ministry pending their assignment to a legation. In the 1820s there were only two officials employed at the Ministry who came from the southern Netherlands; when the court was in Brussels a southern junior clerk and porter were added to the establishment. The situation was no different in the diplomatic and consular service. The recruitment of the overwhelming majority of civil servants from the northern provinces was one of the major grievances of the south.

The demotion of the Netherlands to a third-class power after 1830 had far-reaching consequences for both the Ministry and the diplomatic service. Parliament thereafter lost no opportunity for criticizing the disproportionate grandeur of the machinery for foreign affairs. Fuel was gradually added to the fire of this criticism by lack of confidence in the King's foreign policy, opposition to which could only be expressed in budgetary measures. These were the first indications of an attitude that most liberals were to maintain until the end of the century in debating the foreign affairs budget. As they saw it, the Netherlands had no need to take part in power politics, and consequently did not require an expensive diplomatic service. In their eyes the country was better served by chargés d'affaires with sound economic training, and in the less important posts a consular official who could also act as diplomatic representative would be sufficient.

Partly as a result of these criticisms, the number of missions was reduced by five between 1825 and 1850; four diplomatic missions were down-graded and the remuneration of all diplomats was gradually reduced by an average of 25 per cent. The consular service, by contrast, was augmented during the same period. The number of consuls-general was almost doubled, fifteen new consuls were appointed and the number of vice-consuls rose from four to thirty-six. As a result of all these measures the expenditure on diplomatic and consular services was reduced by 50 per cent in the space of twenty years. The Ministry, on the other hand, had increased its staff to cope with the extra work entailed by the addition of the national industry department referred to above and by the closure of the general state secretary's office in 1840. In 1849 the establishment comprised the secretary-general; one chief clerk *(referendaris)*, one first clerk *(hoofdcommies)* acounting section, one senior clerk *(secretaris)* coding (all administrative class); eight clerks in two ranks – four *commiezen* and four *adjunct-commiezen* – (executive class); seven junior clerks in two ranks – three *eerste* and four *tweede klerken* – (clerical class). The four additional junior clerks *(tweede klerken)* had to be engaged to replace the temporary clerks who had been recruited up to that time to assist when there was a particularly heavy workload. In 1849 the budget for Ministry personnel was 370 000 guilders; in 1824 it had been 270 000.

The Ministry during the years of passivity and neutrality (1848–1918)

The year 1848 was a turning point for the Netherlands in both foreign and domestic policy. In 1840 William II had repealed his father's order that the King was to receive a copy of all dispatches. Since then the Minister for Foreign Affairs had given the King a review of incoming diplomatic reports by means of 'morning reports'. William II and then his son, William III (1849–90), continued this practice even after 1848; a formal implementation of the provision in the Constitution to the effect that the ultimate responsibility for foreign affairs remained vested in the King, although the Minister had full political responsibility for the conduct of foreign affairs. The budget was now debated annually. Treaties relating to the exchange or relinquishment of territory had to be approved by the States General; the King merely had to notify them of other treaties. From 1887 onwards, agreements with financial ramifications also had to be submitted to Parliament for approval.

Under the influence of the revolutionary events of 1848, a reconciliation took place between Belgium and the Netherlands that laid the foundations for good relations between the two states and their royal houses. The Netherlands resigned itself to the fact that it was a small power. The unification of Italy and of Germany represented a threat to the smaller states but the Netherlands maintained an even more passive position in these power politics. It proceeded from the principle that respect for international agreements was the best protection for a small country, and for this reason emphasized in its policy the need to reinforce the international legal order. This interest in international law was given a further stimulus at the turn of the century when two peace conferences were held in the Netherlands, and The Hague became the centre of international justice.

In addition considerable attention was given to defending the principle of the freedom of the seas and to combating protectionism, two points of vital importance to a commercial and maritime nation. The Netherlands was the second largest colonial power in the world. When, in the second half of the nineteenth century, colonial possessions took on increased significance there was a revaluation of the international position of the Netherlands. It is symptomatic of this that half the international issues in which the Netherlands was involved between 1870 and 1914 were connected with its colonial position.

Dutch policy at this time was in every way pragmatic: both the strict principle of non-involvement and the predilection for a legal foundation for international relations were fully consistent with the Netherlands' interests. Nonetheless, the conviction grew that this policy was inspired by ethical motives, and that the Netherlands, by its selfless neutrality and its rejection of power politics and secret diplomacy, was called upon to maintain the international legal order and to act as an example to other nations. This conviction was strengthened in the First World War because many people thought the country was left in peace because of its principle of neutrality.

This policy of standing aloof and maintaining neutrality demanded little initiative or activity on the part of diplomats and the officials at the Ministry. Indeed, they often behaved as though the Netherlands was merely an observer of international events. The continual paring down of the budget, and some doubts among members of the Second Chamber about the usefulness of diplomacy, contributed further to the rigidity of the entire structure. Furthermore, after 1830 the Ministry had become a closed shop, with clerk (commies) posts being handed down from father to son, uncle to nephew. The civil servants were not only related by blood or marriage to one another but also, remarkably often, to the lower echelons of the royal household. A significant proportion of them belonged to the ranks of the Huguenots who had fled to the Netherlands and who spoke French at home, at school and in church. Ever since the eighteenth century Huguenots had been employed at the Ministry because of their facility for French, first at the Office of the Greffier of the States General and later within the Ministry.

Recruiting civil servants from this small Hague community ultimately meant that the civil servants' view of the Netherlands and the world was extremely limited. It is also striking that none of them originated from or had ties with an environment in which livings had to be made in trade, shipping or industry. Owing to poor personnel mobility the average age of civil servants increased, coming to a head in 1840 and 1860 when all the top-ranking staff were over sixty. After 1860 staff gradually began to be recruited from other social circles, and at the same time the number of graduates began to increase.

The number of foreign missions, twenty at the start of the nineteenth century, cut back to sixteen in 1850, was increased in 1914 to twenty-two, largely because a number of consulates-general were reclassified as diplomatic posts. Despite poor remuneration, the foreign service had little difficulty in recruiting personnel. From 1846 onwards there was a committee to select applicants; 1860 saw the introduction of an examination for attachés, who spent a year at the Ministry before being posted abroad. From 1840 to 1860 especially, the intake of attachés was so limited as a result of the economies practised that in the following decades staff mobility was non-existent. Ageing and incompetent diplomats had to be kept on for years, which gave Parliament still further grounds for criticism. The attitude of the liberals, who on the one hand did not wish to spend money on the diplomatic service, and on the other had complained of the number of aristocratic diplomats, in fact brought about the opposite of what they wished to achieve: the poor remuneration made private income a more important criterion for admission to the Foreign Service than personal capacities.

Partly as a result of pressure from Parliament, more attention was devoted to the consular service, and the consular department in the Ministry saw spectacular growth during the period from 1870 to 1900. This development was entirely consistent with the Netherlands' requirements as a commercial and maritime power. After a decision, in 1864, to publish the consular reports, the competence of the consuls was reviewed in 1871. A course was set up in 1875, which marked the beginning of the process of professionalization of the consular service. Consuls had to spend a period of in-service training at the Ministry before being posted to the chancellery of an embassy or to a consulate.

The Ministers for Foreign Affairs who had not themselves graduated from the foreign service had a particular need for a member of staff in their immediate vicinity who was familiar with diplomacy from the inside and who could to some extent counterbalance the influence of the civil service. For this purpose, the Office of the Minister *(kabinet)* was established in 1861. The rank of the diplomat who headed it became a bone of contention between the Minister and Parliament in the following years. The Minister wanted a diplomat with experience as head of a mission, while Parliament considered that an embassy secretary with some experience would suffice. Wherever possible, trainee attachés and embassy secretaries who were temporarily available while awaiting a posting would be placed in the Office of the Minister, which thus became an island of the diplomatic service within the Ministry. Against this background it is not difficult to understand why Parliament in 1880 urged the appointment of a top Ministry official as head of the Office of the Minister. The Minister did not comply with this request: he considered diplomatic experience an essential qualification for the post. The duties of the Office were vaguely defined as 'dealing with secret affairs'. The division of labour between the Minister and the head of the Office was informal and was generally determined by the experience of each in the matter in hand. It was easy for the head of the Office, particularly where the Minister was weak, to acquire considerable power. Despite the confidential relations between some Ministers and their Office heads, the Office has remained an integral part of the Ministry and has not become a specific instrument of the Minister.

In 1876 a functional organizational structure was introduced in the Ministry under Van der Does de Willebois. In addition to junior clerks, porters, etc., there were seventeen officials employed at the Ministry. The role and duties of the secretary-general remained unchanged. An adviser was appointed for the first time: the prominent lawyer T. M. C. Asser, who advised the Minister, on request, on matters of international law. The Minister's Office was maintained, and in addition to dealing with secret affairs it was also allocated the following duties: control of code keys, appointment and dismissal of personnel in the diplomatic service and contact with foreign envoys insofar as these were not dealt with by the Protocol Department. A General Secretariat *(Algemeen Secretariaat)* was set up, comprising three offices: 'A' for the work schedule, the archives and records in general, 'B' for protocol and the library, and 'C' for dispatch. In addition, there were new departments: the First for political affairs, the Second for consular and commercial affairs, and the Third for accounts. The division of work between the First Department and the Office of the Minister, which officially came under this department, was more dependent on the officials concerned and the personal preferences of the Minister than on any functional scheme. In 1889 section B of the General Secretariat became the independent Protocol Department. In 1909 the General Secretariat was renamed the Dispatch Secretariat.

The most important changes were effected in the Second Department, attracting a great deal of interest from Parliament. They included a large increase in the establishment. The name of this department was changed in 1886 to Trade Policy and Consular Affairs, indicating that it was expected to make an active contribution to the preparation of foreign trade policy. In 1909 this function was further underlined by the division of the department into two bureaux: one for consular affairs and one for trade policy. The shift in emphasis related on the one hand to the rising tide of protectionism, over which a careful watch had to be kept, and on the other hand to changes in the Dutch economy, where attention now had to be given to agricultural exports and industry as well as to the more traditional interests of the country, trade and shipping. During this period, inter-ministerial coordination of foreign trade policy and the involvement of industry by means of advisory bodies were continually under discussion.

It is interesting to note here that most secretaries-general between 1840 and 1940 came from the Trade Affairs Department. They formed a counterbalance both to the Ministers and to the head of the Minister's Office and the head of the First (political) Department, who were usually complete laymen in the field of economics.

In the meantime, international law was burgeoning in the Netherlands, partly as a result of the peace conferences. The diplomatic service, the Ministry of Foreign Affairs and the Ministry for the Colonies witnessed the influx of a generation of qualified lawyers with a keen interest in international legal questions. At the outbreak of the First World War, the Ministry had specialized civil servants at its disposal who could defend the country's neutrality in expertly worded notes to the belligerent powers. On the other hand it may be said that the principle of non-involvement and standing aloof had weakened awareness of the reality of foreign policy both in the diplomatic service and at the Ministry.

If we compare the 1914 Ministry with Van Hogendorp's creation a century before, we see that though the establishment had risen to forty-five, the functional structure had lost none of its simplicity. At the outbreak of the First World War the Netherlands declared its neutrality and at the same time set about mobilizing its military forces. During the war years the army was kept at full strength, leaving the belligerent powers in no doubt about the country's readiness to defend itself. However, it was not its consistent policy of neutrality that kept the Netherlands out of the war, but rather the strategic and economic interests of the belligerents. The German government attached more importance to maintaining contact with countries outside Europe via the neutral Dutch ports than to seizing military control of the Rhine–Scheldt delta, which the German military command urged on a number of occasions. Britain, traditionally averse to operations on the Continent, and in any case lacking the necessary means, was content as long as the delta did not fall into German hands.

It was above all the economic aspects of the war that posed great problems for the Netherlands. The country was wholly dependent on Germany for imports of chemicals and coal and its exports of agricultural produce, while its lines of communication with the rest of the world, and thus with its colonies, were controlled by Britain. While Germany did its utmost to exploit Dutch neutrality in its imports and exports, Britain in turn continually tightened its contraband regulations. As the war continued the belligerents made such a mockery of the law of neutrality that eventually nothing remained of the Netherlands' policy but a series of tactical concessions that enabled the two sides to reap equal benefits from Dutch neutrality. Germany's declaration of unrestricted submarine warfare in 1917 and the commandeering of Dutch ships in British and US ports in 1918 effectively put an end to the Dutch claims to neutrality at sea.

Maintaining neutrality meant a considerable increase in the activities of the Ministry of Foreign Affairs. The numerous protests about violations of neutrality, while having little or no effect, were nonetheless significant as a contribution to the interpretation of the law of neutrality. Although Loudon, the Minister for Foreign Affairs, and his staff ably defended Dutch neutrality in their notes, the policy as a whole was not always a convincing one, as the Minister adhered too strictly to the letter of the law in critical situations and paid too little heed to political reality. He was supported in his conduct of affairs by his Ministry officials who, after many years of the non-involvement policy, had only a tenuous grasp of power politics. Thus a tendency emerged at the Ministry to view the strict observation of neutrality based on international law as an end in itself, rather than a means of staying out of the war. On a few occasions the chairman of the Council of Ministers had to step in to persuade the Minister for Foreign Affairs to make tactical concessions on the point of the law of neutrality to prevent military intervention by Germany.

In the early stages of the war there was disagreement between the First (political) Department and the Second (consular and commercial affairs) Department about the allocation between them of the many new tasks facing the Ministry. It was soon normal practice for the First Department to be responsible for diplomatic notes about violations of neutrality, and the Second Department for consultation on matters relating to blockades and transit traffic. As the Dutch government did not wish to give its support to any measures that were at variance with the law of neutrality, the NOT (Netherlands Overseas Trust Company) was founded. Though it controlled practically all foreign economic relations, it was officially only an instrument of cooperation for trade and industry. The NOT gradually developed into a state within a state in the foreign trade area. The many new tasks assigned to the Ministry led to a gradual increase in the establishment, which was partly effected by temporarily transferring officials from the diplomatic and consular services to the Ministry in The Hague.

The Ministry in the inter-war years and during the Second World War (1918–1945)

The end of the war in 1918 coincided with a change of government. Now a capable and resolute figure made his entrance into the Ministry of Foreign Affairs in the person of H. A. van Karnebeek. Van Karnebeek had decided political views and, in addition, considerable experience from previous posts in public administration and the conduct of foreign policy. He was confronted at once by three major problems: the international isolation of the Netherlands as a consequence of its neutrality; the annexation demands of Belgium (for South Limburg and Zeeland Flanders); and the need to restore foreign trade relations. By effecting a rapid transition to active diplomacy and allowing for the direct participation of Dutch trade and industry, van Karnebeek achieved success in all three areas. He wished to accede to the Belgian request for a revision of the 1839 Treaty of London (which governed the partition of the Low Countries), while rejecting Belgium's territorial demands. He was convinced that stable relations with Belgium would benefit the political equilibrium of Western Europe as a whole. The revision treaty was rejected by the Upper House in 1927, however, and van Karnebeek resigned. In the meantime the Netherlands had joined the League of Nations. The judicial organs of the League of Nations were established in The Hague, and Dutch nationals filled a number of important posts in the League's organization, which enhanced the international standing of the country.

On assuming office, van Karnebeek at once set to work on the radical reorganization of the Ministry necessitated by the vastly increased workload and the substantial changes in the nature of its work. The division into two departments, which had existed since 1876, was phased out in 1918 and 1919. The greatest change was to the Second Department (consular and commercial affairs), which had been severely criticized during the war by both Parliament and trade and industry. An Economic Affairs Directorate took the place of the Second Department. The new directorate was allotted additional staff to cope with the large amount of work in the economic field occasioned by the end of the war. A Council of Assistance, in which prominent figures in Dutch trade and industry had seats, was set up to facilitate cooperation between the directorate and the world of trade and industry. The Council in fact continued the work of a previous advisory body that had existed during the war. During van Karnebeek's years in office the Economic Affairs Directorate was the focal point for the coordination of foreign economic policy. Here the Ministry of Foreign Affairs took precedence over the ministries responsible for finance, trade, industry and shipping. The directorate's independent position was further strengthened by the fact that it was accommodated in a separate building for a number of years, owing to lack of space in the main building, and had its own secretariat and archives.

The First Department (political affairs) was split into three sections: a Diplomatic Affairs Department responsible for political affairs and the diplomatic service; a Legal Affairs Department; and, after Dutch entry into the League, a League of Nations Department. This last department was assisted by the Advisory Committee on Questions of International Law, which was composed of civil servants and specialists in this branch of law. In the preceding years the committee had been concerned with the organization of the Third Peace Conference; after 1920 it became an advisory body on matters relating to the League of Nations. The influence of the head of the Minister's Office was restricted: he retained responsibility for the codes section, the classified archives and certain administrative duties, but his unofficial function as adviser to the Minister now fell to the head of the Diplomatic Affairs Department. From 1920 onwards the Minister had a secretary, the post being filled by young diplomatic service officers.

By joining the League of Nations the Netherlands had abandoned its policy of non-involvement and neutrality. A more active foreign policy took its place, which van Karnebeek described as a 'policy of independence'. After his resignation the policy was pursued unchanged until the 1930s, when the League of Nations lost its credibility as an instrument for collective security and the Netherlands returned to its traditional policy of non-involvement, which meant that the work of the Ministry also took on a more passive character. The establishment (forty-five in 1914; eighty in 1940) was cut back at the beginning of the thirties, partly as a result of the world economic crisis. In order to economize, the posts of head of the Minister's Office and head of Protocol were combined.

In the course of the thirties responsibility for foreign economic relations was removed in various stages from the Ministry of Foreign Affairs and transferred to the Ministry of Economic Affairs. There were two reasons for this radical change: first, the world economic crisis prompted vigorous efforts on the part of the government to improve the economy and hence trade relations with other countries, which meant a considerable expansion of both the activities and the staff of the Ministry of Economic Affairs; second, van Karnebeek's successors lacked his prestige in the Cabinet, and were no match for forceful colleagues like T. J. Verschuur, the Minister for Economic Affairs, and the financial expert H. Colijn, who headed successive governments in these years. Trade negotiations were thereafter conducted and handled in Parliament by the Minister for Economic Affairs. This change was characteristically expressed in the renaming of the Ministry of Foreign Affairs' Economic Affairs Directorate, which in 1933 reverted to its 1876 name of Consular and Commercial Affairs Department. This shift of authority, which was naturally accompanied by the necessary changes in competence, also had long-term consequences. Both in the recruitment of new staff, which was already restricted to the minimum by the economy drive, and in personnel policy in general little attention was henceforth paid to expertise in economics. Almost two decades later the effects of this oversight were felt in full.

In fact the expertise of the Ministry staff was limited on the whole to the political and legal aspects of foreign policy. There was little conception of ideology or social relations as the driving force in political action, or of the political forces that were becoming apparent in the world outside Europe. Although more than a quarter of the documents handled by the Ministry since the end of the nineteenth century had related to the position of the Netherlands as a colonial power, no specialists had been recruited to deal with this work. The thoughts and actions of the Ministry and foreign service personnel were based entirely on the situation in Europe, even in matters concerning the vital interests of the Netherlands in Asia. Communications in this sector also left much to be desired: reports from the Dutch diplomatic mission in Australia containing important information on behalf of the government of the Dutch East Indies reached the governor-general via the Ministries of Foreign Affairs and of the Colonies in The Hague.

Even when, towards the end of the thirties, it became obvious that war was inevitable, the Netherlands clung to its policy of non-involvement. There was a vague hope that the country might yet manage to stay out of the war, as it had done twenty-five years earlier, and in any case there was no real alternative. Alignment with France and Britain, who were themselves not prepared for armed conflict with Germany, would have offered no effective protection; on the contrary, it would have furnished Berlin with a pretext for launching an attack on the Netherlands. However, whatever illusions The Hague may still have cherished, the German offensive of 10 May 1940 was the hour of truth. The fighting lasted five days, and its course surprised both sides: the Dutch had hoped to be able to hold out until France and Britain could come to its aid, while the Germans for their part had underestimated Dutch resistance and were unable to take the seat of government on the first day as had been planned.

On 13 May 1940, two days before the capitulation, Queen Wilhelmina and her Ministers left for London to continue the struggle from Britain. Immediately after the capitulation the Germans closed the Ministry of Foreign Affairs in The Hague. The staff, dispersed among the other ministries, for a time continued its work, which consisted mainly of promoting the interests of Dutch nationals in countries occupied by the Germans, under the direction of the State Secretary. The Ministry also maintained contact between Dutch authorities and the German Auswärtiges Amt in The Hague. On 11 June 1942 the Ministry of Foreign Affairs was officially abolished by the Germans. The remaining employees were given posts in other government departments.

In London, the Minister of Foreign Affairs E. N. van Kleffens (1939–46) established new administrative machinery in the course of 1940. Its nucleus was the Dutch diplomatic mission in London; later it was extended to include foreign service officers who became available as diplomatic posts elsewhere were closed. When the United States entered the war, the Dutch embassy there was reinforced, Washington now having become a war centre equal in importance to London. Forty-two people were employed in the Ministry in London, eleven of whom were top-grade officials.

On paper, the organization of the Ministry in London was practically identical to the pre-war establishment; in practice, however, the small number of officials there had to carry out the most divergent tasks. For most of them this did not present problems as they nearly all came from the diplomatic service and were not accustomed to the strict division of labour that was the rule in the Ministry. Only the League of Nations Department was omitted from the new structure. In its place came the Post-War Questions Section, which grew in importance as the end of the war approached.

Political reorientation and reorganization (1945–50)

The way in which the Ministry of Foreign Affairs resumed its activities after its return to the Netherlands in 1945 was characteristic of the dilemma then facing the whole of Dutch political and social life. On the one hand there had been a radical break with the pre-war situation in numerous areas – certainly in the conduct of foreign affairs – while on the other hand there was a nostalgic yearning for a return to pre-1940 conditions. This applied in particular to senior officials who in 1945 resumed their former functions.

This ambivalent attitude was also apparent in the rebuilding of the ministerial structure. Although the Netherlands' position in the world had undergone radical changes that had completely altered the nature of the Ministry's work, no fundamental reorganization of the Ministry took place. The pre-1940 structure remained the basis, and the areas of activity and working methods of some departments and sections were modified only when and to the extent that was absolutely necessary.

The most radical change in foreign policy came with the final abandonment of neutrality by working together with other Western countries and, finally, joining NATO. Other areas of foreign policy demanding attention immediately after the war were cooperation within Benelux, membership of the United Nations and participation in Marshall Aid. Although the first steps in this new direction had been taken during the war, it was not until the end of the 1940s that the politicians and the bodies concerned with foreign policy finally came to accept the change after an almost unbroken tradition of two and a half centuries of non-involvement.

Up to 1949 the diplomatic aspect of the liquidation of the Netherlands' colonial relationship with what was to become Indonesia formed an important part of foreign policy. The Ministry and its foreign service had difficulty in finding the right approach to convincing international public opinion of the legitimacy of Dutch policy on the Republic of Indonesia. Once again the Ministry had to face the consequences of its strong European bias and the fact that it had hitherto shown so little interest in Asian affairs. To facilitate consultations between the Ministry in The Hague and the colonial administration in Batavia (Jakarta), the Ministry appointed a special adviser in 1945 to assist the deputy-governor-general. From 1947 to the transfer of sovereignty in 1949 the Ministry maintained its own agency in Batavia, the Far East Department, which had extensive powers. This department provided the Minister for Foreign Affairs with a direct link for consultation with the governor-general, without needing to involve the Minister for the Colonies.

Another change in the organizational structure was the establishment of a separate 'Germany Department' which was responsible for the preparation of a peace treaty with Germany. When developments in Germany took a different turn in 1946, the department was disbanded.

The rest of the Ministry was adapted by stages to suit the new circumstances, culminating in a division into eight departments under the direct authority of the secretary-general. First, the responsibility for matters relating to diplomatic and consular officers, which had been in the hands of the Political Affairs and of the Consular and Commercial Affairs Departments respectively, was transferred to the new Foreign Service Department as part of a plan to combine diplomatic and consular officers and interpreters in a single foreign service corps. The Minister's Office and the Protocol Department, already headed by one person, were now fused to form one department. In addition, a Communications Division, an Internal Affairs Department and an Information Department were set up.

Changes were also made to the two departments dating from 1876: the Diplomatic Affairs and the Consular and Commercial Affairs Departments.

The former was renamed the Political Affairs Department and the latter was split into the Transport and Major Rivers and the Economic Affairs Departments. The Economic Affairs Department, however, had only a very modest role to play in the preparation and implementation of foreign economic policy: the foremost policy centre for economic affairs was the Directorate-General for Foreign Economic Relations, an inter-ministerial agency in which the Ministry of Foreign Affairs was represented alongside other ministries, but which was effectively controlled by the Ministry of Economic Affairs.

As has already been said, the oversights of the pre-war period now took their toll: before the Second World War scarcely any new staff had been recruited for either the Ministry or the diplomatic service, and little care had been taken to ensure that the few who were recruited were interested in financial and economic matters. At a stage when economic ties with other countries were being restored many Netherlands missions experienced a desperate shortage of diplomats with expertise in this field. The need was temporarily met by seconding civil servants from the Directorate-General for Foreign Economic Relations to the missions abroad. In 1950 these people were taken into the foreign service on a permanent basis. The personnel policy of former years was not the only reason that the Ministry of Foreign Affairs did not function as the centre for policy on foreign economic relations: equally important was the fact that the Ministers for Foreign Affairs of this period (1944–8) did not actually regard economic matters as diplomatic territory. Furthermore, from 1946 onwards much of their attention was taken up by the Indonesian question.

The Legal Affairs Department, which had been set up in 1918, was closed down. In practice a separate legal approach to problems, divorced from their political or economic contexts, was not conducive to a balanced or alert foreign policy. Lawyers were now attached to the various departments to advise on the legal aspects of the issues at an early stage of policy preparation. A legal adviser was given the task of coordinating the work of the lawyers in the various departments.

The only motives advanced for closing down the Legal Affairs Department in 1950 related to efficiency: the Ministry was too involved in the prevailing situation to see that the measure could also have been based on reasons of principle. The abolition of the department in fact also marked a change of course in foreign policy, bringing to an end the long period of non-involvement and neutrality. It was also the end of the era in which the Netherlands deemed the strengthening of the international legal order its best guarantee of safety – a belief from the middle of the nineteenth century onwards, which had led to ever-increasing emphasis being placed on the legal aspects of international relations. By paying too much attention to the law, with its tendency to preserve the *status quo*, the Ministry had sometimes overlooked the dynamics of world events. Experts in international law had gradually come to occupy a dominant position at the Ministry, and some of them saw the law not as a means but as an end in itself. Dutch neutrality during the First World War had, however, shown the risks involved in basing policy exclusively on the law without taking the political implications into account.

A Legal and Administrative Affairs Department was set up, but not to carry on the work of the old Legal Affairs Department: the new department was largely limited to dealing with Netherlands citizens abroad or foreigners in the Netherlands.

Organizational structure and personnel in 1949 was as follows: General Management, Secretariat of the Minister 13, Transport and Major Rivers Department 11, Economic Affairs Department 33, Political Affairs Department 34, Information Department 18, Protocol Department 11, Legal and Administrative Affairs Department 23, Foreign Service Department 21, Home Service Department 182, Communications Division 50; total, 396.

The 1950 reorganization

There were two turning points in Dutch foreign policy in 1949: accession to NATO and the transfer of sovereignty over colonial possessions in Asia to the Republic of Indonesia.

After the Second World War no one in the Netherlands wanted to revert to the policy of neutrality that had failed in 1940. The preference was for a world security system within the framework of the United Nations, and the reinforcement of the world legal order that this entailed was perfectly in keeping with the traditions of Dutch foreign policy. The Netherlands would have liked the legal basis of the United Nations reinforced and the elements of power politics within it weakened, partly by increasing the influence of the smaller states (meaning those in Europe and Latin America).

The alternative method of guaranteeing national security – by forming a military or political bloc – did not yet tie in with Dutch thinking. It was only after it had become apparent in central Europe that Russian expansion could not be restrained by the instruments of international law that the Netherlands joined NATO. Since then it has remained a loyal member, and has supported the policies of the most important of the allies, the USA, with conviction. With the exception of Communists, pacifists and in recent years some left-wing social democrats, no single political grouping has questioned NATO membership.

The second event was the loss of colonial possessions in Asia in 1949, together with the West Irian question, which remained unresolved until 1962. After 1945 the Dutch economy, which had hitherto been based on trade and shipping, revolving around transit to and from the German hinterland and the colonies, turned its sights to industrial production. The loss of the colonies spurred on this development. Interest in the overseas world declined, and the significance of European states as trading partners increased. Dutch participation in European economic cooperation should be seen against this background. Although Parliament often professed supra-national ideals for Europe, official policy on this point was less committed. The Minister for Foreign Affairs, Joseph Luns, who put his personal stamp on policy from 1952 to 1971, championed British entry into the European Economic Community to counterbalance West Germany and France. In the sixties the question of whether the Netherlands should orient itself towards the Atlantic or towards Europe became a topic for debate.

Slight shifts in emphasis can be discerned in Dutch foreign policy from 1950 to 1980. Human rights and development cooperation received increased attention as a result of periods of office of two social democrat Ministers from 1973 to 1977: Max van der Stoel at Foreign Affairs and Jan Pronk at Development Cooperation.

In 1950 a general reorganization of the Ministry took place. The rapid increase in personnel after 1945 had completely overwhelmed the organizational structure, which dated from 1919: there were 118 staff in 1946 and 455 in 1950. The workload and the organization were out of step, with the result that it was impossible for the Minister and his senior civil servants to obtain a clear overall picture of the work. Two things operated in favour of the reorganization: the Minister, Dirk Stikker (1948–52), had come from industry and combined clear insight into organizational matters with great drive. In addition, retirement and appointment to posts elsewhere resulted in top jobs at the Ministry becoming vacant, which facilitated the reallocation of responsibilities.

Two organizational models were used in the new structure. As far as possible, policy-making, advisory and administrative functions were kept separate. Where appropriate, work was divided on a regional rather than functional basis. At the same time, the post of State Secretary, sharing full political responsibility with the Minister, was created, as was already the case at other ministries. The aspects of policy for which the State Secretary is responsible depend on his own particular areas of expertise.

The secretary-general remained head of the civil service within the Ministry under the new arrangements. Several new senior posts were created. Two assistant secretaries-general were appointed, one for political and one for administrative affairs. One transport and two legal advisers formed an advisory group. The reorganization took into account the fact that advisers would need to be appointed for other sectors in subsequent years. The Ministry as a whole was divided into three parts: policy departments under the assistant secretary-general for political affairs, administrative divisions under the assistant secretary-general for administrative affairs and the remaining departments directly under the secretary-general.

The policy sector consisted of six departments (the figures in brackets indicate the number of independent sections within the department or division): Information Department (3), European Affairs Department (5), Eastern Affairs Department (3), African and Middle Eastern Affairs Department (2), Western Hemisphere Department (3), International Organizations Department (4). The administrative sector consisted of five divisions: Home Service and Personnel Division (3), Communications Division (4), Mail and Filing Division (3), Accounting Division (4), Research and Documentation Division (3) (set up as part of the reorganization). The following departments came directly under the secretary-general: Foreign Service Department (6), General Affairs Department (5), Protocol Department (3). The head of one of these departments, usually the Protocol Department, also acted as deputy secretary-general. With staff increases from 500 in 1950 to 1600 in 1980, the Ministry has undergone some important changes with the establishment of new departments and sections, but the basic structure has not fundamentally altered since 1950.

Directly after the reorganization the assistant secretary-general for political affairs was appointed director-general, a post that already existed in other Ministries. In 1953 two more directors-general were appointed, one for Indonesia and one for the Economic and Military Aid Programme, which were key areas of policy at the time. These posts were rendered obsolete by subsequent developments and have now been abolished. During the fifties, dozens of officials who had been in service in the former Dutch East Indies joined the Ministry, so both the Ministry and overseas posts were staffed by people who had knowledge and experience of Third World problems, at the very time that the young states in Asia and Africa were beginning to play an independent part in world politics. These officials were not replaced after their retirement in the seventies by experts in the same field.

The present division of labour in the policy sector dates from 1965, when, in addition to the director-general for political affairs, two new directors-general were appointed, one for European cooperation and one for international cooperation. The first controlled all the departments concerned with Dutch relations with European organizations such as the EEC, Euratom and the OECD. The second director-general was in charge of all those departments concerned with international cooperation, such as the United Nations, and the various forms of development cooperation. Further changes affected the advisory posts: in 1971 a roving ambassador was appointed and in 1972 a policy-planning adviser.

In 1974 the civil service side was extended with the appointment of a deputy secretary-general, who took over the work of the assistant secretary-general for administrative affairs. A separate post of Minister for Development Cooperation was created in 1965 and in 1978 an assistant secretary-general was appointed to prepare the way for the integration of Ministry personnel with foreign service personnel.

The organizational emphasis within the existing structure has shifted, particularly in the past decade, as a result of political developments and changing policy. Both directorates-general in the multilateral sector have seen an increase in the scope of their work at the expense of the regional sections, which form part of the Directorate-General for Political Affairs. The Directorate-General for International Cooperation is now by far the largest single unit in the Ministry.

The advent of the development workers and the revolt of the 'referendarissen'

In 1965 a Minister without Portfolio was appointed to be responsible for development cooperation, with several branches of the Ministry of Foreign Affairs at his disposal to carry out his duties. In the 1970s development cooperation came to occupy an important place in foreign policy. The number of civil servants working in this sector increased rapidly and new sections and departments were established under the director-general for international cooperation. Today a quarter of the Ministry's staff is employed in the development cooperation divisions. The budget for development cooperation has become a bone of political contention, and for years now has been at a set rate of 1.5 per cent of net national income, making the Netherlands a front runner in the Western world. Cuts have been made in the Ministry of Foreign Affairs estimates in the last few years, but not in spending on development cooperation.

During the term of office of the Social Democrat, Jan Pronk, as Minister for Development Cooperation (1973–7), the Netherlands sometimes adopted a position in international consultation that was at variance with the policies of other Western European countries. On occasion this gave rise to friction between development policy and general foreign policy, which was the responsibility of the Minister for Foreign Affairs, Max van der Stoel. Among the younger civil servants there was even an ideological rift between the politically committed development cooperation workers on the one hand, and the pragmatic and conservative civil servants of the more traditional branches of the Ministry on the other. Closely bound up with this was the matter of the powers of the foreign service officials in Third World countries *vis-à-vis* the young volunteers working in their areas. The volunteers sometimes claimed that they met with more understanding from the development cooperation divisions at the Ministry than from the staff of the diplomatic missions and the Ministry's regional sections. A decree issued in 1976 by the Minister, which provided for experts from the Ministry to be posted to developing countries – a measure intended to increase the expertise available at the missions – helped to ease the tension. However, there are still organizational problems relating to development cooperation, and it will only be possible to resolve them once it is clear where the experts at the Ministry and the missions, whose promotion is based on performance, stand in relation to the foreign service officials trained for more general work, who are promoted automatically.

Foreign service and Ministry employees have formed two separate units since 1814. A practice has evolved in recent years of detaching a small number of Ministry officials (forty in 1979), often specialists, to missions abroad. Foreign service officials (totalling 500 in 1980) are posted to the Ministry for a few years at various points in their careers (there were sixty-five at the Ministry in 1979). A large number of top posts for which diplomatic experience is required are reserved for them in the policy sector – generally from the rank of 'directeur' upwards.

There are two weaknesses in this system: first that foreign service officials grow out of touch during long absences from the Netherlands and, apart from their diplomatic experience, do not always have the managerial qualities that are indispensable in high Ministry positions; the other is that the promotion prospects of Ministry employees are limited as a result. Minister for Foreign Affairs Joseph Luns, who had little interest in the organization of the Ministry, paid no attention to the widening gulf between the foreign service and the Ministry itself.

The latent dissatisfaction with this state of affairs came into the open in 1971 when younger civil servants *(referendarissen)* mounted a campaign to focus attention on the increasing rigidity in the structure of the Ministry. The revolt of the *referendarissen*, as it was called, even drew attention from outside the Ministry.

The new Minister, the experienced politician Norbert Schmelzer (1971–3), decided in principle in 1972 to abolish the distinction between personnel of the Ministry and of the foreign service, which had already been done in most Western European countries. An assistant secretary-general was appointed in 1978 to take charge of the integration. However, there is still little prospect of forming a single unit in the near future. The motivation for Ministry staff to spend a few years in a distant foreign post is weak, and there are increasing doubts in an age of rapid and intense communication and increasing consultation between experts (within the EEC, NATO, the UN and the North–South dialogue) about whether the all-round diplomat who is re-posted every few years is still what is needed. The indications are that the discussion of integration of the foreign service with the Ministry will thus be influenced by the question of whether the entire system needs to be adapted in order to be able to cope with the needs of the 1980s. This is apparent from criticism from other ministries, political circles and the press, about the present system in areas where particular expertise is required, such as trade promotion, financial consultation and cultural cooperation.

The Ministry and party politics

Apart from exceptional cases in the development cooperation sector, civil servants at the Ministry have never played a political role. As a matter of form civil servants are discreet about their own political views, in keeping with the special position of the Ministry. Their political views generally range from moderate to conservative. The Ministers and State Secretaries of whatever party have always been able to rely on completely loyal civil servants.

Foreign policy has usually played a subordinate part in Dutch politics. Parliamentary debates often concentrate on details, though in recent years there has been growing interest in formulating broad policy on such themes as human rights and the North–South dialogue. The Minister for Foreign Affairs was usually the last to be chosen when a government was being formed. Even long after the Second World War foreign policy was still regarded as a matter that should remain above party politics and the same went for the Ministers. They were always independent of political parties and, if anything, tended to be conservative. It is true that after 1945 the political allegiance of the Minister was taken into consideration, but real 'party Ministers' remained an exception. Only Dirk Stikker (1948–52) the Liberal leader, was a prominent politician, but his appointment as Minister related more to the Indonesian question than to foreign policy as a whole. The various parties have little interest in the foreign affairs portfolio, which rarely offers an opportunity to realize political ideals that would also appeal to the electorate.

Since they did not have a party base, the Ministers for Foreign Affairs were always in a fairly weak position in both government and parliament. Joseph Luns was the exception to this rule, but his strong position was primarily due not to his party ties but to the great personal popularity built up during his seventeen years as a Minister, which he exploited at election time. His successor, Norbert Schmelzer, was the first Minister for Foreign Affairs who had had a long parliamentary career. Now that relations with Third World countries and respect for human rights have become important issues of political debate, it is to be expected that the Ministry will become more politicized. Both in this century and the last, nearly all the Ministers have been products of the diplomatic corps. Because they were unfamiliar with the civil service set-up, and also had little party-political sway, they were often in an isolated position. In such circumstances some Ministers tended to turn to those people with whom they felt at home: their ex-colleagues at the foreign missions. They preferred telephoning a few ambassadors to reading reports by their civil servants or consulting the parliamentary foreign affairs committee.

It is a remarkable fact that all the organizational changes carried out at the

Ministry since 1813 were initiated by the small number of Ministers who had not been in the foreign service. The 1824 reorganization under van Nagell, an ex-diplomat, appears at first glance to be an exception, but in fact the Minister for Foreign Affairs was merely implementing the terms of a royal decree that provided for the reorganization of all the ministries.

Personnel and recruitment
The Ministry and the diplomatic corps, being separate organizations, since 1814 have each recruited their own personnel. For members of the Ministry (administrative class) a university training has been usual since about the middle of the nineteenth century. They do not participate in a competitive examination, and until 1979 had only on-the-job training, though in that year a special two-month training programme was started. Law as a specific subject used to be the norm for members of the Ministry. In the 1970s the figures were approximately: law 56 per cent, economics 16 per cent, political sciences 11 per cent, sociology, history and philology 10 per cent, other subjects 7 per cent; but by 1979 only 33 per cent had law as a subject. Most members of the Ministry come from Leiden University: up to 60 per cent before 1940, about 26 per cent between 1972 and 1976; and in 1979 their number increased again to 38 per cent.

For the diplomatic service a university training has been essential since about 1830. A competitive examination was introduced in 1846, and on admission to the foreign service prospective diplomats stay for a one-year training in the Ministry. Since the 1950s there has been a special 9-month training programme for attachés, who are posted abroad immediately after their examination at the end of the course. Until 1940 nearly all diplomats studied law, although since 1950 their number has gradually been diminishing. The specific subjects of the applicants admitted to the diplomatic service in the 1970s were: law 55 per cent, economics 15 per cent, political sciences 9 per cent, sociology, history and philology 16 per cent, other subjects 5 per cent. By 1979 only 25 per cent of the attachés admitted to the service had law as a specific subject. Leiden University has been the cradle for diplomats for a long time: of the attachés admitted in the 1970s 40 per cent were educated there, and in previous decades the figure was often more than 50 per cent. This number has now (1979) diminished to 18 per cent.

Ministry buildings
In 1813 the Ministry occupied the 'Huis aan de Bassecour', a seventeenth-century house adjacent to the houses of parliament. During the second half of the nineteenth century the building was clearly too small: civil servants often had to work in pitifully cramped conditions. However, in those days the working day was only about five hours, which was less than in the other ministries. The fact that it took so long to resolve the accommodation problem can only be attributed to the lack of interest in foreign policy and the weak position of the Ministers for Foreign Affairs in the government.

Since 1912 the Ministry has been housed in an impressive eighteenth-century building on the Plein in the centre of The Hague. Until 1945 this building was large enough for the relatively small establishment, but the rapid increase in staff after the war made it necessary to move departments elsewhere. The building on the Plein now contains only the offices of the

Ministers, State Secretaries, and a few departments and some reception rooms.

Work has now started on the construction of a large office block to house the Ministry, with room for 1800 civil servants. The new building, which is due for completion in 1984, is situated near Central Station, close to other ministries, the Royal Library and the General State Archives. In a few years the Ministry will have a fine, purpose-built building, fully capable of meeting all the demands made on the central foreign policy organization at the present time.

The reorganizations in perspective

If we compare the organizational model of 1950–65 with the present system, the most striking feature is how little now remains of the former regional set-up. Organization along functional lines has once again gained the upper hand through the concentration of duties into the Directorates-General for European and International Cooperation.

There is now in fact a division of labour according to regions, international frameworks for cooperation and subject matter. This means that the senior staff have to meet periodically to coordinate the activities of the various departments. Such institutionalized methods of consultation, which have gradually come into being, function less efficiently where unexpected political developments require rapid action. This can sometimes mean that embassies are left too long without instructions. Furthermore these frequent consultations are a burden on the senior officials of the Ministry, especially for the secretary-general, who does not have his own department or staff.

It is also true to say that long-term policy planning facilities have been left behind in the overall development of Ministry organization. This is undoubtedly bound up with the fact that top-level officials at the Ministry, who are already overburdened with implementing the details of policy, do not always have sufficient opportunity to draft long-term policy. Moreover, Dutch foreign policy has traditionally responded to events outside the Netherlands, so that in the past there was little scope for autonomous planning. There are also indications of a certain amount of conflict between the extensive expansion of the multilateral sector of the Ministry and the growing nationalism in many parts of the world, which responds well to the bilateral approach.

These difficulties, which have only been sketched briefly here, together with the problems already mentioned in connection with integration and the position of the development cooperation sector, may well mean that the Dutch Ministry of Foreign Affairs will be faced with major organizational problems in the 1980s.

BIBLIOGRAPHY

Little has been published on the subject of the foreign policy institutions of the Republic of the United Provinces of the Netherlands in the seventeenth and eighteenth centuries or of the Ministry of Foreign Affairs in the nineteenth and twentieth centuries. The most comprehensive study is the official report published on the occasion of the structural reorganization in 1950: *Organisatie en reorganisatie van het*

Det.artement van Buitenlandse Zaken (The Hague 1950). Information on the institutional aspects of foreign policy during the Republic is to be found in various chapters of J. Heringa's *De eer en hoogheid van de staat. Over de plaats der Verenigde Nederlanden in het diplomatieke leven van de zeventiende eeuw* (Groningen 1961), M. A. M. Franken's *Coenraad van Beningen's politieke en diplomatieke aktiviteiten in de jaren 1667–1684* (Groningen 1966), and J. Aalbers' *De Republiek en de vrede van Europa, I, Achtergronden en algemene tendenties* (Groningen 1980).

For a survey of the composition and background of foreign service personnel in this century, see J. Niezing's article: 'Diplomatie: een organisatie in beweging' in *Acta Politica*, IV (1969), 139–172 and 248–274. Biographies of nineteenth-century Ministers are contained in M. W. Jurriaanse's *De Nederlandse Ministers van Buitenlandse Zaken 1813–1900* (The Hague 1974). There is also a small book by the same author on the buildings in which the Ministry has been housed since 1813 entitled *Het Logement van Amsterdam. De behuizing van het Ministerie van Buitenlandse Zaken in verleden en heden* (The Hague 1965).

Detailed information on personnel policy has been compiled by the committee appointed to advise on the integration of Ministry and foreign service employees, and is published under the title *Rapport van de commissie van Advies voor de Integratie geïnstalleerd op 8 april 1976 door de Minister van Buitenlandse Zaken* (The Hague 1976).

The State Commission for Dutch History (Rijkscommissie voor Vaderlandse Geschiedenis) has published the most important documents relating to Dutch foreign policy since 1848 in *Bescheiden betreffende de buitenlandse politiek van Nederland 1848–1919* (The Hague 1957–) and its sequel *Documenten betreffende de buitenlandse politiek van Nederland 1919–1945* (The Hague 1976–). In each of the many volumes, each covering a period of a few years, the documents are preceded by an introduction providing information on Ministry and diplomatic service personnel in the period concerned.

English language publications include J. H. Leurdijk (ed.), *The Foreign Policy of the Netherlands* (Alphen aan de Rijn 1978), a collection of articles on various aspects of foreign policy with an extensive bibliography. The T. M. C. Asser Institute in The Hague has published a standard work on the subject of international law: *International Law in the Netherlands* 3 vols (Alphen aan de Rijn, Dobbs Ferry, N.Y. 1978/1980). The most recent work is J. J. C. Voorhoeve's *Peace, profits and principles. A study in Dutch foreign policy* (The Hague, Boston, London 1979). The author also devotes a chapter to the 'Dutch foreign policy system (Ministry of Foreign Affairs, cabinet, parliament, public participation)' and provides a very comprehensive bibliography, including all English-language publications since 1945.

NETHERLANDS – APPENDIX A

THE MINISTRY OF FOREIGN AFFAIRS
(January 1980)

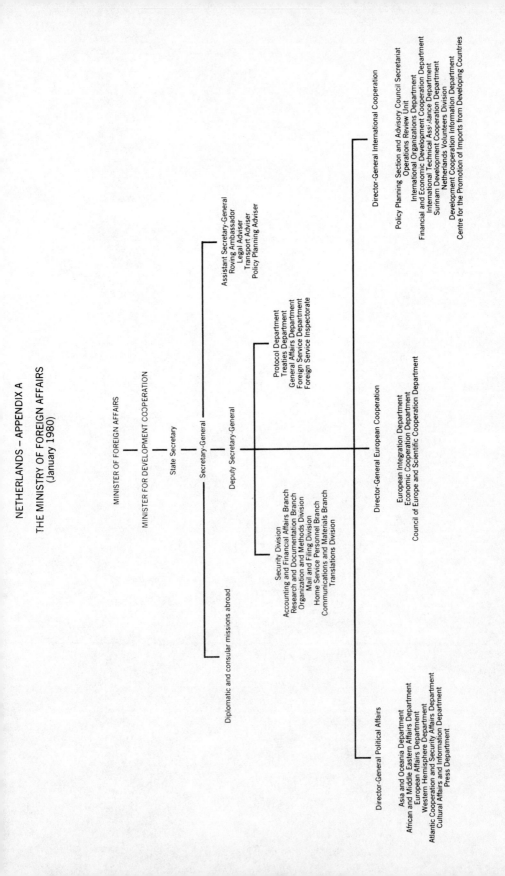

MINISTER OF FOREIGN AFFAIRS

MINISTER FOR DEVELOPMENT COOPERATION

State Secretary

Secretary-General

Deputy Secretary-General

Assistant Secretary-General
Roving Ambassador
Legal Adviser
Transport Adviser
Policy Planning Adviser

Protocol Department
Treaties Department
General Affairs Department
Foreign Service Department
Foreign Service Inspectorate

Diplomatic and consular missions abroad

Security Division
Accounting and Financial Affairs Branch
Research and Documentation Branch
Organization and Methods Division
Mail and Filing Division
Home Service Personnel Branch
Communications and Materials Branch
Translations Division

Director-General Political Affairs

Asia and Oceania Department
African and Middle Eastern Affairs Department
European Affairs Department
Western Hemisphere Department
Atlantic Cooperation and Security Affairs Department
Cultural Affairs and Information Department
Press Department

Director-General European Cooperation

European Integration Department
Economic Cooperation Department
Council of Europe and Scientific Cooperation Department

Director-General International Cooperation

Policy Planning Section and Advisory Council Secretariat
Operations Review Unit
International Organizations Department
Financial and Economic Development Cooperation Department
International Technical Assistance Department
Surinam Development Cooperation Department
Netherlands Volunteers Division
Development Cooperation Information Department
Centre for the Promotion of Imports from Developing Countries

Norway

The Royal Norwegian Ministry of Foreign Affairs

ERIK-WILHELM NORMAN

Erik-Wilhelm Norman has been head of the Archives Division of the
Royal Norwegian Ministry of Foreign Affairs since 1960. He was
born in 1922 at Andenes in northern Norway and studied at the
University of Oslo. He joined the Archives Division in 1952.

When on 7 June 1905 the Norwegian Parliament (Storting) passed the resolution that broke up Norway's ninety-year Union with Sweden, it had with one bold stroke brought the country back into the family of fully sovereign nations. As one of the more far-reaching results of this sudden change of status, Norway was for the first time in nearly five hundred years faced with the problem of shaping a foreign policy of its own and of setting up an administrative machinery to that end. In view of the limited financial resources available and the noticeable shortage of experienced personnel this was indeed a formidable task. However, the Norwegians were not entirely unprepared for it.

First, it is important to bear in mind that within the framework of the Union Norway had been a separate state, even if its position could not be described as one of full equality with its Swedish partner. Enjoying a very considerable measure of autonomy, Norway had retained its own parliament, government and judicial system as provided for by the constitution of 1814. It had also maintained its own army and navy, together with a strictly separate civil service. The supremacy of Sweden had thus been restricted to the realm of foreign policy.

Considering unity in the conduct of foreign affairs as the very cornerstone and *raison d'être* of the Union, the Swedes had always insisted that the King should exercise his prerogatives in that field through his Swedish Minister of Foreign Affairs and the Swedish diplomatic and consular services acting on behalf of both kingdoms. While it is true that towards the end of the Union the Swedish government had reluctantly agreed to discuss the establishment of a separate Norwegian consular service, it had done so on the clear assumption that the ultimate control even of that service was to rest with the Swedish Foreign Minister.

However, Norway's subordinate position in this particular respect had not excluded it from all influence on the conduct of external affairs. According to the constitution of 1814, three members of the Norwegian ministry were to reside in Stockholm to provide Cabinet counsel on Norwegian affairs for the King. By virtue of a royal decree, from 1835 the presiding member of that body (the Minister of State) had attended all formal sessions between the King and his Swedish ministers at which external affairs affecting Norway were discussed. Since 1836 all consular appointments had been handled in joint sessions of Swedish and Norwegian ministers, and since 1858 there had been within the Norwegian Ministry of the Interior in Christiania (Oslo) an office for consular and commercial affairs. Towards the end of the century the problem of Norway's share in the conduct of foreign affairs had grown into a major issue, and in 1899 the Norwegian government had decided to set up within the same Ministry a new Department for Commercial, Consular and Foreign Business, through which all official correspondence between the Norwegian public administration and the joint Ministry of Foreign Affairs in Stockholm was to be channelled. This step had been taken partly with a view to establishing a firmer and more coordinated control of the transaction of Norwegian foreign business, partly in anticipation of the contemplated setting up of a separate Norwegian consular service. But it could, undoubtedly, also be construed as an opening move towards the establishment of a wholly separate ministry to handle foreign affairs. Swedish suspicions in this respect had seemed to be amply confirmed when two years later the

Ministry of the Interior was officially redesignated, the Ministry of Foreign Affairs, Commerce, Shipping and Industry.

Equally important was the fact that during the closing stages of the Union a number of Norwegians had been attached to the joint foreign services as well as to the Ministry of Foreign Affairs in Stockholm, some of them attaining fairly prominent positions. Thus, during the years from 1900 to 1903 the highest administrative office of the Ministry, that of permanent under-secretary of state (secretary-general) had been occupied by Thor von Ditten, who upon the dissolution of the Union was to play a very active part in the efforts to provide independent Norway with equivalent services of its own.

As a result, when the day finally came for Norway to assume complete control of foreign affairs it had at its disposal an admittedly small, but still significant, nucleus of experienced personnel, together with a skeleton organization that could be developed without too great difficulty into a fully fledged Ministry of Foreign Affairs. The first step in this direction was taken on the very day of the parliamentary resolution that sealed the fate of the Union, when the Provisional Government decreed that as of 15 June 1905, Jørgen Løvland, Minister of State, was to take charge of the Department for Commercial, Consular and Foreign Business, from then on officially designated the Ministry of Foreign Affairs.

The beginning was indeed a very modest one. The Department had been made up of three divisions, and its staff had consisted of one director-general, two heads of division, nine executive officers and a number of clerks. Only a few immediate changes of any importance took place as a result of its trans-formation into a Ministry. Norway had not yet been recognized as a sovereign and independent state by any foreign power and was therefore still unable to enter into any formal diplomatic or consular relations with the outside world. Thus, having no regular foreign service to administer, the new Ministry was for some time compelled to lead a somewhat shadowy existence, devoting most of its time and energy to planning and preparing for the services that would have to be created as soon as the world at large was ready to accept Norway's new identity.

During this initial stage the work of one man in particular left a clear imprint on the organizational structure that was gradually taking shape. Thor von Ditten, former permanent under-secretary of state at the Swedish Ministry of Foreign Affairs, was temporarily assigned to the Foreign Minister as personal adviser, and was soon charged with responsibilities closely resembling those of a secretary-general. However, his most important con-tribution was to provide the blueprint for the future organization of the Ministry. He visualized the Ministry as being made up of two departments, the first of which was to be responsible for the administration of the diplomatic service and for the handling of political affairs, protocol and ciphers, while the other was to be charged with consular and commercial affairs. The Archives Division was to be placed between the departments as a separate and autonomous unit. This plan was adopted by the Provisional Government with only a few alterations, the most important of which was the introduction of the post of secretary-general, which was to be combined with that of director-general of the Department for the Diplomatic Service, Political Affairs and Protocol. A bill to this effect was submitted to the Storting as soon as the other powers had on 26 October 1905 recognized

Norway's independence and had agreed to an exchange of diplomatic missions.

As mentioned earlier, Swedish resistance to Norway's demand for a foreign representation of its own had proved to be one of the most disruptive issues during the closing years of the Union and had provided the Norwegians with their main argument for bringing the Union to an end. One might, therefore, quite reasonably have expected the Storting to take a most favourable view of the first budget proposals for the new Ministry and its supporting services. But the final outcome of the parliamentary handling of these matters during the spring of 1906 did not quite measure up to such rosy expectations. The post of secretary-general was erased from the budget; the Storting was not even prepared to accept the setting up of two departments on a permanent basis, as it was widely believed that the workload would diminish considerably once the breaking-in period was over. As a result, one of the two directors-general had to proceed with an interim appointment only. Similar arrangements were made for other posts, bringing the total number of temporary appointments up to six. This preference for provisional solutions was motivated by a desire not to be tied down by some rigid pattern until more experience had been gained.

Nevertheless, the organizational structure that emerged from this process did bear a strong resemblance to von Ditten's blueprint. The Diplomatic and Political Department had two divisions: the First Division was mainly responsible for the administration of the Ministry and of diplomatic missions abroad, for relations with foreign diplomatic missions in Norway and for all matters of ceremony and protocol; the Second Division was charged with political affairs, questions regarding the national territory and international law, Arctic affairs, etc. The Consular and Commercial Department was likewise organized into two divisions: the Third Division was responsible for the administration of the Norwegian consular service abroad, relations with foreign consular establishments in Norway, emigration and immigration, and seamen's affairs; while the Fourth Division was charged with business relating to foreign trade, shipping, communications, finance, and the national economy generally. As planned originally, the Archives Division was placed outside the departmental structure. A director-general presided over each department, and to each of the four departmental divisions a head and two or three executive officers were assigned, while a first archivist and a deputy archivist were placed in charge of the Archives Division. Technical operations such as typing, copying, mailing, etc. were taken care of by seven clerks. The entire ministerial staff thus numbered 23 members.

If the Ministry may be described as having had a very modest beginning, much the same can be said for the foreign service over which it was to preside. The appropriation bill approved by the Storting in March 1906 provided for only eight diplomatic missions (six legations in Europe, one in Washington DC and one in Buenos Aires) and 20 career consular establishments of varying size and rank.

A distinctive feature of the first organizational set-up was the sharp dividing line between the diplomatic service and the consular service. As previously mentioned, the administration of the two services had been assigned to different departments of the Ministry, and the personnel attached to them were on the whole supposed to have entered upon separate careers.

This may seem odd in view of the fact that during the period in question the trend in most other European countries was decidedly towards an integration of those services. An explanation may be found in those special circumstances that form the historical background to the establishment of such services in Norway. It must be remembered that their birth came right after a long and bitter argument between Norwegians and Swedes on the question of the extent to which it would be practicable to set up a wholly separate and independent Norwegian consular service. As long as the joint diplomatic service was under Swedish control the Norwegians found it to their advantage to think in terms of a sharp distinction between the diplomatic and the consular services and to play down the need for political coordination and control. The organization that emerged during the early months of 1906 was to a considerable degree cut from a pattern drawn up by several official commissions that had examined the matter and made their recommendations during the period immediately preceding the abrogation of the Union. Thus shaped to match political conditions that had now ceased to exist, it was in this particular respect not too well suited to meet the new situation facing the country after 1905.

For this and a number of other reasons, the Ministry and its supporting services soon came under heavy political fire. The sometimes rather heated debates that took place in the Storting as well as in the press for a number of years concerned not only the administrative arrangements of the new services but also the very goals that were to be set for their operation. It was generally accepted that Norway was to keep clear of all foreign political entanglements and that top priority was to be given to the promotion and safeguarding of foreign trade and shipping. But there was also considerable support for the more extreme view that the foreign services should concentrate on looking after Norway's economic interests, to the virtual exclusion of all other activities normally associated with foreign policy. 'We want no foreign policy!' was a battle-cry often sounded from influential quarters, and while it was met with strong reservations on the part of the Minister of Foreign Affairs, its supporters were still a force to be reckoned with.

The attitude thus described stemmed from various and sometimes conflicting motives. In the minds of many liberals and radicals foreign policy was a term closely associated with unscrupulous power-politics. There was a widespread feeling that conflicts of interests between states could best be settled by moving them from the realm of foreign policy to that of international law, and that traditional diplomacy ought to be replaced by legal procedures laid down in arbitration treaties or similar arrangements.

Other motives seemed more earthbound. The period in question had been one of unprecedented industrial, commercial and maritime expansion, bringing to the fore a set of manufacturers, exporters and shipowners whose special interests inclined them towards rather a narrow concept of the objectives to be pursued by the foreign services. From their key positions in the economic life of the country they were able to bring considerable political influence to bear on the administration of external affairs.

This faction harboured a certain predilection for the consular service, which in their view was 'useful', hardworking and businesslike, as opposed to the diplomatic service, which they tended to associate with pomp and circumstance, tedious protocol, time-consuming ceremonies, lavish entertainment and general extravagance. So they wanted to reduce the diplomatic service to the minimum considered necessary to assert Norway's new position as a sovereign state. Moreover, they wished to tear down the barrier between the services by adding consular duties to those normally assigned to diplomatic missions as a step towards full integration. As for the question of recruitment to the services, they desired to break the apparent predominance so far enjoyed by lawyers in order to make room for men of practical business experience.

As a matter of fact, the recruitment policies soon came under attack from many different quarters. There were under the prevailing system three main ways of gaining admission to a foreign service career. The speediest and most direct approach would be as a first step to obtain an appointment as a grade II executive officer at the Ministry of Foreign Affairs or at some Norwegian consular establishment abroad. As a method of recruitment it met with universal approval, even if the criteria used in selecting candidates for such posts were often exposed to severe criticism. Objections usually centered on the alleged preference given to members of the legal profession.

An alternative opening was sometimes provided by the award of so-called attaché scholarships, which enabled the recipients to work at a foreign service station on a temporary basis with a view to qualifying for permanent employment. However, scholarships awarded under this arrangement entailed no formal guarantee of such employment.

Another back door into the career was available to those who could afford to work for some time without pay as volunteers at diplomatic missions while waiting for vacancies to occur. As was to be expected, this arrangement soon came under vehement criticism for unduly favouring the privileged few who were able to draw on a private income, and it was abolished after only a few years. Even so, attacks on the recruitment policy continued with unabated intensity, accompanied by repeated demands that more importance be attached to mercantile education and business experience.

No wonder that amidst all this clamour it took considerable time and effort to knock the foreign services into a more durable shape. In 1909 the two departments of the Ministry of Foreign Affairs were abolished, leaving one director-general in charge of the entire organization. This step was motivated partly by considerations of economy and partly by the need for a more uniform administrative control of the two external services. However, the day-by-day management of those services remained split between two divisions. For a few years this arrangement was left undisturbed, and was even formally confirmed as permanent by a royal decree of 14 June 1912. Nevertheless, as early as the following year the departmental system was reintroduced with the transfer of the Department of Shipping from the Ministry of Commerce to the Ministry of Foreign Affairs, where at the same time a General Department was created to provide an administrative superstructure for the four divisions that had originally constituted the Ministry. This arrangement proved as makeshift as the preceding ones, because in 1916 the Department of Shipping was retransferred to the Ministry of Commerce as part of the ministerial reform of that year.

Meanwhile, the Norwegians had woken up to the harsh realities of the First World War. It was a rude awakening in more ways than one, not least for those who had believed that Norway could do without a foreign policy. Bitter experience soon came to foster a growing realization that mere protestations of strict neutrality and some measure of military preparedness might not be sufficient to keep the nation out of the war. In fact, the defence of neutrality soon turned out to be more a political problem than a military or a legal one, thus confronting the Ministry with a number of new tasks for which it did not seem too well prepared.

An immediate effect of the new situation was a rather drastic increase in the workload. During the first year of the war the number of incoming letters and cables more than tripled, and the whole level of activity was raised in a way that nobody had foreseen when the organization had been geared mainly to the promotion of commercial and maritime interests.

The answer to the many problems arising out of this state of affairs took the form of a series of improvisations. These, while involving considerable increases in personnel strength, did not appear to entail any fundamental change in the organizational structure, but there was more to them than met the eye. For one thing, many of the new employees received temporary appointments only, their presence in the organization being camouflaged in the budget proposals under such inoffensive labels as 'extra work'.

By the end of 1915 the staff had already been increased by no less than 50 per cent, the Political and Commercial Divisions had both been subdivided under some temporary arrangement and deputy heads had been assigned to each of them. Moreover, since the beginning of the same year, a new Export Control Division had been in operation, though only on a provisional basis. Towards the end of 1916 the Ministry was further strengthened by the addition of yet another division, charged primarily with the handling of commercial treaties and customs agreements. What seemed the only departure from this steady process of growth was the retransfer in 1916 of the Department of Shipping to the Ministry of Commerce, which again left only one director-general in charge of all operations at the Ministry of Foreign Affairs.

Of considerable importance were the changes made in the allocation of business within the Ministry in order to meet the exigencies resulting from the trend towards the integration of the diplomatic and consular services. It had become standard practice to combine the office of envoy with that of consul-general, thus entrusting the incumbent with the supervision of all Norwegian consular activities within the territory of the receiving state. As this development also called for a greater measure of administrative coordination at home it was decided in 1917 to assign the responsibility for the administration of both services to a single division of the Ministry. This was a significant step towards the creation of a unified foreign service.

Another innovation occurred when a regular press service was organized in 1920. A press officer had been attached to the Ministry as early as 1909, but this arrangement had, for a number of reasons, proved to be rather short-lived. The somewhat vaguely defined duties assigned to the officer seemed to be a curious blend of information work and intelligence gathering, and as those activities were supposed to entail a certain amount of secrecy the entire arrangement caused considerable suspicion and ill-will in political quarters as well as in the press; few tears were shed when the post was abolished in 1912. The new service that took shape during the early months of 1920 was organized along lines drawn up in close consultation with the Norwegian Press Association. The direction of the service was entrusted to a press counsellor assisted by a press secretary, while operations abroad were assigned to four correspondents stationed in London, Paris, Berlin and

Washington DC. These correspondents were not formally attached to any legation, nor did they enjoy the diplomatic privileges normally accorded to press attachés. However, in dealing with matters considered to be of political importance, i.e. matters affecting Norway's relations with foreign powers, they were supposed to act under orders from the local Norwegian envoy.

The steady process of integration was formalized in the Foreign Service Act of 1922. A royal commission appointed in 1919 had been entrusted with the task of working out proposals for a complete overhaul of the foreign services, and the new organization that emerged in the wake of these efforts was largely based on the recommendations put forward by that body.

The most salient feature of the reform was the final merger of the three existing services – the Ministry, the diplomatic and the consular services – into a single, fully integrated foreign service. From now on no formal obstacles could be put in the way of transferring personnel from ministerial and diplomatic posts to consular ones or vice versa. Career officials were thus obliged to accept transfer to any position of equivalent or superior rank within the new service, unless otherwise stipulated. Important innovations were introduced even within the Ministry itself. For one thing, the office of secretary-general finally came into being, thus placing the whole Ministry under the professional direction of one administrative head who was also supposed to act as chief counsellor to the Foreign Minister on diplomatic affairs.

Moreover, two departments were now set up, each under the supervision of a director-general. The Administrative Department had four divisions: the Administrative Division, the Protocol Division, the Successional and Legal Affairs Division and the Archives Division. The Political and Commercial Department probably owed its existence to the new awareness of the close interdependence of foreign policy and foreign trade that had been fostered by wartime experience. This department was made up of six divisions based largely on a regional 'desk' system, the General Division and the Press Division being the only units not organized on this basis.

Noteworthy improvements were also achieved in the field of recruitment policy. A set of rules was drawn up for the admission of probationers to the service. University level education was to remain an important factor in the selection of candidates, but openings were now made available to candidates possessing only a secondary school education, providing that they had gone through a minimum of three years' practical business training. Moreover, before being finally admitted to the service for permanent employment probationers were required to pass an entrance examination arranged by the Ministry. The training period was set at three years, and a number of grants were made available to enable candidates possessing no private means to embark upon a foreign service career. Finally, the whole admission process was placed under the control of a Probationers' Commission made up of career officials and representatives of various organizations in trade, shipping and industry.

Considered as a whole the reform of 1922 seemed a substantial step forward. Even to more pessimistically inclined observers it now might look as though the period of improvisations and makeshifts was finally to be succeeded by one of orderly progress. However, what happened during the years immediately following the reform turned out to be rather a far cry from the visions nurtured by those who initiated it.

No sooner had the service been steered on its new course than Norway, like so many other countries, was hit by the cold winds of post-war recession. During the period of financial crisis, social and political upheaval and general economic malaise the Ministry of Foreign Affairs received its full share of the burden of cuts in public spending. One of the first positions to fall victim to the inexorable economy drive was that of first archivist, which was left vacant from 1924 to 1935. One post of head of division had to be abandoned in 1926, followed by the two positions of director-general in 1927. As a result, some divisions had to be placed under the immediate direction of the secretary-general. Among those left to the care of the secretary-general were the Political Division and the League of Nations Division, the latter having been formed in 1930 to cope with Norway's ever-increasing involvement in League affairs. Thus, to the duties normally assigned to the secretary-general were added those of a director-general.

Some attempt at redressing the balance was made towards the end of 1934, when the two positions of director-general were restored, one being assigned to the Administrative and Legal Department, the other one to the Commercial Department. But the direction of political and League of Nations affairs, as well as those of the Press Division, remained with the secretary-general until 1938, when under the pressure of the looming international crisis another director-general was appointed to take charge of a new Political Department. On the very eve of the Second World War the Ministry had at last been brought up to the minimum strength necessary to carry out its task in an ever more strife-torn world.

This relative strength was soon to be turned to good account when, in September 1939, Norway was for the second time in twenty-five years confronted with the challenge of maintaining its neutrality in relation to an armed conflict between the great powers of Europe. To many of the older employees life at the Ministry during the first months after the outbreak of hostilities seemed a rough repetition of something they had been through at an earlier stage in their careers. As in 1914, their workload grew drastically, calling for increased tempo as well as many extra hours to cope with an abnormal situation. Even so, staff enlargements far beyond those provided for in the 1939/40 budget became unavoidable. By the end of March 1940 the staff numbered 119, which exceeded by 29 the total of 90 covered by the budget. Whatever pangs those responsible may have felt in that respect were soon to be entirely forgotten in the turmoil of dramatic events that was about to follow.

During the first months of 1940 there had been at the Ministry an increasing awareness of the fact that the efforts to uphold Norway's neutral position had entered a very critical stage and that the country might at any moment be exposed to actions that would draw Norway into the war. Some quite rudimentry administrative preparations for such a contingency had even been made, the most important of which were the plans drawn up for the evacuation of the ministerial archives during an emergency. But in spite of the growing uneasiness that had for some time troubled the initiated, the massive invasion of German armed forces that took place during the early morning hours of 9 April came as an almost total surprise.

Nevertheless, thanks to a combination of sheer luck and remarkable resolution and energy on the part of certain key persons, the King, the

Government and members of the Storting succeeded in escaping from the capital just as it was on the point of being occupied by the invading forces. Temporary seats of government came into existence in various places north-east of Oslo, from where the Government tried to organize some armed resistance in anticipation of the military assistance that had been promised by the Allies.

A small group of career officials of the Ministry of Foreign Affairs and some members of the clerical staff accompanied the Foreign Minister in this evacuation, taking with them quite a substantial part of the Ministry archives, which were subsequently taken across the Swedish border and placed in the custody of the Norwegian legation in Stockholm. However, as the military situation in south-eastern Norway rapidly deteriorated the Government was soon forced to strike camp and seek refuge in the valleys further north, leaving behind most of the makeshift administrative apparatus that had surrounded it so far. Except for the tiny band of officials accom-panying the King and his Ministers in their vagrant existence, the central administration of the realm had now virtually disintegrated. Not until, after week of restless roaming from one place to another, the Government was finally able to gain what seemed to be a somewhat firmer foothold near the city of Tromsø in northern Norway could the semblance of a central state administration be restored, even if its authority did not exceed beyond those parts of the country that had still not been occupied by the invaders. A small detachment of the Ministry of Foreign Affairs now established itself in the vicinity of Tromsø in order to serve as the Foreign Minister's secretariat. Meanwhile, the secretary-general had arrived in Stockholm, where he organized within the Norwegian legation another detachment called the B-Department, to which was assigned the task of transacting Ministry business that could not in the circumstances be handled on Norwegian soil.

Events took another disastrous turn when at about the beginning of June the Allies, now faced with a serious new threat by the German offensive in the west, found themselves compelled to withdraw their forces from Norway. As any further military resistance now seemed to be of no avail, the King and the Government decided to leave the country in order to continue the struggle from Great Britain, while the Norwegian army commander was authorized to surrender to the Germans all forces remaining on Norwegian territory.

Having established itself on British soil, the Exile Government lost no time in building up a provisional administration. As a part of this process a Ministry of Foreign Affairs in exile gradually took shape during the summer months of 1940. At the outset a tiny staff of seven persons moved with the Foreign Minister into the Old Manor at Bracknell in Berkshire (once the hideout of Dick Turpin, the notorious highwayman). Little by little there grew out of this core an organization that by the end of the war was to employ no less than 72 persons. This growth was greatly facilitated when, towards the end of 1940, the Ministry was permitted to move into larger and more convenient office premises at Kingston House, Princes Gate, in London's West End. When fully developed the wartime structure of the Ministry included a General Department covering administrative affairs, archives, cipher, accounts and mailing, a Political Department, a Commercial

Department, a Protocol Service, a press counsellor and a counsellor on political history. Although it had been established under difficult circumstances, it was a fairly effective and well-oiled machinery that in the spring of 1945 could be transferred to a liberated Norway.

As of 1 June 1945 the Ministry was again at work on Norwegian soil after nearly five years in exile. A new era began, during which the Ministry had to adjust to the many profound changes in international relations produced by the war. For one thing, the continuous dismantling of colonial empires taking place during the post-war period made it highly desirable to enter into diplomatic relations with many new nations emerging from that process. As a result, a number of new foreign service stations came into existence, which again led to an increased demand for a strengthening of the administrative establishment at home.

The traumatic experience provided by the war had fostered a deeper consciousness of the close interdependence now prevailing within the family of nations and a growing realization of the fact that even a small nation living on the northernmost fringe of Europe could not afford to stand aloof from world affairs. So for Norway, as for so many other countries, this period was one of unprecedented involvement in international matters. This trend manifested itself in Norway's active participation not only in the multifarious activities of the United Nations but also in various regional arrangements, the most important of which were the economic cooperation instigated by the Marshall Plan and embodied in the OEEC, the military and political cooperation that followed in the wake of Norway's accession to NATO, and last but not least the manifold fields of Scandinavian and Nordic cooperation. Furthermore, many questions that had formerly been settled on a bilateral basis now called for multilateral solutions, while at the same time bilateral forms of cooperation in new fields became increasingly common. Such a radical expansion in the field of foreign policy, particularly when it occurred during a period marked by post-war reconstruction problems and very limited resources, put a severe strain on the apparatus responsible for the day-to-day execution of that policy.

The first post-war organizational structure was provisionally outlined in a royal decree of 27 July 1945. It included four departments. The General Department was to cover administration and personnel, accounts, inheritance cases and legal affairs, archives and library, cipher and mailing. The Political Department was set up with two divisions, while three divisions were assigned to the Commercial Department. Moreover, a War Reparations Department consisting of two divisions was established on a strictly temporary basis. Outside the departmental structure and placed under the direct control of the secretary-general were the Protocol Service, the Press Service, one counsellor for international law and one for political history. The entire staff of the Ministry were supposed to number 156.

In its broad outlines this pattern was to remain unchanged for some years, though the War Reparations Department, as planned, was closed down in 1948 and its duties entrusted to the Inheritance and Legal Division of the General Department. By the end of 1950 another Legal Division was set up within the General Department, leaving only inheritance cases and matters of family law with what was now renamed the Inheritance Division. In 1954 all legal matters were transferred to the new Department of Legal Affairs.

However, since 1979 the Foreign Minister's international law adviser has taken charge of some special legal matters, particularly those concerning the law of the sea. For a few years (between 1973 and 1978) the political direction of these matters was even entrusted to a special Cabinet Minister.

Another major addition to the post-1945 Ministry appeared in 1950, when an Office of Cultural Relations was established with a view to promoting Norway's cultural contacts with other nations. Like the Press Service, the new office was at first placed outside the departmental structure, but in 1967 it was converted into a fully fledged Department of Cultural Affairs, staffed on the executive level with career officials. Meanwhile the Press Service had been integrated into the regular foreign service as early as 1958, and in 1961 had been transformed into a Press Department. Finally, in 1973 the two departments were merged under the name of the Press and Cultural Relations Department, which comprised the Press Division, the Information Division and the Cultural Relations Division.

The Ministry moved into a new field of activity when it assumed the overall direction of Norway's aid to developing countries. It began with contributions to multilateral aid institutions during the early post-war period; bilateral aid followed from 1953. At the Ministry these matters were handled by the Political Department, but after some years the direct administration of bilateral aid was left to the Norwegian Agency for International Development, which was established by an act of the Storting in 1962. In 1968, the Agency was replaced by the Directorate for Development Aid. Like its predecessor, the Directorate was to act under the authority of the Ministry of Foreign Affairs, but while the Agency had mainly been responsible for bilateral technical assistance, the Directorate was now entrusted with the overall planning and coordination of all Norwegian aid activities. At the same time a new Department of International Economic and Social Development was established within the Ministry.

However, in 1978 the powers accorded to the Directorate under this arrangement were visibly modified when important elements of the planning function were transferred to the Department. This was accompanied by some transfer of personnel to permit the Foreign Minister to exercise greater political control over aid operations. As it stands today, the Department has five divisions organized partly on a functional and partly on a regional basis.

Meanwhile the Commercial Department had undergone an expansion more or less in step with the rather breathtaking pace set by the post-war growth in international economic cooperation. True enough, the increase in the number of divisions covered by that Department from three in 1945 to five in 1975 did not appear too impressive, at least not when measured by an international yardstick. But judged in terms of manpower employed and output achieved the growth was far from negligible. Such was the situation in 1978, when the Department reached an important turning point.

In order to avoid work being duplicated and to enable the Ministry to devote more time and resources to the political coordination of various international activities pursued even by other Ministries or government agencies, it was decided to transfer a substantial part of the commercial business to the Ministry of Commerce. This move entailed the transformation of the Commercial Department into a Department of External Economic Affairs embracing six divisions. The First Division was to deal with external economic problems in general and was often referred to as the Signals Division, as one of its tasks was to pick up information and ideas from abroad and have them relayed to interested parties within the government apparatus. To the Second Division were assigned all matters with a bearing upon international cooperation in the sphere of oil and energy. The Third Division was made responsible for the handling of matters regarding the bilateral economic relations with Eastern European countries and with countries outside Europe; this Division was also to undertake coordination of the international activities of other Ministries in various fields not covered by other divisions within the Ministry of Foreign Affairs. The Fourth Division was to take care of Norway's participation in the OECD as well as of matters relating to international cooperation in the fields of technology and research. The Fifth Division was to handle questions regarding multilateral cooperation with a view to establishing a New Economic World Order, while the Sixth Division was to cover shipping and aviation.

It is, however, important to note that this new arrangement did not exclude the Ministry of Foreign Affairs from participating in foreign commercial affairs whenever such interference might appear necessary for political reasons. Thus the Ministry retained its right to instruct the Norwegian foreign service stations in such matters if need be, while the Ministry of Commerce was expected to channel its instructions through the Ministry of Foreign Affairs whenever questions of a non-routine character were involved.

Another fairly recent addition to the organizational structure is the Department of Policy Planning and Research, which came into existence in 1973 in reply to a long-standing demand for an improved planning capacity. Though small in size, harbouring two divisions only, the Department has acquired a steadily growing importance during a period when other departments, entirely absorbed as they are in day-to-day operations, have found it increasingly difficult to spare time and resources for thorough analysis and long-range planning. The Research Division meets this particular need, while the Reports Division has been given the no less important tasks of preparing excerpts of selected Foreign Service stations' reports and of selecting material for publication.

Attention has been focused on the new formations within the Ministry. It is also necessary to have a last look at some of the 'old' departments, which have all undergone varying degrees of growth and change. However, as readers can refer to the organizational chart (Appendix A) there is little point in describing in detail the distribution of business between the various divisions. Attention will instead be drawn to a few salient facts.

The Protocol Department, which until 1978 had officially been designated the Protocol Service, has remained a fairly small organization. As recently as 1978 its staff numbered only 10. This seems quite remarkable in view of the rather drastic increase there has been in the number of tasks that normally devolve onto a protocol organization – such as, for instance, the technical arrangements in connection with official state visits. Because of the limited capacity of the Protocol Department many of these arrangements must be left to the departments concerned. In order to remedy this somewhat unsatisfactory state of affairs, since 1979 a high-ranking official has been attached to the Department and placed in charge of the preparation of official visits.

Furthermore, plans for the establishment within the Protocol Department of an official visits secretariat are now under discussion.

On the other hand, the Department of Political Affairs (previously referred to as the Political Department) has expanded in a way that largely reflects the growth in international political commitments that Norway has taken upon itself since the end of the last war. Starting out with two divisions in 1945 the Department today includes six divisions, some of which have been organized on a regional basis, others on a functional one, while a third category may best be described as mixed.

The Department of Administrative Affairs (previously referred to as the General Department) has also moved forward in step with the rest of the foreign service. The strongest motivation may have come from the needs of the ever-growing number of career foreign service stations which come under the administration of this Department. Factors pointing in the same direction are the steady increase in the number of people employed at the Ministry itself and the repeated calls for more sophisticated technical procedures, particularly within the sphere of communications. By 1979 the Department had under its wing 76 career foreign service stations with 399 professional foreign service officers in addition to locally engaged staff and 308 employees serving at the Ministry in Oslo. Six divisions now share the workload.

In order to relieve the directors-general of some pressure of work, deputy directors-general have gradually been appointed for all departments. Apart from these additions, some new positions were created outside the departmental structure, and under the direct control of the Foreign Minister or the secretary-general. The post of inspector-general for the foreign service was established in 1965 to facilitate the Ministry's control over its foreign service stations. The inspector-general was to serve as a link between those stations and the Ministry, to obtain for the Ministry a better insight into their problems through inspections on the spot and to submit to the secretary-general recommendations aimed at improving their standard of efficiency. During the last twenty years a number of special advisers have also been attached to the Ministry in order to provide the Foreign Minister with expert counsel on a variety of matters, particularly those that do not fit easily within the established division of labour between the departments. The advisers will thus often serve as coordinators of business being handled by several departments. So far most of them have been picked from the career foreign service.

It remains to have a brief look at the top political leadership of the Ministry. Up to 1948 the Minister of Foreign Affairs had no politically appointed assistant. While it is true that the counsellor on political history had unofficially functioned as a kind of top political adviser, and that the counsellor's office had to some extent served as a political secretariat, this practice was never formalized. But in 1948 the first Under-Secretary of State was appointed to serve as the Foreign Minister's top assistant and adviser on political affairs. Though a political appointee whose term of office must necessarily end with that of his or her Foreign Minister, the Under-Secretary is not a member of the Government in terms of constitutional law, but only a top-ranking official. In the course of the last fifteen years the top political apparatus has been further strengthened by the appointment of a political private secretary as well as by the establishment of a Foreign Minister's Secretariat.

The future of the Ministry has recently been discussed by several officially appointed commissions. The problem causing most concern seems to be that of providing the maximum political coordination in the conduct of foreign affairs within the Ministry of Foreign Affairs as well as between that Ministry and other government agencies. One alternative suggestion is that the present departmental structure should be replaced by one made up of three departments only; there would be one department for bilateral business organized in five regional divisions or 'desks' covering Africa, Asia, Latin America, Western Europe and North America, and Eastern Europe respectively. Another department reserved for multilateral business would cover United Nations affairs, UNCTAD, EEC, OECD, etc., while a third unit organized along functional lines could look after business that does not fit into the bilateral/multilateral concept. These ideas are still being discussed, but a first cautious step in the direction of a desk system has already been taken, as the budget proposal for 1981 provides for the establishment of three geographic units covering Latin America, Africa and the Arab world. (The Latin American unit has in fact been in operation since 1979). It remains to be seen whether or not this move is really a foretaste of things to come.

During the seventy-five years of its existence the Ministry of Foreign Affairs has occupied a variety of premises. As the Ministry took shape during the summer of 1905 it moved into rented premises at Victoria Terrasse 7, a centrally located tenement building that had been erected during the 1880s. For some years the Ministry had to share the building with private tenants until the house was bought by the Government and turned over to the Ministry in 1913. Here the Ministry remained until the building had to be evacuated on 9 April 1940 as a result of the German invasion. During the years of German occupation the building acquired some notoriety as the headquarters of the Gestapo. After the period of exile in Great Britain and its return to Oslo in June 1945 the Ministry was given temporary quarters in a new office building at Solplassen 1 (now Kronprinsess Märthas plass 1). Like so many makeshift arrangements this one proved rather long-lasting. Not until 1963 was the Ministry finally allowed to settle down in permanent quarters at 7 Juni-plassen 1, only a few steps from where it was first housed in 1905. Here the Ministry occupies a modern office building in addition to premises located in an adjacent building dating from the 1880s.

(Bibliography appears on page 408)

THE ROYAL MINISTRY
OF FOREIGN AFFAIRS
(March 1979)

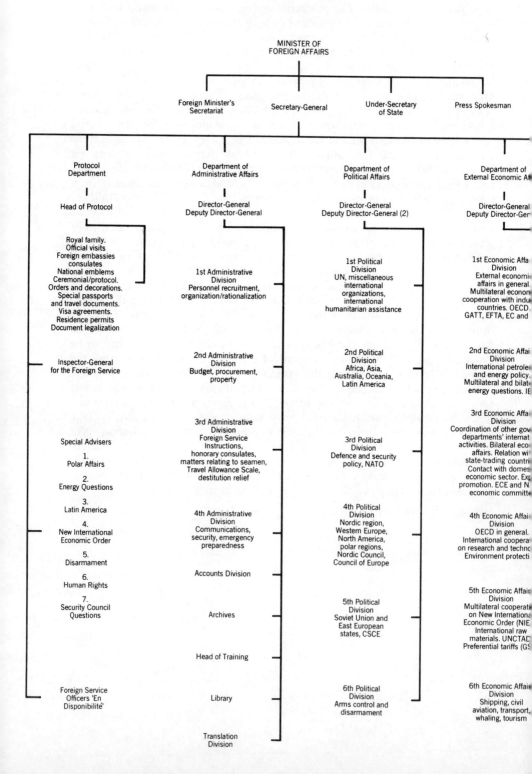

MINISTER OF
FOREIGN AFFAIRS

Foreign Minister's
Secretariat

Secretary-General

Under-Secretary
of State

Press Spokesman

Protocol
Department

Head of Protocol

Royal family.
Official visits
Foreign embassies
consulates
National emblems
Ceremonial/protocol.
Orders and decorations.
Special passports
and travel documents.
Visa agreements.
Residence permits
Document legalization

Inspector-General
for the Foreign Service

Special Advisers

1.
Polar Affairs

2.
Energy Questions

3.
Latin America

4.
New International
Economic Order

5.
Disarmament

6.
Human Rights

7.
Security Council
Questions

Foreign Service
Officers 'En
Disponibilité'

Department of
Administrative Affairs

Director-General
Deputy Director-General

1st Administrative
Division
Personnel recruitment,
organization/rationalization

2nd Administrative
Division
Budget, procurement,
property

3rd Administrative
Division
Foreign Service
Instructions,
honorary consulates,
matters relating to seamen,
Travel Allowance Scale,
destitution relief

4th Administrative
Division
Communications,
security, emergency
preparedness

Accounts Division

Archives

Head of Training

Library

Translation
Division

Department of
Political Affairs

Director-General
Deputy Director-General (2)

1st Political
Division
UN, miscellaneous
international
organizations,
international
humanitarian assistance

2nd Political
Division
Africa, Asia,
Australia, Oceania,
Latin America

3rd Political
Division
Defence and security
policy, NATO

4th Political
Division
Nordic region,
Western Europe,
North America,
polar regions,
Nordic Council,
Council of Europe

5th Political
Division
Soviet Union and
East European
states, CSCE

6th Political
Division
Arms control and
disarmament

Department of
External Economic Af

Director-General
Deputy Director-Ger

1st Economic Affa
Division
External economi
affairs in general.
Multilateral econom
cooperation with indu
countries. OECD
GATT, EFTA, EC and

2nd Economic Affai
Division
International petrole
and energy policy.
Multilateral and bilat
energy questions. IE

3rd Economic Affa
Division
Coordination of other gov
departments' internat
activities. Bilateral eco
affairs. Relation wi
state-trading countri
Contact with domes
economic sector. Exp
promotion. ECE and N
economic committe

4th Economic Affai
Division
OECD in general.
International coopera
on research and techno
Environment protecti

5th Economic Affair
Division
Multilateral cooperati
on New Internationa
Economic Order (NIE
International raw
materials. UNCTAD
Preferential tariffs (GS

6th Economic Affair
Division
Shipping, civil
aviation, transport,
whaling, tourism

Department of Legal Affairs	Press and Cultural Relations Department	Department of International Economic and Social Development	Department for Policy Planning and Research
Director-General Deputy Director-General	Director-General Deputy Director-General	Director-General Deputy Director-General (2)	Director-General Deputy Director-General
1st Legal Affairs Division Human rights, territorial land boundaries, claims for compensation, double taxation	Press Division Contact with Norwegian and foreign press broadcasting services etc.	1st Division Multilateral development cooperation. Development policy questions in UN. Science and technology for development	Research Division Research on foreign policy questions of significance for Norwegian foreign policy
2nd Legal Affairs Division Territorial sea, legal aid, private international law, legal aspects of maritime activity	Information Division General information via publications, films, exhibitions, pictorial service, Norwegian events abroad etc.	2nd Division UNDP and UN specialized agencies, World Food Council, World Food Programme, World Bank, regional development banks	Reports Division Foreign service stations' reports. Selected report extracts
3rd Legal Affairs Division Inheritance, family law, service of legal documents, rogatory commissions	Cultural Relations Division Multilateral and bilateral cultural agreements, exchanges, Norwegian teaching posts abroad	3rd Division Bilateral development cooperation, medium-term programmes and budgets. Multi-bi cooperation. DAC. NORAD	
4th Legal Affairs Division Treaty Law questions, diplomatic and consular immunities and privileges, outer space	Editor	4th Division Development cooperation Africa	
Foreign Ministry's International Law Adviser		5th Division Development cooperation Asia, America, Oceania, Portugal, Turkey and Jamaica	
		Deputy Director-General UNCSTD	

BIBLIOGRAPHY

Rolf Andvord, *Med hånden på hjertet* (Oslo 1964).

Erik Colban, *Femti år* (Oslo 1952).

Kjell Colding, 'Organisasjonsspørsmål i Utenriksdepartementet', in *Norsk Utenrikspolitisk Årbok* (Oslo 1975), 99–115.

Hans Fay, *På post i fem verdensdeler* (Oslo 1959).

Innstilling om Utenrikstjenesten. Hovedoppgaver og organisasjon (Oslo 1970).

Fritz Wedel Jarlsberg, *Reisen gjennem livet* (Oslo 1932).

Reider Omang, *Utenrikstjenesten* (Oslo 1954).

——, *Norsk utenrikstjeneste. Grunnleggende år* (covering the period from 1905 to 1912 (Oslo 1955).

——, *Norsk utenrikstjeneste. Stormfulle tider* (covering the period from 1913 to 1929) (Oslo 1959).

Gudrun Ræder, *De uunnværlige flinke* (containing information from the period of the Second World War) (Oslo 1975).

Reformutvalget for Utenrikstjenesten, 1946. Innstilling (Oslo 1947).

Portugal

The Ministry for Foreign Affairs

FRANCO NOGUEIRA

Dr Alberto M. Franco Nogueira was Minister for Foreign Affairs in
Portugal from 1961 to 1969 and a member of the Portuguese parliament from 1969 to 1973. He was born in 1918 in Lisbon and graduated
from the Faculty of Law at Lisbon University in 1940. He entered the
foreign service in 1941 and served as chargé d'affaires in Tokyo from
1946 to 1950 and as consul-general in London from 1955 to 1958. He
also served in the Ministry, first as assistant political director (1958)
and then as director-general for political affairs from 1959 to 1961.
He has written a number of books, *United Nations and Portugal: a
study of anti-colonialism* (1963), *The Third World* (1967) and more
recently, a four-volume study of *Salazar: estudo biografico* (1977,
1978, 1979, 1980). A fifth volume is in preparation.

International relations, as opposed to foreign policy, have existed for thousand of years. Tribes, groups of tribes, peoples, were in reciprocal contact on the same continent and sometimes across continents – Asia, Europe, Africa – through territorial expansion or nomadism. These relations were established at random and did not have a coherent meaning or a sustained purpose, except in so far as they sprang from the basic issues common to all: war and peace, alliances, trade. However, if we concern ourselves solely with Western history, one may say that a more stable system of international relations only emerges with Alexander's empire, the Greek cities and the Roman Empire. More than a thousand years were to elapse until, with the Peace of Westphalia in the middle of the seventeenth century (1648), the system was fully developed and widely adopted. Throughout the various historical phases of the development of true international relations one feature stands out as common to all: its conduct was the exclusive province of the emperor, king or ruler; it was a personal prerogative, which he would usually delegate at his discretion and as a matter of personal trust to members of his family, the aristocracy or the military class. There was no question of a department or office of the state, or of a body of professional civil servants, to deal with international relations.

Portugal became an independent kingdom in 1140 under Afonso I. In the field of international relations the new nation followed the established usage of the times; but there was already the beginning of a real foreign policy. Military considerations were of course paramount: to expel the Muslims from the southern part of the territory and push them back across the sea; this aim took centuries to achieve and implied almost constant warfare. For this purpose, Afonso I and his successors endeavoured to enlist the support of other European forces, namely the Crusaders; they also established close relations with the Papacy, then the highest spiritual and political power, even though there were many sharp disagreements, as the Portuguese kings never accepted the jurisdiction of the Holy See in secular and civil matters; and there were relations with the other kingdoms of the Iberian Peninsula, a field in which Portugal had to tread carefully in order to assert its independence and sovereignty and at the same time avoid arousing hostility which would drive its neighbours to a hostile coalition. Such, then, was the foreign policy of Portugal. There was, however, no office or department of state entrusted with the conduct of external relations, nor were there officials of any rank to deal with them. The king alone directed everything; the envoys were selected by him, appointed on a personal basis and bound by personal devotion to the monarch. It was to the sovereign alone that they reported, in utmost secrecy, the outcome of their missions and negotiations. Usually, the king would share the problems of foreign policy with a single man, the chancellor, in whom he placed his full trust and whose advice he would seek in confidence; otherwise that man, whose modern equivalent would be the chief minister, played no part in the conduct of international relations.

At the end of the fourteenth century Portuguese international relations underwent a considerable expansion. Two important new factors came into play: the increased power of some of the Iberian kingdoms (which later became Spain) and the first dreams of Portuguese expansion across the oceans. It seems appropriate to stress that these two factors are at the roots of the Anglo–Portuguese alliance (the first treaty was signed in 1373). At the great and decisive battle of Aljubarrota a small British contingent fought alongside the Portuguese army against the Castillians. Under João I a new Anglo-Portuguese treaty was signed in England at Windsor (1386) confirming an alliance that was both defensive and offensive and covering all aspects of relations between Portugal and Britain. The two nations, facing the sea, had found common interests, and each undertook to provide help in case of attack from a third party; an undertaking that has lasted until the present day. (It is also of interest to recall that under the terms of the Treaty of Windsor Philippa, daughter of John of Gaunt, Duke of Lancaster, was married to João I and became Queen of Portugal; from this marriage Henry the Navigator was born.

At the beginning of the fifteenth century the Portuguese embarked on their great, epoch-making oceanic voyages. It was far more than an adventure. It was a carefully pondered decision, a deliberate policy, based on strategic considerations: to attack from the rear the Eastern peoples who were pressing Western Europe, to seek overseas support to balance the growing power of Spain, to spread Christianity and Western ideals and to break the monopoly of trade in the hands of the eastern and central Mediterranean peoples. A hundred years later, Vasco da Gama had sailed around Africa and reached India (1497), and Alvares Cabral had crossed the Atlantic and landed in Brazil (1500).

During this time the Portuguese central government was expanded. Numerous bodies were created to provide for the increasing needs of the administration, both at home and overseas. Starting at the end of the fourteenth century a new high office of state emerged: that of the Privy Secretary or Privy Minister (Escrivão da Puridade – literally, the *one who writes in secrecy*). This man was personally appointed by the king, and gradually became the highest ranking official, serving at the king's pleasure; in his hands was concentrated all the most delicate and confidential business of state, including international relations and negotiations with foreign powers. The functions and powers of the Escrivão da Puridade were larger and had a wider scope than those of the former chancellors. The king was surrounded by a council of advisers, but the Escrivão ranked higher than all the others, and the most important issues were dealt with between him and the king, in great secrecy, and were not shared with the other members of the Council. Still, there was no department or office entrusted with the specific task of conducting international relations even though they were by then very complex and diversified.

During the sixty years of the Spanish occupation of Portugal, international relations were of course carried out by the King of Spain, nominally in his capacity as King of Portugal although Madrid was the centre of all decisions. When Portugal recovered its independence in 1640 a new era opened up for Portuguese foreign policy and diplomacy. There was the Spanish war against Portugal, as Madrid did not accept the fact that the Portuguese had regained their sovereignty; and Lisbon had to seek support – military help, financial aid, political alliances – in the subsequent struggle. João IV of Portugal sent ambassadors to France, Holland, Denmark, Sweden, the Holy See and, of course, to Britain. The Anglo-Portuguese alliance once again played a major role. Oliver Cromwell had confirmed the old treaty by signing a new one, very profitable to British trade. In 1661, disregarding strong Spanish opposition, Charles II again sustained the alliance; through new agreements he married a Portuguese princess, Catherine of Braganza, who thus became Queen of England.

In the meantime the Congress of Westphalia took place, and there was a general settlement in Europe following the Thirty Years War. Portugal was present at Westphalia. International relations followed a new pattern, and the government in Lisbon kept abreast of the times. Two important developments have to be stressed: first, among the king's advisers, who formed the Council of State, one was specifically entrusted with the conduct of foreign relations, with the official title of Secretary of State; second, the envoys or ambassadors were not sent abroad to deal with a specific problem but became resident and were accredited on a permanent basis. Although decisions ultimately rested with the king, the Secretary of State drafted the instructions, subject to the king's approval, and envoys corresponded directly with the Secretary of State. The latter was considered the king's chief adviser, and had a small number of trusted assistants to help him in his work. The king devoted a good deal of attention to foreign relations: he would receive the Secretary of State three or four times each week, and the Secretary of State was the only adviser who was allowed to interrupt the monarch when he was engaged with other advisers on some other business of state. It was a rudimentary Ministry of Foreign Affairs.

On 28 July 1736 King João V issued an order or decree (alvará) creating three large departments of state: the Secretariat of State for Home Affairs, the Secretariat of State for the Navy and Overseas, and the Secretariat of State for Foreign Affairs and War. What was later to become the Portuguese Ministry of Foreign Affairs had come into being. The first head of the new department was Marco António de Azevedo Coutinho, an experienced diplomat who had been envoy extraordinary to Paris from 1721 to 1728, and was later to be ambassador to London from 1737 to 1739. The second head of the department was Sebastião de Carvalho e Melo, who had been envoy extraordinary to London from 1739 to 1745 and to Vienna from 1745 to 1749, and who later, with the title of Marquis of Pombal, became Principal Secretary of State (or Prime Minister) under King José for twenty years.

It should not be overlooked that the new department was to deal with both foreign affairs and war. In the mind of Portuguese kings at the time, the issues of war and peace and of foreign policy were intimately related. For political and practical reasons, responsibility for the conduct of international relations and the preparation for defence rested with the same person. It was a perfectly logical step at a time when the monarch was both commander-in-chief of the armed forces and sole master of the nation's alliances. Friends and foes were personal friends and foes of the king.

This structure of the new department was maintained until 1801, in which year it was divided into the Secretariat of State for War and the Secretariat of State for Foreign Affairs. However, after only six months the old set-up was restored and the two departments were merged. Twenty-one years later, by the law of 12 June 1822 after the liberal revolution, the department was again divided. This separation of the two Secretariats has been retained ever since. During the rest of the nineteenth century, and even though Portuguese politics showed great instability both internally and externally, the basic organization of the Secretariat for Foreign Affairs did not undergo significant changes. At the turn of the century, in 1910, with the demise of the monarchy and the proclamation of a Portuguese Republic, the old Secretariat of State for Foreign Affairs was named the Ministry for Foreign Affairs, the name by which it is known today.

Most of the old structures were retained after 1910. Continuous political crises at home, weakness and instability of governments, inexperience of the new republican administration, prevented the new regime from devoting the required attention to international relations. Even though there were problems of the utmost importance in the international field – the First World War, in which Portugal took part; the Anglo–Portuguese alliance; the League of Nations; world economic crises, etc. – the Ministry for Foreign Affairs was neglected and was not equipped, from the point of view of organization and staff, to deal with the issues that the country had to face. After the liberal revolution in the early nineteenth century, the career staff were recruited on merit, and this was accentuated after the proclamation of the Republic in 1910; family, social or financial background was irrelevant to entry into the foreign service. However, many of the most important posts abroad were filled by political appointees who lacked knowledge and experience, distinguished as they were in other activities; much was improvised; and it seems accurate to say that between 1910 and 1930 Portugal was devoid of a coherent and efficient foreign policy. As a result, both during and after the war much damage was done to Portuguese interests. Portuguese participation in the war itself was carelessly planned and not really discussed in political terms with the Allies; the part played by Portugal, both in the French and in the African battlefields, was not properly established, and was rather minimized or ignored after the war. At the Peace Conference in Versailles, Portugal did not receive the reparations to which it was entitled, nor did it secure from the principal Allies the political commitments and assurances concerning Portugal's place in international bodies, its territorial integrity, etc., that were to be expected. Much blame should be placed on the shoulders of the Portuguese delegation at Versailles – or rather the various successive Portuguese delegations. Led by political appointees, and even though it had the technical support of some junior foreign service officials, the delegation displayed great inexperience, lack of preparation, and an amateurish approach to problems and situations, and this partly explains the poor results achieved.

As it is well known, in 1926 there was a military coup in Portugal, the outcome of which was a new political and social regime. Two years later, António de Oliveira Salazar was asked to take over the Finance Ministry and try to solve the country's serious economic and financial condition. His efforts were successful, and because of the prestige and authority he thus acquired Salazar was entrusted with the formation of a government. In 1932 he became Prime Minister. He then drafted a new constitution, which embodied the ideological, political, economic and social expression of the new regime. This constitution was approved by national referendum and came into force in April 1933.

In accordance with the constitution of 1933, the overall direction of foreign policy was vested in the President of the Republic as a matter of political principle; but the head of state had to conduct it through the government; and it was the government that took political responsibility both for decisions and for their implementation.

In the meantime, after the outbreak of the Spanish Civil War and as the international atmosphere over Europe was darkening, Salazar took over the Ministry for Foreign Affairs in 1936. He then found out for himself what had been obvious for a long time to those directly concerned: the inadequacy of the Foreign Ministry. In 1938 (by decree-law 29319 of 30 December) the Ministry for Foreign Affairs was completely reorganized. It was the first real attempt to have a modern, up-to-date and operational department to deal with the international relations of the country.

In line with the constitution of 1933, the law of 1938 entrusted the Foreign Minister with the execution of foreign policy, and the Foreign Minister was the effective head of the department. From 1936 to 1947 Salazar was both Prime Minister and Minister for Foreign Affairs. During this period, of course, the decision-making process was simplified. If there were decisions that could not or should not be taken by the Foreign Minister alone, in view of their national importance or implications, the Prime Minister was entitled to take them, assuming full political responsibility before the Cabinet, the President and the nation. However, Salazar always kept a sharp separation between the responsibilities of the Prime Minister and those of the Foreign Minister. While he held the two offices, of course, he took upon himself the responsibilities of both. He would report to the President regularly. Every Sunday morning, during a two- to three-hour meeting, he would devote a large part of the time to foreign affairs. He also frequently reported in writing, addressing to the President short letters on topical problems. For major problems of policy – granting facilities to the British in the Azores during the war, the reoccupation of Portuguese Timor, which had been invaded first by Australians and then by Japanese, the military defence of Portuguese strategic positions – Salazar would place the issue before the Cabinet and there would be a debate, sometimes requiring several Cabinet meetings.

In 1947, Salazar handed over the Ministry for Foreign Affairs to a minister. From that moment on, even though he was always deeply interested in international relations and foreign affairs, Salazar did not interfere in the running of the Ministry for Foreign Affairs or in the direct conduct of foreign policy. As Prime Minister, he received a copy of all the incoming and out-going cables; he received the Foreign Minister whenever the latter requested it; he dealt with and discussed the issues raised by the Minister; but except under exceptional circumstances or when some problems were closely linked with internal political life, he refrained from raising any issues himself. Decisions were made in the Ministry, or it would be decided that, because of its importance, the issue should be placed before the Cabinet. At Cabinet meetings the problems were presented and the solutions argued by the Foreign Minister; before the debate took place Salazar might make a comment or expand on some detail, but then participated in the discussion as any other minister. As Prime Minister, Salazar never asked any foreign ambassador to see him, and received members of the foreign diplomatic corps in Lisbon very seldom and only at their own request. In conversation with foreign ambassadors, Salazar would never commit the Government, unless the issue had already been decided in Cabinet or cleared with the Foreign Minister.

The Foreign Minister reported directly to the President and to the members of the National Assembly.

The Minister for Foreign Affairs was, then, in accordance with the law of 1938, the political head of the Ministry. However, under that law, how was the department organized? The Ministry had a permanent head: the secretary-general, a career official holding the rank of ambassador. The secretary-general was the coordinator of the work of the department, and he could on his own authority address any other Portuguese authority; he could give instructions to Portuguese representatives abroad; and he was the only official, besides the Minister, whose answers to foreign ambassadors would commit the Government. A number of specialized departments came under the direct authority of the secretary-general: protocol, code room, press service, mail room, inspectorate and control. The secretary-general was also chairman of the Council of the Ministry, a body created to advise the Minister on promotions, transfers, appointments to posts abroad and disciplinary action.

Below the secretary-general, but under the direct authority of the Minister, there were two main departments: the Directorate-General for Political Affairs and Administration and the Directorate-General for Economic and Consular Affairs. Each department was headed by a director-general, a career official, with the rank of minister of first class. The directors-general reported directly to the Minister. The secretary-general attended their meetings if he so wished or was invited by the Minister. The two directors-general could receive and confer with the heads of foreign missions, but their answers would not, in principle, engage the responsibility of the Government. They could send instructions to Portuguese representatives abroad, but only in the name and on behalf of the Minister. However, the bulk of the Ministry's work was in fact carried out by the two directors-general and the various smaller departments under each of them. They handled all the detailed work, directed the preparation of position papers, drafted the important dispatches and cables and submitted recommendations for the Minister's approval.

Under the law of 1938 Portuguese representation abroad was provided for by the establishment of embassies, legations and consulates. There were embassies only to the Holy See, London, Rio de Janeiro, Madrid and Washington. The legations, headed by a minister, could be of first or of second class depending on the importance of the country. There were four categories of consulates: consulates-general, and first, second and third class consulates. Where required, honorary consuls could be appointed. According to the conditions of the post, special staff could be attached to the various missions: military, cultural, commercial, press attachés.

This basic structure, with minor improvements, lasted for nearly thirty years. After the Second World War, however, Portuguese international relations became increasingly complex and diverse. The multiplicity of international organizations, the emergence of new nations, the complexity of the issues at stake, the difficulties inherent in Portuguese policies themselves, all imposed heavier responsibilities on the Ministry of Foreign Affairs. In terms of both staff and structure the Ministry was clearly inadequate, and fundamental reforms were essential. These were enacted by decree-law 47 331 of 23 November 1966.

An entirely new concept (for Portugal) was introduced by this law. Whereas the law of 1938 had established the competence of the various departments according to the *nature* of the problems – political, economic, administrative – the law of 1966 gave priority to the *area* where the problems originated. The old system was not altogether abandoned: at the higher levels the nature of the problem would again be considered in order to ensure the required global perspective and coordination. But the new mixed system encouraged better specialization, a deeper understanding of problems, a clearer picture of local situations, a more sustained follow-up of the various issues, a better utilization of opportunities and possibilities. A second important feature of the reform of 1966 was that it brought under the control and direction of the Ministry many external activities – cultural, commercial, etc. – that used to be handled by other Government departments. Thirdly, the reform gave the Ministry a more important voice, even a final say, in matters pertaining to international relations. Finally, the old-fashioned distinction between embassies and legations for countries of different rank was abolished, in line with the concept accepted by the international community that all nations are equal.

In the new structure, the Minister is of course still the political head of the department (see Appendix A). As before, the secretary-general is the professional head, and his duties, responsibilities and rank are the same as they were in 1938. However, the services under the secretary-general have been considerably expanded. The secretary-general has under his direct authority the following: Legal and Treaty Division, Information and Press Service, Protocol, Archive and Library, Inspectorate and Control, Code Room, Mail Room. Below the secretary-general, but under the authority of the Minister and reporting directly to him, are three major departments: the Directorate-General for Political Affairs, the Directorate-General for Economic Affairs and the Directorate-General for Central Administration. These three departments together carry the bulk of the work of the Ministry.

The director-general for political affairs, who may hold the rank of ambassador or minister of first class, has two assistants, both with the rank of minister of second class. The director-general for political affairs has under his direct authority the following five divisions: Europe and America; Africa, Asia and Oceania; Foreign Cultural Relations; International Organizations; the Atlantic Pact (NATO). The director-general for economic affairs, who also has two assistants, has under him the following three divisions: Europe and America; Africa, Asia and Oceania; International Economic Organizations. Finally, the director-general for central administration, who has only one assistant, has under him three divisions: Consular Affairs, Administration, and Personnel. A fourth department, the Directorate-General for International Cooperation, has recently been created, the main purpose of which is the conduct of negotiations and the establishment of closer links with former Portuguese overseas territories.

Abroad, Portugal has 106 embassies and 53 consulates; the number of honorary consulates changes from time to time, as required. A number of permanent delegations are also accredited to international organizations such as the United Nations and its specialized agencies, NATO, the European Economic Community, etc.

In the department in Lisbon there is a supporting staff, who are civil servants but non-career officials, who fill the positions of clerks, typists, accountants, etc. Abroad, many of the supporting staff are locally recruited except for those handling confidential matters, who are sent from Lisbon. The numbers depend, of course, on the nature of the work to be done and the size of the embassy.

Who can be admitted to the Portuguese foreign service? Various conditions have to be fulfilled. Any Portuguese citizen, male or female, who has never had any other citizenship, may seek admission. He or she has to have a university degree in law, history, philosophy, economy or finance. Then, after submitting his or her application, the candidate is invited to a social test. He calls at the Ministry, is interviewed by senior officials, engaged and scrutinized in conversation both alone and in a group. If he succeeds, then the candidate presents himself for an examination, both written and oral, lasting several days. The candidate has to draft documents, make a précis, and answer questions before a panel of senior officials and university professors. The tests are conducted on the basis of a list of subjects covering history, international politics, international law, diplomatic history and world economy. Marks are given to each candidate, and only those who obtain twelve or fourteen marks out of twenty (the number is altered from time to time) qualify for admission.

Having succeeded in their tests, the candidates are appointed in accordance with the marks they were given. The order of appointment establishes their seniority for the future. They are appointed on a provisional basis for two years, as embassy attachés. During these two years they undergo intensive training; they are rotated through the various divisions within the department; they are entrusted with minor responsibilities such as drafting simple documents or studying old files that are to be reopened because new problems have arisen in connection with them. After two years the final decision is taken by the Council of the Ministry, which recommends to the Minister the definite admission or the rejection of the candidate. If admitted, a candidate becomes a third secretary of embassy and a career official.

The Portuguese diplomatic service has the following ranks: third, second and first secretary of embassy; counsellor of embassy; minister of second class; minister of first class; ambassador. Each official has to serve at least three years in his rank before promotion. There was a time when the diplomatic and consular careers were entirely separate, though consuls-general and counsellors of embassy could both compete to become head of mission. But this concept was abandoned, and for a very long time now the two careers have been merged. Any official can serve indifferently as consul or secretary, being transferable from one to the other with equivalent rank, and having equal access to the rank of minister or ambassador. Promotions up to the rank of counsellor or consul-general are made on the basis of distinguished service and seniority, and are recommended to the Minister by the Council of the Ministry. If the Minister does not accept the Council's recommendations he must justify his own decision in writing. The promotions from first secretary to counsellor or consul of first class were until recently made in accordance with the outcome of a competitive examination among the first secretaries, but this procedure has now been abandoned. Promotions to the three higher ranks – ministers and ambassadors – are made solely on the basis of distinguished service. In fact the majority of Portuguese foreign service officers end their careers as ministers of second class. At any given time, the number of officials holding the personal rank of ambassador cannot exceed twelve on active duty. Ministers of first and second class have the title of ambassador when *en poste*, and they are locally accredited as such, but that does not mean that they have been or will necessarily be promoted to the rank of ambassador. Most of the Portuguese embassies are headed by ministers, except in recent times, when the head of mission may be a political appointee, who is given the provisional rank of ambassador.

The usual retiring age is seventy years, though for those serving abroad it is sixty-five years, which when convenient may be prolonged to sixty-eight. Those reaching that age will be transferred to the Department if there is a vacancy for their rank; otherwise, they retire on pension.

There are about 400 career officials in the Portuguese diplomatic service, and about 300 administrative and bureaucratic staff, not including those locally recruited. Taking into account the technical and specialized attachés (cultural, military, press, commercial), the diplomatic establishment of Portugal has about 750 officials, again not including foreign staff locally recruited.

The career officials are freely transferred from diplomatic to consular service, and vice versa.[1] The categories of third, second and first secretaries and of counsellor, rank equal to those of consuls of third, second and first class and of consul-general. Promotion to minister of second class is available equally to counsellors and consuls-general.

As an institution, what is the nature of the Portuguese Ministry for Foreign Affairs? Sociologically, does it have any special characteristics?

A first point should again be stressed: the Ministry is entirely open. That is to say, the recruitment of its staff is based on merit, and on merit alone. Since the beginning of this century a tradition has been firmly established that admission to the foreign service depends solely on the outcome of the examination to which candidates are subjected, and promotion and access to the highest ranks depend on personal achievement. For both admission and promotion the family background is entirely irrelevant: there is no tradition whatsoever connecting any families or their members with the foreign service. The social background and financial situation of candidates are also immaterial. If the Portuguese foreign service is related to an institution, it is to the university; and as all classes of Portuguese society have access to university, so are all classes represented in the foreign service. In other words, one cannot identify the Portuguese foreign service with any class of society. Nor can one identify it with a particular university: candidates to the service come from all the Portuguese universities. But it is true to say that the university influences the foreign service, in the sense that all candidates must have a university degree. It gives the service an intellectual outlook and a sense of elitism, which is sometimes criticized by the civil servants of other departments and by public opinion, and the service is looked upon with a certain amount of both envy and contempt. Possibly as a reaction, the service tends to isolate itself from Portuguese daily life, and may sometimes overlook some realities of that life. On the other hand the foreign service, more than any other, looks upon the nation as a whole, has a global perception of its problems and objectives, and is in a good position to coordinate various points of view and, if necessary, to arbitrate among conflicting sectional interests.

Since the Second World War foreign relations seem to have acquired a new dimension. The multilateral diplomacy of the United Nations, the mushrooming of international organizations, the conduct of negotiations in the 'market place', the public debate of important issues among governments and nations – all this has brought about a style requiring new methods and a new approach. However, the fundamental nature and scope of international relations remain, and though the style of diplomacy has changed its substance is the same. One must not always take appearances – public negotiations, press conferences, summit meetings, etc. – for reality; the reality is the same as before, that is, bilateral contacts, secret negotiations, the debate of real issues among governments, which are not necessarily those debated before the public eye.

The Portuguese Ministry for Foreign Affairs has adapted itself to the new style. The turn from classical and traditional to modern methods took place after 1956, under the impact of Portuguese membership of the United Nations. Since then, Portuguese foreign service officials have been able to ensure Portuguese participation in all the international organizations of which Portugal is a member, and have accustomed themselves to public speaking and debate and to multilateral negotiations. From 1956 onwards there was a shortage of staff to meet all the new requirements, but the number of officials authorized by law was gradually increased so the foreign service was able to expand its recruitment. It may be said that by 1960 the crisis had been overcome. As the Ministry's officials are nowadays more in the limelight, and are seen to deal with both national and international problems, some of which arouse wide interest and publicity, there is among the Portuguese public a better appreciation of the part played by and the usefulness of the Portuguese foreign service.

In theory, members of the foreign service are expected to cover all aspects of international relations, be they political, cultural, military, economic, financial or commercial. In point of fact, of course, the various delegations and missions are assisted, as required, by experts and technicians familiar with the particular problems under discussion. The head of a delegation or a mission is a Foreign Minister's official; he seeks the guidance and advice of the experts, but responsibility for the presentation of the Portuguese point of view and for final decisions rests with him, and to him and to the Ministry are ascribed the success or failure of a mission or negotiation.

The long tradition of the Portuguese Ministry for Foreign Affairs, of which it is very proud, can be traced through the nation's various historical periods. In addition, during its history many prominent Portuguese – historians, writers, poets – have come from within its ranks. For more than seventy years now, the Portuguese Foreign Ministry has been housed in the same building. In earlier times, it was the Convent of Nossa Senhora das Necessidades (Our Lady of the Needs); then it became, late in the eighteenth century until the proclamation of the Republic, the Lisbon residence for the royal family; since 1910, it has housed the Foreign Ministry. Much work has been done to improve, expand and adapt the building. It is now known as the Palacio das Necessidades (Palace of the Needs). Apart from the functional area which looks rather austere and cold, the building may be considered rather luxurious with many salons, galleries and reception rooms full of charm and tradition.

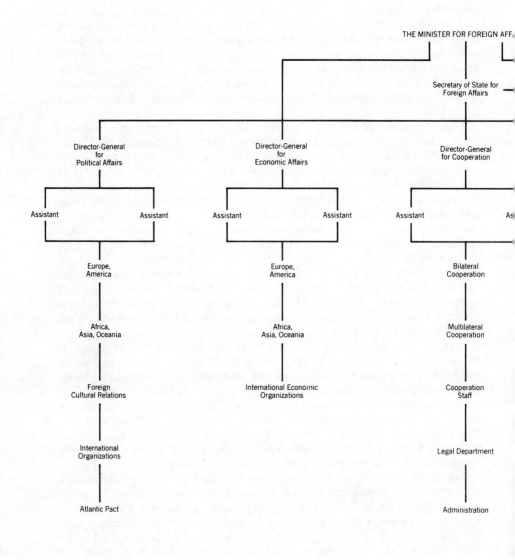

THE MINISTER FOR FOREIGN AFF

Secretary of State for
Foreign Affairs

Director-General
for
Political Affairs

Director-General
for
Economic Affairs

Director-General
for Cooperation

Assistant   Assistant

Assistant   Assistant

Assistant   As

Europe,
America

Europe,
America

Bilateral
Cooperation

Africa,
Asia, Oceania

Africa,
Asia, Oceania

Multilateral
Cooperation

Foreign
Cultural Relations

International Economic
Organizations

Cooperation
Staff

International
Organizations

Legal Department

Atlantic Pact

Administration

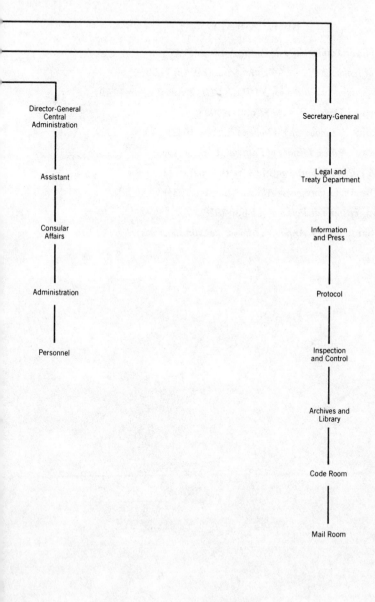

Director-General
Central
Administration

Assistant

Consular
Affairs

Administration

Personnel

Secretary-General

Legal and
Treaty Department

Information
and Press

Protocol

Inspection
and Control

Archives and
Library

Code Room

Mail Room

NOTE

[1] It has long been customary for career officials to serve alternatively at home and abroad though some ambassadors have been kept at a single posting for extended periods of time (even over twenty years in the case of the ambassadors in Brussels and Paris after the Second World War).

BIBLIOGRAPHY

Eduardo Brazão, *História diplomática de Portugal* (Lisbon 1932).

——, *A Secretaria de Estado dos Negócios Estrangeiros* (Lisbon 1978).

——, *A diplomacia portuguesa nos séculos XVII e XVIII*, 2 vols (Lisbon 1978).

Hugh Kay, *Salazar and Modern Portugal* (London 1968).

Marquês do Lavradio, *A diplomacia e o Império* (Lisbon 1943).

Harold V. Livermore, *A New History of Portugal* (London 1969).

Charles Nowell, *A History of Portugal* (New York 1962).

Edgar Prestage, *The Anglo-Portuguese Alliance* (London 1934).

J. Veríssimo Serrão, *Historia de Portugal* (Lisbon 1978).

Luiz Teixeira de Sampaio, *O Arquivo Histórico do Ministério dos Negócios Estrangeiros* (Lisbon 1925).

Spain

Spain's First Secretariat of State, Ministry of State and Ministry of Foreign Affairs

DENIS SMYTH

Dr Denis Smyth is Lecturer in Modern History at University College, Cork. He was born in Dublin in 1948, obtained his first degree at University College, Dublin and his doctorate at Cambridge, where he held a Research Studentship at Peterhouse from 1973 to 1976. He is the author of a forthcoming work on 'British policy and Franco's Spain during the Second World War'.

One of the most prominent features of modern Spanish history has been the number of contrasts, even contradictions, that it has embodied. Uneven economic development and disparate social evolution cut across, and exacerbated, divisions that already existed, producing an idiosyncratic national community in the modern era – an asymmetrical composition of the archaic and the advanced. These diverse factors and factions have often uneasily coexisted; sometimes they have associated in unexpected symbiosis; occasionally they have come into sharp conflict, most spectacularly in the nationwide Civil War of 1936–9, in which the many structural tensions of the modern period were reduced to one all-embracing antagonism: a combat between progressive Republican and conservative 'Nationalist' Spain. Such internal disarray was the result of overlapping historical processes of growth and decline. From the eighteenth century onwards, Spain was characterized by an upsurge in some areas and activities, by decay or fossilization in others. The economic expansion and regional dynamism of the north and east of the country stood in shaky equilibrium with the rural stagnation and cultural backwardness of the centre and south. By the twentieth century the country was partially modernized and partially traditional, an organic imbalance rendered all the more serious by the failure of the Spanish monarchy to reestablish around itself any political consensus. Only an agreed political system could have provided the representatives of the old and the new Spain with an acceptable mechanism by which to resolve their differences without injury to a fragile social and national unity. However, Spaniards not only differed over particular political problems, they also disagreed as to the proper rules for the conduct of political life. The champions of the 'two Spains' espoused irreconcilable constitutional schemas for the ordering of national politics. Governments have changed often enough in modern Spain but so, too, have regimes. Since society was too riven to rally for long to any of the political contestants, power tended to fall to those who exerted superior force or exhibited more cohesion or less exhaustion at a given moment.

No government ministry, not even one whose concern was the management of foreign affairs, could be immune to, or isolated from, such protracted domestic instability. The inevitable vicissitudes inherent in any pattern of governmental growth were greatly exaggerated in Spain by the erratic and rapid rate of political changeover and systemic uncertainty. In the last two centuries the Spanish Foreign Ministry has advanced, then retreated, has prospered, then retrenched, has been neglected and ignored, and even once abolished altogether. Its stamina has been impressive but its institutional evolution has been laborious and, perhaps, less than complete. As recently as 1977 one commentator remarked that it has not been a proper political ministry, but merely and 'essentially a diplomatic department', a bureaucratic office rather than a mature ministry exercising proper authority in the formulation and execution of Spain's foreign policy.[1] It seems a heavy historical irony that Spain's Foreign Ministry should be so described, when that country is distinguished from its European neighbours by the precocity of its innovations in managing its external affairs. However, a brief survey of the early phase of modern Spain's organized action in the realm of international relations will demonstrate that its foreign policy administration has had long experience of the halting, interrupted and incomplete character of Spain's institutional development.

The vigour that the 'Catholic Kings', Ferdinand and Isabella, displayed in the later fifteenth and early sixteenth centuries in gathering in Spain's peninsular territory and launching its imperial enterprise in the New World, was also expressed in administrative growth and refinement. Accrediting the 'first non-Italian resident envoys outside Italy' in European history, they proceeded to deploy one of the most widespread diplomatic networks of the day.[2] Moreover, their diplomatic corps was staffed by men of a calibre, competence and conscientiousness much superior to those serving other powers.[3] The central administration of the early Spanish monarchy was no less active in its attention to foreign policy matters. As the secretaries of the King came to a working division of royal business, some among them generally handled foreign affairs. Royal favour usually raised one of this latter group of officials to a predominant position, vis-à-vis his peers, in the administration of Spain's foreign relations, leading to his being regarded as 'first' secretary.[4] By Ferdinand's death in 1516 Spain possessed a rudimentary central office for the management of its external affairs. The secretary who headed this office, however, operated only as a functionary, administratively facilitating the foreign policy decisions that remained the exclusive preserve of his royal master.[5]

The Emperor Charles V continued the good work begun by his illustrious grandparents. He established a Council of State as a common administrative organ for all his vast and diffuse territories, an institutional creation whose purpose was to aid him, inter alia, in the resolution of high international policy and issues of war and peace, the conclusion of alliances and matrimonial unions, and the unification of general policy. The secretary of this council became the secretary of state charged with guiding Spain's foreign relations.[6]

A more precise definition of administrative jurisdiction and a greater specialization of bureaucratic function developed within the managerial structure of Spain's international relations as the sixteenth century progressed. The two leading governmental appointments made by the new king, Philip II, in 1556 crystallized the evolution of a distinct department of Spanish government whose focus was the field of foreign affairs. On 6 February 1556 Gonzalo Pérez was instructed to undertake the secretaryship of state, with the following brief: '(To supervise) affairs of peace and war and matters dependent on them and the correspondence which each minister of a province conducts with those of the others, and with princes, potentates, states and ambassadors . . .'.[7] Shortly afterwards, Philip II named Juan Vázquez de Molina as secretary of state and war of the kingdoms of Spain, thereby effecting a formal split between internal and external, foreign and domestic affairs. In fact, Gonzalo Pérez presided for ten years over a specific entity solely concerned with international policy.[8]

After his secretary's death, Philip II acted to hone further the foreign policy instrument that he wielded. On 8 December 1567 he distributed the business of the Secretariat of State between two appointees. One was entrusted with all matters pertaining to the Imperial, English and French courts, while the other was assigned responsibility for all Italian diplomatic matters. These departmental divisions came to be entitled, respectively, the Secretariat of State of Northern Affairs (Secretaría de Estado de la negociación del Norte) and the Secretariat of State of Italian Affairs (Secretaría de Estado de la negociación de Italia), and were normally directed by two different people, though they were sometimes placed in the care of one official.[9] Initially, each of the Secretariats of State possessed an establishment, in addition to the secretary himself, of one chief clerk and three ordinary clerks, but later this staff was enlarged to include a couple, each, of grade two and grade three clerks. Each secretariat also employed a *derechero* to collect the fees owed to it under various headings, an unspecified number of general employees (*entretenidos*) and an often substantial number of supplementary clerks.[10]

However, this early bureaucratic development rather lost its way in the late sixteenth century. From 1587, Philip II used the Secretariats of State only as organizations for the transaction of the routine administrative business falling within their respective competence. For advice and assistance in foreign policy decision-making, he turned to some of his counsellors of state. This became normal practice in the seventeenth century, with the secretaries relegated to a narrowly bureaucratic role, their former position in the inner circle of Spanish foreign policy-making being assumed by a chief minister.[11] The individuals occupying the latter post (*validos*) usually owed their political ascendancy to the support of a court faction and a temporarily won royal favour.[12] In terms of organizational coordination and concentrated institutional control of foreign policy, this represented a considerable falling off from the solid achievements of the sixteenth century. Moreover, this decline in the active function of the secretaries of state in the policy-making process was reflected in internal decay. A sure sign of institutional atrophy was the habit, which first arose in the reign of Philip IV (1621–65), of assigning two individuals to take up the Secretariat of State for Italy (regarded as senior to that for the north in the seventeenth century). One of these appointees would actually perform the practical tasks involved in the job, whereas the second, already always serving the monarch in another capacity, would receive the emoluments, honours and prerogatives pertaining to the position.[13] The fact that the premier Secretariat of State in foreign affairs had so diminished in stature as to be considered primarily as a sinecure for another official provides proof of the depth of administrative regression in this area. The central governmental device that Philip IV forged to rescue the sinking fortunes of an increasingly embattled seventeenth-century Spain, the Secretariat of the Universal Office (Secretaría del Despacho Universal), had neither the incipient specialization of function nor the embryonic ministerial responsibility in the management of the state's external affairs evident in sixteenth-century developments.

The accession of the Bourbons to Spain's throne in 1700, for all that it generated internal turmoil and external conflict in the War of the Spanish Succession, brought much-needed reserves of executive energy and resources of administrative inventiveness.[14] The field of foreign policy administration was at the heart of the governmental restructuring undertaken, early in his reign, by Philip V. On 30 November 1714 he created, by royal decree, a new administrative base for Spanish government in the form of four Secretariats of the Office (Secretarías de Despacho) and a Universal Treasury Intendancy (Intendencia Universal de Hacienda). The secretariats were endowed with exclusive control over particular aspects of government with the express purpose of ensuring a departmental specialization and managerial expertise that would improve the efficiency of the whole state machinery. As *ex officio* members of the Cabinet Council (Consejo de Gabinete), the secretaries of state (secretarios de estado), as the chiefs of the reshaped secretariats were to be called, would mutually benefit from the greater knowledge and skill regarding particular branches of the royal government, which they could bring, individually, to the deliberations of the supreme royal council.[15]

Among the Secretariats of the Office was established one for Affairs of State (Negocios de Estado) which was assigned direction of 'transactions and correspondence with the other sovereigns, and with their ministers and those of foreign countries, which are to be handled and tended by a single person'. The fact that this Secretariat was mentioned first in the royal decree of November 1714 caused it to be referred to as the First Secretariat (Primera Secretaría) and its incumbent to be dubbed the Primer Secretario de Estado y del Despacho, designations that survived until the later part of the nineteenth century.[16] This First Secretariat proceeded to thrive in the more bracing administrative atmosphere of Bourbon Spain and was soon elevated by royal sponsorship into a veritable principal ministry. Over the course of the eighteenth century this Secretariat expanded its competence beyond the boundaries of foreign affairs, absorbing existing or new government activities. For example, the Madrid General Superintendency of Police, which was set up in March 1782, was placed under the stewardship of the First Secretariat of State.[17] Although this institutional trend rather subverted the original aim of its initiation, namely to focus departmental effort exclusively upon the area of foreign relations, the accumulating authority of the First Secretariat was asserted in the field of its principal charge as well.

Under Philip V the First Secretariat had, for all its bureaucratic energy, remained an agency devoted solely to translating his policy choices into action. Its holders played no creative part in foreign policy formulation. With a new king, however, this state of affairs was transformed. A new phase in the evolution of the First Secretariat set in with Ferdinand VI's ascent to the throne on 9 July 1746. From that time until virtually the end of the century the First Secretariat operated, according to some Spanish historians, as a genuine ministry. This change was wrought by the successive nomination to the first secretaryship of tried and tested diplomats, men with a long record of service in their country's interest abroad. The patent professionalism of these individuals was sufficient to turn them into active collaborators with the monarch in the determination of Spain's foreign policy.[18]

The pioneer of this process of departmental maturation was José de Carvajal y Lancaster, who cooperated with Ferdinand VI in the endeavour to promote a peaceful European equilibrium that would leave the Spanish government free to pursue domestic reforms and uphold Spain's empire in Latin America. Carvajal also sought to widen the professional experience of the First Secretariat's personnel and to standardize their income. He introduced the procedure of appointing to the posts of secretaries of the embassies, and officials of the Secretariat, individuals who had already been employed in some diplomatic role at home or abroad. This practice aided the formation of a specialist team of civil servants who alternated in action between the central foreign policy administration and Spanish diplomatic missions abroad. Carvajal also, for the first, time, officially specified the salaries for the various grades of employment within the Secretariat.[19]

The reign of that most enlightened of eighteenth-century Spanish despots, Charles III (1759–88), was marked by further progress in the delineation of a diplomatic career in Spain. In 1760 the First Secretariat's establishment comprised ten officials, two chief clerks, and two each of a subordinate hierarchy of clerks ranging from the second to fifth grades. Moreover, it was laid down at this time that the secretaries of the Spanish embassies at 'the four principal courts of Europe' should be selected from these clerical officials of the central administration. This decree lent royal sanction to a custom that already existed, but it marks the formal birth of the Spanish diplomatic career.[20] For instance, out of the ten individuals employed by the First Secretariat of State in 1763, five had attained ambassadorial rank by the end of their administrative careers and two had become ministers (of legations).[21] The salaries of the Secretariat's employees were also increased substantially in the early 1760s.[22]

The Spanish diplomatic service received a further fillip from the actions of the leading 'enlightened' governmental figure of the later eighteenth century, José Moñino y Redondo, Count of Floridablanca. Floridablanca, who held the First Secretariat and acted as the King's First Minister for a lengthy period starting in 1776, increased the establishment of the department by four additional officials (including a translator and an archivist). These were generally chosen from among either the clerks of embassy or legation (a new category created during Floridablanca's tenure of office) or the secretaries of the diplomatic missions. He continued that interchange of personnel between central secretariat and the diplomatic representations that was fostering such technical competence and corporate consciousness among Spain's foreign policy bureaucrats. In the later 1780s he created a form of diplomatic apprenticeship by dispatching young men, between the ages of fifteen and twenty, to Spain's embassies and legations abroad, where employment in junior functions would give them a basic grounding in diplomatic skills and practices.[23]

Five classes of official had become defined by the last years of Floridablanca's sojourn at the head of the First Secretariat. These were, in order of ascent, diplomatic attaché or acting employee, clerk of embassy or legation, secretary of embassy or legation, minister (of legation) or envoy, and ambassador. When a representation was left without a chief, for any reason, the secretary of the mission adopted the role of chargé d'affaires.[24] A regular mode of entry to, and promotion within, the ranks of the 'employees of the First Secretariat for the Diplomatic Career' (as they had come to be called by the start of the nineteenth century),[25] developed naturally without the need for legal provision. Moreover, it is a measure of the corporate consciousness that had arisen within the Spanish foreign service that when Mariano-Luis de Urquijo, who held the first secretaryship at the turn of the century, attempted to revise the conditions governing membership of, and ascent within, the profession, he had to abandon the effort in the face of tenacious resistance, offered especially by José García de León y Pizarro, then chief clerk or official in the Secretariat.[26]

One avenue of access to the Spanish diplomatic service in the late eighteenth and early nineteenth centuries was through the position of diplomatic attaché. Progression to the level of clerk of a diplomatic mission's secretariat would occur after a few years. The next step was transfer to the central administration of the First Secretariat as clerk of the eighth or ninth grade. The diplomat could then expect reintegration into the service abroad with the status of secretary of a diplomatic representation. The summit of the diplomatic career, open to both the secretaries of the missions abroad and those who had pursued an administrative career exclusively within the central organization of the First Secretariat of State and had attained the rank of chief clerk, was the post of minister (of legation) or ambassador. Aspirants to the diplomatic service might enter at the advanced level of secretary of a mission if they had already served time in one of the royal government's Secretariats of the Office, particularly the First Secretariat itself. Those bureaucrats who sprang from the latter secretariat generally returned to work again in the central machinery of Spain's foreign policy before being nominated minister or ambassador in a foreign country. Those officials emanating from other central government departments usually remained on service abroad, achieving ambassadorial or ministerial status without any period of participation in the central foreign policy administration. Finally, the possession of high office, social prestige or wealth could enable one to short-circuit the whole process. Leading civil functionaries, senior military personnel and prominent nobles were appointed directly to head embassies and legations.[27]

The first head of the Secretariat to specify the educational requirements and fix a minimum age for entrants to the diplomatic service was Pedro Ceballos Guerra, an otherwise undistinguished first secretary. On 17 July 1816 it was decreed that aspirants to the diplomatic career should have reached twenty years of age, and have been engaged in set studies for some years before. At the age of fourteen they should have completed their basic education in religion and the humanities, and were then charged with attendance at a Spanish university to study philosophy for one year, geography and 'national' history for another, 'natural' international law for two years more, and administrative law and political economy for a final two years. Their progress over this course of studies was to be duly certified by the university authorities. The purpose of this precise definition of the educational preparation of Spain's diplomats was affirmed to be the formation of a pool of apprentices in the diplomatic service, 'fit servants of the state', who could fill the junior positions in the missions abroad. Army and naval officers, 'distinguished for their knowledge and talents' were also appointed, as armed service attachés, to Spain's representations in the major military powers at this time in an effort to keep abreast of the latest advances in military affairs.[28] This was a response in diplomatic organization to the revolution in the technology and techniques of warfare, so recently and so brutally visited upon Spain by the Napoleonic occupation and the war that it engendered, between 1808 and 1814.

For all that the Spanish diplomatic service had consolidated the working conditions and corporate identity of its members in the last years of the eighteenth and the first decades of the nineteenth centuries, the central government department that it served was rudely treated in those tumultuous times. As the shock waves spilled over the Pyrenees from revolutionary and Napoleonic France, and the unity of the Spanish *antiguo régimen* was irrevocably broken, all Spain's governing institutions, including the First Secretariat of State, registered the impact of this traumatic experience.

The first secretaryship entered into a phase of decline from 28 February 1792 when Charles IV, to appease revolutionary France, dispensed with the services of Floridablanca, who had been striving to seal Spain off from political contagion.[29] Charles IV did place the First Secretariat under the control of his trusted favourite, Godoy, for a period. However, the increasingly intractable nature of Spain's foreign relations at this time, dominated as they were by a dynamic France, the rather variable proficiency with which the unpopular and untrained Godoy managed them, and the fact that after March 1798 the latter exercised his virtual dictatorship over Spanish state policy without occupying the first secretaryship, all contributed to a diminution in the power and prestige of that department.[30]

The Napoleonic incursion into Spain in 1807–8, produced by French expansionism and compounded by Spanish monarchical ineptitude, precipitated a bitter conflict which incidentally further reduced the significance of the First Secretariat. The spontaneous armed resistance that broke out against the French from the spring of 1808 was eventually organized under provincial *juntas* that in turn created a Supreme Central Junta. This latter body met for the first time on 25 September 1808, and from that moment all the Secretariats of the Office (the First Secretariat of State included) were demoted to purely administrative roles, with their secretaries restricted to a passive, bureaucratic function. For the total power of political decision and policy choice rested with the Supreme Central Junta and its successors, the Regency and the Cortes (parliamentary assembly) to Cadiz. No less than thirteen people headed this diminished Secretariat during the five years of the War of Independence, an intensity of change in directorship that allowed it little opportunity to adjust to varying leadership styles or priorities.[31] This administrative recession was, of course, a reflection of the general national disarray that the Napoleonic essay in forced modernization had caused in Spain. From this point right up to the end of the Franco regime, Spain sought to exorcize the internal divisions and social contradictions uncovered by the shock of combat and ideological upheaval. With pardonable hyperbole, Salvador de Madariaga summarized the profound consequences of this structural crisis thus: 'In foreign, as in home affairs, Spain had to start in the nineteenth century from the bare ground. There was nothing.'[32]

Ferdinand VII was hardly the man to react imaginatively to a *tabula rasa*. His reflex reaction to royal absolutism revived the worst, not the best, practices of the old regime, a reversion all the more detrimental in that his initial appointees to the first secretaryship were singularly lacking in managerial talent or personal initiative. The royal favourite, Miguel Carvajal y Vargas, third Duke of San Carlos, who held the First Secretariat between May 1814 and November 1815, exerted himself so little in the direction of foreign policy that Spain's representatives abroad were left without any proper instructions about the current policies governing the state's external relations. Even when San Carlos bestirred himself to reply to their urgent pleas for guidance, his advice was hardly helpful. He answered one anxious enquiry in these tautological terms: 'His Majesty decides in favour of what could be most conducive to the interests of the Monarchy.'[33]

Pedro Ceballos (who succeeded to the headship of the First Secretariat in 1815, when European statesmen were still engaged upon the momentous task of restructuring European politics after the turbulent Napoleonic era) proved a no more vigorous departmental chief. Again, heads of mission were deprived of central government counsel, and those who did receive instructions from Ceballos were only confused by the contradictory and rambling nature of his missives. The fall of Ceballos from office in October

1815, in part engineered by the Russian minister plenipotentiary to Spain, Dmitrii Paulovitch Tatistchev, demonstrates the extent to which the politics of the court camarilla had come to affect the departmental leadership, and even the content, of Spanish foreign policy under Ferdinand. Tatistchev had so ingratiated himself with Ferdinand that he was also able to contribute to the unseating in September 1818 of the man who succeeded Ceballos, José García de León y Pizarro, a distinguished long-serving diplomat.[34]

However haphazard the procedure that had lifted Pizarro to the top of the First Secretariat, he did avail himself of the opportunity to reform and revivify the administration of Spain's foreign relations while he lasted in office. The abuses that he sought to correct indicate the scale of institutional inanition in the First Secretariat. Pizarro abolished five chief clerkships that had been created by his two immediate predecessors, probably as sinecures. He enforced upon the Secretariat's employees regular attendance at work, and its conscientious performance, to remedy the pervasive slackness that had characterized departmental life in the preceding period. He also required Spain's representatives abroad to enter into frequent and systematic communication among themselves, so that their diplomatic strivings in the national interest might be properly concerted.[35] Not for the first or the last time, however, this administrative renewal was to be interrupted by political disturbance.

The short-lived liberal revolution of 1820–3, forcing Ferdinand to rule as a constitutional monarch in tandem with an elected Cortes, ushered in another phase of governmental confusion. Between 1819 and 1826 as many as twenty-six secretaries acted, in title or in practice, at the head of the First Secretariat.[36] This pace of bureaucratic replacement at the topmost level in the Secretariat removed pattern and purpose from its proceedings. During the liberal triennium, 1820–3, Ferdinand even conducted his own clandestine foreign policy, as he sought behind the backs of his constitutional government, the assistance of the Holy Alliance for the restoration of his absolute power.[37]

The ultimate success of this strategy, thanks to the assistance of his fellow Bourbon, Louis XVIII of France, did not induce Ferdinand to preside over any great political or governmental resurgence in the last decade of his rule, 1823–33. Political and economic pressures did eventually persuade him to permit some administrative changes, in the hopes of ensuring the survival of the absolute monarchy amid a less homogeneous society and a more diversified economy.[38] Although not at the heart of these developments, the removal in 1832 of virtually all its statutory duties, other than those relating to the conduct of Spain's foreign relations, from the First Secretariat, was one example of the governmental streamlining in progress.[39] However, as the Spanish historian Joseph Fontana has argued, it is a mistake to concentrate overmuch upon the royal role at this juncture in the country's history.[40] For the middle decades of the nineteenth century saw the birth of a new social and governmental order, which even if it did not persist for long unchallenged was clearly the product of novel economic and political forces of a strength sufficient to induce the monarchy and other traditional interests to share power with them.

The protagonists of this new liberal bourgeois order erected a constitutional monarchy, initially, through the Regency of María Cristina.[41] The impulse came from them, and they were also the dynamic element in the renovation of government departments that was effected during this period. The First Secretariat, or as it increasingly came to be called from the 1830s, the Ministry of State, was thoroughly overhauled by a series of liberal ministers. It could hardly escape this fate, as Ferdinand had coupled the prime ministership (presidency of the Council of Ministers) with it in 1823, and although the posts were formally separated in 1840 the chief minister did often also assume responsibility for foreign affairs in later decades.[42] The Secretariat of State, which title remained its legal description until 1868, was too much at the centre of the web in the 1830s–1850s not to be the focus of efforts at governmental reform and regeneration.

On 16 June 1834, the Prime Minister and secretary of state, the playwright Francisco Martínez de la Rosa, began this process of departmental renewal. He created the administrative position of subsecretary in each of the Secretariats of State in order to facilitate the transaction of government business in a more methodical and expeditious manner. The subsecretary was to be nominated by the Minister and act as his immediate subordinate, relieving him of routine clerical functions. The departmental head would thus be free to concern himself with the 'important reforms' being projected in the various branches of governmental activity, and to attend the sessions of the Cortes. All the secretariats were also then subdivided into administrative sections and 'definitively reconstituted as ministerial departments'.[43] Martínez de la Rosa also fixed the establishment of the Ministry of State at a modest level: apart from the secretary and subsecretary, it was to be made up of eight officials, two acting employees, four assistants, five filing clerks and five porters.[44]

It was the next chief Minister of State, the Count of Toreno, who, acting on the royal authority granted the previous year to rationalize internal departmental structures so as to expedite and regularize the flow of government business, fundamentally reshaped the internal organization of Spain's central foreign policy machinery in August 1835. He abandoned the traditional system whereby officials collated business for action exclusively according to its geographic origin. Now topics were to be shared out among officials on the basis of subject-matter, not provenance. The officials were themselves grouped into new ministerial sections distinguished by particular subject, rather than by region. Thus two of the new ministerial sections, the first and the second, were assigned responsibility for diplomatic and political correspondence with the representatives of foreign powers in Spain, and with Spanish diplomats and consuls abroad. The third section was to process cultural, industrial and scientific matters, as well as to establish a diplomatic dialogue with the new states that had emerged from the dissolution of Spain's Latin American empire. A fourth and final section, that of Accounting and Internal Affairs, was mainly entrusted with the administration of matters pertaining to the Ministry's own employees, and to those in the diplomatic and consular services.[45]

The Ministry of State was left little time to adjust to its internal reordering before being subjected to the economies in government expenditure that were dictated by liberal ideology and the state's financial exigencies in the later 1830s. In October 1836 the Minister of State, José María Calatrava, suppressed the position of subsecretary, allocating his duties to a chief clerk/

official, reduced the sections of the Ministry to only two and lowered the salaries of its employees. However, this cut in state expenditure proved counterproductive, as bureaucratic duties were less distinctly defined than they had been under the previous ministerial structure, and the resultant confusion of administrative competences was detrimental to the orderly working and efficiency of this government department. Moreover, the reduction in their salaries aggravated the collective frustration of the Ministry's functionaries.[46] This internal dissatisfaction was assuaged in July 1838, when a provisional, specific distribution of ministerial business among individual officials reestablished an effective division of labour. Injured bureaucratic sensibilities were also mollified by the assignation of authority over all matters relating to the Ministry's personnel to the chief official who had assumed the duties of the subsecretary. Control by one of their number over their own internal affairs had been a long-standing ambition of the functionaries in Spain's foreign service, an aspiration that they now realized.[47] That all was still not well, however, is indicated by a complete reversion, in May 1847, to the ministerial structure that the Count of Toreno had established in 1835, with the subsecretary and fourfold sectional division of the Ministry fully restored.[48] The Spanish government did not long remain content with these revived arrangements, and in December 1851 a new ministerial structure was enacted, which in the recent words of a senior official of the Ministry of Foreign Affairs (Ministerio de Asuntos Exteriores) constituted 'the immediate precedent for the current organization of the Ministry'.[49]

This major renovation was the work of the aristocratic Minister, Manuel de Pando Fernández de Pinedo, Marquess of Miraflores, a parliamentarian, a politician of the Moderado party, and, although not a professional diplomat, a man who had often performed successfully in a diplomatic capacity for his country. His brief tenure of the Ministry of State from 1851–2 proved to be a milestone in the development of its interior configuration and the elaboration of its internal procedures. The reforms were motivated by the desire to promote greater efficiency in the Ministry's practice, while maintaining 'the stability of the employees' whose expertise and experience were also vital for administrative competence. These innovations were contained in two royal decrees of December 1851 and January 1852, the effect of which was to divide the Ministry of State into six broad branches: the subsecretariat, three sections, a chancellery and (section for the) interpretation of languages, and an archive and library.

The subsecretariat was defined as 'the centre of the Ministry where all the actions of the service must conjoin in order to impart the necessary unity to their direction and dispatch'. The subsecretariat was to take charge of all current ministerial files and to ensure that the problems they raised were appropriately resolved. It was also to handle decisions based upon existing laws or regulations, matters relating to the Ministry's personnel, as well as the direction and inspection of its services. Ministerial control over policies and proceedings was secured by the stipulation that the subsecretary had to present to his political chief for decision any 'serious or significant' topic that might affect existing dispositions or established policy. The Ministry's sections were placed under the immediate authority of the subsecretary. These sections were structured according to a pattern that allowed for a degree of both regional and thematic specialization. The first section was to focus on business arising from foreign diplomatic representations in Metropolitan Spain, or from Spanish agents (excluding consular and economic ones) resident in Europe, the Levant, Barbary and Morocco. The second section was to deal with affairs emanating from the American states' legations in Spanish territory, or from Spain's agents overseas. It also looked after the remaining Spanish colonies and the consular representations established in them. The business of the third section consisted, *inter alia*, of commercial and navigational matters, as well as those pertaining to the internal administration and accounting of the Ministry. The drafting of treaties, agreements and credentials fell within the competence of the Chancellery and Interpretation of Languages (Cancillería e Interpretación de Lenguas), as did the issuing of passports and supervision of translations. The archive and library had to retain and preserve all the files, documents, correspondence and other official papers, the books, maps and globes of the Ministry.[50]

The complementary rules and regulations that were laid down on 12 January 1852 for the orderly and efficient operation of the Ministry were no less significant than this institutional reorganization, and some of the practices established at this time have survived right up to the present day. The subsecretary was to keep the Minister informed on all matters and relay his wishes and directions to the chiefs of the sections, except where the latter cared to establish direct contact with his other subordinates. In addition, detailed specifications were outlined for the execution of the Ministry's paperwork. When files were being drawn up systematic references were to be made to the antecedents on record of the business in hand. These cross-references were to be placed after an abstract of the relevant documents. Each abstract was to carry a complete date, and be signed by the sectional chief. Current files were to be maintained in the following fashion: documents were to be located in files in a sequence determined by date of receipt; each document was to carry an abstract of its contents on its folder and be appropriately numbered; each file was to bear an index on its cover; when any original file was requested by another ministry it was to be accompanied by an index, of which a copy, along with one of the file's abstract, was to be retained, duly signed by the subsecretary, 'so that its history can be conserved'.

No important memorandum was to be signed by a chief of ministerial section without its having previously been submitted to, and approved by, the subsecretary. The sectional heads were enjoined to ensure that such documents were properly prepared and written in a style that was 'pure, correct and worthy of the person or authority to whom it was directed'. The number of registers to be kept in any given section was left to the discretion of its chief but a minimum set was specified as 'indispensable'. The subsecretariat was directed to maintain a register of the state's diplomatic and consular employees with full career details; a book comprising a record of the business being conducted by the various sections, compiled from the documents forwarded to the subsecretariat by the sectional heads; and a book of 'precedents' containing the established subsecretarial procedures for the treatment of important affairs such as treaties and extradition. The first section of the Ministry was instructed to keep a book of 'acknowledgements of receipt', noting in systematic fashion the numbers and dates of dispatches received from each mission. The second section was ordered to maintain an indexed book of overseas correspondence. The third section was commanded to maintain a statistical register detailing Spain's maritime commerce, and another book recording all payments made by the sections. Finally, a collection of formulae and a record of passports issued were the chief registers deemed necessary for the chancellery.[51]

As it happened, this thorough revitalization of the Ministry of State coincided with the birth of a modern, professional career bureaucracy in Spain. Influenced by the French example, Juan Bravo Murillo used his brief premiership in 1852 to create a 'career open to talents' proven in a competitive exam or *oposiciones*. The *ancien régime* habit of selling offices in the government employ attracted to the state service many who were more anxious to exploit their purchase to their own profit than to serve their government in a disinterested and honest fashion. The practice indulged in by nineteenth-century politicians, once in power, of rewarding their followers with a division of the spoils of office also militated against conscientiousness and continuity in the administration. Bravo Murillo managed to establish, at least in principle, a civil service recruited and promoted by merit and hierarchically organized. The opposition to Bravo Murillo's policies forced him to effect this reform by 'provisional decree', which meant that no effective machinery was set up to implement the change in practice. However, the value of a bureaucratic meritocracy gradually imposed itself upon those inside and outside government as the decades passed, especially after the restoration of the Bourbon monarchy in 1874. The 'new' middle class professionals who entered government service became grouped in separate special administrative corps, securing their conditions of work and guaranteeing their opportunities for promotion. These specialist corps were joined by a full range of general corps in 1918, the latter made up of the 'other ranks' of the civil service.[52]

By an organic law of 1900, Spain's diplomatic and consular services were entrusted to two 'technical special' corps, respectively entitled the diplomatic career and the consular career. However, the similarity of matters with which both services dealt, and the feeling that the representation of Spanish interests in any given foreign country would benefit from a unified structure and command led to a fusion of these administrative corps into one in September 1928. Spain's diplomatic career was formally defined as the preserve of a 'special and professional corps of the state', whose function was the service of the nation in the central administration, in Spanish diplomatic representations abroad and in international organizations. Since then, Spain has possessed a single, united diplomatic service at home and abroad.

The development of a modern bureaucracy in the later nineteenth and early twentieth centuries, however imperfect and inchoate some of its features, represented an immense improvement upon the arbitrary political favouritism of previous practices of recruitment to the civil service. The preconditions of a takeoff into self-sustained governmental growth appeared to have been established in the early 1850s in Spain's foreign policy administration. The central machinery had been completely overhauled and the ground rules had been laid for the systematic formulation of a professional group of bureaucrats to administer Spain's foreign relations. Yet, once again, these promising developments failed to reach full fruition. The Ministry of State did not achieve an appropriate autonomy in, and authority over, the determination of Spain's foreign policy, nor did it forge a coherent international strategy for the country. A later Foreign Minister has described the Ministry of State in the early twentieth century as a 'dependency' of the royal palace, with the King, Alfonso XIII, actually conducting foreign policy.[53]

It was the continuing political instability in Spain that thwarted administrative progress. The liberal Isabeline monarchy was assailed by Carlist 'ultras' and radical Republicans on each flank. Moreover, the inability of the monarchy and constitutional parties to establish a peaceful and regular mode of change of government – the sign of genuine political consensus – integrated the military *pronunciamiento* into the political system as the motor of governmental transition. This volatile pattern produced a change of regime to a more radical constitutional monarchy in 1870 under Amadeo of Savoy, and after the collapse of that experiment, in its turn, to the short-lived Republic of 1873, which did not possess sufficient resilience to survive the actions of its opponents and supporters. The restoration of the Bourbons in the person of Alfonso XII marked a peace of exhaustion, but the carefully constructed political system of Cánovas del Castillo, which sought to assimilate all major interests into the existing order without endangering the hierarchy of property and power, also eventually broke down in practice. Spain was even more divided than before, as the Basque country and Catalonia boomed and the socio-political aspirations of workers and peasants found expression in the mass anarcho-syndicalist and socialist movements.[54]

This unresolved crisis of power continued to confound administrative evolution. The Ministry of State had no natural immunity against the debilitating effects of national political disorder. The provisional government of 1868–9 sacked some officials of the Ministry and cut the salaries of others. The subsequent Savoyard monarchy reduced the whole ministerial budget, depressing employees' wages across the board and forcing a cutback in administrative operations. The reforming ambitions of the Republic of 1873 encompassed the internal structure of the Ministry of State. On 3 March 1873 the Subsecretariat of the Ministry of State, along with those of other ministries, was transformed into the Secretariat General. After further altering some administrative arrangements, the Republican regime pared the whole organization down to a bare minimum on 9 July 1873. The Secretaría General was not only to perform the duties that had previously been the concern of the Subsecretariat, but its competence was widened to include all the tasks hitherto accomplished by the political sections and the chancellery. Only a commercial section, a section for accounting and general affairs, and a few other technical sections survived to function under this swollen general secretariat.[55]

The Bourbon restoration and the relative political stability of the last decades of the nineteenth century afforded breathing-space for administrative resuscitation. Thus in 1888 the Ministry of State was again amplified generously into ten sections, including a subsecretariat (which had been revived as early as 1875), separate political sections for Europe, America and (one) for the other three continents, and individual commercial and consular sections.[56] However, internal institutional resurrection was not sufficient to guarantee development. The political system of the restoration allowed an assertive monarch like Alfonso XIII to play a powerful, even prominent, role in affairs of state. It has been noted above that his intrusions into the realm of Spanish foreign policy-making hampered the growth of a responsible Foreign Ministry. Indeed, the nature of the restoration political system militated against any development of responsible government. For ultimate power of governmental appointment rested with the monarch, and there was no real practice of popular sovereignty, since reigning governments always won elections through the widespread employment of bribery and intimidation. Such political arrangements allowed Alfonso XIII considerable scope to act out the self-styled role of the nation's 'first ambassador', but impeded representative political control over, and the consequent development of public accountability in, the Spanish foreign policy-making process.[57]

The administrative aftermath of 1898, when Spain's remaining imperial jewel, Cuba, was wrenched away in war with the United States of America, had produced structural retrenchment within the Ministry even before Alfonso XIII came of age in 1902. General government economies reduced the extent of its organization. By the royal decree of 30 December 1901 a new ministerial pattern was fixed, and detailed rules for the conduct of administration were published. Doubtless the specification of procedural rules was undertaken in an effort to remedy the administrative sclerosis assumed to have been one of the causes of the disaster of 1898. Under the new scheme the subsecretariat was retained, but there was to be only one political section. A commercial and consular section, a colonial section, a general registry and cipher sections, archive and library, diplomatic and telegraphic cabinets, along with some other technical departments, now formed the other subdivisions of the Ministry of State. This reorganization was to prove durable enough, lasting in its essentials for almost three decades. The rules outlined for the transaction of ministerial business proved even more long-lived, being reaffirmed in September 1932, and indeed surviving in many instances right up to the present day.[58]

The 'general rules' for the dispatch of business contained the following provisions. The chiefs of sections and ministerial departments were directed to ensure the collection, at the start of each working day, of the documents awaiting their attention in the subsecretariat. Reception of these in the sections was to be duly registered in a book, uniformly divided in every department into five parts, corresponding to the sources of diplomatic communications from ministries, Spanish legations, foreign legations, etc. Once this was done, the sectional chief was directed to relay to his staff the instructions of the Minister and subsecretary as to the tasks requiring fulfilment, and he was to ensure that these duties were properly completed. The sectional chief was himself to draw up the reports requested by his superiors, though he was permitted to delegate this duty to a senior subordinate unless specifically told to refrain from doing so. Any such report should start with references to the matters or documents upon which it was based, then expound its argument, citing supporting evidence of any relevant kind, and finish with its opinion as to the appropriate decision or action to be taken. When presenting subjects to the subsecretary for decision, the sectional chiefs were reminded to inform him, also, of other current business ready for immediate completion in their departments. The subsecretary could reserve some of these matters for his personal resolution, leaving the others to the departmental chiefs. Precise rules for the drafting of different kinds of documents and special regulations for particular intradepartmental procedures were also set down.[59]

Such growing internal bureaucratic orderliness, however, could not always compensate the Ministry of State for its situation in an increasingly dysfunctional political system. This was dramatically demonstrated in the later 1920s. Alfonso XIII had accepted the *pronunciamiento* of General Miguel Primo de Rivera in 1923 as a last resort to rescue the dwindling fortunes of the Spanish monarchy. The potential contradiction between administration by relatively sophisticated bureaucratic organization and political rule by crude military dictatorship was realized by Primo de Rivera's characteristically extreme action in November 1928: he abolished the Ministry of State outright, absorbing its services into the Presidency of the Government (Presidencia del Gobierno), which he held.[60] It is probably best to view this latter deed as less a flamboyant gesture and more as one of the moves in the direction of a radical, right-wing, authoritarian regime, which appears to have been his political goal.[61]

The Second Spanish Republic, which emerged in 1931 from the sudden, successive demise of the *dictadura* and exile of Alfonso XIII, seemed a context more conducive to the maturation of the Ministry of State, which had already been fully restored in 1930. The Ministry certainly experienced a measure of reorganization during the Republican period, one reshuffle being that effected in December 1932. This divided the Ministry into two major subdivisions: the Directorate of Foreign Policy and Commerce and the Directorate of Administration. In September 1935 these were suppressed and two ministers plenipotentiary were placed at the head of the separate services that the directorates had embodied.[62] However, it is not the administrative rearrangements of the Republic that really require comment so much as the failure of the Ministry, yet again, to establish itself firmly as a primary political and managerial institution in the determination of a comprehensive national foreign policy.

Some aspects of Republican government policy towards the Ministry of State necessarily caused disturbance and discontent within that body. The change of regime entailed a purge of the most prominent pro-monarchist ambassadors. The nomination of a series of literary personalities to head Republican Spain's leading embassies is explained by the fact that these individuals were loyal to the new regime and possessed the requisite linguistic skills. Some, however, suspected that there was an ulterior motive behind these appointments. The Spanish humorist Julio Camba was concerned at not being invited to assume an ambassadorial post, until he consoled himself with the conclusion that the real object of the exercise was to rid Spain of these tiresome figures. He was already abroad, so the government did not have to tempt him into exile.[63] Anyway, the mass defection of Spain's diplomatic corps to the anti-Republican side in the Civil War of 1936–9, noted below, shows that this purge was less than thorough.

The quality of leadership given by Republican Ministers to the Foreign Ministry was uneven. The first incumbent was the demagogic Alejandro Lerroux, 'than whom fewer Spanish public men could have been found less competent for such a task', according to one of the new ambassadors.[64] However, aware of his incompetence and inexperience in this field, as in others (on one occasion he confessed that he understood none of Spain's problems deeply), Lerroux tended not to interfere much with the bureaucrats at home or the diplomats abroad.[65] Some of the other Republican Ministers of State were not particularly distinguished either, although the socialist Fernando de los Ríos, for one, performed effectively.[66] Moreover, the Republican governments also lacked the financial resources to conduct any ambitious foreign policy.[67]

However, what prevented any real development in Spain's foreign policy-making process was the recurrence of political polarization and growing class conflict. Politics and passions were directed inwards, leaving little time or energy for the consideration of foreign policy practices or principles. The Republican parliamentary democracy was also too racked by inner dissension to provide the mature political milieu necessary to round off the evolution of the Ministry of State and entrench its position as a responsible authority within a foreign policy-making process. Niceto Alcalá-Zamora, the first President of the Republic, singled out Spaniards' 'fatal propensity to discord' as the most important obstacle to the fashioning of national foreign policy.[68]

In the dying days of the first reforming Republican governments, Fernando de los Ríos did establish a Junta Permanente de Estado to function as a permanent advisory council of state to successive governments, coordinating their foreign policy and endowing it with 'indispensable continuity'. This consultative body was to be composed of all past and present Presidents of the Republic, Presidents of the Council of Ministers, Presidents of the Cortes, Ministers of State and one serving and one ex-ambassador of the Republic. This attempt to ensure some consistency of purpose in Spanish foreign policy rapidly fell victim to the intensity of internal political divisions. Some members refused to attend while in opposition. The socialist representatives had to abandon attendance when their party colleagues demanded that they report on the Junta's deliberations. Moreover, since the Junta could be convened only by the government, as and when it saw fit, the party in power could leave it in abeyance at any time, denying its opponents any political opportunity and prestige it conferred on them. Finally, as merely an advice-giving entity its counsel could be, and often was, ignored by the Minister of State who received it.[69] The depth of socio-political antagonism in Spain was too profound for such flimsy devices to generate compromise or cooperation, as the outbreak of civil war in July 1936 demonstrated.

The military rebellion against the elected Republican government was to have immediate and long-term consequences for the Ministry of State that reflected its momentous impact on the country as a whole. The most dramatic initial result of the start of civil war for the Ministry was the mass resignation of career diplomats and consuls, perhaps as many as 90 per cent of their entire number.[70] Some were reluctant to represent their country while their fellow citizens were slaughtering each other at home, but most were active partisans of the rebel 'Nationalist' cause.[71] The non-career (usually non-Spanish) employees in Spain's embassies were often willing to remain at their posts, as in London,[72] though some who stayed on acted as agents for the insurgents – like the Spanish telephonist in the Paris embassy, who betrayed many secrets.[73] The desertion and purge of officials from the Ministry's central administration during the Civil War caused a virtual collapse in the orderly conduct of the Republic's foreign affairs. The transfer of the seat of the Republican government from besieged Madrid to Valencia also contributed to the disruption of ministerial routine and records.[74]

Eloquent testimony to the scale of the problem, and to the gallant efforts made to solve it, was contained in the decree published by the Republic's government in April 1937, where the 'treachery of the great majority' of Spain's diplomats, necessitating an 'almost total' renewal of the Ministry's personnel, was noted. The new ministerial employees, characterized by their 'republican fervour' and 'modernity of spirit', were exhorted to collaborate with the 'select nucleus' of loyal career officials in the 'sacred duty' of constituting an instrument capable of managing a 'genuinely republican international policy'. The decree had a reminder for those obsessed with revolutionary spontaneity:

> 'A number of our present diplomats – and this is natural – are unaware of the fundamental norms relating to this Ministry, norms that are not in any way survivals of bureaucratic routine but imperative functional rules of collective organic and methodical work, refined by centuries of experience, whose infraction is paid for immediately in inefficiency and disorder.'

The primary rule of good administrative behaviour in foreign relations was described as 'constant and active communication between Spain's representations and the Ministry of State'. Detailed instruction was provided on the proper drafting and forms of such regular diplomatic communication. The Republic's front line troops in the diplomatic theatre of the Civil War were informed of the significance of their historic mission:

> 'We have the obligation, not only for today but also for the future; the duty to found a school and a tradition, and for this it is imperative to leave established a system that will not only permit us and our successors to study, on the basis of living documents, questions up for decision, but also create in the Ministry and in the Representations the documentary sources of knowledge that today we lack, the archives in which is collected the history of our time, without which our work will want for continuity, and, as a result, the possibility of purification and progress.'[75]

That the new ministerial servants needed such inspirational and practical advice, and that it was not always heeded, is indicated by the fact that José Giral, who became Minister of State in May 1937, had to resort frequently to newspapers to keep himself informed, in some degree, on foreign affairs.[76]

However, in the field of foreign policy administration, as in so many others, what is remarkable about the Republic's efforts and improvisations is not their shortcomings but their relative success. Amidst a bloody civil war, and subjected to acute internal social and political struggles, Republican Spain maintained a diplomatic network that represented its interests in a largely indifferent or hostile world. If the Western democracies failed to come to the aid of the Republic in any sustained or substantial fashion, that was not because its case was not adequately presented to them, but because of their resolve to ignore it, for their own reasons. Spain's Ministry of State died an honourable death in 1939.

Its successor had already come into being in the Nationalist civil war camp. The administration erected to manage the Nationalist war effort and govern the territory they conquered had all the simplicity dear to a group of army officers with their preference for direct and uncomplicated chains of command. By the autumn of 1936 the Nationalist military *junta* had established a Technical Committee in Burgos to administer their zone. Colonel Francisco Serra was appointed to the position of Secretary General of External Relations, but with no real authority in policy formulation or execution.[77] Real power remained at the Nationalist military headquarters in Salamanca, where General Francisco Franco functioned as the main decision-maker in foreign relations. In these early days Franco was advised on, and assisted in, diplomatic matters by his friend José Antonio de Sangróniz, Marquess of Desio, who drew on his professional experience to impress upon the General, and on others, the principles and practices of orderly diplomacy.[78] Moreover, the investment of Franco with complete political and military command by his fellow insurgent generals on 1 October 1936 endowed him with full diplomatic power.[79] Franco combined the absolute authority of the headships of state, government, armed forces and political *movimiento* to reign supreme as 'Caudillo of Spain by grace of God' for almost the rest of his life.

Franco was always his own chief diplomatist. Juan Peche, subsecretary of Spain's Foreign Ministry, described the policy-making process in the 1940s thus: 'The Chief of State is the one who carries, personally, the total responsibility for these matters of international policy. He hears everybody and meditates at length; then, it is he who takes the decision.'[80] Franco, of course, soon had an ample bureaucratic support for his foreign policy initiatives. On 30 January 1938 the Ministry of Foreign Affairs (Ministerio de Asuntos Exteriores) was created, its function being defined in December 1945 as the 'realization' of Spain's foreign policy. Franco's foreign policy leadership style was not such, however, particularly in the first years of his rule, to afford it an opportunity to develop any genuine autonomy or rhythm in its diplomatic efforts. This was so because of the intimate connection between Franco's domestic hold on power and the configuration of the international context that surrounded him. Foreign aid was vital to Franco's civil war victory and he had to manoeuvre carefully through the maelstrom of the Second World War and the demise of his former friends, Hitler and Mussolini, in order to survive. One Spanish commentator has defined Franco's foreign policy as 'a long game of adaptations to global political conjunctures in order to retain power'.[81] The fascist-style Caudillo became the 'organic democrat' and 'free world' warrior to adjust to changes in the pattern of international power relations.

He was active, too, in not only the determination but the actual conduct of his regime's foreign policy when he deemed it necessary. Thus, he dispatched his Minister of the Interior, Ramón Serrano Suñer, to Berlin in September 1940 to negotiate a Spanish entry into the war on the Axis side, which would secure territorial profit and his survival in Hitler's 'New Order'. He also corresponded directly with the Nazi leader on this matter and himself took the eventual decision to turn down the German terms.[82] He also initiated a correspondence with Churchill towards the end of 1944 in an effort to obtain an Anglo-Spanish *rapprochement* that would ease his passage through the difficult days looming up with the impending defeat of Nazi Germany.[83] Apart from these definite *démarches*, Franco for many years routinely exercised his supreme authority over international matters by beginning meetings of his Council of Ministers (Consejo de Ministros) with personal reports on, and summaries of, current foreign policy and problems.[84]

The implications of Franco's personal tutelage over the shape and course of Spain's foreign policy for the Ministry of Foreign Affairs may be briefly stated. Once more the general governing system, for all that it enforced political stability on the nation as a whole, did not encourage the development of a regular ministerial responsibility in the foreign policy-making process. Franco was in practice willing to delegate some authority to Ministers for Foreign Affairs to pursue policies consonant with the international aims that he set. Moreover, he also tolerated a greater degree of individual action on the part of his Foreign Ministers in his later years in power, when his position was too secure to be much jeopardized by diplomatic indiscretions.

However, the broad lines of policy remained his to define, even if he chose to follow the counsel offered by Foreign Ministers. Certainly, the ministerial moves made in the 1960s and early 1970s for closer association between Spain and the European Economic Community had Franco's full approval.[85] Moreover, Franco was always prepared to intervene directly in the execution of policy if it was too dilatory or contrary to his wishes. Thus, for example, he ordered his diplomats to wind up the negotiations over the United States–Spanish Base Agreements of 1953, even though they had not secured all their desiderata.[86] Again, Franco revealed his reluctance to relax his ultimate hold on foreign policy-making when he excluded the general area of international relations from the government committees that he set up in 1957 to group relevant ministers for greater executive coordination in particular fields.[87]

For all that the Spanish Ministry of Foreign Affairs remained too much subject to the Caudillo's direct influence to evolve as an independent and authoritative agent in the policy-making process, its personnel did not fare too badly under his rule. There was a drastic purge of employees of the Ministry of State in 1939, with even the hall porters in the Ministry itself and the servants of the embassies abroad being dismissed by the civil war victors.[88] However, the great majority of career diplomats who had rallied to the rebel banner were restored to official active service. Their special administrative corps, the *Carrera diplomática*, was permitted the same degree of indulgent autonomy in maintaining its own recruitment, promotional and social security practices that was afforded the other special corps units by a regime grateful for the support of so many professional bureaucrats in the Civil War. One measure of the success of a special corps in preserving its corporate identity was the extent to which it gained control over admission into its own ranks. The corps that became self-recruiting could be self-perpetuating. One of the surest ways of operating a stranglehold on entry into a special corps was control of an educational institution that trained and qualified aspirants for particular branches of the governmental service. The Foreign Ministry's Diplomatic School (Escuela Diplomática), founded in 1942, has perpetuated a dynastic element in the foreign service. As recently as 1978, out of a class of 55 in the school, nine were directly related to diplomats, and the majority bore names firmly associated with service in high governmental positions.[89]

However, the Diplomatic School has produced a corps of professional diplomats educated as generalists within the framework of some specialization (international affairs, economics, consular affairs, etc.). The diplomats' work has been supported by the employment of outside experts (often recruited from the other relevant ministries) to perform certain specialist functions, for example as commercial or labour attachés in Spanish embassies abroad. Still, the Francoist schooling of Spanish diplomats was far from perfect. Moreover, the large-scale reform of administrative corps enacted in 1964 did not in practice greatly impinge on special and elite corps, like the diplomatic career.[90] Nevertheless, the need to groom genuine specialists in geographic and thematic fields for the Spanish diplomatic service itself has been recognized by modern spirits inside the Diplomatic School in the post-Franco period. These reformers are being supported by leading functionaries of the Ministry of Foreign Affairs, as well as by its Foreign Service Directorate.[91]

Franco's personal mastership over Spain's foreign policy did not prevent an administrative regrowth in the Ministry of Foreign Affairs. For, as one commentator has emphasized, the growing complexity of modern international affairs inevitably evoked a corresponding organizational elaboration in Spain's foreign policy adminstration, however elemental may have been the initial diplomatic priority of the Franco regime, i.e. survival. The gradual reintegration of Francoist Spain into the international system of political and economic relations (for instance, through Spanish entry into the United Nations in 1955, and by economic agreement with the European Economic Community in 1970) produced periodic rearrangements and amplifications of the ministerial machinery. One feature of the restructurings was an alternating preference for geographic or functional specialization as the predominant feature of ministerial organization. Thus, in February 1970, the various regional directorates of the Ministry of Foreign Affairs were absorbed into a monolithic Directorate-General of Foreign Policy, which was to operate along with a number of functional sections. However, the regional general directorates were restored in November 1973, although it was left to the first post-Franco government to abolish the Directorate-General of Foreign Policy in April 1976.[92]

The other noteworthy aspect of later Francoist foreign policy administration was the institutional effort to respond to the increasingly multidimensional character of international relations. Thus, the Foreign Ministry's Directorate-General of International Economic Relations was reshaped in March 1971, through the creation of a Subdirectorate-General of Multilateral Economic Relations and one of Organizations for European Integration. Nevertheless, the failure to define precisely the respective competences of the latter entities, and the opposition that their establishment provoked from within the Ministry of Commerce, demonstrate that the ineptitudes of Franco's last years characterized administrative as much as general national policy.[93]

However, Franco did perform one vital service for the Ministry of Foreign Affairs in the 1960s and 1970s by allowing the economic change that, in those years, facilitated the rapid development of an industrial sector in the Spanish economy. This economic transformation has so altered the balance of social forces in the country as, apparently, to make consensus-based democracy a viable and appropriate political system for contemporary Spain. The transitional government of Carlos Arias Navarro, for all its political inefficacy, did act to restructure the Ministry of Foreign Affairs in April 1976. This reordering reasserted the importance of geographic specialization as a primary principle of internal departmental divisions, introducing the regional general directorates and subdirectorates specified in Appendix A and fixing the functional directorates displayed thereon as well. This revitalization of the regional directorates in the Foreign Ministry should better equip it to meet the realities of a global system still dominated by the operations of nation-states. The distribution of functional competences, however, seems to entail some over-lapping of authorities and potential duplications in administration.[94] More important than this internal refashioning of the Ministry was the establish-ment of a democratic political system in Spain during 1977–8. With a govern-ment responsible to a freely elected parliament, and a state presided over by a genuinely constitutional monarchy, there has emerged the liberal political atmosphere in which the Ministry of Foreign Affairs has some chance of acquiring real and proper status in the formulation and execution of Spain's foreign policy.

Indeed, the Foreign Minister of the first democratically elected government after Franco, Marcelino Oreja, did hope to place his Ministry in the vanguard of Spain's international endeavours. He wanted to use the occasion of Spain's negotiations for membership of the European Economic Community to begin overhauling the entire structure of the Ministry of Foreign Affairs in a manner that would endow it with authentic influence in the policy-making process. His notion was to establish a secretariat of state within the Ministry charged with managing relations and negotiations with the EEC. Oreja's plan, seemingly, was to gather relevant experts from other ministries on to the 'platform' constituted by this secretariat in order to position his Ministry in a commanding height from which to control Spain's foreign commerce.[95] This project was frustrated by intragovernmental opposition, which led instead to the appointment of Leopoldo Calvo Sotelo in February 1978 as Minister without Portfolio, charged with supervising Spain's relations with the EEC. He was provided with a small bureaucratic apparatus to support his handling of the negotiations with the EEC.[96] The success that crowned the Spanish negotiating team's efforts, with a favourable report by the European Commission in November 1978 on the Spanish request for membership, was well earned. For it was acknowledged in Brussels that it was the competence and efficiency of the Spanish negotiators, and their back-up services, that enabled the Community authorities to reach their affirmative response so swiftly.[97]

However, the Ministry of Foreign Affairs appears to have been strengthened by subsequent administrative developments. The recent creation of a Secretariat of State within the Ministry should ensure senior supervision of ministerial operations while relieving the Minister of the crushing burden of administrative routine, which prompted one latter-day incumbent to describe his charge as an 'infernal machine for producing papers'.[98] The Minister for Foreign Affairs should, therefore, have more time to participate in parlia-mentary and democratic political life, and also to play his due part in the collective ministerial management now enshrined in the Spanish constitution as the expression of responsible government.[99] That government also seems to be developing in the direction likely to complete the Foreign Ministry's long march to political maturity and real authority in the decision-making process. On 14 August 1979 a Delegate Committee of the Government for Foreign Policy was set up, 'an innovation of extraordinary potential importance'. It was constituted as an 'open entity' to be composed of the President of the Government (Prime Minister), one of the vice-presidents, the Minister for Foreign Affairs and his secretary of state (to act as the committee's secretary), as well as such other ministers, high functionaries and individuals whom the Prime Minister should summon to attend any meeting.[100] Although this development entails the loss of the feudal-style autonomy enjoyed by the Ministry under Franco, it should signify its integration into a genuinely authoritative and responsible foreign policy-making process.

Again, the Ministry of Foreign Affairs has managed to regain administrative control over Spain's relations with the EEC. For one of the first acts of the government formed in February 1981 under the premiership of Leopoldo Calvo Sotelo was to abolish the independent Minister without Portfolio (lately held by Eduardo Punset Casals), which had negotiated on Spain's behalf with Brussels. In its place a new Secretariat of State for Relations with the EEC was established inside the Ministry of Foreign Affairs. It is problematic whether such a governmental readjustment will fulfil the foreign ministerial ambition to control the directing organ of Spain's foreign commerce, assimilating personnel and powers from the financial and economic ministries. For the intragovernmental contest for supreme authority over Spain's external commercial policy has been of long duration and is not susceptible of easy resolution, however urgent the need for administrative rationalization in this area.[101] A more sophisticated system of interdepartmental coordination might better secure administrative coherence in Spain's international economic policy than any mere expansion of an individual ministry's authority.

Indeed, the exigencies of democratic politics and bureaucratic proficiency both now point up the need for a modernization of Spain's foreign policy administration. An ever more complex international environment requires a corresponding organizational elaboration and evolution of expertise in Spain's diplomatic machinery. It will be no easy task to effect such changes while also practising the more open and consensus-based diplomacy required by contemporary Spain's democratic polity. Yet Spain's foreign policy machinery has already promoted one project crucial to the consolidation of that democratic regime. The successful conclusion of Spain's bid for acceptance in principle of its application for membership of the EEC has gratified virtually all the prominent political and economic interests in the country. The support of some major social and economic forces for the democratic system in Spain stems, at least in part, from the knowledge that such a political order is a precondition of entry into the EEC. The achievement of European recognition of modern Spain's democratic credentials was one source of the socio-political consensus that helped to isolate and defeat the attempted military *coup d'état* of 23 February 1981. The diplomatists have secured breathing space, at least, for Spainish democracy, the very political system that seems most likely to foster the full maturation and modernization of Spain's foreign policy-making process. If they can persuade France to abandon its reservations concerning an early Spanish entry into the EEC,.

they will have completed a mission potentially vital to the entrenchment of democracy in Spain's government and politics. Spanish Foreign Minister, José Pedro Pérez Llorca, acknowledged this in March 1981: 'Full integration into the European Community is an inseparable and corollary part of the construction of the State's democratic institutions.'[102]

The author wishes to acknowledge the assistance of the Spanish Embassy, Dublin, and the Research Department of the Foreign and Commonwealth Office, London, in locating material for the preparation of this chapter. Neither body, of course, bears any responsibility for the contents and conclusions of this piece.

NOTES

[1] Pablo Sebastian, 'Reestructuración del Ministerio de Asuntos Exteriores', El País (Madrid), 29 October 1977.

[2] Peter Barber, Diplomacy: The World of the Honest Spy (London 1979), 14; Carlos Fernández Espeso and José Martínez Cardós, Primera Secretaría De Estado; Ministerio De Estado: Disposiciones Orgánicas (1705–1936) (Madrid 1972): Estudio Preliminar by José Martínez Cardós, x–xviii.

[3] Barber, op. cit., 23–4.

[4] José Antonio Escudero, Los Secretarios de Estado y del Despacho (Madrid 1969), I, 25.

[5] Martínez Cardós, op. cit., xxiii.

[6] Ibid., xxiv–xxv.

[7] Escudero, op. cit., III, 747–49.

[8] Martínez Cardós, op. cit., p. xxxiii.

[9] Ibid., xxxiii–xxxvii.

[10] Ibid., xlv.

[11] Ibid., xxxvii.

[12] Henry Kamen, A Concise History of Spain (London 1973), 95.

[13] Martínez Cardós, op. cit., xlv.

[14] G. E. Aylmer, 'Bureaucracy' in Peter Burke (ed.), The New Cambridge Modern History, XIII, Companion Volume (Cambridge 1979), 172.

[15] Martínez Cardós, op. cit., lxviii–lxix.

[16] Ibid., lxix, lxxi.

[17] Ibid., lxxi, cvii.

[18] Ibid., xcv.

[19] Ibid., xcvii–xcviii.

[20] Archivo General del Ministerio de Asuntos Exteriores (hereinafter cited as A.G.M.A.E.), Palacio de Santa Cruz (Madrid), Organización, legajo 3. 542.

[21] Fernández Espeso and Martínez Cardós, Primera Secretaría De Estado; Ministerio de Estado: Estudio Preliminar by Martínez Cardós, ci–cii.

[22] Ibid., cii.

[23] Ibid., cvii–cviii.

[24] Ibid., cxxxiii.

[25] *A.G.M.A.E. Personal* leg. 175, número 9. 294.

[26] Martínez Cardós, op. cit., cxxxiii.

[27] Ibid., cxxxiii–cxxxvi.

[28] Cited in ibid., cxxxviii–cxxxix.

[29] Ibid., cix; Richard Herr, *An Historical Essay on Modern Spain* (Berkeley 1971), 1974 edn, 66.

[30] Herr, op. cit., 66–9; Martínez Cardós, op. cit., cxi.

[31] Herr, op. cit., 70; Martínez Cardós, op. cit., cxiii–cxiv.

[32] Salvador de Madariaga, *Spain: A Modern History* (London 1961), 277.

[33] Martínez Cardós, op. cit., cxvii–cxviii.

[34] Ibid., cxx–cxxi.

[35] Ibid., cxxii.

[36] Ibid., cxxiv.

[37] Herr, op. cit., 80–1.

[38] Ibid., 81–2; Raymond Carr, *Spain, 1808–1939* (Oxford 1966), 146–54.

[39] Martínez Cardós, op. cit., cxxxi–cxxxiii.

[40] Joseph Fontana, *La crisis del Antiguo régimen, 1808–1833* (Barcelona 1979), 49.

[41] Herr, op. cit., 82–98; Carr, op. cit., 155–210.

[42] Martínez Cardós, op. cit., cxxix, cxxxix–cxl.

[43] Fernández Espeso and Martínez Cardós, *Primera Secretaría de Estado; Ministerio de Estado: Disposiciones Orgánicas*, 63–4; Kenneth M. Medhurst, *Government in Spain: The Executive at Work* (Oxford 1973), 119.

[44] Martínez Cardós, *Primera Secretaría de Estado; Ministerio de Estado: Estudio Preliminar*, cxliii.

[45] Ibid., cxliii–cxliv.

[46] Ibid., cxlvi.

[47] Ibid., cxlvii; *A.G.M.A.E. Organización*, leg. 3. 542.

[48] Martínez Cardós, op. cit., cxlviii.

[49] Ibid., v.

[50] Ibid., cxlviii–cli; and *Real Decreto de 16 de diciembre de 1851 por el que se fija nueva planta en la Primera Secretaría del Despacho de Estado*, Fernández Espeso and Martínez Cardós, op. cit., 111–13; *Reglamento interior de la Primera Secretaría de Estado de 12 de enero de 1852*, ibid., 114–23.

[51] *Reglamento Interior de la Primera Secretaría de Estado de 12 de enero de 1852*, Fernández Espeso and Martínez Cardós, op. cit., 114–23.

[52] Medhurst, op. cit., 102–5; Carr, op. cit., 243–5; Migel A. Albaladejo Campoy, 'Pasado, presente y futuro de la Función Pública Española', *Cuadernos Economicos de Información Comercial Española*, No. 13 (1980), 36–9. Diplomatic employees on service

abroad were exempted from the application of the royal decree of 18 June 1852 (ibid., 90).

[53] José María de Areilza, *Diario de un Ministro de la Monarquía* (Barcelona, 2nd edn, November 1977), 50.

[54] Herr, op. cit., 99–141; Carr, op. cit., 169–563.

[55] Martínez Cardós, op. cit., cliii–cliv.

[56] Ibid., clv–clvi.

[57] Gerie B. Bledsoe, 'Spanish Foreign Policy, 1898–1936' in James W. Cortada (ed.), *Spain in the Twentieth-Century World: Essays on Spanish Diplomacy, 1898–1978* (Westport, Connecticut 1980), 7.

[58] Martínez Cardós, op. cit., clvii.

[59] *Real Orden de 30 de diciembre de 1901 por la que se aprueban las instrucciones para el régimen y despacho del Ministerio de Estado,* Fernández Espeso and Martínez Cardós, op. cit., 271–313.

[60] Martínez Cardós, op. cit., clx.

[61] Shlomo Ben-Ami, 'The Dictatorship of Primo de Rivera: A Political Reassessment', *Journal of Contemporary History,* Vol. 12 (1977), 65–84.

[62] Martínez Cardós, op. cit., clxiii.

[63] Salvador de Madariaga, *Morning Without Noon: Memoirs* (Westmead, Farnborough, Hampshire, 1974), 165 and *Spain: A Modern History,* 462–3. See also Niceto Alcalá-Zamora, *Memorias (Segundo texto de mis Memorias)* (Barcelona 1977), 332.

[64] De Madariaga, *Memoirs,* 178.

[65] Ibid., 198; and de Madariaga, *Spain,* 462.

[66] De Madariaga, *Spain,* 474; Alcalá-Zamora, op. cit., 319.

[67] Manuel Azaña, *Obras Completas,* IV: *Memorias Políticas y de Guerra* (Mexico 1968), 313.

[68] Alcalá-Zamora, op. cit., 318.

[69] Ibid., 319–20; de Madariaga, *Spain,* 474; *Decreto de 7 de Noviembre de 1933 por el que se crea la Junta Permanente de Estado,* Fernández Espeso and Martínez Cardós, op. cit., 607–9.

[70] Charles R. Halstead, 'Spanish Foreign Policy, 1936–1978' in James W. Cortada (ed.), op. cit., 44.

[71] Pablo de Azcárate, *Mi embajada en Londres durante la guerra civil española* (Barcelona 1976), 23–4; Jill Edwards, *The Brtish Government and the Spanish Civil War, 1936–1939* (London 1979), 17.

[72] De Azcárate, op. cit., 30.

[73] Halstead, op. cit., 88, note 49.

[74] Ibid., 56. See also Azaña, op. cit., IV, 617.

[75] *Circular del 10 de abril de 1937 en la que se fija la nueve organización del Ministerio de Estado,* Fernández Espeso and Martínez Cardós, op. cit., 654–61.

[76] Halstead, op. cit., 88, note 47.

[77] Ibid., 43, 84, note 3.

[78] Ibid., 43; José Mario Armero, *La Política Exterior de Franco* (Barcelona 1978), 66.

[79] Halstead, op. cit., 43.

[80] José María Doussinague, *España Tenía Razón (1939–45)* (Madrid 1950), 22.

[81] Mario Armero, op. cit., 9.

[82] Denis Smyth, *Diplomacy and Strategy of Survival: British policy and Franco's Spain, 1940–41* (Cambridge, forthcoming).

[83] Viscount Templewood, *Ambassador on Special Mission* (London 1946), 300–6.

[84] Mario Armero, op. cit., 66.

[85] Medhurst, op. cit., 69, 88; Teniente general Francisco Franco Salgado-Araujo, *Mis Conversaciones Prividas con Franco* (Barcelona 1976), 334, 362, 368.

[86] De Areilza, op. cit., 45, 55.

[87] Angel Viñas, 'La Administración de la política económica exterior en España, 1936–1979', *Cuadernos Economicos de I.C.E.,* No. 13 (1980), 199; Medhurst, op. cit., 96.

[88] Halstead, op. cit., 61; de Azcárate, op. cit., 36.

[89] Medhurst, op. cit., 107–8; Soledad Gallego-Diez, 'Cómo se fabrica un embajador', *Cuadernos para el diálogo,* 25 February 1978, 47.

[90] Medhurst, op. cit., 115–17; Albaladejo Campoy, 'La Función Pública Española', *Cuadernos Economicos de I.C.E.,* 44–5.

[91] Viñas, op. cit., 238–9.

[92] Ibid., 172–5, 223–6, 229.

[93] Ibid., 225.

[94] Ibid., 228–9.

[95] Pablo Sebastian, 'Reestructuración del Ministerio de Asuntos Exteriores', *El País,* 29 October 1977.

[96] Viñas, op. cit., 234.

[97] *Bulletin of the European Communities, Supplement 9/78,* 'Opinion on Spain's application for membership' (Brussels 1979).

[98] De Areilza, op. cit., 51.

[99] *The Spanish Constitution* (approved by popular referendum and enacted as law in December 1978), Article 108.

[100] Viñas, op. cit., 242.

[101] Ibid., 159–247.

[102] *Cambio 16* (Madrid), No. 486, 23 March 1981, 31.

BIBLIOGRAPHY

I. General, Historical and Bibliographical

Peter Barber, *Diplomacy: The World of the Honest Spy* (London 1979).

Raymond Carr, *Spain, 1808–1939* (Oxford 1966).

James W. Cortada, *A Bibliographical Guide to Spanish Diplomatic History, 1460–1977* (Westport, Connecticut 1977).

Salvador de Madariaga, *Spain: A Modern History* (London 1961).

J. H. Elliott, *Imperial Spain, 1469–1716* (London 1963).

Manuel Fraga Iribarne and Rafael Rodríguez-Moñino, *Los fundamentos de la Diplomacia* (Barcelona 1977).

Richard Herr, *An Historical Essay on Modern Spain* (Berkeley 1971, 1974 edition).

Henry Kamen, *A Concise History of Spain* (London 1973).

II. Official Documentary Sources

Archivo General del Ministerio de Asuntos Exteriores, Palacio de Santa Cruz, Madrid.

Bulletin of the European Communities, Supplement 9/78. 'Opinion on Spain's application for membership' (Brussels 1979).

Carlos Fernández Espeso and José Martínez Cardós, *Primera Secretaría de Estado; Ministerio de Estado: Disposiciones Orgánicas (1705–1936): Estudio Preliminar* by José Martínez Cardós (Madrid 1972).

III. Memoirs and Diaries

Niceto Alcalá-Zamora, *Memorias (Segundo texto des mis Memorias)* (Barcelona 1977).

Manuel Azaña, *Obras completas,* 4 vols (Mexico 1966–8).

José Maria de Areilza, *Diario de un Ministro de la Monarquía* (Barcelona 1977).

Pablo de Azcárate, *Mi embajada en Londres durante la Guerra Civil Española* (Barcelona 1976).

Salvador de Madariaga, *Morning Without Noon: Memoirs* (Westmead, Farnborough, Hampshire 1974).

Manuel Fraga Iribarne, *Memoria breve de una vida pública* (Madrid 1980).

Carlton Hayes, *Wartime Mission in Spain, 1942–1945* (New York 1946).

Francisco Franco Salgado-Araujo, *Mis Conversaciones Privadas con Franco* (Barcelona 1976).

Ramón Serrano Suñer, *Entre Hendaya y Gibraltar,* 2nd edn (Barcelona 1973).

——, *Entre el silencio y la propaganda, la Historia como fue: Memorias* (Barcelona 1977).

Viscount Templewood, *Ambassador on Special Mission* (London 1946).

IV. Selected monographs, etc.

José Mario Armero, *La Política Exterior de Franco* (Barcelona 1978).

Raymond Carr and Juan Pablo Fusi, *Spain: Dictatorship to Democracy* (London 1979).

Jill Edwards, *The British Government and the Spanish Civil War, 1936–1939* (London 1979).

José Antonio Escudero, *Los Secretarios de Estado y del Despacho*, 4 vols (Madrid 1969).

Ramón Garriga, *La España de Franco: Las Relaciones Secretas con Hitler*, 2nd edn (Puebla, Mexico 1970).

——, *La España de Franco: De la División Azul al Pacto con los Estados Unidos, (1943 a 1951)* (Puebla, Mexico 1971).

Paul Preston, *The Coming of the Spanish Civil War, 1931–1936* (London 1978).

Denis Smyth, *Diplomacy and Strategy of Survival: British Policy and Franco's Spain, 1940–41* (Cambridge, forthcoming).

Hugh Thomas, *The Spanish Civil War*, 3rd edn (London 1977).

J. W. D. Trythall, *Franco: A Biography* (London 1970).

Angel Viñas, *La Alemania nazi y del 18 de julio*, 2nd edn (Madrid 1977).

——, *El Oro de Moscú* (Barcelona 1979).

——, *Política Comercial Exterior en España, 1931–1975*, 2 vols (Madrid 1980).

V. Articles and Essays

Miguel A. Albaladejo Campoy, 'Pasado, presente y futuro de la Función Pública Española', *Cuadernos Economicos de Información Comercial Española*, No. 13, 1980, 19–121.

G. E. Aylmer, 'Bureaucracy' in Peter Burke (ed.), *The New Cambridge Modern History, Vol. XIII: Companion Volume* (Cambridge 1979), 164–98.

Gerie B. Bledsoe, 'Spanish Foreign Policy, 1898–1936' in James W. Cortada (ed.), *Spain in the Twentieth-Century World: Essays on Spanish Diplomacy, 1898–1978* (Westport, Connecticut 1980), 3–40.

Soledad Gallego-Diez, 'Cómo se fabrica un embajador', *Cuadernos para el diálogo*, 25 February 1978, 46–7.

Charles R. Halstead, 'Spanish Foreign Policy, 1936–1978' in James W. Cortada (ed.), *Spain in the Twentieth-Century World: Essays on Spanish Diplomacy, 1898–1978* (Westport, Connecticut 1980), 41–94.

Pablo Sebastian, 'Reestructuración del Ministerio de Asuntos Exteriores', *El País*, 29 October 1977.

Angel Viñas, 'La Administración de la política económica exterior en España, 1936–1979', *Cuadernos Economicos de Información Comercial Española*, No. 13, 1980, 157–272.

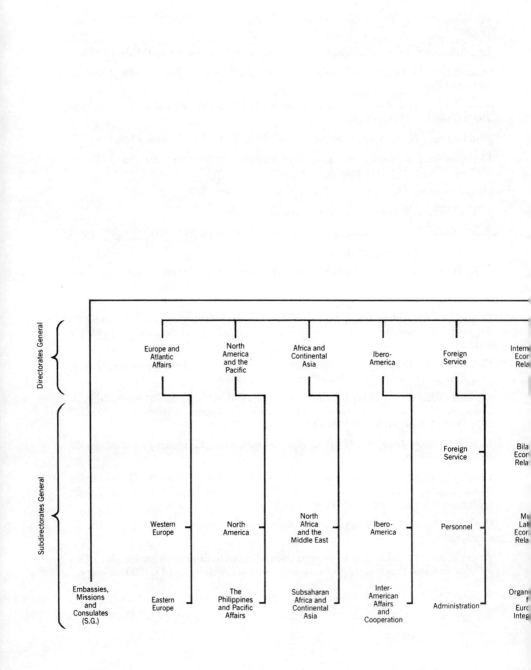

SPAIN – APPENDIX A

THE MINISTRY OF FOREIGN AFFAIRS (1981)

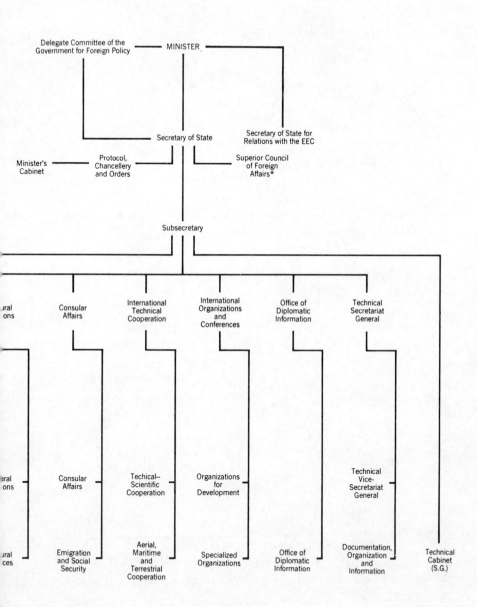

(*an advisory Council composed of selected diplomats and experts)

Sweden

The Ministry
for Foreign Affairs

WILHELM CARLGREN

Professor Wilhelm Carlgren has been Director of Archives in the
Ministry for Foreign Affairs since 1965. He took his doctorate in
history at Stockholm University. He has published studies about
Russian and Austro–Hungarian policy from 1906 to 1908 and about
Swedish foreign policy, *Svensk utrikespolitik, 1939–1945* (1973),
translated by A. Spencer, *Swedish Foreign Policy during the Second
World War* (1977).

The King's Office for Foreign Correspondence and its predecessors

Sweden's present Ministry for Foreign Affairs came into existence in 1840. In that year the old central office of governmental power, the Chancellery (Kansli), was converted into seven separate ministries, with the Ministry for Foreign Affairs ranking second after the Ministry of Justice.

The Ministry for Foreign Affairs was also officially known as the King's Office for Foreign Correspondence, the name of its immediate predecessor, which had been in existence since 1791. During its first decades the Ministry retained many of the Office's traditional forms and practices. An outline of its history could therefore quite appropriately start with a sketch of the King's Office for Foreign Correspondence during the half-century 1791–1840. But first of all it may be of interest to present a brief summary of the central administration of foreign affairs in Sweden during its age as a great power (1632–1718) and during its 'Age of Liberty' (1718–72).

'In older times the external affairs of the Realm were discharged by the Chancellery with the Chancellor of the Realm, later the President of the Chancellery, as chief. Under him there were in the Chancellery at first two and then four councillors, presiding over the various departments of the Chancellery and assisted by secretaries of state and under-secretaries. According to the Constitution of 1634 the Chancellery consisted of two departments: the one, in which all external affairs as well as internal affairs not belonging to any other authority or collegium of the Realm were managed, the other, the archives, in which the documents of the Realm were kept. Since, however, under Queen Christina and King Charles X the Realm had risen to the power and importance lost under the grandson of this King, it proved as a consequence of the vast quantity of business necessary to divide the first department, or the so-called daily chancellery. The Chancellery Regulations of 1661 stipulated that there should be four instead of two councillors in the Chancellery and that it should consist of four departments – the first one covering Swedish and Danish affairs, the second one German affairs and foreign affairs in general, the third one affairs concerning Poland and Russia and the countries on the other side of the Baltic, the fourth one the archives of the Realm.

There were two secretaries of state, dividing between themselves the business of the four departments and assisted by four under-secretaries. For the assistance of the Chancellor of the Realm for matters to which he wanted to attend himself there was a private secretary.

These regulations continued to be valid until 1713, when they were abrogated by new ones, issued by King Charles XII from Timurtasch and altogether transforming the Chancellery. They were, however, after the death of the King replaced by regulations issued in 1719. Instead of the two external and four internal divisions, which according to the 1713 Regulations formed the Chancellery, three divisions, one for external and two for internal affairs, were set up, at the head of each a secretary of state responsible for preparing the matters, for presenting them to the Collegium of the Chancellery and then for dispatching them.

During this time, as well as henceforth during the Age of Liberty, in the Chancellery external affairs as a rule were dealt with collegially, i.e.

they were sent to the Collegium of the Chancellery to get its opinion on them. The humble opinion of the Collegium was then presented by the Secretary of State for the External Division to the Council of the Realm. It was inevitable that such slow progress should give rise to a wish that issues, many of which could not wait for such lengthy deliberations, should be settled more promptly. During the Age of Liberty, therefore, the former private secretary of the Chancellor of the Realm, after 1713 called presidential secretary, had more and more important matters to deal with, while the Collegium of the Chancellery was disregarded. Because of this it was possible for secret matters to be handled with much greater security, as not only the Collegium but also a considerable part of the Council of the Realm and the King could be kept in ignorance of them.' (Taken from the introduction to the bill dealing with the reform of the Ministry for Foreign Affairs in 1858.)

After the reign of Charles XII Sweden was only a second-rate power, yet it had by no means withdrawn from European politics. Swedish foreign affairs were still dominated by negotiations about alliances, subsidies, war and peace. But instead of the supreme will of earlier kings or chancellors there now began a rule of the Riksdag – the Parliament – or rather of competing parties in the Riksdag. Consequently, foreign policy became an important arena in the struggle for power between parties, politicians and officials. This struggle naturally tended to make decisions more protracted. Speedy and resolute actions, necessary in the time of classical cabinet diplomacy in Europe, were more delayed or obstructed than could even be expected because of the rather unwieldy bureaucracy and the collegium system. The satisfactory conduct of foreign affairs required machinery that worked more speedily and secretly than the Chancellery, and the management of really important and vital matters was gradually left more or less exclusively to the prime minister of the time, i.e. to the president of the Chancellery. The President had at his disposal his private secretary and other assistants in his office.

Gustav III's *coup d'état* in 1772 completely altered the management of foreign affairs in Sweden. The Riksdag, which during the Age of Liberty had directed and controlled the country's foreign policy, was compelled to relinquish that role to the King. The councillors of the realm and their principal, the president of the Chancellery, who hitherto had carried out the instructions of changing Riksdag majorities, were now advisers or only assistants to the King, who in fact acted as his own Foreign Minister. As time passed, the King increasingly preferred to rely upon the support of the staff of the Office of the President of the Chancellery, which came under his direct control. It was consequently, in 1791, renamed the King's Office for Foreign Correspondence. Only unimportant and ceremonial matters were delegated to the Chancellery.

A comparatively small and smooth-running office had taken the place of the rather unwieldy and cumbersome bureaucracy of the Chancellery. In 1791 the Office had eight officials: one permanent secretary, two first and five second secretaries. They were to be mere assistants to the King, kept busy with ciphering, deciphering, copying, filing and the packing and dispatching of diplomatic bags. Even the permanent secretary was more a secretary than an adviser.

The machinery created by Gustav III persisted in all essentials even after his death in 1792. The old aristocratic bureaucracy won back some nominal positions – the Office was declared part of the Chancellery and made subordinate to its president. But all important matters were still handled by the King's Office, as a rule under the direct orders of the King. Nor were procedures altered by the Constitution of 1809, according to which the Prime Minister for Foreign Affairs (until 1876, when the post of Prime Minister and Head of the Government was established, there was also a Prime Minister for Legal Affairs) was also head of the Office and of the Directorate of the Chancellery, where ceremonial and less important questions concerning commerce and Swedish citizens abroad were still dealt with, as well as of Swedish missions abroad. Yet even under the new Constitution the real maker of foreign policy was the King, who was explicitly given the right to prepare and handle affairs of foreign policy in the way he saw fit, with the exception of the declaration of war and the conclusion of peace. Marshal Jean Baptiste Bernadotte, who after being elected Swedish Crown Prince in 1810 immediately took over the direction of Swedish foreign policy and retained undisputed control until his death in 1844 as King Charles John, certainly made full use of the power thus accorded the Crown. After 1811 the reports of Swedish missions abroad, although addressed to the Foreign Minister, were written in French (which continued to be used until 1876) in order to enable the Crown Prince 'all the sooner to know the zeal with which His Majesty's ministers fulfilled their duties'.

Bernadotte employed his own secretaries and agents in addition to those of the Office, and he obviously often kept matters from Swedish ministers and officials. However, as he was successful in both war and peace – as well as being a dynamic personality – no revolt or even opposition to this system arose. 'The real and only Foreign Minister is and remains Papa himself', wrote the Swedish Minister in Paris in 1837.

At the end of the 1830s the staff of the King's Office for Foreign Correspondence, despite all the violent events in Europe and Sweden during the revolutionary and Napoleonic wars of intervening years, was exactly the same as it had been in the 1790s: one permanent secretary, two first and five second secretaries. (Two assistants and three Cabinet couriers were also on the staff list.) Some extra help had been called in on various critical and busy occasions, but on the whole the staff must have merited high marks for efficiency. One reason for this was undoubtedly that the salaries and prospects for promotion in the foreign service were better than those in other government departments and agencies, where junior civil servants often had no salaries at all to start with, and even when they rose in the ranks had to take assignments outside their official duties in order to make ends meet. (The consequence was, of course, that a great deal of their time and energy was spent on tasks not pertaining to their regular employment.) Only in the King's Office for Foreign Correspondence, one reads in a committee report in 1822:

> 'do all have salaries, probably because it has been found necessary to obtain further security for the silence required than a promise of secrecy. How much work is done there compared to what is performed in other offices. How are the officials there honoured above others in the Chancellery. And how happy are deemed those who are admitted to it.'

It was thus easy for the Office to find suitable recruits. They were usually serving in other offices of the Chancellery as extras or copyists, after reading Latin, philosophy, history or political science at a university and then passing entrance tests for the Chancellery service (which included written examinations in French and Latin). For security reasons all appointments were permanent. Once appointed, officials enjoyed additional renumeration and could look forward to a safe career as there was only one Swedish diplomatic service, comprising both posts in the Office and those overseas.

In 1840 the Swedish diplomatic service abroad numbered some twenty persons, half of them envoys, the rest secretaries and attachés. Most important were the legations accredited to the great powers of the time – Berlin, London, Paris, St Petersburg and Vienna. With the exception of Washington all posts were in Europe. Sweden was still a small agrarian country without enough foreign trade to warrant transoceanic diplomatic representation.

The Swedish state was traditionally a rather ungenerous employer. Even if a Swedish diplomat was better paid than members in other branches of the bureaucracy, he could hardly function satisfactorily, especially abroad, without private means to supplement his salary. This qualification, as well as language proficiency, familiarity with worldly matters and the manners required in international society, was rarely found outside aristocratic circles. Members of the Swedish foreign service were consequently recruited almost exclusively from the high nobility of the country.

The Ministry for Foreign Affairs until the end of the Union between Sweden and Norway (1905)

In 1840 the various offices of the old Chancellery were reorganized into seven ministries, the external division of the Chancellery and the King's Office being merged into the Ministry for Foreign Affairs. As already mentioned, this reform changed little in the management of Sweden's foreign affairs. Foreign policy was still directed by the King himself and the new Ministry was also still called the King's Office for Foreign Correspondence. The negotiations between Sweden and the western powers during the Crimean War were conducted primarily by King Oscar I in person, who also sent personal agents on some missions. The general situation at the time, however, increasingly demanded a ministry that was something more than a secretariat for the King. Expanding international communications brought states and their citizens into closer touch with one another; legal and commercial questions also had to be kept under review and be dealt with by the foreign service; while political questions were less predominant than before. The organization of the Ministry, which had remained practically unchanged for sixty to seventy years, was too old-fashioned to manage the increasing amount of work. A few years after the Crimean War, in 1858, a major reorganization was carried out.

One main aim of the reform was to lighten the workload of the permanent secretary, who was the sole senior official. He was responsible for all details and was also often the only person who had served in the Office long enough to have a thorough knowledge of routine and of the matters that came under its jurisdiction. In order to spread decision-making responsibilities and to make posts sufficiently attractive for competent officials to stay in Stockholm, the Ministry was divided into three departments – the political, the legal and trade, and the administrative departments, each with a chief who held a rank between permanent secretary and first secretary. One first secretary would assist the permenant secretary and also be responsible for the minutes of Government sessions and ciphers; four senior second secretaries were to assist in the three departments; and three more junior secretaries were to work mainly as copyists. But the Ministry, with fifteen officials (including the grand master of ceremonies) and five assistants, was still small.

The reform was launched in a vigorous and optimistic mood. After having devoted themselves exclusively to their own affairs for some time, Sweden and Norway should, the Government declared, resume their rightful place in the deliberations of the European powers. To be sure, politics played an essential role in the activities of the Ministry during the following half-century until the dissolution of the Union between Sweden and Norway in 1905 and the subsequent reorganization of the Swedish foreign service in 1906. But its concern was Union politics, not international politics; the main aim was to keep away from European affairs, not to participate in them.

Bernadotte's principal aim in bringing about the Union between Sweden and Norway in 1815 was to keep the two countries together and out of conflicts between other states, above all those between Britain and Russia. This obviously required a joint foreign policy and, in consequence, he let his Swedish ministers and officials handle Norwegian foreign affairs too.

The Norwegians at first resigned themselves to this. Soon, however, they began to demand the right for Norwegian ministers to participate in decisions concerning Norway or Norwegian matters, as well as opportunities for Norwegian citizens to enter the foreign service. Their wishes were gradually heeded, but in the long run even far-reaching concessions did not suffice. It became increasingly obvious that the Norwegians were eager to end the Union, to break loose from Sweden. During the latter part of the nineteenth century Norwegian opposition to the common crown and the joint foreign service gathered momentum; initially, their aim was to weaken the power of the Swedes, but later to be rid of them altogether. The Swedes, wanting to maintain the Union, which in their opinion was likely to deter the great powers from intervention on the Scandinavian peninsula, resisted what they considered to be a risky Norwegian separation. They succeeded in preserving the Union, though it became weaker and weaker, until 1905.

The King – or in the case of the first Bernadotte, the Crown Prince – had played a leading part in shaping Swedish foreign policy since the reign of Gustav III. During the second half of the nineteenth century this royal role began to diminish. An attempt by Charles XV in 1863 to enforce an alliance with Denmark, which failed because of opposition in the Swedish and Norwegian governments, was the last really important royal initiative in Swedish foreign policy. From then on the government took over, though the name of King's Office for Foreign Correspondence lived on in the Constitution until the 1960s. True, Oscar II and Gustav V may later have contemplated or perhaps even attempted to make moves on their own. But they no longer had enough power to impose their will upon their ministers. This placed the Foreign Minister in charge of foreign policy, not just ostensibly but now also in reality. As a rule all Foreign Ministers – sixteen out of the eighteen who held the office during the period 1809–1905 – were diplomats or had at least served for some years as heads of missions abroad. Usually they had no political aspirations and were content with a policy of muddling through. Their performance at the Ministry was not always brilliant. Nevertheless, they seem to have had a better sense of proportion than some of their successors.

The continuous quarrels over the Union and the consequent deliberations and reports required to settle them, at least temporarily, had rather crippling effects. The 'Norwegian question' became the Ministry's most important problem. The recurrent disputes about the correct interpretation of the Union Statute of 1815 and of other regulations and clauses furthered a formal and legalistic approach to foreign affairs in general. In 1878 and in 1899 new instructions were issued, which contained more detailed rules than the 1858 one though hardly altering them. The working burden of the Ministry (measured in letter statistics) increased steadily. To meet the new requirements, from the 1870s female assistants were engaged to help with the routine Chancery business in order to make the secretaries available for more demanding tasks, and at about the end of the century a few new officials were added to the Ministry's staff. Thoroughgoing administrative reforms, however, were held back in order not to present the Norwegians with openings to break up the Union.

Even with the Norwegian question, politics did not have the same precedence in the activities of the Ministry as they had before. Towards the end of the nineteenth century Swedish industry made its first attempts to capture foreign markets, while at the same time protectionism was becoming a predominant feature of the trade policy of many countries. As a result, the foreign service was being constantly called upon to assist in overcoming various trade barriers, through negotiations or other diplomatic activity. Furthermore, the steadily developing international contacts between states, authorities, organizations and individuals gave diplomats far more to do in the legal field than before – arbitration treaties, international conventions, inheritances from emigrants and other cases of international law.

Yet the Ministry remained much the same as it had been in 1858. The number of officials rose very slowly, from fifteen in 1858 to nineteen in 1905. Old customs and traditions persisted from the times when the Ministry had been ruled patriarchally and when almost all the officials were members of the nobility and were related or moved in the same circles. The day's work still began at 11 o'clock to give officials time to recover from the social activities of the previous evening. The cipher was kept in an easily burgled wooden cupboard secured with a locking device for which the opening code was a fairly open secret – the word 'Mosel'. The drafts prepared by the young secretaries were mostly scrutinized by heads of department, those dealing with more important matters also by the permanent secretary.

There were still no special examinations for admission to the foreign service. As before, some proficiency in languages was required, particularly in French, and some years of academic studies, mostly resulting in the usual degree for entrance into the civil service. The earlier aristocratic dominance was obviously receding but had not yet quite disappeared. The career possibilities for a new second secretary were comparatively good in that he could reckon upon ultimately becoming a Swedish envoy abroad. His financial position in the course of his career could, however, be difficult at times. The Riksdag was not more open-handed than in earlier times towards the foreign service, and while a private fortune was perhaps no longer a necessity it was still a very desirable qualification for the Swedish diplomatic profession.

In 1905 representation abroad – as well as the Ministry for Foreign Affairs at home – remained essentially the same as it had been half a century before. Legations were established only in European capitals and in Washington. Short-lived diplomatic representations had, however, existed in Caracas and in Rio de Janeiro, and a few salaried consulates-general or consulates were to be found in North America and in the Far East. Behind these transoceanic advances lay not only Swedish trade but also, perhaps more importantly, Norwegian shipping. Nonetheless, the contacts between Sweden and countries far from the foreign service's traditional European field of action had grown considerably during the last decades of the Swedish–Norwegian Union.

The Ministry for Foreign Affairs through the World Wars

The end of the Swedish–Norwegian Union in 1905 left the door open for long-postponed changes and reforms. In 1906 both the Ministry and its overseas representations were given a new organization and corresponding new instructions. In the eagerness for modernization, however, a precariously free hand was given, and before long the 1906 scheme was to show serious deficiencies.

The principal aim was to meet the wishes of Swedish industry and shipping by giving more help and support, 'trade expansion' being the watchword of the day. Commercial and legal questions had hitherto been handled in the same department: now one commercial and one legal department were established. As to politics, the leading theme was quite the reverse: Sweden should keep aloof from the affairs of Europe as much as possible and try to dodge international conflicts and tensions. Accordingly it was no longer deemed necessary to have a special department for political affairs. Political affairs should be handled by the Foreign Minister himself, assisted by the permanent secretary. The administrative department remained practically as it was, as did the number of officials, of whom there were between fifteen and twenty.

Thus the Ministry's working capacity did not increase, and the permanent secretary, and even the Foreign Minister himself, became burdened with routine work. Some remedy was obtained when, in 1911, a new press department was set up with instructions not only to handle the ministry's relations with the press but also to assist the permanent secretary in the management of political matters. But no more was done, and in 1914 the Ministry was ill-equipped to meet the great demands made on Swedish foreign policy by the First World War. Of course, no adequate scheme for an organization called upon to cope with lengthy wartime conditions could have been set up in 1906. A far-sighted assessment should nonetheless have given the Ministry resources enough to follow international developments and the ways and means of great power policy.

The Ministry was thus ill-prepared to handle the strain of wartime conditions. The legal department to some extent served a political function, but without much success; a more flexible, less legalistic course would often have been an advantage. Certainly an experienced political department would have prepared several important questions more thoroughly before they were submitted to the government for decision. The trade department did not have adequate resources to execute the government's foreign trade policy, and in fact surrendered its direction to commissions outside the Ministry. As a further handicap the Ministry became involved in the bitter power struggle between right and left. Affairs were somehow kept going through temporary arrangements, including considerable reinforcements. Reforms were obviously necessary but had to await more normal times to be put into effect.

Immediately after the war, in 1919, a thorough reorganization took place. In 1914 the first non-diplomatic Foreign Minister – at the same time the first commoner in this post – had been appointed. His two successors during the war years were likewise non-diplomats (and commoners). The permanent secretary, no longer the Minister himself, was thus the chief professional in the Ministry. To enhance his position he now had a higher rank than before, and to give him more time for direction and supervision the heads of department were given greater powers to decide matters themselves. The establishment of a well-staffed political department was, after the experiences of the war years, an obvious reform. The new department became, however, something of a super-department: it had three geographical bureaux, the old press department was transformed into political bureau number four, and questions concerning trade agreements and trade policy were referred to the political department. To a small special commercial department were relegated matters regarding economic and commercial information. The legal and administrative departments were reinforced and each was divided into two bureaux. Altogether, the staff of the Ministry grew considerably – in 1918 it totalled 88 and by 1920 numbered 120.

The 1919 reorganization provided a welcome stimulus for the Ministry. Yet it was too much influenced by impressions from the war years, above all from the momentous negotiations over trade agreements with Britain and Germany. These had no doubt been crucial to the general foreign policy of Sweden, but in normally peaceful times there was no need to divide the handling of trade questions between the political and commercial departments. Moreover, even without these questions the political department, and particularly its chief, had quite enough to do, as business relating to the League of Nations (which Sweden joined in 1920) and international conferences increased considerably during the 1920s.

In 1928 some of the innovations of 1919 were cancelled and conditions reverted to their previous status. Trade policy and trade negotiations were again referred to the trade department, which was simultaneously reinforced and divided into two bureaux, one for negotiations and treaties and the other for commercial information. The press bureau left the political department and again became independent. The political department was organized into two instead of three bureaux, one for questions relating to the League of Nations, the other for 'political questions in general'. This 1928 scheme was still in force when the Second World War began in 1939, the only important change being the establishment of a third bureau at the trade department. Between these three bureaux, affairs were divided according to geography, and the separation that had existed between treaty and information matters was abolished.

For the Ministry's officials the inter-wars years meant a livelier and wider degree of domestic and foreign intercourse. Because of changes in the

Constitution at the beginning of the 1920s, the Riksdag's connections with foreign policy questions, and thus with the Ministry for Foreign Affairs, had been broadened. The League of Nations enabled small states to play a more active role in international politics, and international conferences demanded Sweden's participation. In managing these extended external contacts Swedish governments (in the 1920s swiftly superseding one another, in the 1930s more stable) had to rely on the Ministry to provide professional competence and to maintain continuity. This led to closer and better contacts than before between leading politicians and officials, and at the same time offered the staff of the Ministry greater opportunities for professional training and international experience.

The old aristocratic stamp of the Ministry began to fade away. Recruitment to the foreign service had been widened and improved, not least thanks to raised salaries and better promotion prospects since not only the Ministry but also the representation abroad had been enlarged, both to adjust it to the new political map of Europe after 1918 and to further Swedish commercial interests in transoceanic countries. Indeed, a modest expansion of Swedish representation in foreign countries had begun in 1906, in connection with the reorganization of the Ministry for Foreign Affairs. Now after the First World War the expansion was extended to include posts not only for envoys but also for counsellors and secretaries. Special entrance examinations had been introduced in 1913, giving some guarantee of efficiency and capability in new diplomats; moreover, admission to the career was confirmed only after a probationary period of two years.

The years of the Second World War strained the Ministry, and especially its senior officials, to the utmost. There were some differences of opinion about how far concessions to the belligerent great powers should go, but there was unanimity about the main aim of the policy: to keep out of the war. Foreign policy during the war meant continuous hard negotiations with the belligerents, the careful sifting of often vague information, and declarations and discussions about the rights and duties of a neutral state. Yet on the whole the 1928 scheme stood the test – in the political department the League of Nations bureau turned to really vital matters, and in the trade department a special bureau for shipping was established. The shortcomings of the 1914–18 period were not repeated: the all-important trade negotiations were controlled by the Ministry, and political questions were handled with more deftness and routine than during the earlier war. All things considered the Ministry, led very competently by two outstanding diplomats as Foreign Minister (Christian Günther) and permanent secretary (Erik Boheman), must be praised for a remarkable achievement. Indeed, in retrospect the war years 1939–45 can be seen as something of a peak period in the annals of the Swedish Ministry for Foreign Affairs.

During the inter-war years, Swedish missions in transoceanic countries had increased, above all in South America. This expansion proved to be of great importance for the small but extremely valuable transoceanic trade during the war. A further development of Sweden's foreign service after the war was definitely contemplated, and had in fact already been planned. The war had changed the map of Europe and many lines of communications were broken, yet on the whole missions abroad had been able to look after Swedish interests as far as war or occupation allowed. The reports coming into Stockholm from abroad were of a far higher calibre than those received during the First World War. During the 1920s and 1930s the Swedish foreign service had become by international standards competent and effective, and was well able to withstand the hard tests of the war years.

The present Ministry for Foreign Affairs

In 1945 the Swedish Ministry for Foreign Affairs had been in existence for a century, to be exact for 105 years. During that time it had undergone three major reorganizations – in 1858, in 1906 and in 1919, with several minor adjustments in between. The staff employed at the Ministry had been doubled over and over again and in 1945 (admittedly still a war year, so with extra help and reinforcements) numbered about 275. Reforms and expansion reflected Sweden's increasingly active role in international politics and in the world economy. Yet in 1945 Sweden was still a country on the periphery of Europe, rather remote from the centres of world events. In the years to come, distances between centres and peripheries were to be reduced as international interdependences deepened and international cooperation in various fields steadily grew. How frequent would be the reforms and what scale of expansion would the Ministry for Foreign Affairs – and the foreign service in general – now find necessary to keep pace with these developments?

In 1945 there was not the same pressing need to reorganize the Ministry as there had been in 1918. On the contrary, the 1928 structure had come out of the war years quite well. The strains of the early post-war years were thus borne by furnishing the existing structure with new units or particular posts. In 1949 a new bureau was added to the political department, principally to handle questions concerning Sweden's relations to and actions within the United Nations. The trade department, strictly occupied at first with bilateral trade negotiations and then with steadily increasing contacts with new international trade organizations such as GATT, the OECD, etc., was given some new posts, but in the main had to rely on temporary arrangements and reinforcements to cope with its growing amount of work. The legal and administrative departments remained largely as they had been when the war ended.

At the beginning of the 1960s, however, the time had come for more extensive changes. The amount of time that Ministry officials had to spend in preparing and attending more or less regular sessions of international organizations, as well as a large number of international conferences, was out of all comparison to that required during the inter-war years. Other countries were becoming more interested in Sweden, and people in Sweden also became more interested in foreign countries. The Ministry was expected to possess, or in any case be able speedily to produce, particulars about conditions at home and abroad. Assistance to developing countries became a more and more time-consuming concern.

In 1963, after a thorough survey of the Ministry's tasks and resources, the Riksdag granted several reinforcements. New units were established: a negotiation group to relieve the ordinary departments of some negotiation work and similar assignments handled in addition to their regular duties, and a reports secretariat to manage the editing and distribution of information about foreign countries sent in from Swedish missions abroad. The administrative department was considerably reinforced. A special office to handle questions concerning assistance to developing countries, which had at first come under the political department, had been in existence for some time but was now reinforced. Together with the additions made to other departments this meant an appreciable increase in Ministry staff, from 350 in 1962 to 412 in 1963. However, the structure was essentially the same as in 1928; the intention was to acquire more resources and a greater degree of flexibility, not to remodel the Ministry.

In the years that followed, more thorough-going changes were recommended in the fairly lively debate on the best model for the Government's administrative machinery as a whole. In some of the suggested schemes, the Ministry was to be a super-ministry, with a senior minister responsible for foreign policy and some junior ministers handling external trade, assistance to the developing countries and disarmament. Other proposals aimed to reduce the Ministry, in particular one that intended to transfer the Ministry's trade department to the Ministry of Commerce. The international secretariats, which in the 1960s were established in other ministries, wanted to manage the special external questions of their ministries themselves, i.e. to keep them out of the hands of the Ministry for Foreign Affairs, which had dealt with most of them up to that time. One also often heard criticism of the Ministry: its organization was out-of-date; it was not only a government office for preparing and effecting the government's political decisions, but the only ministry that was also a civil service office handling a lot of rather trivial routine matters, such as assistance to tourists, the accounts of the Swedish diplomatic missions abroad, all kinds of information, exhibitions, etc. It would be more suitable – so it was argued – to divide it into two large entities, a ministry for essential foreign policy questions and a civil service office for consular, legal, administrative and information matters.

Most of these suggestions have gone no farther than the paper on which they were written. One, however, has partially been realized. In 1973 the Ministry's trade department was transferred to the offices of the Ministry of Commerce, to merge with corresponding divisions there. The staff of these divisions coming from the Ministry for Foreign Affairs are still part of this Ministry, not of the Ministry of Commerce. Amalgamation is thus not yet complete, but should it take place, it would be the logical conclusion of a long development: since the beginning of the 1930s the Minister of Commerce and not the Minister for Foreign Affairs has been responsible for foreign trade, and his Ministry has assumed the management of more and more foreign trade questions that were previously handled by the Ministry for Foreign Affairs.

The Ministry's sphere of activity has, however, also been broadened. The Government's handling of assistance to developing countries has been concentrated in the Ministry for Foreign Affairs, and the office for dealing with these affairs has thus developed into a large department comprising three divisions. New bureaux have been added: to the political department for disarmament, the long-range planning of Swedish foreign policy and Asian and African questions, to the legal department for treaty matters, and to the press unit for information matters.

In 1974–5 a new survey of the Ministry's tasks and functions was undertaken. Recommendations for a thorough restructuring were not adopted; instead, it was decided to streamline the existing structure – still based on the

1928 design – as well as to strengthen it with a number of new posts. Two innovations of 1963, the negotiation group and the reports secretariat, were dismantled and most of their posts incorporated in the political department. At present, January 1981, the Ministry employs 600 persons.

The most important changes within the Ministry over the last ten years concern not its organization but the staff policy of the foreign service. The staff were formerly divided into different categories: diplomats, consular staff, clerical staff and messengers. Admittedly some staff had transferred from, say, consular to diplomatic careers. For a long time this was very much the exception, but in the 1950s and 1960s these transfers gained momentum. In 1976 a decision was made to favour a general integration of the different careers. This staff policy has meant that the principles for recruitment to the foreign service have been somewhat modified. Theoretical education and university studies are no longer such dominant qualifications, and greater emphasis is placed on practical experience. This approach should lend to a wider net of recruitment.

Swedish representation abroad has been redoubled in the last thirty years: in 1947 there were 53, in 1981 115 salaried embassies, delegations and consulates; there are some 1400 foreign service staff employed abroad, most of whom are still stationed in Europe and North America, though in recent years a great many embassies have been established in African and Asian states.

The present organization of the Swedish Ministry for Foreign Affairs is given in Appendix A. Two departments – the trade department and the department for international development cooperation – are led by special under-secretaries of state; the others all come under the permanent under-secretary of state. This post thus remains the key office at the ministry, as it has been since 1840, or rather since 1791. The 1928 scheme, now fifty years old, has on the whole stood the test of time, though in recent decades there has been a tendency to take less account than before of rigid spheres of responsibility and to rely more on general flexibility and a readiness to meet sudden crises and contingencies. This was, of course, an approach to the management of foreign affairs that had some relevance in the late eighteenth century when the King's Office for Foreign Correspondence, the present Ministry's predecessor, came into existence. There is nothing new under the sun! Nevertheless, the Ministry is no longer the only caretaker of Swedish interests in foreign countries. Other ministries, and a great many civil service offices, have established increasing direct contacts abroad. The exclusiveness of the Ministry is by no means what it was, and it is constantly diminishing. Each society, of course, has its own ways and means of handling its foreign affairs. An absolute monarch makes his own mark on their administration, a mark quite different from that of a parliamentary democracy, which functions at a time and in a country where foreign policy is no longer the prerogative of kings and aristocrats but a concern of all levels of society.

BIBLIOGRAPHY

Sources for the early development of the Swedish foreign service are dispersed in various Chancellery files. Particulars can be found in the standard work: S. Tunberg *et al.*, *Den svenska utrikesförvaltningens historia* (Uppsala 1935); French version: *Histoire de l'administration des affaires étrangères de Suède* (Uppsala 1940). This book covers the period up to 1935. Useful information is also contained in the various volumes of *Den svenska utrikespolitikens historia* (History of Swedish Foreign Policy) 1–5 (Stockholm 1951–61). There are very few special studies in the field; one covering a wider theme and longer period is Kjell Emanuelson, *Den svensk-norska utrikesförvaltningen 1870–1905* (Lund 1980).

About life and work in the Ministry for Foreign Affairs in the late 1880s there is an interesting day-to-day report in the diaries of the then chief of the Political Department, Carl Fleetwood: *Fran studieår och diplomattjänst 1879–1892*, 1–2 (Stockholm 1968).

For the development after 1900, committee reports of 1906, 1909–21, 1928, 1963 and 1975, completed by the resulting bills and Riksdag decisions (in the parliamentary print) are very valuable. The unprinted material in the files is not easy to survey.

Among the memoirs of later years should be mentioned particularly Erik Boheman, *På vakt, Från attaché till sändebud* and *På vakt, Kabinettssekreterare under andra världskriget* (Stockholm 1963–4), and Gunnar Hägglöf, *Möte med Europa 1926–1940* and *Samtida vittne 1940–1945* (Stockholm 1971–2), English edition: *Diplomat, Memoirs of a Swedish envoy in London, Paris, Berlin, Moscow and Washington* (London 1972).

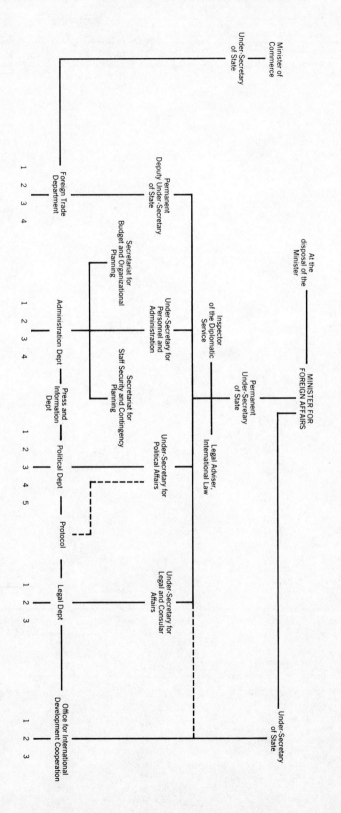

SWEDEN – APPENDIX A

THE MINISTRY FOR FOREIGN AFFAIRS (1981)

Switzerland

The Federal Department of External Affairs

BERNARD FREYMOND

Bernard Freymond is currently First Counsellor at the Swiss embassy in Athens. He was born in Saint Cierges, Vaud, in 1941 and studied at the University of Lausanne where he took his *licence* in political sciences in 1965. After working in industry in the Federal Republic of Germany, he joined the Federal Department of External Affairs in 1967 and has seen service in Belgrade, Washington, Bern and temporarily at the United Nations in New York. He was head of the Personnel section of the Administrative Directorate from 1978 to 1980.

The present organization of the department in charge of Switzerland's external relations and the defence of its interests abroad results from a long process that paralleled the changes characterizing the creation of Switzerland itself over the centuries. The establishment of the present federal state marks the completion of a slow evolution that began in 1291, the year in which the populations of Uri, Schwyz and Unterwald decided to unite in order to throw off the yoke of their suzerain, Duke Rudolph of Habsburg. In order to get a picture of this evolution, one must bear in mind that it took over 500 years for the Confederation of three small sovereign states, covering 2700 sq.km around Lake Lucerne, to reach its present form as a federal state that comprises twenty-three cantons (of which three are divided into half-cantons) and cover an area of more than 41 000 sq.km from the Lake of Geneva to the Bodensee, between the Alps and the Jura.

Historical introduction

Because Switzerland was from the outset composed of sovereign states that only gradually granted to a central body the authority to represent them abroad, it acquired a department charged exclusively with external relations relatively late in comparison with the great European powers. For quite a long time, the states (cantons) of the Confederation were anxious to keep for themselves the prerogative of settling relations with foreign powers, though they acknowledged the right of the Federal Diet to send embassies abroad.

Under the *ancien régime*, that is until the creation of the Helvetic Republic in 1798, the right of legation belonged to each canton individually. The question of representation of the Confederation abroad was settled separately in each case: the Confederation would decide whether to send an embassy to a foreign power, an embassy that would return once its mission had been accomplished. The embassies were thus entrusted with limited assignments and had not yet gained any permanent features. These special missions still exist, in the appointment of a delegation – headed by an ambassador and lasting for a limited period of time – to represent the Government on ceremonial occasions.

The fall of the *ancien régime* was brought about by the intervention of French troops in Switzerland (following an incident evidently caused by French officers), which served the purposes of First Consul Bonaparte. The France born of the Revolution was very keen to have control over the Alpine passes, and thus over the strategic roads linking Paris and Milan, as well as to put an end to the reactionary influence of English agents active in the aristocratic governments of some influential Swiss cantons. The occupying power enforced a unitary constitution, which changed Switzerland into a republic similar to France. From the creation of this first state, endowed with real central power, dates the sending of the first permanent diplomatic representatives from Switzerland: with the opening, in 1798, of permanent legations in Paris and Milan, and in Vienna in 1802.

Following the political events that took place in Italy, the Swiss legation in Milan was transformed into a consulate-general in 1816, while the Swiss legations in Paris and Vienna were left as special cases until 1848.

Although the 1798 Constitution had planned for national or federal rights of legation, apart from the three cases mentioned above it was not until the institution of the 1815 Federal Pact, which marked the return to the *ancien régime*, that the first permanent representations abroad were established.

However, strictly speaking, these representations did not constitute diplomatic missions but were rather consular posts established in capitals or commercial towns according to the commercial interests that Switzerland wished to protect. The Federal Pact established that the Diet would run the external politics of the Confederation (now twenty-two cantons) but in essential matters only; the individual states retained their right to sign military treaties with foreign countries in order to provide soldiers, and to negotiate about economic and legal matters.

Up to this point, the various Swiss constitutions never expressly prevented the individual states from sending diplomats abroad on certain occasions. At the Congress of Vienna, for instance, some cantons were represented by a large number of official or semi-official agents; such circumstances did not ease the task of the diplomats who made up the delegation of the Federal Diet.

The 1848 Constitution marks a turning point in the history of Switzerland, which from a confederation of states became a federative state complete with a central power. It meant the disappearance of certain privileges reserved to the cantons, notably with regard to foreign relations. This Constitution established the principle of the exclusive authority of the federal state with regard to external relations. The Federal Council, a collegiate board of seven members each appointed as the head of a department (ministry), was entrusted with the handling of all questions of external relations. Since that time, the conduct of foreign affairs has been entrusted to one of the seven departments, called until 1978 the Federal Political Department, the first Ministry of External Affairs as such, which was also made responsible for maintaining order and peace within the Confederation. The Constitution of 1874, still in force today, confirmed this principle.

As a direct consequence of this important structural change, relations with foreign countries were considerably increased. The network of representation was going to be organized and developed. Until 1900 the Swiss diplomatic system remained small and only a few new missions were established: Turin (from 1861 to 1865), transferred to Florence (1865) until the opening of a legation in Rome in 1871, Berlin (1865), Washington (1882), Buenos Aires (1891) and London (1891). Paris and Vienna included, the diplomatic network comprised only seven legations, and the consular network thirty-six posts (fifteen of them overseas) that were opened between 1815 and 1848, mainly in Europe and America. Before 1914 five new diplomatic missions were opened: The Hague (1904), St Petersburg and Tokyo (1906), Rio de Janeiro (1907) and Madrid (1910).

Until 1848 the Confederation, really a cluster of sovereign states that minted their own coinages, raised their own troops, levied taxes and collected customs duties at their borders, did not of course possess a permanent central administration, except for the brief period of the Helvetic Republic (1798–1803). As soon as the cantons decided to transform the Confederation into a real federative state, they agreed to concede part of their sovereignty to the central administration established by the Constitution of 1848. The tendency towards centralization was further reinforced with the new Constitution of 1874.

A collegiate government of seven members elected by the Parliament was created and received the name of Federal Council. Each of its members in turn was to hold the presidency of the Council for one year. As representative of the Confederation to the world, this member of the collegiate board was given the title of President of the Confederation, but without fulfilling the functions of a head of state. In fact, his role was and still is today a limited one. It is that of *primus inter pares*, restricted to the presidency of the Federal Council and the exercise of different functions of a ceremonial kind, such as the acknowledgement of the credentials of newly accredited heads of missions or of the good wishes presented by the diplomatic corps at New Year. From the point of view of constitutional law the supreme power, which is usually held by the head of state, falls within the competence of the collegiate government as a whole.

For many years after the creation of a federal administration in 1848 the administration of foreign affairs was considered to be the least absorbing area for a federal councillor (minister); it was therefore decided to entrust its direction to the member who was holding the presidency of the Confederation. Thus, from 1848 to 1914 (with an interruption between 1887 and 1897), and again from 1917 to 1920, under exceptional circumstances, the President of the Confederation was in charge of the Federal Political Department, which meant that the Minister of External Affairs changed each year. This lack of continuity had obvious disadvantages as far as the running of the Department was concerned.

In the law on the organization of the federal administration passed on 26 March 1914 it was decided to entrust foreign affairs permanently to one member of the government, following the example of other areas under central authority. The Federal Political Department thus lost its involvement with presidential affairs, but there was a notable widening in the scope of its activities. The Division of Commerce (which corresponds to the ministry of external trade in many countries) had since 1895 been part of the Federal Department of Commerce, Industry and Agriculture, but was now attached to the Federal Political Department. The Political Department was also put in charge of matters bearing no direct relationship to foreign affairs, such as naturalization and options, the organization and running of the work of the federal authorities, elections and voting, the question of cantonal frontiers, intercantonal assistance for the needy and emigration. In order to fulfil its mandate, the Federal Political Department was organized into three divisions. These were the Division of External Affairs, the Division of Commerce and the Division of the Interior.

The First World War brought many new duties to the Political Department, resulting in various administrative innovations. Among these tasks one finds, for instance, the exercising of mandates as the protecting power, problems relating to the internment of foreign soldiers who had taken refuge on Swiss territory, and the protection of Swiss citizens abroad.

By a decree of the Federal Council of 25 June 1917, the President of the Confederation was again assigned the conduct of the Political Department, and the Division of Commerce was attached to the Department of Public Economy as had already been the case from 1895 to 1914.

In 1918 four offices were created and attached to the Division of External Affairs. They were the bureau for the study of questions of international law, the legal bureau, the press bureau and the correspondence bureau. In 1920 it was once again decided to abandon (this time for good) the system requiring the Political Department to change its head (in the person of the President of the Confederation) each year.

On 3 October 1923 the Federal Chambers (Parliament) decided provisionally to leave the Division of Commerce to the Department of Public Economy, an arrangement that has been kept until today, although the possibility of uniting foreign affairs and external commerce under a single head of department has been raised several times.

For reasons of economy, the Federal Council decided on 19 February 1926 to suppress the Division of the Interior by dividing its duties between the Federal Chancellery and the Federal Department of Justice and Police. The Office of Emigration was kept for a few more years until it was attached to the Federal Office for Industry, Crafts and Engineering and Labour. From then on, only one division remained within the Department, the Division of External Affairs. This structure was an anomaly and soon led, in the 1914 law on organization, to the actual disappearance of the distinction between the duties of the Department and those given to the Division of External Affairs as a subordinate authority. The Division of External Affairs had gradually come to arrange and settle matters that should have fallen within the field of the Political Department. By 1930 all distinctions had disappeared, and the head (chef) of the Division of External Affairs had taken over the running of all affairs. He had become the necessary intermediary between the head of the Department and the offices that made up the Division. This structure soon became too cumbersome; some sections of the Division created over the years had become almost as important as actual divisions.

The Department grew very rapidly during the Second World War, increasing from 603 to 1917 employees between 1939 and 1941. This growth was largely the result of Switzerland assuming, as a protecting power, numerous mandates for representing the interests of the belligerent powers in the countries with which they had broken off diplomatic relations as a normal consequence of war. An important section of the staff appointed under private contract during the war was gradually dismissed as normal diplomatic relations were resumed between the various warring states. Furthermore parliament imposed a total freeze on appointments from 1947 to 1955 to allow the overall strength of the federal administration to be stabilized, and the strength of the Department was reduced to about 1300 people in 1951.

The post-war period
After the end of the Second World War the foreign policy of Switzerland, which had been spared the horrors of this unprecedented conflict, became increasingly inspired by the idea of neutrality and solidarity, which resulted in a wider opening to the world and the application of the principle of 'universality of diplomatic relations'. One consequence of the war had been to stop the development of the external service of the Confederation, which had been planned in order to guarantee Switzerland's presence in a number of extra-European states where there was either insufficient representation or none at all.

The hostilities forced neutral Switzerland to keep an extreme check on these plans, which were postponed until better days. An important report delivered by the Federal Council to the Chambers emphasized that the time had come for Switzerland to abandon this reserve and emerge from its isolation. Great upheavals had taken place in the world, politically, socially and economically, certain tendencies could already be distinguished as far as international commerce was concerned, especially with regard to the increasing responsibilities of the state towards the private sector of the economy.

Economic needs have of course played a leading part in this movement to establish closer links with other countries, as foreign trade is vital for Switzerland, which lacks all natural resources. At the same time it was increasingly felt that intellectual and artistic relations with foreign countries should be developed. Between 1945 and 1979 diplomatic relations were established with about a hundred states, among them Canada and China in 1945 and the USSR in 1946. (In this last instance, it was a case of reestablishing relations that had been broken in 1919.)

The rearrangement of the country's external affairs after the war, and the requirements of the Federal Political Department with regard to Switzerland's presence abroad, which raised problems of vital importance, meant that the external service needed to adapt to the new circumstances. This adjustment could only take place with the simultaneous reorganization of the central office. Because of this the head of the Department provisionally ordered a new distribution of the offices, approved by the Federal Council on 20 March 1946. After a four-year trial and with a few minor alterations based on a survey made by experts, the Federal Council adopted the new organization of the Department by a decree of 20 January 1950 (see diagram).

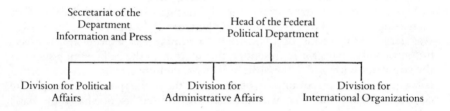

The close links between nations during the post-war period, and the adoption of the San Francisco Charter (which set the foundations of the United Nations Organization and thus significantly contributed to the rapid development of multilateral diplomacy) reduced, if not *de facto* at least *de jure*, the earlier difference between the great powers and other states. The Charter of the United Nations established the principle of the equality of votes among its members. Previously, only the great powers exchanged ambassadors, who according to accepted practice took precedence over plenipotentiary ministers representing lesser powers. The latter, convinced that they possessed the same rights as the representatives of the great powers, one after another raised their legations to the rank of embassies. Switzerland resisted this movement for a long time and remained attached to the old system, until it became obvious that this peculiar status sometimes placed Switzerland in a position of inferiority. In order to protect its interests abroad more effectively, the country was in the end forced to imitate the others and decided in 1957 to raise its legations to the rank of embassies. At present, only a very few small states still keep legations.

The Federal Department of External Affairs today

According to the terms of the Constitution of the Swiss Confederation of 25 May 1874, it is the duty of the Federal Council to protect the interests of the Confederation abroad, to watch over the external safety of the country and to maintain its independence and its neutrality.

From the point of view of the internal administrative organization of the Confederation, the Federal Political Department has been entrusted to carry out the foreign policy tasks described in the Swiss Constitution, under the provisions of the federal law of 19 September 1978 on the organization of the federal administration, which replaced that of 1914 and changed the name of the Department to the Federal Department of External Affairs (Département fédéral des affaires étrangères, DFAE). The principal intention behind the new law was to alleviate the burdens of the seven federal councillors. This was done by modifying some of the Department's duties and by introducing a new title, that of secretary of state, to head the Directorate of Political Affairs within the DFAE, to replace the previous title of secretary-general. (The same title was also introduced for the head of the Federal Office for External Economic Affairs (formerly the Division of Commerce) of the Federal Department for Public Economy.) The legislator's will was that this should not be a new post, but rather the conferment of a title that would enable the recipient better to assert, in his relations with foreign countries, the importance of his office and his standing in the administrative structure; coming immediately after the head of the department he represents, the secretary of state has a quasi-ministerial rank, and is thus able to deal with foreign representatives on the same terms as a vice-minister and hence usefully relieve the head of his department.

The 1978 law also introduced new denominations for several federal offices. The Federal Political Department, as we have seen, became the Federal Department of External Affairs, which corresponds better to the terminology now generally adopted. The Administrative Directorate was now called the General Secretariat, and its director consequently became secretary-general in an attempt to keep a certain consistency in the names of the administrative offices of the seven federal departments. In unifying the organization and structure of the federal departments in this way, no account was taken of the fact that in the foreign affairs ministry of other countries the title of secretary-general is often reserved for the civil servant highest in grade, who in the DFAE is called the secretary of state.

If there was once a time when Switzerland could live in a state of self-sufficiency, putting its main effort into the consolidation of its internal equilibrium, that period is over. The country has already had to open out into the world because of the smallness of its territory, the poverty of its soil, its distance from the sea and the fact that it is part of cultures that are centred in neighbouring nations.

The preservation of Switzerland's identity, its economic survival and the remarkable development of its industries depend essentially on the relations Switzerland is able to maintain with foreign countries: they in turn condition its foreign policy, which is characterized by permanent neutrality, solidarity and participation in world affairs. Since the end of the Second World War especially, Swiss foreign policy has entered an active phase based on multiple relations with other countries. It is obvious that the permanent neutrality that enabled it to avoid two world conflicts made it Switzerland's duty to associate closely with the activities of countries involved in the reconstruction of a devastated world and dedicated to the reestablishment of international relations in a spirit of peace and equality of rights.

Thus, within a span of about thirty years, the duties of the Federal Department of External Affairs have increased substantially in many areas. In bilateral diplomacy the number of states with which Switzerland maintains relations rose from 36 in 1945 to 145 on 1 January 1980; at the same time Switzerland played its part in the relatively new phenomenon in international relations, multilateral diplomacy, which sprang from the need felt by different states to coordinate their efforts to solve problems that in different ways concern them all. Humanitarian aid is a traditional element of neutrality (along with good offices) whose importance was underlined by the creation of an assistance unit that in 1980 had a total budget of 44 million francs, including aid to international organizations and missions of assistance in case of catastrophies abroad. Cooperation for development was fostered by the creation of the Office of the Delegate of the Federal Council for Technical Cooperation, which was modified into the Directorate for Cooperation for Development and Humanitarian Aid. This is responsible for the conception, management and supervision of work in the Third World, which in 1980 amounted to 340 million francs, multilateral aid included. The development of the system of social security benefits for Swiss citizens living abroad, as well as the considerable increase in the numbers of Swiss travelling abroad who need occasional assistance, have also added a noticeable load to the work of the external service. In scientific and technical affairs Switzerland has for many years followed developments abroad. Scientific attachés have been posted to Washington and Moscow and, for a few years, to Tokyo, in order, among other things, to establish closer relations between the scientific circles of the country of residence and Switzerland. The active part played by Switzerland in the different multilateral programmes for scientific research that have been undertaken by European countries also deserves mention (the European organization for nuclear research in Geneva, the European Space Agency in Paris, the European Conference on Molecular Biology and the Laboratory of Molecular Biology, both in Heidelberg).

The last thirty years have been marked by a development of international relations unequalled in our history. They were and will no doubt long remain characterized by an intensification of bilateral and multilateral contacts; by an increasing recourse to roving diplomacy; by the duty of diplomatic and consular representations to grant protection in the economic and social fields; by international scientific cooperation in the sectors that fall within the competence of the state (sectors that are continually expanding); by cooperation for development and humanitarian aid, which is bound to retain its importance; and by the need to promote abroad a comprehensive image of the country's cultural, social, political and economic life. To these traditional areas of foreign policy should be added new problems of world importance, some of which are also vital for Switzerland: for instance, monetary questions, demographic problems, environmental problems, nutrition, exploitation of raw materials and energy supplies. This general movement necessarily impels Switzerland to cooperate with other states to a far greater extent in order to assert its presence and defend its interests.

For a very important part of their activities, the Swiss diplomatic and consular representations in fact act as an extension of the various federal departments and offices, and not just of the Federal Department of External Affairs. In the consular area, for instance, the duties that derive from the civil and military registration of Swiss citizens (an obligatory formality for Swiss citizens residing abroad for more than twelve months) are made on behalf of the cantons and of the military administration, which receives an income-based tax for military exemption from every Swiss citizen with military obligations who resides abroad. The cashing of money for the optional social security and the payment of old age pensions also come under the ordinary duties of Swiss representations abroad, and these are effected on behalf of the Swiss Equalizing Fund, which comes under the Federal Department of Finances. In the case of assistance to needy Swiss citizens, the diplomatic or consular representations act on behalf of the Federal Department of Justice and Police.

It is probably in the economic and commercial spheres that the DFAE and its representations abroad are most clearly seen in their role of intermediary or representative. Indeed, the Federal Office for External Economic Affairs, in charge of foreign trade, has no representatives abroad, so both diplomatic missions and consular posts are directly subordinate to this office, which comes under the Federal Department for Public Economy, for everything relating to economic matters and commercial affairs – notably the promotion of exports, which has become increasingly important in the last few years since the development of the energy crisis and the upheaval of the international monetary system. In this area, the diplomatic and consular representations are effectively an extension of the Federal Office for External Economic Affairs, and through it, of the higher economic organizations, as well as of the Swiss Office for the Development of Trade, a semi-state body in charge of assistance to private enterprises interested in foreign markets.

Finally, there is a traditional activity of the Federal Department of External Affairs that deserves special mention, its good offices, which results among other things in the keeping (as of 1 January 1980) of fifteen mandates as protecting power by which the Swiss diplomatic and consular service represents the interests of Iran, the United States of America, Guatemala, Great Britain, Honduras, Brazil, Ecuador, Israel, Poland, the Ivory Coast, Egypt and South Africa in the states with which these nations have broken off diplomatic relations. Moreover, since 1919 Switzerland has represented abroad the interests of the Principality of Liechtenstein.

Appendix A shows the organization of the DFAE as it appeared after the three partial reorganizations, of 1976 (reorganization of the Office of the Delegate for Technical Cooperation), 1977 (suppression of the Directorate of International Organizations) and 1978 (reorganization of the Administrative Directorate, at present the General Secretariat – see below).

When preparing the affairs of the Department, those for the Federal Council and for Parliament, the head of the Department is assisted directly by a secretary, as a general rule a young diplomat, and by a personal assistant, actually a political appointee. The post of personal assistant is an innovation introduced in 1978. The secretary is essentially in charge of the affairs of the Department and of those of the Federal Council when they concern the DFAE, while the personal assistant is mainly responsible for relations with

Parliament and for the affairs of the government concerning the six other ministries.

The legal adviser to the Department, who has the rank of ambassador, is among other things in charge of questions arising from Switzerland's policy of neutrality, and general problems of the laws of neutrality, disarmament, and international jurisdiction.

The General Secretariat, which employs about 150 people, is responsible for staff policy, for the appointment and training both of civil servants of the diplomatic, consular and chancellery services and also of the other staff needed to run the central office and the external service; for security questions; for management and organization problems; for administrative and consular inspection; for real estate, bookkeeping, the diplomatic bag, and tele-communications. Since its partial reorganization in 1978, the Secretariat has consisted of fourteen sections, grouped into two divisions.

Under the responsibility of the secretary of state (until 31 January 1979 known as the secretary-general), the Political Directorate (Direction politique) is the most important board, in the context of the mission that the DFAE must fulfil according to the Constitution. The partial reorganization of 1977 saw the disappearance of the Directorate for International Organizations, and aimed at bringing together all questions of a political nature under the responsibility of a single director, while abandoning the formal criterion that separated multilateral from bilateral affairs. The Directorate now comprises three divisions, which employ a total of 90 people: Political Division I (Europe and North America, Council of Europe); Political Division II (Africa, Latin America, Asia and Oceania); Political Division III (international organizations, scientific, cultural and UNESCO affairs). The distribution of bilateral affairs, roughly between the northern and southern hemispheres, replaced, in 1973, a division that separated the world into east and west.

There are two sections simultaneously attached to both Division I and Division II: the Section for Consular Protection, which is in charge of the safety of Swiss citizens established permanently or temporarily abroad; and the Service for Foreign Interests, which administers the mandates of protecting power entrusted to Switzerland (15 mandates by 1 January 1980).

In addition to the three major divisions, a number of administrative staff services are directly answerable to the secretary of state. They employ about 60 people. The Political Secretariat examines the fundamental questions of international politics and their effects on Switzerland. The Service for Swiss Citizens Abroad deals with questions arising from the presence of Swiss citizens abroad (about 300 000 reside permanently abroad) and the policy of the Confederation towards them. It also acts as a link between the representa-tions of the external service and the Commission for Coordination for the Presence of Switzerland Abroad. The Economic and Financial Service acts in close collaboration with the Federal Office for External Economic Affairs, so that the financial and economic elements in Swiss international policies can be taken into account. This service also handles certain questions concerning invisible investments and transactions. Finally, the Economic and Financial Service is in charge of energy questions. The Information and Press Service has a double function. It keeps in close contact with the Swiss and international press accredited in Bern by providing information of interest to them; and it keeps the external service informed about problems essential to the Department and the main international events covered in the press. The Integration Bureau, which comes under the authority of both the Federal Department of External Affairs and the Federal Department of Public Economy, coordinates the Swiss position over problems deriving from European integration. It prepares agreements that are then negotiated with the European Community, and is the customary interlocutor of the permanent Swiss mission to the EEC in Brussels.

Apart from responsibility for the services described above, the secretary of state must also coordinate the activities of the other directorates, in so far as the latter have a political aspect that influences Switzerland's external relations. Moreover, as seen above, the secretary of state, having quasi-ministerial rank, can relieve the head of the Department in his relations with foreigners. In his directorial functions, he is assisted by a private secretary. The Directorate of International Public Law, which includes about 50 assistants, is in charge of general questions of international public law and its modification, of neutrality law and neutrality policy. The Office for Maritime Navigation, whose head office is in Basle, comes under the authority of this Directorate. The head of the Directorate is a member of the Central Commission for Navigation on the Rhine, for which the Directorate acts as secretary. The Directorate is, moreover, in charge of relations with the Principality of Liechtenstein. The Directorate of Cooperation for Development and Humanitarian Aid (formerly known as the Office for Technical Cooperation) was a simple section at its creation in 1961; it has become increasingly important as the necessity of aiding Third World countries has imposed itself on the industrialized nations. The federal law of 19 March 1976 established the limits of the mandate granted to this Directorate for the assistance of the most underprivileged countries and of the victims of natural catastrophes, war, etc. This area of activity involves about 120 assistants at the central office and about 300 experts under private contracts abroad. The Directorate's budget allocation amounts to about 340 million francs for 1980 (bilateral cooperation and contributions to international organizations included).

When the question of gathering together within the Directorate of Political Affairs all political questions, bilateral and multilateral, was discussed, it was decided that humanitarian aid should be grouped with problems of cooperation for development, so as not to overburden the head of the Directorate of Political Affairs. At the same time the opportunity was taken to raise the Office for Technical Cooperation to the rank of a directorate, and its denomination was modified accordingly. The Division of Humanitarian Affairs, which employs 20 assistants out of the total number of 120 mentioned above, comprises two distinct sectors of activities: the organizations for humanitarian assistance (budget for 1980 of 36 million francs), and the assistance unit in case of catastrophe abroad (whose credit for 1980 amounted to 8 million francs).

The expansion of the Swiss diplomatic and consular representations in the post-war period was necessitated by the increase in the number of independent states following the post-war decolonization process and also by the Swiss desire, in addition to its policy of neutrality, to share in the rebuilding of the post-war world. Most of the consulates-general that Switzerland maintained in former colonial states were raised to the rank of embassies, in parallel with the opening of new representations. By 1 January 1981 Switzerland maintained

88 embassies and two bureaux dependent on a main embassy (one in Abu Dhabi, the other in Riyadh), seven missions and delegations to international organizations, 39 consulates-general, 53 consulates, and 68 consular-agencies, among which seven were vacant.

Switzerland maintains diplomatic relations with almost all member states of the United Nations, with the exception of a number of very small states who have only a limited diplomatic structure and therefore maintain a very small number of representatives abroad. Official contacts between these countries and Switzerland are organized on an *ad hoc* basis or take place in New York, as these states are generally represented, if not permanently, at least during the General Assemblies of the United Nations.

It is worth noting in this connection that Switzerland gives only a relative value to the principle of reciprocity. Thus ambassadors are accredited to a number of states in which the defence of Swiss interests may require close contacts and regular visits from an official representative, though these same states do not themselves have accredited ambassadors in Bern, either because of their restricted interests in Switzerland or because of a lack of professionally trained staff. Conversely, a few countries keep a permanent embassy in Bern as a centre of multiple accreditation for a number of European countries, though Switzerland is represented for them only by an ambassador residing in a third country.

There are a few cases that deserve mention. These are states officially represented in Switzerland, where they have an ambassador or an extra-ordinary and plenipotentiary minister, but to which Switzerland does not have an accredited diplomatic representative. This is the case for Liechtenstein and the Vatican. It is further only represented in Monaco by the Swiss consul in Nice, in San Marino by the consul-general in Florence, and in Andorra by the consul-general in Marseilles.

Swiss diplomatic relations at the bilateral level are handled by three different kinds of embassies. The first are embassies headed by an extraordinary and plenipotentiary ambassador; there are 67 such missions. Given the limited number of resident ambassadors it can afford to keep, Switzerland often makes use of the multiple accreditation system, by which a resident ambassador is often simultaneously accredited to several countries. There he is sometimes represented by a chargé d'affaires *ad interim*.

The second category consists of embassies administered by a chargé d'affaires holding an appointment. This office, which had fallen into disuse, was reintroduced in Switzerland a few years ago. The receiving countries have in some cases shown a preference for this form of representation, rather than having an embassy run by a chargé d'affaires representing a head of mission who is resident in a third country. In January 1981 there were five missions of this kind: in Singapore, Wellington, Conakry, Tripoli and Colombo. There is a precise distinction between these categories. An ambassador is accredited to the head of state to whom he presents his credentials; the chargé d'affaires holding an appointment, for whom an agreement is also required, is accredited to the Minister of External Affairs. The chargé d'affaires holding such an appointment comes directly under the central office in Bern.

The third kind of embassy is that run by a chargé d'affaires *ad interim*. These embassies, 16 in number, are directly dependent on an ambassador residing in a third country, to whom they are subordinate in the hierarchy. The chargés d'affaires, who belong to the consular service and on whom a diplomatic title is conferred for the period of their assignment, are chosen from among agents who have at least the rank of first secretary of embassy. When their administrative rank corresponds to that of a second secretary of embassy, they are usually granted the title of first secretary. These chargés d'affaires are given instructions not only by the responsible head of mission but also directly by the central office in Bern, which must ensure that the main embassy receives copies of all instructions.

As a result of the considerable development of multilateral diplomatic relations since the Second World War seven permanent diplomatic missions have been established. These are in New York (for the United Nations), in Geneva (the United Nations and international economic organizations such as the General Agreement on Tariffs and Trade and the European Free Trade Association), in Paris (Organization for Economic Cooperation and Development and UNESCO), in Brussels (the EEC) and in Strasbourg (the Council of Europe).

In some instances the Swiss ambassador is not only accredited to the host nation but is also made permanent representative to the international organization residing there. For example, the Swiss ambassador at Vienna is also accredited to AIEA and ONUDI, and the ambassador at Nairobi to PNUE.

The consular network comprises 56 posts run by professional chefs de poste (35 consulates-general and 21 consulates) and 36 posts run by honorary chefs de poste (4 consulates-general and 32 consulates) without professional staff.

According to the 1963 Vienna Convention on consular relations, honorary consuls should exercise their jurisdiction over a district whose size is determined by agreement between the sending and the receiving states, and this is generally the case. These posts are granted the usual administrative authority, but as the head of the post cannot give all his time to consular matters (he is, by the way, not paid for his services, and only receives a nominal allowance) he must be assisted by somebody, usually a secretary, who deals with the affairs of the consulate, if necessary with the help of the professional representation to which the honorary post is subordinate. For the most part the staffs of these honorary positions are not linked to the Federal Department of External Affairs through administrative regulations, but are exclusively dependent on the head of the honorary office, who gets an allowance from the Department for his expenses.

The above rule has a few exceptions, particularly in the United States where the Swiss consular network was reorganized about ten years ago. A number of consular districts dependent on professional consulates, which existed before this reorganization, have been brought together and placed under the jurisdiction of a few large consulates-general. This rearrangement allows administrative work to be rationalized and has created large centres of influence, especially in economic and cultural matters. The consuls-general, relieved from administrative routine by the appointment of adequate staff, including a deputy with the rank of consul, are better able to concentrate their efforts on the promotion of Switzerland's image in their consular district. In order to help them in their duties and to facilitate contacts at a local level outside their towns of residence, a series of honorary consulates has been created, to a certain extent replacing the former career consulates. The difference is, however, that these posts have no consular districts and are not granted any administrative jurisdiction. In this respect, there is little distinction between them and the consular agencies, which are discussed below.

In distinction to those of other nations, Swiss consular agencies are like small supporting establishments in important towns, serving the interests of the diplomatic mission in the capital. A consular agent is a local representative of the ambassador, and can also be asked to lend his support to the distant mission in some urgent and exceptional cases. Appointed by the head of the Federal Department of External Affairs, these consular agents have no direct contacts with the head office, but only with the mission on which they are dependent. They are given the title of vice-consul or consul *ad personam*. On 1 January 1981, Switzerland maintained 68 consular agencies, of which seven were vacant.

Appointed by the head of mission with the permission of the DFAE, and chosen from among influential compatriots, correspondents are the most informal Swiss representatives abroad. The number of correspondents has varied considerably; there are at present about 200. A correspondent is granted neither official status nor diplomatic immunity. He is not given a title and does not receive an allowance.

In spite of the importance of its interests throughout the world and the relatively large number of citizens who have emigrated to other continents, Switzerland possesses a modest federal administration and cannot afford the luxury of a highly developed diplomatic and consular system. Out of the total of 33 750 civil servants and other employees who make up the general administration of the Confederation (excluding the railway (CFF) and the post, telegraph and telecommunications (PTT) networks), external affairs employs only 1756 people, that is 5 per cent of the total federal administrative staff. About one-third of them work in Bern, and the rest in the external service. The budget allocated to the Confederation's external relations amounted to 602 million francs for 1980, only 3.47 per cent of the Confederation's total costs (CFF and PTT again excluded). When comparing this percentage with that of other countries, it must be remembered that the expenses of the Confederation constitute only a part of the overall expenses of the public authorities because of the country's federal structure. In order to give a precise account of the funds spent on foreign relations in proportion to public expenditure, one should include the public expenditure of the cantonal governments. For comparison, let us say simply that the Confederation's share of Switzerland's public expenditure represents about 39 per cent of the total, that of the cantons 33 per cent, and that of the communes 28 per cent (figures for 1976).

The Swiss diplomatic and consular service includes roughly 280 diplomats (university graduates) and 280 consular officers (consuls-general, consuls and vice-consuls). The chancellery service includes approximately 280 officers and the secretarial service 330 secretaries. In addition to these three career services, whose civil servants are subject to the discipline of transfers, there are 580 non-transferable other civil servants and employees (e.g. experts, specialists, radio operators, locally recruited secretaries, translators) at the central office and abroad.

This number of staff, relatively small in comparison with those of other countries of equivalent importance, is of course not sufficient to carry out completely the duties of the network maintained by Switzerland. Like many other countries, Switzerland sometimes entrusts its consular representations to honorary agents who carry out their duties part-time in addition to their normal professional activities. Generally relieved from activities of a purely administrative nature, these honorary consuls must fulfil duties of representation and can intervene in certain consular matters at the request of the diplomatic mission to which they are answerable, thus providing support for the professional system. With the increase in the duties of some of these honorary representatives, it has become necessary to appoint professional staff to take on the usual administrative duties (registration, military taxes, social security, occasional assistance to tourists in difficulty, etc.). When such representations have taken on sufficient importance, the present tendency is to replace the honorary consul by a professional consul. This policy makes it possible to compensate, to some extent, for the severe reduction in promotion possibilities for professional consular civil servants that took place when many consular posts were transformed into diplomatic missions as former colonies achieved independent statehood.

At present the DFAE suffers from a significant imbalance in the age of its staff. This situation results from the numerous appointments made during the Second World War in response to the large amount of work undertaken by Switzerland acting as protecting power on behalf of belligerent powers. It is also the result of a total freeze on appointments from 1947 to 1955 decreed by Parliament. The gap represented by this nine-year period will be greatly felt in the coming years, during which an exceptionally large number of heads of diplomatic or consular representations who entered the DFAE before 1947 are due to retire.

The fact that this will result in a considerably lower average age for executives in higher positions is not in itself a bad thing. But the preoccupying factor for the Department is that the recruitment of new agents to replace those due to retire has not taken place during the last twenty years. Indeed, in the sixties the competition of a private sector in full expansion, which offered considerably higher salaries than the state, has kept away from public service a significant number of the young university graduates who might have been expected to take an interest in a diplomatic career. In the early seventies the salaries of public servants were readjusted to set right a situation that had been deeply felt by the whole of the federal administration, and more candidates entered the annual competitive examination for the diplomatic and consular service, but in 1974 Parliament decided to freeze once more the numbers of the Confederation's federal administration as part of an economy measure intended to restore the balance of federal finances.

Today the DFAE is far from having reached the desired balance, and the present freeze on federal staff (32 750 civil servants and employees) will be maintained for at least the next few years. With the numerous departures of diplomatic officers holding an academic degree (88 diplomats, that is 30 per cent of the present strength of this category of officer, between 1979 and 1984) and of consular and chancellery officers (187 civil servants, 33 per cent of the strength of these categories, between 1980 and 1989), as well as the insufficient recruitment during the last few years, the Department is in great danger of seeing its numbers regularly diminished. Its duties, however, have been increasing constantly since the Second World War because, as already demonstrated, of the intensification of international relations, both bilateral and multilateral, and because of the increasing role of the state in a range of activities where the Swiss citizen desires it to intervene more or less directly.

To avoid this problem, recruitment in recent years should have exceeded the Department's immediate needs in order to ensure that trained and experienced agents would be available to fill the gaps. However, by imposing a strict limit on the number of staff in the DFAE (which since 1974 may not exceed the current total of 1756 people), Parliament has decided otherwise. One can only hope that if real difficulties occur it will draw the necessary conclusions and accept full responsibility for the situation it has created by imposing a freeze on numbers for a long period and for the second time in thirty years.

Until the end of the Second World War no specific standards were applied in the admission of staff to the diplomatic and consular service or to the chancellery. The salaries paid to civil servants who went abroad were insufficient. These officials were always recruited from the same restricted circle, a practice that was far from democratic. When the 1947 freeze on staff appointments ended, it became urgent to put recruitment on a wider and more objective basis, the more so as it was necessary to prepare for increasing duties and to plan for the long term in the recruitment and vocational training of diplomatic and consular agents, who would in due course be called upon to replace staff appointed before 1947.

In 1956 a new recruiting system was introduced with the adoption of two regulations that established examinations for admission to the diplomatic and consular service as well as to the chancellery service. These examinations evaluate the candidate's aptitude for a career in the service of his choice, his intellectual adaptability, solidity of character, presentation, physical and moral stamina, etc., and assess his knowledge of languages, history, economics, law and general culture. Future diplomats must have completed their university training with a *licence* or a doctorate. There is also an examination of a more technical kind for those aspiring to careers in the chancellery, for which only a vocational non-university training is required (commerce, banking, secretarial work, administration, for example).

Candidates who pass the entrance examination are appointed as non-permanent employees and follow a two-year practical course, divided between the central office and the external service. In addition, a complete winter term is spent, in the case of the future diplomats, at the University Institute for Higher International Studies (IUHEI) in Geneva. A final examination assesses the knowledge acquired on this course. Candidates who pass their training course are then appointed as civil servants to the diplomatic and consular service on the one hand, and to the chancellery service on the other.

The evaluation that can be made after the twenty-five years that this system has been in operation (it has not been modified substantially since 1955) is highly positive. The introduction of competitive examinations has, among other things, considerably widened the range of civil servants in the diplomatic service, with regard both to their social origins and, in the case of diplomats, to their previous academic training. The aims of democratization in recruitment set by the Department have been well fulfilled, thanks to the conditions established by admission regulations adopted in 1955 and also to the improved financial opportunities offered to civil servants. The administration is responsible for providing the staff of its external service with the means to fulfil their social obligations, particularly in the area of representation, and for covering the costs that accompany a travelling life – children's schooling, periodic returns to the home country, wear and tear of furniture, etc. – so the staff no longer need substantial private means.

In order to secure objective conditions for admission, the commissions for admission to training courses for the diplomatic and chancellery career are composed not only of higher civil servants from the Federal Department of External Affairs, but also of representatives from the Federal Office for External Economic Affairs, the universities, and Parliament.

It is interesting that the question of a fair linguistic representation between the representatives of the different official languages within the Federal Department of External Affairs has never been a problem for the Department, as can be the case in countries where two or more languages are spoken. Since 1948 the proportion of French-speaking civil servants at all levels of the hierarchy has almost always been larger than the actual proportion of the French-speaking Swiss population. Foreign affairs have traditionally appealed to representatives of the French-speaking cantons, though French-speakers appear to be under-represented among civil servants in the other federal departments. On the other hand, unfortunately, the proportion of Italian-speaking civil servants is below the proportion at a national level.

Since 29 December 1964 the position of the staff of the Federal Department of External Affairs has been regulated by a special ordinance of the Federal Council, distinct from the administrative regulations for other civil servants of the federal administration. This ordinance is partly a codification of unwritten rules already in use. It has contributed notably, thanks to the substantial improvement in the material situation of both civil servants and employees, to the democratization of the system.

In the career services of the Department, which comprise all civil servants subject to transfer regulations, including the secretarial section, promotion is linked both to the individual's ability to fulfil a higher position and to the needs of the service. Two commissions for promotion (internal bodies consisting of senior civil servants appointed by the head of the Department) annually consider for promotion all agents who have served the requisite number of years in each grade and therefore comply with the formal conditions for promotion. The commissions put forward their recommendations to the appropriate authority (secretary-general, head of the Department or Federal Council, depending on the rank of the agent) who makes the final selection. There is a possibility of appeal in cases of non-promotion.

In January 1974 the Department organized an internal study group, which studied the Federal Department of External Affairs for over a year, examining its articles, conditions and work methods. It formulated recommendations destined to make the best use of existing means in the interests of Swiss foreign politics. This study proceeded from an analysis of the structures and duties of the Department based on the experience accumulated since the Second World War, while attempting to make short- and long-range forecasts of the most appropriate ways in which the Department might increase its efficiency without unduly increasing its numbers and costs.

Most of the working party's recommendations have been put into practice. For instance, the network of the external service has been restructured by various means: a number of diplomatic and consular missions have been closed; some multiple accreditations have been redistributed in a more rational (and therefore more economical) way; embassies run by chargés d'affaires have been opened in Kuwait, Maputo and Luanda, new consular agencies in Manama, Dubai, Nantes and Porto, and resident ambassadors have been appointed to Baghdad and Damascus. Work has been rationalized by simplifying the duties of the administrative sector and of the chancellery service abroad. Benefits have been increased through a more logical and systematic use of the tariff applied by the embassies and consulates for the services they provide to trade companies and to individuals. Precise instructions about the expenses in the field of social representation have been laid down in order to increase efficiency and improve cost effectiveness in maintaining useful contacts. Finally, an increased effort has been made to promote the image of Switzerland abroad.

Conclusion

At the risk of being accused of lack of modesty, one cannot remain silent about the high degree of efficiency and professional conscientiousness at the heart of the Swiss diplomatic and consular service. The tasks to be carried out are often difficult, not only because of the modest means at its disposal but also, even more importantly, because its agents abroad represent the interests of a tiny state that is not part of any great alliance and does not belong to the United Nations. Switzerland's position is not always understood by other members of the society of nations; its representatives abroad must make tireless efforts to ensure that their country's position will be understood in the context of its complex character, which results from the combination of three great European cultures (French, German and Italian) and of different nations, as well as the important part played both by its leaders and by Parliament in the foreign policy-making process. Nowhere else in the world, indeed, do the people themselves exercise such wide rights, through the referendum, on subjects that elsewhere come exclusively within the sphere of parliamentary or governmental control. These peculiarities sometimes create misunderstandings in relations between Switzerland and other countries. It is the duty of its diplomatic agents to dispel them and to make the voice of their country heard when its interests, which are considerable despite its size, are at stake.

The Federal Department of External Affairs has the merit of having turned its hand, without being asked by anyone else, to its own internal problems; the reasons justifying its existence, its present and future aims and the means it must employ to achieve them. Numerous improvements in its functioning have resulted from this examination, which have increased its efficiency and have no doubt strengthened its credibility with the Government, and with Swiss public opinion.

The versatility of the agents in the professional services, who are subject to the discipline of transfers as a condition of their employment, has given the service great flexibility, and ensures that new blood is brought into the central administration at regular intervals. This dynamism is envied by the other ministries, who are characterized by a greater rigidity in their structures and personnel policies. These movements, which encourage constant reexamination of the Department's organization and tasks, permit the service to remain in a state of continuous evolution, able to adapt itself rapidly to new situations created by the vicissitudes of international relations.

The emphasis on the various tasks that fall to the service can be moved from one area of activity to another according to the needs of the moment. For example, the cultural contribution of the Swiss presence abroad, which was regarded for a long time as being of minor importance, is today considered worthy of greater attention on the part of the diplomatic and consular services, and praiseworthy efforts are being undertaken in that direction. At the same time, the importance and urgency of finding solutions to the problems of developing nations are increasingly recognized, and it is expected that the diplomatic service should play a more active role in the north/south relations that are crucial to the long-term survival of industrial nations. The problem is now understood to be not only of an ethical nature but also an extensively economic one; it is in the interests of the industrialized nations to fill as rapidly as they possibly can the gap that separates them from their partners in the southern hemisphere.

In the world of today, which is characterized by an unprecedented intensification of interstate relations springing from the ever closer inter-dependence of states in areas ever more numerous and complex, the role of the Department of External Affairs, far from diminishing in importance because of modern communications systems, is increasing. This is as true for its bilateral activities as it is for its multilateral dimensions.

BIBLIOGRAPHY

'Loi fédérale du 26 mars 1914 sur l'organisation de l'administration fédérale' and its amendments, and 'Loi fédérale du 19 septembre 1978 sur l'organisation et la gestion du Conseil fédéral et de l'administration fédérale', in *Recueil des lois fédérales* and *Recueil systematique du droit fédéral*, published by the Swiss Federal Chancellery, Bern. The Chancellery also publishes *Rapports de gestion du Conseil fédéral pour les années 1973 à 1979*.

Etienne Bourgnon, 'Service diplomatique suisse et Service consulaire suisse', in *Fiches juridiques suisses* (Bern 1977).

——, *Die diplomatischen und konsularischen Vertretungen der Schweiz seit 1798* (Bern 1968, n.p.).

——, *Un Ministère des affaires étrangères s'interroge*. Report of a working party to the head of the Federal Political Department (Bern 1975).

Bernard Freymond, 'Département politique', in *L'administration fédérale: ses tâches et son activité* (Bern 1975–6), 13–16.

Julien Rossat, Pascal Frochaud and Jean Bourgeois have written several internal studies and open examinations of the work and organization of the Federal Political Department (unpublished works).

SWITZERLAND – APPENDIX A

THE FEDERAL DEPARTMENT OF EXTERNAL AFFAIRS

HEAD OF THE FEDERAL DEPARTMENT OF EXTERNAL AFFAIRS ———————— Legal adviser

Secretary of State
Head of the Political Directorate
Head of Central Services

Protocol

Information
and press

Political
secretariat

Economic and
financial service

Service for Swiss
citizens abroad

European
integration
bureau
DFAE/DFEP

General
Secretariat

Personnel division

Personnel
section

Legal service

Recruitment and
formation

Salaries

Journeys and
transport

Indemnities

Library

Administrative
division

Accountability

Courier

Archives

Radio

Telegrams

Administrative
inspectorate and
consular affairs

Furnishings

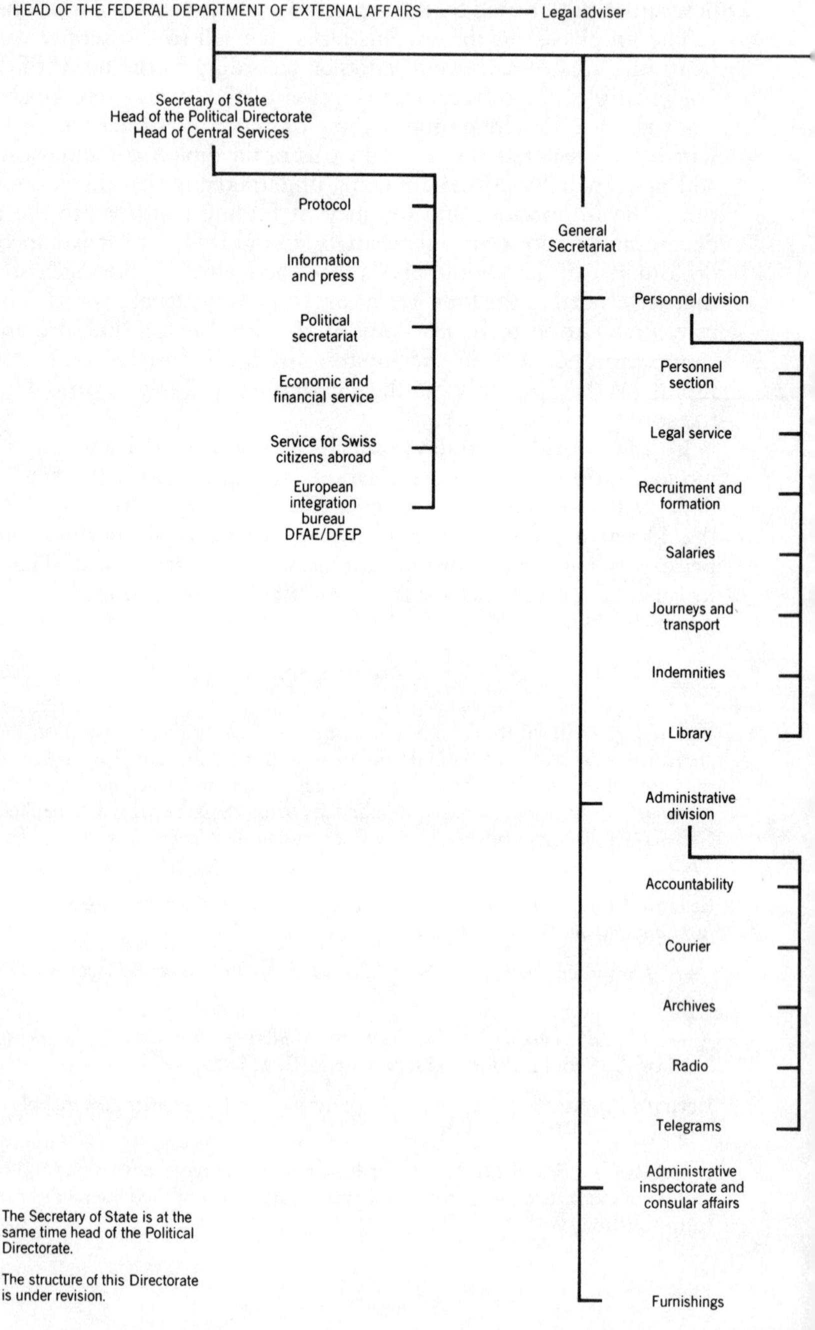

1. The Secretary of State is at the
   same time head of the Political
   Directorate.

2. The structure of this Directorate
   is under revision.

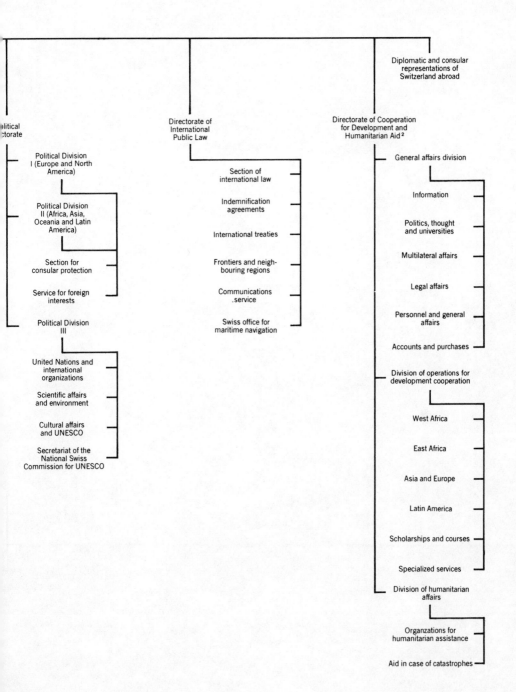

Diplomatic and consular
representations of
Switzerland abroad

Political
Directorate

Directorate of
International
Public Law

Directorate of Cooperation
for Development and
Humanitarian Aid [2]

Political Division
I (Europe and North
America)

Political Division
II (Africa, Asia,
Oceania and Latin
America)

Section for
consular protection

Service for foreign
interests

Political Division
III

United Nations and
international
organizations

Scientific affairs
and environment

Cultural affairs
and UNESCO

Secretariat of the
National Swiss
Commission for UNESCO

Section of
international law

Indemnification
agreements

International treaties

Frontiers and neigh-
bouring regions

Communications
.service

Swiss office for
maritime navigation

General affairs division

Information

Politics, thought
and universities

Multilateral affairs

Legal affairs

Personnel and general
affairs

Accounts and purchases

Division of operations for
development cooperation

West Africa

East Africa

Asia and Europe

Latin America

Scholarships and courses

Specialized services

Division of humanitarian
affairs

Organzations for
humanitarian assistance

Aid in case of catastrophes

Turkey

The Ministry of Foreign Affairs under the Ottoman Empire and the Turkish Republic

SINAN KUNERALP

Sinan Kuneralp has published several papers on the foreign relations of the Ottoman Empire and is currently preparing a handbook on the Ottoman diplomatic service. The son and brother of diplomats, Mr Kuneralp was born in Ankara and studied at the University of Paris. He is project manager in a private company in Istanbul and Ankara.

From the day they first emerged as a world power at the battle of Malazgirt (Manzikert) in 1071, when the Seljuk Turks defeated a Byzantine army and penetrated for the first time into Asia Minor, until the victorious advance of the Ottoman Turks was decisively checked at the gates of Vienna in 1683, the Turks had very little use for diplomacy as an implement to conduct foreign policy. Their conception of international relations was fairly straightforward and single-minded: to wage war and then dictate their own peace conditions. With the decline of their military power came an increasing awareness of the existence of the hitherto scorned European powers, which gradually evolved into an attempt by the Ottoman Empire to forestall any real or imaginary policy of encroachment on the part of these powers. Thenceforth, diplomacy came to be regarded not as the pursuit of war by other means but as a way to preserve the conquests made by Ottoman armies in an earlier age. If Ottoman diplomacy failed to achieve these aims this was due more to the spirit of the age than to any shortcomings of its own. Its relative success is described by a contemporary observer not noted for an overwhelming sympathy towards Turkey: 'Très habile, la Sublime Porte a toujours su opposer les puissances; tantôt penchant pour l'une, tantôt pour l'autre suivant les besoins du moment. La Sublime Porte accepte tout, promettant beaucoup mais ne se livrant jamais. On peut affirmer avec assurance qu'à aucun moment nulle puissance n'a pu se flatter d'avoir joui d'un credit complet dans ses conseils. La Turquie n'a jamais cédé qu'aux suggestions qui étaient conformes à ce qu'elle croyait son intéret ou à ses vues particulières.'[1] In the meanderings of the foreign policy of the Turkish Republic one can sense the same preoccupations.

As intimated above, a state of war was the only one that Ottoman rulers at the height of their power in the fifteenth and sixteenth centuries could envisage for their relations with foreign states. The *Sharia* or Islamic Law stipulated that no definite peace could be concluded with a non-Moslem power as long as its rulers did not acknowledge the primacy of the Moslem faith. Catholic Spain's refusal to treat with Moslem states is to be viewed in the same perspective. However, accommodations could be and were found to this precept as commercial considerations or the shifting of the sixteenth-century balance of power triumphed over strict adherence to canonical rules. Temporary suspensions of hostilities were arranged and renewed, though there were still intervals during which bloody fighting took place. Some time after the conquest of Istanbul, Venice, which had extensive trading interests in the Levant and Black Sea area signed an agreement with the Turks by which Venetian nationals were granted the same commercial rights as they had enjoyed under Byzantium; in exchange, large tracts of territory in the Balkan peninsula that belonged to the Republic devolved to the Ottoman Empire. A year after this agreement was signed the Ottoman Sultan Mehmet II sent an envoy to Venice, where he was received with great honour. The agreement did not lead to the establishment of a permanent Venetian mission in Istanbul, but it did provide favourable conditions for the development of economic and political relations as Venice made use of her privileged links with the Ottoman state against her own rivals. Mehmet II was too shrewd a statesman to let religion interfere with this opportunity to foster dissension between the European powers; in the picturesque language of a French writer quoting a contemporary Ottoman chronicler, he was content to 'soutenir les chiens contre les porcs et les porcs contre les chiens'.[2] Similar trading rights were conceded to the other Italian city-states during the following decades, and in 1495 a special envoy of the Russian Tsar Ivan III, Michel Pletscheiff, also obtained large concessions for Russian fur traders.

Until the middle of the following century no permanent ambassador took up residence in Istanbul. The usual procedure was for the European powers to send special missions with limited instructions, such as to negotiate a truce or announce the accession to the throne of a new ruler. In 1530 the Doge of Venice was represented by a special envoy called Mocenigo at the circumcision celebrations of Suleyman II's sons. In 1528, Ferdinand of Habsburg sent a representative to Istanbul in an unsuccessful attempt to forestall the signature of an agreement between his Hungarian rival and the Ottoman Empire.

Permanent embassies were gradually established by European powers on the shores of the Bosphorus during the sixteenth and seventeenth centuries after France concluded a treaty with the Ottomans in 1535 that amounted to the first definite political settlement between them and a European power. This agreement provided *inter alia* for reciprocal freedom of navigation and the establishment of French consuls in Ottoman ports. The Habsburgs followed suit after a Turkish envoy bearing peace proposals to end the state of war between the two countries had been received in state in the Austrian capital in 1533. A Venetian *bailo*, as the Republic's ambassadors were known, had preceded by a short time the Austrian internonce in Istanbul. England had from 1583 a permanent representative in the Ottoman capital, mainly handling commercial matters though Queen Elizabeth had toyed with the idea of a joint Anglo-Turkish attack on Catholic Spain. Holland's representatives looked after their country's extensive trade interests from 1612 onwards; and one of them, J. Coljer, who served for forty-one years in Istanbul, often acted as a mediator in disputes between the Ottoman Empire and another power. As for the Russians, the Treaty of Carlowitz in 1699, which first secured for them direct access to the Black Sea, also provided for a Russian representative to be permanently stationed in Istanbul. Permanent missions were opened in the Ottoman capital by Sweden in 1734, the Kingdom of the Two Sicilies in 1740, Prussia in 1749, Spain in 1779, Sardinia in 1824, the USA in 1830, Tuscany in 1834, Greece in 1835 and Portugal in 1843. Istanbul became one of the pivots of the diplomatic circuit. However, for almost three centuries after the first foreign embassies were opened in Istanbul the Turks for various reasons failed to reciprocate. They were not, first of all, very much interested in foreign countries, for whose inhabitants they felt mostly scorn and contempt. Then Turkish traders had no commercial interests abroad that would justify the existence of diplomatic missions to look after them.[3] Furthermore, Turks were also loath to live for long periods in foreign parts, and this unwillingness to expatriate themselves would render difficult the task of finding suitable staff for such missions. But perhaps the most important single factor that delayed for centuries the formation of a proper Ottoman diplomatic service is to be found in the structure of the imperial administrative machine, with its heavily centralized nature, which demanded that every question of importance be dealt with in Istanbul. Thus the Ottomans, in conducting negotiations with foreign powers, preferred as a rule to use the latter's envoys in Istanbul.

At the head of this centralized ruling machinery were the sultans. During the fifteenth and sixteenth centuries a line of exceptionally gifted and able sultans succeeded each other on the Ottoman throne and supervised personally the conduct of state affairs both at home and in military and foreign matters. The fairly limited scope of the view prevailing about the conduct of foreign affairs did not necessitate the existence of an extensive department assisting the sultans in the drawing-up of foreign policy. There was no separate section in the Ottoman chancery dealing exclusively with foreign affairs, and the official in charge of the Empire's foreign affairs combined this position with responsibilities relating to financial or internal matters until well into the nineteenth century, when a separate Ministry of Foreign Affairs was set up. The fusion between internal and external affairs is best illustrated by the choice of messengers commissioned to deliver the sultan's notification to a foreign ruler. These were chosen from among the Cavuses, a corps discharging the duties of couriers to provincial governors. The sultan was content to let his will be known to foreign rulers, and declared war if they did not comply with it. Even though the Cavuses despatched to foreign countries were mere couriers, they were nevertheless bearers of the imperial word, and their safety was not a matter to be trifled with – as the Hungarians discovered to their cost when in 1521 they murdered Behram Cavus, who had been sent to Buda by the sultan to demand the payment of a tribute. This incident precipitated an attack by the Turkish armies on Belgrade which eventually led to the conquest of Buda.

A court official called the Nisanci, whose principal duty was to stamp the sultan's cipher (Tuğra) on official documents after having examined and corrected them, supervised matters connected with foreign relations at a time when the Turkish armies, led in person by the sultan, were advancing triumphantly through central Europe and the Near East.

Towards the close of the sixteenth century the succession of remarkable sultans who had largely contributed to the establishment and aggrandizement of the Empire during the preceding two centuries came to an abrupt end. Their successors preferred to leave the conduct of state affairs to the Sadrazam or grand vizier, who was the sultan's representative in both civil and military matters. The grand vizier's Chancery, known as the Divan-ı Hümayun Kalemi, was headed by an official called the Reis–ül Küttab, who besides supervising the work of the Chancery prepared the reports presented by the grand vizier to the sultan and assisted the former in matters related to foreign affairs over which he (the grand vizier) had overall control. Even so, the Reis–ül Küttab or Reis Efendi was not, initially at least, very important, and as only a minor figure in the grand vizier's suite did not actually take part in negotiations with foreign envoys but merely kept a record of them. However, the burden of running the Empire increased with the passing of time and the emergence of new issues, leaving the grand vizier less opportunity to handle personally all matters of government. At the same time as relations with foreign states entered a more complex phase that demanded constant attention and a more subtle approach, the task of conducting foreign affairs was gradually delegated to the Reis Efendi. This was formalized during the Carlowitz peace conference, when the Reis Efendi assumed responsibility for the conduct of the negotiations that led to the conclusion of a peace treaty with Russia.

From now on the Reis Efendi became a Foreign Minister of sorts, though this was not his only attribution and he still had no subordinate office dealing exclusively with foreign affairs. Most of the offices coming under the Reis Efendi were of a more or less hybrid nature, dealing with both foreign and domestic affairs, some of which were not even remotely connected with the conduct of foreign policy. The former included (1) the Beylikci, a sub-section of the Divan in charge of issuing and recording various documents such as treaties made with foreign states and those concerning their execution; (2) the Mektubî sadr Âli, which dealt with the incoming and outgoing corres-pondence of the grand vizier and thus could occasionally cover foreign affairs; (3) the Amedî, which as the personal secretariat of the grand vizier kept records of the meetings between the Reis Efendi and foreign envoys; (4) the Divan-ı Hümayun Tercümanı or Dragoman, the Translator of the Imperial Divan, together with his assistants, the Dil Oğlanları, one of the most important offices under the Reis Efendi. Among the offices not related to foreign affairs were the Tahvil and the Rüus, which issued and recorded warrants for the investiture of provincial governors, holders of feudal landholdings, etc..

The Ottoman Chancery was a highly complex body of in-bred, paper-generating clerks who scribbled away happily for generations. At the lower echelon of the hierarchy were the *hülefa* or clerks of first, second and third class, with the *tesvidci* (maker of rough copy), the *hülasaci* (précis writer) and the *tebyizci* (maker of final draft). Their work was checked first by the *kanuncu*, a legal expert who ensured that the measure which was the subject of the document conformed to the administrative law of the Empire, then by the *mümeyyiz*, who examined the documents in order to maintain uniformity and correctness of official style, and lastly by the *kesedâr* (purse-bearer), who intervened at the final stage to collect fees charged for the issue of documents. The Reis Efendi, while supervising the work of the officers under him, also performed various other functions. He was personally responsible, as already stated, for drawing up the reports that the grand vizier regularly submitted to the sultan on all affairs of state, and he read the messages the sultan sent to the grand vizier during council meetings. But gradually the conduct of foreign affairs became his main occupation, and it was through him that the foreign representatives in Istanbul transacted their diplomatic business. He was, however, always assisted by the Empire's head jurist, the Kazasker, whenever important points were raised in order to safeguard the interests of the state. The Reis Efendi would also make the necessary arrangements when a foreign representative had express instructions from his own government to deal directly with the grand vizier. Moreover, the Reis Efendi was also expected to accompany the grand vizier on campaigns, as the latter led the Ottoman armies in the field after the sultans abandoned the practice of going on campaigns themselves. A substitute would be appointed in the Reis Efendi's place for the duration of the campaign, and though the substitute's tenure of office was temporary he exercised all the powers and fulfilled all the functions of the Reis Efendi himself.

Though the volume of diplomatic activity increased over the centuries, the status of the Reis Efendi in the Ottoman hierarchy remained fairly modest. Foreigners sensitive to the importance of diplomatic relations came to consider him as a fully fledged minister for foreign affairs, and consequently attributed to his office an importance that paradoxically was denied to it by the Ottomans

themselves. They persisted in their determination not to attach great importance to their relations with the European states, about whose politics, laws
and occasionally even geographical locations they often had only the vaguest
of notions. Their sources of information were quite meagre as their own
nationals did not bother to learn European languages. The little intelligence
they did obtain was derived from a few limited sources. The earliest and most
short-lived had been, in the second half of the sixteenth century, the network
of *marrano* merchants, the crypto-Jews, who had established trading
counters in Amsterdam, London and Bordeaux and who maintained a close
correspondence with one of their flock, Joseph Nassi, a favourite of Sultan
Selim II. The Ottomans were thus provided with some precious information
on the internal situation of the European states. The few and infrequent
special embassies despatched by the Ottomans to European courts were not
very successful as a means of gathering information, partly because they were
not meant to perform this duty. Nevertheless, the head of one such embassy
sent to Paris in 1669, Süleyman Ağa, has won the eternal gratitude of the
Parisian coffee drinkers for having introduced this beverage to France.

The translator to the Imperial Divan, the dragoman, whose office came
under the direct supervision of the Reis Efendi, served throughout as the
principal source of information on Europe at the disposal of Ottoman rulers.
Until the middle of the seventeenth century this office was held by a
European renegade, usually of Italian, Hungarian or German origin, who
would usually know, besides his mother tongue and the language of his new
country of adoption, Latin and one or more other European languages. From
the 1650s onwards, members of Greek Orthodox families from the Phanar
quarter of Istanbul who had begun to acquaint themselves with European
ways and languages assumed this responsibility. The dragoman's duty was to
translate the notes and communications exchanged between foreign envoys
and the Reis Efendi, and to interpret during negotiations or when foreign
ambassadors were received in audience by the sultan or the grand vizier.
Because of his direct access to European sources of information the dragoman
did not simply serve as a go-between but was often used on special missions,
and although he was given specific instructions he nevertheless enjoyed considerable latitude. However, some of these dragomans proved unreliable and
a number were beheaded for having compromised Ottoman interests by
divulging confidential information to foreign representatives in Istanbul.

By the end of the eighteenth century some of the more articulate Ottoman
observers of the Empire's decline had reached the conclusion that the
regeneration of the Ottoman state structure could be achieved only through
administrative and military reforms along European lines. One of the
leading advocates of this school of thought was no one less than the reigning
sultan himself, Selim III, who had distinguished himself even before
ascending the throne by his keenness to keep himself informed about the
fluctuations of European politics. Thus his decision to open permanent
embassies in various European capitals during the early 1790s had a twofold
objective. First, they were to provide first-hand information about the
upheavals that, following the French Revolution, threatened to embroil the
Empire in the European crisis. Second, these missions were expected to serve
as training grounds where young officials would be instructed in European

languages and practices connected with the administration of the Empire.

Starting with London in 1793, permanent missions were established in Paris, Vienna and Berlin. The missions each consisted of an ambassador, two or three young secretaries, and one or two interpreters who were usually Greek or Armenian subjects of the Empire. The heads of mission and their staff were expected to serve three years in their places of residence. More or less simultaneously with the opening of permanent diplomatic missions, consuls were also appointed in various trading centres abroad to look after the commercial interests of Ottoman subjects. The newly nominated consuls were usually Greek Orthodox subjects of the Empire who had long been established as merchants in the places that now came under their jurisdiction. As a matter of fact, the first consulates were opened in places where Ottoman Christians had been known to trade since the beginning of the eighteenth century – Malta, Messina, Naples, Genoa, Marseilles and Alicante. Amsterdam followed in 1804 and London in 1806. To complete the opening of permanent embassies and consulates, some steps were taken to reform and rationalize the office of the Reis Efendi in an effort to meet the increase in official business resulting from the creation of an Ottoman permanent diplomatic corps. As such, a special section of important affairs was created (Mühimme Odası), staffed initially by fifteen clerks to implement policies formulated by the sultan. However, this should not be read as an attempt to create a central bureau for the conduct of foreign affairs but only as a realization of the necessity for an effective direction of the diplomatic relations of the Empire in view of the prevailing turmoil caused by the Napoleonic wars in Europe.

Opposition to the reform programme initiated by the sultan, lack of qualified personnel for the embassies and the failure to coordinate the activities of the embassies efficiently all hindered the proper development of a network of diplomatic respresentation. By 1811, barely twenty years after the first embassies opened, all ambassadors were recalled and chargés d'affaires were left in charge of skeleton missions.

When the Greek uprising that was to lead to the creation of an independent Greek kingdom started in Morea during the summer of 1821, the Greek subjects of the sultan who were by now acting as chargés in Ottoman missions abroad became security risks and were dismissed. The embassies and consulates were soon closed down altogether.

At the same time, the Ottoman Government took measures to combat its dependence on the Greeks. A Moslem was appointed dragoman of the Divan and an office, the Tercüme Odası (Translation Room) was inaugurated with the dual purpose of instructing Ottoman officials in European languages and translating into Turkish articles published in the European press about the Ottoman Empire. This establishment was to grow into one of the essential elements of the Foreign Ministry when this institution was founded a decade later. It also served as a nursery for a new breed of officials, conversant with European languages, who had wholeheartedly adopted the reform policies advocated by Selim III. Sultan Mahmud II, who succeeded to the throne in 1809 after a brief spell of reaction, pursued the same policies and reestablished permanent diplomatic representations abroad. Mahmud's aim was to try to obtain assistance from Europe at a time when his empire, barely recovering from the loss of Greece, was fighting for survival against a powerful provincial governor who had rebelled against the Sultan's authority in Egypt.

Permanent embassies were reopened in Paris, London and Vienna in the course of 1834; soon after, consular nominations were resumed. Lessons had been learned from the failure of the earlier attempt to establish permanent embassies. The importance of the Translation Room as a training school for budding diplomats was emphasized by a series of regulations. More meaningful was the change made in the title of the Reis-ül Küttab, who became in March 1836 Hariciye Nazırı (Foreign Minister) to bring the position in line with its European counterparts.

Though this change in title can serve as a convenient landmark to date the foundation of a Foreign Ministry in the modern sense, it was only over the following decades that the Ministry acquired the structures needed for the proper functioning of such an institution. There was no deliberate effort to provide the necessary administrative basis for the efficient functioning of the Ministry, which was run on more or less *ad hoc* lines. Regulations were passed relatively late in its history.

When the Reis Efendi was given the title of Foreign Minister in March 1836, no alterations were made to the fabric of his old office, which only changed its name. In November of that year the position of under-secretary (Müstesar) was established to assist the Minister. After a few years of confusion caused by the lack of any clear distinction between offices (a Foreign Minister combined his ministerial post with the ambassadorship in London, while his under-secretary did the same in Paris), things settled down in the 1840s when the post of under-secretary, which had been abolished in 1842 upon the appointment of its incumbent to the embassy in London, was reestablished in 1845 to serve as the mainspring of the Ministry. The office of secretary-general (Hariciye Katibi) was also created as a move to decentralize the internal administration of the Ministry by delegating some of the responsibilities of the under-secretary to this new official. This post was abolished in the 1870s, and the *mektupcu* (an official inherited from the office of the Reis Efendi) was promoted to replace him as the administrative head of the Ministry.

During and after the Crimean War the Ministry acquired a clear identity. This was partly achieved by the establishment of separate archives, the Hariciye Evrak Odasi, which were run in a more rational way and were later to serve as a repository for the archival material of most other civil service departments.

The Ministry of Foreign Affairs preserved until the 1880s the dual character of the office of the Reis Efendi, continuing to handle various matters relating to the internal affairs of the Empire alongside the Chancery of the grand vizier (the Divan-ı Hümayan Kalemi), which issued and recorded all imperial orders, restrictions, notifications, etc. Moreover, the Ministry had general control over the non-Moslem subjects of the Empire through a department divided into separate sections for each community. Though the Ministry lost these two responsibilities in the 1880s, it did retain some additional duties not usually associated with the conduct of foreign affairs, such as the supervision of the mixed courts established in the Empire through the Capitulations granted to foreign powers. The Minister for Foreign Affairs was also the *ex officio* chairman of the Board of Health, established to coordinate the quarantine services of the Empire and to prevent the spread of contagious diseases. The Board, composed of both Turkish and foreign members, acted as a ministry of public health and was as such subordinate to the Ministry of Foreign Affairs.

It was only in 1913 that an organic law was passed regulating the working of the Ministry and giving a clear indication of its subdivision into specialized departments. These had come into existence gradually in response to specific needs.

The department of the Ministry that handled political affairs was the Tahrirat-i Hariciye Kalemi, or as it was known in French the Direction de la Correspondance Etrangère. The department was responsible for the drafting of all political and diplomatic dispatches sent to Ottoman missions abroad. In 1877 an inner section was inaugurated in this department to deal exclusively with important affairs; it was reminiscent of the Mühimme Odası that had been established in the office of the Reis Efendi at the close of the eighteenth century.

Both the Translation Room and the Press Department remained under the supervision of the Ministry. The Press Department controlled the national press, published locally both in Turkish and in other languages, and also foreign journals circulating in the Empire; it was one of the busiest and most crowded sections in the Ministry, as a very strict censorship was maintained.

Another important section was the Department of Nationalities, known in French as the Bureau des Sujétions. It was established in 1869 to check on the real nationality of a great number of individuals living in Turkey who claimed to have foreign nationality in order to benefit from the advantages given by the Capitulations to foreign nationals. Foreigners who had business transactions to conduct with any official Turkish department had to present a paper stating that they were not Turkish subjects. The Bureau des Sujétions, which had branches in all the main provincial centres, delivered this document in exchange for a fee; these fees constituted the main revenue of the Ministry.

In addition to the departments already mentioned, others handling consular, commercial, legal, etc. affairs were gradually opened. With the advent of the telegraph, a telegraphic cipher department was established. The Introducteur des Ambassadeurs, who acted as the head of court protocol, and the dragoman of the Divan came also under the Ministry of Foreign Affairs and ranked among its most senior officials. In 1896, the Minister was given a private secretariat headed by a chef de cabinet. The Council of the Ministry, which met twice a week to discuss administrative matters, was composed of the under-secretary, the secretary-general, the chief of the ministerial cabinet and the heads of departments.

The 1913 Organic Law replaced this rather shadowy organization with another more akin to the structure of a contemporary Foreign Ministry. The powers of the under-secretary, who was given a deputy, were reinforced as the office of the secretary-general was abolished. Two directors-general were established; the first handled political matters, supervising three sections, whose specific activities were clearly defined, as well as the by now institutionalized section of important affairs. The second director-general dealt with consular and legal matters and commercial affairs. The under-secretary had direct control over personnel, press, nationalities, archives, translation and accountancy departments. The office of the government's chief legal adviser had earlier been incorporated into the Ministry, while the head of court protocol had been transferred to the palace.

This set-up, inspired by a study of similar European institutions, was to be adopted in its broad outlines by the Turkish Republic when the Ottoman Empire was overthrown in 1922.

At the same time as the expansion of the Foreign Ministry was taking place, and perhaps even the reason for its development, a string of permanent diplomatic missions was opened in foreign capitals in the course of the nineteenth and early twentieth centuries starting with the embassies in Paris, Vienna and London established in 1834. These were followed by missions in Berlin (1837), Athens (1840), Tehran (1849), Brussels (1854), The Hague (1854), Turin (1854), Naples (1856), Madrid (1857), St Petersburg (1857), Washington (1867), Bucharest (1878), Belgrade (1879), Cetinje (1880), Stockholm (1898), Sofia (1909), Bern (1915), Copenhagen (1917) and Kiev (1918).

In 1860 drastic economy measures aimed at curtailing public expenditure forced the government temporarily to close down its missions in those countries that had not been a party to the Paris Peace Treaty of 1856. The Ottoman government made an exception for its missions in Athens and Tehran, capitals of two neighbouring countries. Those missions that were closed down in 1860 were reopened in the 1880s. In the meantime, Ottoman envoys in the remaining capitals were also accredited to those countries where permanent missions had been abolished. The ambassador in London, for instance, was accredited to The Hague and Brussels, the ambassador in Paris to Madrid.

In 1886 a regulation was passed dividing Ottoman diplomatic missions abroad into four categories. To the first category belonged the embassies – London, Paris, Vienna and Tehran – that had been opened initially as such, St Petersburg (which was raised to embassy status in 1873), Berlin (embassy in 1874), Rome (replacing Turin, embassy in 1883). To these seven embassies Washington was added when the post was raised to an embassy in 1914. The staff of each embassy, according to the 1886 regulation, was composed of one counsellor, one first secretary, one second secretary and one third secretary, in addition to the ambassador himself. The missions in Athens, Bucharest and Belgrade were first-class legations each with one first, one second and one third secretary, plus the head of mission. Cetinje and Washington were second-class legations, with one first and one second secretary, while Madrid, Brussels and Lahej, being third-class legations, had only one third secretary in addition to the minister. There was no restriction on the number of unpaid attachés. Though this regulation determined the number of personnel assigned to each mission, appointments were made without any regard to its stipulations – some representations had more than their allotted number of secretaries while others were understaffed.

The opening of diplomatic missions abroad was justified by the necessity for the Ottoman Empire to integrate itself into the European community of states. The proposers of this change argued that the Empire could no longer afford to pursue its policy of 'splendid isolation'. As a matter of fact the Crimean War, during which the Ottoman Empire had been allied to the two great western powers, and the ensuing Congress of Paris, which had admitted Turkey into the European concert, had made it imperative for reasons of both prestige and policy that the Empire be represented in as many capitals as possible.

As diplomatic missions abroad became a permanent feature of Ottoman administration, there appeared in the Empire a new type of civil servant, the career diplomat, who having a sound knowledge of at least one European language and having acquired familiarity with European ideas, thoughts and mores, served as an essential channel for the diffusion of these concepts, which were to be instrumental in the modernization of Ottoman society.

During the first decades that followed the establishment of permanent missions, the selection of personnel appointed to serve abroad reflected the newness of the institution. Mahmud II was reported to have said, in order to convince reluctant would-be appointees, that it was more glorious to be an ambassador to a foreign court than Minister for Foreign Affairs in Istanbul. The first heads of missions were either military officers who had been trained abroad or leading apologists for the policy of opening the Empire to European influences. Their staffs were composed of young trainees from the Translation Room, who were sent abroad to complement the instructions they had received in Istanbul. Then, in the late 1860s and early 1870s, these first graduates from the Translation Room, having risen through the ranks, and having climbed through the various echelons of the diplomatic hierarchy both abroad and at home, themselves became heads of missions and created a professionally trained diplomatic corps. One of the first to achieve this was Esat Pacha, who having undergone a period of training at the Translation Room was sent, at government expense, to Paris to complete his studies in the late 1850s, was later appointed as secretary to the Paris embassy and then transferred to St Petersburg as first secretary. After a prolonged period of duty as counsellor again in Paris, Esat was sent as consul-general to Buda, from where he was promoted minister to Athens in 1872. Having subsequently served as head of mission in Rome and in Vienna he was called back to Istanbul in 1878 as under-secretary at the Foreign Ministry before being appointed in 1880 to Paris, where he remained as ambassador for fourteen years.

This brief summary of the career of a professional diplomat is useful, as it provides an insight into the Ottoman diplomatic service as a working institution, with all the paraphernalia of promotions, changes of residence, etc. However, there was no rule that clearly regulated any of these. Admission into the Ministry, for instance, was based more on patronage than anything else, with the children or other relatives of the reformist administrative elite being given preference. Esat Pacha, for example, was the younger brother of Emin Muhlis Pacha, who was serving as dragoman of the Divan when Esat himself entered the foreign service. Nepotism and favouritism were perhaps inevitable, at least in the early years, as the reformist movement did not have a large following and the young men entering the Translation Room were already politically engaged either through family links with the reformists or from personal conviction. One of the most blatant cases of nepotism was Musurus Pacha, who distinguished himself by remaining ambassador in London for thirty-five years. This worthy had at one time staffed the entire embassy with his sons, nephews and sons-in-law.

In 1885 a commission, presided over by the under-secretary and comprising all the heads of departments, was appointed to examine prospective candidates, who were required only to show their proficiency in French, which since the late 1830s had been the official working language of the Ottoman Ministry of Foreign Affairs. The commission was also to check on the morality and personal ability of the candidates. The successful candidate would be admitted for a probationary period of two years, at the end of which his appointment was confirmed. The same commission also decided on the nominations and appointments, both in the Ministry and abroad, of the secretaries, attachés and consuls. The appointments of the counsellors and the consuls–general were decided by the Minister himself, while heads of mission were appointed by the sultan upon proposals from the Minister.

There was no clear–cut rule determining the tour of duty either abroad or at home. Diplomats served for indeterminate periods, and nominations and movements from one post to another depended principally on connections. As a rule, heads of mission were moved less often than their subordinates, and though none equalled Musurus Pacha's record-breaking stay in London, several Ottoman ambassadors remained for more than fifteen years in the same post. The same body of personnel provided staff to serve in missions abroad and in posts at home; generally, its members were frequently inter-changed, though there were instances of senior officials acceding to the highest positions in the Ministry without ever having served abroad. Similarly, other diplomats were never on duty at home; after completing their two-year probationary period in the Ministry, they spent their whole official lives abroad.

Despite the emergence of a professional body of foreign service officers, outsiders continued to be appointed heads of embassies and legations. Some of these appointments were meant to be golden exiles for their incumbents, whose presence in Istanbul had, for one reason or another, become undesirable to the powers of the time. Other non-professional appointments were destined to reward loyal servants of the sultan. The great majority of non-professional envoys came from the military. One of these soldiers-turned-diplomat, Major-General Ibrahim Fethi Pacha, served successfully as Ottoman envoy to Belgrade for ten years; then during the Balkan wars he commanded an army corps that, according to the calculations of the Ottoman general staff, was meant to capture the capital where he had earlier represented his sovereign. Ibrahim Fethi failed to storm the Serbian capital, and died in the attempt. His body fell into the hands of the Serbians, who retained good memories of the Ottoman envoy and gave him a state funeral in Belgrade.

Consulates, which had begun as honorary posts to which local dignitaries or Ottoman resident merchants were appointed, underwent tremendous development and mushroomed throughout the world during the nineteenth century. Nominations of honorary consuls were continued, and there were few towns that could not boast of the presence of an Ottoman consul, some of the more unlikely places being Jerez de la Frontera in Spain and Bradford in England. Simultaneously, a network of consulates headed by officials from the Ottoman Ministry of Foreign Affairs was established in the main industrial and commercial centres of the world. Neighbouring countries were the object of special attention, and in some cities of southern Russia and Persia officers from the general staff were appointed as consuls. The consulate in Kermanshah, for instance, was regarded as being on the same level as a minor legation while during the First World War the Ottoman consul in Harrar had a distinctly political role, gun-running in the Red Sea and fostering unrest in Italian Eritrea and the Sudan.

Although most of the career heads of mission had earlier done a stint in one of the major consular posts, and although there was – at least on paper – no distinction between the diplomatic and consular services, there existed an *ipso facto* specialization, and some officials rotated from one consular post to another without ever being appointed to a diplomatic mission.

For most of the period covered the Ottoman Empire was governed in an autocratic way, and ministerial appointments were the reflection of either the sultan's or the grand vizier's will; in this they did not differ greatly from other administrative appointments. The ministerial seat was the highest position a career official could aspire to; it is interesting to note that in the period from the creation of the Ministry in 1836 to the overthrow of the Empire in 1922, of the thirty-eight Ministers for Foreign Affairs only six were career diplomats, twenty-one had in one capacity or another served either in the Ministry or in missions abroad, while the remaining eleven had had no connection with foreign affairs before or after their nomination as head of the Ottoman diplomatic service.

One interesting aspect of the Ottoman diplomatic service was its racial and religious composition. The Ottoman Empire was a multinational state comprising many different ethnic and religious groups. One of the aims of the nineteenth-century Ottoman reformists was to build up an Ottoman commonwealth out of this motley collection, and one way of creating a feeling of solidarity and loyalty was to open the service of the state to members of all communities. This well-meant but obsolescent policy was applied relatively successfully in the foreign service, which admitted to its ranks members of all the major ethnic groups in the Empire. Four non-Moslems served as Foreign Minister, the last of them, a Maronite Christian, as late as 1922. Orthodox Greeks and Armenians were appointed to embassies and consular posts and served as heads of department in the Ministry. Dadian Pacha, an Armenian, filled the post of under-secretary for almost twenty years. By the second half of the nineteenth century a large number of Moslem Turks were acquainted with foreign languages and were willing to mingle with foreigners, so one can assume that the admission of non-Moslems to senior posts in the diplomatic service reflected a genuine intention on the part of the Moslem reformist elite to let their non-Moslem subjects participate in the conduct of affairs.

The Nationalist Movement that rose against the very stiff clauses of the Sèvres Peace Treaty, dictated after the First World War by the Allied Powers to the vanquished Ottoman Empire, and that ultimately toppled the imperial regime, conducted its struggle on both the military and the diplomatic fronts. During the early stages of the Movement its Foreign Ministry was housed in a single room on the second floor of a derelict building in the provincial city of Ankara, which was to become the capital of the new regime. The Ministry consisted of four people under a Minister who had served in a junior capacity in the Ottoman diplomatic service before holding some important appointments in the imperial provincial administration. The revolutionary character of the new regime was indicated by the fact that one of the four people working for the Ministry was a young woman.

Despite this rather unassuming start, the Ministry of Foreign Affairs is today one of the most important public departments, attracting some of the brightest young graduates entering the service of the state. This importance is a reflection of the considerable place foreign relations still occupy in the minds of Turkish policy-makers because of the country's geopolitical situation.

Recruitment to the Ministry in the early days of the Republic was a fairly simple matter. Though there were many former imperial officials who were transferred to the Republican diplomatic service (Ahmet Muhtar Mullaoğlu, who served as the first Republican ambassador to the United States, had been the Ottoman envoy to Athens before the First World War; Münir Ertegün, who held some of the key embassies after the proclamation of the Republic, had taken part in the Brest-Litovsk peace negotiations as legal adviser to the Ottoman delegation), there was nevertheless an acute need to fill up the ranks of the Ministry, which had been depleted both by the losses in human lives sustained during the war and by the departure and emigration of many members of the non-Moslem communities who had hitherto served in the diplomatic service. Admission was therefore a mere formality. No educational requirements were expected from candidates, who were only asked to have a fairly good knowledge of French. Needless to say, strong family connections were an added bonus. However, during the early 1930s, as a result of the emphasis placed by the Republican leaders on formal education, admission to the Ministry was now conditional on the candidate passing an entrance examination. This exam, which was open only to university graduates, barred the way to the amateurish dilettantes. Officials without university degrees who had been admitted earlier were barred from further promotion, as an unwritten law restricted appointments to ambassadorial posts to university graduates.

The entrance examination in its present form is open to male and female graduates in law, political sciences and economics. It takes place once or twice a year, depending on the requirements of the Ministry for new personnel. These requirements also determine the number of candidates admitted, which usually averages twenty at each session. The first part of the exam is a written test to judge the candidate's ability to express himself on paper on a given topic both in Turkish and in either French or English. A fairly stiff selection process takes place at the end of this test, the main criterion for success being mastery of a foreign language. Candidates who survive the first selection are invited to an oral examination which takes the form of an informal interview, with senior officials from the Ministry testing the examinee's academic knowledge. Successful candidates are then admitted to the Ministry and distributed among the various departments according to the grades they obtained in the examinations; those who come top of the list are recruited into one of the political or economic departments.

After a probation period of six months, the new recruit is given the title of third secretary, but there still remains a hurdle on his way to the top. Six years after his admission to the Ministry he has to pass another exam to be promoted to first secretary. In contrast to the entrance examination, this exam aims at assessing the professional ability and skills the candidate has acquired. Questions are very much to the point and are limited almost entirely to service matters.

The Republic inherited the basic structure of the imperial Foreign Ministry, to which additions were made with time to meet rising needs. The central figure of the Ministry remained the secretary-general, who has always been a career diplomat. Though the secretary-general is appointed from among the senior ambassadors, there have been instances of secretaries-general acceding to the post who had not previously served as heads of mission abroad. The secretary-general has a varying number of deputies (see Appendix A). The three sections of the Direction de la Correspondance Etrangère of the imperial Ministry handling political affairs were promoted to independent departments under separate directors-general and were known by numbers, the First Department covering Western Europe and the Americas, the Second, Eastern Europe, Asia and Africa, and the Third, international organizations. In the early fifties a Fourth Department was created to handle cultural relations with foreign countries, a NATO Department was established after Turkey joined in 1952 and a Department of International Economic Affairs was set up to coordinate foreign financial relations. The conflict with Greece over Cyprus led to the creation of a separate department covering the issue, and a Research and Planning Department was established to serve as a ministerial 'think tank'. In 1967 an administrative reshuffle redistributed the business of the various departments (e.g. the NATO Department was renamed the Department of Mutual Security Affairs as a sign of changing times) and still serves as a basis for the present structure; there are a few minor modifications, the most notable being the abolition in 1973 of the post of senior deputy secretary-general. Following the series of terrorist attempts against the lives of Turkish diplomats serving abroad and their families, a special section was established to deal with security matters for the protection of diplomatic staff.

The secretary-general presides over the administrative structure of the Ministry and is assisted by his deputies, each of whom is responsible for specific departments. These departments, headed by directors-general, are in turn subdivided into various divisions under a head of division, the divisions being composed of a varying number of desks each assigned a specific country or topic. The desks, the lowest administrative units in the Ministry, are headed by a first secretary.

Promotion from a position to a higher one is now by seniority. Every official in the Ministry can today reasonably aspire to the rank of ambassador if he has completed the required terms in the lower echelons though whether he will get a nomination to an ambassadorial post corresponding to the title is another matter. This rather awkward system was devised in order to prevent meteoric ascensions, which are thought to undermine the corporate morale of Ministry officials.

There is no specialization in the foreign service, neither in the diplomatic and consular fields nor in serving at home or abroad. As a matter of fact, officials alternate regularly between a posting abroad and a nomination at the Ministry and the policy of the Ministry is to ensure, particularly at the lower levels, maximum interchangeability among its staff. Regulations currently in force provide for a two-year stint of home duty for each five years of service abroad, which can take place either in a consulate or in a diplomatic mission. Junior secretaries on their first posting abroad spend three years in a mission in Europe or North America and two years in an Asian or African capital and are also expected to serve at least once in a consulate. The movements of heads of mission are less clearly determined, but an ambassador is expected to remain three years in one post.

The distribution of Turkey's permanent missions abroad is as follows

(1979). Europe: all capitals with the exception of Iceland and Malta; the two North American states; Latin America: Argentina, Brazil, Chile, Cuba, Mexico, Venezuela; Black Africa: Ethiopia, Ghana, Kenya, Nigeria, Somalia, Zaire; all member countries of the Arab League with the exception of Mauritania, Oman and the two Yemens; Asia: Afghanistan, Bangladesh, People's Republic of China (since 1972), India, Indonesia, Iran, Japan, Malaysia, South Korea, Thailand. Turkey, who recognized the state of Israel in 1948, has since that date had a diplomatic mission in Tel Aviv. There are also Turkish delegations accredited to the main international organizations. Following general practice, Turkey has raised the level of its diplomatic representations to the status of embassy with the exception of its representation in Tel Aviv, which remains a legation headed permanently by a chargé d'affaires.

The tendency nowadays is to restrict nominations to ambassadorial posts abroad to career diplomats. A retired senior officer from the armed forces is occasionally sent to serve as ambassador, but this practice is becoming exceedingly rare, much to the relief of Ministry officials. In 1979 only one embassy was held by a retired army officer, in contrast to four a few years earlier. The heads of the State Planning Organization are as a rule appointed to one or the other of Turkey's mission to international economic bodies upon completion of their tour of duty.

This practice of closing the Ministry to outsiders has ensured that it has remained politically independent of the various governments, especially important in recent years, which have witnessed frequent changes of government because of parliamentary disequilibrium. The relative stability of the Ministry's senior personnel offsets the frequent changes of Minister, who are nowadays parliamentarians with little or no practical experience of the conduct of foreign affairs. Two recent Ministers were academics, and one a senior politician with a long experience of provincial administration. At times of parliamentary crisis, when caretaker governments are appointed as temporary stopgaps, a senior ambassador is usually chosen as Foreign Minister. In the early forties the creation of the post of parliamentary under-secretary, to be held by a member of parliament, proved to be a short-lived attempt to introduce direct parliamentary control in the Ministry. Today parliamentary control is effected through the Foreign Affairs Commissions of both houses of parliament, who must table their approval of the Ministry's budget and who take this opportunity to express their views both on the Ministry's record and on foreign affairs.

Besides the diplomatic personnel, the Turkish Foreign Ministry's staff includes three other categories: legal advisers, some of whom are officials of the Ministry while others are seconded on a part-time basis from universities; the administrative class, whose members look after the accounts of the missions and similar matters; the technical class, which includes a multitude of specialists ranging from cipher clerks to wireless experts and others who may be recruited on a contract basis for specific assignments.

The compulsory retirement age for all categories is sixty-five; civil servants are entitled to retire on pension after twenty-five years of service. Ministry officials who are getting married must have the Ministry's approval beforehand, and an unwritten law prevents marriages with foreign nationals.

The Foreign Ministry is regarded with mixed feelings. Turkish diplomats are accused of having been unable to keep abreast of the rapid evolution of Turkish society in recent years and to have lost touch with it. At the same time, they are criticized for failing to present the Turkish case on various issues properly on international platforms. There is also some feeling of resentment against the Hollywood image of the diplomat as a 'social butterfly', an image that is hard to erase. The emphasis on foreign languages, which is the qualifying factor for admission, severely limits the number of applicants; only the scions of well-to-do families educated in private schools have the necessary linguistic qualifications to pass the exam. Further, the increasing number of children of diplomats entering the service reinforces the image of an elite corps closed to outsiders. This in turn generates a feeling of clannish pride that is shared by many Foreign Ministry officials.

In 1968 an Academy of Foreign Affairs was established within the Ministry to serve as a training school for probationary officials. Its curriculum has been devised to equip the young diplomats with a more balanced knowledge of local realities, with lectures on economic and social questions. It has also been suggested that foreign service officials should serve for a limited period in the provincial administration so that they may acquire a first-hand knowledge of local conditions. Nothing has come of this proposal since its logical corollary would be that provincial administrators should serve in the diplomatic service.

There is now a growing tendency among junior diplomats at mid-career, attracted by better working conditions, to request secondment to one or other of the international organizations. But Foreign Ministry nominees represent only a small proportion of the Turkish nationals working in these organizations. Still, it is from the Ministry's ranks that hail the two Turks who have held the most senior appointments in such organizations (Ambassador O. Olçąy as deputy secretary-general of NATO and Ambassador F. Berkol as assistant under-secretary of the United Nations).

As a concluding note, one may say that the Ministry of Foreign Affairs, established in 1836, is in fact the oldest public administration in Turkey; all the other ministries in their present forms were set up at a later date. In 1986 the 150th anniversary of its inception will be commemorated – one hopes in a manner befitting the importance both of the Ministry's past role as a channel for the introduction of reforms and of its present one of formulating a policy that will steer Turkey through the delicate course of international relations in the 1980s.

NOTES

[1] B. Bareilles, *Rapport Secret sur le Congrès de Berlin* (Paris 1919), 15.

[2] J. M. Jouannin, *La Turquie* (Paris 1840), 126.

[3] The treaty of Passarowitz, signed with Austria in 1717, provided for an Ottoman consul (Shehbender) to reside in Vienna to look after trade matters. The consul, one Osman Ağa, was recalled at the request of the Austrian govi ıment when he claimed recognition as a diplomatic agent, with the ensuing immunities and privileges.

BIBLIOGRAPHY

Very little has been published either in Turkey or elsewhere on the Turkish foreign service. A useful study of the office of the Reis-ül Küttab is to be found in Carter Findlay's article 'Origins of the Ottoman Foreign Ministry' in *International Journal of Middle East Studies*, I (1970), 334–57, while the same author's 'Foundation of the Ottoman Foreign Ministry' in *International Journal of Middle East Studies*, vol. 3, no 4 (1972), 388–416 is explicit enough.

Thomas Naff, 'Reform and the conduct of Ottoman Diplomacy' in *Journal of the American Oriental Society*, vol LXXXIII (1963), 292–315, covers the establishment abroad of the first permanent missions, and J. C. Hurewitz, 'Ottoman Diplomacy and the European State System' in *Middle East Journal*, 15–2 (1961), 141–52, discusses the working state of the Ministry during the nineteenth century.

Even less is available on the present state of the Ministry of Foreign Affairs. Metin Tamkoc discusses briefly the influence exercised by career diplomats in policy formulation in his *Guardians of the National Security and the Modernization of Turkey* (Utah 1976), 254–8.

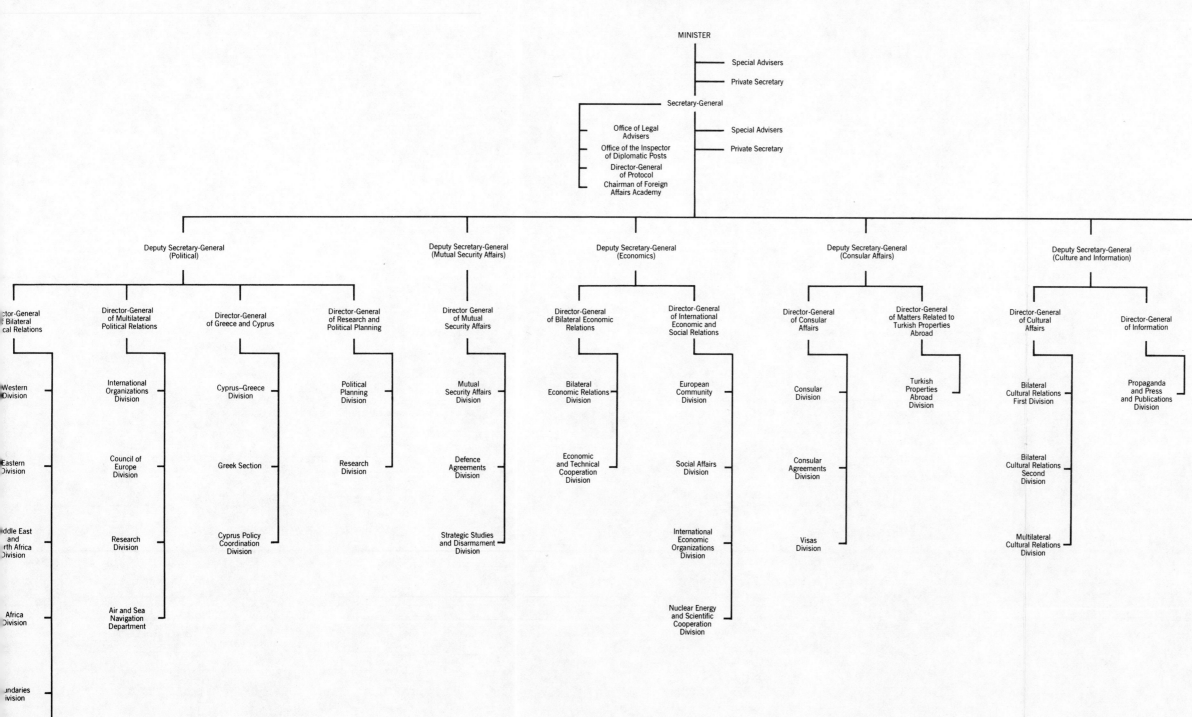
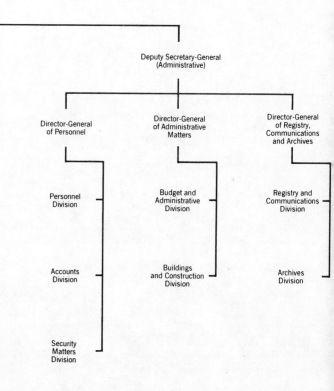

MINISTER

- Special Advisers
- Private Secretary

Secretary-General

- Office of Legal Advisers
- Office of the Inspector of Diplomatic Posts
- Director-General of Protocol
- Chairman of Foreign Affairs Academy

- Special Advisers
- Private Secretary

Deputy Secretary-General (Political)

- Director-General of Bilateral Political Relations
  - Western Division
  - Eastern Division
  - Middle East and North Africa Division
  - Africa Division
  - Boundaries Division
  - Demarcation Boundaries Division
- Director-General of Multilateral Political Relations
  - International Organizations Division
  - Council of Europe Division
  - Research Division
  - Air and Sea Navigation Department
- Director-General of Greece and Cyprus
  - Cyprus–Greece Division
  - Greek Section
  - Cyprus Policy Coordination Division
- Director-General of Research and Political Planning
  - Political Planning Division
  - Research Division

Deputy Secretary-General (Mutual Security Affairs)

- Director General of Mutual Security Affairs
  - Mutual Security Affairs Division
  - Defence Agreements Division
  - Strategic Studies and Disarmament Division

Deputy Secretary-General (Economics)

- Director-General of Bilateral Economic Relations
  - Bilateral Economic Relations Division
  - Economic and Technical Cooperation Division
- Director-General of International Economic and Social Relations
  - European Community Division
  - Social Affairs Division
  - International Economic Organizations Division
  - Nuclear Energy and Scientific Cooperation Division

Deputy Secretary-General (Consular Affairs)

- Director-General of Consular Affairs
  - Consular Division
  - Consular Agreements Division
  - Visas Division
- Director-General of Matters Related to Turkish Properties Abroad
  - Turkish Properties Abroad Division

Deputy Secretary-General (Culture and Information)

- Director-General of Cultural Affairs
  - Bilateral Cultural Relations First Division
  - Bilateral Cultural Relations Second Division
  - Multilateral Cultural Relations Division
- Director-General of Information
  - Propaganda and Press and Publications Division

Deputy Secretary-General (Administrative)

- Director-General of Personnel
  - Personnel Division
  - Accounts Division
  - Security Matters Division
- Director-General of Administrative Matters
  - Budget and Administrative Division
  - Buildings and Construction Division
- Director-General of Registry, Communications and Archives
  - Registry and Communications Division
  - Archives Division

Union of Soviet Socialist Republics

The Tsarist and Soviet Ministry of Foreign Affairs

TEDDY J. ULDRICKS

Professor Teddy J. Uldricks is Professor of Russian and Modern European History at the University of North Carolina at Asheville. He holds an A.B. in history from the University of California, Berkeley, and M.A. and Ph.D. degrees in Russian history from Indiana University. Professor Uldricks is the author of *Diplomacy and Ideology: The Origins of Soviet Foreign Relations, 1917–1930* (1979) as well as several articles on Soviet diplomacy and on the Russian Revolution.

The direction of foreign affairs had been one of the primary tasks of the tsars since the foundation of the modern Russian state. During the so-called 'gathering of the Russian lands' in the fifteenth century, the foreign policy of the state and the personal fortunes and ambitions of the Muscovite grand princes were indistinguishable. Diplomacy was the province of the grand prince and a small coterie of favourites surrounding him. Gradually, during the reign of Ivan III, an administrative system of departments or chancelleries developed out of the institutions of the royal household. While the tsar decided matters of high policy, the administration of foreign affairs was handled either by clerks *(d'iaki)* of the exchequer (Kazennyi dvor) or, at times, by other clerks especially concerned with foreign matters. The increasing extent and complexity of Moscow's external relations in the sixteenth century necessitated a more elaborate state apparatus.

Evolving out of the tsar's treasury, the first official Russian diplomatic agency, the Ambassadorial Department (Posol'skii prikaz) was created by Ivan IV in 1549. The powerful Muscovite *d'iak* Ivan Viskovatyi headed the new organization. The Ambassadorial Department was originally charged with merely administrative responsibilities such as conducting foreign correspondence, keeping diplomatic archives and provisioning foreign guests in Moscow, but it subsequently played a significant role in the formulation of foreign policy. The senior officials of the Department, meeting in 'tribunals', deliberated on major policy issues and made recommendations to the sovereign.

The Ambassadorial Department was housed in the Kremlin where, in addition to the archives, it maintained a library with extensive holdings of foreign books. By the 1590s the Department employed seventeen clerks. These clerks were divided into senior and junior ranks and some of them held functional titles such as signatory clerk or document clerk. They received no formal preparation for their work, only on-the-job training. Because of the higher qualifications of clerks in the Department (mainly knowledge of foreign languages and cartography in addition to basic literacy), they were better paid than other clerks. The Department received its budget from vodka excise taxes and fees from certain towns. By 1689 the Ambassadorial Department, now employing forty clerks, comprised five sections: a first department for dealing with the Holy Roman Empire, the Papacy, Spain, France, England, dynastic questions and the commercial quarter of Moscow; a second department for Persia, Armenia, India, the Kalmyks, the Don Cossacks, couriers and foreign merchants; a third department for relations with Poland, Sweden, Turkey, the Crimea, the Balkans, Holland, free cities and Greece; a fourth department for Denmark, Brandenburg, Kurland, and interpreters and translators; and a fifth department for Georgia, China, Khiva, Bukhara, the Siberian Kalmyks and textile mills. The Ambassadorial Department also controlled some lesser departments such as the Little Russian (Ukrainian) Chancellery and the Chancellery for the Ransom of Military Captives.

In the seventeenth century foreign policy decision-making was a complex process that involved the tsar, his courtiers, the bureaucracy, the Boiar Duma and even the Zemskii Sobor. Up to 1667 the Ambassadorial Department was usually headed by a senior clerk *(dumnyi d'iak)*, but after that date it was run by men of higher rank and greater political influence. Under such able diplomatists as A. L. Ordin-Nashchokin, A. A. Matveev and V. V. Golitsyn the Ambassadorial Department occupied an important position in affairs of state. Despite its growing influence, the Ambassadorial Department never had sole charge of foreign affairs. It had to share authority in this sphere with the Great Exchequer (Prikaz Bol'shoi Kazny) and the Department of Secret Affairs (Prikaz Tainykh Del). Besides advising the tsar on international problems, the Ambassadorial Department dispatched and instructed Russian representatives abroad, dealt with foreign merchants in Russia and supervised the affairs of some minority populations (for instance, the Don Cossacks and the Kazan Tatars) living in the borderlands of the realm.

Although Muscovy had frequent contact with a number of foreign states during the sixteenth and seventeenth centuries, the tsars usually employed temporary envoys for this purpose rather than establishing permanent missions abroad. Similarly, representatives of foreign powers were not normally accorded the right to remain indefinitely in Moscow. Distrust of things foreign and fear of contamination by alien influence were strong in pre-Petrine Russia. Muscovite envoys were of three sorts. A grand ambassador *(velikii posol)* was dispatched to great powers, while lesser countries received an ordinary ambassador *(legkii posol, posol* or *poslannik)*. The former posts were customarily held by members of the boiar elite, whereas the latter were regularly staffed by functionaries of the Ambassadorial Department. Envoys of the lowest rank, gonets or herold, were simply message carriers. Because of the importance of diplomatic work and also because of its educational and linguistic prerequisites, the Department was freed, at least in part, from the stultifying grip of the *mestnichestvo* system (i.e. appointment by social precedence). It was able to recruit its personnel according to merit to a much greater extent than could other segments of the bureaucracy. Many foreigners were employed by the Department because of their knowledge of languages and of conditions abroad. Nevertheless, Russian diplomacy was all too often hampered by the climate of suspicion, xenophobia and ideological rigidity, and the tendency to put form ahead of substance, that characterized Muscovite society.

Tsarist diplomats were closely bound by minutely detailed instructions. They seldom had much latitude in negotiation and they were often stymied when diplomatic situations evolved beyond the narrow confines of their commissions. Upon returning from their missions, they were required to file lengthy reports, not about conditions in the lands they had visited but on the ways in which they had carried out their instructions. In a practice subsequently duplicated in the Soviet era, Muscovite representatives were sometimes accompanied by agents of the secret service (Tainyi Prikaz) to ensure precise execution of their charges. In yet another analogue with later Soviet experience, Russian diplomats occasionally 'defected' to the service of a foreign power.

Russia did not maintain permanent missions abroad until the time of Peter the Great. Before 1700 the only established embassy was in Warsaw, but by the end of Peter's reign there were regular missions in all the European capitals. Peter wished to pursue an expansionist foreign policy, driving the Swedes from the Baltic shores and simultaneously striking south against the Ottoman Turks, but he initially lacked the means to achieve these ambitious goals. He had neither the military power, nor the diplomatic leverage, nor the basic socio-economic organization needed for such undertakings. Traditional Muscovite institutions, including the Ambassadorial Department, were not sufficiently well organized to exploit efficiently Russia's human and material resources. Peter's solution to this problem was a sweeping reform of the governmental structure in an attempt to introduce rational and efficient administration based on European models. A new central apparatus was created in which the various administrative functions (e.g. state finance, army and navy, commerce) were assigned to a number of 'colleges'. The colleges were administered by the six or eight highest-ranking civil servants or military officers in each field, and the staff of each college bore collective responsibility for all the problems submitted to it. A College of Foreign Affairs was among the original nine colleges decreed in 1717, and was subsequently established in new quarters on the banks of the Neva in St Petersburg. The College was divided into a Chancellery, where documents were executed, and a policy-making Office *(prisutstvie)* where the president and vice-president of the College, four or five counsellors and as many 'assessors' met daily to make decisions and recommendations on foreign policy.

The College of Foreign Affairs was one of the most important organs of government during the eighteenth century. Its chairman usually held both the highest civil rank, that of *kantsler,* and membership in the Senate, and he sat in the highest councils of state which deliberated on the most important issues. The Foreign College, together with those of War and the Admiralty, were the only colleges exempt from senatorial control, and they were distinctly larger and more prestigious than the domestic affairs colleges. This simply reflected the priority given by Peter to the expansion of his empire. Despite this royal patronage, however, it would be many years before the College of Foreign Affairs developed the sort of sophisticated procedures, extensive intelligence system, adequate financial resources and reliable communications network enjoyed by its foreign rivals.

To fill the ranks of his expanding diplomatic service, Peter actively recruited young men from among that small portion of the Muscovite nobility which shared his westernizing zeal. Many of the new Russian diplomats had some minimum of experience abroad and some acquaintance with a foreign language. They also adopted western dress and manners, and they ceased to seclude themselves while abroad as their predecessors had done. Yet while the quality of Russian representation had improved, it was still far from ideal. In one case, Ambassador A. A. Matveev's incomprehension of the relatively free press in England, and of the legal limits on the power of the Crown to abridge that freedom, led to a temporary break in Anglo-Russian relations. Peter sought to overcome this lack of suitable foreign service officials by employing a large number of foreigners, especially Dutchmen and Germans, in the College of Foreign Affairs. These men often had previous diplomatic experience, but, in the words of one British ambassador in Moscow, they were all too commonly men 'such as come discontented from the allies and have no true knowledge of the Czar's empire or interest with respect to other nations'.[1] The College, both under Peter I and throughout most of the century, continued to offer promising careers for Russians of the middle and lower orders as well. P. P. Shafirov, for instance, advanced by his merit from the post of translator to that of vice-chancellor of the

College of Foreign Affairs. The quality of Russian diplomacy did rise gradually during the eighteenth century, but personnel recruitment remained a serious problem. The College was seldom fully staffed in this period.

The modern Imperial Ministry of Foreign Affairs dates from 1802. The old College of Foreign Affairs was found increasingly inadequate as both the volume and importance of diplomatic activity grew dramatically during the period of the Napoleonic wars. The new Imperial Ministry possessed a more streamlined structure than its predecessor and a Minister with both authority over and responsibility for all diplomatic matters. This development did not, however, lessen the pivotal role of the autocrat in foreign policy formation. The first Minister and Acting Minister under this system, Aleksandr Vorontsov and Adam Czartoryski respectively, were both part of the tsar's personal staff (the Unofficial Committee) and were directly responsible to him. Despite these attempts at reform, the Russian diplomatic establishment still remained unwieldy and inefficient. The Ministry underwent minor reorganization in 1810 and again in the reign of Nicholas II, but its overall structure remained basically unchanged down to 1917. From 1828 until the fall of the Romanov regime the Ministry occupied spacious offices at 6 Dvortsova Street near the Pevchii bridge in St Petersburg.

In the nineteenth century the Ministry of Foreign Affairs was headed by a Foreign Minister who was appointed by the tsar and responsible solely to him. In 1906 a Council of Ministers was created on which the Foreign Minister sat along with the heads of the other departments. The chairman of the Council (a pale reflection of the British Prime Minister) acted as an intermediary between the Minister and his monarch, but the basic flows of command and responsibility remained the same.

The 1906 statute spelled out four separate functions for the Foreign Ministry: it conducted political relations with all foreign governments; it sought to protect Russian interests, especially trade, in foreign lands; it actively worked on behalf of Russian citizens to further their affairs in other countries; and it assisted foreigners with their affairs in Russia. The structure of the Ministry included, in addition to the Minister, a deputy minister, the organs of the central ministry in St Petersburg and the foreign missions, as well as some local offices scattered throughout Russia, which were added in 1906 to fulfil consular functions and to provide reports on conditions in frontier and border areas. The Minister's staff comprised the chief councillor of the Ministry, the councillors of the Ministry and officials for special tasks. The deputy minister had charge of the overall direction of all current affairs. The central institutions of the Ministry were its Council, the Chancellery, the Asiatic (or First) Department, the (Second) Department for Internal Communications, the Department for Personnel and General Management, and the archives.

The Council of the Ministry, on which sat the deputy minister, two *ex-officio* members and other Ministry officials appointed by the tsar, met to discuss an agenda prepared by the Minister and also to administer oral examinations to candidates seeking positions in the Ministry. The Chancellery handled most diplomatic correspondence in its two Expeditions (sections) and it also had a special Lithographic Section for the Ministry's own publications. The functions of the Asiatic Department included correspondence in Asian languages, translation of Eastern language materials, processing of any documents in those languages, and the operation of the Eastern Languages Training Section.

The Department for Internal Communications prepared all documents and other messages to foreign powers (except those covered by the First Department), supervised the accrediting of foreign consulates within the Empire, looked after the navigational rights of Russian ships, administered legal affairs, and served as an information bureau for international affairs. The Department for Personnel and General Management was charged with the administration of personnel matters, preparation of the Ministry's budget and overseeing of government property allocated to the Ministry, supervision of the financial accounts of the diplomatic service, custody and use of the Seal of State, and responsibility for defending the interests of Russian churches abroad. From the early nineteenth century the Ministry also included an 'expedition' for consular affairs. However, there was no rigid distinction between diplomatic and consular posts in Russia as there was in Great Britain. N. K. Giers, for example, served successively as the Russian first secretary in Constantinople, consul in Jassy, consul-general in Bucharest and minister in Persia.

The great expansion of the Russian Empire during the eighteenth and nineteenth centuries, which came to include Finland, most of Poland, Bessarabia, the Caucasus, all of Siberia and much of Central Asia, made it necessary for the Imperial Ministry of Foreign Affairs to establish branch offices throughout the Empire. These local institutions of the Ministry were to mediate in disputes and to facilitate agreements between visiting foreigners on one hand, and Russian citizens and government organs on the other. Such officials were attached to the Amur governor-general, the Warsaw governor-general, the chief of the Trans-Caspian region and the viceroy of the Caucasus. The Ministry also operated an office at Odessa.

Following the practices established by the Congress of Vienna in 1815, the foreign missions were of two kinds: embassies, legations and missions whose grades corresponded to the rank of their chief; and consulates-general, consulates and agencies that were administered under separate consular rules. During the nineteenth and early twentieth centuries imperial decrees and statutes had established, on paper, an elaborate and modern foreign office, outwardly resembling the French and British establishments. However, the lack of capable and disciplined personnel greatly hindered the operation of the Ministry. The cultural backwardness of the Russian population in general, as well as the special interests and attitudes of those groups that supplied most of the recruits for the foreign service, greatly affected both the ability of the Foreign Ministry to carry out its tasks and the style of Russian diplomacy.

In 1913 the Ministry of Foreign Affairs employed 689 officials. Entry into the diplomatic service in the early twentieth century was by examination – an oral examination in political economy, international law and geography, as well as a translation exercise in French. These tests were administered by the Council of the Ministry. Admission to diplomatic posts required further written and oral examinations in political economy, international law, the history of treaty relations and the consular code. Places in the diplomatic corps were generally reserved for men born into the gentry. In fact a diplomatic career was often passed down through the family. The education of such young gentlemen varied greatly, from those few sent to the best

European universities to the majority instructed either at home by tutors of varying quality or in the military regiments. To compensate for the lack of native education and talent in the early nineteenth century, foreigners were often brought into the imperial Ministry (e.g. Prince Adam Czartoryski, John Capodistrias, Count Pozzo di Borgo). These men spoke French – the language of diplomacy – with ease, and possessed all the social graces. They brought with them both a wide knowledge of world conditions and a background of considerable experience in the relatively more efficient government bureaucracies of western Europe. The use of foreigners, even in the most sensitive posts, was not at all unusual in the cosmopolitan era of Metternich and Alexander I. Count Karl Nesselrode, German born and educated, continued to head the Ministry under Nicholas I despite that sovereign's cult of 'official nationality'. To be sure, foreigners were not always constant in their loyalty to the national interests: both Czartoryski and Capodistrias left Russian service to join their respective Polish and Greek causes.

The rise of national consciousness that characterized the nineteenth century disposed many Russians to 'purify' their government. The nationalist press blamed the foreign or 'German' element in the Ministry of Foreign Affairs for various setbacks suffered by tsarist diplomacy during the century. Count Nesselrode was the frequent object of such chauvinistic vilification because of his German name and his supposed lack of 'national spirit'. As the century progressed, the proportion of Great Russians in the Ministry increased and foreigners played a sharply diminished role in the foreign service. Yet names like Benckendorff, Meyendorff, Lamzdorff and Mohrenheim continued to occupy important places on the diplomatic list, and at the opening of the twentieth century such prestigious posts as the embassies in London, Berlin, The Hague and Peking were held by Russified Germans.

There is considerable controversy over the degree of freedom of initiative accorded to nineteenth-century tsarist diplomats and over the nature of their relationship to the emperor. Friedrich Engels, writing in 1890, maintained that 'The Russian diplomatic corps forms, so to speak, a modern Jesuit order, powerful enough in case of necessity to overcome even the whims of the Tsar and to become master of the corruption within Russia, in order to disseminate it abroad the more plentifully; a Jesuit order recruited originally and preferably from foreigners.'[2] More recently, many scholars have taken the opposite position on this question. They have emphasized the power of the autocrat to determine foreign policy, to bend the diplomatic corps to his will, and even to influence the nature and quality of Russian perceptions of the outside world.

The Ministry of Foreign Affairs certainly had no constitutional or customary right to formulate Russian foreign policy. That was entirely the prerogative of the tsar. The Ministry, like the Department and the College before it, had been created simply to execute the will of the sovereign. That does not mean, however, that the Minister and his staff were merely unimportant functionaries. In practice the policy-making powers of the Foreign Minister varied directly in proportion to the abilities and strengths of character of each tsar and each Minister. For instance, the six successive Foreign Ministers who served under Alexander I appear to have been little more than his secretaries. This powerful tsar personally dominated both the

formulation and execution of policy. Yet, given the difficulties of communication that plagued diplomacy in the early nineteenth century, even this
strong-willed monarch had to allow his representatives considerable latitude.
Friedrich von Gentz, Metternich's assistant, was particularly struck by the
'attitude of independence which the Russian ministers and agents assume
everywhere in their opinions, in their language, and very often in their
actions, even in regard to the most important affairs.'[3]

Nicholas I, like his predecessor, also strove to retain personal direction of
foreign affairs. He regarded his Foreign Minister, Count Nesselrode, as little
more than his agent. But Nesselrode, working quietly behind the scenes, did
exert a significant influence on the course of imperial policy. He helped to
restrain the impetuous tsar from rash actions and he fought constantly against
various nationalist factions that demanded a more aggressive, even
belligerent, foreign policy. Under Nesselrode's guidance, Russian foreign
policy remained oriented toward cooperation with the other powers of
Europe until the Crimean War. Alexander II and his Foreign Minister, A. M.
Gorchakov, worked well together, carrying out a cautious foreign policy
imposed on a weakened Russia in the wake of the Crimean *débâcle*. Towards
the end of the reign, however, the old and feeble Gorchakov lost control of
the situation and allowed the country to drift against his will into another war
with the Ottoman Empire.

N. K. Giers, Foreign Minister under Alexander III, struggled to regain the
control of imperial foreign affairs that Gorchakov had lost. The tsar firmly
believed that he alone determined foreign policy, but Giers was shocked to
discover how little attention the Emperor actually paid to international
affairs. Giers, despite his own and others' statements to the contrary, to a
great extent directed Russian foreign policy during his term as Foreign
Minister. By the force of his logical and sensible analysis of events, he
persuaded Alexander to follow a moderate policy of cooperation among the
eastern empires.

Giers' retirement in 1895 marked a turning point for the Foreign Ministry
and Russian diplomacy. A succession of four strong tsars and three able
Foreign Ministers (Nesselrode, Gorchakov and Giers) had dominated Russian
foreign policy for most of the nineteenth century, but the situation
deteriorated rapidly as the incompetent and ill-fated Nicholas II let the whole
administrative apparatus of government gradually distintegrate. Nicholas
clung to the notion of autocratic prerogative to such an extent that he actually
attempted to prevent any discussion of foreign policy by his own Council of
Ministers, but in spite of these pretentions the last Romanov could not
control the course of affairs. Russian diplomacy suffered through seven
changes of Foreign Minister under his reign. Some of the Ministers, like
V. N. Lamzdorff, were docile nonentities. The French ambassador in St
Petersburg, M. Bompard, described Lamzdorff as '. . . a minister of foreign
affairs *à la russe,* which is to say that he does not have control of the foreign
policy but only of the diplomacy of Russia, with the mission of adapting the
latter to the former.'[4] Other Foreign Ministers under Nicholas, such as the
ambitious A. P. Izvolskii, pursued aggressive – even reckless – policies, but
accomplished little. The tsar could not provide strong leadership, and he
would not long tolerate it from others.

The Ministry of Foreign Affairs also had to share its authority with certain other departments of government – most notably the Ministries of War, the Admiralty and Finance. Powerful bureaucrats from outside the Foreign Ministry would on occasion completely usurp the Ministry's diplomatic functions. Thus Sergei Witte took personal command of the negotiations for the Treaty of Portsmouth. The army also frequently initiated actions that entailed serious diplomatic repercussions without first consulting the Foreign Ministry. General M. G. Cherniaev, for example, stormed Tashkent in 1865 against the instructions of the Foreign Ministry and without any sort of authorization from St Petersburg. To make matters worse, the tsars often completely circumvented the Ministry by employing military men and other agents outside the foreign service on important diplomatic missions. These special envoys, such as Prince Menshikov who was sent to Constantinople in 1853, often behaved in a high-handed and uncontrolled way, in this case helping to bring on the Crimean War. Similarly, Admiral E. I. Alekseev's meddling in foreign affairs during the reign of Nicholas II contributed to the onset of the Russo-Japanese War.

The Ministry's own representatives were not always an improvement over the special envoys. All too frequently they worked against each other or failed to carry out their instructions, substituting instead their own policies for those of the government. In one instance A. S. Griboedov, the Russian chargé d'affaires in Persia, conspired with the governor-general of the Caucasus, General A. P. Ermolov, to pursue a policy quite different from that contained in his instructions issued by the Ministry. Griboedov and Ermolov encouraged the Persians to attack the Ottoman Empire. This breach of discipline brought a reprimand from Nesselrode, but he could not go further in disciplining the unruly Griboedov, who enjoyed Ermolov's powerful protection. This kind of unreliability on the part of some of its diplomats plagued the Ministry throughout its existence.

Such diplomatic irresponsibility in the Russian foreign service was minimized in part, however, by the relatively high degree of ideological cohesion among its members. The overwhelming majority of Foreign Ministry officials were entirely loyal to the autocracy and rather conservative in outlook (though certainly not averse to an occasional bribe). There has been much discussion about the supposed impact of pan-Slavism on Russian foreign policy. During the nineteenth century, anti-Russian propagandists, especially in Great Britain, frequently raised the spectre of a Slavic or 'Asiatic' menace to civilization. They accused Russia of attempting to create a great Slavonic empire in eastern Europe at the expense of the Ottoman, Habsburg and Hohenzollern empires. In reality, though, pan-Slavic sentiments did not penetrate deeply within either the upper echelons of the imperial administration or the Ministry of Foreign Affairs. In contrast to the ambitions of the pan-Slavs, Russian diplomats in the Balkans often attempted to dampen revolutionary enthusiasms among the Turkish sultan's Slav subjects, making it clear that support from St Petersburg would not be forthcoming. Even when Alexander II and Gorchakov declared war on the Turks in 1876, pan-Slavic ideology had nothing to do with their decision. They would have preferred to solve the Balkan problem in concert with the other European powers.

It has been suggested that the Asiatic Department of the Foreign Ministry was a hotbed of pan-Slavist sentiment, and that this Department often championed pan-Slavic expansionist goals in contrast to the general policy of the Ministry. This was true only in certain instances. The Department did advocate an aggressively expansionist Balkan policy under the leadership of the notorious pan-Slav, N. P. Ignat'ev, but this was certainly not the case during the subsequent directorships of Stremoukhov and Giers. Within the foreign service generally, only a few diplomats held pan-Slav beliefs. N. Hartwig and A. V. Nekliudov, who were in part responsible for the Balkan war of 1912, are examples, but their actions are evidence of the persistent diplomatic irresponsibility within the corps rather than of any widespread sympathy for the pan-Slav ideology among tsarist officials.

In addition to its problems with independent-minded diplomats, the Imperial Ministry of Foreign Affairs had a reputation for inefficiency and disorganization. It was vastly overstaffed, due both to featherbedding and to the dearth of really competent men in the Russian service. It was not uncommon early in the nineteenth century for the Ministry's rolls to carry many names of persons not really employed. The foreign office thus provided genteel sinecures for a number of Russian literary figures. Pushkin nominally joined the Ministry after graduation from the Tsarskoe Selo Lycée in 1817, but he apparently had no duties. Similarly, the dramatist Griboedov did not receive an actual assignment for more than a year after he took service with the Ministry. Such practices, however, appear to have been eliminated by the end of the century. The Ministry must have become somewhat more efficient, as well, since the size of its staff had decreased slightly between the reigns of Alexander I and Nicholas II, despite the institution's increased workload. Under Alexander I the Ministry employed well over 700 diplomats and officials, while for 1913 the figure was only 689. Yet even in the twentieth century, Ministry officials worked at a leisurely pace and had long respites for tea.

The February revolution of 1917 wrought few structural or personnel changes in the old tsarist Ministry of Foreign Affairs. The Ministry was now responsible to the Provisional Government, of which the Foreign Minister was a prominent member. P. N. Miliukov, of the liberal Kadet party, replaced the last tsarist appointee, Nikolai Pokrovskii, in that position. Of the two Deputy Ministers, Anatoli Neratov remained in office while A. A. Polovtsev retired, to be succeeded by Boris Nol'de, a man with both diplomatic experience and Kadet affiliations. Miliukov carried out a minor reorganization of the Ministry in March to improve its operating efficiency, and Petr Struve, the prominent liberal publicist, became head of the newly created Economic Department. Otherwise, things remained almost unchanged at the Ministry's central offices in Petrograd.

The same was true at Russian embassies abroad. The new Minister published an appeal on 5 March 1917 asking the staff of the imperial diplomatic service to stay at their posts. Most of them responded favourably to this request. Only a handful of intransigent monarchists resigned their positions or were fired by Miliukov. The great majority of tsarist diplomats proved completely willing to serve the Provisional Government. The notorious Izvolskii retained the ambassadorship in Paris until just before the Bolshevik revolution, and the chargé in London, Konstantin Nabokov, enthusiastically welcomed the new regime. The Ministry was severely criticized by left-wing groups for its failure to effect a more thorough housecleaning. Viktor Chernov and his Socialist Revolutionary Party led the attack. They argued that such reactionary tsarist functionaries as Izvolskii, Sazanov, Neratov and Paklevskii-Kozel were completely unsuited to conduct a democratic foreign policy for the new Russian republic.

It is little wonder that many of the former tsarist officials remained to serve under Miliukov, given the way he described his own policy: 'It was carried on in the spirit of traditional union with the Allies, excluding the thought that the Revolution could weaken the international significance of Russia by a sharp change of orientation and by a change of viewpoint in regard to agreements which had been concluded and obligations which had been assumed. . . . In all his declarations the Foreign Minister vigorously emphasized the pacifist aims of the liberating war, but always placed them in close connection with the national problems and interests of Russia.'[5] Since tsarism had been discredited by its bungling of the war effort and by the rumours of treasonable Germanophile tendencies at court, many diplomats actually regarded the Provisional Government as an improvement over its imperial precursor. The new administration would at least prosecute the war vigorously.

Miliukov so strongly and outspokenly opposed the anti-war sentiments of the Petrograd soldiers and workers that his pronouncements on foreign policy brought on a crisis, with huge protest demonstrations filling the streets on 21–22 April. On this account a new cabinet was formed on 5 May with another Kadet, M. I. Tereshchenko, replacing Miliukov as Foreign Minister. However, Tereshchenko effected no major changes in foreign policy or within the Ministry. He continued to follow the same course as his predecessor, which included a refusal to publish the secret treaties revealing the tsarist and Entente war aims. Thus when the Bolsheviks took over the Ministry of Foreign Affairs in October they inherited an institution that was the product of a gradual evolution throughout the nineteenth century, and which the Provisional Government interregnum had done little to change.

Following the Bolshevik seizure of power, the Second All-Russian Congress of Soviets established a new regime for revolutionary Russia, the Council of People's Commissars. Included on the list of departments for the new government was a commission for foreign affairs, which was renamed the People's Commissariat for Foreign Affairs (its Russian acronym, Narkomindel) a few days later. The Bolsheviks did not expect their recently created diplomatic service to shoulder much responsibility, however. On the contrary, they confidently anticipated that the victorious proletarian revolution would soon sweep away the capitalist states, and with them the need for formal (i.e. bourgeois) diplomacy. Lev D. Trotskii accepted the post of Foreign Commissar because that supposedly undemanding job would allow him plenty of time for party work and writing. He told a comrade that as Narkomindel chief he would, 'issue a few revolutionary proclamations to the peoples of the world and then shut up shop.'[6]

The first major task facing Trotskii was the problem of bringing the Foreign Ministry and diplomatic missions of the former Provisional Government under Soviet control. The Bolsheviks hoped that the experienced foreign office officials and diplomats would remain at their posts, but the majority of the staff proved totally unwilling to cooperate with the new regime. Most of these officials, whether veterans of the tsarist diplomatic service or post-February recruits, wished to continue the war against Germany and were thus opposed to Lenin's foreign policy. They therefore readily joined their colleagues in other ministries in proclaiming a general strike of government employees against Soviet power. The Council of People's Commissars then discharged the striking officials without pensions, arrested their leaders and forcibly occupied the Foreign Ministry building. Only about a dozen staff members of the Ministry and a few Russian diplomats serving abroad joined the new Commissariat. Because of the general hostility to the October revolution among foreign governments, the Bolsheviks were not able to take control of Russian embassies around the globe. The overwhelming majority of Russian diplomats stationed abroad opposed the Soviet regime and were therefore also dismissed. The Western governments to which they were accredited, however, continued to honour the credentials of these anti-Bolshevik diplomats, in some cases for many years.

Trotskii delegated responsibility for reopening the foreign office and creating new machinery for the Narkomindel to an assistant, Ivan Zalkind. Zalkind proceeded to set up the new Commissariat on an *ad hoc* basis, salvaging as much of the structure of the old Ministry as possible and creating new organs wherever necessary. Correspondence and general paperwork were handled, as before, by the Chancellery, now renamed a Secretariat. The two major geographic divisions were the Department for Relations with the West and the Department for Relations with the East (the latter a recreation of the old tsarist Asiatic Department). Control over foreign visitors and immigration was placed in the hands of a Visa Department, while a Bureau of Prisoner of War Affairs was created to carry out the double assignment of maintaining contact with Russian prisoners in enemy hands and propagandizing German and Austrian army captives in Russia. The most novel Bolshevik creations were two information agencies, a Press Bureau under Karl Radek and a Bureau of International Revolutionary Propaganda staffed by Boris Reinshtein and two Americans, John Reed and Albert Rhys Williams. Radek's operation was soon transferred to the Soviet Central Executive Committee and Reinshtein's group became the Narkomindel Press Department. The Commissariat also included departments for legal matters, personnel, economic affairs, ciphers, currency exchange, publications, archives and public lectures. Most of these departments must have been very small and several of them probably shared the same personnel. By the end of December 126 people were employed by the Narkomindel, which was, surprisingly, the first commissariat to be fully established. In March 1918 the Foreign Commissariat, along with the rest of the Soviet government, transferred its operations to Moscow, where it occupied the top floors of the old Hotel Metropole, renamed the Second House of Soviets.

Although the recreation of the central foreign office was carried out with dispatch, the Bolsheviks were not initially successful in their attempts to establish Soviet missions abroad. The Narkomindel tried to displace the non-cooperating diplomats of the former Provisional Government by simply appointing in their places Bolsheviks who happened to be abroad or sympathetic foreigners. Thus Maksim Litvinov, who was still in London, was named Soviet representative to Great Britain; while V. V. Vorovskii, in Stockholm at that time, was appointed ambassador to Sweden, Denmark and

Norway; and L. K. Martens, who was then in New York, was accredited to the United States. Similarly, John McLean, a leader of the radical Independent Labour Party, was nominated as Soviet consul at Glasgow and P. Simonov, a former ore miner and union leader, was made consul-general in Australia. These and other would-be Bolshevik representatives were soon arrested and deported by the states to which they were accredited. During its formative period the Narkomindel remained a central organ without the usual diplomatic outposts. The Soviet government had to rely on the foreign diplomatic corps resident in Petrograd and on radio broadcasts in order to make its views known to the outside world.

Except for the publication from tsarist archives of the Entente powers' secret treaties, the Narkomindel had few tasks of real significance during the period of civil war and foreign intervention in Russia. The party Central Committee took direct charge of the crucial Brest-Litovsk peace negotiations, leaving only a minor role for the Foreign Commissariat. The onset of intervention by the Allied powers in 1918 led to the nearly complete isolation of the Bolshevik regime. The foreign diplomatic corps in Russia departed *en masse* in July, while those few European states that had admitted Soviet representatives (Sweden, Denmark, Switzerland) soon expelled them. Even the Germans, perhaps hoping to curry favour with the victorious Allies, broke relations with the Soviet republic and forced Soviet ambassador Adolf Ioffe to leave Berlin. By early 1919 Narkomindel envoys remained only in Persia, Afghanistan and Turkey. In this situation the Bolsheviks were forced to rely on various informal and unofficial channels of communication with other states. The Russian Red Cross, several prisoner of war relief and repatriation organizations, trade missions and the Central Union of Cooperative Societies were each utilized, under the covert direction of the Narkomindel, as vehicles for quasi-diplomatic activity. As a mark of revolutionary egalitarianism, the Foreign Commissariat also abandoned the traditional diplomatic ranks (ambassador, minister, etc.). Heads of the few existing Soviet foreign missions were now simply styled plenipotentiary representatives.

The year 1921 marked a turning point in Soviet foreign relations and, therefore, a change in the status of the Commissariat of Foreign Affairs as well. The Bolshevik victory in the civil war and the collapse of Allied intervention compelled the Western powers to recognize the continued existence of communist Russia. Similarly, the failure of revolutionary movements in western Europe forced upon the Bolsheviks the equally unpleasant realization that, for the immediate future at least, the Soviet republic would have to coexist with the capitalist states. The economic crisis of 1920–1 further necessitated an accommodation with the imperialist powers. Lenin's New Economic Policy required not merely a period of peace but also foreign trade, credits and technical assistance. The efforts of Soviet diplomacy to attain these goals were at least partially successful. Between 1921 and 1924 the USSR secured formal recognition and trade relations with all of the great powers except the United States. The Rapallo treaty of 1922, which forged an alliance of sorts between the Soviet Union and Weimar Germany, was the greatest accomplishment of the Narkomindel in the 1920s.

The formerly sleepy Commissariat of Foreign Affairs found itself the centre of hectic and vitally important activity after 1920. Trotskii, who was always too preoccupied with the most urgent matters of state and party policy to spare much time for the Narkomindel, had left the Commissariat in 1918. His replacement, G. V. Chicherin, was ideally suited to command the Soviet foreign service. Chicherin was a dedicated Bolshevik, well educated and knowledgeable about international affairs, who had once served in the tsarist Foreign Ministry. The new commissar presided over the rapid expansion of the Narkomindel. By 1921 the staff of its central apparatus in Moscow numbered over 1300, and the following year the Commissariat was moved to more comfortable and spacious quarters at the corner of Lubianka Avenue and Kuznetskii Most. A Collegium, which consisted of the Commissar, his deputy and several other top officials, had been created in the foreign office to provide a forum for discussion and collective decision-making. In order to handle the increased workload, the technical departments of the Commissariat (finance, personnel, etc.) were streamlined and combined into a single Chancellery Department, and the Secretariat, having lost most of its managerial functions, was attached directly to the Collegium. The Department of the West was reorganized, with sub-departments for Central Europe, the Anglo-American and Romance countries, and the Baltic and Scandinavian states, while the Department of the East now included sub-divisions for the Near East, Far East and Middle East. The enlarged Collegium included Commissar Chicherin (with special responsibility for overall policy, relations with the East, and public relations), Deputy Commissar Litvinov (with special responsibility for relations with the West), V. P. Menzhinskii (with special responsibility for relations with border states), P. P. Gorbunov, S. S. Piliavskii, Iakov Davtian, Lev Karakhan, Iakov Ganetskii, Viktor Kopp, Fedor Rotshtein and Khristian Rakovskii.

The Narkomindel also began to publish its own journal of international affairs, *Mezhdunarodnaia zhizn*, in addition to occasional reports, monographs and documentary collections. The Press Department also assumed responsibility for censoring the dispatches of foreign correspondents in Russia. With the formation of the USSR in 1923, the Narkomindel became an All-Union Commissariat, and it absorbed the small diplomatic services of the Ukraine and other Soviet republics. In 1926 the Eastern and Western Departments were abolished and their sub-sections were made into separate departments (i.e. Departments for the Anglo-American and Latin states [covering Britain, the USA, France and Italy], Scandinavia, the Baltic States and Poland, Central Europe, the Balkans, the Near East, the Middle East, and the Far East).

Soviet diplomacy was a dangerous profession in the 1920s. Nationalist and anti-Communist groups assassinated three Soviet ambassadors and a number of lesser diplomatic personnel during the decade. The Narkomindel's foreign missions were also frequently the victims of harassment by the police forces of hostile governments.

The Foreign Commissariat gathered its personnel from several distinct sources during the first years of its existence. The handful of officials from the former Ministry who consented to serve the Bolshevik regime was augmented by cadres of party workers who possessed no special competence in diplomatic work, but who were assigned in large numbers by the party Secretariat simply to fill the many vacancies in the Narkomindel. Few of these latter recruits ever achieved high rank in the Commissariat and most of them remained in the foreign service for only a short time. Foreign radicals, like John Reed or the Polish Communist Julian Marchlewski, provided a small but valuable contingent of staff members. The most important component of the Soviet diplomatic service, however, was comprised of Russian radicals who had been forced by tsarist persecution to flee abroad and who now returned to serve the revolution. They were especially suited to diplomatic work as most of them spoke several foreign languages, had acceptable European manners and were familiar with the political and social dynamics of the Western states.

The diplomatic service that emerged under Chicherin's guidance was unique among both Soviet commissariats and European foreign offices. Bolsheviks comprised over half of the organization, but the Narkomindel also included numerous officials who had formerly professed Menshevik, Socialist Revolutionary and even Kadet sympathies. Although representing a workers' state, there was nothing proletarian about this Commissariat. Almost three-quarters of the Soviet diplomats came from middle-class backgrounds, while most of the remainder laboured to conceal their noble lineage. The overwhelming majority of Narkomindel officials had received some instruction at university level. Advanced degrees in medicine, law, engineering and the liberal arts were relatively common among Soviet representatives in the 1920s and 1930s. The Foreign Commissariat drew its personnel from all the major nationality groups of the USSR, but Great Russians accounted for almost half of its employees. Finally, the Narkomindel was an almost entirely male organization. Women held only four per cent of the high and middle level posts in the foreign office.

At first, on-the-job training was the only possible remedy for the lack of experienced diplomats. The more conscientious Narkomindel employees attempted to make up for their deficiencies through reading programmes and conversation with Chicherin and the few remaining veterans from the former Ministry. The Narkomindel also provided a number of scholarships each term for potential foreign service recruits to study in the diplomatic section of the social science faculty at Moscow State University. In addition, the Foreign Commissariat joined forces with the War College to create a special faculty of Oriental languages, which later spawned the Institute for Eastern Studies. By 1925 the majority of Narkomindel representatives in Asia had received some training in this school. Towards the end of the decade a few formal courses on foreign affairs were instituted within the Commissariat, but it was not until the founding of the Institute for Training Diplomatic and Consular Workers in 1935 that the Narkomindel possessed an adequate facility for preparing the diplomatic cadres.

The Commissariat of Foreign Affairs was responsible for carrying out the foreign policy of the Soviet government and for providing that government with detailed reports on the international situation. The constitution divided the task of policy formulation between the Congress of Soviets, which was to determine the overall objectives of Soviet diplomacy, and the Council of Commissars, which framed specific policy directives and provided practical instructions for the Narkomindel. In practice, however, the Central Committee, and subsequently the Politburo, of the party dealt with all major foreign policy questions. The Foreign Commissariat played a significant role, nonetheless. Its leading officials (Chicherin, Litvinov, Sokolnikov,

Karakhan, Krasin, etc.) were part of the regime's small foreign policy-making elite that determined the course of Soviet diplomacy. The Commissariat's crucial function of reporting and interpreting the behaviour of the outside world gave it added influence.

The Narkomindel never had the same significance in Kremlin politics as it had in the realm of foreign policy formulation. Unlike many other state and party organs, the Foreign Commissariat remained relatively detached from the succession struggle of the 1920s. Trotskii's tenure as commissar was very brief, and he failed either to staff the Narkomindel with his supporters or to develop any significant following within the organization. Chicherin was certainly no oppositionist, though he disliked Stalin. The Soviet foreign office, by its very nature as an organ of formal diplomacy, was predisposed to support Stalin's policy of socialism in one country, which implied the stabilization of relations with the Western powers and the diminution of Russian aid for foreign revolutionary activities, which embarrassed and handicapped Soviet diplomacy. While a few prominent political figures (e.g. Rakovskii, Antonov-Ovseenko, Kamenev) apparently received diplomatic posts abroad as a means of eliminating them from domestic struggles, the Narkomindel never became an active centre of oppositional activity as did the *Gosplan* apparatus or the Leningrad party organization.

Soviet commentators have often claimed that the Narkomindel gave birth to a radically new, proletarian form of diplomacy. Such claims are, at the very least, overstatements. Soviet diplomacy in this period did emphasize the public relations value of diplomatic activity in seeking to reach broad audiences and it did effectively utilize the modern communications media. It could scarcely have been otherwise, given the policy of non-recognition and active hostility towards the Bolsheviks initially pursued by the Western powers. Nor were Soviet proclamations of open and honest diplomacy entirely novel. To a great extent they echoed Wilsonian principles. If anything, the Bolsheviks were merely quicker than most of their rivals to perceive the new styles of diplomacy demanded by the age of mass politics and mass communications. Moreover, the Narkomindel soon began to balance its propaganda offensives with more traditional diplomatic initiatives whenever possible. Diplomatic notes, formal negotiations, even secret treaties, increasingly replaced the earlier style of diplomacy by proclamation and denunciation. The necessities of protecting the USSR imposed the usages of bourgeois diplomacy on the Kremlin's representatives.

Soviet diplomatic practice was exceptional in one respect. For the first few years after the revolution Soviet representatives often attempted to assist revolutionary movements in the countries to which they were accredited. Adolf Ioffe once boasted that his embassy in Berlin during 1918 was the 'staff headquarters for a German revolution'.[7] Soviet diplomatic pouches occasionally carried instructions and funds for foreign radicals. By 1921, however, the Kremlin had begun to learn that revolutions could not be provoked by the intrigues of diplomats and that such attempts undermined the relationship between the Soviet representative and the government to which he was accredited. Thereafter the Narkomindel began to dissociate itself from such activities. Chicherin laboured valiantly to deny any connection between his Commissariat and the Comintern.

Chicherin stepped down as Commissar of Foreign Affairs in July 1930, having lost both his health and his former influence in the foreign policy-making process. His successor, Maksim Litvinov, proved to be an equally talented diplomat. The new commissar distinguished himself as the most eloquent advocate of collective security at the League of Nations. Under his leadership the USSR was recognized by several more countries, including the United States, and the size and complexity of the Narkomindel grew apace. The political-geographic divisions of the Commissariat now included the first Western Department (for Scandinavia, the Baltic and Finland), the Second Western Department (for the Balkans, Czechoslovakia, Austria, Germany, Switzerland, Luxembourg and the Low Countries), the Third Western Department (for France, Italy, Great Britain, the Commonwealth and the Americas), the First Eastern Department (for the Near and Middle East), and the Second Eastern Department (for Mongolia, Tannu Tuva and the Far East). A Department of International Problems was formed in the early 1930s to deal with international diplomatic conferences and a Service for League of Nations Affairs was attached to the Narkomindel Secretariat after the Soviet Union joined the League in 1934.

Chicherin, and subsequently Litvinov, created an efficient foreign office and recruited a capable corps of diplomats who were in every sense a match for their bourgeois counterparts. Their work was almost completely undone, however, by the great purges of the late 1930s. Almost two-thirds of the Soviet ambassadors and high level Narkomindel officials were purged. The list of victims included deputy commissars Nikolai Krestinskii and G. Ia. Sokolnikov and such prestigious diplomats as Lev Karakhan and M. I. Rozenberg. Despite the grim rumours that circulated about the fate of their colleagues, most Soviet representatives abroad obeyed their recall orders and went voluntarily to their doom, although the NKVD may well have kidnapped a few of them from their embassies. Even the handful of survivors (e.g. Litvinov, V. P. Potemkin, Aleksandra Kollontai, Ivan Maiskii) lost their influence and suffered demotions. The Soviet consulates were another victim of the purges. A Consular Section had been organized in the Narkomindel Economic and Legal Department in the early 1920s and it had subsequently evolved into a Consular Branch and then a Consular Department. The consulates had, upon occasion, been important in Soviet diplomacy, especially in countries that did not yet recognize the USSR *de jure* or that had broken formal diplomatic relations with Moscow. In spite of their usefulness, the Soviet consulates abroad were abolished and foreign consulates in the USSR were closed during the period of the great purges.

Stalin's lieutenant, V. M. Molotov, replaced Litvinov as Commissar in May 1939. This radical displacement of personnel, combined with the atmosphere of terror, severely crippled the functioning of the Narkomindel. The Commissariat was flooded with inexperienced recruits (e.g. Andrei Gromyko, Valerian Zorin, Iakov Malik). The profile of this second generation differs markedly from the old diplomatic corps of the Chicherin and Litvinov years. These new men often came from lower-class back-grounds and many of them either had no post-secondary education or had attended technical institutes. Few of them had been abroad or knew any foreign languages. Perhaps more importantly, the two groups of diplomats differed in their formative experiences. Many of the purge victims had belonged to the revolutionary intelligentsia in tsarist times. The typical member of the new diplomatic generation, however, had been only twelve years old in 1917. These men had reached maturity while Stalin was besting his rivals for Lenin's mantle. Such changes in personnel created problems for Soviet diplomacy. Foreign diplomats noted that the new Soviet representatives were often unfamiliar with foreign affairs, rigid and lacking in initiative. There is no evidence to indicate that the purge of the Foreign Commissariat was related to changes in Soviet foreign policy.

The demands of global war and then of the Cold War strained the capacities of the ravaged Commissariat to their limit. Molotov (aided by a small band of survivors from the Litvinov years) laboured with considerable success to train his corps of neophyte diplomats and to exclude the cadre of secret police officials who had assumed important positions in the Narkomindel during the purges. It was also in these years that the Commissariat was renamed the Ministry of Foreign Affairs and that formal diplomatic ranks and uniforms were reintroduced. Although the purges had been curtailed in 1939, Kremlin power struggles continued to disrupt the rebuilding of the foreign service. In March 1949 Molotov was forced to relinquish the Foreign Ministry to Andrei Vyshenskii, and at the same time Molotov's wife was arrested and exiled from Moscow. Stalin may have been preparing a new purge of his own no longer trusted élite, since Nikolai Bulganin lost the Defence Ministry and Anastas Mikoian forfeited the Foreign Trade Ministry simultaneously. At a Central Committee plenum in 1952 Stalin directly attacked Molotov and Mikoian, but the prospective purge was abruptly cancelled when the ageing dictator died the following year.

Although Molotov immediately reclaimed the Ministry of Foreign Affairs, he soon ran afoul of the political ambitions of Nikita Khrushchev. By engaging in personal summit diplomacy (e.g. his state visits to China, India, Burma, Yugoslavia, England and Afghanistan), and by flooding the Foreign Ministry with men from the party apparatus, which he controlled, Khrushchev gradually squeezed Molotov out of Soviet foreign affairs. The cautious, conservative Molotov, who wanted to make no concessions and take no risks in the diplomatic arena, strongly opposed Khrushchev's peaceful coexistence campaign, as well as his reckless attempts to expand Soviet influence abroad. Khrushchev accused Molotov of using the diplomatic service to subvert the party's policies in favour of his own. In June 1956 Molotov was ousted from the Politburo (Praesidium) and forced to resign as Foreign Minister. Dmitrii Shepilov, formerly a Central Committee Secretary, temporarily took charge of the Ministry until February 1957, when the post was entrusted to a professional diplomat, Andrei Gromyko.

The function of the Foreign Minister, and of the Ministry generally, in making and implementing Soviet foreign policy varied greatly during these politically tumultuous years. Stalin dominated both the formulation and the execution of policy. Inexperienced Soviet diplomats, operating in a paralyzing climate of fear, tended to carry out their instructions mechanically and to refer even the most minor matters back to Moscow. After Stalin's death Molotov, now a key figure in the new collective leadership, exercised a powerful influence over policy, both domestic and foreign, until his defeat by Khrushchev. The role of Foreign Minister Gromyko and his professional diplomats was inferior not only to that played by the flamboyant personal diplomacy of Khrushchev, but also to that of the powerful party figures who were brought into the central Ministry apparatus and into the Soviet embassies in Communist countries. The appointment of N. S. Patolichev, party First Secretary in Belorussia, as Deputy Foreign Minister in 1955 is a good example. Khrushchev also weakened the integrity of the Ministry by using it as a place of exile for his defeated opponents (e.g. the nomination of I. F. Tevosian, deputy chairman of the Council of Ministers and a Malenkov ally, as ambassador to Japan in 1956). Khrushchev made the subservient position of the Foreign Minister brutally clear when he told Averell Harriman that 'Gromyko only says what we tell him to. At the next Geneva meeting he will repeat what he has already told you. If he doesn't we'll fire him and get someone who does.'[8]

Khrushchev's tenure in power was not, however, entirely negative for the Foreign Ministry. The stultifying, fearful Stalinist environment gave way to a more open situation in which Soviet diplomats were relatively free to engage foreign colleagues in meaningful discussion, to attend or sponsor diplomatic social events, and to explore the realities of life abroad – in short, to function as professional diplomats. The training of foreign service personnel was also markedly improved. The Institute of International Relations (frequently referred to by its Russian initials, IMO) was created under the Ministry's jurisdiction as the primary institution for educating prospective diplomats. Now, as then, secondary school graduates who survive the rigorous selection process are admitted to a demanding five-year curriculum in history, international law, economics, Marxism–Leninism, foreign languages and foreign area studies. From the very beginning the students are required to specialize in a particular geographic area. A sixth year is taken up with a six-week internship at the Ministry, six months of field training at an embassy abroad and, finally, the preparation of a thesis. Candidates are then reassigned as probationers to an embassy where, after an apprenticeship of one or two years, about half of them are accepted into the diplomatic corps as attachés. The Higher Diplomatic School, also run under Foreign Ministry auspices, has been reorganized as an international affairs graduate programme to which experienced diplomats return for advanced training and further specialization. The Khrushchev years also witnessed the founding of several important new institutions, and the up-grading of some older ones, for the study of world affairs. The Institute for World Economy and International Relations, the Institute for the Study of the USA and the Institute of Oriental Studies are especially significant in this regard.

Like Stalin and Khrushchev before him, Leonid Brezhnev established direct control of foreign policy and diplomacy when he consolidated his position as leader of the Soviet political system in the early 1970s. He sought to implement a policy of détente with the West in meetings with President Pompidou of France, Chancellor Brandt of West Germany, and American Presidents Nixon and Ford. He also personally negotiated and signed a number of important international agreements, even though he was not until recently formally an official of the Soviet government. Brezhnev's ascendency in foreign affairs has not, however, meant the eclipse of the Foreign Ministry. Far from treating the Foreign Minister as a glorified errand boy as Khrushchev did, Brezhnev has taken Gromyko to all his summit meetings and apparently relies on his Minister as an indispensable aide in dealing with Western leaders. Gromyko's influence is symbolized by his elevation to the ruling Politburo in 1973. Since that time the Soviet Foreign Minister has exhibited much more latitude and initiative in negotiating with foreign powers. Most importantly, the Foreign Minister serves on the Politburo Foreign Policy Commission and on the USSR Defence Council. Gromyko has firmly established his position in the Soviet foreign policy-making élite, which in 1979 also included Brezhnev, Premier Alexei Kosygin (recently deceased), Mikhail Suslov and Andrei Kirilenko (two powerful party officials), Dmitrii Ustinov (the Defence Minister) and KGB chief Iurii Andropov. Besides Gromyko, twenty-three other senior Soviet diplomats sit on either the party Central Committee or the Central Auditing Commission. The most important diplomatic posts, such as the ambassadorship in Washington, seem to carry virtually *ex-officio* Central Committee membership. Thus although the Foreign Ministry certainly does not dominate the formulation of Soviet foreign policy, or even hold a monopoly of world affairs information and expertise, its influence in that process has never been greater.

Since the Second World War the Ministry of Foreign Affairs has grown enormously in both organizational complexity and numbers of personnel. Three factors account for this growth: the emergence of the USSR as one of the two global super-powers, the rapidly expanding number of newly sovereign Third World countries, and the active diplomatic campaigns (pursued by both Khrushchev and Brezhnev) to achieve peaceful coexistence with the West while at the same time extending the world wide influence of the Soviet Union.

As Foreign Minister, Andrei Gromyko participates in policy formulation in the Politburo, conducts high level diplomatic negotiations and supervises the functioning of his Ministry. He also signs certain types of diplomatic agreements, issues credentials and letters of recall for his diplomats, and certifies the competence of special envoys. Gromyko is assisted by two first deputies – Georgii Kornienko, a professional diplomat and arms control expert, and Viktor Mal'tsev, a veteran party official turned diplomat, and by seven more deputy ministers.[9] In addition, a general secretary is in charge of administrative operations for the Ministry. The Ministry Collegium, comprised of the above officials plus nine of the more important department heads, meets several times each week to advise Gromyko on foreign policy and administrative matters. Almost all these men are experienced diplomats who have entered the Collegium since Khrushchev's fall.

Under the Collegium, the Ministry is organized into seventeen geographic departments, nine functional departments, eight administrations and three schools. The geographic departments consist of: the First African Department (for northern Africa excluding Egypt), the Second African Department (sub-Saharan west coastal countries), the Third African Department (eastern and southern African countries), the First European Department (Benelux, France, Portugal, Italy, Spain and Switzerland), the Second European Department (Australia, Canada, Ireland, Malta, New Zealand, United Kingdom), the Third European Department (Austria and Germany), the Fourth European Department (Czechoslovakia and Poland), the Fifth European Department (Bulgaria, Cyprus, Greece, Hungary, Rumania and Yugoslavia), the First Far Eastern Department (China, Korea and Mongolia), the Second Far Eastern Department (Indonesia, Japan and the Philippines), the Latin

American Countries Department, the Middle Eastern Countries Department, the Near Eastern Countries Department (Egypt, Iraq, Israel, Jordan, Kuwait, Lebanon, Syria, Yemen and the Sudan), the Scandinavian Countries Department (Denmark, Finland, Iceland, Norway and Sweden), the South Asian Department (Bangladesh, Burma, India, Nepal, Pakistan and Sri Lanka), the South-east Asian Department (Kampuchea, Laos, Malaysia, Singapore, Thailand and Vietnam), and the United States of America Department.

The functional departments comprise the Department for Cultural Relations with Foreign Countries, the Information Department (for cryptography and communication between the Ministry and its missions abroad), the International Economic Organizations Department, the International Organizations Department (for the UN, etc.), the Press Department (which also monitors the foreign press and accredits foreign journalists in the USSR), the Protocol Department, the Treaty and Legal Department, the Bureau of Translations, and the Tenth Department (for gathering foreign political, economic and military intelligence). This last department is operated jointly by the Ministry and the KGB.

The Ministry also houses the Administration of Affairs (for general management), the Archives Administration (which provides research services and publishes the *Dokumenty vneshnei politiki SSSR* series), the Consular Administration, the Currency and Finance Administration (which is responsible for the Ministry budget), the Administration for Foreign Policy Planning, the Administration for General International Problems, the Personnel Administration (which works closely with the party Secretariat's cadres department), and the Administration for Servicing the Diplomatic Corps (for provisioning the foreign diplomatic and consular missions in the USSR). The Ministry operates three schools: the Higher Courses of Foreign Languages, the Diplomatic Academy (or Higher Diplomatic School), and the Moscow State Institute of International Relations (IMO). Since the early 1950s the Ministry has been housed in a 26-storey skyscraper on Smolenskaia Square in Moscow which it shares with the Ministry of Foreign Trade.

Since its origin in 1917, the Soviet Foreign Ministry has undergone numerous reorganizations. Some of these reforms stemmed from the changing position of the USSR in world affairs (e.g. the creation of a service for League of Nations Affairs after the USSR joined that body in 1934), while other reorganizations reflected changing global realities (e.g. the proliferation of departments concerned with Asia and Africa after the Second World War). On a few occasions, such as the abolition of the Collegium in 1934, structural changes within the Ministry occurred as part of broader reorganizations throughout the government apparatus. Organizational reshuffling has been noticeably less frequent and less sweeping during the Brezhnev years. It is not clear whether such bureaucratic remodelling has, on balance, hindered or aided the execution of Soviet foreign policy, since Soviet diplomats do not publicly criticize their Ministry.

The Soviet regime, unlike some Western governments, does not operate its central Foreign Ministry apparatus, its diplomatic missions abroad and its consulates as three separate services. Thus there is no practical distinction between the Ministry and the diplomatic service. On the contrary, Soviet diplomatic officers specialize in a particular country or geographic region and their careers show a pattern of assignments alternating between diplomatic appointments to the country or area of their expertise and service in Moscow in the corresponding Ministry desk or department. The same is true for Soviet consular representatives. Except for a brief period during the great purges, the USSR has maintained a network of consulates and consulates-general around the globe. These consular operations are an integral part of the Ministry of Foreign Affairs. Soviet consuls-general, consuls and vice-consuls are always experienced diplomats, though their staffs at the consulates are usually specialized in consular work. The consulates share responsibility for facilitating foreign commerce with the Ministry of Foreign Trade, which also maintains a world-wide system of trade representatives. Furthermore, in countries with communist regimes that are allied to the USSR, economic relations are regulated, in part, by direct contact between the communist parties and various economic ministries of the respective governments.

The USSR constitution was amended in February 1944 to permit each of the Soviet Union's sixteen constituent republics to establish its own foreign office. These republican foreign ministries operate under the close supervision of the Soviet Foreign Ministry and only a few of them have even a small diplomatic corps. The Belorussian and Ukrainian republics were admitted as charter members of the United Nations in 1945, but since that time Moscow has been unsuccessful in its attempts to seat any of its republics on other international bodies. Soviet UN delegations, however, typically include a representative of the Uzbek republic's foreign office. Such republican diplomacy may be marginally useful in propitiating nationalist sentiment within the minority republics and in impressing the peoples of Asia and Africa with the ethnic equality that supposedly pervades the Soviet system. Despite the policy of recruiting diplomats from among the ethnic minorities of the USSR, especially for sensitive UN and Third World posts, the overwhelming majority of Soviet Foreign Ministry and embassy personnel are males of Great Russian nationality.

In addition to the greatly expanded central Ministry institutions in Moscow, the Soviet Union now has 113 diplomatic missions abroad (a twofold increase since 1960) as well as a revived network of consulates. Its embassies are staffed, for the most part, by talented and thoroughly knowledgeable professional diplomats, virtually all of whom are members of the Communist Party. Two generations are discernible within the Soviet foreign service: a second (or post-purge) generation, which was recruited in the 1937–47 rebuilding period and which, through long experience, has overcome its initial handicaps of foreign affairs ignorance and fear-induced rigidity, and a third generation of younger men who entered the Ministry since the mid-1950s and who have benefited from the rigorous training programmes of the IMO and the Diplomatic Academy. Besides their background in international relations and diplomacy, many of these younger diplomats posted to Third World countries have additional technical training in such subjects as agronomy or hydraulic engineering. Moreover, the relative disinclination of Brezhnev to use the Foreign Ministry as a place of exile for opponents has also facilitated this trend toward greater professionalization. The stability of the Foreign Ministry in the last two decades has become both a strength and a weakness for the USSR. On the positive side, Soviet Russia's representatives are among the most experienced diplomats in the world. But on the negative side, the continual domination of the most desirable embassies and Ministry offices by the Gromyko generation must be highly frustrating to the no-longer-young third generation in the diplomatic corps. Soviet law specifies a minimum retirement age (sixty) at which an able-bodied male government employee may retire at full pension, but the code does not designate any age at which retirement is mandatory. Given the rather low pensions available to them, Soviet diplomats tend to hold their appointments as long as they can. Some senior diplomats have been rewarded with semi-retirement at full pay as 'consultants' within the Foreign Ministry.

Gromyko's professional diplomats do not control one set of embassies, however – those in other communist countries. There the Soviet ambassador is normally a senior official from the party apparatus who functions as the representative of the Soviet Communist Party to the local ruling party. Such party-state 'diplomats' are usually Central Committee members who, especially in countries where Soviet troops are stationed, assume the right to meddle in local party politics. The enunciation of the Brezhnev Doctrine (i.e. the limited sovereignty of satellite states) has given this practice ideological justification. In dealing with other communist states, whether in the Soviet bloc or not, the Foreign Ministry shares responsibility with the party Secretariat's Department of Relations with Communist and Workers' Parties of the Socialist Countries.

The embassies of the USSR frequently have the largest foreign mission staff in the country to which they are accredited. This has given rise to speculation that the Soviet missions house large numbers of KGB officials, some of whom enjoy immunity as diplomats. Estimates of the percentage of intelligence agents in the Soviet missions range from 40 to 45 per cent in certain Western countries up to 75 per cent in some Third World countries. One of the functions of these KGB officials is to monitor the performance and loyalty of the embassy staff. Another objective is to gather intelligence. Recently, for example, members of the Soviet embassy in Mexico City were implicated in an attempt to procure sensitive technical data from a defence contractor, the TRW Corporation, in southern California. Sometimes these KGB diplomats are active in the political life of the country to which they are assigned. This was apparently the case when S. M. Kudriavtsev (who had previously operated an atomic spy ring in Ottawa) was appointed ambassador to Cuba in 1960, the year of Castro's consolidation of power. Normally, however, the KGB and military intelligence (GRU) officials occupy less conspicuous posts as third secretaries or attachés. Political policemen have not held top posts at the Foreign Ministry in Moscow since the late 1940s.

In summary, the contemporary Soviet Ministry of Foreign Affairs is a sophisticated and thoroughly professional organization capable of meeting the increased demands that Brezhnev's active foreign policy places upon it. Its diplomats are well trained and highly competent, though still very cautious in negotiation. The leading officials of the Ministry play a significant role in the formulation of Soviet foreign policy.

I wish gratefully to acknowledge the help in completing this chapter which I have received from Igor N. Belousovitch, Valentin M. Berezhkov, Peter B. Brown, John Paton Davies, Ben Fischer, Jerry F. Hough, Barbara Jelavich, Ann Kleimola, Morton Schwartz, and J. Owen Zurhellen.

NOTES

[1] *Sbornik imperatorskago russkogo istoricheskago obshchestva,* vol. L (1888), 304.

[2] Karl Marx and Freidrich Engels, *Werke* (Berlin 1972), vol. XXII, 14.

[3] Quoted in Patricia Kennedy Grimsted, *The Foreign Ministers of Alexander I: Political Attitudes and the Conduct of Diplomacy 1801–1825* (Berkeley and Los Angeles 1969), 18.

[4] Quoted in G. H. Bolsover, 'Aspects of Russian Foreign Policy, 1815–1914', in Richard Pares and A. J. P. Taylor (eds), *Essays Presented to Sir Lewis Namier* (London 1956), 325.

[5] P. N. Miliukov, *Istoriia vtoroi russkoi revoliutsii* (Sofia 1921), vol. I, 84.

[6] Leon Trotsky, *My Life* (New York 1960), 341.

[7] Louis Fischer, *Men and Politics: An Autobiography* (New York 1966), 26.

[8] W. Averell Harriman, 'My Alarming Interview with Khrushchev', *Life,* vol. XLVII, no. 2 (13 July 1959), 33.

[9] For information on the current holders of these and other high level Ministry posts see *Directory of USSR Ministry of Foreign Affairs Officials,* published frequently by the US Central Intelligence Agency and available to non-government users through the Document Expediting (DOCEX) Project at the Library of Congress.

BIBLIOGRAPHY

Viacheslav P. Artem'ev, *Selection and Training of Soviet Personnel for Trade Missions Abroad and the Soviet Trade Mission in Iran* (New York 1954).

Vernon Aspaturian, *Process and Power in Soviet Foreign Policy* (Boston 1971).

A. S. Bakhov, *Na zare sovetskoi diplomatii* (Moscow 1966).

A. S. Belokurov, *O posol'skom prikaze* (Moscow 1906).

Avis Bohlen, 'Changes in Russian Diplomacy under Peter the Great', *Cahiers du Monde Russe et Sovietique,* vol. VII, no. 3 (July–September 1966), 341–58.

G. H. Bolsover, 'Aspects of Russian Foreign Policy, 1815–1914', in Richard Pares and A. J. P. Taylor (eds), *Essays Presented to Sir Lewis Namier* (London 1956).

Peter B. Brown, 'Early Modern Russian Bureaucracy: The Evolution of the Chancellery System from Ivan III to Peter the Great, 1478–1717' (Ph.D. dissertation, University of Chicago 1978).

Edward L. Crowley, *The Soviet Diplomatic Corps, 1917–1967* (Metuchen, N.J. 1970).

Richard K. Debo, 'Litvinov and Kamenev – Ambassadors Extraordinary: The Problem of Soviet Representation Abroad', *Slavic Review,* vol. 34, no. 3 (September 1975), 463–82.

Raymond Dennett and Joseph E. Johnson (eds), *Negotiating with the Russians* (Boston 1951).

L. Fedorov, *Diplomat i konsul* (Moscow 1965).

M. F. Florinskii, 'Soviet ministrov i Ministerstvo inostrannykh del v 1907–1914gg.', *Vestnik Leningradskogo Universiteta: istoriia, iazyk, literatura,* 1978, no. 2, 35–9.

Sunray Gardiner, 'Old Russian Diplomatic Vocabulary: A Study Based on the Documents of the Posol'skiy Prikaz Relation to the Holy Roman Empire, 1488–1699' (Ph.D. dissertation, University of London 1965).

E. N. Gorodetskii, *Rozhdenie sovetskogo gosudarstvo, 1917–1918gg.* (Moscow 1965).

Patricia K. Grimsted, *The Foreign Ministers of Alexander I: Political Attitudes and the Conduct of Diplomacy, 1801–1825* (Berkeley and Los Angeles 1969).

Andrei A. Gromyko *et al.* (eds), *Diplomaticheskii slovar*, 3 vols (Moscow 1971–3).

Constantin de Grunwald, *Trois Siècles de Diplomatie russe* (Paris 1945).

M. P. Iroshnikov, 'Iz istorii organizatsii narodnogo komissariata inostrannykh del', *Istoriia SSSR,* 1964, no. 1, 105–16.

——, *Sozdanie sovetskogo narodnykh komissarov i narodnye komissariaty oktiabr 1917g–ianvar 1918g* (Leningrad 1967).

Barbara Jelavich, *St Petersburg and Moscow: Tsarist and Soviet Foreign Policy* (Bloomington, Indiana 1974).

Aleksandr Kaznacheev, *Inside a Soviet Embassy: Experiences of a Russian Diplomat in Burma* (Philadelphia and New York 1962).

Eugene L. Magerovsky, 'The People's Commissariat for Foreign Affairs, 1917–1946' (Ph.D. dissertation, Columbia University 1975).

—— (ed.), 'Organization and Administration of Soviet Foreign Relations', in Thomas Hammond (ed.), *Soviet Foreign Relations and World Communism* (Princeton, N.J. 1965).

Boris Meissner, 'The Foreign Ministry and Foreign Service of the USSR', *Aussenpolitik,* vol. 28, no. 1 (1977), 49–64.

——, 'Die zaristische Diplomatie: A. Die Gesandtschafts-Prikas (Posol'skij Prikaz)', *Jahrbücher für Geschichte Osteuropas,* vol. IV, no. 3 (1956), 237–45.

Drew Middleton, 'The New Soviet Man – In Diplomacy', *The New York Times Magazine,* 7 December 1958, 23, 107.

P. N. Miliukov, *Istoriia vtoroi russkoi revoliutsii* (Sofia 1921).

Ocherk istorii ministerstva inostrannykh del (St Petersburg, n.p., 1902).

Vladimir Petrov, 'The Formulation of Soviet Foreign Policy', *Orbis,* vol. 27 (Fall 1973), 819–50.

—— and Evdokia Petrov, *Empire of Fear* (New York 1956).

V. A. Polenov, 'Obozrenie prezhniago i nyneshniago sostoianiia ministerstva inostrannykh del', *Sbornik imperatorskago russkogo istoricheskago obshchestva* (St Petersburg 1867–1917), vol. XXXI, 163–96.

Herman Pörzgen, 'Im Hochhaus am Smolensker Platz', 'Die sowjetische Diplomatie und der Kreml', and 'Moskaus Diplomaten', *Frankfurter Allgemeine Zeitung,* 15, 16 and 17 January 1969.

Galen B. Ritchie, 'The Asiatic Department during the Reign of Alexander II: 1855–1881' (Ph.D. dissertation, Columbia University 1970).

V. I. Savva, *O posol'skom prikaze v XVIv* (Khar'kov, n.p., 1917).

Hans Schawohl, 'Die Geschichte beginnt mit Cromwell', *Christ und Welt,* 9 March 1962.

Morton Schwartz, *The Foreign Policy of the USSR: Domestic Factors* (Encino, Calif. 1975).

Robert M. Slusser, 'The Role of the Foreign Ministry', in Ivo Lederer (ed.), *Russian Foreign Policy* (New Haven 1962), 197–239.

Jan F. Triska and David D. Finley, *Soviet Foreign Policy* (New York 1968).

Robert C. Tucker, 'Ruling Personalities in Russian Foreign Policy', in Tucker, *The Soviet Political Mind* (New York 1963).

Teddy J. Uldricks, *Diplomacy and Ideology: The Origins of Soviet Foreign Relations, 1917–1930* (London and Beverly Hills 1979).

US Central Intelligence Agency, *Directory of USSR Ministry of Foreign Affairs Officials* (Washington 1978).

US House of Representatives, Committee on Foreign Affairs, *Soviet Diplomacy and Negotiating Behavior* (Washington 1979).

Theodore Von Laue, 'G. V. Chicherin, People's Commissar for Foreign Affairs, 1918–1930', and Henry L. Roberts, 'Maxim Litvinov', in Gordon A. Craig and Felix Gilbert (eds), *The Diplomats, 1919–1939* (Princeton, N.J. 1953).

Rex A. Wade, *The Russian Search for Peace, February–October 1917* (Stanford, Calif. 1969).

Valerian A. Zorin, *Osnovy diplomaticheskoi sluzhby* (Moscow 1964).

——, et al. (eds), *Istoriia diplomatii* (Moscow 1959).

UNION OF SOVIET SOCIALIST REPUBLICS – APPENDIX A

THE SOVIET MINISTRY OF FOREIGN AFFAIRS

COLLEGIUM

Minister

Two First Deputy Ministers

Seven Deputy Ministers

Secretary-General

Nine other Collegium members

GEOGRAPHIC DEPARTMENTS	OTHER DEPARTMENTS	ADMINISTRATIONS	SCHOOLS
First African	Department for Cultural Relations with Foreign Countries	Administration of Affairs	Higher Courses of Foreign Languages
Second African	Information Department	Archives Administration	Diplomatic Academy
Third African	International Economic Organizations Department	Consular Administration	Moscow State Institute of International Relations (MGIMO)
First European	International Organizations Department	Currency and Finance	
Second European	Press Department	Administration for Foreign Policy Planning	
Third European	Protocol Department	Administration for General International Problems	
Fourth European	Tenth Department (Covert Intelligence)	Personnel Administration	
Fifth European	Treaty and Legal Department	Administration for Servicing the Diplomatic Corps	
First Far Eastern	Bureau of Translations		
Second Far Eastern			
Latin American Countries			
Middle Eastern Countries			
Near Eastern Countries			
Scandinavian Countries			
South Asian			
Southeast Asian			
United States of America			

United Kingdom

The Foreign
and Commonwealth Office

VALERIE CROMWELL

Valerie Cromwell is Reader in History at the University of Sussex.
She was educated at the University of London. She taught at Bedford
College, London, 1960–1, and at Newnham College, Cambridge
University, where she was Fellow and Director of Studies in Modern
History from 1961 to 1964. She has published several articles on the
British Foreign Office; a study of the diplomatic service in
V. Cromwell, B. Keith-Lucas, C. O'Leary and K. C. Wheare, *Aspects
of Government in Nineteenth Century Britain* (1978) and *Revolution or
Evolution: British Government in the Nineteenth Century* (1977).

The British Foreign and Commonwealth Office is the office of Her Majesty's Secretary of State for Foreign and Commonwealth Affairs, who is responsible for Britain's relations with all other countries. It has existed in its present form only since 1968, when the Commonwealth Office was merged with the Foreign Office. The history of the Foreign Office begins in March 1782, when Charles James Fox was appointed Secretary of State 'with the sole Direction of the Department of Foreign Affairs'. Before then, no single department of state was wholly responsible for the administration of British foreign policy.

The conduct of foreign policy before 1782

Foreign policy lay – and lies – within the prerogative of the Crown. In constitutional theory neither House of Parliament in the eighteenth century had any share in either the formulation or the execution of foreign policy. It was generally agreed that the making of treaties, the declaration of war and the signing of peace treaties were royal prerogatives. Any treaty requiring new legislation, alteration in customs and excise duties or subsidy for a foreign state required parliamentary approval and might provoke debate. Probably a more important opportunity for parliamentary involvement in foreign policy lay in the growing practice of presenting to Parliament selected and edited extracts from official correspondence with diplomats abroad and foreign representatives in London, which often created an opportunity for major debates on foreign policy. Despite these occasional opportunities for parliamentary discussion, which tended to be retrospective in character, and the legislative and financial sanctions that Parliament could impose, the formulation and day-to-day administration of foreign policy in practice remained within royal prerogative and, until Anne's reign, were largely controlled by the sovereign. Although the Hanoverian kings were all keenly interested in the making of foreign policy, that policy became, as did all others, progressively the responsibility of ministers answerable to Parliament. In particular, it was the responsibility of the Secretaries of State.

The post of King's Secretary had emerged in the medieval period and acquired considerable significance and influence under the Tudor monarchs. After 1540 it was customary for the post and the work to be shared by two people, although the office has been and remains a single unit, however many Secretaries of State might be appointed at one time. Any Secretary can perform the duties of his colleagues. Throughout the centuries the allocation of work has reflected contemporary administrative convenience and can be easily adjusted. From 1640 it is possible to distinguish a rough geographical division in the foreign work of the Secretaries; after 1689 these divisions became known as the Northern and Southern Departments or Provinces and lasted until 1782. The Northern Secretary corresponded with British representatives in Holland, Scandinavia, Poland, Russia and what was known as the Empire; the Southern Secretary was responsible for France, Italy, the Iberian Peninsula, Switzerland, Turkey, and also Ireland, the Channel Islands and most of the colonies. Both dealt randomly with home affairs, except that the Northern Secretary usually handled Scottish business. The distinction between the two departments was not sharp and the distribution of work by country varied with special circumstances. A third Secretaryship of State was established in 1768 with responsibility for the colonies, but that office was abolished in 1782.

In the years before 1782 the making of foreign policy decisions was achieved by discussions between the sovereign and his most influential advisers. Those decisions were only rarely disapproved by a parliamentary majority. A number of proposals for radical change in the method of conducting foreign affairs were occasionally made. The favourite idea appears to have been that of setting up an *ad hoc* council of professional diplomats with at least seven years' service abroad to advise the king. In practice, foreign affairs remained the formal concern of the Privy Council and less formally of the various forms taken by the eighteenth-century Cabinet. These bodies took decisions and made recommendations to the king. Once these decisions were accepted, it was the job of the Secretaries to send the requisite instructions to diplomats abroad. All British diplomats were instructed to follow the orders sent them by the Secretaries and to correspond regularly with them. The Secretaries could also communicate in London with the representatives of foreign governments there, but were often handicapped in such negotiations since they could rarely speak or even understand any foreign language except French. In addition, foreign diplomats in London were often poorly equipped to converse in English. The Secretaries of State therefore tended to prefer to negotiate through British representatives abroad.

By the eighteenth century, the two Secretaries were coming to be accepted as the only proper means of communication between the government and its overseas representatives. Only very occasionally were they bypassed by the king or by a particularly influential minister such as the Duke of Newcastle. The importance of the Secretaries in the determination of foreign policy often placed one of them in a dominating position in his Cabinet.

The creation of the Foreign Office, March 1782

The difficulties caused by the geographical division of ministerial responsibility between the two Secretaries became more obvious and more significant as effective royal direction of foreign policy declined. Personal friction could lead to one Secretary attempting to press his ideas and schemes at the expense of the other. Rivalry between them was not uncommon, and occasionally representatives of both Secretaries and their views were accredited to foreign courts. Serious conflict in a particular issue between the Secretaries could always be resolved by a decision of the king or his chief minister, but persistent personal tension was not so easily smoothed away. Multiplicity of duties diverted the Secretaries from single-minded concentration on foreign affairs. The offices of the Secretaries also had to share responsibility for foreign communications with other departments: the Board of Trade had to be consulted on commercial treaties and dealings with consuls; the joint postmaster-generals controlled the interception of letters of foreign ministers to and from their representatives in London.

As early as 1771 George III had seriously considered a reorganization of the work of the Secretaries, very similar to the arrangement eventually made in 1782. He again suggested it in 1781, so may have been influential in the introduction of the new scheme. Little evidence survives of the creation of the Secretaryship of State for Foreign Affairs or of the founding of a separate Foreign Office. The only official records appear to be the circular letters issued by Charles James Fox to foreign envoys in London and British representatives abroad, which announced his appointment with sole responsibility for foreign affairs. Although the division of authority for foreign affairs had proved a source of friction over a long period, the strong personalities of Fox and Shelburne and their obvious mutual suspicion and jealousy must have looked singularly unpromising for shared responsibility in foreign affairs in 1782. Against this background of probable ministerial animosity and royal pressure for reform the rearrangement of business may have resulted directly from the abolition of the Secretaryship of State for the American Colonies when Rockingham's ministry took office in March 1782. It must also be remembered that a group of the new ministers, including Shelburne, had already shown themselves concerned to reform both the finances and the administration of government offices.

Although little is known of the background to, and little contemporary comment was apparently evoked by, the reorganization, described by D. B. Horn as 'much the most important administrative change in the sphere of foreign policy during the eighteenth century', the effects of the change were rapidly seen. The new Home Office under its new Home Secretary relinquished responsibility for foreign affairs, except for business relating to Algiers, Morocco, Tripoli and Tunis, where it supervised consuls until the mid-nineteenth century, and also executive responsibility for the conduct of the war in the American Colonies. It was also to retain control of the Russian and Nootka Sound mobilizations and government reactions to the opening stages of the French Revolution. 'Mr Fox's Office', as the Foreign Office was first commonly known, soon settled down in its new role. Fox inherited his staff from the old Northern Department, which had varied very little in size from the late 1750s, that is two under-secretaries and usually eight clerks. These clerks were divided into three classes; a chief (or first) clerk, senior and junior clerks. The first chief clerk in the new office was Jeremy Sneyd, who had worked in the Northern Department since 1750. All the clerks in the offices of the Secretaries had been appointed by them and were paid from the fees received when certain documents passed through the office and from the right to frank letters and newspapers. A parliamentary enquiry in 1786 reported that the under-secretaries were receiving an annual salary of £500 each, with additional fees and gratuities; the chief clerk depended entirely on fees and gratuities for his income. Not only did the Secretary have to meet the clerks' salaries, varying from £410 for the 'second clerk' to £80 for the 'tenth clerk', from fees, but he was also responsible for the general expenses of the Office. Income from fees was supplemented by his own emoluments, a patent salary, additional allowance and special grants. From 1699 until 1782 fees were pooled and divided equally by the Northern and Southern Departments, and were again in 1795 after the creation of a third Secretaryship in 1794 with the consequent need for an equitable distribution of revenue. A fee fund was established in each office, superintended by the chief clerk. As the fees became progressively more inadequate for the needs of the office, they were reinforced by parliamentary grants.

The task of the new Office was described by Sneyd in 1785 as 'conducting the correspondence with all Foreign Courts, negotiating with the Ambassadors or Ministers of all the Foreign Courts in Europe, as well as of the United States of America, and receiving and making representations and applications to and from the same, and in corresponding with the other principal Departments of the State thereupon.'[1] Work was not made easy by the continuance of the long-accepted practice that a Minister might remove any papers he wanted on leaving office. Also no systematic practice of recording in and out letters existed. Burges, who became under-secretary at the Foreign Office in 1789, ruefully commented: 'the immense number of dispatches which come from and go to foreign courts are piled up in large presses, but no note of them is taken, nor is there even an index to them; so that if anything is wanted the whole year's accumulation must be rummaged over before it can be found, and frequently material concerns must be forgotten for want of a memorandum to preserve their memory. As to the past it would be an Herculean task to put things right.'[2]

It was also expected that the work could be done by a staff hardly bigger than that found in the Secretaries' offices in the mid-eighteenth century. By comparison with the contemporary French Foreign Ministry, the British Office remained very small and simply organized. In addition to the two under-secretaries, who were responsible for all aspects of the administration and functioning of the Office, there were eight clerks in 1782. One oddity, which became exaggerated with the years, was that the position of chief clerk, held by the most senior clerk at the time of the vacancy, carried prestige but did not involve him in the political work of the Office. The chief clerk was responsible for the financial work of the Office, a responsibility that was underlined by the arrangements of 1795, which gave Sneyd's successor, Thomas Bidwell, Senior, the job of paying the messengers employed by the Office in addition to the handling of the fee fund. He was so heavily involved in book-keeping that he had little time to concern himself with the political work of the department. The other clerks prepared the political and inter-departmental correspondence of the Office by copying dispatches, recording correspondence in registers and making fair drafts and copies of important papers. They also ciphered and deciphered dispatches. They usually only worked from eleven to four o'clock daily and in the evening on foreign post nights. The most noticeable change in the new Office for the clerks of the old Northern Department was in the amount of work. As early as 1787, they complained that the volume of work had doubled and there were signs of growing absenteeism. They were nevertheless hard-working, despite their low levels of pay which persisted until 1795.

The Foreign Office in the nineteenth century

The new Office took over not only the staff of the old Northern Department but also its premises in Cleveland Row. In 1786 it was moved to a house belonging to the Duke of Dorset, part of one of the old tennis courts at Whitehall, and in December 1793 it moved again to Lord Sheffield's house in Downing Street where it remained for almost seventy years. Other houses on either side were slowly acquired. The inadequacy of accommodation there was well known long before an official decision was taken in 1861 to demolish the buildings. A new Foreign Office building was planned as part of the general redevelopment of Whitehall. George Gilbert Scott's original massive Gothic design (1858) was refused by Palmerston, who admitted that he 'could not contemplate without alarm the idea of filling up with gloomy-looking buildings in the Gothic style, the whole of the space between Downing Street and Great George Street'.[3] Divided opinion in both Parliament and the press on possible styles was overcome by Palmerston. Scott's final design for the exterior was essentially Italianate with 'an occasional infusion of Gothic': he managed, however, to use many of his original designs for the interior. While it was being built, the Office was housed at 7 and 8 Whitehall Gardens; it moved into the new building, which it has occupied ever since, on 1 July 1868.

It is important to see the changes in the functioning of the staff of the Office against a background of steadily increasing pressure of work. In 1826, the number of dispatches and papers received and sent was 12402. By 1900 that total had increased to 101515. If the establishment was to be able to handle this increasing business competently and speedily, changes had to be made in organization. The growth in the size of the establishment did not match that in business. Sir Edward Grey's staff (1906–16) was hardly different in size and classification from that of Canning (1822–27). By 1822 the establishment had become one chief clerk, four first class or senior clerks, six second class clerks, six third class clerks or junior clerks, three assistant junior clerks, a supplementary clerk in the chief clerk's department, a private secretary and a précis writer, a librarian and sub-librarian, a translator, two office keepers, a door porter and a printer. This establishment only marginally increased in the second half of the century. Clarendon's reforms took the total number of staff from thirty in 1853 to forty-three in 1858; the number was only forty-one in 1902–3. A large increase only came with the intro- duction of the registry system in 1905, when the number of second division clerks jumped from eighteen to fifty-nine. On the eve of the First World War Grey had, in addition to the under-secretaries, one controller of commercial and consular affairs, one chief clerk, seven senior clerks and twenty-eight junior clerks.

For a long time after 1782 the Foreign Secretary needed little more than efficient clerical assistance. He was able to manage the diplomatic corres- pondence and administer the general routine of the Office, aided by his private secretary and his précis writer, who were both placed on the office establishment by Order in Council in 1795. Neither post was necessarily filled by one of the Office clerks until the mid-nineteenth century, by which time one or more assistant private secretaries were being appointed. Until 1812 the précis writer appears to have been the senior of the two, but slowly the private secretary acquired greater influence and became involved in appointments and promotions within the Office and the diplomatic service. The précis writer became in effect an assistant private secretary. From 1875 both under-secretaries also had private secretaries. Only very slowly was the work originally done by the Secretary of State himself delegated in the first place to the under-secretaries and eventually to other staff in the Office.

The Secretary of State implemented policy formulated in the Cabinet. As the Cabinet became a more cohesive body, it became clear that a small group of ministers, comprising the Prime Minister, the Foreign Secretary and one or two others, was better informed and more involved in foreign policy decision-making than other Cabinet members. In practice it was only rarely that the views of the Foreign Secretary were overruled, and then only by the Prime Minister.

The post of Foreign Secretary retained great political prestige throughout the nineteenth century. Often the same man appeared as Foreign Secretary in successive ministries, thereby acquiring extensive and valuable experience. Palmerston was intermittently Foreign Secretary in total for seventeen years. There were only seventeen Foreign Secretaries between 1815 and 1914, and most of them were appointed after considerable experience of political office. At the end of the century Salisbury was so reluctant to leave the Foreign Secretaryship that he combined it with that of Prime Minister. It was constitutionally proper that the sovereign could play an active part in the making of foreign policy, but the level of involvement varied very much with individual monarchs. William IV regularly expressed opinions and nearly achieved the level of daily supervision of business maintained by his father, George III. After the early years of her reign Victoria, supported by her husband, insisted on being fully informed of foreign developments and attempted to ensure that important dispatches were always submitted to her for approval before they were sent out. Intermarriage by her children with other European royal families and the length of her reign equipped her with invaluable channels of private communication and considerable expertise, which strengthened her position in consultations with her ministers. In the last resort, however, the making of policy rested with the Cabinet, and in particular with the Foreign Secretary.

In addition to his very independent position in the Cabinet, the Foreign Secretary remained relatively free from parliamentary control. Only rarely did he sit in the Commons. Canning and Grey were unusual in that they were neither peers nor the sons of peers. As in the eighteenth century, the constitutional position was clear: any parliamentary involvement in foreign policy derived from a government's need either to raise finance or to get new legislation passed, both of which functions required the cooperation of the Commons. An important example was the defeat in the Commons of the Conspiracy to Murder Bill, which had been introduced by Palmerston in 1858 after the Orsini Plot. The bill was defeated and the Government fell. Interest in foreign politics was keen in both Commons and Lords; it was often used as a convenient diplomatic excuse by Foreign Secretaries in their negotiations. Publication of parliamentary papers on foreign affairs expanded in both size and volume, but the content of those Blue Books was always approved by the Office. Motions for papers by the Commons were often successfully resisted with the words 'not in the public interest'. As party allegiance strengthened, such motions became less common and the initiative for publication came more and more from the Office.

Throughout the century the Office existed to serve the Foreign Secretary in his work in implementing foreign policy and in his parliamentary responsibilities. As in the eighteenth century, there continued to be two under-secretaries in normal circumstances. They were responsible for sharing the work of the Office among the clerks and for preparing draft dispatches for the Secretary of State. At first both held office through political favour, but after 1795 it became customary for only one under-secretary to be replaced at a change of ministry. As this practice became established, the office of permanent under-secretary emerged, though holders of it long persisted in seeing themselves as the senior under-secretary. John Backhouse ensured that his successors should have virtually exclusive responsibility for the management of Office affairs and his successor, Henry Unwin Addington, was described by the chief clerk in 1842 as permanent under-secretary of state. In

1831 a salary differential had been established between the two under-secretaries. The other under-secretary was identified closely with the Secretary of State and left office with him. In the first half of the century he was by no means expected to be a member of either the Lords or Commons: as many as ten were not. His was, however, a political appointment and was called the junior under-secretary. When it became important to have an under-secretary in the Commons because Foreign Secretaries were successively peers, the title of parliamentary under-secretary came into use, and it was underlined by his assumption of all the parliamentary business of the Office in 1876.

Neither under-secretary had much influence on policy until late in the century. From 1782 each was allocated responsibility for correspondence with particular countries, assigned much on the lines of the old Northern and Southern Departments. It was only in the 1820s that a distinction began to emerge in the work each did, and that distinction was often blurred by the capacities and inclinations of particular individuals. The next forty years saw great fluctuations in the allocation of countries, with a perceptible tendency to concentrate diplomatic business on the permanent under-secretary. Edmund Hammond's tenure of office (1854–73) witnessed not only a clear acceptance of the permanent under-secretary's authority in the Office, but also the beginnings of his advisory function. Under him the political departments established their primacy and the organization of the Office looked much more like its twentieth-century form. Not only was the permanent under-secretary now the recognized head of the Office, but also his advisory function was established. The use made later of this function varied considerably. Currie (permanent under-secretary 1889–94) commented on his predecessor Pauncefote's failure even to comment on political dispatches, yet he and his successor Thomas Sanderson (1894–1905) were both very cautious in offering advice. Since Hammond's time, apart from Pauncefote (1882–9), his successors have previously served in the Foreign Office or in the diplomatic service or in both. Hammond was a vigorous administrator and was able to exploit the parliamentary involvement of his political colleagues to strengthen his own internal position.

The growing pre-eminence of the permanent under-secretary had by 1876 limited the work of the parliamentary under-secretary to the administration of parliamentary business and occasionally of the Commercial Department. Pressure of work eventually forced the appointment of a third under-secretary. In 1858 the situation was particularly difficult and the post of assistant under-secretary was created. The holder of this post was closely supervised by the under-secretaries except for his responsibility for the Consular Department. After an experiment with a second assistant under-secretary with special legal responsibilities in 1876, the need for a second assistant under-secretary with a share in diplomatic business was accepted. In 1895 a third assistant under-secretary was appointed.

By the 1830s the chief clerk and the senior clerks had almost completely lost any involvement with the political work of the Office. As the Foreign Secretary's decisions on policy were political, the work of the 'political' departments of the Office consisted largely in file-keeping and the provision of information. Until the 1840s and 1850s these political departments remained inferior to the administrative departments. In these the chief clerk administered all financial matters; the senior clerks headed departments that had emerged in the 1820s: the Treaty and Royal Letter Department, the Consular Department and the Slave Trade Department. The political divisions were administered by the clerks assistant. Palmerston became more and more dissatisfied with this practice of using second-class clerks to fulfil duties 'which are in their nature sufficiently important and confidential to be assigned to the five persons of longest standing and of the highest rate of salary'.[4] He consequently ordered a review of the duties of the chief and senior clerks. Change came but slowly. Business increased enormously between 1829 and 1838 and the clerks themselves were discontented with the slow rate of promotion. The first stage of reform proposals involved the addition of two clerks and an adjustment in the size of the classes. The Chancellor of the Exchequer, Francis Baring, accepted the former but hesitated over the latter in case the proposal encouraged the Home and Colonial Office clerks to make similar demands. He attempted in return to secure the abolition of the agency system, by which Office clerks were employed by members of the diplomatic service as bankers. He was forced to give way on both counts. The early 1840s saw the second stage of the reforms with the promotion of the heads of the political divisions to the senior class and the reduction of the second class. Palmerston in 1841 also emphasized the need to promote the best qualified clerks without reference to seniority but could effect little change. Another attempt to abolish the Foreign Office agencies failed in the 1850s. They were finally abolished in 1870.

Slowly the political departments increased in importance and prestige. Edmund Hammond's consolidation of the permanent under-secretary's authority in the Office involved his near monopoly of political business. By 1865 he supervised four of the five political departments. He controlled the French Department (France, Switzerland, Italy, Madagascar and Miscellaneous), the Turkish Department (Russia, Greece, Turkey, North Africa and the Middle East), the Spanish Department (Spain, Portugal, Mexico, South and Central America) and the American Department (China, Japan, Siam, USA and Mosquito). The parliamentary under-secretary only administered the German Department (Austria, Prussia, German states, Belgium, Denmark, Netherlands and Sweden). By 1882 the political departments were reduced to three, all under the control of the permanent under-secretary: the Western (Europe) Department (Austria, Germany, Portugal, Spain, France, Italy, Madagascar, North Africa, Belgium, Denmark, Netherlands, Sweden, Norway, Switzerland and Miscellaneous), the Eastern (Europe) Department (Greece, Montenegro, Romania, Serbia, Russia, Turkey, Egypt, Persia and Central Asia) and the American and Asiatic Department (North, South and Central America, China, Japan, Siam). This last department was subdivided in 1899 into a Far Eastern (or China) Department and an American Department. In practice there was considerable flexibility in the distribution of business. By the end of the century the departments had also acquired individual styles. The Western Department was considered the most important in the Office and the Eastern Department the most aristocratic. Both occupied three rooms: the first room for the senior clerk and his assistant; a second room for the junior clerks with longest service, who kept the registers and organized the confidential print, the regular means by which dispatches were copied and circulated to ministers and selected ambassadors; and a third room for the rest of the junior clerks.

Throughout the century the Office was able to resist external pressures – chiefly from the Treasury – for reform either of its organization of work or of its methods of recruitment. The work of the clerks remained largely mechanical. The 1850s witnessed the first major skirmish between the Office and the Treasury, which pressed for uniformity of practice in all government departments. Long after other departments had accepted open competitive entry and a distinction between intellectual and mechanical work, the Office was still arguing successfully that its work was confidential and therefore completely different from that of other departments. It was asserted that such work could only be done by completely trustworthy staff who were known or recommended to the Secretary of State and whose social position excluded the possibility of introducing two classes of clerks doing different work and being paid on two different salary scales. The major recommendations of the 1855 Northcote–Trevelyan enquiry – open competitive examinations and the differentiation between intellectual and mechanical work – were thus resisted by Clarendon and Hammond. The Office's own solution to the problem of increasing pressure of work was to suggest the introduction of a new class of clerks assistant to help the senior clerks. The Treasury reluctantly accepted this in 1857, having lost its campaign to persuade the Office to accept copying clerks at least in the Consular and Slave Trade Departments. Later the Office permitted a little adjustment in the shape of unestablished clerks in the administrative departments and the library, but in 1871, when Robert Lowe was urging a unified civil service, Clarendon and Hammond repeated their victory of 1855. The supplemental clerks were relatively well paid but restricted to non-confidential work. In 1881, when the number of 'political' departments was reduced, four lower division clerks were employed in the Commercial and Consular Departments. Although only a small change, this proved to be of major importance in the future development of the Office. These lower division clerks were called second division clerks after 1890 and in 1896 the supplementary clerks in the administrative departments were merged into the second division. A few senior second division clerks were appointed staff officers. In 1889 a lady typist (known as a lady typewriter) was introduced into the Office. As yet, it must be emphasized, none of these changes involved the political departments.

In a similar way, the Office retained its own methods of recruitment. In 1856 Clarendon, faced with the strong Northcote–Trevelyan recommendation for examinations, accepted a qualifying examination for both junior and supplementary clerks. Before then the Foreign Secretary had appointed to all posts, and it was to be a long time before the recruits via examination reached senior positions in the Office. The examination was separate from that used for the other government departments. A candidate had to be nominated by the Secretary of State, be a man of honour and of good health and have the ability 'to write a good bold hand forming each letter distinctly, to write quickly and correctly either English or French from dictation, to understand French well and to be able to make an accurate and good translation of any French paper, and also to make a correct and clear précis or abstract of any set of papers placed in his hands.'[5] The age limits were to be 18 to 24 years, there was to be one year's probation and promotion was to be by merit. A slight element of competition was introduced by Clarendon in 1857 when it was accepted that three nominated candidates should compete for each vacancy.

When candidates achieved equal marks, a German translation and reading test were used to break the deadlock. Standards were not high, and although Clarendon won exemption from the 1870 Order in Council, which enforced open competition, he bowed slightly to outside pressure and introduced more stringent examinations in 1871. There were now to be eight compulsory papers, including arithmetic and French translation, and a range of optional subjects. Apart from a few minor alterations, including changes in subject matter, this examination pattern continued into the twentieth century.

At the end of the century, the Foreign Office remained a socially exclusive preserve. The continuing need for nomination ensured that young men from families unknown to the Foreign Secretary or to his private secretary did not apply. The examination reflected the kind of education expected of upper class young men. Almost all candidates had either been educated at one of the major public schools, which grew in importance during the second half of the century, or had been tutored privately. Only a relatively small number had received a university education. The great preponderance of recruits came from aristocratic and gentry families. It was by no means uncommon for successive generations of a family to enter the Office. To succeed in the new examinations with the tougher tests in languages and secretarial skills school leavers often needed extra tuition. A year or two in France and Germany helped to perfect school languages and was usually followed by a course at a 'cramming' establishment, most commonly Scoones of Garrick Street. Even university graduates found it necessary to resort to crammers. There is some evidence that the educational homogeneity of the Office narrowed at the end of the century. Although academic standards for admission to the Office had been raised, the work expected of the new recruits remained largely mechanical. Arthur Ponsonby reminisced in 1914 that he 'had been nearly nine years in the service, and my work was still to copy out dispatches, to put numbers on papers, to sort confidential prints, and, more especially, to do up dispatch bags with sealing wax and red tape'.[6] The system could only continue as long as an able permanent under-secretary could cope with his departments and the Secretary of State could handle the problems facing him each day.

The nineteenth-century diplomatic service

Although the establishment of regular diplomatic representation in the place of occasional and special missions had become the normal practice of European states in the second half of the fifteenth century, it was not until the eighteenth century that a marked development of professionalism had occurred in the British diplomatic service. All the features of a structured profession – a regular gradation of ranks, agreed salaries and allowances and promotion from grade to grade – appeared in some form before 1789. By 1789 Britain was regularly represented in north-eastern Europe and had an adequate network of missions elsewhere in Europe, especially in Italy and Germany, though only after this time was there regular diplomatic representation in the United States of America and in other states beyond Europe. By then British missions were staffed by a regular hierarchy of officials ranging from heads of mission, including ambassadors, through secretaries of embassy and secretaries with creditive letters to unpaid staff and private secretaries. By 1815 a basic distinction had emerged between those placed on the establishment, who would expect to be paid by the Treasury from Civil List funds, and those, as yet unestablished, who might receive a small salary or only board and lodging from the established staff employing them. This sharp dividing line could be crossed, and often was, in the course of a diplomatic career. This pattern of employment was to continue well into the nineteenth century.

It must be emphasized that until 1919 the diplomatic service was quite separate from the Foreign Office. Levels of pay and pensions, methods of recruitment and career structure differed noticeably between the two services. Some small interchange of staff was tolerated. Faced with a strong recommendation by the 1861 Select Committee on the diplomatic service that exchanges should be possible, Russell introduced regulations on exchanges in 1862. Temporary exchanges were to be allowed at the discretion of the Foreign Secretary, but were to be restricted to the lower ranks of the services. In practice, such exchanges proved very difficult to arrange and, when achieved, were usually justified on personal grounds. In no sense were they encouraged. The Select Committee that sat in 1870 and 1871 pressed for wider interchange, but although the number of exchanges increased between 1870 and 1890, rarely were they arranged for other than short periods that were of little advantage to the two services. The Ridley Commission in 1890 firmly recommended a much more extreme change, the amalgamation of the two services. Its proposals were referred to a departmental committee, which concluded its survey of all the obstacles in the way of amalgamation with the mild suggestion that the introduction of common grades for the two services would make transfer of staff much easier for the Secretary of State. In the event nothing was done to ease such transfers.

Apart from official coolness to interchange of staff between the two services, diplomatic posts offered little attraction to Foreign Office staff. The cost of living abroad was high, and despite the repeated encouragement of select committee reports no positive inducement in the form of either pay or promotion was available to ease exchanges. Members of the diplomatic service, on the other hand, had usually experienced, if only briefly, work in the Foreign Office. By the end of the century newly appointed attachés spent about six months in one of the Foreign Office departments, but not more than a handful of diplomats were working in the Office at any one time. It was only at the top level of both services that transfers were easily arranged, particularly from the Office to the diplomatic service. A number of assistant under-secretaries became ministers or ambassadors; three permanent under-secretaries, Addington, Hardinge and Nicolson, had been ambassadors.

The diplomatic service had expanded steadily since 1815, when it had been reconstituted after the dislocation caused by the wars with France. The Protocol of Vienna in 1815 had regulated diplomatic rank: it placed ambassadors in the first and ministers plenipotentiary in the second rank. In the 1840s the status of embassy was accorded by the British government only to the five most important missions – Paris, Vienna, St Petersburg, Constantinople and Brussels. As Britain entered into diplomatic relations with more and more countries, the number of embassies hardly increased. The vast majority of British missions abroad were legations headed by a minister. Between 1815 and 1860 the number of missions grew from twenty to thirty-seven; numbers employed in the service also increased. In 1833 there were eighty-one paid members of the service; in less than fifty years the number had doubled.

The nineteenth century witnessed a further stage in the professionalization of the diplomatic service. Over half of the total of 119 heads of mission serving in the period 1812–60 had passed their entire careers in the service from the lowest grade, that of unpaid attaché, and only nineteen of them had no diplomatic experience before appointment. In response to increasing pressure of work in missions abroad, secretaries of legations were appointed to all missions after 1815. The job of these secretaries was to copy dispatches and keep records. The new workload after 1815 also resulted in the regular appointment of attachés. In the eighteenth century ministers had occasionally been helped in their work by friends or the sons of friends or relatives staying in their households. Such people were still to be found in the 1820s and later, but in 1825 Canning ruled that such people could only be attached to a mission with the written approval of the Secretary of State. Despite this ruling the Secretary's control of these unpaid attachés remained weak, and would remain so as long as young men became unpaid attachés with no intention of pursuing a career in the diplomatic service. A spell as unpaid attaché was still seen as a useful stepping stone to a political career. In addition to the unpaid attachés, the number of paid attachés also increased. In 1838 Palmerston began the practice of employing all new paid attachés briefly in the Office to prepare them for the kind of work expected of them.

From the 1830s the normal diplomatic career pattern began with service as an unpaid attaché, followed by the posts of paid attaché, secretary of legation, secretary of embassy, head of mission and, very rarely, ambassador. In response to criticism by the Select Committee of 1861, the ranks of first, second, and third secretary were introduced and that of paid attaché abolished. Examinations had been introduced in 1856 for unpaid attachés, which tested handwriting, dictation in English and French, languages (French and one other), geography, précis and modern history. A second, more advanced group of examinations for promotion to paid attaché was from 1862 taken between the third and second secretary grades. Entrants to the diplomatic service, who remained unpaid until after 1919, were appointed third secretary after probation. A £400 a year income qualification was not removed until 1919.

The required period of unpaid service, together with the fact that diplomatic examinations were tougher than those for the Foreign Office, led to a decline in the number of candidates in the late 1860s. The introduction by the Foreign Office of a more challenging examination in 1871 made entrance to the diplomatic service relatively easier. In 1880 a scheme of 'limited' competition was introduced for the diplomatic service on the lines of that already practised by the Foreign Office. The highly critical report of the Ridley Commission (1889–92) resulted in the same examination being given to both sets of candidates, though they were still separately graded. However, success for one group meant an immediate salary, while for the other only probationary unpaid service. The Select Committee of 1870–2 had recognized in its report how far changes in the administration of the diplomatic service in 1861 'have materially altered the character of the service, and have tended to make it a closed profession, which is entered, chiefly, by those who mean to make it the occupation of their lives, and in which, promotion in ordinary circumstances, goes by way of seniority.' It recommended a number of improvements: minimum salaries for the different grades were specified; junior members should stay at least three years in a post before being moved; and heads of mission should be given permanent residences. Despite these encouragements to reform, tremendous variety persisted in the salaries of diplomatic posts, outfit and rent allowances. It was not until well into the twentieth century that the diplomatic service could offer a candidate the promise of something approximating to the career pattern emerging in the Foreign Office in the late nineteenth century. The diplomatic service remained the preserve of the landed classes. Though the percentage of recruits coming from the aristocracy diminished during the latter part of the century, there were few representatives from the commercial and industrial strata of British society. A substantial private income was essential for a young man to survive the financial uncertainties of a diplomatic career.

Throughout this period the consular service remained very much the 'Cinderella service'. Three separate branches composed it: the general consular service, the Levant consular service and the Far Eastern consular service. The general consular service was only organized fully as a career service in 1903. An attempt had been made in 1825 in Canning's Consular Act to regularize the service by the institution of a proper system of salaries and a fixed scale of fees. A Consular Department was set up at the Foreign Office. Development on these lines was rapidly stunted in the wave of government financial retrenchment that arose in the 1830s. Throughout the nineteenth century the consuls remained second-class citizens in the diplomatic world. The problems of patronage and the appointment of unsuitable candidates to consular posts persisted. Such promotion as there was depended simply on seniority. As the political work of the Foreign Office increased, the chance of consular reports being seen by even an assistant under-secretary was very small; by the end of the century the Foreign Office was acting simply as a post office forwarding consular reports to the Board of Trade. Limited opportunities for informal contact between the consuls and the Foreign Office were further curtailed, somewhat paradoxically, by the abolition in 1870 of the agency system, by which consuls had paid heavily for Office clerks to collect their salaries and forward their mail. The consuls entered the twentieth century very differently from the French consular service: they were in isolated posts and had no systematic recruitment, grades, opportunities for transfer or promotion: they lacked coherent overall control.

The twentieth-century Foreign Office and diplomatic service
Political developments in Britain since 1900 have extended the independence of the executive in the making of foreign policy in the narrow political sense. Occasional attempts to render the Foreign Office more responsive to outside opinion by the institution of a parliamentary standing foreign affairs committee were easily resisted until 1979, when the introduction of a number of Commons select committees on what was seen as a trial basis included a Foreign and Commonwealth Committee. Often intense pressure for more 'open' diplomacy has resulted in little more than the more frequent laying before Parliament of the texts of treaties and other major international documents. Faced with the critical report by the Central Policy Review Staff in 1977 and a general campaign for 'open' government, the Government

declared its intention in 1978 to publish two new series of papers, a regular series of Foreign Policy Documents and an occasional series of Background Briefs on policy-making.[7] A general acceptance that governments should seek a bipartisan approach to foreign politics has prevailed, with some notable exceptions of which the Suez Crisis and the controversy over Britain's entry to the EEC are possibly the most striking.

It can be argued that by 1914 the Foreign Office had become a modern department of state. Yet while its bureaucratic growth was to continue, its actual role and importance were to shrink. The pressures and effects of two world wars combined with rapid scientific and technological advance have fundamentally altered the international environment and led to major adjustments in the functions of the Foreign Office. These changes have been clearly reflected in the altered role of the Foreign Secretary. He was no longer to be the dominant member of the Cabinet nearly equal to the Prime Minister, as was his nineteenth-century predecessor. Many more individuals held the position both between and after the wars and, only rarely, as in the case of Eden, had they the opportunity to acquire extensive experience. Moreover, the Office was finding important competitors in the decision-making process. During the inter-war years, the Treasury, the Board of Trade and the service departments as well as the Colonial Office and the India Office with their expanded jurisdictions could not be ignored. The decline in Britain's status as a world power and the reduction in its imperial role after 1945 forced even more radical adjustment. In 1968 the Office was merged with the Commonwealth Office. It subsequently had to face persistent criticism of its size, methods of recruitment, wastage of talent and political preoccupation. Not only has the Office had to adapt to the swift growth of multilateral diplomacy conducted through permanent international organizations, but it has also been persuaded towards a broader definition of foreign policy, which has involved a closer dialogue with those concerned in the making of economic, social and defence policy. Britain's membership of the North Atlantic Treaty Organization has introduced new elements into the work of the Office and new lines of communication have been developed with the Ministry of Defence and the representatives of NATO. Membership of the EEC has resulted in a vastly expanded range of international activities for which the Office has a number of ministerial rivals in the control of negotiations with the Community. Against a background of pressure from those who believe that support for Britain's trading and financial position must take priority over purely political concerns, the Office has had to enlarge its competence while negotiating with domestic departments more experienced in such matters. Since 1945 the external roles of home departments have continued to expand. A particular example is the way in which the Department of Trade, with whom the Office has achieved a successful working relationship, has responded to the implications of Britain's membership of the Community. The demands of both the British and the European parliament have required an active response; it will be noticed from Appendix A that the Office now has a Parliamentary Commissioner and Committees unit. Political, economic and technological developments since 1945 have helped to blur the traditional distinction between domestic and foreign policy built up since 1782. The FCO has thus lost its nineteenth-century pre-eminence in the making of foreign policy.

In the nineteenth century there had already been signs that the Office could not restrict itself to a political role if it was to retain that pre-eminence in the management of Britain's external relations. Successive experiments with commercial departments indicated persistent confusion in the minds of Foreign Secretaries and senior officials about how the Office should relate to the activities of the Board of Trade and how the consular service, that 'Cinderella service', should be managed. In April 1912 a controller of Commercial and Consular Affairs became responsible for both the Commercial and Sanitary Department and the Consular Department. The negotiation of commercial treaties was thus in the hands of the Foreign Office, which at the same time was obliged to rely on the Board of Trade for advice and information on commercial matters and policy. Correspondence by the Board with diplomatic and consular officials on commercial matters was conducted through the Foreign Office. In the period before 1914, and to a certain extent up to 1939, senior Foreign Office officials continued to consider such matters as of only minor importance.

Another indicator of the broadening definition of foreign policy has been the steady growth in the appointment of specialist attachés to overseas missions. Commercial attachés were first appointed in 1880 and commercial secretaries after 1906; they worked under the direction of the Commercial Department. Military and naval attachés had first appeared in 1857 in the form of serving officers seconded for short periods. These were joined by air and press attachés between the two world wars and by cultural, scientific and labour attachés after 1945.

In what was the chief concern of the Office – the political work – the deficiencies of the existing system were apparent in 1900. For the junior staff, the bulk of their time was still spent in registering, docketing, ciphering and deciphering papers and in preparing dispatch bags for embassies and legations. The first major steps towards reform in the organization of work were initiated from within by Francis Villiers, an assistant under-secretary, in 1903. His diagnosis of the difficulties of the Office was that once able young men were recruited no real use was made of them, a diagnosis that belatedly echoed the Northcote–Trevelyan report of 1855. His constructive solution was many-pronged. It included the creation of a ciphering room, the removal of all non-political miscellaneous work to the non-political departments, the rationalization of 'Blue Book' work under a parliamentary under-secretary and the transfer of the chore of making up dispatch bags from the clerks to office keepers. T. H. Sanderson, the permanent under-secretary, accepted most of these proposals, which were then warmly endorsed by the Foreign Secretary, Lord Lansdowne (1901–5); once Treasury approval had been received for the necessary additional staff the relevant instructions were issued. These changes were important preliminary steps if devolution of political work was to be effected.

Lansdowne's aims were to adjust the system of recruitment in the hope of attracting more university graduates and to ensure that younger men received a larger share of the political work. As a preliminary step, in 1903 he initiated discussions on the handling of papers. A committee reported in 1904 that a General Registry was needed and that it should be staffed and worked by second division clerks as it was in the Colonial Office. There should be a central registry and three sub-registries. It was estimated that about twenty clerks would be needed. Papers were to be kept flat (an innovation) and telephones should be installed throughout the Office to facilitate the complex system of paper movement. Despite tough Treasury opposition the new registry system began on 1 January 1906 with a registrar, an assistant registrar,. two staff officers, nine second division clerks and four boy clerks. The work of the first division staff was fundamentally transformed. Virtually all the simple secretarial work, which had been their lot since the days of Palmerston, was taken over by second division staff. The first division staff were thus liberated to share in the policy-making process and even the most junior of them were encouraged to do so. Before 1906 it had been customary for only the briefest comment to be added by the permanent under-secretary or an assistant under-secretary to drafts and dispatches. After January 1906, when papers were sent to the Foreign Secretary a sheet was attached giving the opinions of departmental officials. The practice was established that once the Foreign Secretary initialled his own or any other minute, the Office was authorized to carry it out. Sir Edward Grey enjoyed discussing policy questions with his staff. He was prepared to delegate such work as the semi-official correspondence with diplomats abroad and minor negotiations, but retained his responsibility for all major decisions, depending heavily for advice first on his permanent under-secretary, Charles Hardinge (1906–10), and then on his private secretary, William Tyrrell. The devolution aimed at by Lansdowne had been achieved, though in the years before 1914 this largely meant that the burden of work fell on the senior members of the hierarchy. Eyre Crowe, later permanent under-secretary, proved the driving force behind the implementation of the reform scheme.

By 1914 much had indeed changed in the Office. In 1904 Lansdowne had succeeded in broadening the educational backgrounds of candidates by raising the age of entry to twenty-two and expecting them to take the same examination papers as for Class I of the Home Civil Service. Competition increased especially after 1907, when earlier restrictions on the number of examinees were removed. From the point of view of school, educational homogeneity persisted. Of fourteen senior officials in 1898, ten had been educated at a leading public school, mostly Eton. Between 1908 and 1913, nine of the sixteen candidates were Etonians. What had changed was that they had now also attended a university, normally Oxford or Cambridge. Another change in 1907 was the transfer of nomination for both the Foreign Office and the diplomatic service from the Foreign Secretary to a selection board comprising the permanent under-secretary as chairman, the Foreign Secretary's principal private secretary, one or more members of the diplomatic service and one of the heads of a Foreign Office political department. This selection board seems to have nominated much the same sort of candidate as before. Only in 1912 and 1913 are there hints of a slight widening in the social background of candidates. Slowly the Office routine had become less flexible, although long weekends and holidays reflected the social life and expectations of first division staff. The hours of second division staff, 10.30 a.m. to 6 p.m., slowly came to determine working hours for all. Telephones were installed in all departments and the number of typists rapidly increased. New responsibilities encouraged a greater degree of specialization by first division staff.

Despite these important reforms in the functioning of the Office, external pressure for change in both the administration of external relations and the recruitment of staff intensified. The Ridley Commission had already presented evidence to support the importance of amalgamating the Office with the diplomatic service. In 1914 the Union of Democratic Control, led by E. D. Morel, supported the attack by radical backbenchers and Labour party members on Grey's methods of conducting foreign policy. They repeated the criticisms given in evidence to the MacDonnell Commission on the Civil Service (1914). The Foreign Office again argued against amalgamation, but the Commission's recommendations were firm and well-supported by evidence: a single foreign service should be created and ways must be found to remove social and financial handicaps on candidates; membership of the selection board should be extended, the £400 income qualification abolished and all candidates should take the same examinations as for Class I of the Home Civil Service; the commercial role must be strengthened by more efficient use of commercial attachés and a general reform of the consular service. The outbreak of war delayed any attempts to implement any part of these recommendations, though a series of departmental committees was created to consider them.

The stresses and strains of the 1914–18 war forced major changes in the working of the Office. A large number of temporary assistants was recruited. The experience of the wartime Contraband Department and the Ministry of Blockade led to negotiations with the Board of Trade and the creation in 1917 of the Department of Overseas Trade, which was to be shared by both Departments and to administer a new commercial diplomatic service. This was very much a compromise arrangement, which left the Board of Trade responsible for the formulation of commercial policy and the Department of Overseas Trade for its implementation. Confusion in the direction of the Foreign Office in the immediate post-war period with, in effect, one office in London and one in Paris, and persistent Treasury resistance to schemes that involved increased expenditure, ensured that any implementation of the pre-war MacDonnell reforms would be, at best, partial. The wartime structure was gradually dismantled. The War Department was dissolved in October 1920 and its work redistributed between the Eastern, Western and the new Central and Northern Department. The American and Far Eastern departments continued. The functions of the disbanded Commercial department were shared by the Department of Overseas Trade and the political departments, thus strengthening their economic role. In 1922 League of Nations affairs were transferred from the Cabinet to the Office.

Amalgamation of the staff of the Foreign Office and the diplomatic service was finally accepted after long and difficult negotiations with the Treasury. These negotiations were complicated by questions of recruitment. Treasury determination to force open competition on the Office was finally deflected by a compromise settlement. The selection board was to be widened by the addition of a Civil Service Commissioner and one or two public members; it was to interview candidates only after the examination, which was to be open to all. The desire of the Office to provide special payments for the diplomatic service and to get Office salaries on the same scale as Treasury staff was finally achieved. The scheme was to be introduced on 1 April 1919, though negotiations continued on rent and special allowances for diplomats. A new career structure, with diplomatic titles for most ranks and new salary scales, was introduced; a new promotion board made the first appointments from the combined list. By the summer of 1920 doubts within the promotion board resulted in a special sub-committee recommending a joint list only up to first secretary level. Both the permanent under-secretary, Lord Hardinge, and the Foreign Secretary, Lord Curzon, supported these views, and without further ado the joint seniority list of an amalgamated foreign service was reduced to a joint list of only second and third secretaries. Public interest in the Foreign Office had died away, and although many in the Office and in the diplomatic service resented amalgamation as an unnecessary reform imposed from outside, the arguments that carried the day appear to have been based on the unique needs of each service. This defeat for the reformers was not complete; transfers between the two services, for example, noticeably increased. It has been established that by 1930 only 16 out of 74 diplomats and six out of 77 clerks were considered non-interchangeable,[8] a very different situation from that customary before 1914.

Pressures for some democratization of the foreign service were only marginally successful. The end of the private income requirement, the new salaries and allowances and more open examination procedures widened recruitment. In the years 1925–9 there were nine Etonian entrants out of the thirty-eight recruited into the amalgamated service. In 1932 in the group of seven recruits, only one was an Etonian; in 1938 of eleven recruits, three were Etonians. A larger number of other public schools were represented in the entry and a handful came from state grammar schools. Oxford and Cambridge remained dominant. There appears to have been a continued widening of the social background of candidates: in particular, the number of entrants from professional families rose. It was stated in answer to a parliamentary question in January 1930 that of the 110 admitted to the service since 1919, five were ex-elementary (state) schoolboys.

The other major change of the post-war period was the restructuring and reform of the Registry system, which had been introduced in 1906 and which rapidly proved inadequate for Foreign Office needs. Requests to increase the number of Registry staff had been repeatedly rejected by the Treasury and even before the war the Central Registry had proved a bottleneck..The number of papers handled by the Office leaped from 58 790 in 1913–14 to 146 846 in 1921. Alwyn Parker, the librarian, worked out a new system in 1918 that depended on new Registry accommodation near the ciphering and typing department and a 50 per cent increase in staff. These changes were eventually adopted. A single Registry divided into three branches, Classification, Archive and Despatch, was established. Experience at the Peace Conference produced adjustments to the new system. Classification became Opening branch and much of its work was transferred to the Archive branch, which became the most important, subdivided for each department and then further subdivided for each country. A new Main Index branch was added. These changes meant simplified processes and staff reduction. New grades of staff were needed, clerical staff for the routine work and executive clerical staff for the Archive branch and other key positions. Thus skilled staff and a relatively large number of clerks, typists and messengers had to be recruited once the Treasury had approved the scheme in January 1920. No further second division clerks were appointed after 1920: new staff were recruited into the executive and clerical grades, as in the Home Civil Service departments. By 1921, there were 117 male clerks and 94 typists. Slowly, department by department, the new system was introduced. The improved clerical system and the new overseas clerical service facilitated the policy-making process but made no difference to the responsibilities of first division staff on the diplomatic establishment, who continued to prepare minutes and drafts much as they had in the pre-1920 period.

Although the post-war diplomatic service retained much of its pre-war character, having grown from fifty-four in 1913–14 to seventy-five in 1921–2, the Foreign Office presented a very different picture. Even with reductions of staff forced by Treasury pressure, the Office establishment had risen from 185 in 1913–14 to 880 in 1926. The building was enlarged but remained inadequate. The limited reforms of 1918–20 enabled the Office to handle its increased responsibilities in a very different political world. The dying away of external pressures for reform in the making of foreign policy removed the impetus for further change and ensured the survival of old practices. The assumption of a dominating role in the making of foreign policy by the Prime Minister, Lloyd George, not only in the latter years of the war but also in all the stages of peacemaking, had seriously eroded Foreign Office prestige. In the years immediately after the war extensive criticism of the official policy-makers in 1914 reduced the confidence of senior staff. It would take some time for that confidence to be restored.

After the dismantling of the wartime structure, the permanent senior establishment of the Office was one permanent under-secretary, one assistant under-secretary, eight assistant secretaries (later called counsellors) similar to the nineteenth-century senior clerks but equivalent in rank to the pre-war assistant under-secretaries. By 1922 there were three assistant under-secretaries and in 1925 the senior of them was called deputy under-secretary. Assistant clerks had become first secretaries. In the 1930s the number of under-secretaries continued to increase, a forerunner of the post-war expansion in the senior hierarchy of the Office. By 1936, there was a deputy and six under-secretaries. In 1935 a second parliamentary under-secretary was appointed and in 1938 a new post created (chief diplomatic adviser) for Robert Vansittart, whose strong views on European questions and independent stance irritated both Eden and Neville Chamberlain and who was replaced by Alexander Cadogan. By 1925 three assistant legal advisers were working with the legal adviser, and in 1929 one of them became claims adviser. In addition to the existing Eastern, Central, Western, Northern, American and Far Eastern departments, two additional political departments were formed: the Egyptian Department (1924), which covered Egypt, the Sudan, Abyssinia (except 1935–6 when a separate Abyssinian Department existed), the Italian colonies in Africa and Africa general (from 1930), and the Southern Department (1933), which covered Austria, Hungary, Italy and Albania, Yugoslavia, Romania, Bulgaria, Greece, Czechoslovakia (till 1938) and Switzerland (from 1936). These changes in 1933 as well as important staff movements would seem to have been manipulated by Vansittart who was anxious to strengthen the Central Department. Wartime propaganda and press activities, including the separate Ministry of Information, were disbanded after the Armistice, but a News Department was reconstituted, using in part the staff of the Political Intelligence Department. After 1935 the head of this department, Sir Reginald Leeper, actively encouraged the newly formed, independent British Council's propaganda role abroad.

With the disappearance of the Commercial Department in 1920 and the assumption of its major functions by the Department of Overseas Trade, economic work was supposed to be done in the political departments. The Western Department (and in 1938 the library) assumed charge of sanitary and health matters. Also in 1920 the Consular department passed in part to the Department of Overseas Trade. The Foreign Office's commercial attaché service had been disbanded in 1919 and the Department of Overseas Trade administered the newly established commercial diplomatic service. The commercial counsellors sent their reports direct to the DOT. The division of duties between the Office and the DOT prevented any real possibility of serious political consideration of economic and commercial developments. Attempts in the 1930s to create an Economic Relations section in the Office that would collect economic information and coordinate the views of interested government departments foundered in the face of interdepartmental rivalries. Although the section was created in 1931 (due to the efforts of Victor Wellesley and Frank Ashton-Gwatkin, its first head), it was allowed only a minimal role. The Treasury proved suspicious of any hint of Foreign Office interference in economic policy-making. At the same time the Foreign Office, unwilling to take expert advice from outside its walls, failed to hold its own in discussions with the Treasury about subjects that had the most far-reaching diplomatic consequences. The Chief Clerk's Department (briefly known as the Financial Department, 1900–13) became the Establishment and Finance Department with the chief clerk becoming principal establishment officer in 1933. In 1938 the post of finance officer, which had been created in 1922, was merged with that of principal establishment officer. The chief clerk came to rank as assistant (and in one case as deputy) under-secretary in the inter-war period. A Dominions Information Department was formed in 1926 to deal with relations with and between the Dominions where they affected the Office. The Dominions were by now pursuing more and more independent foreign policies and developing their own diplomatic establishments. After 1918 the Library assumed responsibility for Parliamentary Papers from the dissolved Parliamentary Department; it also inherited the Historical Section, which had been set up during the war.

In the inter-war period the senior staff of the Office never completely recovered their pre-war position or prestige. After the fall of Lloyd George in 1922, the Office began to re-emerge from the shadows. Lord Curzon, Austen Chamberlain, Ramsay MacDonald (who like Salisbury combined the office of Prime Minister with that of Foreign Secretary), Eden for a short time, and Lord Halifax in the spring and summer of 1939 all left their marks on the course of British diplomacy. Under Austen Chamberlain (1924–9), Office confidence was restored. Like his nineteenth-century predecessors, Chamberlain managed to keep up regular personal correspondence with his ambassadors; the Prime Minister's relative lack of interest in foreign politics enabled the Foreign Secretary to achieve a certain independence in policy-making. In Eyre Crowe, permanent under-secretary (1920–5), the Office had an administrator of the highest order and a man devoted to the service. By contrast, Robert Vansittart was in some ways more a statesman than a civil servant. Less interested in administrative matters than Crowe, he exerted an important influence on his successive political chiefs and even after 1936, when Eden began to pursue an independent line in policy, he continued to play a central role. Vansittart's sharp differences with the new Prime Minister, Neville Chamberlain encouraged the latter's tendency to look elsewhere for advice and support. The Treasury, which had already gained in influence on foreign policy during the 1920s, strengthened its position in the aftermath of the financial crisis of 1929–31 and jealously guarded its role in international financial and economic relationships. Its pressure together with the strongly held views of the service departments considerably curtailed the independence of the Foreign Office, which was itself seriously divided on the policies to be pursued towards Germany and the other European nations. Differences between Chamberlain and Eden (Foreign Secretary 1935–8) and the tendency of Eden's successor, Lord Halifax, as well as other members of the Cabinet to yield to Chamberlain on questions of foreign policy further reduced the authority of the Office.

There was little change in the balance between the Office and the diplomats abroad during the inter-war period. Though the Office remained the more powerful element in the decision-making process, ambassadors could still play a determining role. D'Abernon and later Henderson in Berlin, Miles Lampson in China, Robert Craigie (whose advice was in the end ignored) in Japan and Lindsay in Washington were obvious examples. There is also some evidence that the Consular Department took on new life under the direction of David Scott, though persistent demands for economy prevented long overdue reforms. Increasing public criticism and a series of parliamentary questions led to a reconsideration of the amalgamation of the consular and diplomatic services. David Scott's memorandum of 1938 and a departmental committee began the process that was to lead to the large-scale Eden reforms in 1943. Already in 1934, the independent Levant service had been absorbed in the general consular service and in 1935 a compromise arrangement was reached with the China service. Until 1943 there was little interchange between the consular and the diplomatic service except in the Levant and the Far East where local expertise was valued more highly by the Office than in other areas. Even the Eden reforms did not meet the basic problem of the need to upgrade commercial and consular work. Both the Plowden (1963) and Duncan (1968–9) enquiries revealed continued differences and distinctions between types of posts and the kinds of people recruited to fill them.

The demands of the 1939–45 war proved an even greater test for the Foreign Office than that of 1914–18 but the Office was better placed to face it. The Foreign Secretary was made a member of the War Cabinet. Departments proliferated from sixteen in 1938 to twenty-four in 1944 and twenty-nine in 1945. Some had been divided so that key areas or countries (North America, France and later Germany) could be dealt with individually. There were special war problems, a separate Refugee as well as a Prisoner of War department. The main areas of new expansion were in the intelligence and economic fields and, in 1942, Gladwyn Jebb was given a few attic rooms at the top of the Foreign Office building to create an Economic and Reconstruction department to deal with post-war planning. It is perfectly true that the Office was just one among many institutions concerned with wartime planning and strategy whether in the areas of defence, economics, intelligence or propaganda.

Nevertheless, the position of the Office was far stronger than in the 1914–18 war partly as a result of the strong links (despite differences) between

Churchill and Eden and partly from the critical need for continuing negotiations with both the Soviet Union and the United States of America. The British embassy in Washington became almost a Foreign Office in itself. Also in contrast with Office attitudes to criticism in the 1914 war, it was in June 1941 that Eden announced to the Commons his intention to carry out wide-ranging reforms which both the public and his officials had been urging for some time past. These would include the creation of a combined service distinct from the home civil service, the broadening of the field of entry into the new service to meet the critics of ivory tower élitism and the provision of special retirement pensions for those staff in the middle ranks of the service who were clearly unsuited for the highest posts in either the Office or the diplomatic service. A major change was to be the inclusion in the new service of the consular service, which had been kept at arm's length for so long.

At the same time as these far-reaching plans for the reform of the Office and the diplomatic service were being worked out, the political departments were intensively employed in contingency planning for whatever might be Britain's role in the post-war world and participation in whatever international security organization might be devised to succeed the League of Nations. The Foreign Office was thus able to influence Churchill's wartime policies and post-war plans. The opening of official records for the post-war period is enabling research to be done on the functioning of the Office after 1945. It is already clear that under Bevin the influence of the Office was considerable. Attlee's choice of Ernest Bevin, the doughty ex-trade unionist and successful Minister of Labour, initially surprised the Office but rapidly proved a very happy one. He brought to the post of Foreign Secretary a flair for negotiation and administration that was to be necessary for the Office in the taxing years after 1945. He was to preside with great skill over the difficult period of major reform, which had been inaugurated by his predecessor. Recruitment on a permanent basis to the staff of the Office and the diplomatic service had ceased with the outbreak of war, the wartime pressure of work had been met by the appointment of temporary staff who departed at the end of the war. Entry to the service was now to be open to women. Obstruction to the admission of women had been maintained by senior staff of the Office in the face of persistent external pressure during the 1930s and early 1940s. A shortage of suitable male candidates for temporary posts and the availability of highly qualified female candidates for administrative work forced the Office to accept women on a temporary basis in late 1941. The competence of female recruits to the wartime service effectively ensured the impossibility of a return to the pre-war restriction.

In 1943 outline plans for a new structure were published and what became known as the Eden Reforms were effected gradually in the later 1940s and the 1950s. The main aims were to adapt the structure of the service to new responsibilities and to offer a worthwhile career to its staff. Most important was the amalgamation and complete integration of the Foreign Office, the diplomatic service, the commercial diplomatic service and the consular service into a single unified foreign service. Senior positions in the Office and abroad were open to all staff who could be called on for any type of work. The process of amalgamation was completed in 1946 by the inclusion of the overseas information services from the Ministry of Information. Examinations for entry into the unified service were to be special variants of those used for the home civil service. Two schemes were proposed for Branch A (equivalent to the home administrative class): Method I, virtually identical to the home examinations but with a language requirement, and Method II, soon known as the 'Country House Party', with three days of group tests under a chairman, an observer and a psychologist who were all members of the selection board. Method II came to be the normal method for recruitment to Branch A. Methods of recruitment to Branch B, Grade 5 (equivalent to the home executive class) and to Grade 6 (equivalent to the home clerical class) were similar to those for the home civil service. Branch C, the typing class, recruited only women. Branch D consisted of overseas established staff such as chancery messengers, office keepers and night guards. Branch C recruits usually spent time in a 'training pool' at the Office before being sent abroad.

These fundamental changes for the personnel of the Office were to prove only the beginning of a series of major administrative reorganizations. The India Office was closed in 1947. Such of its functions as remained were merged with the Dominions Office to form the Commonwealth Relations Office. As more colonial territories became independent, the functions of the Colonial Office diminished. A new Department for Technical Cooperation acquired some of its responsibility for economic development in 1961 and even more in 1964 when it expanded into the Ministry for Overseas Development. In 1966 the vestigial Colonial Office joined the Commonwealth Relations Office to form the Commonwealth Office, which in 1968 merged with the Foreign Office. Major structural changes in other government departments, in particular the creation of a unitary Ministry of Defence by means of a merger of the three service departments, the rapid growth of the Cabinet Office and the successive changes since 1968 in the role of the Department of Trade, have widened and complicated the range of Office activity: at the same time they have also tended to diminish the Office's central coordinating position.

In addition to the major administrative reorganization forced upon the Office by these shifts of responsibility in the post-1945 period, steady pressure of work resulting from continuous adjustment to change in the international world, the increasing number of overseas missions and persistent Treasury appeals for reduction in expenditure resulted in an enlarged service but with recurrent shortages of staff. Lord Strang estimated that in 1957, after the disbandment of the German Section, which had been responsible for the Control Offices in Germany and Austria, the total staff in Grades A, B and C was 'only about 3000'.[9] Even at the highest level, staffing problems have persisted, although frustrations have occasionally been expressed by those in mid-career postings. The 1943 reform proposals had recommended extensive in-service training for new recruits, but the continued shortfall in staff has repeatedly discouraged its development. The reports of the Plowden Committee (1964) and Duncan Committee (1969) both underlined the increasing need for specialized training, especially to provide for the Office's need for area and language expertise, but their recommendations coincided with yet more demands on foreign service staff as Britain became steadily more involved with the European Community. In 1977 the Central Policy Review Staff returned to the problem and suggested various ways in which the development of much needed expertise could be financed by Office and diplomatic economies. The Government's White Paper on Overseas

Representation, published in 1978, while not accepting the Review Staff's solution, indicated firm support for the encouragement of staff management specifically aimed at the building up of additional expertise.

After the dislocation of functions caused by the Second World War the Office settled down to a threefold distinction of its activities: (1) political departments, each dealing with a distinct geographical area – there were nine of these in 1957; (2) functional departments, which dealt with certain types of questions irrespective of geographical area, e.g. the Treaty and Nationality Department and the Information Department – 19 of these existed in 1957; (3) administrative departments responsible for the internal organization of the service at home and abroad – seven, apart from the Research Department and Library, were functioning in 1957. (The Passport Office and Passport Control Department also retained a tenuous link with the Office.) This was the structure by which foreign policy had to be formulated at all levels and by which contacts had to be maintained with other government departments in any way involved with other states and international organizations. Since the late 1950s the Office has been forced into a defensive stance to protect its right to coordinate a foreign policy very different in nature from that of the nineteenth century. Since Bevin, no other Foreign Secretary has achieved his kind of authority in either the Cabinet or the Office. The signs are, however, that Lord Carrington has been able to build on the authoritative position he established after the resolution of the Rhodesian tangle. The failure of the Office to impose its policy at the time of the Suez crisis demonstrated the limits of its capacity to influence major decisions. Office support for Britain's entry to the EEC met repeated Cabinet resistance. Failure to develop economic expertise in response to political needs allowed other government departments to take the initiative, especially in relations with the EEC.

The Office has found itself under repeated attack for its persistent social exclusiveness and lack of sympathy with the commercial needs of the country. Many of the accusations were exaggerated and ill-founded, but they reinforced other assaults on Office confidence, which were to result in the appointment of the Plowden and Duncan enquiries, whose main purpose seemed to be the reduction in the status of the Office to match the changed position of Britain in the world. It should, however, be pointed out that similar criticisms had been made of the home civil service and departments in the late 1950s and early 1960s, which led to the appointment of the Fulton Committee and its reform proposals (1966–8).

In 1964 the Government accepted the main recommendations of the Plowden Report, in particular that the separate foreign and Commonwealth services should be merged. The single service came into existence in 1965, but the institutional adjustments took several years. The Duncan enquiry was aimed specifically at the need to find possible economies in overseas representation. The persistent failure of the Office to allocate staff to the consideration of even short-term forward planning and the definition of foreign policy aims was severely criticized in both the Plowden and Duncan reports. Both committees recognized the difficulties encountered by the Office as its dominating position in the direction of foreign policy was being assailed by the home departments. The Plowden committee understood very well that interdepartmental committees usually resulted in 'the highest common factor of interdepartmental agreement and no more' and appealed for a 'clear and comprehensive definition of government strategy'. The Office set up a group of assessments staff to meet this recommended reconsideration of assumption and forecast in foreign policy. This proved to be too weak to play an active role. By 1972 the Office had a planning staff that reported to the Planning Committee, which comprised the permanent under-secretary and deputy under-secretaries and which was attended by the head of the planning staff. This committee gave the planning staff access to senior officials, but it could also eliminate proposals considered in some way unacceptable to ministers. Informal access to ministers by planning staff was thus not reinforced by the Office's structure. The need for adequate planning resources has been reinforced by Britain's entry to the EEC, which has further intensified the intermixture of the 'political' aspect of foreign policy with economic, industrial and social policy and encouraged an even greater proliferation of interdepartmental committees.

Though both the Plowden and Duncan reports had recommended changes, they also acknowledged the adjustments already being made within the Office as it came to represent the needs of 'a major power of the second order'. The rapid reduction of Britain's international status in the years after 1945, combined with the ever-accelerating trend towards complex bilateral and multinational diplomacy, had forced the Office into new functions and attitudes. By the 1970s the bulk of the staff had been recruited since 1945, including the permanent under-secretary and five of the ten deputy under-secretaries. Nevertheless, many old traditions and practices continued and provided ammunition for critics. The new Foreign and Commonwealth Office has remained, in many characteristics, the Foreign Office as it absorbed other departments. Its retention of the old Foreign Office building, while it has extended into other office buildings (even the Home Office) in the same complex and elsewhere, has underlined this survival. By 1972 there were sixty-eight departments, each headed by a counsellor (equivalent to assistant secretary in the home civil service) reporting through fifteen assistant under-secretaries and nine deputy under-secretaries to the permanent under-secretary and Foreign Secretary. Of these, twenty-two geographical departments represented the traditional political role of the Office, each with between six and twelve administrative grade staff organized by country or countries and one or more senior first secretaries to assist the head of department. Five departments dealt with information and cultural policy, working with the Central Office of Information, the British Broadcasting Corporation and the British Council. One department, the News Department, conducted relations with the press. Fifteen departments responsible to the chief clerk (a title interestingly revived in 1970) managed the Office's executive functions and administered the Office and diplomatic service. The Research Department library and records, legal advisers, economists, India Office library and records with their specialized staff, serviced the other departments. The main growth area in the Office had been in the functional departments, which numbered twenty in 1972. Their number was reduced in 1973 on entry to the European Community but has risen since. The relative weight of work between the different types of department is represented by the numbers of staff. The 1972–3 estimates listed geographical departments 347; functional departments 850; administrative departments 707; information, cultural and news 126. (These numbers include administrative, executive and secretarial grade staff.)

The present (1981) structure is given in diagrammatic form (see Appendix A). It will be noticed that the chain of command and report within the Office is highly complex and not easily mapped. Departments and units report sometimes via the same assistant under-secretary to different deputy under-secretaries. Despite the hopes of the Duncan committee that the merger of the Foreign Office with the Commonwealth Office would result in a reduction in the number of supervising under-secretaries, the extension of functional departments and special-purpose units – as, for instance, the Conference on Security and Cooperation in Europe unit linked to a specific conference – together with increasingly complex relationships with home departments, has encouraged more senior appointments. The setting up of the enquiry by the Central Policy Review Staff, which had previously dealt almost exclusively with domestic policy, underlined the tighter interweaving of the Office with the home departments in the making of policy. Overseas representation was to be reviewed, whether 'performed by members of Her Majesty's Diplomatic Service, by members of the Home Civil Service, by members of the Armed Forces or by other agencies financially supported by Her Majesty's Government'. The investigators asserted that the major thrust of British external relations was economic in character and that institutional machinery should be fashioned to meet this pressing need. The report underlined the crucial importance of coordination and good communications between the large number of agencies and departments concerned in the making and supporting of Britain's overseas economic policy if constructive and coherent policies were to be followed. Having argued strongly for extended overseas service for staff concerned in overseas economic work, whether from the Foreign Office or from the Department of Trade, it pressed for a much wider interchange with all home departments to increase the overseas expertise in the recipient departments as well as to provide specialist training for foreign service staff.

These recommendations, together with the Herbecq report (Civil Service Department, 1978) on interchange of staff, encouraged the development of an interchange programme designed to correct the imbalance between exchanges into and out of the foreign service (138:46 in 1977). Interchange has increased, directed on the part of foreign service staff but voluntary for home civil servants, to the level of 159:61 in 1981. The Government had agreed in 1978 to work towards a closer working relationship between the diplomatic and home civil services and to improve the level of co-ordination of British overseas representation by increasing the resources available for it in Whitehall and abroad. The success of an exhortative exchange scheme was to be monitored by the Civil Service Department. External economic and political pressures have reinforced the need for such co-ordination. Symptoms of these pressures are to be found not only in the increased level of staff interchange but in the large number of visits abroad (3528 in 1975) made by members of staff in home departments such as Trade, Industry and Consumer Protection and the significant statistic that almost half the senior staff of the office of the United Kingdom permanent representative to the European Community, including the deputy permanent representative in 1978, came from home departments. There have also been a few examples of staff interchange with organizations outside the civil service such as merchant banks and commercial firms where specialist skills have been required.

The generally negative response of the government to the CPRS report indicates the difficulties that hinder any attempt to reduce the numbers of senior staff. At a public level, in the House of Lords and the press there were loud denunciations of the investigators' attempts to downgrade both the political and cultural work of the Office: the defenders of the BBC World Service and the activities of the British Council, both of which were to be curtailed, managed to focus on those aspects of the report at the expense of many of the more important recommendations. The increasing complexity of external relations has, however, within the Office reinforced the need for a certain streamlining. There are now 59 departments, which include 20 geographic, 19 functional, 11 administrative and 9 specialist and supporting departments or units (see Appendix A). The location of different types of department in different buildings further highlights their different roles.

These changes of function and organization must also be seen against a background of Cabinet pressure for reductions in government spending that has been sustained since 1976. There can be no doubt that the rationalization of the Office and its overseas missions during the 1970s has reflected external pressures. New financial restraints will encourage further attempts to reduce the status of some missions to what are now described as 'mini-missions' with a handful of staff, and the withdrawal of missions altogether leaving local responsibility for British nationals with honorary vice-consuls. Since 1979 35 missions have been closed, and others are likely to be eliminated. Appendix B shows the typical staff structure of a medium-sized embassy. The maintenance and even increase in senior staff levels stands against a background of a 9 per cent reduction in staff since the amalgamation of departments in 1968. At the beginning of 1981 staffing levels stood at 4700 in the diplomatic service at home and abroad, supported at home by 2000 home civil servants.[10] The total of 4700 diplomatic service staff included representational, administrative and technical staff. About 2760 were overseas. Representational staff counted for approximately 3000, of which 1900 were overseas. Nearly 7000 locally engaged staff are employed overseas mainly in support roles; they are not members of the diplomatic service. A Government White Paper of 1979 planned more major change. Detailed reviews of manpower needs have been undertaken, which allow for training margins and possible reductions in the number of posts. A desire has been expressed for the introduction of annual leaves in order to prevent overseas personnel feeling remote from the policy-makers in London. Staff reductions are planned in the areas of research, information and defence services with the aim of rationalization and coordination. Various technological innovations have been adopted. Computerized accounting began in 1979 and the Government agreed to undertake long-term planning of communications development. The skills and power of the inspectorate have been enhanced in the last few years in order to reduce overseas costs and to improve standards of office efficiency in missions abroad.

The social background of entrants into the Foreign and Commonwealth Office has been vastly widened. In the 1950s only one in seven of the administrative entrants (the highest class) came from a state school and only one in ten had not attended Oxford or Cambridge University. By the 1970s, one in two came from a state school and one in three had not attended Oxford or Cambridge. Methods of recruitment now follow the pattern developed for the home civil service in the 1960s and closely resemble, for the administrative grade, Method II of the 1950s. The number of applicants vastly exceeds the number of posts available. Despite the difficulties of economic recession, which press hard on a relatively small government department, staff morale is high. The Office hopes that over the next few years structural changes of a gradual nature will be made, with the aim of providing an overseas representation able to adapt 'to the future on the basis of a realistic but confident assessment of Britain's role in the world'. It remains to be seen how far the Office is able to throw off some of its remaining outdated traditions and can continue to recruit, train and keep staff with the capability and flexibility to meet the challenges of the last twenty years of the twentieth century.

The author wishes to acknowledge the assistance of Zara Steiner in the preparation of this chapter and to thank the staff of the Personnel Policy and Personnel Operations Departments of the FCO for information and advice on the current organization of the Office.

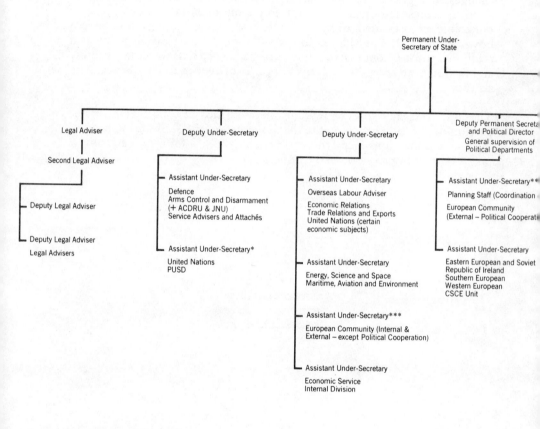

Permanent Under-
Secretary of State

Legal Adviser

Second Legal Adviser

Deputy Legal Adviser

Deputy Legal Adviser
Legal Advisers

Deputy Under-Secretary

Assistant Under-Secretary

Defence
Arms Control and Disarmament
(+ ACDRU & JNU)
Service Advisers and Attachés

Assistant Under-Secretary*

United Nations
PUSD

Deputy Under-Secretary

Assistant Under-Secretary

Overseas Labour Adviser

Economic Relations
Trade Relations and Exports
United Nations (certain
economic subjects)

Assistant Under-Secretary

Energy, Science and Space
Maritime, Aviation and Environment

Assistant Under-Secretary***

European Community (Internal &
External – except Political Cooperation)

Assistant Under-Secretary

Economic Service
Internal Division

Deputy Permanent Secreta
and Political Director
General supervision of
Political Departments

Assistant Under-Secretary**

Planning Staff (Coordination

European Community
(External – Political Cooperati

Assistant Under-Secretary

Eastern European and Soviet
Republic of Ireland
Southern European
Western European
CSCE Unit

KEY

ACDRU	Arms Control and Disarmament Research Unit
JNU	Joint Nuclear Unit
PUSD	Permanent Under-Secretary's Department
CSCE	Conference on Security and Co-operation in Europe
ADP	Automatic Data Processing

*/**/*** = posts occupied by
the same person

Note

1. Each Deputy to the Permanent Under-Secretary is primus inter pares.

2. Although there is already a considerable flexibility in the
organisation, the new system is designed to increase
flexibility. It is not a strict hierarchical system. It is
not yet clear how the two Deputy Permanent Under-Secretaries
will divide office responsibilities in the Permanent
Under-Secretary's absence.

3. The post of Deputy Permanent Secretary and Political
Director is a new position from April 1982. Precise
responsibilities still to be defined.

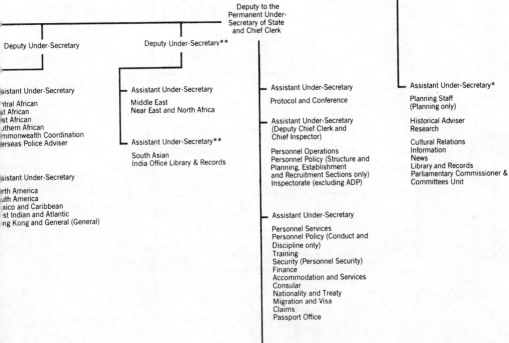

Deputy to the
Permanent Under-
Secretary of State
and Chief Clerk

Deputy Under-Secretary

Deputy Under-Secretary**

sistant Under-Secretary

ntral African
st African
st African
uthern African
mmonwealth Coordination
erseas Police Adviser

sistant Under-Secretary

rth America
uth America
xico and Caribbean
st Indian and Atlantic
ng Kong and General (General)

Assistant Under-Secretary

Middle East
Near East and North Africa

Assistant Under-Secretary**

South Asian
India Office Library & Records

Assistant Under-Secretary

Protocol and Conference

Assistant Under-Secretary
(Deputy Chief Clerk and
Chief Inspector)

Personnel Operations
Personnel Policy (Structure and
Planning, Establishment
and Recruitment Sections only)
Inspectorate (excluding ADP)

Assistant Under-Secretary

Personnel Services
Personnel Policy (Conduct and
Discipline only)
Training
Security (Personnel Security)
Finance
Accommodation and Services
Consular
Nationality and Treaty
Migration and Visa
Claims
Passport Office

Assistant Under-Secretary
(Director of Communications)

Communications Administration
Communications Engineering
Communications Operations
Communications Planning Staff
Communications Technical Services
Inspectorate (ADP only)
Security (Technical)

Assistant Under-Secretary**

Far Eastern
South East Asian
Hong Kong and General (Hong Kong)
South Pacific

Assistant Under-Secretary*

Planning Staff
(Planning only)

Historical Adviser
Research

Cultural Relations
Information
News
Library and Records
Parliamentary Commissioner &
Committees Unit

UNITED KINGDOM – APPENDIX B

A TYPICAL EMBASSY STRUCTURE

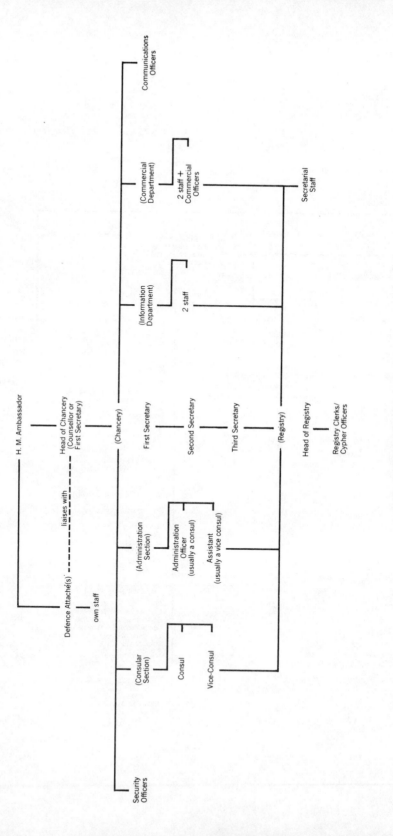

H. M. Ambassador

Defence Attaché(s) — — — liaises with — — — Head of Chancery (Counsellor or First Secretary)

own staff

(Chancery)

(Consular Section)

Consul

Vice-Consul

(Administration Section)

Administration Officer (usually a consul)

Assistant (usually a vice consul)

Security Officers

First Secretary

Second Secretary

Third Secretary

(Registry)

Head of Registry

Registry Clerks/ Cypher Officers

(Information Department)

2 staff

(Commercial Department)

2 staff + Commercial Officers

Communications Officers

Secretarial Staff

This plan shows members of the foreign staff.
Locally recruited staff work in most sections other than the Chancery.
The Head of Chancery has a pivotal position. He or she may
be a Counsellor or First Secretary.

NOTES

[1] *Appendix to the 1st Report of Commissioners on Fees, Gratuities, etc. of Public Offices*, HC. 1806 (309) XI, 27.

[2] J. B. Burges, *Letters and Correspondence* (J. Hutton ed.), (London 1885), 131–2.

[3] Palmerston Papers, National Registry of Archives, GC/SC/21, 28 July 1859.

[4] Public Record Office, F.O. 366/386, Minute by Palmerston, 26 April 1836.

[5] Public Record Office, C.S.C. 2/5, Foreign Office to Civil Service Commission, 25 June 1855.

[6] *Fifth Report of the Royal Commission on the Civil Service*, HC 1914 [7749], Q 39, 397.

[7] *The United Kingdom's Overseas Representation*, HC 1978 [7308], 4.

[8] Christina Larner, 'The Amalgamation of the Diplomatic Service with the Foreign Office', *Journal of Contemporary History*, VII (1972).

[9] Lord Strang, *The Foreign Office* (London 1957), 56.

[10] In comparing staff numbers with other countries' equivalents, it must be emphasized that many different objectives, responsibilities and practices are reflected in the means of calculating them. For instance, unlike France, it is not the practice in the United Kingdom to include officers responsible for cultural relations because they are in most countries the responsibility of the British Council. Unlike West Germany, the United Kingdom does include staff employed in export promotion and other commercial work.

BIBLIOGRAPHY

Valerie Cromwell, 'The Diplomatic Service', in V. Cromwell *et al.*, *Aspects of Government* (Dublin 1978).

D. B. Horn, *The British Diplomatic Service, 1689–1789* (Oxford 1961).

Ray Jones, *The Nineteenth Century Foreign Office* (London 1971).

Charles R. Middleton, *The Administration of British Foreign Policy (1782–1846)* (Durham, North Carolina 1977).

D. C. M. Platt, *The Cinderella Service: British Consuls since 1825* (London 1971).

——, *Finance, Trade and Politics in British Foreign Policy, 1815–1914* (London 1968).

Report of the Committee on Representational Services Overseas, 1962–3 (Plowden Report), HC. 1964 [2276].

Report of the Review Committee on Overseas Representation 1968–9 (Duncan Report), HC. 1969 [4107].

Review of Overseas Representation. Report by the Central Policy Review Staff (London 1977).

Zara Steiner, *The Foreign Office and Foreign Policy, 1898–1914* (Cambridge 1969).

Lord Strang, *The Foreign Office* (London 1957).

Mark A. Thomson, *The Secretaries of State, 1681–1782* (London 1932).

Sir John Tilley and Stephen Gaselee, *The Foreign Office* (London 1933).

The United Kingdom's Overseas Representation, HC. 1978 [7308].

William Wallace, *The Foreign Policy Process in Britain* (London 1975).

United States of America

The Department of State and American Foreign Policy

HUGH De SANTIS

Hugh De Santis is special assistant for European regional affairs (Bureau of Intelligence and Research) at the Department of State in Washington, D.C.* He was educated at the University of Chicago, receiving his Ph.D. in diplomatic history in 1978. He has just published *The Diplomacy of Silence* (1981) which analyses the perceptions of the USSR formed by American career diplomats during the period 1933–1947.

*This paper was prepared before Mr De Santis began his State Department service.

WALDO HEINRICHS

Professor Waldo Heinrichs is Professor of History at Temple University. He studied at Harvard University, taking his Ph.D. in 1960 and at Oxford. He has published *American Ambassador: Joseph C. Grew and the Development of the United States Diplomatic Tradition* (1967) as well as other books and numerous articles on professional diplomacy and American–East Asian relations.

The era of free security

During most of the nineteenth century the United States enjoyed what the historian C. Vann Woodward has described as the age of 'free security'. Since foreign states rarely posed a threat to America's existence, political relations with other governments were not of critical importance. This fortunate circumstance of geography left its imprint on the organization of American foreign relations then and, indeed, well into the twentieth century, long after free security had disappeared. The nation did not devote a significant portion of its talents or treasure to the maintenance of a strong diplomatic establishment.

At the beginning the reverse had been true. Surrounded by colonies of Great Britain, France and Spain, the new nation of the eighteenth century took a keen interest in European rivalries and their consequences. The finest minds of the Republic led missions to Europe or otherwise preoccupied themselves with diplomatic affairs. Benjamin Franklin, John Jay, John Adams, Thomas Jefferson, George Washington, Albert Gallatin, John Quincy Adams, Henry Clay and James Monroe gave their best efforts to protecting the nation in a dangerous, war-torn world. Then the defeat of France in 1815 and the collapse of the Spanish empire in the new world opened the way to generous years of international solitude and continental expansion for the United States.

Circumstances favoured American reclusiveness. The remoteness and vast reaches of the nation made foreign invasion difficult; American disengagement from European affairs made it unnecessary. The one nation capable of threatening American security was Great Britain, but the vulnerability of Canada, the value of trade with America, and the generally benign, commercial orientation of British policy encouraged tolerance. The British navy, dominating the seas, underwrote American security.

Deeply-rooted popular suspicion of Europe also affected American foreign policy and its organization. America meant freedom from Europe, from intolerable religious and political systems. At first Americans hoped that their society would serve as a model for others, but Europe proved unregenerate. Better then, they concluded, to preserve their experiment in democracy, republicanism and individual freedom from contamination by Old World influences. Everything wrong with Europe seemed reflected in its diplomacy: dynastic ambitions and rivalries, aristocratic privilege, intrigue, deceit and incessant war. For Americans, the less diplomacy the better.

This suspicion of diplomacy did not include consular affairs. Americans believed in trade, for the benefit of their pockets and the well-being of all mankind. Foreign trade contributed substantially to American economic growth. Merchants needed the assistance of consuls, and these the parsimonious Congress was prepared to authorize. Trade assistance became a traditional and valued function of the State Department.

The structure of the American government heavily affected the conduct of foreign relations. Constitutional powers in foreign affairs, when they do not reside in the Congress, belong to the President, who is also commander-in-chief of the armed forces. The Secretary of State, while first in precedence among Cabinet officials and principal adviser to the President on foreign affairs, enjoys no constitutional stature. The influence he can exert depends entirely on the wishes of the President. Early Presidents established their primary role in the conduct of foreign relations, but Congress persistently and jealously guarded its rights. The price of democratic scrutiny is a cumbersome procedure. Both houses of Congress rule how much money the State Department should get. No bureau or humble clerkship can exist without the approval of Congress. Treaties require the consent of two-thirds of the Senate, and all presidential appointments are subject to Senate approval. The State Department soon became a 'patronage orchard' ripe for plucking by each party as it came to power.

Suspicion of diplomacy, and indeed of central government, a benign foreign environment, constitutional checks and balances, and the lack of a large, natural constituency made the State Department a relatively insignificant organ of government in the nineteenth century. It was small, passive if not inarticulate in policy, preoccupied with mundane matters. At least it was economical, and the nation expected little more.

Emergence as a world power

Toward the end of the nineteenth century this modest diplomatic establishment became increasingly inadequate for the management of American foreign affairs. The State Department and its foreign service began to change fundamentally in size, structure and function. Three developments determined and shaped these changes.

In the first place, American economic growth required better servicing of foreign trade. Vast industrial expansion in the post-Civil War years led to a surge of exports that established the United States as the world's second largest trading nation. At the same time, cyclical fluctuations, especially the severe depression beginning in 1893, led the American business community to believe that expanding exports would provide critical relief from idle factories and social tensions at home. To manage and expand this trade Americans travelled abroad in increasing numbers. The result was an overwhelming burden on American officials in the State Department and abroad who performed the bureaucratic chores attendant on trade and travel abroad and now were expected to drum up new markets for American goods.

A second determinant of change was the increasingly dangerous and competitive world environment. Beginning in the 1880s great power rivalries in Europe spilled over into a race for empire in Africa and Asia. The generous era of free trade, open markets and informal empire gave way to higher tariffs, colonial acquisition, spheres of interest and closed trading systems. Americans not only worried about maintaining existing markets in Europe and the outer world but also feared European political and economic penetration of neighbouring Latin America. A threatening world made them more aware of the need for better defences, in particular a modern navy, and also better official representation in foreign capitals. The protection and advancement of growing American interests abroad required skilled diplomacy and accurate intelligence. Furthermore, international rivalries enhanced the importance of national prestige, and Americans found their amateurish diplomats and shabby legations humiliating. Citizens demanded the upgrading of American representation abroad to the quality and status of a great power.

A third factor shaping the new American diplomatic establishment was the bureaucratic mode of organizing work in modern societies according to functional skills integrated by elaborate systems and routines. The stress was on efficiency, expertise and experience, all dependent on career commitments. The bureaucratic mode, taking hold in American business in the late nineteenth century, became the model for government reform. By bureaucratic criteria the State Department and its overseas missions appeared woefully mismanaged and inept, and the demand rose for fundamental reorganization and the provision of attractive careers for able young Americans.

Originally, the State Department was the principal executive office of the United States government, responsible for a host of domestic duties in addition to foreign affairs – such as patents, the census, pardons, and even at one time the mint and the mail. Over time these duties moved to other agencies, leaving the Department of the 1870s with thirty-one clerks, six bureau chiefs, two assistant secretaries and the Secretary of State. The First Diplomatic Bureau and First Consular Bureau, supervised by an assistant secretary, dealt with most European countries, China and Japan. The Second Diplomatic and Second Consular Bureau took care of the rest of the world, principally Latin America. The diplomatic service was exceedingly small, with no ambassadors and fewer secretaries of legation than ministers. The consular service was much larger, reflecting the trading interests of the nation. In 1890 the United States had, apart from regular consulates, 437 consular agencies scattered in cities around the world, staffed by part-time, ill-paid merchants, American and foreign. Only exceptionally did American ministers, secretaries and consuls serve longer than the term of the President who appointed them. It was this ramshackle, miniscule foreign affairs establishment that became the target for reform in the 1890s.

Reform came slowly and piecemeal; Congress grudgingly relinquished patronage. The United States began exchanging ambassadors in 1893, but little else except a gradual increase in authorized personnel occurred until the presidency of Theodore Roosevelt. Beginning in 1906 the pace quickened, especially for the consular service which, with its trade promotion function, was nearest to the hearts of American businessmen.

Between 1906 and 1915 legislation, executive orders and strong, persistent leadership within the State Department radically reorganized the consular service and established it as a career. Replacement of consular agents with salaried American consuls and clerks enhanced the American character of consulates. Classification of consulates according to importance, assignment of specific territory to each, and an increase in the numbers and supervisory functions of consulates-general brought about a more rational division of labour and tighter control. Standardized procedures and a roving inspection corps improved accountability and efficiency. Entrance into the consular service only at the lower grades and by examination, promotion on the basis of merit and experience, appointment to grade rather than post and higher salaries offered substantial career inducements.

Diplomatic reform lagged. Pressure for change was not as great; obstacles were greater. Old prejudices survived, associating diplomacy with aristocracy, intrigue and entanglement in Europe's wars. Little awareness existed of the interdependency of the modern world, the indivisibility of peace, and the need for expert representation of widening national interests. Affluent Americans travelling abroad were less interested in the skill of American diplomats than in the impressiveness of their entertainment and social standing. In the appointment of envoys the amateur ideal prevailed: businessmen, educators and above all 'men trained in the practical school of American politics' seemed more representative of America and more likely than career diplomats to reflect the President's views.

To be sure, the diplomatic service changed. Diplomatic secretaries tripled in number between 1898 and 1918; counsellors of embassy and second and third secretaries appeared on the rolls; larger embassies organized subdivisions with senior secretaries emerging as administrative officers. Promotion of some secretaries to minister and even ambassador occurred. Like the consular service, the diplomatic service offered entrance by examination, promotion by merit, and appointment to grade rather than post. But careerists lacked any assurance that merit and experience would open the way out of the humble secretarial world into the higher service of ministers and ambassadors.

The reforms of the Roosevelt, Taft and Wilson presidencies, and especially the more active role in world affairs resulting from the First World War, greatly enlarged and altered the State Department itself. Until the war, three executive departments – State, War and Navy – occupied the large, grey office building just west of the White House (now White House offices). In time the others moved out, leaving the State Department supreme in its elegant Victorian setting with pillars, porticoes, mansard roof, bronze stair balustrades and red mahogany doors two inches thick.

After several decades of rapid growth 'old State' settled down during the inter-war years. A staff of 82 at Washington in 1898, including messengers, labourers and porter, increased to 210 in 1909, 714 in 1921, and 753 in 1936. Additionally some 3600 foreign service officers and their staffs manned 57 missions abroad and 288 consular offices. In the 1920s the organization dealt with close to a million pieces of mail and over twenty thousand cables and telegrams annually. Its net cost to the taxpayer, after returns from passport and consular fees, was $1 200 000 in 1925.

The Department gradually shook off the age of quill and inkstand. It acquired better facilities for disseminating information within and to the field, a modern filing system and, grudgingly, telephones, typewriters and telegraph operators. It persisted in sending handwritten diplomatic notes until the British Foreign Office switched to typing them. A quaint and musty air clung to the Department, partly no doubt because of the extraordinary longevity of certain key officials. Alvey A. Adee, for example, who presided over the Department's prose and precedents, died in harness in 1924 after fifty-four years of service.

The office of the Secretary of State faced south toward the Washington monument on the second floor. By 1924 he had a substantial executive secretariat, including an under-secretary, four assistant secretaries, a counsellor and a resident diplomatic officer. With the exception of the Latin American area, however, assistant secretaries did not directly supervise relations with other nations. Rather they dealt with administrative, legal, economic and fiscal matters. This left policy direction to the Secretary of State, the under-secretary and the six geographic divisions.

The geographic divisions replaced the old diplomatic and consular bureaux. First to appear was the Far Eastern Division in 1909, followed by the Latin American, Mexican, Western European, Eastern European, and Near Eastern Divisions. These precursors of the present geographic bureaux, staffed by civil servants and foreign service officers detailed home from the field, became the key echelon in management of ordinary relations with other nations. Long incumbency of division chiefs, their assembled regional expertise and inadequate supervision gave these divisions a large voice in policy formulation and management as well.

Tradition and system militated against good policy. The Secretary of State had too much to do. The last to fill the job successfully in 'old State' was Charles Evans Hughes, and it proved overwhelming even for him. The problem was not so much inadequate staffing as misconception of the task. The nineteenth-century practice persisted of building policy case by case, from the particular to the general, like the common law. American leadership had simply not reached the point of seeing foreign policy as high policy, requiring sustained attention at top levels, broad conception, and management and coordination from the top down, from the general to the particular. Foreign problems were still the exception rather than the rule. Lacking a modern sense of the task, harried Secretaries of State let policy control slip away to lower, parochial levels, comforted by the belief that the ordinary need not concern them and that problems they were unaware of did not exist. The well-known inertia of the modern State Department derives in no small way from this condition.

The reform movement that had begun in 1906 culminated in the Foreign Service Act of 1924, which amalgamated the diplomatic and consular services into one unified career system. Existing diplomats and consuls were recommissioned as foreign service officers. A single personnel system controlled entry by examination, promotion from grade to grade and retirement. Henceforth, assignment to diplomatic or consular work depended on an officer's capabilities, the stage of his career and the needs of the government. To make the career more attractive, salaries were substantially raised to a maximum of $9000, retirement and disability funds were provided, and home leave and representation allowances were authorized. Ministers and ambassadors were still not included in the classified service, but foreign service officers could now be formally recommended for appointment as minister. At the same time, officers whose performance was judged inferior could be retired early.

Amalgamation was more easily legislated than effected. The diplomatic and consular services were quite different, not only in the type of work performed but in the type of person performing it. In its short span as a career organization from 1906 to 1924, the diplomatic service developed a strong cohesiveness and a distinct culture, which persisted in spite of the directive to amalgamate, and indeed lingered on into the post-Second World War era. As this strain is of great importance in understanding the modern foreign service, its origins and development need to be examined.

Diplomacy was an attractive prospect to young men of wealth at the turn of the century: secretaryships of embassy and legation were opening up; Theodore Roosevelt was calling sons of the best families to serve the nation; a career diplomatic service was taking shape. New recruits of the Republican years managed to survive the transition to a Democratic administration in 1913, and their ranks swelled during the war. They learned the ropes of diplomacy and moved quickly upwards through the ranks. A few secured ministerships. By the 1920s, back in the comfortable times of peace, 'normalcy' and Republicanism, careerists staffed all embassies and legations and held key policy posts in the Department.

The old diplomatic service was an extraordinarily homogeneous group of less than one hundred officers. Inherited wealth was a prerequisite, as salaries were a fraction of what was considered necessary to support a diplomat socially. The recruits came from upper-class families and mostly from boarding schools and Ivy League colleges (Harvard, Yale, Princeton, etc.). Where family acquisition of wealth was recent, these élite schools and colleges provided a means of upper-class acculturation. Abroad, these favoured sons of America became closely acquainted with each other as they moved from post to post. Since most secretaryships were in Europe at capitals near each other, a close social grouping – an informal subculture – formed with many of the attributes of an exclusive private club.

Socially adept, these diplomatic secretaries moved easily in European social and diplomatic circles. Exposure to the European sense of diplomacy as a profession encouraged them to work at solidifying the career principle in the United States. But they had difficulty defining precisely how diplomacy qualified as a profession: especially in their day, and to some extent today, diplomacy was a matter of instinct, personality, and talent for dealing with people. It was more of an art than a distinct field of knowledge like law or medicine. Nevertheless, they persisted in the idea of diplomacy as a profession because it tended to legitimize a still tenuous career.

By amalgamating the diplomatic and consular services, the Foreign Service Act presented a direct challenge to this socially élite corps. To the American public they seemed snobbish dilettantes, more European than American in background, manners and values – the very antithesis of suitable American representatives. One object of the Foreign Service Act was to dissolve this clubby service by mixing in consuls of more average background.

The administration of the new foreign service in the 1920s largely defeated the intention of Congress. Diplomats managed to keep their old service relatively intact by exercising a veto over transfers of consuls. One foreign service existed with two types of officers: those from the old diplomatic service, who tended to monopolize traditional diplomatic functions and political reporting, either from embassies or consulates; and those from the consular service, who remained chained to the routine tasks of caring for Americans and American trade.

Over time the social complexion of the foreign service changed as the first generation of professionals moved on, up or out. Recruits attracted by the personal and material rewards of the new service were more broadly representative of American society and better equipped intellectually. However, the older generation imparted to their younger colleagues the élitist spirit of the original service, the sense of comradeship, of professional calling, and of diplomacy as a subtle art that few were qualified to practice. As the State Deparment and foreign service grew in typical bureaucratic fashion – functionally and hierarchically – an invisible web of professional intimacy and *esprit de corps* persisted, providing support and encouragement in an occupation that was often lonely, dreary, uncomfortable and dangerous. At the same time, by presenting a closed front to those who would alter it, the foreign service ran the risk of failing to adapt to changing circumstances and practices in diplomacy.

The era of independent internationalism

Modernization did not ensure the State Department increasing influence over foreign policy. During the period of American neutrality, the war and the Paris Peace Conference, Woodrow Wilson reserved all major policy questions for himself, consulting his personal adviser, Colonel Edward M. House, far more than his successive Secretaries of State. In the 1920s Secretaries Charles Evans Hughes and Henry L. Stimson exerted strong influence on policy. Indeed, the decade was perhaps the high-water mark of State Department prestige, morale and influence. Even then, however, it had to battle with the Departments of Commerce, Agriculture and the Interior, which briefly established separate foreign services.

Franklin D. Roosevelt's foreign affairs establishment was far more skilled than his cousin Theodore's at the turn of the century. Promising officers such as George Kennan, Charles Bohlen and Llewellyn Thompson were rising through the foreign service. More than half the chiefs of mission were career diplomats, including such veterans as Joseph Grew, William Phillips, Hugh Wilson and John MacMurray. These diplomats had a keen sense of the relation of power to diplomacy, a healthy scepticism and caution in foreign dealings, and a well-developed sense of the limitation of American influence in a complex and turbulent world. Nevertheless, political reporting, so far as it was influenced by old school diplomats, tended to deal with leading figures of government rather than deep social and economic forces, and with leading powers rather than emerging nationalities. Further, it reflected the anti-Communist bias of American upper-class thinking, thereby closing off from objective appraisal a most significant factor in the world scene.

Cordell Hull was a powerful and determined Secretary of State, but he relied heavily on his subordinates and was vulnerable to flattery. As a result, the geographic divisions of the Department developed into what Dean Acheson described as feudal baronies over the long course of Hull's secretary-ship. Deeply set in both their ways of looking at the world and their policy guidelines, they were not receptive to new challenges. Hull was successful in reasserting State's control over competing foreign services of other departments, and made every effort to retain primacy in policy-making. Yet the sharp distinction Hull and his staff drew between the classic diplomatic functions of the State Department and those of other departments had the effect of narrowing the scope and influence of the Department just when new substantive areas of foreign relations, such as economic and military assistance and propaganda, were becoming significant. State also failed to cooperate with the military in developing joint strategic policy. Given the extraordinary scope of the challenges posed by a world verging on war, and the President's habit of circumventing obstructive bureaucracies and bureaucrats, new tasks more often than not passed to agencies outside State, with the result that the Department lost influence relatively over the course of the thirties and the war years.

The foreign service was prescient in forecasting war with Japan, though it failed on the whole to understand the immensely complex inner workings of Japanese policy-making. With notable exceptions, foreign service officers underrated the menace of Hitler and were over-complacent about European developments of the 1930s.

The fortunes of the State Department declined further during the Second

World War. The foreign service, highly selective in recruitment, grew very slowly, too slowly, before the war. During the war, with appointments suspended and, beginning in 1944, officers subject to military service, it actually declined in strength. The forced resignation of Under-Secretary Sumner Welles, the illness and retirement of Hull, and the brief, unsatisfactory secretaryships of Edward R. Stettinius Jr. and James F. Bynes left a leadership vacuum. The Department held its own in post-war planning for Japan and for international organizations. Otherwise it moved into the new era of American power and responsibility, in the words of Dean Acheson, 'breathless and bewildered like an old lady at a busy intersection during rush hour'.[1]

II

The era of politico-military confrontation

The expanding nature and scope of America's post-war obligations imposed new responsibilities on the State Department in addition to its traditional focus on the political aspects of the nation's foreign policy. By way of illustration, there were 113 administrative units (bureaux, offices, divisions) within the Department in 1948, as opposed to 62 in 1943 and only 36 in 1931. At the end of 1945, the Office of International Information and Cultural Affairs that had been established during the war was reorganized into ten divisions, including five geographic divisions, to promote American policies and ideals among foreign peoples. By President Truman's executive order of 20 September, 1945, State further inherited the duties of intelligence gathering and analysis undertaken by the Office of Strategic Services (OSS) during the war. Administration of this functional area rested with the newly created post of special assistant to the secretary in charge of research and intelligence. Responsibilities in the economic sphere similarly multiplied. Besides coordinating with economic agencies such as the International Monetary Fund and the Bank for International Reconstruction and Development, the Department, by another executive order, absorbed a host of activities previously performed by the Foreign Economic Administration and other war agencies. Finally, the State Department retained its politico-military status on the State–War–Navy Coordinating Committee, which continued to operate for a short time after the war. When, in consideration of Washington's growing concern with national security, the Department of Defense was formed in 1947, State assumed a still greater coordinating role with defence officials in the formulation of post-war foreign policy.[2]

To bring some organizational cohesion to this welter of change General George C. Marshall, who became Secretary of State in January 1947, created an executive secretariat that centralized in one coordinating unit the Department's various administrative bodies. He also formalized the Department's planning function, hastened by the breakdown of relations with the USSR, by establishing a policy planning staff that replaced the informal and ineffective Secretary's Staff Committee. Headed by George Kennan and joined by other career diplomats, the planning staff provided the Secretary with long-range policy options and objectives that also served as a guide for current policy decisions.

Despite Marshall's innovations, the Department did not successfully integrate its new responsibilities with its traditional political role. Obviously, part of the problem lay in the sheer magnitude of the post-war duties it was assigned, for which it had little prior preparation. However, there was also considerable resistance within the Department to its broader mandate. This derived largely from the attitudes of career diplomats, who nurtured the belief that the most important foreign-policy decisions were political ones, for which, not incidentally, the most relevant experience was gained in the foreign service. They maintained that economic, cultural-ideological and strategic questions were of secondary value; rigorous objective analysis less important than intuition and political judgement tempered by experience. The service's ingrained professional élitism and its insular point of view about State's wider role in foreign policy formed a powerful subculture that influenced the attitudes and norms of other officials within the Department. This took on all the more significance in view of the fact that foreign service officers held many of the key positions in the geographic bureaux and on the country desks. Opposition within this 'informal culture' to the Department's assimilation of the OSS's research and analysis branch (reminiscent of the observation made by former Secretary Henry Stimson that gentlemen did not open other people's mail), which was briefly placed in the political offices, led to the institution of a separate Central Intelligence Agency under the National Security Act of 1947.[3]

The Foreign Service Act of 1946, which purported to make the service a more functionally diverse organization, actually reinforced the institution's élitist self-image. Without diluting the professional identity of the career diplomat as political expert, 166 staff and reserve officers laterally entered the service under this legislation to perform administrative, cultural and economic tasks in token recognition of the American government's expanding objectives abroad. Moreover, the act gave the career service statutory control of its own administration by establishing a director-general of the foreign service, who reported directly to the Secretary and the assistant secretary for administration. Appeal mechanisms bureaucratically prolonged and therefore weakened the act's provisions for weeding out ineffective diplomats; and although some lateral entrants rose to the top of the foreign service hierarchy, most did not fare well in the competition for promotion with career officers. In the end, the service remained institutionally impermeable to the changing nature of American foreign affairs and the eventual effects of this metamorphosis on its own vitality. As one veteran diplomat put it, the career officer sought a return to a less complicated era in American diplomacy, 'when the Cold War was unknown, when nationalism was self-contained, when foreign aid was remote as the Milky Way from our thoughts'.[4]

Despite the rearguard action fought by career diplomats and others at State against the force of modernity, in 1948 a special commission under the chairmanship of Herbert Hoover formulated recommendations to make the Department more responsive to its changing role. The Hoover Commission's findings, which called for closer supervision from the top of the Department hierarchy, greater delegation of responsibility and more effective administration of the foreign service, won the acceptance of Dean Acheson, who had served as vice-chairman of that body when he replaced Marshall as Secretary in 1949. Acheson reorganized the regional bureaux, making them accountable for all foreign-policy decisions in their areas – social, economic and administrative as well as political; he elevated to the assistant secretary level the heads of the geographic divisions, the division of international organization affairs, congressional relations, economic affairs and public affairs; and he created two deputy under-secretary positions to deal with administrative and substantive matters. Furthermore, he established a single office for personnel, budgetary and foreign service matters. In so doing, he made the director-general of the foreign service a staff assistant in the office of the deputy under-secretary for administration, thereby closing the service's separate access to the Secretary.[5]

As it turned out, however, coordination of effort within the Department was still lacking; such organizational cohesion that existed was mainly a result of Acheson's capable leadership and personality. And the informal culture of the Department still served as a barrier to the successful implementation of formal organizational changes. Foreign service officers continued to be bureaucratic saboteurs, unwitting or not, of the modernizing trend within the Department, biding their time in Washington until they could be transferred abroad. Acheson himself found the career service excessively cautious, unimaginative and insecurely confined to bureaucratic routine.[6]

Coming at a time when fast-changing world developments demanded fresh policy initiatives, the State Department's inertia proved bureaucratically self-destructive. As the Department chafed at its new duties, competing agencies increasingly gained influence within the foreign affairs bureaucracy. To be sure, this competition had existed, with no small duplication of function, since the end of the Second World War. The Departments of Defense, Treasury, Commerce, Agriculture, and Labor, the Joint Chiefs of Staff, the CIA, the AEC, and the Council of Economic Advisers, among other agencies, all shared in the formulation of post-war foreign policy. In addition, the National Security Council (NSC), established under the 1947 defence act partly as a check against the discretionary authority exercised by Franklin Roosevelt in determining foreign policy, advised the President on the integration of domestic, foreign and military developments affecting national security. While the Secretary of State shared equally in the body's deliberations, the collective voice of the NSC, which weighed heavily in favour of the defence community, superseded that of any one of its members.[7]

Cold War tensions and the government's preoccupation with national security questions contributed to the ascendancy of the defence establishment in the globalized foreign affairs agenda. Alarmed by the fall of Nationalist China in 1949, the outbreak of the Korean War and the perceived linkage between Soviet expansionism abroad and suspected Communist subversion within the United States, Congress encouraged the growing influence of national security agencies. Intent on preserving and aggrandizing their political leverage within the foreign affairs bureaucracy, the Department of Defense, the CIA and the NSC consequently expanded their functional jurisdictions at the expense of the State Department and its theoretical role of *primus inter pares*.

With the advent of the Eisenhower years, the Department's foreign policy mandate markedly deteriorated. To respond more quickly to current developments, President Eisenhower established within the NSC a Planning Board and an Operations Coordinating Board to implement the former's policy directives. Indicative of the growing crisis management of American foreign affairs, this move effectively reduced the utility of the policy planning staff. The appearance of new agencies further encroached on State's political domain. An assistant secretary of defense for international security affairs (ISA) was appointed in 1953 to coordinate the Defense Department's participation in foreign policy. Symbolic of its prominent politico-military role in the foreign affairs complex, ISA was later dubbed the 'little State Department'. The creation of the United States Information Agency in the same year diminished the Department's cultural and propaganda agenda. This organization grew out of Senator William Fulbright's insistence that cultural and educational programmes should be separated from propaganda activity. Accordingly, the agency's foreign service, USIS, was divided into two groups: one operating autonomously, that engaged in propaganda, and a second, reporting to the State Department, that focused on educational and cultural matters. In 1954 the Department of Agriculture reinstated its foreign service. While this elicited no cry of protest from career diplomats, it removed a functional area from the State Department's foreign service. Furthermore, the Department of Agriculture, along with USIA and the International Cooperation Administration (the latter the most recent in a series of independent agencies that administered foreign aid), undercut the authority of career diplomats in the field by stationing their officials abroad on an equal level with the heads of diplomatic missions.[8]

Between 1953 and 1960 morale in the Department sank to a low exceeding that of the 1930s. The economy drive initiated by the Eisenhower administration produced a major reduction in the personnel force (known as a RIF in governmentese) and halted new recruitment to the foreign service. The personal style of John Foster Dulles hardly lifted depressed spirits. A strong Secretary in the mould of Marshall and Acheson, Dulles enjoyed a close working relationship with Eisenhower. But much preferring policy analysis to administration and, further, tending to play his cards close to the chest, he was a poor executive. When Dulles was in Washington, which was infrequently, he conferred with Department officials selectively and desultorily, ignoring staff proposals in some cases and ridiculing them in others. Obviously, none of this raised the confidence level of his subordinates.[9]

Far more injurious to the psychological well-being of Department officials were the twin bogeys of McCarthyism and Wristonization. Loyalty investigations initiated by Truman to ferret out Communists or Communist sympathizers within the Department intensified following the 'loss' of China. Historically regarded as suspect by the American public and Congress, Department officials were now viewed by many either as Moscow's dupes or as an insidious fifth column. The harassment perpetrated by Senator Joseph McCarthy, who felt that the Department was full of 'bright young men who are born with silver spoons in their mouths', subsequently received the support of the Secretary of State. While Dulles may not have personally labelled Department officials – and particularly foreign service officers – homosexuals, 'com-symps' or 'incompatibles', in an effort to placate Republican nabobs in the Senate, he opened State's portals to the McCarthy inquisition. The security investigations, where they did not destroy careers and reputations, extinguished whatever initiative that existed in the Department, fostered the very conformism that had exercised administration officials and engendered in the survivors a lasting Cold War mentality. Beaten into institutional submission by the ravages of McCarthyism, the Department, as opposed to Dulles, deferred to other actors in the foreign affairs complex, notably the Department of Defense, the JCS and the NSC.[10]

The committee headed by Brown University president Henry M. Wriston assembled to implement the recommendations of the Hoover Commission and the later Rowe–Ramspeck–DeCourcy Committee: to integrate into a single administrative entity civil service employees, foreign service staff and reserve personnel and career diplomats; and to improve the Department's specialized competence in the new foreign policy agendas dealing with cultural, economic and politico-military issues. Unfortunately, the massive programme of integration that followed, which Dulles endorsed, effectively reduced the Department's capabilities within the foreign affairs bureaucracy; many employees with technical skills were summarily transferred from Washington to the field, while career diplomats with more traditional political orientations returned to the Department. Wristonization demoralized nearly everyone. Apart from those with exceptional talent, most civil service employees and technical support personnel in the foreign service felt that competition for promotions with career diplomats had jeopardized their growth potential. Despite the fact that Wristonization created more jobs in the Department for which foreign service officers could compete, careerists apathetically trekked back to their Washington confinement, resentful about the dilution of their professional status. Personnel integration backfired in still another way. In order to advance their careers, a large number of Wristonees gradually became coopted into the traditional values of the foreign service, which led to an under-utilization of their specialized expertise.[11]

Ideologically tainted by the scourge of McCarthyism, ignored by Dulles and mired in the bureaucratic morass of Wristonization, the ship of State drifted listlessly through the remaining years of the fifties, little stirred by the brief and lacklustre secretaryship of Christian Herter.

When John Kennedy assumed the presidency in 1960, the crisis atmosphere that characterized US–Soviet relations during the 1950s was still running strong in official circles and throughout the public. Kennedy himself campaigned as a cold warrior, branding the Eisenhower administration with the 'loss' of Cuba in the same way that Republicans had denounced Harry Truman's acquiescence to Communist rule in China after the Second World War. And animadversions on the State Department's performance and allegiance had little abated. Senators Lyndon Johnson and Henry Jackson deplored the 'depressing lack of new ideas' in the Department, without which the United States could not 'regain the initiative in the struggle against Communism'. Representative John Pillion, a Republican from New York, condemned State's lack of planning and the policy of 'appeasement' promoted by 'an influential minority in the upper ranks of the Department to obstruct policies and strategies to eliminate the communist menace'.[12]

Though sceptical of the Department's capabilities, Kennedy set out to inject new life into its role in the policy process. Uncomfortable with Eisenhower's formalized approach to policy-making, he abolished the rigidly structured Operations Coordinating Board and relied far less on the NSC.

Conversely, he restored the State Department's status as the primary coordinating agency in the foreign affairs bureaucracy and removed the distinction created by Dulles between policy and operations. He further tried to revive the policy planning staff, now the policy planning council, by bringing in an outsider, W. W. Rostow, as its director. Analogously, he instituted the 'country team' concept, which made the chiefs of diplomatic missions the single authoritative voice for all American activities abroad save military operations. Personnel programmes under Kennedy stressed specialization, planning and minority recruitment. Much of the Kennedy approach to personnel management found its way into the 1962 report of the Herter Commission, which was formed to put the President's 'new diplomacy' into practice.[13]

But the Kennedy reforms were never systematically carried out. Part of the difficulty lay in the President's style. Preferring to receive quick answers to emerging crises, Kennedy chose to work through *ad hoc* interagency task forces rather than to depend on the more cumbersome and slower processes of the State Department. He also greatly relied on his personal staff – Rostow, Averell Harriman, and academics like McGeorge Bundy, John Kenneth Galbraith and Roger Hilsman – which further tended to circumvent bureaucratic channels in the Department. In addition, the shifting of 'players' by Kennedy in the so-called 'Thanksgiving Day Massacre' of 1961 – George Ball's replacement of Chester Bowles as under-secretary as an example – and his penchant for dealing personally with country desk officers created a state of psychological suspense and bureaucratic instability in the Department. And the emergence of yet more new agencies – AID, the Defense Intelligence Agency and the Arms Control and Disarmament Agency – further circumscribed the Department's role in the policy process and aggravated the condition of functional redundancy in the foreign affairs complex. As a case in point, State's politico-military bureau, which was formed in 1962, essentially replicated the functions of ISA.[14]

A second difficulty lay in Kennedy's designation of Dean Rusk as Secretary of State. The appointment of Rusk, which came after Kennedy had chosen the Secretary's key subordinates, was dictated by domestic political considerations rather than by Rusk's experience in the State Department or by the President's regard for his capabilities. Given his razor-thin margin of victory and the Cold War mentality of the times, Kennedy was reluctant to select Chester Bowles, spokesman for the liberal foreign policy wing of the Democratic party and advocate of closer ties with the developing countries, or Adlai Stevenson, who favoured an accommodationist posture with the USSR. While less hard-line than Acheson, say, or Paul Nitze, who served under McNamara as assistant secretary for international security affairs, Rusk's conservative stance on US–Soviet relations made him politically more marketable to the electorate and to Congress.

Rusk's forte as Secretary, unlike that of Dulles, reputedly lay in the area of operations rather than policy formulation. But he did not turn out to be an effective administrator. For one thing, he did not maintain good lines of communication with the Department. Although he delegated authority to the assistant secretaries of the geographic bureaux, he generally removed himself from their activities, thereby setting himself apart from the Department bureaucracy. Moreover, Rusk was not a 'take charge guy', a trait

Kennedy valued highly, as was Secretary of Defense Robert McNamara, who was permitted to make his own top appointments and whom, according to recently released documentary data, Kennedy had tabbed as his successor in 1968. Consequently, Rusk was less the forceful proponent of the Department's mandate in the foreign affairs establishment and more one of the 'players' – and not a particularly influential one – on Kennedy's personal staff.[15]

Finally, exogenous factors adversely affected the success of the Kennedy reforms. Not the least of these was the relentless advance of technology, which made it increasingly more convenient for heads of state to telephone their counterparts directly or to hop onto an aeroplane if the exigency of business demanded immediate attention. As a corollary to this development, technology has facilitated the centralization of policy-making, which, reinforced by Kennedy's personal style, grew apace in his administration. A second external inhibitor of the Kennedy reforms was the Bay of Pigs fiasco in April 1961. Embarrassed by the faulty intelligence he had received from all sources in preparation for the filibuster of Cuba, Kennedy narrowed his circle of policy advisers, thereby further abridging State's role.[16]

The distance between Kennedy and the Department – and really between the President and a good part of the foreign affairs bureaucracy as a whole – widened in the months ahead. The Cuban missile crisis of 1962, which drew the United States uncomfortably close to the precipice of nuclear war, and the sharply escalating arms race with Moscow deeply disturbed Kennedy. He also had to contend with the anxiety of the American public, which clamoured for a ban on nuclear weapons testing. Having overcome his initial inexperience and insecurity in the presidency, Kennedy, even as he was stepping up American involvement in Vietnam, privately began to rechart the course of American foreign policy. In restrospect, the year 1963 proved to be a turning point; although it was not perceptible at the time, the policy of politico-military confrontation began to give way to negotiation and peaceful coexistence, in short, the policy of accommodation. Suspicious of the foreign affairs establishment, particularly the State Department, whose lingering defensive conservatism from the 1950s precluded such a major policy initiative, Kennedy effectively became his own Secretary of State, trusting in the counsel of his closest advisers, notably his brother, Attorney-General Robert Kennedy, Bundy, McNamara, and staff aide Theodore Sorenson. The earliest manifestation of this shift in policy came in August of that year, when the United States and the USSR agreed to ban atmospheric testing of nuclear weapons.[17]

Kennedy's tragic death leaves to speculation how the accommodationist alternative would have fared under his leadership. It must also be left to conjecture how Kennedy would have dealt with Vietnam, although insiders such as Roger Hilsman have suggested, and not unpersuasively, that his intention was to liquidate American involvement there.[18] In any event, the devolution of the policy of negotiation awaited the administrations of Lyndon Johnson and Richard Nixon, and, more importantly, the disruptive and demoralizing effect of the Vietnam War on American foreign relations.

The era of negotiation

Like Harry Truman two decades earlier, Lyndon Johnson was catapulted into the presidency at a crucial moment in the history of American foreign relations.

Both men found their predecessors hard acts to follow. For one thing, neither Truman nor Johnson possessed the charismatic appeal of Roosevelt or Kennedy. For another, neither was experienced in international affairs. Withal, both had been kept in the dark on foreign-policy developments. Truman had misunderstood Roosevelt's receptivity to spheres of influence, which the latter had carefully concealed to avoid public and congressional opposition. Amid pressure from Congress, Truman singlemindedly pursued the policy of containment. Influenced by the national temper of the 1950s, the need to reassure an American public traumatized by Kennedy's assassination that the administration's policies would be continued and the Goldwater challenge from the right, Johnson sustained the course of confrontation in Vietnam to the impoverishment of the emerging policy of negotiation.

Despite their obvious personality differences, Johnson also adhered to Kennedy's informal management of the foreign affairs bureaucracy. While the NSC met with greater regularity under Johnson, its agenda and attendance remained unstructured. Owing to Johnson's limited background in foreign policy and, *ipso facto*, his lack of confidence in this area, comprehensive policy planning received even less attention from Johnson than Kennedy gave it. Sceptical of professional advice, Johnson discarded the use of special task force groups. But his famous 'Tuesday lunches', which informally brought together the Secretaries of State and Defense, the special assistant for national security affairs and a handful of aides for discussions on Vietnam, simply continued his predecessor's 'ad hockery' in a different form.[19]

Despite his criticism of the State Department while he was a member of the Senate, Johnson similarly stressed the importance of the Department's coordinating role in the formulation and implementation of policy. Johnson appointed the under-secretary for policy coordination as chairman of the Senior Interdepartmental Group (SIG), which he formed to direct the coordination of interagency affairs in foreign countries; and he designated assistant secretaries of the geographic bureaux as chairmen of the Interdepartmental Regional Groups (IRG), which accorded with Rusk's view that the latter should be responsible for formulating and recommending policy. Johnson further endorsed Kennedy's emphasis on minority recruitment and on specialization. Efforts undertaken at the end of 1963 to convert generalists into specialists through a series of planned work assignments led, two years later, to the institution of an elaborate Manpower Utilization System and Techniques programme. By the end of the Johnson years, a new personnel category of Foreign Service Reserve Unlimited (FSRU) had been created, which, following a similar change in USIA, brought to fruition Kennedy's desire to establish a permanent foreign service reservoir of skilled specialists.[20]

There was only one major bureaucratic change during the Johnson administration, and this, the Planning-Programming-Budgeting System (PPBS), ended in failure. Introduced at the end of the Kennedy years upon the recommendation of the Herter Committee report and modelled on the systems analysis approach employed in the Defense Department by McNamara, the purpose of the PPBS was to streamline policy and operations in the State Department by defining options in cost-benefit terms. Programmed planning and budgeting won the support of management analysts outside the government and of some officials within the Department, especially William Crockett, a Wristonee and the deputy under-secretary for administration.

But however effective it proved to be in determining new weapons systems, it could not measure subjective values such as political judgement that remained the Department's stock in trade. Recognizing this as well as the resistance PPBS met from the Department's subculture and from other budgetary agencies, the Johnson administration laid it to rest in 1967.[21]

As was the case during the Kennedy years, the larger organizational mandate Johnson envisioned for the State Department did not translate concretely into real bureaucratic gains. Like his predecessor, Johnson did not exercise the executive control required to carry through the organizational reform. Nor did Rusk, who enjoyed a much closer relationship with Johnson than he had with Kennedy, demonstrate the necessary leadership to strengthen the Department's role in the foreign affairs bureaucracy. For that matter, neither Under-Secretary George Ball nor his successor, Nicholas Katzenbach, effectively represented the Department's bureaucratic interests as chairmen of the SIG. The absence of direction from the executive office and the lack of leadership from the Secretary and his key subordinates simply reinforced the Department's passivity and institutional insularity. Its dilatoriness in carrying out presidential orders and its sloppy staff work induced Johnson, in reciprocal fashion, to rely more on his personal staff and on other agencies in the foreign affairs complex, particularly the Defense Department.[22]

These factors, combined with the economic retrenchment programme undertaken in 1968, contributed to a new cycle of demoralization within the Department. Depressed by the inflated levels of reserve and staff personnel, the FSRU category, the special effort made by Kennedy and Johnson to help minorities enter the service, and the inflation-induced economic cutbacks, foreign service officers closed themselves within their private world. However, a number of younger diplomats, critical of the service's traditional élitism, conformism and resistance to change, formed the vanguard of a 'Young Turk' movement in 1967 to foster a spirit of activism. Their report, *Toward a Modern Diplomacy*, released in the waning months of Johnson's presidency, advocated a number of administrative changes, including better staff support for high Department officials, improved communications, increased delegation of responsibility from the top of the organizational hierarchy, and a broader mandate for the foreign service.[23]

A fundamental reason for Johnson's lack of attention to organizational reform in the Department was, of course, his preoccupation with other matters. Intent on developing and implementing his predecessor's domestic objectives, he invested considerable time and effort in what became the 'Great Society' programme. Moreover, by 1965 he found himself politically bogged down in the quagmire of Vietnam. Just as the embarrassing Bay of Pigs episode and the spiralling US–Soviet arms race prompted Kennedy to retreat into his inner circle of personal advisers, the débâcle of Vietnam evoked the same response from Johnson. Johnson's decision to intensify American military involvement in South-East Asia coincided with the views of Rusk and McNamara, JCS chief General Maxwell Taylor and emeritus advisers like Dean Acheson. Their political leverage, which, with the exception of McNamara, would probably have diminished had Kennedy pursued the course of disengagement, accordingly increased. So did the role of national security adviser Rostow, a hardliner as well, and the NSC. The centralization of foreign affairs decision-making, in turn, contributed to a somewhat more structured policy process. Johnson made greater use of the NSC's National Security Action Memorandums, which originated in the Kennedy administration, to help formulate current policy. A lesser, but not insignificant, informational conduit for policy-making was also provided by the State-chaired interdepartmental committees that Johnson formed in 1966.[24]

Barraged by the American public's increasingly virulent opposition to Vietnam policies, Johnson, a vain man who received criticism, however objective, as a personal affront, confined himself to the counsel of his advisers. Gatherings at the 'Tuesday lunches' resembled a kind of staff command post where the President sought consensus support for his views. Dissident opinions were considered obstructionist by Johnson. When McNamara, who in 1967 began to advise against further escalation of hostilities, presented his altered views on Vietnam to the Senate Armed Forces Committee, Johnson portrayed himself as a 'man trying to sell his house, while one of the sons of the family went to the prospective buyer to point out that there were leaks in the basement'. But such breaches of secrecy were uncommon. The confidentiality of the Tuesday sessions insulated the President from public censure, from the reproaches of the 'Young Turks' in the State Department, who opposed the enlargement of hostilities, and from Congress, which had in any case acquiesced in Johnson's management of the war after the 1964 Gulf of Tonkin resolution.[25]

The deluge of criticism at home and abroad, however, would not be stemmed. While he had convinced himself that American objectives in Vietnam could be realized, Johnson was not oblivious to this public outcry. At another level, the President now realized that the Cold War struggle the United States was waging with the USSR in Vietnam had eroded American international prestige. No less disturbed than Kennedy by the mounting Soviet build-up of nuclear weapons, Johnson further recognized that the policy of politico-military confrontation stood to threaten rather than strengthen national security. Indeed, Soviet President Alexei Kosygin, concerned about losing prestige in the Communist world, had unequivocally stated to Johnson in 1964 and at their Glassboro, New Jersey meeting the following year that the proposed discussions on mutual limitations of force levels could not proceed as long as the United States continued to prosecute the war in Vietnam.[26]

Thus it was, in 1965, that Johnson seized upon the Christmas lull in the fighting to send a phalanx of emissaries – Harriman, United Nations Ambassador Arthur Goldberg, Vice-President Hubert Humphrey, among others – on a global peace mission. Bureaucratically, this grandiose gesture of personalized diplomacy, so reminiscent of Franklin Roosevelt, served to widen the distance between the President and the State Department and to undermine the role of American diplomats abroad. Moreover, tactically it failed to change the situation in Vietnam. Nor did the renewal of American bombing. As the later TET offensive made all too clear, the enemy's spirit was not broken.[27]

By the beginning of 1968, Johnson knew full well that Vietnam had become a political albatross irreparably damaging his chances to succeed himself. In an effort to salvage his dwindling political stock at home and his place in history, regain American prestige abroad and lessen tensions with the USSR, he decided to abandon the policy of politico-military confrontation in favour of that of negotiation. This shift necessitated a corresponding loss of influence among 'hawks' like Rusk and Rostow and created a mandate for a new group of 'dovish' policy advisers such as Clark Clifford and the other so-called 'wise men'. But, unable to disentangle the United States quickly from the predicament of Vietnam he had perpetuated, and sensing the political disaster at home he personally could not have accepted, Johnson withdrew his candidacy for the presidency, which now passed, along with Vietnam and the policy of negotiation, to Richard Nixon.

It hardly seemed likely in 1969 that a veteran cold warrior such as Nixon would be inclined to terminate America's struggle against a 'third-rate' Communist power, the same Nixon who, in an earlier time, had accused Truman and the State Department of cowardly accepting Communist control of China. But precisely because of his credentials as a hardliner, because of his campaign commitment to 'peace with honour', because, as a Republican, he was not associated with the emergence of Red China and the Korean War, he was in a position domestically to do what Johnson could not. Now willing to admit that the spectre of a monolithic Communist world had dissipated, and recognizing – certainly after the disastrous invasion of Cambodia in 1970 – that the policy of politico-military confrontation had failed to prevent the emergence of a Communist-dominated Vietnam, he further pursued the course of negotiation and accommodation in US–Soviet relations that had been initiated in 1963 and resumed in 1967. Even more astonishing, Nixon buried the axe of resentment between Washington and the Chinese People's Republic by establishing diplomatic relations with Peking in 1972.

As enunciated in the Nixon Doctrine of November 1969, which called for greater restraint in US foreign relations and urged America's allies to share in the burden of assistance to the Third World, the President reversed the Cold War-inspired Truman Doctrine. While emphasizing the importance of maintaining American military security, Nixon redefined the nation's foreign policy in terms of negotiation, not confrontation; in so doing, he proceeded to liquidate America's global commitments. Nixon elaborated on this new strategy in his February 1970 report to Congress, in which he stressed the theme of peace through international partnership in relations with the Third World, in economic development, in the exploration of science and technology, and in the control of nuclear weapons.[28]

The policy of negotiation was endorsed by Henry Kissinger, the Assistant to the President for National Security Affairs in the Nixon White House. Indeed, such a supporter of *Realpolitik* as Kissinger considerably reinforced the new directions in foreign policy the President was taking, including discussions on trade and strategic arms limitations and the *apertura a sinistra* with Peking. He perceived SALT I and the US–Soviet trade talks as the key links in a mutually reinforcing process of collaboration that would induce the Soviets, in their own national interest, to cooperate with the United States in political areas, especially with the developing countries.

To be sure, Secretary of State William Rogers fully supported the Nixon Doctrine and the emerging rhetoric of détente, noting in a December 1969 speech that the administration would continue 'to probe every available opening that offers a prospect for better East–West relations'.[29] But his status in the foreign affairs bureaucracy was dwarfed by the charismatic Kissinger, whose Metternichian style of diplomacy curiously charmed the American public. Despite his *ex officio* position of national security adviser, Kissinger was functionally the President's *de facto* secretary of state for policy analysis, which left Rogers and the State Department the responsibility for programme implementation.

The separation of policy from operations and the NSC's designation as the primary foreign policy-formulating agency revived the bureaucratic forms of the Eisenhower years. Critical of Kennedy's and Johnson's informal style of decision-making – 'catch-as-catch-can talkfests' – in which the President sought advice from conflicting channels and regularly intervened in the policy process, Nixon favoured a more structured and formalized approach. He was opposed at the same time to Eisenhower's preference for concurrence among his advisers, which he believed limited the President's options to choose from alternative points of view. Under the Nixon system, the NSC became the formal clearing-house for policy papers prepared by other agencies or by inter-agency committees, which it synthesized for the President in National Security Study Memorandums. Policy papers on SALT drafted by the State Department's politico-military division, ISA, the CIA and ACDA serve as a case in point. As the word *study* denotes, these papers were more analytically oriented than the National Security *Action* Memorandums used by Kennedy and Johnson. Although Nixon did retain certain bureaucratic structures from the previous administration – Johnson's SIG and IRG as examples – they were controlled by the NSC Review Group, which was in turn dominated by Kissinger.[30]

For all its rhetoric of openness, however, the Nixon approach was really a closed system; information regularly flowed up the communications network from the line departments and other foreign affairs agencies to the White House, but only intermittently back down from the executive office. The 'White House-centred' system of foreign policy, as I. M. Destler has called it, thus failed to coordinate decision-making at the top of the foreign affairs pyramid with its subordinate parts, which, administratively neglected, grew still more bureaucratically obese. The State Department's role, like that of the Defense Department, was limited to proffering considerable information but only generalized policy advice. The critical counsel on major issues (SALT, for one, and the normalization of relations with China, for another) came from the NSC and the various specialized groups it spawned – all chaired by Kissinger – such as the Washington Special Actions Group, which assumed primary responsibility for crisis management.[31]

Kissinger's increased involvement in operations, which he found necessary to ensure the implementation of his policies, badly disrupted communications and organizational continuity in the State Department, and with it morale as well. Actually, morale was on the upswing when Nixon entered the Oval Office. The impetus provided by reform-minded diplomats in 1967–8 stimulated a major internal effort to improve the organizational effectiveness of the Department. Under the direction of William Macomber, deputy under-secretary for administration, and later under-secretary Elliot Richardson, some 250 foreign affairs professionals within and without the Department worked intensely in thirteen task force groups. Their report, published in December 1970, presented more than 500 recommendations to upgrade the Department's performance. These included increased functional specialization, better recruitment and training, the development of new evaluation measures to emphasize creativity, and the revamping of promotion and retirement policies to infuse the 'living system' with new blood.[32]

But the attempt at management reform failed to improve State's dwindling bureaucratic leverage. In the first place, Macomber's good intentions aside, the proliferation of specialized agencies had by this time made it unlikely that the State Department would ever reclaim the mandate it received – and rejected – after the Second World War to exercise its authority as the primary actor in the foreign affairs bureaucracy. Furthermore, the informal culture of the Department remained impervious to the Macomber report's recommendations. Notwithstanding changes in the social composition of the diplomatic community – broader social-class and educational representation, the increasing recruitment of women and minorities, a greater degree of professional specialization – the values and norms of the service continued to stress the primacy of politics in foreign policy and to favour the generalist in both the selection and assignment processes. Newcomers, one Department official observed, were still socialized into a way of life rather than a job. Institutionally constrained by the traditional subculture of the foreign service, the State Department persisted in defining its role in the foreign affairs complex as an essentially political one. Activities that deviated from this traditional role were frequently considered illegitimate, and tended to be left for other agencies to perform. Apart from these considerations, the reform thrust never received the support of Secretary Rogers, a weak Secretary whose portfolio as minister of state Nixon had substantially given to Kissinger from the start. Finally, the extreme centralization of the foreign-policy process under Nixon militated against any real change. Faced with a demoralized Department, and one that had become in some quarters outspokenly critical of the administration's policies – notably the Cambodian invasion – Nixon and Kissinger further distanced themselves from the bureaucracy.[33]

Disclosures during the Watergate hearings on the administration's secret bombings of Cambodia in 1969 intensified the centralization of foreign policy in the Nixon administration. Public and congressional aspersions on the President's conduct exacerbated his oft-demonstrated psychological predisposition to suspect the external world of baleful motives. Partly for this reason, but also in a frantic effort to divert national attention away from Watergate, he appointed Kissinger Secretary of State in 1973. By now a prisoner in the White House-centred world he created, Nixon really trusted only Kissinger's counsel on foreign policy. No less mistrustful of other 'players' in the foreign affairs bureaucracy who might encroach on his prerogatives, Kissinger, too, had minimized his communications with the State Department, which he sometimes treated as his personal baronial estate from which he periodically plucked talented professionals for the NSC staff. For a time, Under-Secretary Richardson inhibited the NSC from violating the Department's jurisdictional turf. An unexpectedly strong performer and a worthy adversary for Kissinger, Richardson had succeeded in breathing life into the policy planning staff, which thence became the policy coordinating staff, until he left State to head the Department of Health, Education and Welfare. Even the NSC staff, frustrated by Kissinger's reluctance to delegate authority and by their inaccessibility to the President, suffered a major breakdown in morale; halfway through Nixon's first term, two-thirds of the original members had quit. As time would show, Kissinger's style as Secretary would no more ingratiate him with officials in the State Department, which, with some exceptions, languished in a condition of bureaucratic desuetude.[34]

Kissinger's presence as Secretary and, briefly, national security assistant as well, was quite reassuring to Gerald Ford, who succeeded the embattled but impenitent Nixon to office in 1973. Having limited interest in and knowledge of foreign affairs, Ford, who preferred strong figures in his Cabinet anyway, depended on Kissinger, in the same way that Johnson depended on Rusk and McNamara, to provide continuity with his predecessor's policies. Heeding Kissinger's advice, Ford sustained the course of détente in US–Soviet relations, completing a trade agreement with Moscow in 1974 and, at the Vladivostok summit meeting in November of the same year, tentatively agreeing with Soviet party leader Brezhnev on a new strategic arms treaty. With Kissinger again as chief architect, Ford also continued Nixon's efforts to resolve the Arab–Israeli conflict.

Given the enormous mandate he received from the President, easily exceeding that of Dulles, who was kept in closer check by Eisenhower than it appeared, Kissinger exercised an historically unprecedented degree of power to formulate foreign policy. His control over the State Department bureaucracy, which he bypassed rather than managed, was equally remarkable. Because of his political leverage and the respect he was accorded as a policy strategist, morale within the Department and the foreign service somewhat improved when he became Secretary. This was particularly so for the policy planning staff, which enjoyed a renaissance during his secretaryship. But the staff, directed by Kissinger loyalist Winston Lord, functioned less as a bureaucratic entity within an integrated department and, not unlike the NSC staff, more as the Secretary's private 'brains trust'. Moreover, Kissinger's reliance on the policy planning staff served to insulate him from competition with senior Department officials. Staying personally abreast of the cable traffic from the field, he minimized his encounters with senior Department officials in the geographic bureaux. Middle- and lower-level bureaucrats were virtually ignored, frequently completely uninformed about substantive matters. This centralization of authority worsened the Department's already low morale, generally aggravated its bureaucratic inertia and, in those instances when officials openly opposed Kissinger, fostered organizational disintegration.[35]

So long as Kissinger enjoyed the confidence of Ford, however, friction within the foreign affairs bureaucracy little affected American foreign policy. But the bloom on the Nixon–Kissinger and now Ford–Kissinger policies was fast fading. Intent on reasserting their constitutional authority in foreign affairs, Senate and House leaders of both parties demanded further reductions in the force ceilings agreed to at Vladivostok. In the Jackson–Vanik amendment to the 1974 Trade Act, they tied increased US trade with Russia to more liberal emigration policies for Soviet Jews. Disturbed by the expansion of Soviet influence in Third World countries such as Angola and by Moscow's development of MIRVed missiles, congressional conservatives, having overcome the national guilt associated with Vietnam, began to part company with détente. For their part, liberals expressed fears that the *Realpolitik* strategy of the Nixon–Ford years, revelations that Nixon had used the CIA to overthrow the Allende government in Chile and Ford's attempted covert intervention in Angola threatened to undermine American democratic traditions and to create another Vietnam.[36]

Weary of the national divisions Vietnam produced, gravely concerned about inflation and other domestic problems and suspicious of establishment politicians – especially those associated with the Vietnam–Watergate era – the American public sought respite from the turmoil of the previous decade. They registered their disaffection by electing an outsider – Georgia Governor Jimmy Carter – as the new President.

Between confrontation and negotiation

The foreign policy of the Carter administration reflected the uneasy union of three different points of view, each of which paralleled the policy alternatives John Kennedy confronted. Having pledged to continue the process of détente in US–Soviet relations, Carter, supported by Secretary of State Cyrus Vance and Vance's successor, Edmund Muskie, sustained the policy of negotiation advocated in the 1950s and early Kennedy years by Adlai Stevenson. This line was manifest in Carter's commitment to the successful culmination of the SALT II talks. At the same time, mindful of mounting congressional opposition towards Soviet policies at home and abroad, notably in the cause of human rights that he had personally championed, the President, with the backing of national security adviser Zbigniew Brzezinski, simultaneously engaged in periodic hard-line rhetoric. Without linking the human rights campaign to the arms talks, Carter attempted to establish a broader form of cooperation with Moscow that was consonant with American ideology as well as American interests. The President increasingly embraced the hard-line approach in the latter half of 1979 as a result of the embarrassing discovery of a Soviet brigade in Cuba and the Russian invasion of Afghanistan. Finally, notwithstanding the Iranian seizure of American diplomats in November 1979, Carter attempted to improve US relations with the Third World, particularly the developing states of Africa. This cord, identified during the Kennedy years with Chester Bowles and more recently endorsed by American liberals still afflicted with the guilt of Vietnam, was patronized by the President's erstwhile ambassador to the United Nations, civil rights activist Andrew Young.

Despite the lack of cohesion to Carter's foreign policy – a condition that led to no small disaffection in the State Department – the bureaucracy welcomed the change of Secretary. First, Vance was an insider trusted by Department officials and respected as both a policy adviser and a manager. In contrast to the bureaucratic centralization imposed by Kissinger, Vance decentralized the Department's operations. By delegating authority to subordinates and keeping them informed of substantive matters, he contributed to the development of a more functionally integrated organization. Under Vance the State Department played an important role in sensitive areas of foreign policy. For one, it helped to prepare Carter for the Camp David meetings with the heads of state of Israel and Egypt; for another, policy papers drafted by the Department contributed to the formulation of the US position in the SALT II talks with the USSR.[37]

Vance also took a keen interest in the new Foreign Service Act, which received congressional approval in October 1980. This bill, which took effect in February 1981, seeks to simplify the present cumbersome administration of the service in order to make it more responsive to the changing circumstances of American foreign relations. Among other things, it will reduce the various personnel categories to a generalist class of foreign service officers and a body of foreign service specialists; limit the number of non-career appointments and ensure that those officers who reach career status undergo a more rigorous tenuring process; dismantle Wristonization by distinguishing, like the British system, between foreign service and civil service employment; and create a senior foreign service, analogous to the executive ranks in the civil service and armed forces. Reflecting the growing centralization of foreign affairs activities, the Foreign Service Act will expand the permanent base of civil service employees, including policy-oriented personnel, from roughly 3200 to 3800. The permanent overseas staff will comprise foreign service officers, who will continue their rotational tours of duty in Washington, and a support group of foreign service specialists.[38]

In spite of all this, morale in the Department continued to deteriorate during the Carter presidency. Because Vance spent so much time shuttling about the globe, and because he was thrust into the role of crisis manager by the international turmoil of 1979, he did not devote sufficient attention to his administrative responsibilities. To make matters worse, Deputy Secretary Warren Christopher was also frequently away from Washington. More serious was the feeling that Vance's (and later Muskie's) influence in the foreign affairs complex had been overshadowed by Brzezinski and the NSC staff, and even at one time by Andrew Young.

Certainly Brzezinski affected Carter's views on foreign policy, particularly after the onset of the Afghanistan crisis. Brzezinski perceived his position as national security adviser more as that of an 'ideas man', an inheritance from Kissinger, rather than as the executor of a process that served the President by presenting him with competing interpretations among other foreign affairs agencies, preparing policy options and facilitating Cabinet-level relations. Hardly a shrinking violet, Brzezinski tried (unsuccessfully) to out-Kissinger Kissinger. For a time this earned him a certain degree of presidential mistrust. Significantly, Carter did not give the NSC – or, for that matter, any other agency – the mandate it received from Nixon. Indeed, according to some officials, the President sought advice from Vance and Secretary of Defense Harold Brown to minimize the NSC's power base within the bureaucracy. Following the Cuban imbroglio and the Soviet invasion of Afghanistan, however, Brzezinski increasingly played a dominant role in the formulation of US foreign policy.[39]

Young's position in the administration proved even more nettlesome to Department officials, particularly foreign service officers who felt that the ambassador had attempted to poach on their diplomatic preserve and hence had undermined their status in the foreign-affairs complex. Resentment focused less on substantive matters – Young's success in ameliorating American relations with the developing African states in fact won praise from some quarters – than on style. Young's free-wheeling behaviour and frequent *ex cathedra* pronouncements in derogation of official policy flew right in the face of the Department's informal culture, which historically has stressed the importance of silent, discreet, anonymous diplomacy. Largely because of domestic political considerations, Carter was loath to muzzle Young. However, objections from Vance and Congress in the summer of 1979 over the ambassador's indiscretions on the Palestinian question forced the issue. Subsequent personal comments by Robert Strauss, at the time Carter's special emissary to the Middle East talks, provoked similar irritation among Department officials.[40]

A number of other factors exacerbated psychological tensions in the State Department during the Carter presidency. Once more, inflation-induced economy measures left the Department understaffed and overworked. Over the years, the Department's work force has shrunk as a percentage of total employment in the mushrooming foreign affairs bureaucracy. At the end of 1979 some 10500 people worked for the Department, 60 per cent of whom served abroad. Foreign service officers composed approximately 40 per cent of the total complement and two-thirds of those posted outside the United States. Roughly 25 per cent of all career diplomats were political officers; another 20 per cent were economics officers. Lacking a domestic constituency to support its case before congressional appropriation committees, and still stigmatized as an élitist, Eurocentric institution, the Department's budget has declined relative to other foreign affairs agencies. A condition that has nagged the Department since the Kennedy years, it has recently provoked particular discord in view of mounting inflationary pressures.[41]

For all the management reform proposals that have attempted to restore its primacy in foreign affairs, the Department has consistently lost ground to competing agencies. The formation of the International Communications Agency in 1977, which divested State of its responsibilities in the cultural area, and the creation of an under-secretary of defence for policy – the latter at the urging of Congress – were simply the most recent examples of bureaucratic centrifugalism that have attenuated the Department's status in the foreign affairs bureaucracy. Not surprisingly, Department officials have become cynical about the many efforts at reorganization and modernization. The senior executive service created by the civil service reform bill has produced considerable anxiety among Department functionaries who face the social and professional embarrassment of being demoted to a lower civil service grade if they receive unsatisfactory evaluations in the executive class. The new Foreign Service Act has provoked the same distress among diplomats, who fear that the stringent 'selection-out' provision attendant with the new executive rank will jeopardize their career status at a point in their lives when they are least likely to find alternative employment easily. For a variety of reasons – inflation, unhealthy and (as evidenced by events in Iran and elsewhere) dangerous posts, familial problems associated with working wives who may not be able to pursue their careers abroad, and the decreasing likelihood of reaching the ambassadorial level – a foreign service career has lost much of the allure it had in the era of George Kennan or Charles Bohlen, when the diplomat was, in the words of one official, 'the beau ideal rather than the head of the company store'. In the light of the growing centralization of policy-making, the closest to that ideal tomorrow's career diplomat can hope to come is a middle-grade post, one large enough to receive attention in the State Department but not important enough for the diplomat's function to be preempted at the top of the foreign affairs bureaucracy.[42]

It is possible, of course, that the State Department's diminished role in the foreign affairs complex will change. As a host of studies during the past three decades have almost truistically pointed out, a strong Secretary of State would surely strengthen the Department's influence in the bureaucracy.[43] But the combined impact of technological change, the new problems that north–south relations pose for international relations and the multiplication of foreign affairs agencies with their own agendas and bureaucratic interests to safeguard make it improbable that the mandate the Department received after the Second World War will be wholly restored. New issues such as energy, ecology, human rights and the scientific exploration of the ocean beds have further complicated traditional formal political relations among nations. While the present State Department organization includes separate divisions for these new functional areas, without the requisite technical expertise and the institutional acceptance of the changing nature of American foreign affairs the Department may increasingly be forced to assume, in contrast to more specialized agencies, a smaller role in the formulation of foreign policy.

NOTES

[1] This account of the history of the Department of State and the foreign service has been drawn particularly from Waldo Heinrichs, 'Bureaucracy and Professionalism in the Development of American Career Diplomacy', John Braeman et al. (eds), *Twentieth-Century American Foreign Policy* (Columbus 1971), 119–206; ibid., *American Ambassador: Joseph C. Grew and the Development of the United States Diplomatic Tradition* (Boston 1967); Warren Frederick Ilchman, *Professional Diplomacy in the United States, 1779–1939* (Chicago 1961); William Barnes and John Heath Morgan, *The Foreign Service of the United States* (Washington 1961). See also Thomas S. Estes and E. Allan Lightner, Jr, *The Department of State* (New York 1976); Robert D. Schulzinger, *The Making of the Diplomatic Mind* (Middletown, Conn. 1975); Richard Hume Werking, *The Master Architects: Building the United States Foreign Service, 1890–1913* (Lexington 1977).

[2] Acheson, Dean, *Present at the Creation* (New York 1969), 39; Graham, H. Stuart, *The Department of State* (New York 1949), 424–41; James L. McCamy, *The Administration of American Foreign Affairs* (New York 1950), 49.

[3] Although only about 6 per cent of all Department personnel were engaged in political affairs by 1948, more than a fifth of these were foreign service officers. See McCamy, page 57. For an enlightening discussion of the Department's 'informal culture', see Andrew M. Scott's two articles, 'The Department of State: Formal Organization and Informal Culture', *International Studies Quarterly*, 13 (March 1969) 1–19; and 'Environmental Change and Organizational Adaptation: The Problem of the State Department', *International Studies Quarterly*, 14 (March 1970), 85–95.

[4] Henry S. Villard, *Affairs at State* (New York 1965), 219.

[5] McCamy, 67–82.

[6] Dean Acheson, 'The President and the Secretary of State', in Don K. Price (ed.), *The Secretary of State* (Englewood Cliffs, N.J. 1960), 48–9.

[7] See Paul Y. Hammond, 'The National Security Council as a Device for Interdepartmental Coordination: An Interpretation and Appraisal', *American Political Science Review*, 54 (December 1960), 899–910.

[8] Interview.

[9] Townsend Hoopes, *The Devil and John Foster Dulles* (Boston 1973), 141–8.

[10] John F. Campbell, *The Foreign Affairs Fudge Factory* (New York 1971), 117. Hoopes, *Dulles*, 151–8. For the historical origins of the loyalty investigations, see Richard M. Freeland, *The Truman Doctrine and the Origins of McCarthyism: Foreign Policy, Domestic Politics, and International Security, 1946–1948* (New York 1972); see also O. E. Clubb, *The Witness and I* (New York 1974), 282.

[11] Wristonization has been treated in a number of monographs. See Zara Steiner, *Present Problems of the Foreign Service* (Princeton 1961); also see John E. Harr's *The Anatomy of the Foreign Service: A Statistical Profile* (New York 1965) and his *The Development of Careers in the Foreign Service* (New York 1965).

[12] Excerpts from the Congressional Record of 30 June 1960, 19 November 1961 and 3 October 1962, in 'Congressional Comments Regarding the Foreign Service and the Department of State, 1960–1966', Research Project No. 57, July 1966, The Historical Office, Department of State. Kennedy was also influenced by the findings of the Jackson Subcommittee hearings on the conduct of American foreign policy. See Sen. Henry M. Jackson (ed.), *The Secretary of State and the Ambassador* (New York 1964).

[13] Kennedy's reaction to the Eisenhower approach and his relationship with the NSC is examined in I. M. Destler, 'National Security Advice to U.S. Presidents: Some Lessons from Thirty Years', *World Politics*, 29 (January 1977), 143–76. See also Richard A. Johnson, *The Administration of United States Foreign Policy* (Austin 1971), 118–19, 136–7. Robert Rossow discusses specialization in the Kennedy administration in 'The Professionalization of the New Diplomacy', *World Politics*, 14 (July 1962), 561–75. On the country director–country team concept, see William I. Bacchus, *Foreign Policy and the Bureaucratic Process: The State Department's Country Director System* (Princeton 1974). The emergence of the 'country director' during the Johnson administration was an attempt to replicate the 'country team' concept in Washington.

[14] Interview.

[15] I. M. Destler, *Presidents, Bureaucrats, and Foreign Policy* (Princeton 1972), 98, 117, 152. See also Smith Simpson, *Anatomy of the State Department* (Boston 1967); and Burton Sapin, *The Making of United States Foreign Policy* (Washington 1966). The documentary data referred to, as reported in the *Washington Post* of 24 September 1979, derives from Robert F. Kennedy's oral history of 1964, located in the John F. Kennedy Library in Boston.

[16] Interviews.

[17] Interviews. See also Robert A. Divine, *Blowing on the Wind: The Nuclear Test Ban Debate, 1954–1960* (New York 1978).

[18] Roger Hilsman, *To Move a Nation: The Politics of Foreign Policy in the Administration of John F. Kennedy* (Garden City, N.Y. 1967), 536–7.

[19] Destler, *Bureaucrats*, 168–90.

[20] Destler, 'National Security Advice', 157; Johnson, 120–1, 137, 148.

[21] Campbell, 74–84; see also John E. Harr and Frederick Mosher, *Programming Systems and Foreign Affairs Leadership: An Attempted Innovation* (New York 1970).

[22] Johnson, *passim*; Destler, *Bureaucrats, passim*.

[23] Frances Fielder and Godfrey Harris, *The Quest for Foreign Affairs Officers: Their Recruitment and Selection* (New York 1966); Chris Argyris, *Some Causes of Organizational Ineffectiveness* (Washington 1967); *Toward a Modern Diplomacy: A Report to the American Foreign Service Association* (Washington 1968).

[24] Destler, 'National Security Advice', 154, 157–8; interviews.

[25] Townsend Hoopes, *The Limits of Intervention* (New York 1969), 90.

[26] See John H. Barton and Lawrence D. Weiler (eds), *International Arms Control* (Stanford 1976), 172–6.

[27] Doris Kearns, *Lyndon Johnson and the American Dream* (New York 1976), Ch. 12; Campbell, *Fudge Factory*, 72; interviews.

[28] 'U.S. Foreign Policy for the 1970s: A New Strategy for Peace', *Department of State Bulletin*, vol. 62, March 9, 1970; see also David F. Trask, *Victory without Peace: American Foreign Relations in the Twentieth Century*, 2nd edn (New York 1975), 174–9.

[29] Rogers' comments in the *Department of State Bulletin*, vol. 61, December 12, 1969, 622.

[30] Destler, 'National Security Advice', 154–9; Destler, *Bureaucrats*, 118–32. For a theoretical view of the Nixon system, that is, the President as adjudicator, see Alexander L. George, 'The Case for Multiple Advocacy in Making Foreign Policy', *American Political Science Review*, 66 (September 1972), 751–85.

[31] See John F. Campbell, 'What Is to Be Done? Gigantism in Washington', *Foreign Affairs*, 49 (October 1970), 81–99.

[32] See *Diplomacy for the 70s: A Program of Management Reform for the Department of State*, *Department of State Publication 8593* (Washington 1970). For an evaluation of this effort, see William I. Bacchus, 'Diplomacy for the 70s: An Afterview and Appraisal', *American Political Science Review*, 68 (June 1974), 736–48.

[33] Interview.

[34] Interviews.

[35] Laurence H. Silberman, ambassador to Yugoslavia during part of Kissinger's reign, has pointed out that morale in the Department gradually improved during the Kissinger years. See 'Toward Presidential Control of the State Department', *Foreign Affairs*, 57 (Spring 1979), footnote 16. Department sources, however, suggest the opposite.

[36] For an interesting essay on the human rights–stability dichotomy in American foreign relations, see William Bundy, 'Who Lost Patagonia? Foreign Policy in the 1980 Campaign', *Foreign Affairs*, 58 (Fall 1979), 1–27.

[37] Interviews.

[38] For more on the 'Bill to Promote the Foreign Service of the United States by Strengthening and Improving the Foreign Service of the United States and for Other Purposes', see the testimony of Secretary Vance and Under-Secretary for Management Benjamin Read before the Subcommittee on International Operations of the House Committee on Foreign Affairs and the Subcommittee on the Civil Service of the House Committee on the Post Office and Civil Service, 21 June 1979.

[39] Interviews.

[40] Interviews.

[41] Interviews.

[42] Interview; see Bacchus, 'Foreign Affairs Officials: Professionals Without Professions?' *Public Administration Review*, 37 (Nov–Dec 1977): 641–50.

[43] Besides the reports of the Hoover Commission, the Herter Committee and the Jackson Subcommittee, a Brookings Institution study of 1951, 'The Administration of Foreign Affairs and Overseas Operations', and the report submitted to President Johnson in 1967 by the President's Task Force on Government Organization, among others, have also stressed the importance of a strong Secretary of State.

BIBLIOGRAPHY

Dean Acheson, *Present at the Creation* (New York 1969).

Graham Allison and Peter Szanton, *Remaking Foreign Policy: The Organizational Connection* (New York 1976).

Chris Argyris, *Some Causes of International Ineffectiveness within the Department of State*. Center for International Systems Research (Washington, D.C. 1967).

William I. Bacchus, 'Diplomacy for the 70s: An Afterview and Appraisal', *American Political Science Review* 68 (June 1974), 736–48.

William Barnes and John Heath Morgan, *The Foreign Service of the United States* (Washington, D.C. 1961).

John F. Campbell, *The Foreign Affairs Fudge Factory* (New York 1971).

I. M. Destler, 'National Security Advice to U.S. Presidents: Some Lessons from Thirty Years', *World Politics* 29 (January 1977), 143–76.

——, *Presidents, Bureaucrats, and Foreign Policy* (Princeton 1972, 1974).

Thomas S. Estes and E. Allan Lightner, Jr, *The Department of State* (New York 1976).

Alexander L. George, 'The Case for Multiple Advocacy in Making Foreign Policy', *American Political Science Review* 66 (September 1972), 751–85.

Morton Halperin, *Bureaucratic Politics and Foreign Policy* (Washington, D.C. 1974).

Paul Y. Hammond, 'The National Security Council as a Device for Interdepartmental Coordination: An Interpretation and Appraisal', *American Political Science Review* 54 (December 1960), 899–910.

Waldo Heinrichs, *American Ambassador: Joseph Grew and the Development of the United States Diplomatic Tradition* (Boston 1966).

——, 'Bureaucracy and Professionalism in the Development of American Career Diplomacy', in John Braeman, Robert H. Brebner and David Brody (eds), *Twentieth-Century American Foreign Policy* (Columbus 1971).

Roger Hilsman, *To Move a Nation: The Politics of Foreign Policy in the Administration of John F. Kennedy* (Garden City, N.Y. 1967).

Warren Frederick Ilchman, *Professional Diplomacy in the United States, 1779–1939* (Chicago 1961).

Richard A. Johnson, *The Administration of United States Foreign Policy* (Austin 1971).

James L. McCamy, *The Administration of American Foreign Affairs* (New York 1950).

Richard Neustadt, *Alliance Politics* (New York 1970).

Robert D. Schulzinger, *The Making of the Diplomatic Mind* (Middletown, Conn. 1975).

Andrew M. Scott, 'Environmental Change and Organizational Adaptation: The Problem of the State Department', *International Studies Quarterly* 14 (March 1970), 85–95.

Andrew M. Scott, 'The Department of State: Formal Organization and Informal Culture', *International Studies Quarterly* 13 (March 1969), 1–19.

Smith Simpson, *Anatomy of the State Department* (Boston 1967).

John Steinbruner, *The Cybernetic Theory of Decision* (Princeton 1974).

Graham H. Stuart, *The Department of State* (New York 1949).

Donald P. Warwick, *et al.*, *A Theory of Public Bureaucracy: Politics, Personality and Organization in the State Department* (Cambridge, Mass. 1975).

Richard Hume Werking, *The Master Architects: Building the United States Foreign Service, 1890–1913* (Lexington 1977).

UNITED STATES OF AMERICA – APPENDIX A

THE DEPARTMENT OF STATE
(October 1979)

SECRETARY

US Ambassador to the United Nations

Deputy Secretary

Arms Control & Disarmament Agency

International Communication Agency

International Development Cooperation Agency

Agency for International Development

Under-Secretary for Security Assistance, Science & Technology

Counsellor

Under-Secretary for Political Affairs

Under-Secretary for Economic Affairs

Under-Secretary for Management

Executive Secretariat

Policy Planning Staff

Protocol

Legal Adviser

Congressional Relations

International Narcotics Matters

Consular Affairs

Combatting Terrorism

Refugee Programs

Intelligence & Research

Politico-Military Affairs

Public Affairs

Comptroller

Inspector-General

Administration

Management Operations

Director-General Foreign Service & Director of Personnel

European Affairs

African Affairs

East Asian & Pacific Affairs

Inter-American Affairs

Near Eastern & South Asian Affairs

International Organization Affairs

Foreign Service Institute

Human Rights and Humanitarian Affairs

Oceans & International Environmental & Scientific Affairs

Economic & Business Affairs

Diplomatic, Consular and other establishments and delegations to international organizations

LIST OF INTERNATIONAL ORGANIZATIONS

INDEX